ITALIANISSIMO 1

BEGINNERS · TEACHER'S EDITION

Denise De Rôme
MA (Cantab), MA (Reading)

Principal Lecturer in Italian
University of Westminster

Teacher's Notes by
Antonio Borraccino
BA (Polytechnic of Central London)

Lecturer in Italian
University of Westminster

Television Producer
Jeremy Orlebar

BBC BOOKS

Language consultant for the Course Book: **Angela Letizia**

This book accompanies the BBC Continuing Education television series *Italianissimo 1* first broadcast from November 1992 to January 1993.

The packs of 4 audio cassettes or CDs are available for sale separately from booksellers. The audio cassettes are also available for sale individually from booksellers.

A teaching kit, containing videos of all the 10 tv programmes, the 4 audio cassettes and the Teacher's edition of *Italianissimo 1,* is available from BBC Training Videos, BBC Enterprises Ltd, 80 Wood Lane, London W12 0TT
UK Sales Office; 081 576 2361
Canada: 416 469 1505
Australia: 02 331 7744
For the rest of the world contact the UK Sales Office

The author and publisher would like to thank Giulio Einaudi Editore for permission to quote a poem by Gianni Rodari from *Il secondo libro delle filastrocche* (1985) and part of a poem by Pier Paolo Pasolini from *Le nuova gioventù* (1975), Garzanti Editore for permission to quote a poem by Primo Levi from *Ad ora incerta* (1982), and Arnoldo Mondadori Editore for permission to quote two poems by Giuseppe Ungaretti from *Vita d'un uomo* (1966).

Course Book © Denise De Rôme 1992
Teacher's Notes © Antonio Borraccino 1992
The moral rights of the authors have been asserted

Designed by Andrew Oliver
Illustrated by Linda Smith, Michaela Stewart, Robina Green, Gary Wing, Jeremy Oliver and Kathy Baxendale
Maps by Linda Smith
Studio photographs by Benedict Campbell

ISBN 0 563 36470 X

Published by BBC Books, a division of BBC Enterprises Ltd
Woodlands, 80 Wood Lane, London W12 0TT
First published 1992

Reprinted 1994

This book is set in Bembo Roman by Selwood Systems, Midsomer Norton, Avon
Printed and bound in Great Britain by Butler & Tanner Ltd, Frome, Somerset
Cover printed by Clays Ltd, St Ives Plc

Contents

Course Menu – Level 1

Communication	Situations	Background	Grammar
1 *Immagini* Pronouncing Italian sounds Saying hello and goodbye Saying who you are and where you are Asking for things Identifying people and objects	Sightseeing Buying an ice-cream and a drink **Vocabulary** Numbers 1–20 Food and drink Places Everyday objects	Italians and their language Dialects and linguistic minorities	Nouns in -*o* and -*a* Nouns in -*à* and *è* Plurals Definite articles Indefinite articles Adjectives Questions and negatives Prepositions *di, a, in* *essere* (to be)
2 *In famiglia e fra amici* Asking someone's name and saying yours Asking what something is; who someone is Asking where things are Making simple enquiries about what's available Speaking formally, informally	Meeting people A picnic lunch party **Vocabulary** The family Food and drink Colours Clothes	Family and family life in Italy Italian names	Nouns and adjectives in -*e* Articles *l', un'* Present tense of -*are* and -*ere* verbs (incl. reflexives) *bere* (to drink) Possessive adjectives *c'è, ci sono* *chi? cosa? come? dove?*
3 *Il tempo libero* Introducing others Asking how someone is Saying where you're from Talking about your family Saying what you prefer and why Offering food and drink Saying what you need	Having fun on the beach At the tennis club **Vocabulary** Hobbies and pastimes Sports Drinks and snacks	Italians and free time Sport and leisure *L'Italiese:* anglicised Italian	Articles *l', lo, gli, uno* Present tense of -*ire* verbs *da* (for, since) More possessives Object pronouns *lo, la* *avere, stare, rimanere* *perché?*
4 *I pendolari* Saying how you travel Describing your day Telling the time Saying when you do things Talking about what you have to do Talking about your job	Getting to work Jobs **Vocabulary** Time People, jobs, work Travel, transport Routine activities	Italians at work Italian railways, roads, and public transport	Present tense review Using *a* and *in* Prepositions combined with definite article *andare, venire, uscire* *fare, dovere* *quando?*
5 *Vivere in città* Asking about prices Buying goods Asking about opening and closing times Saying what you want to do Saying what needs to be done Making enquiries	Shops and shopping At the tourist office Parks and amenities **Vocabulary** Town life, shopping Seasons, weather	City life The environment Bologna	Prepositions review More on *da* Partitive *di* (some) Irregular nouns *lo, la, li, le* *potere, volere, sapere* *dire, dare* *quanto?*

End of Level 1: *Interview – Chiappini family; Poems – Gianni Rodari, Primo Levi; Painting – Ambrogio Lorenzetti*

Course Menu – Level 2

Communication	Situations	Background	Grammar
6 *Il mondo della musica* Talking on the phone Suggesting a meeting Arranging when and where to meet – agreeing this Saying what you like and dislike Saying what you've done and where you've been	Using the telephone Making plans Talking about music **Vocabulary** Arts and the Media	Brief introduction to Italian music Conservatories Musical language	Direct and indirect object pronouns *piacere* The *passato prossimo* Some irregular past participles *quale?*
7 *A casa nostra* More telephone talk Checking if something suits Using dates to make a plan Asking to be shown something Asking and explaining how something works Talking about places you know	Using the telephone Inside the home **Vocabulary** The phone Homes and contents Domestic appliances	Italian homes The Basilicata and Puglia	*Ci* Stressed pronouns Position of pronouns Impersonal *si* *dispiacere* Using *conoscere* and *sapere* Irregular present: *possedere, sedersi*
8 *Che giornata!* Making polite requests – do you mind if? Saying you're mistaken and what's gone wrong Apologising, commiserating Expressing regret, dismay, relief and pleasure Asking and giving directions	Finding your way Accidents **Vocabulary** Documents Crime, accidents The law Personal property	Public services in Italy The police *Il burocratese*: the language of bureaucracy	The pronoun *ne* Prepositions in questions *piacere* with *a* More on *sapere* Double object verbs Double negatives Irreg. past participles
9 *A caccia di funghi* Expressing wishes and intentions Talking about quantity Saying more about places Saying what you're doing Expressing love, hate, fear Mealtime conversation	Mushroom picking expedition Processing factory **Vocabulary** The countryside Trees and plants Animals, birds, insects Feelings	The countryside Hunting Emilia and Romagna Regional food	*Ce n'è, ce ne sono* *un mio amico*, etc. Demonstratives: *quello* Present progressive Past participle agreement with *avere* verbs *conoscere* & *sapere* summary Impersonal verbs *Non … mai/più/niente*, etc.
10 *La moda* Expressing opinions Making judgements and comparisons Talking about price, colours and materials Talking about size, quality and suitability Asking about availability	Clothes design and manufacture Choosing clothes **Vocabulary** Clothes and accessories Jewellery Materials, colours, patterns	Italian fashion and design Language of fashion	Comparatives and superlatives Comparing with *che/di* *bello, buono, grande* Relative pronouns Verbs with *a* and *di* Review of *per, da, fra* Irregular nouns

End of Level 2: *Interview – Giorgio Mazzolini; Poems – Giuseppe Ungaretti; Painting – Vittore Carpaccio*

Using the Course

In each unit you'll be able to:

Interactions
Hear the language in action.

Key Phrases
Look at some basics.

Patterns
See how the language is used.

Practice
Practise what you've just learned.

Vocabulary
Reinforce and widen your vocabulary.

Troubleshooting
Avoid common pitfalls.

At the end of each level you'll be able to:

Systems
Look at the grammar – see how the language works.

Reinforcement
Do some more exercises.

Review
Check up on what you know and assess your progress.

Working on your own
Focus on language learning strategies.

Profile
Reinforce your listening and reading.

Culture
Enjoy some paintings and poems.

At the back of the book you can:

Answers
Find the answers to the exercises.

Basics
Sort out some basic grammar terms.

Reference
Find useful verb lists and other detailed information.

Index to Grammar
Find out where grammar points are explained.

Lexis
Check up on words you don't know.

Italianissimo 1 is a multimedia language learning package designed to meet the varying needs of the beginner or near beginner, whether studying alone or in a group. The course consists of:
* a book comprising 2 levels of 5 units each
* 4 audio cassettes or CDs
* 10 TV programmes and 10 radio programmes
Depending on the nature and inclination of the learner it will take between six months and one year to complete the course, the end of which corresponds roughly to GCSE level standard.

Italianissimo 2 will be published in Autumn 1993 and will take the learner up to a pre A-level stage. It will have a similar structure and components.

Aims and Modes of Study

The course is suitable for all learners as it offers them the opportunity to study at their own pace and in the way that suits them best: the various components of the course make it possible for the learner to study the same material from different angles, and with different degrees of complexity. The course features:
* A twin track system of alternative study modes
* Plenty of reinforcement and repetition
* Help on how to develop language learning skills

Twin track approach

The learner has the option of following one of two tracks:
* **Track 1** is the 'core' course, aimed at learners for whom basic communicative needs are most important. The language needed for this is presented in the Patterns section. This gives learners the opportunity to absorb some of the key language and to extend it a little in conjunction with extra vocabulary and some exercises.
* **Track 2** is for intensive learners requiring more in-depth knowledge, who need to learn to communicate more independently in a wider variety of situations. In addition to the core material, there are extra explanations of key structures in the **Systems** and additional exercises in the **Reinforcement** section at the end of each level.

The keynote of *Italianissimo* is flexibility: a comprehensive system of cross-references makes it possible for the learner following Track 1 to dip selectively into Track 2 and for all learners to use the **Reference** section at the end of the book. After having completed one level learners have the opportunity of assessing their progress in the **Review** section and changing tracks if they wish.

Introduction

Aims

The *Italianissimo* Teacher's Book aims to give the teacher an overview of *Italianissimo* and to suggest ways of exploiting it to the full, using all the course components.

Overview

Italianissimo is a Beginners' to Intermediate course for adults, based on a communicative approach and structured to suit different learning needs. The central concept underlying the design of the course is learner autonomy: it is increasingly widely recognised that learning is most effective when learners are able to take an active part in the learning process and become more independent and self-reliant. The advent of Language Centres which provide open access to resources, the development of student-centred courses, plus the rise in student numbers make it even more desirable for learners to develop language-learning strategies which suit their needs and individual learning styles.

Italianissimo accordingly provides guidance on learning from the start and contains a series of language study skills which can be exploited in conjunction with the different components of the course:

a) The **Introduction** to each unit contains suggestions for examining objectives for learning.
b) In the **Basics** the grammar terminology is set out for learners wishing to familiarise themselves with new or unknown terms.
c) The **Review** provides the learner with the opportunity for self-assessment.
d) In the **Working on your own** section learners are given the opportunity to experiment with different ways of practising their language skills and extending their knowledge independently.

Italianissimo is suitable for students working on their own or with a class and meets the needs of those studying for business or pleasure as well as learners aiming at GCSE (or equivalent level) exams. The range of lexis and situations covered is wider than the normal syllabus but the actual grammar presented is less extensive.

The role of the teacher

The development of effective study skills is a valuable and necessary part of teaching, and these notes aim at encouraging the teacher to become a facilitator of learning, not simply the traditional transmitter of information. The extent to which individual teachers will exploit the study skills section in the book will depend on the nature of the student and the objective of the course. They are nevertheless encouraged to begin by using the Course Introduction to discuss the students' aims. They are also encouraged to familiarise the learners with their tools, namely the course and its overall structure and to discuss the Track chosen.

Contents

The *Italianissimo* Teacher's Book contains a page-to-page guide to the ten units of the Course Book. Here are some general suggestions for each section of the unit:

Unit introduction/Cultura e Parole

The Introduction focuses on aspects of contemporary Italian society. It is intended to complement the introduction and **Cultura e Parole** sections in each unit and stimulate class discussion.

Video corner

In this section you will find different suggestions for the use of the video by way of video worksheets and other exercises to help students understand the video sequence, stimulate active viewing (exploiting the visual element) and encourage their responses, either written or spoken.

Help phrases, questions, commands and instructions

These are to encourage as far as possible the use of Italian as the working language of the classroom. Discuss the meaning of 'help phrases' and classroom commands and establish penalties for non-use of these.

Lesson breaking points

These are only given as a very rough guide for a two-hour lesson with a short 10–15 minute break. The pace should be brisk and lively but this will of course depend on many more factors beyong the control of these notes.

Interactions

The **First Time Round** exercise is aimed at developing listening skills: it is intended to help students make sense of unfamiliar language, using what they know. It is important that each Interaction is contextualised. (Each Interaction begins with a suggestion on using simple Italian to introduce the situation.) Make sure students know the meaning of the prompt words given in the **First Time Round** box and that they read the introduction and questions before listening to the cassette/CD. You may prefer to photocopy these or write them on the board/OHP so that the students keep their books closed. The more you stimulate students' curiosity, the more enjoyable this *fase ascolto* will be. You will also find extra sample questions.

Play each Interaction as many times as required. You should also test students on the **Key Phrases** once they have become familiar with the Interaction.

Suggestions are also made throughout the Teacher's Book on how to re-cycle the Interactions in different ways.

Patterns

This section is intended to help students recognise and learn patterns by explaining and extending the **Key Phrases**. It is also an opportunity for you, the teacher, to summarise what you have covered up to this point and, if you wish, to extend it with any additional information given in the **Systems** or the **Reference** section.

In this section you will find suggestions for classroom activities which practise each pattern specifically.

Practice

The exercises in this section are self-explanatory and can therefore be set for homework. It is often possible, however, to carry out these exercises orally in class and to encourage students to write them up at home. You will find more classroom activities in these notes to provide students with extra practice of the functions, the structures and the vocabulary dealt with in each unit.

Vocabulary

There is no doubt that the single biggest problem in learning a second language is the acquisition of words. Yet it can be relatively easy and enjoyable for the students to increase their capacity to learn and remember words if they are encouraged to develop original/personal ways of learning. This is best achieved in an active rather than in a passive way and that is why this section is not intended for tedious memory tests. Suggestions for vocabulary-learning strategies and classroom activities are given in each unit.

Troubleshooting

In this section you will find a quick revision checklist, to remind you and your students what they have learnt in each unit.

Using the exercises on cassette/CD

The cassette is designed as an independent learning tool and contains extra guidance for independent learners. For this reason, and to save time in class, the tape counter number is indicated next to each Interaction. This is intended as a guide only, as there may be differences between cassette counters. (A count of 500 is equivalent to 36 minutes' playback time.)

Play the cassette or CD as required. Give students time to prepare themselves and ask student A to say what he/she thinks the answer is. Ask the others for different suggestions (or corrections). Then go on. Play the cassette or CD, choose another student and repeat the process. Occasionally ask the same student more than one question so as to maintain a brisk pace and keep general interest alive.

In addition to the page-to-page notes for each of the ten units of *Italianissimo* you will find general suggestions on end of level material (**Systems** and **Reinforcement, Review, Profile** and **Culture**).

Working in class

The guiding principle behind the activities contained here has been to provide suggestions which demand individual effort on the part of the student and shift the emphasis of classroom teaching from teacher's performance to active involvement of learners. This is achieved by:

a) 'hands-on' activities – so that students work with visual aids and realia
b) communicative exercises based on genuine information gaps between teacher and students and among the students themselves
c) worksheets which require students to practise specified skills or structures.

Some of the exercises suggested in the latter part of these notes have the aim of stimulating discussion.

Many exercises ask students to make a choice or come to a decision through discussion in groups or pairs. The teacher should always encourage students to explain and/or justify the reasons for their choice.

Equipment

Although there is no need for any special equipment apart from a board and a tape or CD player, many activities in class will be more easily carried out with an OHP which provides an excellent opportunity to focus the attention of the class immediately and is extremely easy to use, even for the less technically-minded.

The advantages of the OHP over the blackboard are obvious in speeding up the ways in which information is stored and retrieved: for example, when projecting correct answers and letting students check by themselves. Written group and pair work can often be carried out on transparency. This is equivalent to having the students working on the blackboard all at the same time.

Using the Course

TV, cassettes/CDs and radio

Whichever track you choose to follow, you are encouraged to get used to hearing the language from the start, in conjunction with the cassette or CD and if possible with the TV programmes. You will find that the book and cassettes/CDs are closely integrated and can be used independently of the TV. Cassette/CD symbols in the text indicate when there is an accompanying recording; a number is also given so you can find the right track quickly on the cassette/CD. The TV gives additional dialogues and information about Italy as well as all the core dialogues in the book. You are therefore strongly encouraged to make videos of the TV programmes or gain access to them if you can. If you want to follow the TV programmes each week you can get a rapid overview of each unit by listening first to the cassette/CDs which contain helpful explanations. You can go back over the unit in your own time. An additional feature of the course are the Italian radio programmes on Radio 5, which are based on the units of the course and include topical news reports from Italy and study tips from teachers of Italian. Do record these if you can.

Getting Going

Italianissimo provides varied, adaptable material which can be tailored to your individual learning needs. To make the most of the course you need first to define what these are.

Define your goals

Whatever has prompted you to embark on this course, whether work, study or general interest, you'll find that to stay motivated you need to set yourself precise short-term aims. Think about what you will be using your Italian for and try to prioritise the four basic language skills involved.

	Vital	Important	Quite important	Unimportant
Speaking				
Listening				
Reading				
Writing				

Although these skills are all interrelated, your attempt to grade the relative importance of each one for your particular purposes will help you focus more precisely on your goals and enable you to use the course more effectively.

Organise your time

Don't be over-ambitious. You must have realistic expectations. Decide how much time you can regularly devote to learning and stick to it. Bear in mind that most people need plenty of time and practice to build up confidence and proficiency. Research shows that on average learners forget about 80% of what they have studied within a mere twenty-four hours unless they use or review what they have learned!

Structure of the Course

* **Level 1** Introductions and personal information. Basic socialising, enquiries, requests and needs.
* **Level 2** Making arrangements, suggestions and invitations. Expressing basic feelings.

Although new material is introduced in each of the five units within a level, similar areas of language are 'revisited' throughout to reinforce and consolidate the main structures.

Working through a unit

A unit has two main parts and two supplementary parts for reference, and is designed to provide material for several hours study. Each of the two main parts is likely to require at least two to three hours to complete, but this will vary with the individual and the approach chosen:

1 Introduction – aspects of contemporary Italian society
   Interactions 1
   Patterns and Practice 1
2 Cultura e parole – the culture behind the language
   Interactions 2
   Patterns and Practice 2
3 Vocabulary – for reference
4 Troubleshooting – for reference

Using the Course

Interactions

To start with we recommend you listen to the interactions without first reading the text. If you are not used to this approach don't be daunted, as the interactions are meant to be listened to several times to help you build up your listening skills.

Use the **First Time Round** questions to focus your attention. Make sure that you have understood the meaning of the words given at the beginning and that you understand the context by reading the introduction and questions carefully. You can also listen to the introductory material on tape or by-pass this and start your listening with the interactions. With practice you will gain a great deal of confidence by realising that you can grasp the gist through guesswork and by building on what you know. Listen as often as you wish. Then move on to:

Key Phrases

Study them and then see if you can pick them out on tape. Once you are confident that you have got as far as you can by listening, study the written text to fill in any gaps in your comprehension. You can also use it to practise pronunciation in conjunction with the tape. To see how the language fits together, move on to:

Patterns

These provide basic explanations of the Key Phrases, often in conjunction with new vocabulary. You'll find that some of this is used in the Practice exercises, so do look back at the Patterns if you get stuck for a word. If you are following **Track 2** remember to make use of the cross-references in Patterns to the Systems section: those following **Track 1** may also find it helpful at times.

Practice

This section provides lively follow-up activities, some of them on the cassette/CD, in which you can use and begin to adapt the language presented so far. As realistic as possible and often humorous, they are designed to give practice in all the language skills. You'll find the answers at the back of the book.

Suggested study plans

It's a good idea initially to devote two or even three sessions to each of the main parts of a unit. The length of your sessions can vary and, as you progress through the course, you will develop your own study routines.

Track 1	Session 1	Session 2	Session 3
Approach A:	Interactions & Patterns 1	Learn some vocabulary	Practice 1
Approach B:	Interactions 1	Patterns & Practice 1	Learn some vocabulary

Repeat the process for the second language section.

Track 2. Vary your approach until you determine what works best for you. Aim at four or even five sessions, to take account of Systems and the Reinforcement exercises.

Vocabulary

This section is intended to aid gradual, systematic vocabulary acquisition by listing additional words on topics which come up in the unit. Any irregular or unusual stress on a word is marked by a dot so that you can pronounce new words correctly from the start. There are notes on vocabulary learning in the **Working on your own** sections of the book.

Learning to Learn

If you have never studied a language before, dip into the **Working on your own** and the **Basics** section before you start. These will help you to gain the confidence you need to manage your own learning and experiment with the material in the course. Don't forget that there is plenty of material for extending your knowledge at leisure, both in the book, on the cassette/CDs and, of course, in the TV programmes. Do exploit everything to the full and make the most of *Italianissimo!* You don't have to be a linguist to achieve this, so persevere and enjoy the experience. **Buon lavoro e buon divertimento!**

SVIZZERA

AUSTRIA

UNGHERIA

FRANCIA

▲ Monte Bianco
VALLE
D'AOSTA
▲ M. Rosa
Bernina
Aosta

TRENTINO
ALTO ADIGE
▲ Marmolada

FRIULI-
VENEZIA
GIULIA

LOMBARDIA
• Trento
• Milano

VENETO
• Venezia
Golfo di Venezia
• Trieste

PIEMONTE
• Torino

EMILIA ROMAGNA

LIGURIA
• Genova
Golfo di Genova

• Bologna

SAN
MARINO

MAR LIGURE

Arno

• Firenze

TOSCANA

MARCHE
• Ancona

I. Capraia

MARE ADRIATICO

I. d'Elba

UMBRIA
• Perugia

CORSICA

Tevere

▲ Gran Sasso d'Italia
• L'Aquila

Roma
ABRUZZO

LAZIO

MOLISE
• Campobasso

MAR
DI SARDEGNA

CAMPANIA

PUGLIA
• Bari

SARDEGNA

MAR TIRRENO

Napoli
I. d'Ischia

• Potenza

BASILICATA
▲ M. Pollino

• Cagliari

Golfo di Taranto

Canale d'Otranto

ITALIA

I. d'Ustica

CALABRIA

Isole Eolie
• Catanzaro

Isole Egadi

• Palermo

Stretto di Messina

MAR IONIO

SICILIA ▲ M. Etna
Siracusa

TUNISIA

MAR MEDITERRANEO

ix

Immagini

Piazza di Spagna (a sinistra) e il Colosseo (a destra), Roma

In this unit you'll learn basic pronunciation; how to greet people and say who you are. You'll also find out how to order something and ask simple questions.

Italy, with its population of nearly 58 million, is a deceptively familiar country. It is known worldwide for its scenic beauty, its art and architecture, good food and design, cars, clothes, opera, films and football. But the stereotypes and images – **immagini** – tell us little about this varied and surprising country.

Italy has an ancient and influential civilisation, yet as a nation it is a relative newcomer – it was unified in 1861. This helps to explain why it is that, although the foundations of the Italian written language were laid by the poet Dante Alighieri in the early fourteenth century, standard spoken Italian is a phenomenon of the mid twentieth century. Even now some 20 per cent of Italians do not speak Italian as their mother tongue and about two thirds are bilingual and speak regional dialects as well. Italy is in fact the most multilingual and least homogenous of Western European countries. She plays a leading role in international affairs, yet regional or local loyalties still frequently prevail over national ones. It is perhaps significant that there is no single Italian patron saint, but a host of local ones. Small wonder then that over 100 years after unification, one of Italy's top journalists, Enzo Biagi, was moved to write 'There is no such thing as Italians; we are not even unified by spaghetti!'

Immagini

Introduce the topic *la lingua italiana* by saying a few words on *la pronuncia*. Although most beginners will not be too concerned with the way they pronounce words, they will be reassured to know that, in order to speak Italian, they won't need to master totally unfamiliar sounds, because all the sounds in Italian (with the exception of *gli*) are to be found in English too. Even the most difficult words to pronounce (those involving the rolling of the 'r') need not be a problem, because a sizeable minority of Italians cannot give a full sound to the 'r' either.

Tell students that pronouncing the written word in Italian is not half as difficult as it is in English and that the few basic rules of pronunciation will be learned in the first few weeks, after which they will have no problem in recognising any sounds or reading any words. As far as accent, stress and intonation are concerned, it will be largely a question of practice, if their aim is to sound as authentic as a native speaker. Point out that it is not crucial to have a set accent (there are simply too many accents for them to worry about imitating the right one). It is more important to get the stress right to start with.

Break the ice and give students confidence right from the start, by building on what they already know. Ask the class to tell you at least one Italian word they know and write it on the board. Cover the board with these words, which could be anything they have heard or read. More detailed phonetic explanations will come later on but for the moment a short, sharp exercise on the basic rules of pronunciation will make the students realise that they already know lots of Italian words and sounds. It will also help them appreciate the simplicity of Italian spelling and provide an opportunity for practising pronunciation and stress on familiar examples.

Stimulate interest in the language in the way you think most appropriate. What views do the group have on Italians? Most people will have had some exposure to Italian probably in the form of a holiday, and they will be familiar with Italian words through food, thanks in part to the waves of Italian immigrants who have established catering businesses and brought *la cucina italiana* to the world. Someone, one day, had the brilliant idea to make and sell ice-cream and this established a popular Italian stereotype which survives today. Ask the students what images spring to mind when they think of Italians.

Video corner
Spot the objects
Aim: vocabulary building
Video sequence: from the map of Italy up to the point when Anna Mazzotti introduces herself

1   Write some words on the board/OHP. Some of these should be names of things that can be seen in the video's opening sequence.

e.g. *cane   statua   borsa   palla   mela   tazza*
   bicicletta   scooter   radio   persone   vaso   chiave
   quadro   luna   ombrello   finestra

2   Let the students guess the meaning of the words and help them if necessary.

3   Play the video sequence and ask them to tick off all the things you have listed as they spot them on the video.

4   You can repeat this activity at other suitable points in the video, for example soon after Anna buys some ice-cream and before she orders the coffee (Interactions 10–11). The following are some of the things that can be spotted. Add a few more words and ask students to tick off what they can see, or to number them in the order in which they appear.

fontana   tavolini   sedie
ombrellone   lampione   campane

Spot the word
Aim: vocabulary building
Video sequence: just before Anna buys some ice-cream

1   Ask students to look for the word *arcobaleno* (or the 'ice-cream to take away') (*gelati da asportare*) sign and tell you when and where it appears in the video.

2   Play the video sequence.

3   You could repeat this type of activity at any other suitable point in the video.

Tuttifrutti (Ice-cream flavours)
Aim: pronunciation practice/vocabulary building
Video sequence: the list of ice-cream flavours

1   Pause the video on the list of ice-creams and let the students guess the meaning of the words. Help them if necessary and practise pronunciation.

2   Ask students for any other ice-cream flavours they know. (Write these on the board.)

3   Write one of the flavours on a piece of paper, but don't show it to the students. Ask them to guess which flavour it is. Limit them to three guesses. If there's time, students can play this game together in pairs.

What are they saying?
Aim: vocabulary building
Video sequence: the final part, just before the credits

1 Tell the students they are going to watch some people gesticulating in the final sequence.

2 Write a topic of conversation for each of the six sketches on the board and discuss the meaning with students.

e.g. a) *carovita*   b) *macchine*
  c) *donne/uomini*   d) *politica*
  e) *strumenti musicali* e) *calcio/totocalcio*

3 Play the sequence and ask students to match the hand gestures, body movements and facial expressions to the topics.

4 For further practice, ask students, working in twos or in groups, to write down the name of a famous person associated with one of the above topics. One student reads out the name, and the others try to be first to call out the correct topic.

Interactions

> **Structures:** a few basic sounds/singular and plural of masculine and feminine nouns/*un, una, il, la* (non) *sono, sei, è*
> **Functions:** introducing yourself/asking for things
> **Vocabulary:** *ciao, buongiorno, piacere, biglietto, guida, per favore, grazie*

Help-phrases and instructions

Introduce the following phrases to the students. Practise them. Make sure that you use them in class and encourage the students to ask these questions in Italian. Stop them if they don't.

Come si dice in italiano . . .? *Ascoltate.*
Cosa vuol dire . . . in inglese? *Aprite il libro (a pagina . . .).*
Come si scrive . . . in italiano? *Chiudete il libro.*

Tell students they are going to hear a few people introducing themselves in a variety of ways.

Interaction 1   (042)

1 Anna Mazzotti introduces herself. Tell students to fill in the sound boxes as they listen.

2 *Ascoltate.* Play the cassette/CD as required.

3 Check answers and discuss further questions.

Interaction 2   (065)

1 The last of the familiar words given is a way of saying 'cheers!'. Ask students to fill in the sound boxes as they listen.

2 *Ascoltate.* Play the cassette/CD as required.

3 Check answers and discuss any questions.

Interaction 3   (094)

1 Ask students to write down the names of the four girls.

2 *Chiudete il libro e ascoltate.*

3 Play the cassette/CD as required.

4 Check answers and discuss any questions.

Presentazioni (1)

Aim: to reinforce introductions presented so far (in Interactions 1, 2 and 3)

1 Introduce yourself to the class in Italian:
Buongiorno/buonasera, io sono . . . .
Ciao, io sono . . . .

2 Elicit the same introduction from the students (it is not necessary to go round the whole class, especially if it is a large one).

3 Ask the students to introduce themselves to each other.

Interactions

1 📼 💿 2

Some of the people in the series say hello and Anna Mazzotti, the presenter, introduces herself.

First time round

Listen out for two ways of saying hello.

Ciao ... **ci**ao. ... **Buongiorno** ... **buo**ngiorno. Buon**gi**orno, **io sono** Anna Ma**zz**otti.

Key phrases

ciao	*hello [familiar]*
buongiorno	*good morning*
io sono	*I am*

As you listen, look at the text and notice how the highlighted letters are pronounced. Try and put an equivalent English sound in each box.

ci ☐   **buo** ☐   **gi** ☐   **zz** ☐

2 📼 💿 3

Next, some familiar Italian words and a way of saying cheers!

First time round

How many of the following would you eat?

Chianti spa**ghe**tti gorgon**z**ola parmi**gi**ano fettu**cci**ne Fras**ca**ti Gu**cci** Lan**ci**a **cin cin!**

Key phrase

cin cin!   *cheers!*

Read the text as you listen. How are the highlighted letters pronounced? Put the equivalent English sound in each box.

chi ☐   **ghe** ☐   **z** ☐   **gi** ☐   **ci** ☐   **ca** ☐

3 📼 💿 4

A few more hellos from a beach in Liguria and people saying who they are.

First time round

Cover up the text below! You'll hear four girls saying their names. Listen to the cassette/CD. What are they called? If necessary, press the pause button after each one and try to write down the name.

Ciao – io sono Marilina.
Ciao – io sono Giovanna.
Ciao – io sono Stefania.
Ciao – io sono Elisabetta.

4   5

Finally, two more names and a way of saying 'how do you do?'.

First time round

How is the name Walter pronounced in Italian?

Io sono Fran**ce**sca.
Io sono **W**alter Ta**gli**aferri.
Ciao – **piacere**.

Key phrase

piacere	*how do you do?*
	pleased to meet you

Look at the text as you listen. Three new sounds have been highlighted. Can you write an approximate English equivalent?

ce ☐   **W** ☐   **gli** ☐

5   6

L'Italia in Miniatura is a large amusement park just outside Rimini on the Adriatic coast. As its name suggests, the park contains models in miniature of the main sights of Italy from all its twenty regions.

First time round

un biglietto	*a ticket*
undicimila	*11 thousand*

Listen to the cassette/CD without looking at the text. Anna buys a ticket and a guide.
Can you pick out the Italian words for *please* and *thank you*?

Anna   **Un biglietto** e **una guida, per favore.**
Ragazza   Ecco il biglietto e la guida. Undicimila.
Anna   **Grazie.**
Ragazza   Grazie.

ecco   *here is*

Key phrases

un biglietto, per favore	*a ticket, please*
una guida, per favore	*a guide, please*
grazie	*thank you*

---

6   7

A couple go to the ticket-office at the Italia in Miniatura park.

First time round

ventiduemila	*22 thousand lire*

What do you think the word for *two* is?

Uomo   Due biglietti e due guide.
Ragazza   Ecco i biglietti e le guide, ventiduemila. Grazie.
Uomo   **Buongiorno.**
Moglie   Buongiorno.

ecco   *here are*

Key phrase

buongiorno	*good morning.* [Here; *goodbye* not *hello.*]

Interaction 4 (110)

1 Here are two more names and a way to say 'How do you do?' Ask students to fill in the sound boxes as they listen.

2 *Ascoltate.* Play the cassette/CD as required.

3 Discuss any other questions which may arise.

Presentazioni (2)

Aim: to reinforce introductions presented in the previous Interaction

1 Shake hands with a student: *Ciao! Io sono . . . Piacere.*

2 Elicit the same introduction from a student and repeat this a number of times with different students.

3 Ask students to do the same in pairs.

Interaction 5 (124)

1 Tell students that as long as they know the magic word, they can ask for anything. Ask them to listen out for the Italian for 'please'. *Chiudete i libri.*

2 *Ascoltate.* Play the cassette/CD as required.

3 Ask students further questions, for example:

What does Anna buy?

Interaction 6 (151)

1 This time two people buy two tickets and two guides. What is the word for 'two'?

2 *Chiudete i libri e ascoltate.* Play the cassette/CD as required.

3 Discuss any other questions which may arise.

Il Chianti e la Cina

Aim: pronunciation practice, spelling and vocabulary building

1 Write a few words on the board. Start with ones students have heard and add some more.
e.g. *ciao, Chianti, Frascati, chiesa, Gucci, chiave, Lancia, cina, Carlo, fettuccine, Chiara, colla, casa*

2 Tell students to write down the words and to search for the ones containing either the sound *ci* or the sound *chi* circling the letter or letters they think produce that sound.

3 To check answers, ask a *volontario* to come to the board.

4 Repeat the procedure for words containing the sounds *ce* and *che*.
e.g. *certo, panca, perché, piacere, cassetta, caro, collo, buco, cosa, francese, schermo*

5 Advise students to list the words in their notebooks according to the different sound categories.

6 Using all the words on the board, point at random to words, asking students for the pronunciation.

Patterns 1

Saying hello and goodbye

Ask students to think of all the greetings they have encountered so far and elicit any others listed in the **Patterns** section. Practise the different hello and goodbye intonations.

You may also like to discuss the usage of:
buongiorno, buonpomeriggio (very seldom used) and *buonasera* (late afternoon onwards)
salve (slightly less informal than *ciao*)
the origin of *ciao* (formally *sciao*, from the Venetian word for slave, *sciavo*, i.e. 'I am at your service. I am your slave').

Saying who you are

a)

1 *Buongiorno/buonasera, io sono* (your name). *Sono inglese/italiano/a.*

2 Elicit the same introduction from a student (they should all be Italian for the purpose of practice).

3 Repeat this a number of times with different students.

4 Ask students to do the same in pairs.

5 Go round the class checking progress.

6 Write on the board *No, non sono . . .* and ask the students to practise this too, by deliberately getting their names wrong. Say, for example: *tu sei Frances* (wrong name) and elicit the right answer. Let them correct you.

7 Students may move round the class asking, for example: *tu sei Madonna/Michael Jackson?* until they feel they know the names of the other class members.

b)
1 Depending on the group, talk about any other nationality you think appropriate: *Io sono australiano e tu?*

2 Encourage students to guess a few more nationalities: *Benissimo! Student A è cinese/australiano.*

3 Ask students to write down their chosen nationality.

4 Say to student A: *Io sono cinese e tu?*
If the student says, for instance: *Io sono canadese,* ask everyone to write down *canadese,* then ask someone to spell it out loud. Write it on the board for everyone to check the spelling.

5 Ask the students to imagine they are a famous person and tell you only their nationality. The rest of the class try to guess their identity. For example: *Io sono americano. Tu sei Michael Jackson?*

Asking for things

Explain:
Per favore = per piacere, per cortesia, per gentilezza
No, thank you = *no, grazie*
Yes, please   = *sì, grazie*

Points for discussion:

a) How often do you use 'please' in English and *per favore* in Italian?
b) Students will be tempted to say *io sono* every time they want to say 'I am'. There isn't, of course, anything wrong with that but constant repetition of *io* sounds odd: *io sono Alison Jenkins, io sono inglese, io sono di Cambridge . . .* To make students aware of how personal pronouns are used in Italian (i.e. only when they would be stressed in English), you could perhaps compare the two different ways one would say 'What do I know about it?' when
a) talking to yourself
b) talking to someone who wants you to do something you know nothing about.

This point could be the end of the first lesson.
Briefly revise the points covered so far and give students a preview of what you will be doing in the next lesson. The emphasis will still be on different sounds of the alphabet but you will also be teaching numbers and discussing general points of interest in the language.

Structures: sound systems (soft and hard *c* and *g*, *gli, bu, gu, z, f*)
Functions: counting from 1 to 20/spelling using the alphabet of cities
Vocabulary: general words with an emphasis on food

Patterns I

i) Saying hello

How you say *hello* depends on how formal your relationship is and on the time of day.

Ciao!   *Hello [inf. – friends only, all times of day]*
Buongiorno   *Good morning [lit. good day]*
Buonasera   *Good afternoon, good evening [lit. good evening]*

The word for *afternoon* is *pomeriggio*, but it is rarely used in greetings.

If you've already been introduced, you can say:

Piacere   *How do you do? [lit. pleasure]*

ii) Saying goodbye

This also depends on the degree of formality and on the time of day.

Ciao   *[inf.]*   Buonanotte   *Good night [inf. and form.]*
Buongiorno   Arrivederci   *Goodbye*
Buonasera

The intonation of **ciao, buongiorno,** and **buonasera** can be different when you say *goodbye*: the voice often falls at the end of the word. However, among native speakers you will find many differences in intonation.

iii) Saying who you are

The key verb is **essere** *(to be)* [see Systems, note 7, p. 80].

| [Io] sono | Anna Mazzotti, sono italiana | *I am* | *Anna Mazzotti, I am Italian* |
| | Walter Tagliaferri, sono italiano | | *Walter Tagliaferri, I am Italian* |

| [noi] siamo | Anna e Francesca, siamo italiane | *We are* | *Anna and Francesca, we are Italian* |
| | Walter e Carlo, siamo italiani | | *Walter and Carlo, we're Italian* |

For the changes in the word **italiano**, see Systems, note 5, p. 79.

iv) Asking for things

If you ask for one thing, the key words are **un** or **una** *(a, an)* and **per favore** *(please)*.

Un biglietto, per favore   *A ticket, please*   Ecco **il** biglietto   *Here is the ticket*
Un cappuccino, per favore   *A cappuccino, please*   Ecco **il** cappuccino   *Here is the cappuccino*
Una guida, per favore   *A guide, please*   Ecco **la** guida   *Here is the guide*
Una birra, per favore   *A beer, please*   Ecco **la** birra   *Here is the beer*

If you ask for more than one of anything, the endings of the words change:

Due cappuccini, per favore.   Ecco **i** cappuccini
Due birre, per favore.   Ecco **le** birre

Accepting: if you want to say 'Yes, please', use **grazie** not **per favore**:
Sì, grazie   *Yes, please*

See Systems, p. 79 for: plurals (note 2); *the* – **il, i, la, le** (note 3); *a/an* – **un, una** (note 4).

Patterns I

v) Numbers

Below are the numbers 1–20. There is a complete list of numbers in Ref. I, 1, p. 239.

uno	due	tre	quattro	cinque	sei	sette	otto	nove	dieci	undici	dodici
1	2	3	4	5	6	7	8	9	10	11	12
tredici		quattordici		quindici		sedici		diciassette		diciotto		diciannove		venti
13		14		15		16		17		18		19		20

vi) Sound-systems: spelling and pronunciation

To help your pronunciation, irregular stress has been marked by a dot [See Patterns 2, note vi, p. 13]. It is not difficult to pronounce Italian and the spelling is quite easy because the same sounds are always spelt in the same way. Start by noticing the differences – and similarities – with respect to the English:

a) Sounds with 'c'
Ci and **ce** correspond to the English *ch* sound:

> **ci**ao **ci**n-**ci**n Lan**ci**a cami**ci**a *(shirt)* **ci**bo *(food)* Masa**cci**o
> pia**ce**re France**sc**a Botti**ce**lli dol**ce**latte **ce**na *(supper)*

But **c** followed by any other vowel is a hard *k* sound as in English:

> **ca**ffè *(coffee)* pes**ca** *(peach)* **ca**mera *(room)* s**ca**rpe *(shoes)*
> e**cc**o pe**co**rino *(pecorino cheese)* albi**co**cca *(apricot)*
> **cu**pola *(dome)* **cu**cina *(kitchen)* **cu**gino *(cousin)*

Beware: **chi** and **che** are always hard *k* sounds:

> **Chi**anti Pino**cchi**o De **Chi**rico ma**cchi**na *(car)* fino**cchi**o *(fennel)* radi**cchi**o *(radicchio)*
> Mi**che**langelo Mar**che** *[Italian region]*

b) Sounds with 'g'
Gi and **ge** have a soft *j* sound:

> parmi**gi**ano **Gi**otto **gi**acca *(jacket)* **Ge**nova **ge**lato *(ice-cream)* **ge**neroso *(generous)*

But **g** followed by any other vowel is a hard *g* sound as in English:

> **Ga**lles *(Wales)* **ga**rage *(garage)* colle**ga** *(colleague)*
> **go**rgonzola **go**nna *(skirt)* **Gu**cci la**gu**na *(lagoon)* Li**gu**ria *[region]*

Beware: **ghi** and **ghe** are always hard *g* sounds:

> Lambor**ghi**ni **Ghi**rlandaio In**ghi**lterra *(England)* spa**ghe**tti tra**ghe**tto *(ferry)*

c) Sounds with 'gli'
This is a characteristically Italian sound. You don't pronounce the *g*: the sound is more like the beginning of the word liaison:

> Modi**gli**ani ta**gli**atelle bi**gli**etto *(ticket)* ma**gli**a *(jumper)* fami**gli**a *(family)* fi**gli**o *(son)*

Patterns 1

Numbers

1 Write numbers 1–20 in full on the board.

2 Say a few numbers at random and ask students to write each one down in figures.

3 Check answers by asking one student to say, in English, the numbers in order.

4 Ask for a *volontario* to do the same.

5 Practise the instruction phrase: *Aprite il libro a pagina* . . . Ask students to tell you each time what is on the page.

6 Introduce students to the idea of using vocabulary maps. Use numbers as an initial example:

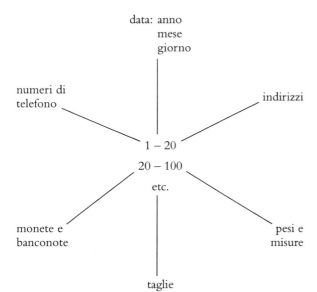

Sound-systems: spelling and pronunciation

Students will be relieved if you tell them that they will be unlikely to struggle much with sounds and that when it comes to writing, the rules are few and simple. Spelling in Italian is not as eccentric as it can be in English (aren't they lucky in comparison with foreign learners of English?).

Start with what the students already know. Ask them to spell sounds they have so far encountered (*Bologna, quadro, Mazzotti, Walter, guida, grazie, bagno, questo*), or to use words they know through food, then ask them to work out a rule.

a) Sounds with 'c'

You may like to mention the following rhyme which emphasises the simple rule. Say it aloud and write it on the board. First explain the meaning of *acca*.

Ca, cu, co   l'acca no.
Che, chi   l'acca sì.

Soft and hard 'c'

1 Ask students to draw four columns, one for each of these sounds:

chi   *ci*   *che*   *ce*

2 Read aloud a list of words and ask them to tick the right columns for the sound they hear. On a second reading, students should attempt to write out the whole word. Most of the words will be entirely new. Elicit their meanings. *Come si dice in inglese?* or *Che cosa vuol dire . . . in inglese?*

3 If the students do not know any of the meanings, make them guess but, if necessary, write the meanings in a different order and ask them to match the Italian word to its English equivalent. Here is a list of examples:

città	*chiesa*	*radicchio*
lenticchie	*spinaci*	*perché*
salsiccia	*cipolla*	*anche*
cibo	*finocchio*	*cena*

4 To check answers, call a *volontario* to the board.

b) Sounds with 'g'

Repeat the same exercise for the sounds:

ghi   *gi*   *ghe*   *ge*

buongiorno	*giardino*	*gentile*
lunghezza	*gelato*	*funghi*
fagioli	*ghetto*	*formaggio*
fagiano	*spaghetti*	*ghiaccio*

Check answers and discuss any questions raised.

c) Sounds with 'gli'

1 Ask students to draw two columns, for these sounds:

li   *gli*

2 Read the following and ask students to write them down in the two columns:

paglia, milione, voglia, moglie, militante, olio, imbrogliare, lieto, imbroglione

3 Check answers and discuss any questions raised.

d) **Sounds with 'bu' + vowel and 'gu' + vowel**
Some students may like a challenge. Go over the
pronunciation of the above sounds, then ask them to
write down the following words: *giusto, chiuso, buio, chiaro,
grigio* – or any other words which contain such sounds.

e) **Sounds with 'w'**
The sign 'W' is often associated with the expression 'long
live . . .' and it is pronounced *viva* at the top of your voice:
e.g. *Viva gli sposi!!!*

f) **The sound 'z'**
Read, and ask students to read, the words in the book.
Add a few more:
zaino, marzo, zucchero, pazzo, pozzo, marziano, stazione

g) **The 'f' sound**
Read, and ask students to read, the words in the book.
Add a few more:
fisico, morfina, fosfato

Uffa! is used to show annoyance. Try to use it in context
at the first opportunity with the appropriate facial
expression.

The alphabet
Make students aware of the importance of linking each
letter of the alphabet with the name of a town (e.g. when
spelling surnames on the phone).

d) Sounds with 'bu' + vowel and 'gu' + vowel

Words with this spelling correspond to an English *bw* and *gw* sound:

buongiorno **buo**no *(good)* **gui**da *(guide)* **gua**nti *(gloves)* li**ngua** *(language, tongue)*

e) Sounds with 'w'

The letter *w* is not strictly speaking part of the Italian alphabet – along with *j k x* and *y*. These letters are found nowadays in words of foreign origin. *W* is pronounced like *v*, so that the *W* in **W**alter is pronounced like the *V* in **V**alentino. See also:

water *(toilet)* **w**altzer *(waltz)*

But the words *weekend* and *whisky*, also used in Italian, are pronounced with the English *w* sound.

f) The 'z' sound

Z can be pronounced in two ways, *tz* or *dz*:
zz tends to have the *tz* sound:

Ma**zz**otti pi**zz**a pia**zz**a mo**zz**arella indiri**zz**o *(address)* raga**zz**o/a *(boy/girl)*

But a single **z** can also be pronounced *tz*:

Gra**z**ie stan**z**a *(room)* pran**z**o *(lunch)* Ti**z**iano *(Titian)* La**z**io *[region]* Sco**z**ia *(Scotland)*

Words with the **dz** sound include:

gorgon**z**ola **z**an**z**ara *(mosquito)* **z**ucchine *(courgettes)*

Words beginning with **z** tend to have the *dz* sound.

g) The 'f' sound

In Italian there is no equivalent of the English *ph* sound, hence the spelling of words like:

Ra**ff**aello *(Raphael)* **f**otogra**f**ia *(photograph)* tele**f**ono *(telephone)*

vii) The alphabet ⌷ ◉ 14

To pronounce this properly, listen to it on the cassette/CD and practise saying it out loud.

A	B	C	D	E	F	G	H	I	L
a	bi	ci	di	e	effe	gi	acca	i	elle

M	N	O	P	Q	R	S	T	U	V	Z
emme	enne	o	pi	cu	erre	esse	ti	u	vu	zeta

The 'missing' letters of the Italian alphabet are: J, known as **i lunga**; K – **cappa**; W – **doppio vu**; X – **eex**; Y – **ipsilon**. They exist in foreign words adopted in Italian: **jazz, karatè, whisky, yoga**.

The vowels are pronounced approximately as follows:

a as in *car* **e** as in *bed* **i** as in *bead* **o** as in *got* **u** as in *souvenir*

e and **o** can vary depending on spelling and regional accents.

Practice I

Cioccolato d'Autore dal 1826

3

L'AMARO DI ERBE MEDICINALI
CHE IN PIU' AIUTA IL FEGATO.

1

2

SCAVOLINI
La cucina più amata dagli italiani

4

5

Caffè Segafredo Zanetti. Calore di casa.

What's on offer?

Can you pronounce the words in these adverts?
Think about the **c**, the **g, gli, z** and **buo** sounds.

1 Amaro medicinale Giuliani. L'Amaro di erbe
   medicinali che in più aiuta il fegato.
2 Select. Fagioli borlotti. I buoni legumi.
3 Caffarel. Cioccolato d'Autore dal 1826.
4 Scavolini. La cucina più amata dagli italiani.
5 Segafredo Zanetti. Tradizione rossa. Caffè
   Segafredo Zanetti. Calore di casa.

Odd one out   8

Below are four sets of words. Practise reading each
word aloud. Can you find the odd one out each
time?

1 chianti   cinzano   cin cin   vodka
2 Lamborghini   Lancia   Olivetti   Ferrari
3 Tiziano   vermicelli   Botticelli   Caravaggio
4 gorgonzola   dolcelatte   dolcevita   mozzarella

Practice 1

1 Make enough copies of the alphabet and distribute it to the students.

2 Dictate a few words students already know, letter by letter, and ask them to read them back to you.

3 Tell them to practise in pairs the Italian spelling of their surnames.

A	(a)	come	Ancona
B	(bi)	,,	Bologna
C	(ci)	,,	Como
D	(di)	,,	Domodossola
E	(e)	,,	Empoli
F	(effe)	,,	Firenze
G	(gi)	,,	Genova
H	(acca)	,,	hotel
I	(i)	,,	Imola
L	(elle)	,,	Livorno
M	(emme)	,,	Milano
N	(enne)	,,	Napoli
O	(o)	,,	Otranto
P	(pi)	,,	Padova
Q	(qu)	,,	Quarto
R	(erre)	,,	Roma
S	(esse)	,,	Savona
T	(ti)	,,	Torino
U	(u)	,,	Udine
V	(vi)	,,	Venezia
Z	(zeta)	,,	Zara

J (*i lunga*)   K (*kappa*)   W (*doppia vu*)   X (*ics*)
Y (*ipsilon* or *i greco*)

Battaglia navale

Aim: to practise the alphabet and numbers from one to twenty-one

1 Give students one copy each of the following grid.

	1	2	3	4	5	6	7	8	9	10	11	12	13	14	15	16	17	18	19	20	21
A																					
B																					
C																					
D																					
E																					
F																					
G																					
H																					
I																					
L																					
M																					
N																					
O																					
P																					
Q																					
R																					
S																					
T																					
U																					
V																					
Z																					

2 Draw on the board objects in everyday use: e.g. *una tazza, una radio, un PC, uno spazzolino da denti, una penna, una banconota,* etc.

3 Divide the students into pairs and tell them to draw the objects anywhere in the grid (give them the exact number of squares needed for each object). Alternatively they could write the word itself in the grid – one letter in each box. Tell them to be careful not to disclose the position of the objects to one another.

4 The students, in turn, should call out a number and a letter, trying to guess the position of the objects in the grid.

5 Tell them to say *Non c'è niente* when their partner draws a blank, and *Hai trovato il/la . . .* when they find an object.

To make this exercise brisk and lively, tell students that they only need to find where the objects are. If they were to define the exact position of each object it could take a whole lesson, much as they would like to carry on playing.

Countdown

1 Students count from 1 to 20 at your prompting (for each number point to any student at random).

2 Follow the same procedure to count from 20 down to 1.

3 Play a game of bingo with students, and, if time, allow them to play in small groups.

This point could be the end of the lesson. Briefly discuss the points covered so far and give students a preview of what is to come.

In the next lesson you will be teaching how to order food and drink, how to ask a question and how to make a simple statement.

> **Structures:** demonstrative pronoun *questo/essere* agreement/prepositions *in, a*
> **Functions:** asking questions/making simple statements, ordering food and drink
> **Vocabulary:** names of towns and regions/*monumento, Trulli, Colosseo, cartoline, famoso*/words linked to drinks and ice-cream flavours

Places

Look at the map. Fill in the names of the three countries you've come across so far in Patterns. What's missing? Unscramble the word below to find out.

D R A I N A L

Nationalities

Now say which of the four countries you come from, using **sono** and one of these nationalities:

scozzese, irlandese, inglese, gallese.

If none of these apply to you, look up Ref. III, 5, pp. 242–3, for more examples.

Spot the city

Here are some people and things associated with five famous Italian cities. Can you name them in Italian?

1 Il papa Michelangelo il Colosseo
2 I Medici Botticelli il Ponte Vecchio
3 Caravaggio Maradona la pizza
4 Il Doge Tiziano la gondola
5 Juventus Fiat *La Stampa*

Hello or goodbye?   8

Listen to the people on the cassette/CD. Are they saying hello or goodbye? Remember to listen for the intonation. Tick your answer on the chart.

	Hello	Goodbye
1 Buongiorno		
2 Buongiorno		
3 Ciao		
4 Ciao		
5 Arrivederci		

Buying breakfast   8

Now test yourself and do some talking. See if you can ask for what you want, not forgetting the words for please and thank you. It's early morning. You go to a **pasticceria** – a cake shop – to buy a cake, that's **una pasta**.

You	[Say, 'Hello'.]
Commessa	Buongiorno. Desidera?
You	[Say, 'A cake please'.]
Commessa	Sì. Va bene questa?
You	[Say, 'Yes'.]
Commessa	Ecco la pasta, mille lire.
You	[Repeat the price to check you've understood and say, 'Thank you, goodbye'.]

Numbers   8

Look over the numbers in Patterns, p. 5. Now listen to the bank-clerk counting her banknotes in Italian. Then answer these questions aloud and repeat the numbers:

1 How many wheels on a car?
2 How many fingers on a hand?
3 How many days in a week?
4 How many legs has a spider got?
5 How many lives does a cat have?
Now for some Biblical clues:
6 How many Wise Men were there?
7 How many Commandments are there?

Phone numbers   8

You have to give someone your phone number in Italian so you practise it in advance. Write it down and say it aloud in single digits (n.b. 0 = zero).

Ordering Drinks   8

There's a group of you in a bar. Can you order the drinks? It's early evening.

You	[Say, 'Good evening'.]
Cameriere	Buonasera.
You	[Say, 'A coffee and three beers, please'.]
Cameriere	Sì, subito.

[You've forgotten to order two cappuccinos. Wait until the waiter comes back . . .]

Cameriere	Ecco il caffè e le birre.
You	[Say, 'Thank you, two cappuccinos, please'.]
Cameriere	Subito.

Cultura e parole

The Italian language – **la lingua italiana** – is fascinating in its diversity. It has existed for centuries as a standard written language, but was only actually spoken by a minority until the advent of television and the spread of mass education in the 1950s. By then about 34 per cent of Italians spoke Italian as opposed to dialect – an improvement on the situation since unification, when it is estimated that the figure was a mere 2.5 per cent. Indeed neither Italy's new king, Victor Emmanuel II, nor her first Prime Minister, Count Camillo Cavour, were fully at ease in Italian: they preferred French or Piemontese. Nowadays standard Italian is of course dominant in all official situations and in education, yet Italian dialects – **i dialetti** – have not died out, though they are spoken mostly at home and among friends, and more in the provinces and the countryside than in the cities. Many of the dialects are extremely different from each other – Friulian and Sardinian are so different from standard Italian that some people class them as separate languages. Apart from the dialect-speaking Italians, most of whom are bilingual, there are linguistic minorities – **minoranze linguistiche** – who speak different languages, for example German in the Alto Adige region and French in the Val d'Aosta region.

But whether Italians speak dialect or not, the way they speak Italian – their accent and sometimes the words they use – is affected by where they come from. In Italy region rather than class determines how you speak: there is simply no equivalent of the Queen's English. Although there is virtually no such thing as a neutral Italian, free of all regional influences, Italians themselves tend to recommend the Italian spoken in central Italy as being the closest thing to a standard model and this is what foreign learners are generally taught.

To give some idea of the regional diversity of spoken Italian here's how some common words and expressions change:

now   adesso (North)   ora (Centre)   mo' (South)

I know your cousin   Conosco tuo cugino (North and Centre)
Conosco a tuo cugino (South)

I have a car   Ho una macchina (North and Centre)
Tengo una macchina (South)

Mi contenti
Ta la sera ruda di Sàbida
mi contenti di jodi la int,
fôr di ciasa ch'a rit ta l'aria

Encia il me côr al è di aria
e tai me vuj a rit la int
e tai me ris a è lus di Sàbida . . .

Mi accontento.
Nella nuda
sera del Sabato / mi
accontento di guardare la
gente / che ride fuori di
casa nell'aria . . .
Anche il
mio cuore è di aria / e nei
miei occhi ride la gente / e
nei miei ricci è la luce del
Sabato . . .

Part of a poem by Pier Paolo Pasolini in Friulian with an Italian translation

Cultura e parole

For centuries the British and the Italians have been attracted and influenced by each other's culture. Italian artists have come to Britain to work and British writers and poets have been drawn to Italy since the Renaissance. Italian was the language of educated young ladies and Italy was the destination of young gentlemen completing The Grand Tour, which was considered an integral part of a gentleman's education.

Il turismo di massa, on the other hand, which began only relatively recently, has brought many more people into contact with Italy. With the rapid increase in commercial and cultural ties, more people than ever now need to understand Italian and Italy's culture.

Discuss and stimulate interest in the language. Why are the students learning it? Which Italian words do they know? Why are there Italian words in the English language (old ones like *stiletto* and more recent culinary ones such as *pizza* and *pesto*)? Again, ask students to list as many as possible. Is Italian older than English? Who learned it in the past? And what for? Talk about the diversity of Italian. If Italian is your mother tongue, or if you have a particular accent, tell students which part or region of Italy it is from. Say a few words of dialect and tell students how these words might change from one village to the other. Have fun with the use of *doppie* – double consonants: nowhere to be found in Venetian, but practically everywhere in Sardinian dialect. Talk about the development of standard Italian in the last half-century. *La tutela delle minoranze linguistiche* is an article of the constitution.

Interactions

Interaction 7 (288)

1 Show students a large map of Italy and mention a few names of cities and regions. Talk about its geographical shape – *a forma di stivale,* and of the almost natural divisions, by pointing out the various areas: *Italia settentrionale, centrale, meridionale e insulare.*

2 *Chiudete il libro.*
Ask students to listen for place names. Ask them to spot the Italian word for cathedral.

3 *Ascoltate.* Play the cassette/CD as required.

4 *Leggete sul libro.*

5 Discuss any other questions which may arise.

Interaction 8 (306)

Anna talks about two famous sights in Rome.
1 *Chiudete il libro.*
How can they tell Anna is asking a question and not making a statement?

2 *Ascoltate.* Play the cassette/CD as required.

3 Varying the intonation, ask students to tell you if you are asking a question or making a statement.
Questo è un libro./? Questa è una finestra./?
Questa è (name of female student)*./? È un registratore./? Questa è una camicia./? È una penna./?*

Interaction 9 (318)

1 Anna is in a shop. Apart from asking for some postcards, what else does she ask and what's the answer?

2 *Chiudete il libro e ascoltate.* Play the cassette/CD as required.

3 Write each line of Interaction 9 on the board in the wrong order.

4 Ask students to put the lines in the right order.

5 *Leggete sul libro.*

Role play

Students can use Interaction 9 as a basis for role play. Discuss with them which items could be changed, for example, names of places. Encourage them to include names of monuments, e.g. *il duomo di Firenze,* and to write a similar dialogue themselves and to practise it in pairs, with the aim of saying it without their 'script'. When they are confident, ask selected pairs to perform in front of the class.

Interactions

7 ▭ ◎ 9

In the Italia in Miniatura park, Anna gets a preview of some of the places she'll be visiting in the series.

First time round

> i Trulli   *ancient conical houses*

Before listening, study the map of the regions on p. ix. Now listen without the text.

How many towns and regions can you spot?

È un monumento famoso. È il duomo di Firenze.
Questi sono i Trulli di Alberobello **in Puglia**.
Questo è un villaggio alpino.
Qui siamo **a Bologna in Emilia Romagna**.

qui   *here*

> ### Key phrases
> | | |
> |---|---|
> | **è** | *it is* |
> | **questi sono** | *these are* |
> | **questo è** | *this is* |
> | **in Puglia,** | *in Puglia,* |
> | **Emilia Romagna** | *Emilia Romagna* |
> | **a Bologna** | *in Bologna* |

8 ▭ ◎ 10

In L'Italia in Miniatura Anna spots two of the sights you can see in Rome.

First time round

How can you tell Anna is asking questions and not making statements?

È la basilica di San Pietro**?**
È il Colosseo**?**

> ### Key phrase
> | | |
> |---|---|
> | **è . . .?** | *is it . . .?* |

9 ▭ ◎ 11

Anna goes to buy some postcards of Portofino: she ends up with pictures of the neighbouring village, San Fruttuoso.

First time round

> le cartoline   *postcards*

Apart from asking for the postcards, what else does Anna ask?

Anna	Buongiorno.
Signora	Buongiorno.
Anna	Queste cartoline . . .
Signora	**Sì**, va bene.
Anna	**Questo è** Portofino? *[she points to a postcard]*
Signora	**No, questo non è** Portofino, è San Fruttuoso.

va bene   *fine*

> ### Key phrases
> | | |
> |---|---|
> | **sì** | *yes* |
> | **questo è . . .?** | *is this . . .?* |
> | **no, questo non è** | *no, it isn't* |

10 ⌷c̄c̄⌷ ◎ 12

Anna chooses an ice-cream in a **gelateria** – an ice-cream shop.

First time round

un gelato	*ice-cream*
il cono	*cone*
cocco	*coconut*

What flavours does Anna choose?

Giovane	**Buonasera.**
Anna	Buonasera. Un gelato, per favore.
Giovane	Sì – il cono?
Anna	Sì, grazie. E, questo è cioccolato?
Giovane	*[pointing to another container]*. No, questo è cioccolato e questo è cioccolato bianco.
Anna	Ah, allora, cioccolato e cocco.
Giovane	Sì.
Anna	Grazie. **Buonasera**.
Giovane	Buonasera.

allora   *then*

Key phrase

buonasera (1) *good afternoon*
         (2) *goodbye*

II ⌷c̄c̄⌷ ◎ 13

Finally, a few more orders. The scene is a bar in Florence.

First time round

un'aranciata	*orangeade*

a What does the waiter say when he brings the drinks?
b What does Anna order?

Cameriere	Buongiorno.
Anna	Un cappuccino, per favore.
[. . . the waiter returns]	
	Grazie.
Cameriere	**Prego**.
[. . .]	
Anna	Un caffè, per favore.
Anna	Un' aranciata, per favore.

Key phrase

prego *don't mention it*

Interaction 10 (327)

1 *Anna è in una gelateria per comprare un gelato.*

2 *Chiudete il libro. Ascoltate.* Play the cassette/CD as required.

3 Write on the board several words relating to food (some of them ice-cream flavours)

e.g. *limone, origano, fragola, lievito, vaniglia, pistacchio, salvia, peperoncino*

4 Ask students to guess which are not ice-cream flavours.

5 Ask students to invent delicious or unusual combinations of two flavours of ice-cream and to ask you for them.

Interaction 11 (340)

1 Anna is in a bar.
What does the waiter say when he brings the drinks?
What does Anna order?

2 *Chiudete il libro. Ascoltate.* Play the cassette/CD as required.

3 Check answers.

4 Play the cassette/CD again. *Leggete sul libro.* Play the cassette/CD as required.

5 Discuss the usage of *prego* or any other questions which may arise.

Patterns 2

This is a . . ., these are

1   Bring to class a map of the town in which you live and, if you can, photographs of some local tourist attractions.

2   Tell students to imagine they are taking some Italian friends around town. Give them the map of the town and ask the students to tell their friends about the things they see on the way. They will need to say:

  Questa è la . . .   *Questo è il . . .*
     una . . .   *un . . .*
  Qui siamo in . . .la . . .

3   Show students pictures of different objects and say, for example:
Questo è un quadro.
Questa è la Torre di Pisa.
Questi sono gioielli famosi.

Give the pictures to the students and ask them to repeat/carry on. Use the pictures in the book.

4   Hold up a picture but have it facing you so that it can't be seen by the students. Make a statement, e.g.:
Questa è la Torre di Pisa. They have to guess *sì* or *no*.

It is a . . ., they are (the)

Carry on showing pictures but add more information. For example:

Questo è un quadro famoso. È un quadro di Raffaello.
Questa è la Torre di Pisa. La Torre di Pisa è pendente.
Questi sono gioielli famosi. Sono i gioielli della Regina.
Give the pictures to the students and ask them to continue.

5   Divide the class into two teams. Divide pictures equally between the teams. One team holds up a picture and states what it is. The other team can score a point if they can give additional information about the picture, and so on.

Amburgo è una città tedesca

Aim: to practise *un, una, è* and adjectives of nationality

1   Write *Amburgo è una città tedesca* on the board.

2   Discuss the meaning.

3   Write the word *Chianti* and ask students to write similar sentences about it,
e.g. *Il Chianti è un vino italiano.*

4   With the help of the dictionary, or with your help if you do this in class, ask students to write down a few more sentences based on the following suggestions:

Paella   Giuseppe Verdi   Edimburgo
Trafalgar Square Cadillac   Mercedes
Porto   Gucci   Bobby Charlton

5   When checking answers for this exercise, you can also practise asking questions, by saying, for example:
Gucci è un designer italiano o francese?

Asking and answering questions

Carry on showing the pictures but this time hold them in front of you so that only the students can see them. Make a point of showing the students that you cannot see the picture and that you are relying on their answers to tell you what it is they see. Ask the question:
Questa è la Torre di Pisa?
Questa è la Torre Eiffel?
Give the pictures to the students and ask them to carry on.

Saying where you are

1   Write the following examples on the board:

Le Piramidi sono in Egitto.
La Torre Eiffel è a Parigi, in Francia.

2   Remind students that they should say:
A Parigi, a Londra, a Pekino but
in Francia, in Inghilterra, in Cina

3   Ask students where these famous buildings or monuments are:

La Fontana di Trevi   La Statua della Libertà
Il Cremlino   Big Ben
Il Colosseo   La Scala
La Torre di Pisa   Il Tempio del Paradiso
La Sfinge   Le Cascate del Niagara

4   Tell them to work in two groups, then compare their answers. The groups can take turns to ask questions and give the answers orally.

This point could be the end of the lesson. In the next lesson you will be teaching the last of the sound-systems. The students will have ample opportunity to practise ordering drinks, making simple statements and asking questions.

Structures: Sound-systems (*gn, qu, du, sci, sce,* double consonant)/word stress
Functions: identifying objects and describing their position
Vocabulary: general vocabulary/Italian artists and film directors/Italian cities/*a sinistra – a destra/in basso – in alto/al centro*

Patterns 2

i) This is a ..., these are ...

The key word is **questo**, and the key verb **essere** *(to be)* [Systems, note 7, p. 80].

quest**o** è	**un** monument**o** famos**o**	*this is*	*a famous monument*
	un quadr**o** famos**o**		*a famous picture*
quest**a** è	**una** chies**a** famos**a**	*this is*	*a famous church*
	una cappell**a** famos**a**		*a famous chapel*
quest**i** sono monument**i** famos**i**		*these are*	*famous monuments*
quest**e** sono chies**e** famos**e**			*famous churches*

See Systems, notes 5 and 6, pp. 79 and 80 for the changes in the endings of the words.

ii) It is a ..., they are (the) ...

There is no word used for *it* or *they*: the verb is sufficient. [See Systems, notes 3 and 4, p. 79 for **un, una; il, i, la, le**]

È un disegno meraviglioso	*It's a marvellous drawing*
È il capolavoro di Leonardo da Vinci	*It's Leonardo da Vinci's masterpiece*
Sono cappelle meravigliose	*They are marvellous chapels*
Sono le Cappelle Medicee	*They are the Medici Chapels*

iii) Asking and answering questions

When you ask a question the word order doesn't change, but the intonation often does. Practise your intonation with these examples:

Questo è il treno per Napoli?	*Is this the train for Naples?*
Sì, è il treno per Napoli	*Yes, it's the train for Naples*
No, non è il treno per Napoli	*No, it's not the train for Naples*
Questa è la strada per Firenze?	*Is this the road for Florence?*
No, non è la strada per Firenze	*No, it's not the road for Florence*

iv) Saying where you are

The key words are **in** and **a**: **a** is for towns, **in** for countries and regions. The other expressions are best learned gradually.

Sono/siamo a	Bologna	*I am, we are in*	*Bologna*
	casa	*at*	*home*
	scuola		*school*
Sono/siamo in	Italia	*I am/we are in*	*Italy*
	Inghilterra		*England*
	biblioteca		*the library*
	bagno		*the bathroom*
	cucina		*the kitchen*
	giardino		*the garden*
	piscina	*at*	*the swimming-pool*

See Systems, note 8 ii, p. 80.

Patterns 2

v) Sound-systems

a) The -gn- sound
This is pronounced like the beginning of the word 'new' in English. It's a familiar sound if you are in the habit of eating lasa**gn**e!

> Bolo**gn**a   Emilia Roma**gn**a   Gran Breta**gn**a (*Great Britain*)
> si**gn**ore *(Mr/man)*   si**gn**ora *(Mrs/lady)*   si**gn**orina *(Miss/young lady)*
> Mante**gn**a   monta**gn**a *(mountain)*   ba**gn**o *(bathroom)*

b) 'qu' + vowel, 'du' + vowel
As with **bu** and **gu** + vowels, you make a *w* sound – *kw* and *dw*:

> **qu**esto *(this)*   **qu**adro *(picture)*   **qu**i *(here)*   **du**omo *(cathedral)*

The same applies to most words where **u** + another vowel follow a consonant:
> s**cu**ola *(school)*   f**uo**co *(fire)*   l**uo**go *(place)*   n**uo**vo *(new)*   s**uo**no *(sound)*   v**uo**to *(empty)*

c) 'Sci', 'sce': the -sh- sound
This is easy to pronounce, but confusing on paper.

> pros**ci**utto *(ham)*   pi**sci**na *(swimming-pool)*   **sci**arpa *(scarf)*   cu**sci**no *(cushion)*
> pe**sce** *(fish)*   **sce**lta *(choice)*   **sce**na *(scene)*

Beware: **schi** and **sche** are hard *sk* sounds:

> **sche**rzo *(joke)*   **sche**letro *(skeleton)*   **schi**fo *(disgust)*   ri**schi**o *(risk)*   **schi**ena *(back)*

d) Double consonants
In Italian double consonants should be stressed more than single consonants, which is not always easy for foreigners. Sometimes, though, the difference is easy to make clear:

> ro**ss**a *(red)*   rosa *(pink)*   ca**ss**a *(till)*   casa *(house)*

The single **s** in the middle of words is pronounced like an English *z*. But with other double consonants it's less straightforward. The important thing is to listen and you'll get the hang of it. A double consonant means the vowel sound is shorter and more open than with single consonants.

> pros**ci**u**tt**o *(ham)*   conos**ci**uto *(well-known)*   se**rr**a *(greenhouse)*   sera *(evening)*
> se**tt**e *(seven)*   sete *(thirst)*   so**nn**o *(sleep)*   sono *(I am)*

vi) Stress patterns

In most words the stress occurs on the last vowel but one. But many common words are exceptions:

> telefono   camera   numero   macchina

The stress falls on the end of a word where there is an accent: città *(town)*   nazionalità *(nationality)*
If a word ends in two vowels the stress pattern varies:

> Lucia   Lombardia   Lucio   Liguria

You'll find irregular or difficult stress patterns marked in the vocabularies at the end of the units and in the Lexis at the back of the book.

Patterns 2

Sound-systems

The –gn– sound

1 Ask students to draw two columns for these sounds:

gn   *n*

2 Read the following and ask students to write them down in the two columns:

ogni, niente, ragno, Agnese, linea, legna, genio, sogno, Regno Unito, signore

3 Check answers and discuss any questions raised.

'qu' + vowel, 'du' + vowel

1 Ask students to draw two columns for these sounds:

qu   *cu*

2 Read the following and ask students to write them down in the two columns:

qui, curioso, quarzo, cubo, scuro, questura, cucire, quattro, quanto, cucina

3 Ask students to work out the rule.

'Sce': the –sch sound

1 Remind students of the rules for pronouncing 'sci' and 'sce', and 'schi' and 'sche'.
2 Write all the following words on the board. Point to them at random and ask students to pronounce them.
3 Write one of the words on a piece of paper and ask students to guess which one you have written.

sciocco   scimmia   piscina   scialle   sciacallo
scherma   mosca   mischia   schiavo   schietto

Double consonants
bocca   braccio   orecchio   ginocchio   capelli

Stress patterns

1 Ask students to repeat these words after you.
2 Next write the written forms on the board.
3 Add further words with double consonants and ask students to pronounce them.
Tell students that it is worth making an effort from the start to get the right stress.

Practice 2

Al bar

Students will be pleased to know that there isn't anything else they should learn about spelling: they just need practice. Ask them to think of all the things they can ask for in a bar. Give them a few minutes to write down what they wish to order and then tell them to compare what they have written with the person sitting next to them. Allow a few more minutes. This time tell them to discuss their suggestions in a bigger group and so on until the whole class is divided into just two groups. Ask each group in turn to tell you what they have written (an order cannot be repeated) and try to engage the two groups in a sort of lively competition. (You could perhaps give a score for each item on the spur of the moment and write it on the board, making comments: *'Un bicchiere di vino bianco. . . . Bene, benissimo, magnifico, eccellente. Ecco quattro punti.'*)

Take the opportunity to discuss all possible combinations of milk and coffee:

cappuccino   caffè   caffelatte
caffè macchiato   caffè corretto   latte macchiato

The image makers

Aim: to practise double consonants and sound systems

Use the names of the following famous Italian film directors omitting the double consonants (which you write separately). Ask students to write the double consonants in the right spaces.

```
BERTOLU__I     LL  CC  SS  LL  LL  FF
RO__E__INI
ZE__IRE__I
FE__INI
```

Geography test

Ask students to think of half a dozen names of cities and say which region they are in by looking at a map.
e.g. *Milano è in Lombardia.*
(You can tell the students to think of the cities used for spelling out alphabet letters.)

Giorgio è in ... a ...

1   Remind students to say: *in Italia, in Puglia – a Bari, a Genova*

2   Ask them to say where five of their Italian friends are **(remind students that practice has nothing to do with telling the truth).**

The box
Aim: identifying objects/vocabulary building

1   Bring a shoe box into the classroom.

2   Divide the students into two or four groups and tell them to gather together a few objects which are available in the classroom and which will fit into the box.

3   Go round each group making sure they know the Italian word for each object they are going to put in the box.

4   Each group, in turn, puts things in the box.

5   After each turn, take the box to another group who will take out all the items they know the name of.
e.g. *Questo è un orologio. Questa è una matita.*

6   The game is won by the team which has taken most objects out of the box.

The tray
Aim: to describe the position of objects/vocabulary building

1   Write the following on the board and discuss their meanings with the students: *a sinistra, a destra, in alto, in basso, in centro.*

2   Choose six small objects, show them to the students and put them on a tray in six different positions. Now describe their positions.

La gomma è in alto a destra.
Le chiavi sono in basso a sinistra.
La cassetta è in centro a destra.
Le caramelle sono in alto a sinistra.
La carta telefonica è in basso a destra.
Il rossetto è in centro a sinistra.

3   Change the positions of the objects and cover up the tray. Describe their positions to students, who have to draw the objects in the right position in a box.

My favourite dish
Aim: vocabulary building

1   Give student A a piece of paper on which he/she has to write his/her favourite dish next to his/her name.

2   Fold the paper so as to conceal what has been written and pass it on to the next student.

3   Let the piece of paper go round the class.

4   Tell students to think of the ingredients of their favourite dish and to look them up in the dictionary for homework.

5   Next lesson, ask student A to list the ingredients while the others guess his/her favourite dish.

Practice 2

Regions

Look at the map of Italy on p. ix with the twenty regions marked. Try to pronounce them. Be careful with the ones ending in **–ia**. Only one has the stress on the final **–i** – Lombardia. Read them aloud.

Where?

Can you say where you are, using **in** or **a** as appropriate?
e.g. [giardino]   Sono in giardino.

1 [bagno] **2** [cucina] **3** [casa]
4 [biblioteca] **5** [scuola]

What's this?

Imagine you are teaching some new vocabulary to a child. You've come across all the words you need in this unit. You'll need to decide which form of **questo** to use.
e.g.   Questo è . . .
        Questa è una birra.

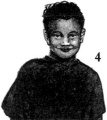

What are these?

Make the above sentences plural, using **questi** or **queste**.
Now practise saying these sentences as questions. Don't change anything except the intonation.

Buying an ice-cream   14

Listen to the cassette/CD and play your part in the conversation.

Whet your appetite!

Which Italian dish do you think you would prefer? Read through the ingredients given below. Try and pronounce each item and then make your choice. The Vocabulary on p. 15 will help, but you don't need to understand every word.

---

1   SPINACI AL PROSCIUTTO

per 4 persone

● *gr 800 spinaci* ● *gr 100 prosciutto crudo* ● *gr 30 burro* ● *aglio sale e pepe*

---

2   AGNELLO IN SALSA

per 6 persone

● *kg.1 agnello* ● *gr. 350 pomodori maturi* ● *aglio, prezzemolo, maggiorana* ● *vino bianco secco* ● *strutto sale e pepe*

What's in a name?

Here are the surnames of some well-known Italians:
   Marconi   Mussolini   Pavarotti   Ferrari

1 Here, in the wrong order, are their first names:
   Benito   Enzo   Guglielmo   Luciano
   Can you match them up with their surnames?
2 What do you associate each of them with?
   a) la lirica   b) la radio   c) la macchina   d) il fascismo
3 These people all have something in common. Do you happen to know what it is?

Identikit   14

Can you say who you are? Start with **Sono** . . .
Now give your nationality. **Sono** . . .
Next give your phone number . . .
Listen to the cassette/CD and the sounds of the Italian alphabet.
Now try to spell your surname.

Vocabulary

Food

il cibo	food
l'agnello	lamb
la bistecca	steak
il pollo	chicken
il prosciutto	ham
la salsiccia	sausage
il vitello	veal
il formaggio	cheese
la verdura	vegetables
l'aglio	garlic
il basilico	basil
la carota	carrot
la cipolla	onion
i fagiolini	green beans
il finocchio	fennel
i funghi	mushrooms
la patata	potato
il pomodoro	tomato
il prezzemolo	parsley
il radicchio	radicchio
le zucchine	courgettes
gli spinaci	spinach
i fagioli	dried beans
la frutta	fruit
la banana	banana
la mela	apple
la pera	pear
la pesca	peach
il gelato	ice-cream
la panna	cream

il finocchio

la cipolla

il radicchio

la cappella

Places

il luogo	place
il posto	place
la biblioteca	library
la cappella	chapel
la casa	house, home
la città	town, city
la chiesa	church
il duomo	cathedral
il giardino	garden
il parco	park
la piscina	swimming-pool
la scuola	school

Meals

il pasto	meal
la prima colazione	breakfast
il pranzo	lunch
la cena	supper, dinner

Drinks

la bevanda	drink
la birra	beer
analcolico	non-alcoholic
il caffè	coffee
il cappuccino	cappuccino
il tè	tea
il vino	wine

People

la persona	person
il bambino [m]	child, baby
la bambina [f]	child, baby

il cameriere	waiter
la commessa	shop assistant
la donna	woman
la signora	Mrs, lady
il figlio	son
la figlia	daughter
i figli	children
il giovane	young man
il ragazzo	boy
la ragazza	girl
l'uomo	man
gli uomini	men

Everyday objects

la borsa	bag
il libro	book
la macchina	car
la matita	pencil
la penna	pen
il portafoglio	wallet
il taccuino	notebook
il quaderno	exercise-book

Rooms

la stanza	room
il bagno	bathroom
la camera da letto	bedroom
la cucina	kitchen
la sala da pranzo	dining-room
il salotto	sitting-room

Adjectives

buono	good
bello	beautiful
meraviglioso	marvellous, wonderful
nuovo	new
vecchio	old
antico	old, ancient
fresco	fresh
lungo	long
stanco	tired
pronto	ready
caldo	hot
freddo	cold

Vocabulary

Guessing words

Encourage students to guess the meaning of words. This
task is even easier if you see the words in written form.
Give students some examples and draw attention to any
pronunciation or stress issues.

vegetariano	*eccetera*	*dizionario*	*disco*
cassetta	*telefono*	*università*	*cattedrale*
stazione	*sistema*	*economia*	*psicologia*
vocabolario	*aereoporto*	*monetario*	*timido*

Tell them that some words have the same spelling in Italian
as in English, but they are pronounced differently:

alibi	*idea*	*radio*	*veto*
video	*cinema*	*automobile*	*micro* (in compounds)

Written in the same way, but pronounced differently, are
some words and expressions which are used in much the
same way, for example:

status quo   *S.O.S.*   *blasé*   *routine*   *persona non grata*

Tell students to be careful of *falsi amici (in senso metaforico)*.
Some words might just be spelled in the same way (or
almost), but their meaning is sometimes very different,
e.g. *cantina, preservativo, educazione, parenti.*

Troubleshooting

If you have not asked the students to do any reading aloud, you can ask them to do it now with the *scioglilingua* and the three words in the boxes. Here is another *scioglilingua: Se non sarà sereno si rassererà.*

This point could be the end of the lesson. Give students a brief summary of the main points in the next lesson, which is set in a vineyard during the grape-picking season:

> a) there is/are, where is/are and what is/are, either as statements or in questions
> b) my, your, his/her
> c) saying your name and asking about others

Review

Here is a checklist of the main points learned in this unit. For each point, ask the students to provide you with one or more examples by asking specific questions.

> alphabet (including spelling with names of cities)
> numbers (1–21)
> all the sound systems
> asking questions and making statements
> ordering food and drink
> greetings
> introducing oneself
> identifying objects and describing their position
> asking for things

Troubleshooting

Culinary confusion

In most languages there are words with several meanings. In Italian this is especially true when it comes to food.

Don't confuse the following:

la pasta	*pasta/small cake*

il pasto	*meal*

Tongue-twisters  14

Try pronouncing the Italian word for *tongue-twister.*

Scioglilingua

Now try pronouncing this well-known Italian tongue-twister. It means, *'Thirty-three people from Trento entered Trento all thirty-three on the trot!'*

Trentatrè trentini entrarono dentro Trento tutti e trentatrè trotterellando.

Sound systems

Can you make the difference between *supper, scene* and *back* clear?

cena CH	scena SH	schiena SK

in famiglia e fra amici

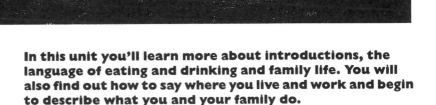

In this unit you'll learn more about introductions, the language of eating and drinking and family life. You will also find out how to say where you live and work and begin to describe what you and your family do.

One of Italy's foremost contemporary writers, Leonardo Sciascia, once said that Italy is not so much a nation, as a collection of families. There is truth in this remark: the family developed as the pivot of society after the Unification of Italy, partly in response to the imposition of the laws and monarchy of the alien Piemontese state upon the rest of the Italian peninsula. This historical mistrust of the state, and the reliance on the family, however, has not prevented radical changes in its structure. On average, Italian families are now very small, with only one or two children. Recent statistics show that the birth-rate in Campania, the region around Naples, is the highest in Italy, but even this is lower than the average birth-rate in Sweden. The second important change is in the legal position of women, inside and outside the home since the 1970s. The **Diritto di famiglia** of 1975 gave partners in a marriage equal economic and legal rights and swept away the longstanding patriarchal supremacy of the man. Divorce was legalised in 1978 and abortion in 1980. Nevertheless, this did not begin a stampede to the divorce courts: Italy's divorce rate is about a quarter of that in Britain. Although Italy is 90 per cent Catholic, remarriage is now increasingly frequent and is no longer frowned upon. Perhaps it is this ability to move with the times which has made the family so durable.

Unità 2

In famiglia e fra amici

The family structure of Italian society will provide many issues for discussion, for it is in the family that the most striking differences between British and Italian society are to be found. Consider the following points, which should give rise to debate in class.

Probably the most traditional, and yet accurate, snapshot of Italy as a family-centred society is one of the family around the table at mealtimes. But the family structure is also reflected in the areas of politics and economics. Public affairs are run on a family and loyalty basis and this naturally opens the way for nepotism and corruption. Public spirit counts for little: Italy has been a unified nation for only a relatively short time and the feeling of nationhood is not perceived in the same way as it is in Britain or in the US, for example. There is scant regard either for privacy (the word cannot be happily translated into Italian), or public goals.

The family is the pivot of society – the formal versus informal address in the language partly reflects this division in society between family and friends on one side and the rest of the community on the other. The position and strength of the family in society also partly explains the underdevelopment of welfare systems. The State often delegates its responsibility and relies on the strength of the family in areas such as care of the elderly. By the same token – to help new families develop – Italy has one of the best child care systems in Europe.

A large number of businesses are run on a family basis. Much of the wealth which is accumulated is shared amongst the family and this partly explains why Italians seem to have such a high standard of living compared to other Europeans.

Video corner

Spot the animal
Aim: vocabulary building
Video sequence: from the scene in the kitchen to the end of the parade in Marino

1 Write some names of animals on the board. Ask students to guess their meanings and help them when necessary.
2 Ask students to note which animals (*un cane e un cavallo*) appear in the video sequence.

Che tipo è?
Aim: vocabulary building on how to describe people
Although this activity is particularly appropriate for this unit you can of course repeat it at any other time
Video sequence: from the beginning until Anna speaks to Bruno Violo

1 Give descriptions of people and ask students to spot them in the video. Here are the descriptions of six people *in ordine di apparizione*. Write them on the board. Ask students to guess the meanings and help them if necessary.

Ha capelli biondi e lunghi. Ha circa 45 anni. (Valentina)
Ha capelli scuri e lunghi, ha occhi scuri, è di media statura e ha circa 25 anni. (Cristina)
Ha capelli scuri e ricci. È molto giovane. (Eleonora)
Ha occhiali ed è un po' calvo con capelli neri ai lati. Ha circa 50 anni. (Antonio)
Ha capelli neri e occhi scuri. È stempiato e ha gli occhiali. Ha circa 50 anni. (Umberto)
Ha capelli neri ma è stempiato. Porta occhiali e ha circa 50 anni. (Bruno)

2 Divide the class into two groups and ask each group to discuss and agree on their answers.

Unscramble the sequence
Aim: vocabulary building
Video sequence: Anna's interview with a boy and his teacher

1 Write each sentence of Interaction 5 on the board but not in the order in which they are spoken.
2 Play the video with the volume turned down and ask the students to put the sentences in the right order.
3 You could repeat this type of activity at any other suitable point.

Tu o Lei
Aim: to practise formal and informal forms of address
Video sequence: Anna interviews people over lunch

1 Play Interaction 4, where Anna is asking people what they eat or drink.
2 Make students aware of the importance of using the right verb endings, which change depending on whether formal or informal forms of address are used.
3 Turn the volume down and pause just before the question. Ask students to repeat what Anna asks each person.

Interactions

Structures: *c'è, dov'è, cos'è/mio, tuo, suo/potere +*
infinitive/reflexive verbs
Functions: checking a list of items/saying your name
and asking about others/saying what there is to do
Vocabulary: *bottiglie, pane, pasta, andare, tesoro,*
contents of a picnic basket, *moglie, sorella, lavoro,*
moltissimo, amica, chiamarsi

Help-phrases and instructions

Che cosa significa . . .?   *Leggete sul libro.*
La domanda è . . .   *Le domande sono . . .*
Qual è la risposta?   *Quali sono le risposte?*
Ci sono altre domande?   *Avete domande da fare?*

Interaction 1   (426)

1 *La vendemmia,* grape-picking and *produzione del vino,*
wine-making, are the themes of most of the Interactions
in this unit. In the first one three people are sorting out
food and drink to be taken on the picnic planned for
lunch: *Valentino, Valentina Muratori e Rossella preparano il*
cestino per il picnic. It isn't quite a ploughman's lunch . . .

2 *Chiudete il libro.*
What four items are being discussed?

3 *Ascoltate.* Play the cassette/CD as required. *Qual è la*
risposta?

4 Ask further questions:

Do they need anything else?
Che cosa vuol dire tesoro in inglese?

5 Play the cassette/CD again. *Quali sono le risposte?*

6 *Leggete sul libro. Ci sono altre domande?*

La lista del picnic
Aim: vocabulary building/discussion

1 Ask students to write down a few items for *una lista*
per il picnic. (Tell them to look at the vocabulary section
at the end of the unit.)

2 Give them a few minutes to write down the words,
then ask them to compare what they have written with
the person sitting next to them. Allow a few more minutes.

3 Ask one pair to tell you what they have written and
write it on the board. The others tick these words if they
already have them on their list. Then ask the class if anyone
has any words that aren't on the board, and write them
too. (If you have an OHP you can give each pair or group
of students a transparent sheet and a pen to write on it.
This will push the students a little harder because they
know they will have to show their work to the others.)

4 Go round the class giving suggestions and answering
questions while everyone is working at their own pace.

5 Collect the sheets and display them on the OHP, or
ask students to read aloud the words they have written.
Correct any mistakes with their help.

C'è bisogno di . . .
Aim: discussion/vocabulary building

1 Make sure the students have understood from the
Interaction the meaning of *c'è/ci sono* and *dov'è/dove sono.*
(Refer them to the Patterns section if necessary.)

2 Explain the meaning of *c'è bisogno di . . .* and of *è*
necessario portare . . . then ask students to make up dialogues
of this type:

C'è il vino?   *Sì, ecco il vino.*
Dove sono i biscotti?   *Ecco i biscotti.*
C'è bisogno di una tovaglia?   *Sì, (no, non) c'è bisogno di . . .*
È necessario portare un ombrello?   *Sì, (no, non) è necessario*
    portare . . .

3 Ask students to work in pairs or in small groups. (You
can follow the procedure for the previous exercise if you
have an OHP.)

Interactions

I 🄲 16

Valentino Muratori, a financial consultant by profession, owns a small vineyard in the Colli Albani hills, not far from Rome. At harvest time his family and friends turn their hands to the picking and get invited to a picnic lunch. In his villa Valentino sorts out the provisions with his wife, Valentina, and a friend, Rossella.

First time round

Pick out the four items of food and drink being discussed.

Valentino	Tesoro, **dove sono** le bottiglie di vino?
Valentina	Sono qui.
Valentino	E qui cosa c'è?
Valentina	**C'è** il pane.
Rossella	E la pasta, **dov'è**, Valentina?
Valentina	È qui. **Ecco** la pasta.
Valentino	**Cos'è questo?**
Rossella	È il caffè, Valentino.
Valentino	Allora, c'è tutto? Possiamo andare?
Valentina	Andiamo.

e qui cosa c'è?	and what's this here? (lit. here what is there?)
c'è tutto?	is that (there) everything?
possiamo andare?	can we go?
andiamo	let's go

Key phrases

dove sono?	where are?
c'è	there is
dov'è?	where is?
ecco	here is
cos'è questo?	what is this?

Dov'è, dove sono? 🄲 🄲 16

Listen to the cassette/CD and ask where certain things are.

2   🔲 🔘 17

Anna greets Valentino Muratori in the vineyard as the grape-picking gets under way.

First time round

molto lavoro	*a lot of work*
oggi	*today*
sua moglie	*your wife*

What two things does Anna want to know?

Anna	Buongiorno, signor Muratori.
Valentino	Buongiorno, Anna.
Anna	**C'è** molto lavoro oggi?
Valentino	Sì, moltissimo.
Anna	E sua moglie, dov'è?
Valentino	Mia moglie è là.

là   *over there*

Key phrase

c'è?   *is there?*

3   🔲 🔘 18

In the vineyard Anna meets some of the grape-pickers. She introduces herself and talks to four girls.

First time round

mia sorella	*my sister*
una mia amica	*a friend of mine*

a Can you spot how to say 'My name is'?
b Pick out their names.

Anna	Ciao!
Daniela	Ciao!
Anna	Io **mi chiamo** Anna. Tu, **come ti chiami?**
Daniela	Io mi chiamo Daniela.
Anna	E **lei, chi è?**
Daniela	Questa è mia sorella.
Anna	Ciao! Tu, come ti chiami?
Rosanna	Mi chiamo Rosanna.
Anna	Lei, **come si chiama?**
Cristina	Io mi chiamo Cristina e lei è Liana, una mia amica.
Liana	Piacere!

Key phrases

mi chiamo	*I'm called*
come ti chiami?	*what are you called?*
lei, chi è?	*who is she?*
come si chiama?	*what are you called? [formal 'Lei' form]*

Phone-in   🔲 🔘 19

Can you spot the names of the callers to a radio phone-in programme and also where they are ringing from?

Interaction 2 (465)

1 The *vendemmia* is under way. *Anna e Valentino Muratori sono nella vigna.*

2 *Chiudete il libro.*
What does Anna want to know from Valentino?

3 *Ascoltate.* Play the cassette/CD as required. *Qual è la risposta?*

4 *Leggete sul libro.*

5 *Avete domande da fare?*

Che cosa c'è da fare?
Aim: vocabulary building

1 Explain the meaning of *c'è qualcosa da fare, mangiare, bere*, etc.

2 Ask students to refer to the vocabulary at the end of the unit to work out the questions from the answers. For example:

....	*Sì, ci sono libri.*
C'è qualcosa da leggere?	*Sì, ci sono libri.*
....	*No, non c'è vino.*
....	*Sì, ci sono panini.*
....	*Sì, ci sono due lettere.*
....	*Sì, c'è un bellissimo castello.*
....	*Sì, ci sono nuove parole.*
....	*Sì, ci sono cassette di musica rock e classica.*
....	*No, non ci sono articoli interessanti.*
....	*Sì, c'è un film.*

3 To give students an idea of what is required, you could ask one or two questions and ask students to read out the correct answer from the list.

Interaction 3 (481)

1 *La vendemmia* is still under way. Anna meets some of the female grape-pickers – *incontra alcune vendemmiatrici.*

2 *Chiudete i libri.* What are the four girls called? (Tell students to try to write down the four names.)

3 *Ascoltate.* Play the cassette/CD as required. *Qual è la risposta?*

4 Ask further questions:
How do you say in Italian 'my name is', 'what is your name?'?

5 Play the cassette/CD again. *Quali sono le risposte?*

6 *Leggete sul libro. Ci sono altre domande?*

Family
Aim: practising *come si chiama?, mio/a, tuo/a* and more vocabulary building

1 Make sure students have understood the meanings of
mi chiamo   ti chiami   si chiama

2 Make sure students understand the meaning of *mio/a, tuo/a* with *fratello, sorella, padre, madre*, etc. Tell them the meaning of *in questo momento* and write on the board a few possible answers for questions you will ask: *a casa, in ufficio, al pub . . .*

3 Ask students at random:

Come si chiama tuo padre/fratello?
Come si chiama tua madre/sorella?

4 Tell students to give their relatives Italian names.

Mio padre/fratello si chiama ....
Mia madre/sorella si chiama ....

Then ask the same student:

Dov'è tuo padre/fratello in questo momento?
Dov'è tua madre/sorella in questo momento?

5 Tell them to answer:

In questo momento mio padre/fratello è ....
In questo momento mia madre/sorella è ....

Variation: Prepare two sets of cards, one of Italian people's names, the other of places. For example: *al cinema, in Canada, a Roma, in Giappone, in discoteca, in campagna, al polo nord.*

By showing the prompt cards you can get students to give less stereotyped answers, e.g. their grannies have gone discodancing. You can also make students practise more Italian names.

This point could be the end of the lesson. Revise points covered so far. In the next lesson students will revise how to say and ask someone's name, how to identify people and objects and learn to describe people.

> **Structures:** *avere*/agreement of adjectives and nouns/formal and informal address
> **Functions:** saying and asking someone's name/ identifying people and objects/learning to describe people
> **Vocabulary:** words which physically describe people

Patterns 1

Naming yourself and others

1   Ask student A *Come ti chiami?* Turn to student B: *Come ti chiami?* Turn to student C and ask him/her: *Come si chiama student B?* and so on.

2   Bring pictures of your family and friends and tell students their names.

Identifying people (and describing people)

1   Bring in photographs of famous people and ask students to say who they are and what they are. For example:

Chi è? Come si chiama?
È il Primo Ministro. Si chiama . . .
È un attore, regista, scrittore famoso. Si chiama . . .

2   Write answers on the board/OHP.

Family album

Aim: to introduce vocabulary used for describing people

1   Carry on showing your own pictures. Your students will be very interested to see and talk about people that have some relevance to you and it will make it easier for them to imagine what you are talking about, even if you speak entirely in Italian.

Questa è mia sorella. Mia sorella si chiama . . .

2   Describe her physical characteristics. Focus the students' attention on the colour of her hair, then the colour of her eyes: *I capelli di mia sorella sono castani. Gli occhi sono castani.*

3   As you proceed to describe more people, start writing on the board the following chart, employing a certain amount of gesticulation in order to be more effective. E.g.: point to your hair or your nose. Make comparisons between the different hair colours of the students.

capelli	occhi	uomo/donna	naso/bocca
biondi	neri	alto/a	grande
lunghi	castani	basso/a	aguzzo
neri	verdi	grasso/a	piccolo/a
corti	azzurri	magro/a	all'in su
castani	chiari	simpatico/a	
lisci		antipatico/a	
rossi			
ondulati			
ricci			

Other words used when describing people:
baffi, barba, occhiali/lenti a contatto, orecchini, neo, lentiggini

4   Ask students to bring in pictures of themselves when babies. Pin all the photos on a board and number them. Students write in Italian next to the numbers: number one is X, because he/she has black hair, a small nose, etc. etc., until all the photos have been discussed and their owners identified.

In treno

Aim: listening comprehension to revise the vocabulary of physical characteristics

1   Tell the students you are going to read a short piece about people on a train. Write the difficult words on the board (e.g. *sacco a pelo/zaino/valigetta*) and explain the meanings if necessary.

2   Copy the statements below on the board and tell students to imagine the situation before you start to read.

3   Read the short Italian passage below at least twice and then ask the students to say if the statements are true or false.

a) At the moment John is on a Naples-bound train.
b) There are many people aboard because it is a local train.
c) There are many Italian and foreign tourists on the train.
d) The two Venetian boys are carrying rucksacks and sleeping bags.
e) One is tall with brown hair and brown eyes.
f) The other one is short with black hair and dark eyes.
g) The child is travelling with the woman from Rome.
h) The Neapolitan gentleman has a big suitcase.
i) The man from Milan is middle-aged.
j) The girl from Turin has short curly hair.

John è un ragazzo inglese, di Liverpool. Adesso John è in Italia in treno per Napoli. C'è molta gente in treno perché è estate e molti sono in vacanza. Ci sono molti turisti, stranieri e italiani. Ci sono per esempio due ragazzi veneziani con zaini e sacchi a pelo. Uno è alto con capelli e occhi castani, l'altro è bassino con capelli rossi e occhi chiari. C'è una signora romana, e con la signora c'è un bambino. C'è un signore napoletano con i baffi e una valigetta piccola e vecchia. C'è anche un giovane signore milanese con capelli biondi e corti. Vicino al signore di Milano c'è una ragazza torinese con capelli castani e lisci. Infine c'è un'altra ragazza con capelli lunghi e neri.

4   Give students copies of the above. Discuss further questions.

Identifying objects

1   Bring in several pictures of different objects (adverts in colour magazines should provide you with ample variety and interest). Hold them up and say:

Questa è la figura numero uno. Che cosa è?

Elicit an answer and write the name on the board.

Patterns I

i) Naming yourself and others

To say *'My name is'* you use the verb **chiamarsi** *(to be called, lit. to call oneself)*.

[Io] mi chiamo ... Anna   *My name is Anna*

When you ask someone their name it's literally *'How do you call yourself?'* [**Come** means *how*].

[Tu,] come ti chiami?   *what's your name? [informal]*
[Lei,] come si chiama?   *what's your name? [formal]*
[Voi,] come vi chiamate?   *what's your name? [plural]*

If you've already introduced yourself you don't need to ask the full question to find out what someone else is called. **E tu? E Lei? E voi?** (lit. *and you?*) is sufficient.

Io mi chiamo	Anna, e tu?	*My name is*	*Anna, what about you?*
	Gianni, e Lei?		*Gianni, what about you?*
	Rosanna, e voi?		*Rosanna, what about you?*

See Systems, note 6 iii, p. 85 for **chiamarsi**.

ii) Identifying people

The key word is **chi?** *(who)*.

Chi è?	*Who is it?*	È	mio fratello/mia sorella	*It's*	*my brother/sister*
			mio cognato/mia cognata		*my brother-/sister-in-law*
			mio figlio/mia figlia		*my son/daughter*
			mio marito/mia moglie		*my husband/wife*
			mio padre/mia madre		*my father/mother*
			mio suocero/mia suocera		*my father-/mother-in-law*

See Systems, note 3, p. 84 for **mio, mia**.

| Chi è? | *Who is it?* | Sono io | *It's me* | Siamo noi | *It's us* |
| | | È lui, è lei | *It's him, her* | Sono loro | *It's them* |

iii) Identifying objects

The key phrase is **che cosa?** *(what?)*. This literally means *what thing?* **Cosa** is often used on its own, without **che**. In front of **è**, **cosa** becomes **che cos'è** and is pronounced as one word.

[Che] cos'è?	*What is it?*	È	un digestivo	*It's*	*an after-dinner drink*
			un dolce		*a dessert*
			una macedonia		*a fruit salad*
			un' insalata		*a salad*
[Che] cosa sono?	*What are they?*	Sono	digestivi	*They're*	*after-dinner drinks*
			dolci		*desserts*
			macedonie		*fruit salads*
			insalate		*salads*

20

Patterns I

iv) Asking and saying where things are

The key words are **dove?** *(where?)* and **ecco** *(here is, here are).*

In front of **è**, **dove** becomes **dov'è** and is pronounced as one word.

Dov'è	il libro?	*Where is*	*the book?*	Ecco il libro	*Here is the book*
	il giornale?		*the newspaper?*		
	la bottiglia?		*the bottle?*		
	la chiave?		*the key?*		
	l'aranciata?		*the orangeade?*		

Dove sono	i libri?	*Where are*	*the books*	Ecco i libri	*Here are the books*
	i giornali?		*the newspapers?*		
	le bottiglie?		*the bottles?*		
	le chiavi?		*the keys?*		
	le aranciate?		*the orangeades?*		

See Systems, note 2 ii, p. 83 for singular endings in **-e** and **l', un'**.

v) Describing what there is

The key phrases are **c'è** *(there is)* and **ci sono** *(there are).*
In front of **è**, **ci** becomes **c'è** and is pronounced as one word.
You can use **c'è** and **ci sono** for describing:

C'è	il bagno	*There is*	*the bathroom*
	la cucina		*the kitchen*

Ci sono	i coltelli	*There are*	*the knives*
	le forchette		*the forks*

vi) Making enquiries

You can turn **c'è** and **ci sono** into questions to make enquiries:

C'è	una banca qui vicino?	*Is there*	*a bank near here?*
	una farmacia qui vicino?		*a chemist's near here?*

Ci sono	ristoranti buoni qui?	*Are there*	*good restaurants here?*
	trattorie buone qui?		*good trattorias here?*

vii) Finding out what's available

If you add **[che] cosa**, to **c'è** and **ci sono**, you can find out what's available, in a restaurant, for example:

Oggi, che cosa c'è?   *What is there today?*
C'è la minestra casalinga e il risotto   *There is home-made minestra and risotto.*
Ci sono fettuccine e lasagne   *There are fettuccine and lasagne.*

Asking and saying where things are

1 Show students some pictures of objects for which they can guess the equivalent in Italian, for example *telefono, giacca, bambini, frutta*. (Alternatively, you can first write some of the words on the board and elicit their meanings.)

2 Put up each of the pictures on the board with a number next to it.

3 Explain the meaning of *nella figura* and ask students:
a) *Nella figura numero* (random numbers) *che cosa c'è?*
b) *Dov'è il telefono? Dove sono i bambini?*

4 Tell students to say:
a) *Nella figura numero . . . c'è . . . (ci sono) . . .*
b) *Il telefono è nella figura numero . . .*

5 Alternatively, you can get the students to ask you the questions initially. When they have had the opportunity to hear you give the correct answers, you can exchange roles and ask them the questions.

Describing what there is

1 Ask students to think of any room in the house and its contents.

2 Go round the class to make sure all the words apply in the context of house and home. Write the names of the rooms in the house on the board.

3 Divide students into pairs. In each pair, students take it in turn to say one object which is in the room they have chosen. The other student has to guess which room their partner has chosen.

4 Encourage students to think of different, more unusual things: *coperchi, libri di ricette* for the kitchen, *mollette, dentifricio* for the bathroom, *giocattoli* or *disordine* for the kids' room, for instance.

In this way some less obvious words will be learned.

Variation: Bring in pictures from colour supplements of several different rooms. You describe one and students say which room is being described.

Making enquiries

1 Give each student a copy of a page from an Italian newspaper, containing a number of different classified advertisements under the heading *Compravendita case e terreni*.

2 It may be useful to go over common abbreviations used in such advertisements.

3 Divide the class into two groups.

4 Ask each group to choose one particular advert and put a circle around it.

5 Ask students to guess which house for sale has been chosen by the other group. (They can only ask questions with a yes or no answer, for example *Ha il garage? C'è il giardino?*)

Finding out what's available

1 Bring in menus from different restaurants.

2 Give copies to students and discuss what is available.

3 Students are the waiters and you are the customer. Ask at random: *Che cosa c'è . . .?*

Practice 1

Formale informale neutrale

Aim: to increase the students' awareness of the use of
different forms of address

Ask the students to put the following expressions into
three categories:
a) those which may only be used in formal situations
b) those which may only be used in informal situations
or
c) those which may be used in either.

Buongiorno.	*Mi chiamo.*	*Sono.*
Come ti chiami?	*Va bene.*	*Buonasera.*
Ciao.	*Come stai?*	*Come si chiama?*
Come sta?	*Sei italiano?*	*È inglese?*

The question of when to use the formal or the informal
address will naturally be asked, because it is something
entirely new to students, though they might guess that, if
in doubt, it is safer to use the formal. Of course, using
the wrong form of address is considered impolite among
Italians, but students will be reassured to know that when
it comes to foreigners, this convention is relaxed a little.

The dividing line becomes even less clear when we take
into account the context of the situation, and not just the
age or relationship of the speakers. For instance, two
people meeting on the beach might address each other
informally, but if the same people met in a work
environment they might at first use the *Lei* form.

This point could be the end of the lesson. Revise
the points covered so far and give a summary of the next
lesson.

> **Structures:** possessive adjectives/present tense
> **Functions:** talking about relatives/asking questions
> using the formal or informal forms of address
> **Vocabulary:** family, relations and neighbourhood/
> recipes /*azienda, proprietario, cantina*/*bere, mangiare,*
> *produrre, lavare,* and any other verbs which you decide
> will be useful

La mia famiglia

Aim: a) vocabulary building (family and relatives)
　　　 b) to reinforce the use of *mio*/*tuo*/*suo* with *fratello,*
　　　　 sorella, padre, madre, etc.

1　Divide the students into pairs.

2　Draw a simple diagram of your family tree and talk
students through it.

3　Tell them to build up their family trees by asking each
other questions such as the following:

Come si chiama tua sorella?　Si chiama Rose.
Come si chiama tuo padre?　Si chiama Stewart.
Come si chiama il marito di tua sorella?　Si chiama George **or**
　Mia sorella non è sposata.
Come si chiama tua zia (la sorella di tua madre)?　Si chiama
　Marie **or** *Mia madre non ha sorelle.*

4　They should be able to make up a family tree. Draw
the following diagram and tell them to fill in the boxes.
(Vocabulary on page 31)

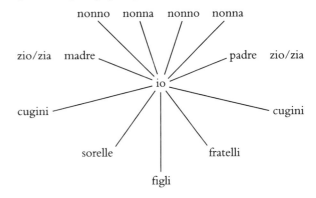

Practice I

What's your name?

Using the clues given in the answers, choose the right question form to ask the following people their names.

1 – Ciao, mi chiamo Nicola.
2 – Buongiorno, piacere, mi chiamo Aldo Bernini.
3 – Io mi chiamo Carla e lei si chiama Rosanna.

What about you?

Now introduce yourself to each of the following people, and then find out what they're called.

1 You meet someone older than yourself on a train.
2 You're at a party given by old friends and meet their young nephew.
3 You come across a young couple in a bar.

Who is it?

Look at the family tree and read the statements made by five of its members. They're all talking about the same person: who is it? – **Chi è?** Check in Patterns 2, note ii, on p. 20 if you've forgotten a word.

Angela	X è mio figlio.
Marco	X è mio padre.
Maria	X è mio fratello.
Giovanni	X è mio cognato.
Bianca	X è il fratello di mio padre.

Spot the relations

Below are all the names of the Cicognani family. Reading downwards, can you discover the words for father-in-law and aunt?

```
    S U S A N N A        P A T R I Z I O
      L U C I A            M A R I A
M A R C O                  B I A N C A
  G I A N C A R L O
    A N G E L A
      B A R B A R A
      G I O V A N N I
```

Now try to use each word in a sentence.

Guess who?

Can you identify four other members of the Cicognani family from what they say about themselves? Use the family tree.

1 Io sono la sorella di Marco e la figlia di Patrizio e Susanna. Chi sono?
2 Io sono la madre di Barbara e Angela e la moglie di Giovanni. Chi sono?
3 Io sono il figlio di Giovanni e Angela e il marito di Susanna. Chi sono?
4 Io sono il cognato di Giancarlo e il padre di Barbara e Angela. Chi sono?

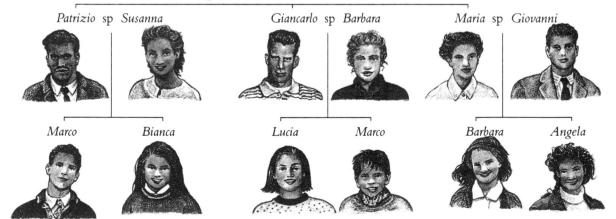

FAMIGLIA CICOGNANI

Giovanni sposato con *Angela*

Patrizio sp *Susanna* *Giancarlo* sp *Barbara* *Maria* sp *Giovanni*

Marco *Bianca* *Lucia* *Marco* *Barbara* *Angela*

What's in it?   19

You've made a wonderful salad and your friend asks you what's in it – **che cosa c'è dentro?** Reply using the cues on tape.

Amico È buona quest'insalata. Che cosa c'è dentro?
You *[Tell him there are tomatoes.]*
Amico E poi, che altro?
You *[Say there's mozzarella.]*
Amico E il basilico, c'è?
You *[Tell him, yes, there's basil.]*

Looking for the bank   19

Listen to the cassette/CD and practise asking for some useful places.

House with all amenities

You are an estate agent trying to sell a house. During the visit to the house your client wants to know what amenities there are in the district. You tell him, picking your adjectives carefully from the list below. You've certainly got all the answers!
e.g. C'è una scuola qui vicino?
   Sì, c'è una scuola nuova.

1 C'è un parco qui vicino?   *vecchio*
2 C'è una piscina qui vicino?   *nuovo*
3 C'è una chiesa qui vicino?   *grande*
4 C'è una trattoria qui vicino? *piccolo*
                   bello

Now can you say what amenities you have in your area?

What's on today?   19

You're in a small family trattoria in the Lazio region. There's no menu, so talk to the owner and sort out what you're going to eat.

Il primo *(first course)*

Padrone Buongiorno.
You *[Say hello and ask him what there is today.]*
Padrone Oggi, per primo c'è la stracciatella e ci sono spaghetti all'amatriciana.
You *[Ask what stracciatella is]*
Padrone La stracciatella è una minestra in brodo con uova sbattute e formaggio.
You *[A clear soup with beaten egg, mmm. What about the spaghetti all'amatriciana; ask what that is.]*
Padrone È un piatto di spaghetti con pomodori, vino bianco e peperoncino.
You *[Order the spaghetti. Say, 'spaghetti, please'.]*
Padrone Va bene.

Il secondo *(main course)*

Padrone Per secondo c'è il pollo arrosto e ci sono i saltimbocca di vitello.
You *[Chicken or veal? Order the chicken.]*

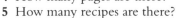

Home cooking

Look at this advertisement for a family cookery book and answer the questions. Try and use guesswork rather than look words up.

1 The title of the book includes a member of the family: which one?
2 What do you think the sentence beginning 'Ecco . . .' might mean, roughly?
3 How many colour photographs are there?
4 How many pages are there?
5 How many recipes are there?

The neighbourhood

Aim: to practise *c'è un/una, ci sono*

1 Ask students to draw a diagram of the area in which they live.

2 Divide them into pairs and ask them to name the items on the diagram and describe them to their partner.

e.g. *C'è un parco. E qui ci sono le aiuole e il campogiochi. C'è una stazione, una libreria . . .*

Variation: Students could do a similar exercise based on a simple plan of their house/flat and its contents.

Che cosa c'è nel tuo piatto preferito?

Aim: to practise *c'è un/una, ci sono* and to recycle vocabulary used previously (in *My favourite dish*)

1 Tell students to describe in writing what is in their favourite dish.

2 In pairs, students take turns to guess the ingredients of their partner's favourite dish.

3 Ask them to swap what they have written.

4 Check answers by asking at random: *Che cosa c'è nel suo piatto preferito?*

5 Write the ingredients on the board and ask the other students to guess the name of the dish.

Cultura e parole

The concept of *la famiglia* is perhaps most clearly reflected in the language itself. You may like to introduce the unit by talking about the origin of Italian and by considering the way *le parole* – words – are structured around a family system. Italian has not borrowed extensively from other languages and students will be pleased to know that it is easy to guess the meaning of a word in Italian just by knowing the root system, the family to which it belongs. Tell them to learn to create their own words by adding prefixes, infixes and suffixes. Take, for example, the word for bread, *pane.* The person who makes it is a *panettiere,* the shop is *panetteria,* a sandwich is *panino; companatico* is something you eat with bread and the traditional Christmas cake is *panettone.* Stimulate interest in the language as a living entity which creates or borrows new words according to need. For instance, the arrival of the fast food restaurant in Italy has brought into the language a new term, *paninaro,* which is loaded with social and cultural connotations, just like the word 'yuppy'. Naturally the connecting thread is not always clear and can sometimes be misleading: *integrale,* the word for wholemeal, for example, seems far removed from the meaning of *integralista,* fundamentalist.

Cultura e parole

When parents register the name of their new-born baby in the registry office – **l'anagrafe** – they can call their child anything they like: there was a brief period under Mussolini when foreign names, or names deemed 'irreligious, ridiculous or subversive', were banned. Yet Italy has a tradition of foreign or politically-inspired names: Mussolini himself was named by his anarchist-republican father after Benito Juarez, a Mexican rebel; while in his native Romagna, names like Napoleone, Bruto, Spartaco or even Anarchico were not unknown! There are many ordinary names, however, which to a foreigner can cause confusion: these are the common boys' names ending in **-a**: Andrea; Battista; Gianmaria; Luca and Nicola. The last is especially confusing, as the stress comes on the **o**, not the **i**.

The closeness of the Italian family is proverbial and the excessively close attachment which can exist between mother and son has given rise to the derogatory term **mammismo**, for which there is no simple direct equivalent in English. However, the term **figli di papà**, which describes pampered children with no need to earn their living, is fairly easily recognisable as 'Daddy's boys'. But are all Italian children really spoilt? Not judging by recent statistics, which suggest that child abuse is as common in Italy as in Britain. And this is not a new trend. The existence even today in the Italian language of the term **padre-padrone** – 'father-owner' would point to that. It was coined and much used to describe the absolute legal power of the father over his children until the changes made in 1975.

Since then the Italian family has evolved and survived. In the 1980s it became the focal point for Italians, disillusioned with politics and politicians. In the 90s, however, partly in response to environmental issues, the signs are that the trend is moving away from individualistic, inward-looking families back to an old tradition of greater involvement in local, but not national, affairs.

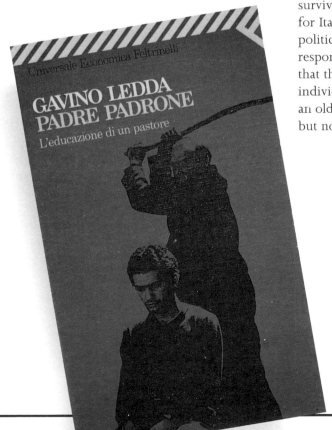

Interactions

4   ⌷⌷   ◎ 20

After the morning's grape-picking, Anna joins the guests at the picnic lunch inside the Muratori's chalet. She asks them what they're eating and drinking.

First time round

la torta	cake

Can you pick out how Anna asks the questions:
a What are you eating?
b What are you drinking?

Anna	**Cosa mangi?**
Ragazza	Mangio pane e formaggio.
Anna	Signora, **cosa mangia?**
Signora 1	Mangio torta di cioccolato e torta di crema.
Anna	**Cosa beve?**
Signora 2	Bevo acqua.
Anna	Signor Antonio, cosa beve?
Sig. Antonio	Bevo vino. Salute!
Anna	Cosa beve?
Uomo	Bevo caffè.

Salute! *to your health, cheers!*

Key phrases

cosa mangi?	*what are you eating?*
cosa mangia?	*what are you eating? [formal]*
cosa beve?	*what are you drinking? [formal]*

5   ⌷⌷   ◎ 21

Anna visits the local wine-making firm – **azienda vinicola** – and meets some pupils and teachers on a tour.

First time round

un po'	*a little*
qualchevolta	*sometimes*

Anna is curious to know:
Do Lorenzo and Maria both drink wine?

Anna	Ciao!
Lorenzo	Ciao!
Anna	**Bevi vino?**
Lorenzo	Sì, un po' con l'acqua.
Anna	E come ti chiami?
Lorenzo	Mi chiamo Lorenzo e **questa è la mia maestra**.
Anna	Signora, Lei, come si chiama?
Maria	Mi chiamo Maria.
Anna	E **beve vino?**
Maria	Sì, qualchevolta.

Key phrases

bevi vino?	*do you drink wine?*
beve vino?	*do you drink wine? [formal]*
questa è la mia maestra	*this is my teacher*

This is ...   ⌷⌷   ◎ 21

Listen to the cassette/CD and see if you can understand who is being introduced.

6   ⌷⌷   ◎ 22

The wine factory is called the Cantine San Marco – the San Marco cellars. The co-owners, Signor Notarnicola and Signor Violo, greet Anna.

First time round

che tipo di?	*what kind of?*
il proprietario	*owner*
questa azienda	*this firm*

a What are the owners' first names?
b What type of wine does the San Marco firm produce?

Anna	Buongiorno.
Sig. Not.	Buongiorno a Lei.
Anna	Lei, come si chiama?
Sig. Not.	Umberto Notarnicola e sono il proprietario delle Cantine San Marco.
Anna	Che tipo di vino produce quest'azienda?
Sig. Not.	Quest'azienda produce un vino bianco e **si chiama Frascati DOC**.

Interactions

Interaction 4 (004)

1 *Dopo la vendemmia c'è il pranzo.*

2 Ask students: *Come si dice in italiano* 'What are you drinking? What are you eating?'?

3 *Chiudete i libri. Ascoltate.* Play the cassette/CD as required.

4 *Quali sono le risposte?*

5 Ask further questions:
Do they eat anything else?
Che cosa significa 'Salute!'?

6 Play the cassette/CD again.

Conjugations

Aim: to practise the conjugations of the given verb, avoiding mechanical repetition

1 In large characters write, on flashcards, names of objects which can be clearly identified with an action. You could write, for example, *vino, acqua, tè* or *caffè* (or *tazza, bicchiere, coppa,* etc.), which are clearly linked with the action of drinking.

2 Show one card to student A and start off by asking: *Che cosa bevi?*

3 Elicit the full answer from student A: *Bevo vino.*

4 Turn to student B and ask: *Che cosa beve (student A)?*

5 Elicit the full answer from student B: *Student A beve vino.*

6 Turn to student C, show him/her a card and tell another student to ask student C a question. Student D will say: *Che cosa bevi?* (and so on).

7 Change the card. If, for example, this time you have written the word *lettera*, start again by supplying the verb: *Che cosa scrivi?*
Student A will say: *Scrivo una lettera.* Turn to student B and ask: *Che cosa scrive (student A)?* Student B will say: *Student A scrive una lettera.*

8 Turn to student C, show him/her a card and tell him/her to ask student D a question. Student C will say: *Che cosa bevi/scrivi/leggi/mangi?* and so on according to the card.
You can repeat this activity at other times using different verbs, and, later on, different tenses (and objects). Make your own cards by choosing the most appropriate verbs. Practise all persons in the singular and plural. (Ask two students together; one answers for both of them.)

Interaction 5 (047)

1 Change of scene: *Anna è in un'azienda vinicola* – wine-making firm – *e parla con due persone, Lorenzo e Maria. La domanda è:* Do they both drink wine?

2 *Chiudete i libri. Ascoltate.* Play the cassette/CD as required.

3 *Qual è la risposta?*

Interaction 6 (083)

1 In the San Marco Cellars: *Anna parla con i proprietari* (owners) *delle Cantine San Marco.*

2 *La domanda è:* What type of wine is produced in the Cantine San Marco?

3 *Chiudete i libri e ascoltate.*

4 Play the cassette/CD as required.

5 *Qual è la risposta?*

6 *Leggete sul libro* Interactions 5 e 6. *Ci sono altre domande?*

This point could be the end of the lesson. Revise the points covered so far. In the next lesson, students will learn how to talk about family, food and the place where they live.

Structures: present tense/formal and informal address/subject pronouns
Functions: introducing people/talking about daily routine/describing the area in which you live
Vocabulary: *gonna, vestito*/colours/family and physical descriptions/daily routine verbs and objects/food

Interaction 7 (115)

1 The harvest is celebrated with a street parade in medieval costumes. *Anna parla prima con una donna e sua figlia e poi con due ragazzi.*

2 *La domanda è: Come si dice in italiano* 'black', 'white', 'red', 'green' and 'yellow'?

3 *Chiudete i libri. Ascoltate.* Play the cassette/CD as required.

4 *Qual è la risposta?*

5 *Ci sono altre domande?*

Interaction 8 (134)

1 *Mentre Anna guarda la sfilata, incontra e parla con Stefano, sua moglie Stefania, e Valentina.*

2 *La domanda è:* Who is Valentina and what is she doing?

3 *Chiudete il libro. Ascoltate.* Play the cassette/CD as required.

4 *Qual è la risposta?*

5 *Leggete* Interactions 7 e 8 *sul libro. Avete altre domande?*

Lavorare sul testo
Aim: reinforcing structures and vocabulary

1 Write any of the Interactions above on the board, omitting some words.

2 Ask students to fill in the gaps.

3 Pair up students and tell them to compare their work.

4 Play the cassette/CD as required.

[...]

Anna	Lei come si chiama?
Sig. Violo	Mi chiamo Bruno Violo e **sono anch'io** un proprietario di quest'azienda vinicola.
Anna	Questa macchina lava le bottiglie?
Sig. Violo	Sì, questa macchina lava le bottiglie e poi con un'altra macchina mettiamo il vino in bottiglia.

e questa macchina?	*and what about this machine?*
poi	*then*

> ## Key phrases
>
> **si chiama Frascati DOC**   *it's called Frascati DOC*
> **sono anch'io . . .**   *I'm also. . .*

7   🔲 ◎ 23

The grape harvest is celebrated in the nearby village of Marino with a parade in Renaissance dress and the colourful costumes of the medieval guilds – **le Arti**.

First time round

portare	*to wear*
la gonna	*skirt*
il vestito	*costume, dress*

Anna speaks to a mother who introduces her little girl and to two young men.

One of the costumes is black and white. What's that in Italian?

[...]

Signora	**Questa è Silvia.**
Anna	Ciao Silvia.
Silvia	Ciao!
Anna	**Che cosa porti?**
Silvia	Un costume tradizionale di Marino, bianco e nero con la gonna a fiori.
Anna	Grazie.
[Anna	**Che cosa porta?**]
Signore	Porto il vestito verde dell'Arte dei Vascellari.
Uomo a cavallo	Porto un costume rinascimentale rosso e giallo.

l'Arte dei Vascellari	*the Vatmakers' Guild*
a fiori	*flowered*

> ## Key phrases
>
> **questa è Silvia**   *this is Silvia*
> **che cosa porti?**   *what are you wearing?*
> **che cosa porta?**   *what are you wearing? [formal]*

8   🔲 ◎ 24

Finally, watching the parade, Anna comes across Stefano, his wife Stefania, and another person.

First time round

figlia	*daughter*

Who is she and what is she doing?

Anna	Buonasera.
Stefano	Buonasera.
Anna	Lei come si chiama?
Stefano	Stefano Bucciarelli e **questa è mia moglie.**
Anna	**Piacere.**
Stefania	**Piacere.**
Anna	Lei come si chiama?
Stefania	Io mio chiamo Stefania Vizzuti e **questa è mia figlia.**
Anna	Ciao!
Valentina	Ciao!
Anna	Come ti chiami?
Valentina	Valentina.
Anna	Cosa mangi?
Valentina	Un gelato.

> ## Key phrases
>
> **questa è mia moglie**   *this is my wife*
> **piacere**   *how do you do?*
> **questa è mia figlia**   *this is my daughter*

Photo call   🔲 ◎ 25

Listen and introduce various members of your family.

Patterns 2

i) Introductions

A simple way of introducing someone is to use **questa** and **questo**:

Questa è	Silvia	*This is*	*Silvia*
	mia moglie		*my wife*
	la mia vicina		*my neighbour*

Questo è	Lorenzo	*This is*	*Lorenzo*
	mio marito		*my husband*
	il mio vicino		*my neighbour*

Questa è la mia amica Paola e questo è suo cugino Marco   *This is my friend Paola and this is her cousin Marco*

Questo è il mio amico Sandro e questa è sua cugina Ida   *This is my friend Sandro and this is his cousin Ida*

For more on **mio, suo, mia, sua** see Systems, note 3, p. 84.

ii) Finding out what things are called

The key verb is **chiamarsi** *(to be called).* [See Systems, note 6 iii, p. 85.]

Come si chiama il vino? Si chiama Frascati DOC.   *What's the wine called? It's called Frascati DOC*

Questo, come si chiama?   *What's this called?*
Questa si chiama zuppa inglese, è un dolce   *This is called trifle, it's a dessert*

Questi, come si chiamano?   *What are these called?*
Questi si chiamano crostini, sono antipasti   *These are called crostini, they're starters*

iii) What you are doing and what you do

To find out what people are up to, the key phrase is [che] cosa? Put this before the verb.

Che cosa	mangi? [tu]	*What are you eating?/what do you eat?*
	mangia? [Lei]	
	mangiate? [voi]	

Mangio	bruschetta	*I am eating/I eat*	bruschetta [garlic bread]
Mangiamo	torta	*We are eating/we eat*	cake

Some verbs have slightly different patterns:

Che cosa	bevi? [tu]	*What are you drinking?/do you drink?*
	beve? [Lei]	
	bevete? [voi]	

Bevo	vino	*I'm drinking/I drink*	wine
Beviamo	acqua	*We're drinking/we drink*	water

See Systems, notes 6 and 7, p. 85 for more on verbs.

Patterns 2

Introductions

1 Show the students a number of pictures of different people. Tell them they are all related to a central character whom you choose and introduce first.

2 Give the central character, and all the others, Italian names: *questo è Marco; questa è Daniela; questo è Luigi; questa è Marina.* Talk about their physical appearances, for example: *I capelli di Marco sono corti, biondi,* etc.

3 Pin up the photographs and tell the students to make up a family from all the people in the pictures.

4 The students are bound to differ in the way they make up their families. Ask them to compare their suggestions.

5 Explain the meaning of *secondo* and tell student A to say:

Secondo student B, Luigi è il fratello di Marco; secondo me, è suo zio.

Finding out what things are called

1 Set geography questions. For example: *Come si chiama la capitale del Brasile?   Come si chiama la moneta della Germania?   Come si chiama il deserto dell'Africa?   Come si chiamano gli abitanti della Giamaica?*

2 Each time explain the key word in the question if it is not understood. (You don't need to give lengthy explanations of new articles or of *di* + article since the students can just formulate the answer in accordance with the question or simply say *si chiama, si chiamono. . . .*)

What you are doing and what you do

1 Give a number of examples from your daily routine which concern eating and drinking (ample gesticulation for better comprehension).

2 Explain the meaning of *al mattino, la mattina, a colazione, a pranzo, a mezzogiorno, la sera, a cena.*

3 Tell students to go round the class and interview each other in order to find out which is the most popular type of drink in the morning or in the evening, and what everyone eats for breakfast, lunch or supper.

4 Write sample questions on the board:

Che cosa mangi al mattino?
Che cosa bevi la sera?

(Toast and cornflakes – *pane tostato e fiocchi d'avena* – will probably be the staple diet for breakfast. Make sure you have a dictionary with you, as people's eating habits vary.)

5 To say what they have found out, students should use the third person singular.

e.g. Student A: *mangia uno yogurt al mattino.*

6 Supervise the whole activity by moving around the class.

7 Expand by repeating the activity and introducing new situations and new verbs:

Che cosa mangi al ristorante?
Che cosa guardi alla televisione? (di solito)
Che cosa ascolti al mattino?

8 Ask students to jot down two or three items that make up their ideal breakfast. Students then ask one another questions to find out what they are.

Identifying with others: me too, you too

When checking answers to the previous activity, encourage students to use the following structure.

e.g. To student A: *Che cosa mangi al mattino?*
Student A: *Mangio muesli al mattino.*
Encourage other students to say: *Anch'io mangio muesli al mattino.*

Practice 2

Il mio quartiere

Aim: vocabulary building/practice of *(che cosa) c'è?/che cos'è?/che cosa sono?*

1 Write the following words on the board and discuss the meanings with students.

libreria	*parco*	*monumenti*
giardini	*supermercato*	*parcogiochi*
palazzo comunale	*piazza*	*piscina*
mercato	*palestra*	*negozi*

2 Draw a sketch of your area on the board, inserting some of the above.

3 Ask students to describe their area through dialogue/role play based on the sketch. This is a sample dialogue. Write it on the board/OHP:

– *Che cosa c'è vicino a casa tua?*
– *C'è una piscina e ci sono dei negozi.*
– *Questo che cos'è?*
– *È un museo.*
– *E questi cosa sono?*
– *Sono aiuole.*
– *Come si chiamano i vicini di casa?*
– *Sono i signori . . .*

4 Ask two students to come to the board to explain the drawing to the others. They could draw their map on a transparency which they can explain, displaying it on the OHP.

Shopping from home

Aim: vocabulary building/to practise reading for gist understanding

1 Obtain an Italian mail order catalogue.

2 Choose a suitable group of items for sale.

3 Copy descriptions of items onto the board.

4 Give students a copy of the page you have chosen from the catalogue with descriptions of the items blotted out.

5 Ask students to identify the objects in the pictures and match them to the descriptions.

6 Check answers and discuss any questions raised.

7 You can repeat this exercise a number of times. The descriptions of the items could perhaps be different and more complex as the students progress through the course.

> **The three forms of *you*:**
>
> **Tu** is informal. It's used with children and people you know well.
> **Lei** is formal. It's used with people you don't know well.
> **Voi** is used to talk to more than one person.

iv) Identifying with others: me too, you too

The key word is **anche** *(also, too)*. You can combine this with **io, tu, lui, lei, noi, voi** and **loro**. In front of **io, anche** becomes **anch'io** and is pronounced as one word:

Sei	australiano anche tu?	*Are you*	*Australian too?*
È	anche Lei?		
Siete	australiani anche voi?		
Sono	americano anch'io	*I'm*	*American too*
Siamo	americani anche noi	*We're*	
È	canadese anche lui/anche lei?	*Is he/she*	*Canadian too?*
Sono	canadesi anche loro?	*Are they*	

You can use **anche** with other verbs:

Lavora in Inghilterra anche Lei?   *Do you work in England too?*

Practice 2

What's this?

Can you identify the objects in the pictures? And can you say what they're called? The answers are in the text.

1 Che cos'è?

'"Orbis" è il nome di questo orologio da parete di DeAgostini in acciaio con fondo marmorizzato: L 76.000 nel diametro di cm 28.'

È un . . .
Si chiama . . .

2 Che cosa sono?

'Si chiamano "La cupola" e sono in fusione d'alluminio con manico e pomolo in poliammide nero, le caffettiere disegnate da Aldo Rossi per Alessi. Da una, tre, o sei tazze, costano rispettivamente, L 37,000, 43.500 e 55.000.'

Sono . . .
Si chiamano . . .

Odd one out

Read these sets of words aloud and see if you can spot the odd one out. To help your pronunciation all irregular stresses have been marked. Check any words you don't know in the Vocabulary on p. 31.

1 utile facile difficile elegante elefante importante
2 patata carota pomodoro pomeriggio cavolo sedano peperone
3 banana uva mela pera pesce pesca arancia
4 gonna camicia vestito giacca giallo scarpa sciarpa
5 bicchiere piatto coltello forchetta cucchiaio acciaio

Where is everyone?

in camera	ascoltare la musica
in salotto	guardare la televisione
a scuola	studiare lingue
in cucina	preparare la cena
a casa	leggere un libro

Match up where everyone is and what they're doing, using the drawings as a guide.
e.g. Sua nonna, dov'è?

Mia nonna è a casa. Legge un libro.

1 Sua madre, dov'è? 2 Suo padre, dov'è?

3 Suo figlio, dov'è? 4 Suo nonno, dov'è?

Friends and neighbours

Imagine the people below are your friends and neighbours in Italy. Introduce them to your visitors from home.

e.g. Your neighbour Pietro and his wife Laura.
Questo è il mio vicino Pietro e questa è sua moglie Laura.

1 Your friend Gina and her brother Paolo.
2 Your neighbour Sandra and her friend Susanna.
3 Your friend Giuseppe and his brother Enrico.
4 Your neighbour Manlio and his cousin Cristina.

Now introduce your real friends from home to your friends and neighbours in Italy.

I too ...

Say what you have in common with other members of your group.
e.g. Studio l'italiano.
Anch'io studio l'italiano.

1 Abito in Gran Bretagna.
2 Lavoro molto.
3 Sono di nazionalità britannica.

You too?

Find out whether your new acquaintances have anything in common with you.
e.g. Io abito qui vicino. Anche Lei abita vicino?

1 Io abito a Bologna.
2 Io lavoro in via Cavour.
3 Io studio lingue.

Now ask a couple the same questions.

Piacere

Aim: practising introducing people

1   Prepare some cards which describe people, for example:

Giuseppina Gualtieri. Sposata. Due figlie. Maestra.

2   Divide the class into groups and distribute cards bearing different names.

3   Tell students to make their group into families (including friends of the family), using the identities of the people on the cards.

4   Go round to be introduced to the friends and relatives, each time feigning a little surprise. (Shake hands, say *piacere* and make the whole experience as real as possible.)

Colour associations

Aim: vocabulary building with the focus on colours

1 Teach students the meaning of *Di che colore è . . .?*

2 Ask students to think of the colours of a list of items which you write on the board, such as the walls in their homes, their front door, their car, their Sunday best, their briefcase, etc.

3 At random, ask students to answer the question: *Di che colore è la tua macchina/la tua valigetta/il tuo miglior vestito?* etc.

4 Ask students what colours are produced if you mix, for example, yellow and red, red and white, white and black.

5 Ask students to jot down two items of clothing. The rest of the class have to guess first the items of clothing and second their colour.

Who's who

Aim: practising personal presentation

1 Show students a copy of an Italian passport or *carta d'identità*.

2 Ask questions relating to the person in the document.

3 Give students a blank front page of a *passaporto/carta d'identità* and ask them to fill it in according to the information you provide.

Rude official

Aim: practising personal presentation in 'difficult' circumstances

1 It can sometimes be quite a task to put across a point to a customs official who has no sense of humour, or to any unpleasant person. Tell students to imagine coming across an unpleasant chap (not like the ones in *Italianissimo*) and to be prepared for a rough ride.

2 Ask students to fill in a form similar to a *passaporto* or *carta d'identità*.

3 Set the scene in an airport (delays, long queues, tempers running high, etc.).

4 Tell students you are a short-tempered official.

5 Collect their forms and ask questions abruptly and rudely. Act in a suspicious and provocative manner but at the same time elicit positive responses from the students.

Colour associations 25

How well do you know your colours?

bianco   nero   giallo   rosso   verde   azzurro

Below are some clues to the colours given here. You'll also hear them on tape. Listen and answer aloud in Italian.

1 What are the colours of the Italian flag shown here?
Answer in Italian: La bandiera italiana è . . .

2 What colour is linked to Italian international sport?
3 What colour is synonymous with a detective story or film?
4 Finally, write down the colours you associate with the following (they are not on the cassette/CD):
a) being in debt; **b)** being in credit; **c)** surrender;
d) ecology?

Identikit

Below is a form for a free catalogue. Check if there are words you don't know, then fill it in, putting your house number after the street name. Leave **C.A.P.** and **Prov.** blank. They stand for the postal code – **codice di avviamento postale**, and the province – **la provincia**.

> PER RICEVERE IL CATALOGO ILLUSTRATIVO, SCRIVETE A:
> **SNAIDERO R. S.p.A. 33100 MAJANO [UD]**
>
> **NOME**
>
> **COGNOME**
>
> **INDIRIZZO**
>
> **TEL**   **C.A.P.**
>
> **CITTÀ**   **PROV.**
>
> **FIRMA**

 25

Now imagine giving your details over the phone to a hotel or campsite. Rehearse your name and address in Italian.

Mi chiamo . . .
Il mio indirizzo è . . . ; abito a . . . *[town]*, in . . . *[country]*

If you need help with the street number, look up Ref. I, 1, p. 239.

Vocabulary

2

Family

il cognome	surname
il nome	name
la famiglia	family
il cognato	brother-in-law
la cognata	sister-in-law
il/la cugino/a	cousin
il genero	son-in-law
la nuora	daughter-in-law
il fratello	brother
la sorella	sister
il marito	husband
la moglie	wife
il nipote	nephew/grandson
la nipote	niece/granddaughter
il nonno	grandfather
la nonna	grandmother
il suocero	father-in-law
la suocera	mother-in-law
i/le gemelli/e	twins
l'amico/a	friend
il fidanzato	fiancé
la fidanzata	fiancée
il signore	Mr, man
la signorina	Miss, young lady

Meals

l'antipasto	starter
il primo	first course
il secondo	main course
il dolce	sweet, dessert

Food

la carne	meat
il maiale	pork
il manzo	beef
il fegato	liver
il pesce	fish
il cavolo	cabbage
l'insalata	salad
il peperone	green pepper
il peperoncino	chili pepper
i piselli	peas
il sedano	celery
l'albicocca	apricot
la fragola	strawberry
il lampone	raspberry
il limone	lemon
il melone	melon
l'uva	grapes
il pane	bread
il burro	butter
la marmellata	jam
il pepe	pepper
il sale	salt

Drinks

l'acqua	water
il digestivo	after-dinner drink
il latte	milk

Tableware

il bicchiere	glass
il coltello	knife
il cucchiaio	spoon
la forchetta	fork
il piatto	plate
la tazza	cup

Places

la capitale	capital
il capoluogo	regional/provincial capital
l'edicola	news-stand
l'isola	island
il mercato	market
il paese	country, village
la nazione	nation
il ristorante	restaurant
l'ufficio	office
la via	street

Verbs

abitare	to live
ascoltare	to listen
assaggiare	to taste
bere	to drink
guardare	to look, watch
firmare	to sign
lavorare	to work
imparare	to learn
leggere	to read
mangiare	to eat
portare	to wear; bring
provare	to try [on]
scrivere	to write
studiare	to study
vedere	to see

Adjectives

grande	big
piccolo	little
simpatico	nice/pleasant
antipatico	nasty/unpleasant
simile	similar
diverso	different
facile	easy
difficile	difficult
utile	useful
elegante	elegant
gratis	free

Colours

arancione	orange
azzurro	blue
bianco	white
giallo	yellow
grigio	grey
marrone	brown
nero	black
rosso	red
verde	green

Clothes

la camicia	shirt
la camicetta	blouse
il cappello	hat
il cappotto	coat
la giacca	jacket
la gonna	skirt
la maglia	jumper
la maglietta	T shirt
i pantaloni	trousers
le scarpe	shoes
la sciarpa	scarf
il vestito	dress, costume

31

Vocabulary

La spesa

1 Here is the week's shopping to be put away. Ask students to divide items into the following categories:

frutta verdura carni farinacei latte

2 Make sure that students know the meaning of the five categories above and then read out the words below, giving students time to write them in the right columns. (You may prefer to give them a photocopy of the words.)

salsiccia	*spaghetti*	*manzo*	*biscotti*
crackers	*ribes*	*fagiolini*	*pane*
burro	*ciliegie*	*cipolle*	*agnello*
riso	*banane*	*cavoli*	*maiale*
pere	*peperoni*	*pollo*	*lenticchie*
arance	*mele*	*piselli*	*tacchino*
gnocchi	*uva*	*sedano*	*salame*

Troubleshooting

Review

Here is a checklist of the main points learned in this unit. For each point, ask the students to supply one or more examples by asking specific questions.

agreement of adjectives and nouns
potere + infinitive
possessive adjectives
present tense
subject pronouns
identifying people and objects (questions/statements)
saying your name and asking other people's names
asking questions using formal and informal forms of address
checking a list of items
introducing people
talking about family and relations
describing what people are like
daily routine verbs and objects
talking about food, recipes and colours
talking about the area in which you live

Troubleshooting

Don't confuse the following:

È, sono   C'è, ci sono

è	*it is*	c'è	*there is.*
è?	*is it?*	c'è?	*is there?*
sono	*they are*	ci sono	*there are*
sono?	*are they?*	ci sono?	*are there?*

C'è is short for **ci è**. The word for *there* is **ci** but in front of **è** it becomes **c'** and is pronounced as one word.

The verbs **è** and **sono** on their own mean *it is* and *they are*. Words for *it* and *they* do exist **(esso/a; essi/e)**, but they are no longer used in spoken Italian.

Chi è? Chi sono?   Chi c'è?

Chi è/chi sono are used for identifying people; **chi c'è** is used for finding out who's around:

Chi è?	*Who is it?*	È Anna.	*It's Anna.*
Chi sono?	*Who are they?*	Sono Anna e Maria.	*They're . . .*
Chi c'è?	*Who's here?*	C'è Anna.	*Anna's here.*
[lit.	*Who is there?*]	Ci sono Anna e Maria.	*Anna and Maria are here*

Cos'è? Cosa sono?   Cosa c'è?

Cos'è/cosa sono are used for identifying objects; **cosa c'è** is used for finding out what's available.

Cos'è	*What is it?*	È	*It's a*
Cosa sono?	*What are they?*	Sono	*They're*
Cosa c'è?	*What is there?*	C'è	*There's*
		Ci sono	*There are*

Dove?   dov'è?

Finally notice the difference between:

Dove?	*where?*	Dov'è?	*where is?*

Dov'è? means **dove è?** In front of the verb **è, dove** drops the

Unità 3

Il tempo libero

*La costa
ligure*

**In this unit you'll be introduced to the language for
socialising and getting to know people. You will also learn
how to say what you enjoy doing in your spare time.**

A glance at the enormous variety of leisure magazines on
sale in Italy should dispel the popular view that Italians
spend all their free time – **il tempo libero** – at football
matches. Whilst it is true that sport, especially football, is a
major leisure interest, there has been an enormous
diversification of hobbies and pastimes in recent years.

Leisure in Italy has come with the prosperity which arrived
after the Second World War during the period known as **il
miracolo economico** – the Economic Miracle. Between
1958 and 1963, Italy's 6.5 per cent growth rate was the fastest
of any major industrialised country except Japan, and nearly
twice that of the UK. Increased spending power brought
radical changes in life-style: sales of domestic appliances and
cars soared. In the late 1950s, 3 per cent of homes had washing
machines, 12 per cent had TV, 13 per cent owned fridges, 25
per cent had bathrooms and there were only about 300 000
cars on the road. By the mid 1960s, over 50 per cent had TV,
fridges and bathrooms, whilst car ownership had risen to over
four and a half million. Nowadays there are few homes without
all these amenities and there are over 25 million cars on the
Italian roads. Although the growth rate has slowed since the
Economic Miracle, Italy is now the third most prosperous
country in Europe.

Unità 3

Il tempo libero

Il tempo libero is big business in Italy. It is part of the service sector, *il terziario,* which has grown rapidly in the last few decades and has become the largest sector of the Italian economy in terms of generation of wealth and number of people employed. Annual statistics, however, show that differences between the rich north and the poorer south, in terms of average income – *reddito pro capite,* and other general economic indicators – have considerable influence on the way Italians spend their leisure time. Bologna, for example, is the city which promotes free time above all others and the one in which people on average spend most on sport. The picture is very different elsewhere. There are more than fifteen libraries in Aosta for every 100,000 inhabitants but only one and a half in Rieti for the same number of inhabitants. Firenze comes top for money spent on the cinema. In Avellino the amount is twenty times less. A quick glance through what is available on television reveals a very large number of private channels. The state monopoly of television was abolished in 1976 and in 1983 the number of private television networks operating at local level was in excess of seven hundred. Most of the local programmes are produced in the north or centre of Italy and those imported from abroad come from the USA. These programmes play a considerable role in introducing cultural influences from outside Italy.

Video corner
True or false
Aim: active viewing
Video sequence: from the garden party to the beach

1   The statements below refer to the first part of the video sequence (from the garden party to the beach). Some are true and some are false.

2   Write them on the board or make enough copies to distribute among the students. Discuss the meaning of each statement.

3   Play the video sequence and ask students to tick the right answers.

4   Play the sequence again and discuss the answers when students are ready.

5   Choose any other sequence and repeat the exercise with more difficult choices.

	V	F

In the garden:
Ci sono molte persone nel giardino.
Barbara è cortese.
Bianca è la madre di Carla Pira.
Angela è una professoressa di inglese.
Il fratello di Chiara è nel giardino.

With the captain of the yacht:
Il capitano è cordiale.
Lo yacht è in altomare.
Il capitano ha meno di trenta anni.

On the beach Anna talks first to Mario and Luca:
Anna Mazzotti è seduta.
Mario ha gli occhiali da sole.
Luca ha i capelli biondi.
Luca sorride.

Then she speaks to two people on the *pedalò:*
La ragazza sul pedalò è annoiata.
Sul pedalò c'è anche il fidanzato.

Soon after, Anna speaks to two girls, then to a mother with two children:
La ragazza bionda è magra.
La ragazza bionda ha un costume a due pezzi.
Ci sono due bambine con la madre.
Valentina ha otto anni.
Matteo ha sei anni.

Interactions

Structures: present + *da*/irregular verbs *stare* and
preferire
Functions: asking and saying how you are/talking
about yourself and your family/stating preferences/
asking why and giving reasons/asking and saying where
you are from
Vocabulary: *prendere il sole, ascoltare musica, giocare a
pallavolo, insegnare, studiare, pedalare, abbronzarsi, avere
bisogno di, professoressa, alunne, divertente, spiaggia, per
fortuna*

Help-phrases and instructions

Hai/avete capito?
Non ho capito. Può/puoi ripetere?
È chiaro?
Non è molto chiaro.
Scrivete.

Interaction 1   (224)

Liguria is a narrow stretch of land between the mountains
and the coast, from the French border to the region of
Tuscany.

1   *Anna è ad una festa nell'Anglo-Ligurian Club e incontra
alcuni invitati.*

2   What are the names of the four people Anna speaks
to?
What is the relationship between the first person and the
other three girls?

3   Play the cassette/CD as required. Ask further
questions:
*Quanti anni ha Bianca? Di dov'è Angela? Da quanto tempo
studia inglese? Quanti fratelli ha Chiara? È lì con la sua famiglia?*

4   Write this Interaction on the board omitting the
questions (or make a copy of the following). For each
word in the question draw one line (*l'* counts as one
word).

ANNA	Signora, piacere, sono Anna Mazzotti.
CARLA	Piacere. Io sono Carla Pira. Insegno inglese qui in Liguria. Queste sono le mie alunne e questa è mia figlia.
ANNA	Ciao.
BIANCA	Ciao.
ANNA	____ ____ ____?
BIANCA	Io mi chiamo Bianca.
ANNA	____ ____ ____ ____?
BIANCA	Ho otto anni.
ANNA	____ ____ ____?
ANGELA	Io mi chiamo Angela.
ANNA	____ ____ ____ ____?
ANGELA	Sono d'Imperia.
ANNA	____ ____ ____ ____ ____?
ANGELA	Studio l'inglese da otto anni con la mia professoressa.
ANNA	____ ____ ____?
CHIARA	Io mi chiamo Chiara.
ANNA	____ ____ ____?
CHIARA	Sì, ho un fratello.
ANNA	____ ____ ____ ____ ____?
CHIARA	No, non sono qui con la mia famiglia ma sono qui con la mia professoressa d'inglese.

5   Tell students: *Scrivete le domande* (individually or in
pairs).

6   Check answers orally then ask students to check the
spellings against those in the book.

Draw the attention of the students to the forms of address
in the following two Interactions. If you are able to show
the video, point out that choosing the right form of
address depends of course on the age, but also on the
situation. (If Anna had met the young boys elsewhere but
on the beach she would have probably chosen the *lei*
form.)

Interactions

I [cc] [CD] 27

In the nineteenth century, Liguria was the haunt of the wealthy British and a favourite leisure spot. Today that past survives in the thriving Anglo-Ligurian club, which meets every Thursday in the seaside town of Bordighera and holds an annual garden party on the Queen's birthday. Anna meets some of the guests.

First time round

inglese	*English*
le alunne	*pupils*

Read the questions below, then listen without the text.

a What are the names of the four people Anna speaks to?

b What is the relationship between the first person she speaks to and the other three girls?

[...]

Anna	Signora, piacere, sono Anna Mazzotti.
Carla	Piacere. Io sono Carla Pira. Insegno inglese qui in Liguria. Queste sono le mie alunne e questa è mia figlia.
Anna	Ciao.
Bianca	Ciao.
Anna	Come ti chiami?
Bianca	Io mi chiamo Bianca.
Anna	E **quanti anni hai?**
Bianca	Ho otto anni.
Anna	Come ti chiami?
Angela	Io mi chiamo Angela.
Anna	E **di dove sei?**
Angela	Sono d'Imperia.
Anna	Da quanto tempo studi l'inglese?
Angela	Studio l'inglese da otto anni con la mia professoressa.
Anna	Come ti chiami?
Chiara	Mi chiamo Chiara.
Anna	Chiara, **hai fratelli?**
Chiara	Sì, ho un fratello.
Anna	Sei qui con la tua famiglia?
Chiara	No, non sono qui con la mia famiglia ma sono qui con la mia professoressa d'inglese.

da quanto tempo ...? *for how long ...?*

> ## Key phrases
>
> **quanti anni hai?** *how old are you? [inf.]*
> **di dove sei?** *where are you from? [inf.]*
> **hai fratelli?** *have you any brothers or sisters?*

2 〔cc〕 〔CD〕 28

Along the coast from Bordighera is Sanremo, famous not only for its song festival and flowers, but also for its beach and luxury yachts.

First time round

Anna talks to the captain of a large yacht. He isn't from Sanremo.
Where does he come from?

Anna	Buongiorno.
Capitano	Buongiorno.
Anna	**Come sta?**
Capitano	Io sto bene, grazie.
Anna	**Di dov'è?**
Capitano	Io sono d'Imperia. È una città qui vicino – a Sanremo.

Key phrases

come sta?	*how are you?*
di dov'è?	*where are you from?*

3 〔cc〕 〔CD〕 29

On the beach Anna meets Mario and Luca.

sposato/a	*married*	Are either of them married?

Anna	Mario, di dove sei?
Mario	Sono di Sanremo.
Anna	**Sei sposato?**
Mario	No, per fortuna non sono sposato.
Anna	Luca, di dove sei?
Luca	Sono di Sanremo e vivo qui.
Anna	E **sei sposato?**
Luca	No. **Non** sono sposato **neanch'io**.

per fortuna   *luckily*

Key phrases

sei sposato?	*are you married? [inf.]*
non ... neanch'io	*me neither*

4 〔cc〕 〔CD〕 30

Anna has four other brief encounters on the beach – with a mother and daughter on a pedalo, a teenage girl, another mother, and a teenage boy.

First time round

perché?	*why?*
perché	*because*
divertente	*fun*
gioco	*I play*

What are these people doing on the beach?

Anna	Ciao.
Ragazza	Ciao.
Anna	*[to the mother]* Buongiorno, signora. **Perché** siete qui?
Signora	Beh, **è** molto **divertente stare qui**, pedalare, andare sul mare, abbronzarsi.
Anna	Ciao, **come stai?**
Ragazza	Bene, grazie.
Anna	**Perché** sei qui?
Ragazza	Sono qui per divertirmi.
Anna	E **cosa preferisci fare?**
Ragazza	Preferisco mangiare il gelato [...].
Anna	Signora, lei **perché** è qui?
Madre	Sono qui **perché** ho bisogno di riposarmi ... [...]
Marco	In spiaggia gioco a pallavolo, sto con gli amici, ascolto la musica e prendo il sole.

andare sul mare	*to go out on the sea*
per divertirmi	*to enjoy myself*
sto con gli amici	*I spend time with my friends*
in spiaggia	*on the beach*

Key phrases

perché ...?	*why?*
perché	*because*
è divertente stare qui	*it's fun being here*
come stai?	*how are you? [inf.]*
cosa preferisci fare?	*what do you prefer doing?*

Sound effects 〔cc〕 〔CD〕 30

Listen to the cassette/CD and say what you prefer doing.

Interaction 2 (275)

1 *Anna parla con il capitano di uno yacht.*

2 Where is he from?

3 Play the cassette/CD as required.

Interaction 3 (290)

1 *Sulla spiaggia Anna incontra e parla con due ragazzi:
Mario e Luca.*
Is either of them married?

2 Play the cassette/CD. Ask further questions:
Di dov'è Luca/Di dov'è Mario?

3 Tell students to re-write Interactions 2 and 3, changing
the forms of address from the formal to the informal and
vice versa.

If you have a video, you can show the students Interaction
4 and draw their attention to the question *Perché siete
qui?*. Stop the video just before Anna asks the same
question in the next two meetings and ask the students
to formulate it correctly for these situations.

Interaction 4 (306)

1 *Anna incontra altre persone in spiaggia e chiede che cosa
fanno.*
Pick out three or four things the people do.

2 Play the cassette/CD as required. Ask further
questions:
For what other reasons do people go to the beach?

Let's talk
Aim: to encourage students to talk about themselves

1 Introduce yourself to one student in more or less the
same way Ms Pira does to Anna Mazzotti in
Interaction 1.

2 Ask the following questions at random in class (but
also stretch students' abilities by asking most or all of the
questions to the same student).

Come ti chiami?
Di dove sei?
Quanti anni hai?
Da quanto tempo studi italiano?
Hai fratelli/sorelle?
Sei sposato?
Hai figli?

3 Students: a) practise the above questions in pairs
            b) change them from informal to formal
            c) think of any more questions
            d) ask you a question each

Some students will be weaker than others and could
perhaps benefit from extra practice. You can at this point
carry on practising the same questions with the weaker
students and ask the rest to do the following exercise
which does not require your involvement.

Giving reasons
Aim: vocabulary building/practising giving reasons

1 Make enough copies of the following list of statements
and distribute them to the class.

2 Ask students to match the right 'location' with the
right action. (You can simply show the exercise on the
OHP if you have one.)

Io sono in spiaggia per	*ballare e divertirsi*
Marco è al bar 'da Luigi' per	*fare sport*
Il signor Franchi è a Milano per	*ritirare un pacco*
Giovanni e Rosa sono in banca per	*vedere una commedia*
Veronica è in discoteca per	*partecipare ad una*
	conferenza
Tu sei all'ufficio postale per	*incontrare gli amici*
I signori Maggio sono a teatro per	*fare la spesa*
Il signor Bauchiero è nel parco per	*portare a spasso il cane*
Franca ed io siamo al supermercato per	*depositare denaro*
Voi siete in palestra per	*riposarmi*

3 Check the exercise orally. Ask ridiculous questions,
e.g. *Veronica è in discoteca per fare sport?*, to elicit the correct
answers.

Patterns 1

Asking and saying how you are

1 Turn to student A and ask the question: *Come stai?*

2 Elicit an answer then ask another student the same question, but this time induce student B to try for a different answer by feigning some terrible toothache.

3 Ask the class: *Come sta student B?* Elicit an answer and repeat the question, varying the number of students directly or indirectly involved each time and the expression on your face.

Asking and saying where you're from

1 Turn to student A and ask the question: *Di dove sei?*

2 Elicit an answer, then ask another student the same question, but this time induce student B to try for a different answer by showing a card of the Eiffel Tower, for example.

3 Then ask the class *Di dov'è student B?* Elicit an answer and repeat the question varying the number of students directly or indirectly involved each time.

4 Encourage students to ask one another the same question.

Talking about the family

1 Turn to student A and ask the questions: *Sei sposato? Hai bambini? Hai fratelli?*

2 Elicit answers and go on to ask another student the same questions.

3 Ask the class: *Student B è sposato? Ha bambini? Ha fratelli?*

4 Elicit answers and repeat the questions, varying the number of students directly or indirectly involved each time.
e.g. Ask two students together: *Avete fratelli?* Tell one of them to answer collectively. Ask a third student: *Hanno fratelli?*

5 At the end, test students' memories by asking them about the family of the first or second student you questioned.

6 Invite them to ask you the same questions.

This point could be the end of the lesson. Revise points covered so far. In the next lesson students will cover the following:

Structures: *da* + infinitive/*preferire*
Functions: asking and stating preferences/agreeing (with others)/asking why and giving reasons
Vocabulary: general/Sunday activities/sport

Patterns I

Exchanging personal information

i) Asking and saying how you are

The key verb is **stare** *(to be, to stay)* [see Systems, note 2, p. 87].

| Come | stai?
sta?
state? | *How are you?* | Come sta?

Come stanno? | *How* | *is he/she?*

are they? |

Sto/stiamo bene, grazie   *I'm/we're fine, thanks*
Sta/stanno bene, grazie   *He, she/they are fine, thanks*
Non c'è male – e tu?/e Lei?/e voi?   *Not bad – how about you?*
　　　　　　 – e lui?/e lei?/e loro?　　　*how about him/her/them?*

ii) Asking and saying where you're from

The key verb is **essere** *(to be)*. The question, literally, is *'of where are you?'*

| Di | dove sei?
dov'è? | *Where are you from?* |

You usually answer by naming your home town:

| Sono di | Imperia
Manchester | *I'm from* | Imperia
Manchester |

If there's an adjective for the inhabitants of a town or region it can be used instead:

Sono romano/sono di Roma   *I'm Roman/from Rome*
Sono ligure   *I'm Ligurian/from Liguria*

But to say what country you're from you always use your nationality and not **di** plus the country:

Sono inglese   *I'm English/from England*

There is a list of nationalities in Ref. III, 5, pp. 242–3.

iii) Talking about the family

Marital status

| Sei
È
Siete | sposato/a?
sposato/a?
sposati/e? | *Are you married?* | Sì

No, non sono sposato/a | sono sposato/a
siamo sposati/e | *Yes*

No, I'm not married | *I'm married*
we're married |

Children

The key verb is **avere** *(to have)* [see Systems, note 2, p. 87].

| Hai
Ha
Avete | figli?
dei bambini? | *Have you got any* | *children?*
young children? |

| Ho
Abbiamo | due figli, un maschio e una femmina | *I've got*
We've got | *two children, a boy and a girl* |

No, non ho figli　　　　　　　　*No, I haven't got any children*

Patterns I

Brothers and sisters

Hai | fratelli?   *Have you got any brothers or sisters?*
Ha |

Sì, ho un fratello e una sorella   *Yes, I've got a brother and a sister.*
No, non ho fratelli,   *No, I haven't got any brothers and sisters,*
    sono figlio unico/sono figlia unica   *I'm an only child*

Age

When you ask someone's age you literally say *'How many years have you?'* The key question word is the adjective **quanto**.

Quanti anni hai/ha? *How old are you?*   Ho sette anni. *I'm seven.*

Quanti anni | ha | tuo figlio?   *How old is your son?*
                   Suo figlio?
                   vostro figlio?

Quanti anni | hanno | i tuoi figli?   *How old are your children?*
                      i Suoi figli?
                      i vostri figli?

See Troubleshooting, p. 48 and Systems, note 6, p. 89 for **Suoi/tuoi**, etc.
See Ref. I, 1, p. 239, for a complete list of numbers.

iv) Asking and stating preferences

The key verb is **preferire** *(to prefer)*. [See Systems, note 1, p. 87.]
To say what you like doing best, just use the infinitive after **preferire**:

Cosa | preferisci | fare?   *What do you prefer doing?*
       preferisce
       preferite

Preferisco | leggere e guardare la televisione | *I prefer* | *reading and watching television*
Preferiamo | chiacchierare e stare insieme | *We prefer* | *chatting and being together*

v) Asking why and giving reasons

The key words are **perché?** *(why?)* and **perché** *(because)*:

Perché | sei/è qui?   *Why* | *are you here?*
         giochi/gioca a pallavolo?   *do you play volleyball?*

perché | è divertente   *because* | *it's fun*
         è interessante   *it's interesting*

You can be more specific by adding a verb in the infinitive:

perché è divertente | stare in Italia   *because it's fun* | *being in Italy*
                      giocare   *playing/to play*

Asking and stating preferences

1 Ask students to carry out opinion polls in class.

2 Choose a topic on which a preference can be expressed, so as to permit a question of the type: *Preferisci A, B o C?* to be asked. For example, if the topic is *genere di film*, tell students to ask: *Che genere di film preferisci guardare?*

3 Here are some suggestions on areas of common interest. Ask students to find out the most popular of the three choices:

hobby e passatempi	*passeggiare, leggere, cucinare*
sport (giocare a)	*tennis, pallone, calcio*
programma televisivi	*attualità, sportivi, telefilm*
musica (ascoltare)	*jazz, classica, pop*
genere di film	*polizieschi, americani, classici*

4 Ask students at random to state the most popular sport, hobby, etc. Tell them to say, for example: *la musica più popolare è il jazz*.

Asking why and giving reasons

1 Go back through the above list of activities with students. Ask briefly why people would do them, e.g. *Perché preferisci cucinare? Perché è divertente.* Gradually elicit as many reasons as possible and write them on the board.

2 Ask students to write down an activity that they do at the weekend. Other students ask what they do and why and give reasons.

Identifying with others: me neither, you neither

1   Ask another student to read out his/her activity.

2   Say that you don't do this activity and invite other students to agree with you and use *ne'anchio . . .*, or agree with the student and use *anch'io.*

Practice 1

Wish you were here
Aim: practising giving reasons in writing

1   On the board draw the back of a postcard. Write a fictitious address on one side and a brief message on the other.

2   Ask students to write a postcard to an Italian friend in which they say where they are and why they are there.

3   Students could then read out their postcards, omitting to say where they are. The rest of the class have to deduce where they are from the reasons they give.

Getting to know each other
Aim: practising asking questions and talking about oneself

1   Ask students to write a dialogue of about a dozen exchanges on everything they can ask each other.

2   Tell them to do some oral practice, then ask one pair of students to role play their dialogue.

3   Take the part of one student but instead of saying what's been written, grossly exaggerate facts, by creating families of up to ten children, for example.

4   When students are more confident, ask them to give the class a short talk (five minutes maximum) about themselves from memory, using only the Italian they have learned so far, and illustrating their talk with photographs, drawings, diagrams, etc.

You can use other adjectives in the same way:

È	importante	imparare l'italiano	It's	important	to learn Italian
	necessario			necessary	
	essenziale			essential	

vi) Identifying with others: me neither, you neither

The key word is **neanche** *(neither)*. You can combine it with **io, tu, lui, lei, noi, voi** and **loro**. In front of **io, neanche** becomes **neanch'io** and is pronounced as one word.

Non sono sposato neanch'io   *I'm not married either*
Non hai fratelli neanche tu?   *Don't you have brothers and sisters either?*
Non ha figli neanche Lei?   *Don't you have children either?*

Practice I

How are you all?

You meet a friend, Roberto, in the street and ask him how he is. Complete the conversation using **stare**.

You	Ciao, Roberto. Come . . .?
Roberto	Bene, grazie. E tu?
You	. . . bene anch'io. E tua moglie?
Roberto	. . . bene anche lei.
You	E i figli?
Roberto	. . . bene anche loro.
You	Allora, voi . . . tutti bene!
Roberto	Sì, . . . tutti bene.

Getting to know you   31

You meet up with Luca in a bar one evening. Find out something about him and his family. You don't know him very well, so use **Lei**.

You	[Say hello and ask how he is.]
Luca	Buonasera. Bene grazie. E Lei?
You	[Say you're fine too.]
Luca	Lei, di dov'è?
You	[Say where you're from and ask where he comes from.]
Luca	Sono di Genova e abito a Sanremo.
You	[Ask if he is married.]
Luca	Sì, sono sposato.
You	[Ask where his wife comes from.]
Luca	Mia moglie è di Genova anche lei.
You	[Ask if he has got any children.]
Luca	Sì, ho una femmina e due maschi.
You	[Ask how old his daughter is.]
Luca	Mia figlia ha dieci anni.
You	[Ask about his sons.]
Luca	I miei figli hanno nove e sette anni.

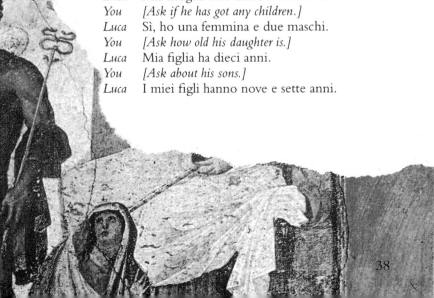

Kindred spirits

You're single, an only child and no good at games!
At parties you tend to feel the odd one out. But the
conversation at this party is different . . .

Non gioco a tennis

To which you can reply, expressing pleasant surprise:

Ah, davvero? Non gioco a tennis neanch'io!

Here are some more phrases welcome to your ears:

1 Non ho fratelli
2 Non sono sposato
3 Non ho figli
4 Non gioco a golf

Can you give an appropriate reply, expressing
solidarity?

Tea or coffee?

You're entertaining Italian guests for the weekend.
First you need to know what refreshments your
guests prefer. Ask each person in turn using the
alternatives suggested below.
e.g. Patrizia, . . .   tè o caffè?
Patrizia, cosa preferisci – tè o caffè?

1 Andrea, . . . vino bianco o vino rosso?
2 Signor Fante, . . . un Cinzano o un Campari?
3 Signori, . . . vodka o whisky?

What you'd rather do

Now you want to know what people would rather
do. The choice is not unlimited, so use the
alternatives given.
e.g. Patrizia, . . . stare a casa o vedere un film?
Patrizia, cosa preferisci fare – stare a casa o
vedere un film?

1 Andrea, . . . guardare la televisione o ascoltare la
radio?
2 Signor Fante, . . . mangiare adesso o aspettare?
3 Signori, . . . giocare a bridge o giocare a scacchi?

Priorities

The symbols below explain the amenities available
in various holiday resorts, being considered by you
and some Italian friends. Pick out a few and put
them in order of importance.
First what do you prefer to have; then what's
important; what's necessary; and, lastly, what's
essential for you.

e.g. In vacanza:
preferisco ottimi ristoranti
è importante avere divertimenti
è necessario avere una spiaggia attrezzata
è essenziale avere giochi per bambini

If you know other Italian speakers, discuss their
preferences too.

Cosa preferisci bere?

Aim: to practise the full conjugation of the present tense of *preferire*

1 Make some cards showing the names of different drinks.

2 Show one card to student A and ask, for example: *Preferisci succo d'arancia o di pompelmo?*

3 Show the same card to student B and ask him or her to ask you or someone else the question.

4 Change the card and address a student formally: *Signor . . . preferisce un caffè o un cappuccino?*

5 Elicit different questions and answers by changing the cards and the number of students you ask each question.

Cosa preferisci fare la domenica?

1 Write the following on the board:

lavare la macchina	*passeggiare*
andare al pub/in chiesa	*fare del giardinaggio*
leggere il giornale	*dormire*

2 Tell students to write a few sentences about what they and the other members of their household would rather do on a Sunday.

3 In pairs, students try to guess what their partner prefers to do on a Sunday. When they get the right answer, they exchange roles.

New words

Aim: vocabulary building

1 Give students a photocopy of a picture (anything which suggests a leisure activity).

2 Ask students to write down at least half a dozen words connected in some way to the picture. (If students do not know the Italian equivalents, tell them to use the dictionary or to ask you or someone else.)

3 Students compare what they have written with someone else and explain the meaning of new words to one another.

4 Students make a note of the new words, which you also write on the board.

5 When the students have studied the words, rub them off the board and give students a time-limit in which to write down as many as they can from memory.

Variation:

Follow **1** and **2** as above.

3 In pairs, students compare words to find ones they have in common.

4 Students compare the remaining words with two more students and carry on until they find out what the most common words are.

Choosing a holiday

Read these descriptions of different holiday resorts.

a

b

c

TESSERA CLUB

obbligatoria in hotel e in residence e per tutta la stagione L. 45.000 per persona per l'intero soggiorno (bambini 3/14 anni L. 35.000), in loco. **Include:** uso del campo da tennis e bocce, windsurf, canoa, vela, catamarano, tiro con l'arco, pedalos, tuffi, nuoto, yoga, ginnastica aerobica, arte applicata, fotografia, mini e junior club, piscina olimpionica e per bambini, piscina con idromassaggi, lezioni collettive degli sports previsti, centro commerciale, discoteca, spettacoli musicali, giochi, feste, cabaret.

TESSERA CLUB

(obbligatoria dal 15/6 al 31/8) per entrambe le formule L. 50.000 per persona (bambini oltre 10 anni) per l'intero periodo di soggiorno, da pagare in agenzia. **Include:** servizio medico, parcheggio, ping-pong, deposito valori, campo calcio, servizio spiaggia, discoteca, piscina, pallavolo e animazione.

d

Decide which one you would go for: **a, b, c,** or **d.** There's no need to understand every word, but look things up if you want to. Be prepared to justify your choice:

preferisco . . . perché

Now unscramble the two words below. They each occur twice in the descriptions. One is linked to the word for saying 'How do you do?'. The other is connected with the verb for 'having fun'.

LEVOIPACE   TENTREVIDE

Your spare time

Can you think of ten words which will help you talk about your spare time? If you need help, there is a list of useful expressions in the Vocabulary on p. 47.

Golf in Italy

Read this article about the history of golf in Italy and for each of the years mentioned see if you can work out how many players and how many golf courses there were. If necessary, check the numbers in Ref. I, 1, p. 239.

Nel 1954 in Italia ci sono diciotto campi e milleduecento giocatori. Nel 1960 i duemilacinquecento golfisti hanno a disposizione venticinque campi da gioco. Nel 1970 gli iscritti alla Federazione sono già settemila con trenta campi.

Nel 1980 a giocare sono tredicimila persone, che diventano venticinquemila nel 1985.

In questi giorni i golfisti praticanti sono quasi quarantamila e i campi da gioco sono centotrentasette.

Cultura e parole

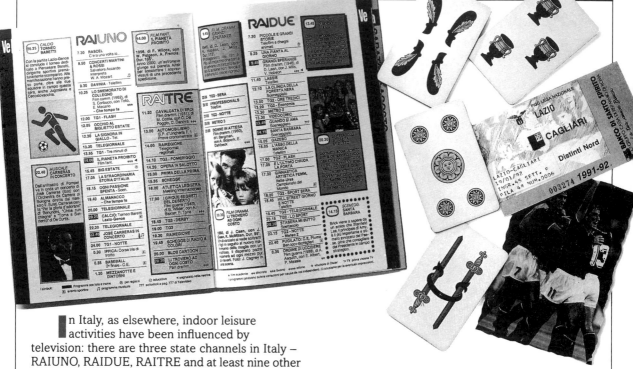

In Italy, as elsewhere, indoor leisure activities have been influenced by television: there are three state channels in Italy – RAIUNO, RAIDUE, RAITRE and at least nine other main channels, one of which, **Retequattro**, offers virtual round the clock viewing. Although nowadays most people have televisions, the habit of watching TV in bars has not died out, particularly when it comes to watching an important football match – **una partita**. Collective rather than solitary leisure activities are still very popular, especially card games – bridge, **il bridge** – and above all **la briscola** and games like **marafone** which are played with a 40-card pack of **carte napoletane**. The four suits are called **bastoni, denari, coppe** and **spade** (some cards are shown above).

Most leisure time is concentrated into the summer holidays – **le vacanze estive** or **ferie. Il mare** – the seaside – has waned in popularity since the 1980s, but is still the choice of over 50 per cent of Italian holidaymakers. Until the 1950s, a seaside holiday was very exclusive. Most people went to Liguria, the first region to develop seaside resorts in the nineteenth century, as it was then one of the few accessible coastal areas where there were no malarial marshes. Nowadays mass tourism has invaded most beaches. There are very few **spiagge libere** – free beaches – because there is an enormous demand for a **spiaggia attrezzata** – a beach with all amenities: a bar, sunbeds – **lettini**, deck-chairs – **sdraie** and umbrellas – **ombrelloni**.

L'Italiese – anglicised Italian. The language of sport and entertainment in Italy has been heavily influenced by English. This is not a new trend: **il jazz**, for example, was used in the 1920s. In the 1930s, under Mussolini, there was an unsuccessful attempt to substitute this with **il giazzo**, but in general Italians have preferred simply to adopt not adapt the words they need: **il rock, la star, i fans, l'hit-parade, lo sport, lo sprint, il fitness, la mountain bike, il windsurfing** and, of course, **il tennis** and **il golf**. The national sport, football – **il calcio**, from the word for kick, has escaped the anglicising trend, though the English word, sometimes spelt **futbol**, is not unknown. Some English words in Italian have unexpected meanings. Take, for example, **lo spot, il golf** and **la spider: lo spot** is an advertising slot on TV and **il golf** first entered the Italian language as a cardigan or jumper (from the English golf jacket) not a game, at a time when golf was not played in Italy. It has only more recently become familiar as a game and is now the up and coming status sport. **La spider** is a convertible sports car and the name came from the spider-shaped framework of the hood.

Cultura e parole

There are no prizes for guessing that football, *il calcio,* is the most popular sport in Italy. It is played by many *per divertimento a livello dilettante* – for fun at an amateur level. Many more are, however, *i tifosi* – the supporters of *le squadre* – the teams. The teams are divided into four main divisions – *in quattro serie: A* to *D.* Horse racing is not particularly popular in Italy, therefore the betting industry is almost entirely based on *Totocalcio,* the national pools linked to the Sunday league football games – *le partite di calcio di campionato.* In order to win the jackpot – *fare 13* – it is necessary to fill in *la schedina,* the pools coupon, and to guess the right result: home win, draw or away win for each of the thirteen matches. For example, if the match is between Napoli and Juventus and the two teams are playing in Naples, 1 would mean a victory for *il Napoli,* X a draw and 2 a victory for *la Juventus* (pronounced 'Iuventus').

The second most practised sport is without doubt *il ciclismo.* There are nearly two million *ciclisti (dilettanti e professionisti)* but cycling is less popular as a way of commuting to work. The *Giro d'Italia* is, like the *Tour de France,* a gruelling and epic race. Only a few *corridori* – riders – have been able to win both races in the same year.

Many more sports are widely practised but the one for which Italians are famous (and perhaps notorious) throughout the world is *automobilismo* – Formula One racing. Names of Italian drivers and car manufacturers are legendary: see how many your students can remember.

Interaction 5 (387)

Although Italians take part in all major international championships, tennis is not so easy to play for many as it is very expensive and finding a court in big cities can be difficult.

1 *Anna Mazzotti è in un tennis club e parla con il vice presidente, Giulio Preti.*

2 *Le domande sono:*
Who else in Giulio's family plays tennis?
How many courts does the club have?

3 Play the cassette/CD as required. *Quali sono le risposte?*

4 Ask further questions:
How long has Giulio been playing tennis?
What types of court are there?
What does Giulio suggest he and Anna should do?

5 *Leggete sul libro. Ci sono altre domande?*

In my neighbourhood . . .

1 Taking their cue from the above interaction, ask students to describe their local gym – *palestra* – or sports centre – *centro sportivo* – through a role play interview.

2 Suggest that students use the following questions:

Dov'è la palestra/il centro sportivo?
Che cosa c'è nella palestra/nel centro sportivo?
Da quanto tempo esiste?
Da quanto tempo giochi/giocate a . . .?
Che cosa preferisci fare?

This point could be the end of the lesson. Revise the points covered so far. In the next lesson students will cover the following:

> **Structures:** *da* + infinitive/question tag *vero?*
> **Functions:** making introductions/offering food and drink
> **Vocabulary:** *spremuta, aperitivo, socio, assistente, Stato, chi?, personale, piacevole, divertente, splendido, prendere, gestire*

Interaction 6 (404)

1 *Anna e Giulio sono nel bar.*
Who is Vincenzo?
How do you say 'What are you having?'?

2 Play the cassette/CD as required. Ask further questions:
Who is there besides Anna and Giulio?
What form of address is used by each person?
What do they all drink?
What does *subito* mean?

Use this Interaction for the following classroom activity:

1 Tell students to list on a large sheet of blank paper, the numbers 1–22.

2 Each of the twenty-two lines corresponds to what each speaker says. Tell students to write down everything they hear.

3 Play the Interaction several times (students will not write much each time). Encourage them to go on.

4 After three or four times, ask students in pairs to compare what they have written. Play the Interaction again, three or four times (the students themselves will now be asking you to play the Interaction again and again), and tell students to compare what they have written, this time in groups of four.

5 Carry on in the same way until the class is divided into just two groups and both have completed the task.

6 Ask each group to tell you what they have written, (one line from each) and write every word on the board.

7 Split students into groups of five – one per character in the Interaction – and tell them to read the Interaction from the board, memorising as much as possible each time. Gradually rub off the Interaction line by line.

8 Invite five volunteers to role play the Interaction and ask everyone to judge the performance (jot down any comments and discuss at the end).

1 Giulio	7 Vincenzo	13 Gino	19 Giulio
2 Vincenzo	8 Giulio	14 Giulio	20 Gino
3 Anna	9 Vincenzo	15 Anna	21 Giulio
4 Giulio	10 Gino	16 All	22 Vincenzo
5 Anna	11 Beppe	17 Giulio	
6 Giulio	12 Giulio	18 Beppe	

Interactions

5 [cc] [CD] 32/33

The very first tennis club in Italy, Il Bordighera Tennis Club, was founded by the British residents of Bordighera in the last century. The club is now all-Italian, with a splendid new bar, gym and games room. Its young Vice President, Giulio Preti, meets Anna.

First time round

il circolo	club
i campi	courts
la terra rossa	clay

Read the words given here and use a bit of guesswork.

a Who else in Giulio's family plays tennis?
b How many courts does the club have?

Anna	Giulio, **da quanto tempo giochi** a tennis?
Giulio	Gioco a tennis da almeno quindici anni.
Anna	E la tua famiglia gioca?
Giulio	La mia famiglia gioca a tennis, i miei genitori, mio fratello . . .
Anna	E il circolo, **da quanto tempo esiste?**
Giulio	Il circolo esiste da cento anni. – Questi sono i campi da tennis.
Anna	Quanti campi avete?
Giulio	Abbiamo sei campi da tennis; quattro in terra rossa e due in sintetico. – Adesso possiamo andar a prendere qualcosa da bere al bar?
Anna	Sì, volentieri.

qualcosa da bere *something to drink*
volentieri *with pleasure*

> ### Key phrases
>
> **da quanto tempo . . .** *how long . . .*
> **giochi?** *have you been playing?*
> **esiste?** *has it existed?*

6 [cc] [CD] 33

In the bar Anna chooses a very Italian drink. She is introduced to two club members, Beppe and Gino, and also to Vincenzo . . .

First time round

il nostro	our
la spremuta	fresh juice
i soci	members

a Who is Vincenzo?
b How do you say 'What are you having?'

Giulio	Questo è il nostro bar. **Ti presento** il nostro barista, Vincenzo.
Vincenzo	Piacere, come sta?
Anna	Molto bene, grazie.
Giulio	**Cosa prendi** da bere, Anna?
Anna	Una spremuta con lo zucchero.
Giulio	Due spremute per favore, Vincenzo.
Vincenzo	Va bene.
Giulio	Beppe? E Gino?
Vincenzo	Oh, eccoli.
Gino	Ciao, Beppe.
Beppe	Ciao.
Giulio	Ciao, Gino.
Gino	Ciao, Giulio.
Giulio	Ti presento due soci del tennis.
Anna	Piacere.
All	Ciao, piacere.
Giulio	Beppe, cosa prendi?
Beppe	Un aperitivo.
Giulio	Gino, cosa prendi?
Gino	Anch'io, grazie.
Giulio	Due aperitivi, per favore.
Vincenzo	Subito.

[...]

eccoli *here they are*

> ### Key phrases
>
> **ti presento** *let me introduce you to*
> **cosa prendi?** *what are you having?*

7   34

Not far from Bordighera, near the French border, are the Hanbury Botanical Gardens, founded in 1867 by an English tea merchant, Sir Thomas Hanbury. Anna first meets Guido Novaro who's in charge, and then Luca, one of his assistants.

First time round

gestire	*to manage*
lo stato	*the state*
all'aria aperta	*in the open air*

Pick out for each of them:
a How long have they been working in the Hanbury Gardens?
b What do they like about their jobs?

Anna	Signor Guido Novaro, Lei è assistente tecnico dell'università di Genova. Chi gestisce questi giardini?
Sig. Novaro	Il giardino è proprietà demaniale, cioè, dello stato.
Anna	E lo gestisce . . .?
Sig. Novaro	Lo gestisce l'università di Genova.
Anna	Da quanto tempo lavora qui?
Sig. Novaro	Lavoro qui da ventinove anni.
Anna	È un lavoro piacevole?
Sig. Novaro	È un lavoro molto bello.
Anna	Perché?
Sig. Novaro	Eh . . . perché lavorare all'aria aperta è molto divertente con tante belle piante.
Anna	Avete molto lavoro?
Sig. Novaro	Sì, abbiamo molto lavoro tutto l'anno.
Anna	**Avete bisogno di** molto personale?
Sig. Novaro	**Abbiamo bisogno di** molto aiuto, sì.

[. . .]

Anna	Luca, da quanto tempo è che lavori qui?
Luca	Lavoro qui da solo sei mesi.
Anna	**È bello lavorare** qui?
Luca	Sì, è molto bello anche perché amo lavorare all'aria aperta.

cioè   *that is to say*

Key phrases

avete bisogno di?	*do you need?*
abbiamo bisogno di	*we need*
è bello lavorare qui?	*is it nice working here?*

8   35

Walking round the gardens Anna meets a holiday-maker who is enjoying the weather.

First time round

il tempo	*the weather*	Can you work out why he is here?

Anna	**Che bella giornata, vero?**
Dott. Savini	Ah, oggi il tempo è splendido . . . meraviglioso.
Anna	Ma Lei, di dov'è?
Dott. Savini	Io sono ligure, di Imperia.
Anna	Ed **è qui in vacanza, vero?**
Dott. Savini	Sì, sono qui perché ho bisogno di riposare. [. . .]

Key phrases

che bella giornata, vero?	*it's a lovely day, isn't it?*
è qui in vacanza, vero?	*you're here on holiday, aren't you?*

Isn't it? Aren't you? etc.   36

Listen to the cassette/CD and see how easily these common phrases are used in Italian. Try and see if you can use **vero**.

Interaction 7 (423)

1 *Anna è nel giardino botanico* (the botanical gardens founded by Sir Thomas Hanbury near Bordighera). *Anna incontra il signor Guido Novaro (capogiardiniere) e Luca (un assistente).*
How long have they been working there?
What do they like about their jobs?

2 Play the cassette/CD as required and ask further questions:
Who owns and manages the gardens?
Is there a lot of work?
How is the work spread out through the year?

The dream job
Aim: to stimulate free writing

1 Tell students to imagine themselves doing the job they would like most.

2 Ask them to write a dialogue of the kind they have just heard/seen.

Interaction 8 (455)

1 *Nel giardino botanico Anna incontra anche il dottor Savini che è in vacanza.*
Why is he there?

2 Play the cassette/CD as required.

Patterns 2

Making introductions

1 Prepare some cards with names of relations.

2 Tell students to practise making introductions by saying:

Ti/Le presento *mio fratello* *mia sorella*
               un mio amico *una mia amica*

3 Depending on the level of the group, you could also use the plural:
i miei cugini *le mie cugine*

4 Ask student A to introduce student B, then ask student B to introduce student C, and so on. Keep a brisk and lively pace.

5 Withdraw the cards and encourage students to make up acquaintances, friendships and relationships on the spur of the moment.

Offering food and drink

1 Divide the class into groups of three or four. One student from each group is the waiter, the others are customers.

2 Practise a sample situation with one group. The waiter takes the orders, then repeats each item at the end:

CAMERIERE:	*Che cosa prende da bere?*
CLIENTE (A):	*Un bicchiere di acqua minerale.*
CAMERIERE:	*Prende qualcosa da mangiare?*
CLIENTE (A):	*Un toast al prosciutto e formaggio per piacere.*
CAMERIERE:	*E Lei che cosa prende?*
CLIENTE (B):	*Un cappuccino e un tramezzino.*
CAMERIERE:	*Va bene. Allora un bicchiere di acqua minerale, un cappuccino, un toast al prosciutto e formaggio e un tramezzino.*

3 In order to add an element of realism, tell them to practise this role play in a brisk and lively manner (it's a busy fast-food bar . . . a lot of noise . . . the waiter makes mistakes in repeating the order).

Saying how long for? how long since?

1 Stress the importance and the simplicity of this pattern (after all, saying what you have been doing in English is much more complex).

2 Ask personalised questions and tell students that it doesn't matter whether it is five minutes or 23 years, the structure is the same.

Da quanto tempo:
studi italiano?   *sei vegetariano?*
bevi vino?   *hai un computer?*
abiti a . . .?   *giochi a tennis?*
sei tifoso del . . .?   *non giochi a tennis?*

3 Tell students that if you add *non* making the question negative as in the last example, it means: 'How long is it since you last . . .?'

Checking and confirming

Tell students to practise the question tag *vero?* by trying to remember as many of the previous answers as possible. e.g. Student A asks student B: *Sei vegetariano da cinque anni, vero?*

This point could be the end of the lesson. Revise the points covered so far. In the next lesson students will cover the following:

> **Structures:** revising the present tense of all conjugations, including *avere* and *essere*
> **Functions:** expressing needs, pleasure and admiration/offering food and drink/talking about hobbies and leisure activities
> **Vocabulary:** hobbies and interests

Expressing need

1 For each of the following situations tell students to work out the right form of *avere* and to choose the most appropriate object of the three available. (Discuss the vocabulary items briefly before you start.)

e.g. You have an envelope, but you haven't got a stamp.
colla/timbro/francobollo
(Ho bisogno di un francobollo.)

1 Your neighbour's car won't start.
candela/pinta/spinta
2 Your friend's pen has just run out of ink.
giro/biro/matita
3 A couple of friends want to make a phone call from a public telephone without a coin slot.
carta di credito/carta telefonica/carta igienica
4 Lucio's portable radio doesn't sound too good.
nuova pila/nuova cassetta/nuovo disco
5 Your football team has not won a game for a long time.
più grinta/meno tifosi/viaggio premio
6 Your account is badly in the red.
fare più spese/guadagnare meno/prendere soldi in prestito
7 You and some friends are planning a sight-seeing tour.
atlante/guida/spartito

2 Ask students to invent a problem. Tell them to explain it briefly and ask the other students to give advice, saying: *Hai/ha bisogno di . . .*

Patterns 2

i) Making introductions

Ti	presento	mia sorella	*Let me introduce*	*my sister*
Le		le mie sorelle		*my sisters*
		mio fratello		*my brother*
		i miei fratelli		*my brothers*

See Systems, note 6, p. 89 for **mie**, **miei**, etc.

The response is usually **piacere** or **molto piacere**.

ii) Offering food and drink

To find out what someone is having, you need the verb **prendere** *(to take)*:

Cosa prendi?/prende?   *What are you having?* [lit. *taking*]

If you want to be more specific you can ask:

Prendi qualcosa	da bere?	*Are you having anything*	*to drink?*
Prende	da mangiare?		*to eat?*

To say what you're having:

Prendo un'aranciata   *I'll have an orangeade*

iii) Saying how long for? how long since?

All you need is the word **da** and the present tense:

Da quanto tempo è qui?   *How long have you been here?*
Da quanto tempo studia l'italiano?   *How long have you been studying Italian?*

Da can mean *for* or *since*:

Sono qui da ieri   *I've been here since yesterday*
Studio qui da sei mesi   *I've studied here for six months*
Gioco a golf da due anni.   *I've played golf for two years*

iv) Checking and confirming

In Italian all you need is the word **vero?** – which means *true?* – on the end of the sentence.

Lei è qui in vacanza, vero?   *You're here on holiday aren't you?*
Lei parla italiano, vero?   *You speak Italian, don't you?*
Studia l'italiano da molto tempo, vero?   *You've been studying Italian for a long time, haven't you?*

v) Expressing need

The expression **avere bisogno di** literally means *to have need of*:

Hai/ha bisogno di aiuto?   *Do you need help?*

Ho bisogno di	riposare	*I need*	*to rest*
	divertirmi		*to enjoy myself*

Patterns 2

vi) Expressing pleasure

The key phrase is **è bello**, literally *it's beautiful,* followed by an infinitive:

| È bello | stare qui
essere in vacanza | *It's nice/lovely* | *being here*
being on holiday |

To express admiration, use the phrase **che bello:**

Che bella giornata!   *What a lovely day!*   Che belle scarpe!   *What lovely shoes!*

In front of masculine nouns **bello** is shortened:

Che bel vestito!   *What a lovely dress!*   Che bei pantaloni!   *What lovely trousers!*

Che bello! on its own means   *How lovely, how nice!*

See Unit 10, Systems, for a fuller explanation.

Practice 2

May I introduce . . .?

You've got plenty of people to introduce. Can you get it right? First introduce the following to your friend Danilo:

1 your mother   3 your sisters
2 your brother   4 your neighbour

Now introduce these people to dottor Rabbiotti:

5 your parents   7 your girlfriend
6 your aunt   8 your grandparents

How lovely!

Everyone likes getting compliments. Practise on the objects pictured here by admiring what you see! Then ask who they belong to, using the **Lei** form of address, and **suo, sua, suoi, sue** (without the article).
e.g. Che bei fiori! Sono Suoi?
   What lovely flowers? Are they yours?

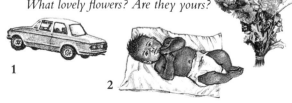

1
2
3
4

Refresh your memory

How many different drinks can you remember? The Vocabulary in Units 1–3 will help. Check out the words for different snacks at the end of this unit.

It's on me   37

You're buying the drinks and snacks for two people: Sandra, who's an old friend, and signor Giustini, whom you've only just met. Ask each of them what they're having.

You	[Ask signor Giustini what he's having to drink.]
Sig. G.	Un aperitivo – un Cinzano.
You	[Ask him what he's having to eat.]
Sig. G.	Un panino con formaggio.
You	[Now ask Sandra what she's having.]
Sandra	Un'acqua minerale, con limone.
You	[Ask her if she's having anything to eat.]
Sandra	Un tramezzino con prosciutto.
You	[Say – me too and I'll have a Cinzano.]

Expressing pleasure

1 You can't account for taste but you can certainly talk about it. Write the following examples on the board OHP:

fare il bagno con acqua molto calda
fare cinque miglia di corsa tutti i giorni
fumare una sigaretta dopo pranzo/cena
uscire tutte le sere
prendere il sole
fare la doccia con acqua fredda
ascoltare musica rock a tutto volume
mangiare cibi salati/dolci
dormire fino a mezzogiorno la domenica
svegliarsi presto tutti i giorni

2 Discuss the meanings as necessary.

3 Ask students to choose one and to express pleasure. For example: *È bello uscire tutte le sere.*

4 Students will naturally also want to express displeasure. Tell them to put simply *non è* before the statement.

Expressing admiration

1 Ask students to express admiration of the following:

giornata, fiori, fotografie, fuochi d'artificio, albero di Natale, canzoni, cartolina d'auguri, pantaloni, poesie, musica, disco, film, negozio, romanzo

2 Read out the items and ask students to write each item in one of four different columns.

bel	bella	bei	belle
(disco)	(cartolina)	(fiori)	(poesie)

3 Ask students to express admiration about something in particular, then discuss the meaning.

Che bel . . .!, if said with a touch of irony, means 'What a . . .! e.g. *Che bel guaio!* What a mess!

Practice 2

Who does what?

Aim: to practise understanding and selecting the right information from spoken Italian

1 Four people taking part in a television quiz introduce themselves and say a bit about their hobbies and spare time activities. Tell students to find out who does what and to fill in the chart below accordingly.

2 Read what each person says, giving the students time to fill in the chart (write it on the board or give them copies).

3 Before you read what each person does, make sure the students understand the words in the chart. It is not necessary for them to understand every word you read, just the main points.

	Lucia Pegrini	Giovanni Mattei	Rita Mantovani	Giacomo Lentini
musica				
chitarra				
passeggiata				
romanzi				
cinema				
piscina				
sport				
ginnastica				
danza				
televisione				
giornale				
amici				

1 Mi chiamo Lucia Pegrini e sono di Pinerolo in provincia di Torino. Lavoro in un ufficio commerciale e di solito torno a casa tardi. Prima di cena, faccio una passeggiata con il cane. Dopo cena, guardo la TV con mio marito o leggo il giornale.

2 Sono un tipo sportivo. Mi chiamo Giovanni Mattei e sono di Trapani, in Sicilia. Sono appassionato di automobilismo e ciclismo. Gioco a tennis e vado spesso in piscina. La sera ascolto musica, o, se c'è un buon film, guardo la televisione.

3 Mi chiamo Rita Mantovani. Lavoro a Milano ma sono di Bergamo. Dopo cena, di solito guardo la televisione o leggo romanzi. Preferisco stare a casa la sera, ma la domenica vado a trovare amici e parenti. Sono appassionata di danza.

4 Mi chiamo Giacomo Lentini e sono di Lecce in Puglia. Sono appassionato di musica e la sera e la domenica suono la chitarra con un gruppo di amici. Di solito, faccio una passeggiata dopo cena e a volte vado a cinema con qualche amico, oppure, prima di cena, faccio della ginnastica in palestra.

4 Check answers, discuss any other questions, then ask students to write out what each person does in their spare time. Tell them to take the information from the chart they have just filled in. Encourage them to use *appassionato/a* and *preferire*.

3

Questionnaire: il tempo libero

Aim: to encourage oral practice of functions and structures learned so far

1   Tell students to carry out surveys on how each student occupies his/her free time.

2   Tell students to copy down a number of likely activities, which you have written on the board. At the top of the page, tell them to write other students' names. For example:

	Student A	Student B	Student C
fai da te			
sport			
cucina			
giardinaggio			
musica			

3   Ask students to go around the class interviewing each other on how they spend their free time. Tell them simply to put ticks on the chart.

4   **Variation:** Students can ask more specific questions. e.g. *Che tipo di attività culturali, sportive o domestiche? Da quanto tempo sei socio di . . .?* and make a note of the answers.

5   Students can prepare a brief report on what they have discovered.

e.g. *Due studenti sono soci di un circolo. Quattro fanno attività sportive. Tre preferiscono svolgere attività domestiche.*

Show off what you know

1   At this point you can tell students that they can say a great deal. Eliciting full answers, ask the following:

T   *Come ti chiami?*   S   *Mi chiamo . . .*
T   *Hai fratelli?*   S   *Sì, uno.*
T   *Come si chiama?*   S   *Si chiama . . .*
T   *Quanti anni ha?*   S   *Ha . . . anni.*
T   *Dove abita?*   S   *Abito a* (name of town)
T   *Hai animali domestici?*   S   *Sì, un gatto.*
T   *Come si chiama?*   S   *Si chiama . . .*
T   *Giochi a tennis?*   S   *Sì, gioco a tennis.*
T   *Da quanto tempo . . .?*   S   *Gioco a tennis da . . .*
T   *Parli francese?*   S   *No, parlo . . .*

2   In order to keep the exercise lively and interesting, involve other students by asking them to repeat (using the third person) one or more answers given previously by someone else.

Il personaggio misterioso

Aim: oral practice of structures learned so far

1   Divide the class into two groups.

2   Tell students to think of a famous person and to write his or her name on a piece of paper.

3   In turn, each group asks a question (only yes or no answers) to the other in order to guess the identity of the famous person.

Lascia o raddoppia (the first Italian television quiz show)

Aim: to practise asking about people's lives, hobbies, etc.

1   Remind students that in quiz shows participants very often have a little chat with the presenter in order to introduce themselves.

2   Ask students to prepare some questions which they could ask as presenters.

e.g. *Come si chiama?*
Ha figli/fratelli/sorelle?
Quanti anni ha . . .?
Che cosa preferisce/preferite fare durante il suo tempo libero?

3   Pair up students and get them to carry on writing questions.

4   Form bigger groups, until you have only two groups.

5   Ask each group to build a 'life' around a character – age, marital status, hobbies, sports, interests – and also build a family around him or her. (To add a touch of realism, tell them that the two characters are called Paolo Brasi and Carla Monte and, if possible, show pictures of them.)

6   One student from each group should be chosen by the other group to answer questions about the character.

7   He/she can consult with the rest of the group but, in order to keep things lively, set a time limit for answering the question. (You should also rule out any unfair questions.)

Il mio tempo libero

Aim: to encourage free writing on the topic of the unit.

Ask the students to write about their free time, providing some examples of activities which they find enjoyable and interesting, saying how long they have been doing these activities, and so on.

You could read some of the work aloud to the class to see if they can guess which student has which hobbies.

How long for?

What activities do the pictures represent? Check in the Vocabulary if you need help with the words. Practise saying how long you've been doing certain activities, starting with the ones shown here:

e.g. an hour; three weeks; eighteen months; seven years

1
2
3
4

Give your reasons!

Can you give two good reasons for doing each activity?

e.g. . . . stare all'aria aperta
   Ho bisogno di stare all'aria aperta.
   È bello stare all'aria aperta.

1 imparare una lingua straniera
2 stare con la famiglia

Now say the following are (1) fun and (2) interesting to do:

3 lavorare in un paese straniero
4 essere socio di un circolo
5 giocare a scacchi

Who does what?  37

Listen to the two people talking about how they spend their leisure time. As you listen, try to mark the chart below for each speaker.

	Speaker 1	Speaker 2
ascoltare: la musica classica		
la radio		
fare: ginnastica aerobica		
del giardinaggio		
yoga		
giocare: a scacchi		
a tennis		
guardare: la televisione		
un video		
leggere: romanzi		
riviste		
stare: con gli amici		

Identikit

Continue to draw up an identikit picture of yourself. Say the answers aloud in Italian, answering as fully as you can.

Quanti anni ha?   Ha fratelli?
È sposato?   Ha figli?
Ha animali domestici?   Di dov'è?
Da quanto tempo studia l'italiano?

Vocabulary

Free time

il passatempo	*pastime*
l'hobby	*hobby*
la gara	*competition*
il gioco	*game*
il torneo	*tournament*
la partita	*match*
lo sport	*sport*
lo svago	*entertainment*
	relaxation
preferito	*favourite*

Verbs

allenarsi	*to train*
ballare	*to dance*
cantare	*to sing*
cucinare	*to cook*
dipingere	*to paint*
disegnare	*to draw*
distrarsi	*to amuse oneself*
tenersi in forma	*to keep fit*
perdere	*to lose*
vincere	*to win*

Sports

l'alpinismo	*climbing*
le bocce	*bowls*
la canoa	*canoeing*
la corsa campestre	*cross-country running*
il ciclismo	*cycling*
il calcio	*football*
l'equitazione	*horse-riding*
la ginnastica aerobica	*aerobics*
il nuoto	*swimming*
la pallavolo	*volley-ball*
il pattinaggio	*skating*
il parapendismo	*hang-gliding*
il tiro con l'arco	*archery*
lo sci	*skiing*
lo yoga	*yoga*

People

la zia	*aunt*
lo zio	*uncle*
lo straniero	*foreigner*
lo studente	*student*
l'amico	*friend*
il turista	*tourist*
l'atleta	*athlete*
il giocatore	*player*
il tifoso	*fan*
il maestro	*coach*

Idioms

avere fame	*to be hungry*
avere sete	*to be thirsty*
avere caldo	*to be hot*
avere freddo	*to be cold*
avere fretta	*to be in a hurry*
aver voglia di	*to feel like*
avere tempo di	*to have time*
avere bisogno di	*to need*

Drinks and snacks

la bibita	*cold drink*
l'amaro	*bitter digestive drink*
lo champagne	*champagne*
l'aperitivo	*aperitif*
la spremuta	*fresh fruit-juice*
lo spumante	*spumante*
il succo di frutta	*fruit juice*
il ghiaccio	*ice*
lo zucchero	*sugar*
fare uno spuntino	*to have a snack*
la brioche	*croissant*
il panino	*roll*
le patatine	*crisps*
il toast	*toasted sandwich*
il tramezzino	*sandwich*

Activities

passare il tempo/ trascorrere il tempo	*to spend time*
appartenere a un circolo	*to belong to a club*
a un coro	*a choir*
essere socio di un circolo	*to be a member of a club*
essere iscritto a un corso	*to be enrolled on a course*
frequentare un corso	*to attend a course*
seguire un corso	*to follow a course*
avere la tessera per . . .	*to belong to, have a ticket for . . .*
la biblioteca	*the library*
una palestra	*a gym*
avere un abbonamento a . . .	*to have a subscription to . . .*
una rivista	*a magazine*
praticare uno sport	*to play a sport*
giocare a squash/	*to play squash*
a calcio	*football*
a carte	*cards*
a scacchi	*chess*
fare del giardinaggio	*to garden*
lavorare a maglia	*to knit*

Vocabulary

Ask students to match the Italian expressions to their English equivalents.

a) *amico di famiglia*   b) *chi trova un amico trova un tesoro*   c) *da amico*   d) *cattive amicizie*   e) *amici per la pelle*   f) *amico del cuore*

1) bosom friend   2) as a friend   3) bad company   4) life time friend/great pals   5) family friend   6) a good friend is worth his weight in gold

Give students tasks for homework. Tell them to:
a) carry a pocket-size dictionary and look up a word whenever it occurs to them.
b) think about the Italian equivalents of the items they use every day. Tell them gradually to compile a list, starting from the morning (*dentifricio, rasoio, tazza, biglietto, autobus,* etc).
c) link these with the actions which form part of their daily routine. For instance:

fare	*sentire*	*leggere*
il bagno	*la radio*	*il giornale*
la doccia	*musica*	*un libro*
colazione	*il notiziario*	*un romanzo*
pranzo	*un rumore*	*un messaggio*

Troubleshooting

Review

Here is a checklist of the main points learned in this unit.
For each point, ask the students to supply one or more
examples by asking specific questions.

present tense of all conjugations, including *avere* and
essere
present + *da*
irregular verbs *stare* and *preferire*
expressing needs, pleasure and admiration
offering food and drink
talking about interests, hobbies and leisure activities
asking and saying how you are
talking about yourself and your family
asking why and giving reasons
asking and saying where you are from
asking and stating preferences
agreeing (with others)

Troubleshooting

Whose is whose?

Getting possessives right can be difficult. The main thing to remember is that in Italian they agree with the *object possessed*, whereas in English they agree with the *owner*.

his/her		*their*	
il suo	libro	il loro	libro
i suoi	libri	i loro	libri
la sua	penna	la loro	penna
le sue	penne	le loro	penne

Questo è il libro di Marco? È il suo libro?   *Is it his book?*
Questo è il libro di Carla? È il suo libro?   *Is it her book?*
Questo è il libro di Marco e Carla? È il loro libro?   *Is it their book?*

The plural forms **suoi**, **sue** indicate *one* owner but *several* objects.

i suoi libri	*his, her books*
i loro libri	*their books*

Don't forget that **Suo** means *your* when you're using the polite form of address:

		your	
il Suo libro	i Suoi libri	la Sua penna	le Sue penne
il tuo libro	i tuoi libri	la tua penna	le tue penne
il vostro libro	i vostri libri	la vostra penna	le vostre penne

Possessives can also be used as pronouns, i.e., without the noun:
    È un bel libro. È tuo?/Suo?/vostro?
The article tends to be dropped in front of the pronoun, except when needed for clarification or emphasis.

Unità 4

I pendolari

Veduta aerea del centro storico, Ferrara

In this unit you'll learn to talk about how you travel and how to describe your routines. You will learn how to ask and tell the time, talk to people about their work and say what job you do.

'Italy is a democratic Republic founded on work'. These are the opening lines of the Italian Constitution which came into force on 1 January 1948. The value of work and its importance as a fundamental right is clearly recognised in the constitution – a fact which may surprise the outsider. The work ethic may not be immediately associated with Italians, and yet it is in part the secret of Italy's economic success since the war. In fact if you ask Italians what job they do, they may well tell you that they have more than one: **il doppio lavoro** – 'double' work is quite common. Sometimes the second job is not strictly official and constitutes what is known as **il lavoro nero** – moonlighting. Italy's submerged economy – **l'economia sommersa** – is actually a vital factor in explaining her prosperity. Despite a huge public debt and high unemployment of over 10 per cent, Italy in the 1990s has so far maintained her place amongst the top nations in Europe. For Italians in regular employment, the wage packet – **la busta paga** – can extend to a thirteenth month's pay – **la tredicesima**, or even a fourteenth – **quattordicesima** – for bankers amongst others. On retirement, on average at fifty-five for women and sixty for men, all Italians receive a pension of 80 per cent of their salary averaged over the final three years. In some professions it is actually 100 per cent – for bankers or journalists, for example.

I pendolari

Introduce the topic by reminding the students to look for the etymology of *pendolare*, in the sense of movement 'to and fro'. Although the trend for working from home is increasing in Italy too, the vast majority of people still travel to and from work every day.

Lavoro is a general term for employment. As far as the Civil Code is concerned, the worker is either *un prestatore di lavoro dipendente*, that is an employee, or *un professionista o prestatore d'opera intellettuale*, – a professional or freelance, and the number of professions has increased since the seventies. A report by CENSIS discovered 163 new professions in the 1980s. There is no doubt that this was largely accounted for by the growth of *il terziario* – the service sector – a trend echoed in many industrialised countries. The percentage of *la forza lavoro* employed in this sector reached 59% in 1990, according to CENSIS, an increase of more than 10 per cent over the previous ten years.

Nearly one hundred bills have been proposed to give professional status to these new jobs. Among the new professions waiting to be given legal status – *legittimazione giuridica* – quite a few do not require an English translation. In the field of tourism, two such new occupations are 'party-manager' or 'visual jockey'; in the financial sector we find the 'cash-manager' and 'logistics manager'. A foreign-sounding profession confers added status.

Video corner

Fisicamente come sono?

Aim: to practise words which describe physical characteristics

Video sequence: interviews at the railway station

1   Three women take part in Interaction 1. They are seen in close-up.

2   Ask students to fill in the grid below, with words to describe each woman's appearance.

	1	2	3
capelli			
faccia			
naso			
bocca			
altro			

How do they travel?

Aim: vocabulary building

Video sequence: from close-up of train on tracks to Daniel going into railway station

1   Four people talk about their journey to work.

2   Elicit words which refer to means of transport and write them on the board.

3   Students write the words in a column and prepare columns alongside for each of the four speakers, as shown below.

4   Play the sequence and ask students to number the order in which each person uses each means of transport.

	1	2	3	4
metropolitana				
macchina				
tram				
bicicletta				
taxi				
treno				
autobus				

La giornata lavorativa di Silvia e Danilo

Aim: listening and note-taking

Video sequence: From Silvia and Anna in the café having breakfast to the end of the scene with Anna and Danilo in the restaurant

1   When Anna meets Silvia for breakfast, and then Danilo over lunch, they talk about their respective working days.

2   Ask students to write down answers to the following questions. (Write the questions on the board or give copies to students.)

	Silvia	Danilo
How long has he/she been commuting?		
What is his/her job?		
How long is his/her working day?		

Interactions

> **Structures:** reflexive verbs *alzarsi,*
> *scusarsi/a* + articles/*andare, venire,*
> *uscire/dovere* + infinitive/relative pronouns *in cui, che*
> **Functions:** talking about your routine/time/asking
> and saying what something's like, how often
> something happens
> **Vocabulary:** travel and daily routines

Help-phrases and instructions

Accoppiatevi.
Lavorate in coppia.
Dividetevi in gruppi di 3/4/5 . . . persone.
Confrontate le risposte.

Interaction 1   (059)

1   *Tre donne parlano della vita del pendolare.*

2   Write on the board:
a) Commuting is very stressful.
b) Commuting is fairly tiring.
c) A commuter's day is tiring and very long.

3   Ask students to match the three voices to the views
expressed on the commuter's life.

4   Play the cassette/CD as required.

Interactions

I [cc] [CD] 2

It's not much fun getting to work in the morning, especially if you have to commute – **fare il pendolare**. Anna talks to early-morning travellers at Ferrara station to find out what it's like.

First time round

il pendolare	*commuter*	You'll hear three
presto	*early*	views expressed – all
tardi	*late*	by women.

As you listen, match the views outlined below with the relevant speaker:

a Commuting is very stressful.
b Commuting is fairly tiring.
c A commuter's day is tiring and very long.

Voice 1	Voice 2	Voice 3

Anna   **Com'è** la vita del pendolare**?**
Signora 1   La vita del pendolare è faticosa e dura perché la giornata **è molto** lunga.
Signora 2   La vita del pendolare **è abbastanza** faticosa. Mi alzo al mattino molto presto e torno alla sera molto tardi.
Signora 3   È molto stressante [. . .]

Key phrases

com'è . . .?	*what's it like?*
è molto . . .	*it's very . . .*
è abbastanza . . .	*it's fairly . . .*

2   [cc]   [CD] 3

Two of the commuters explain how they get from home to work.

First time round

esco di casa	*I leave the house*
prendo	*I take*
vado	*I go*

As well as the car, there are three other means of transport mentioned. They don't sound too different from their English equivalents: can you guess what they are?

[*Anna*   **Come va da casa al lavoro?**]

Signora 1   Esco di casa, **prendo la macchina** perché abito in periferia, parcheggio in stazione, vicino alla stazione, che è difficile perché ci sono molte macchine e molta gente. Prendo il treno, arrivo a Bologna che è la città in cui lavoro e prendo un autobus e vado a lavorare.

Signora 2   Arrivo alla stazione **in macchina** poi in treno vado fino a Bologna e da Bologna **con la bicicletta** vado fino al lavoro.

molta gente	*many people*
in cui	*in which*
da	*from*
fino a	*to, as far as*

Key phrases

come va . . .	*how do you get . . .*
da casa al lavoro?	*from home to work?*
prendo la macchina	*I take the car*
in macchina	*by car*
con la bicicletta	*by bike*

How do you get there?   [cc]   [CD] 3

Listen to the cassette/CD and say how you get around.

3   [cc]   [CD] 4

Silvia Malagò and Danilo Trabecca both live in Ferrara and travel to work together part of the way.

First time round

il treno delle sette e cinquantatrè	*the 7.53 train*
il binario	*platform*

a Do they go to the station together?
b What platform does their train leave from?

Silvia   Mi chiamo Silvia e abito a Ferrara ma lavoro a Bologna. **Ogni mattina** dal lunedì al venerdì **vado in bicicletta alla stazione** di Ferrara e prendo il treno delle 7.53 per Bologna che parte dal binario numero tre.

Danilo   **Tutti i giorni**, tranne il sabato e la domenica, vado alla stazione di Ferrara in macchina e prendo il treno delle 7.53 per Bologna che parte dal binario numero tre.

dal lunedì al venerdì	*from Monday to Friday*
tranne	*except*
il sabato e la domenica	*on Saturdays and Sundays*

Key phrases

ogni mattina	*every morning*
vado . . .	*I go . . .*
in bicicletta	*by bike*
alla stazione	*to the station*
tutti i giorni	*every day*

Interaction 2 (082)

1 *Due donne parlano di mezzi di trasporto.*
Besides the car, which other means of transport do the
women mention?

2 Play the cassette/CD as required. Ask further
questions:
Why does the first woman drive to the station even though
it is difficult to park near the station?
How long does she take to go to work?
In which order do they use the means of transport
mentioned?

Interaction 3 (146)

1 *Anche Silvia e Danilo parlano di treni, macchine e biciclette.*
They both get on the same train.
Do they go to the station together?
From which platform does the train leave?

2 Play the cassette/CD as required. Ask a further
question:
Do they travel on the same days every week?

Days of the week

Aim: oral practice

1   Ask students to think of their weekly routine. Is there anything that they specifically do on particular days? e.g.: *Che cosa fai il martedì?*

2   Write the seven days of the week on the board.

3   Ask students to go round the class to find out the most common activity for each day.

4   Ask for *volontari* to write the most popular activity for each day.

5   When students have had an opportunity to use the days of the week, rub the seven days off the board. Then pick a day and ask a student to tell you the following day, and so on round the class.

Interaction 4 (196)

1   *Anna incontra Silvia e Danilo alla stazione di Bologna. Anna è in ritardo. Danilo ha fretta.*
When does Danilo say he is seeing Anna?
What arrangement do Anna and Silvia make to get to the bar?

2   Play the cassette/CD as required. Ask further questions:
How does Anna apologise for her lateness?
How does Danilo apologise for his early departure?

Days of the week [cc] [CD] 4

Listen to the cassette/CD and try to learn the days of the week.

4 [cc] [CD] 5

Silvia and Danilo meet up with Anna on Bologna station before work and sort out various arrangements. Anna is late and Danilo is in a hurry – he's got to get to his job in Imola, 33 km from Bologna.

First time round

ho fretta	*I'm in a hurry*
a pranzo	*at lunchtime*
fare colazione	*to have breakfast*

a When do Anna and Danilo plan to meet?
b Where do Anna and Silvia plan to meet and how will they get there?

Anna	Scusate, sono in ritardo.
Silvia	Ciao.
Danilo	Ciao, non importa. Come va?
Anna	Non c'è male, grazie.
Danilo	Anna, scusa, ma ho fretta, **devo prendere** l'altro treno per andare a Imola. Ci vediamo a pranzo, allora?
Anna	Sì.
Danilo	Ciao.
Anna	Arrivederci, a presto.
Silvia	Ciao.
	[. . .]

Anna	Silvia, tu hai tempo di fare colazione adesso?
Silvia	Sì, volentieri. Ho una fame da lupo. Conosco un bar in Piazza Maggiore che si chiama Bar Giuseppe. Io però **devo andare** in bicicletta perché dopo devo andare al lavoro.
Anna	Beh, va bene.
Silvia	Va bene?
Anna	Tu vai in bicicletta e **io vengo** in autobus.
Silvia	Va bene.
Anna	Va bene? Andiamo.

scusate, scusa	*sorry*
non importa	*it doesn't matter*
l'altro	*the other*
hai tempo di . . .?	*have you got time to . . .?*
ho una fame da lupo	*I'm starving [I've got a wolf's hunger]*
a presto	*see you soon*
ci vediamo	*see you*

Key phrases

devo prendere . . .	*I've got to catch . . .*
devo andare . . .	*I've got to go . . .*
io vengo . . .	*I'm coming/I'll come*

Odd one out [cc] [CD] 6

Listen to the cassette/CD. Which is the appropriate phrase to use in the circumstances?

Patterns I

i) Getting about

The key verbs are **andare** *(to go)* and **venire** *(to come)* plus the words for *to* – **in** and **a** [see Systems, note 1 i, p. 93.

vado/vengo	a casa	*I go/come*	home
	a scuola		to school
	a messa		to Mass

vado/vengo	in città	*I go/come*	into town
	in periferia		to the suburbs
	in chiesa		to church

It is largely a question of idiom whether you use **in** or **a**. However, there are some rules:

With towns it's always **a**:
Vado/vengo a Ferrara.   *I go/come to Ferrara*

With countries it's **in**:
Vado/vengo in Italia   *I go/come to Italy*

A often combines with **il, l', lo, la, i, le, gli** to form one word:

vado	al lavoro	*I go*	to work
	all' estero		abroad
	allo stadio		to the stadium
	alla fermata dell'autobus		to the bus-stop
	ai giardini pubblici		to the public gardens
	agli istituti di bellezza		to beauty salons
	alle manifestazioni per la pace		to peace demonstrations

At this stage use **a** with the definite article if you're in doubt about how to say *to*.

Look at Systems, note 4 i, p. 94 if you want to know more.

ii) Transport

In Italy, you travel *in* or *with* things: the key words are **in** or **con**:

| vado | in bicicletta | *I go* | by bicycle |
| andiamo | con la bicicletta | *we go* | |

| vengo | in autobus | *I come* | by bus |
| veniamo | con l'autobus | *we come* | |

| vai/va | in treno | *you go* | by train |
| andate | con il treno | | |

| vieni/viene | in metropolitana | *you come* | by tube |
| venite | con la metropolitana | | |

| va/vanno | in aereo | *he, she goes/they go* | by 'plane |
| viene/vengono | in motocicletta | *he, she comes/they come* | by motorbike |

Patterns 1

Getting about

1 Make sure students understand the meanings of:

tutti i giorni   raramente   mai   una volta alla settimana

2 Ask students to put the places you are going to list into the four categories above, according to the frequency of their visits to each place. (Tell them to guess which preposition – *in* or *a* – to use, if they don't know, and also to guess whether or not an article is required.)

scuola	*estero*	*casa*
ufficio	*lavoro*	*parco*
discoteca	*ristorante*	*aereo*
piscina	*palestra*	*banca*
chiesa	*campagna*	*centro*

3 Read out the above list (elicit meanings if not known) giving the students time to write down their answers.

4 Check answers and discuss as necessary.

5 For extra practice, students could work in pairs. Each student asks a partner questions to find out how often he/she goes to the places in the list.

Transport

1 Ask students to go round the class to find out the most common means of transport used for going to work.

2 Tell them to ask: *Come vai al lavoro?*

3 Ask students at random: *Come va student A al lavoro?*

4

Saying how often things happen

Ask students to go round the class finding out the most common everyday activity. Tell students to ask *Che cosa fai ogni mattina/sera?*

What you have to do

1 Ask students to form a sentence using the right form of *dovere* for each of the following situations.

e.g. The policeman has ordered Claudio to stop.
alzarsi/fermarsi/girarsi: Claudio deve fermarsi

a) You and your friend have decided to go on a diet.
mangiare di più/bere in quantità/mangiare di meno
b) The next stop is the hospital. A passenger on the bus asks you when to get off for the hospital.
scendere/salire/girare
c) Gianna and Luciano are often caught out by the rain.
mangiare di meno/dormire di più/portare un ombrello
d) Two new colleagues ask you how best to cope with the mad boss.
ignorarlo/insultarlo/cambiare lavoro
e) Your best friend has just told you an incredible story.
dire meno bugie/fantasticare meno/scrivere un romanzo
f) You have got a severe cold. You tell yourself:
riposare/andare in piscina/andare all'ospedale

2 Ask students to make up rules for the class. For example: you must arrive on time/ask questions in Italian, etc.

This point could be the end of the lesson. Revise the points covered so far. In the next lesson students will cover the following:

> **Structures:** infinitive + *da*
> **Functions:** asking and saying what it's like
> **Vocabulary:** expressing opinions/jobs and professions/places of work/travel/routine activities

Asking and saying what it's like

1 Write the adjectives and activities below on the board.

2 Make sure students know the meanings of the words.

3 Tell students to choose a partner and to ask him/her what each of the activities is like: e.g. *Com'è viaggiare in treno?* The partner should use one of the adjectives in his/her response.

4 Ask questions at random, e.g. to student A: *Secondo student B, com'è viaggiare in treno?*

importante	*divertente*	*interessante*
necessario	*piacevole*	*noioso*
rilassante	*faticoso*	*stressante*

ascoltare la radio
guardare la televisione
andare in palestra
fare sport
viaggiare in treno
leggere il giornale
fare la spesa al supermercato
essere informati
ballare in discoteca
dipingere

If you walk it's **a piedi**:

vado/vengo	a piedi	*I walk, I go/come*	*on foot*

You can also say how you travel by using **prendere** *(to catch)* or *(to take)*:

prendo	l'aereo	*I take*	*the plane*
prendiamo	un tassì	*we take*	*a taxi*

iii) Saying how often things happen

The key word is **ogni** *(every)*.

Vengo qui	ogni mattina/giorno	*I come here*	*every morning/every day*
	ogni sera/pomeriggio		*every evening/afternoon*
	ogni settimana/mese		*every week/month*
	ogni lunedì/domenica		*every Monday/Sunday*
	ogni anno/estate		*every year/summer*
	ogni tanto		*every so often*

Il treno parte	ogni ora/ogni due ore	*The train leaves*	*every hour/two hours*
	ogni dieci minuti		*every ten minutes*

iv) What you have to do

The key verb is **dovere** *(to have to)*. [See Systems, note 1 ii, p. 93.]
It is followed by an infinitive:

Devo	scendere qui	*I must*	*get out here*
Dobbiamo	aspettare l'autobus	*We must*	*wait for the 'bus*
	fare il biglietto		*get the ticket*

Devi	pagare un supplemento?	*Do you have to*	*pay a supplement?*
Deve	fare un abbonamento?		*get a season ticket?*
Dovete	prenotare un posto?		*book a seat?*

v) Asking and saying what it's like

In Italian you say, *'How is it?'* – **Come è? Come** is shortened to **com'** in front of **è** and pronounced as one word:

Com'è	la vita del pendolare?	*What's*	*a commuter's life like?*
	la Sua giornata?		*your day like?*
	il Suo lavoro?		*your job like?*

È	una vita molto stressante	*It's*	*a very stressful life*
	una giornata tanto interessante		*an extremely interesting day*
	un lavoro abbastanza noioso		*a fairly/quite boring job*
	un lavoro poco piacevole		*not a very pleasant job*
	un lavoro un po' faticoso		*a somewhat boring job*

Practice 1

Excuses! Excuses!

There is a particular chore you have been asked to do and you are busy explaining to your friend why you can't do it. You've written your regular appointments in your diary:
e.g. Ogni lunedì vado in ufficio.

lunedì	Ufficio
martedì	Piscina
mercoledì	Super Mercato
giovedì	Ufficio
venerdì	istituto
sabato	Studio
domenica	

Perhaps Sundays are free? Say what *you* normally do on a Sunday.

Refresh your memory (1)   6

Listen again to the first part of Interaction 2 where a woman describes her journey to Bologna. Don't look back at the text, but listen as often as you need to answer these questions:

How does she say:
    I leave the house . . .   I take the car . . .
    I get to Bologna . . .   I catch a bus . . .
    I go to work . . .

Getting to work

Your friends are telling you how they travel. Francesca, for example, takes the train to work.
e.g. Vado in treno. Sì, prendo il treno.

What about the others?

1 Giancarlo

2 Giovanna

3 Luca

4 Stefania

How about you? How do you get to college or work?

How do you get there?   6

Now see if you can describe a journey to a friend.

Amico	Come vai da casa al lavoro?
You	*[Say you leave the house and go to the bus-stop.]*
Amico	Devi aspettare molto?
You	*[Say no, you don't have to wait long.]*
Amico	E poi, quando arrivi a Manchester?
You	*[Say when you arrive in Manchester you walk to the office.]*
Amico	Ah! L'ufficio è vicino alla stazione, allora . . .
You	*[Say yes, it's near the station.]*
Amico	Che fortuna!

Now describe a journey you make regularly, starting with leaving the house and ending with your final destination.

Practice 1

Paolo, Gianna e Chiara

Aim: listening comprehension with a multiple choice

1 In this type of exercise, students will understand more if you can talk about real people (acquaintances/friends/relatives). Write your own material based on people you know. Show pictures to the students. It will help them to visualise/understand/enjoy more.

2 Give students a copy of the questions below.

3 Read the following passage at least three times, giving the students time to choose the right answer.

Paolo, Gianna e Chiara sono molto amici. Paolo è italiano ma in questo momento è a Madrid. Paolo è un giornalista, lavora a Roma ma viaggia molto in Francia, in Germania, in Inghilterra e in Spagna. Gianna invece è americana ma vive in Italia. Gianna, che a dire il vero si chiama Jane, è un'insegnante e abita con Chiara che lavora come libera professionista per una rivista di moda femminile. Gianna insegna a Roma da molti anni: Chiara invece è un designer da solo pochi mesi. Paolo è a Madrid da tre giorni e domani ritorna in Italia.

1 Paolo
parla italiano/è italiano/studia italiano
2 Paolo
scrive per un giornale/è un artista/oggi è in lista
3 Paolo
mangia molto/abita in Spagna/viaggia spesso
4 Gianna
scrive in Italia/viaggia molto/è americana
5 Gianna si chiama veramente
Jane/Vera/Gianna
6 Gianna
vive con Chiara/insegna a Chiara/lavora con Chiara
7 Chiara lavora
in una scuola per donne/come centralinista/nel campo della moda
8 Gianna insegna a Roma
da qualche mese/da molto tempo/da poco tempo
9 Chiara lavora come designer
da qualche mese/da molto tempo/da poco tempo
10 Paolo è a Madrid
da molti anni/da pochi giorni/da domani

4 When you have checked students' answers, give them a copy of the passage you read out and discuss any further questions.

What do you do when?

1 Write the following activities on the board or give students a photocopy.

2 Make sure students know the meanings. Elicit as much as you can.

3 Ask the students to think about each activity and tick one or more of the columns according to how often they carry them out.

4 Ask questions at random: *quando pulisci le scarpe?*

OGNI

	mattina	*sera*	*giorno*	*settimana*	*mese*	*anno*
pulire le scarpe						
lavarsi i denti						
bere il caffè						
mangiare al ristorante						
parlare al telefono						
ascoltare la radio						
passare l'aspirapolvere						
scrivere una lettera						

Where's everybody?

Where do members of the family go to do the following:

e.g. Per comprare un giornale, mio padre . . .
Va all'edicola.

1 Per giocare con i figli, gli zii . . .
2 Per comprare frutta e verdura, mia madre . . .
3 Per prendere un caffè, mio fratello e io . . .
4 Per prendere un autobus, mia sorella . . .
5 Per vedere un film, mio cugino e mia cugina . . .
6 And this evening everyone's going to the match.
Tutti . . .

Memory test

How long does it take you to unscramble the days of the week below?

1 VERDIEN   5 ABATOS
2 LEOCRIDEM   6 VIGEDIO
3 LEUNDI   7 EDITRAM
4 NIDOMECA

What's it like?

Here's what life is like for some people. Read what they say and then make your own comment; use one of the phrases given here to describe each person's situation.

**poco divertente   molto noiosa
tanto interessante   poco stressante**

You don't need to understand every word to answer, so try to guess any words you don't know. You can, however, find them in the Vocabulary.

e.g. 'La mia giornata è piacevole: mi alzo tardi, mi lavo, mi vesto, prendo uno o due caffè, e leggo il giornale. Poi vado a trovare gli amici e pranziamo al ristorante. La sera andiamo al cinema o al bar.'
La sua vita è veramente . . . *(His life is really . . .)*
La sua vita è veramente poco stressante!

1 'La mia giornata è dura e faticosa. Mi sveglio prestissimo, mi alzo subito e vado a lavorare. Lavoro dalla mattina alla sera e torno a casa tardi. Sono stanco e vado a letto. Non ho molti amici.'
La sua vita è veramente . . .

2 'La mia giornata è monotona: mi alzo la mattina alla stessa ora, esco di casa alla stessa ora e prendo lo stesso autobus. Arrivo in ufficio, vedo le stesse persone e scrivo le stesse lettere. Ho lo stesso orario da vent'anni!'
La sua vita è . . .

3 'Ogni giorno è diverso. Viaggio molto e vado in tanti paesi diversi – in Giappone, in India per esempio. Incontro tante persone diverse e imparo sempre cose nuove.'
La sua vita è . . .

Now say what *you* do on: a boring day; on an interesting day.

Cultura e parole

Le Ferrovie dello Stato [FFSS]

In a country as fragmented as Italy, the railways have always been considered an important means of communication. Italy's first Prime Minister, Cavour, was well known for his passionate belief in the power of the railways to unify the nation, while Mussolini's boast that he made the trains run on time is legendary. In actual fact the railways were efficiently run as early as the beginning of the twentieth century and are amongst Italy's oldest nationalised industries. Between 1905 and 1906, most of the 13 000 km of track was taken over by the State. There are now 19 726 km of State-run railway, half of it electrified, and Italy's train service is generally acknowledged to give good value for money. You can go a long way for very little: an ordinary ticket costs about three pounds for a 100-km journey and there are various season tickets which provide discounts. For students and state employees there is an **abbonamento studenti e impiegati dello Stato**, valid all year, and for workers there are weekly seasons – **abbonamenti settimanali e festivi** which are also valid at weekends. Anyone can buy an **abbonamento ordinario** which can be monthly or yearly. Then there are special travel cards: **Carta Famiglia; Carta Argento** and **Carta Verde**, which offer between 20 and 50 per cent discounts for families, the over-60s and 12- to 26-year-olds. Although Italian railways provide a good public service, and are heavily subsidised, they have been neglected and under-used in recent years in favour of the roads: there are now fewer goods trains in operation than in 1938. This has led to recent moves to revamp the railway system.

L'autostrada

Italy has a long tradition of pioneering in road building which goes back to the Romans. The Italian road network of some 300 000 km still follows some of the ancient roads: the Aurelia, the Flaminia, the Via Emilia and the Via Appia. The **autostrade**, first built in the 1920s, cover nearly 7 000 km and represent the great innovation of the twentieth century: the **autostrade**, rather than the railways have unified Italy. To drive on the motorway you pay a toll – **un pedaggio** – for which you get a ticket – **uno scontrino** – at the toll station – **il casello** – except on some routes in the south which are free. The combined price of the petrol – **la benzina** – and the toll makes this a fairly expensive mode of travel, but getting rapidly to one's destination is a priority for many Italians. Airports – **gli aeroporti** – have grown rapidly in number (there are around 50) to accommodate the demand for internal flights – **voli interni**.

Il trasporto urbano

Public transport within cities is mainly confined to the bus. Tickets are not available on the bus: you buy a ticket for a single ride – **una corsa semplice** – or a book of tickets – **un blocchetto** – in tobacconists' – **i tabacchi** –, at a newspaper kiosk – **un'edicola** – or at the bus terminal – **il capolinea**. The tube – **la metropolitana** – operates in a few cities such as Rome (since 1955) and Milan (since 1964) while the tram is a feature of Turin and a few other cities such as Salerno. Finally, in Venice, public transport is, predictably, by boat: not so much the gondola as the **vaporetto** – the waterbus.

Cultura e parole

Besides the new professions which sprang up during the seventies and eighties, there has also been a tendency in the last few years to use euphemistic terms to denote existing types of employment; for instance, in a more environmentally-conscious world, it makes more sense to refer to dustbinmen (*spazzini*) as *operatori ecologici*. Similarly nurses (*infermieri*) are more often called *paramedici*, and caretakers (*bidelli*) are referred to as *assistenti scolastici*. These new terms may not be used in everyday language, but they are eagerly adopted in written documentation, especially in the 'official' language of *circolari ministeriali* – Government documents.

Occupations

Ask students to guess the English equivalents of the following occupations:

cassiere	*operaio/a*	*coltivatore diretto*
dottore/dottoressa	*dentista*	*impiegato/a*
insegnante	*artista*	*designer*
falegname	*architetto*	*direttore/direttrice*
segretario/a	*uomo d'affari/*	*assistente*
ricercatore/	*donna d'affari*	*libero/libera*
ricercatrice	*chirurgo*	*professionista*

Places of employment

1 The following words refer to different places of employment (the last two are more specific). Ask students to say which ones they can't guess the meaning of.

studio	*scuola*	*ufficio*	*laboratorio*
sala riunioni	*fattoria*	*fabbrica*	*società*
ambulatorio	*ospedale*	*sportello*	*scrivania*

2 Ask students to write a few sentences based on the following example:

Gianna, che è insegnante, lavora in una scuola a Roma da molti anni.

Tell students to change everything except:

. . ., che è . . . lavora . . . da . . .

3 Students number the places of employment 1–12. Throw dice: the resulting numbers tell them where they work. Students then have to tell you their occupation.

This point could be the end of the lesson. Revise the points covered so far. In the next lesson students will cover the following:

> **Structures:** *dovere* + infinitive/imperative (second person)
> **Functions:** telling the time
> **Vocabulary:** travel and work

Interaction 5a   (310)

1 *Silvia e Anna sono nel Bar Giuseppe.*
How does Anna ask Silvia what job she does?
How long is Silvia's working day?

2 Play the cassette/CD as required. Ask further
questions:
How often does Silvia have breakfast in Bar Giuseppe?
How long has she been commuting?
Where does Silvia work?
At what time does she have to leave the house?
At what time does she return home?

Interaction 5b   (340)

1 *Anna e Silvia sono ancora nel bar.* Anna asks more
questions about Silvia's working day:
How does she get to work?
Is there anything unusual about her journey?

2 Play the cassette/CD as required. Ask further
questions:
Does Silvia live far from the station?
What does she do in the evening?
What about in wintertime?
How many bikes has she got?

Interactions

5a 7

Anna and Silvia meet up again in the Bar Giuseppe. Anna learns about Silvia's job.

First time round

spesso	*often*
devo uscire	*I have to leave*

Anna wants to know if Silvia often has breakfast in the bar and how long she's been commuting.

a How does she ask Silvia what job she does?
b How long is Silvia's working day?

Anna Vieni spesso qui a fare colazione?
Silvia Ogni tanto quando ho tempo.
Anna Da quanto tempo fai la pendolare?
Silvia Faccio la pendolare da . . . da molto tempo, da cinque anni, però lavoro a Bologna solo da tre anni.
Anna E **che lavoro fai** esattamente?
Silvia **Lavoro** in un ufficio, **nel campo dell'informatica.**
Anna È lunga la tua giornata?
Silvia Sì, abbastanza. Lavoro **dalle nove alle cinque** del pomeriggio in ufficio, però devo uscire di casa **la mattina alle sette e mezza** e torno **la sera** alle sei e mezza.

Key phrases

che lavoro fai?	*what job do you do?*
lavoro nel campo dell'informatica	*I work in the field of computers*
dalle nove alle cinque	*from nine to five*
la mattina	*in the morning*
alle sette e mezza	*at half past seven*
la sera	*in the evening*

5b 8

Anna finds out a bit more about Silvia's journey to work. She asks Silvia if she lives far from the station.

First time round

lontano da	*far from*
quando piove	*when it's raining*
e c'è la nebbia	*and foggy*

a How does she get to work?
b Is there anything unusual about her journey?

Anna Ma abiti lontano dalla stazione?
Silvia No, abito in città, in centro, nel centro di Ferrara.
Anna E come fai per andare a lavorare allora?
Silvia Prendo la bicicletta per andare da casa alla stazione di Ferrara, poi prendo il treno e ho un'altra bicicletta vecchia alla stazione di Bologna per andare al lavoro. Ho due biciclette, insomma. E poi la sera per tornare a casa, faccio la stessa cosa.
Anna Ma **d'inverno** quando piove e c'è la nebbia?
Silvia Faccio quasi sempre la stessa cosa, non cambio programma.
Anna Che coraggio!
Silvia Anna, scusami, **sono** già **le nove** e sono in ritardo per il lavoro e devo scappare. [. . .]

come fai per . . .?	*how do you . . .?*
non cambio programma	*I don't change my routines*
che coraggio!	*you're brave!*

Key phrases

d'inverno	*in the winter*
sono . . . le nove	*it's nine o'clock*

6 9

After lunch with Danilo in Imola, Anna spends the afternoon in Bologna and then boards the train for Ferrara. She talks to a state employee who commutes regularly.

First time round

un impiegato dello stato	*a state employee*
... volte alla settimana	*... times a week*
verso che ora rientra?	*about what time do you return?*

How many times a week does this man travel?

[*Anna*   **Che lavoro fa?**
Signore Sono un impiegato dello stato.]
Anna   E **quante volte** alla settimana, quindi, deve fare Ferrara – Bologna?
Signore Beh, io viaggio praticamente dal lunedì al venerdì per cinque volte alla settimana.

Anna   E verso che ora rientra la sera?
Signore Per tre giorni alla settimana rientro **alle quindici e trenta** e per due giorni alla settimana **alle diciotto e trenta**.

| fare Ferrara–Bologna | *to make the Ferrara–Bologna trip* |
| praticamente | *virtually, basically* |

Key phrases

che lavoro fa?	*what job do you do?*
quante volte?	*how many times?*
alle quindici e trenta	*at 3.30 p.m.*
alle diciotto e trenta	*at 6.30 p.m.*

24-hour clock 10

Listen to the cassette/CD and repeat the numbers from 10 to 30. Now listen to the station announcements and work out what they mean.

Patterns 2

i) Jobs

When you ask people what job they do, you need the verb **fare** *(to do)*. [See Systems, p. 93.]

| Che lavoro | fai? | *What job do you do? [informal]* |
| | fa? | *[formal]* |

The answer is literally, *'I do the ...'*

Faccio	il medico	*I'm*	*a doctor*
	l'assistente sociale		*a social worker*
	la segretaria		*a secretary*

But you can also use **sono** and say *'I am'*, with or without **un** and **una**:

| Sono | (un/un') insegnante | *I'm* | *a teacher* |
| | (un) postino | | *a postman* |

If you are in charge, the word varies according to the profession. Here's one expression:

  È il capo   *He's the boss*

Fare or **essere** are often used interchangeably with all the above professions (with the exception of **operaio**, generally used only with **essere**). However, **fare** is more specific and clearly indicates that you are actually practising your profession. Another way of stating your job is to use **mi occupo di**:

| Mi occupo di | marketing | *I'm in* | *marketing* |
| | pubbliche relazioni | | *public relations* |

Interaction 6 (370)

1 *Anna è sul treno che da Bologna torna a Ferrara, e parla con un impiegato dello stato.*
How many times a week does he travel?

2 Play the cassette/CD as required. Ask further questions:
How many times a week does he get back at three-thirty?
What time does he arrive home the other two days?

Patterns 2

Jobs

1 Ask students to go round the class to find out what job everyone else does.

2 Encourage them to use all the ways of stating your occupation: *faccio, sono, mi occupo di, lavoro nel campo . . .*, etc.

3 You can also ask them to write sentences of the type suggested earlier in the unit. Here is the pattern again:

. . ., che è . . ., lavora . . . da . . .

(This time, however, encourage them to substitute *che è . . .* with *che fa . . .* or *che si occupa di . . .* and to add *. . . nel campo . . .* after *lavora*.)

4 Ask student A: *Che lavoro fa student B?*

5 Stretch students' abilities by asking less obvious questions, for example: *Quante persone ci sono nel tuo ufficio?* or *Come si chiama il tuo direttore o la tua direttrice?* Feign surprise; say that you know him or her. *È un mio caro amico o una mia cara amica.* Go on telling incredible lies that students can understand. Encourage them to challenge you.

Telling the time

1 Make a list of programmes which have a regular slot either on television or radio.

2 Ask students to say what time the programmes begin, e.g. *Che ore sono quando comincia il programma* PM *sul quarto canale della radio? . . .* and end, e.g. *Che ora sono quando finisce il programma* The World at One *sul quarto canale della radio?*

Sample programmes

1	Today	4	Lunchtime News (BBC 1)
2	The World at One	5	Newsnight
3	PM	6	Coronation Street

3 If possible, obtain a list of TV programmes and times from an Italian newspaper or magazine and give students a copy. Read the name of a programme and ask students to say what time it starts.

4 Students then work in pairs. One thinks of a TV programme, the other has to guess it by asking what time it starts/finishes.

Arrivals and departures: at what time?

Ask students to go round the class to find out who gets home the latest after the class.
e.g. *A che ora arrivi a casa dopo la lezione d'italiano?*

To indicate what line you're in, you use **nel campo di** *(in the field of)*:

| Lavoro nel campo | dell'informatica | *I work in* | *computers* |
| | delle comunicazioni | | *communications* |

Sometimes you simply want to say where you work, or who you work for:

Lavoro	in un ospedale	*I work*	*in a hospital*
	alla posta		*at the post office*
	per una ditta		*for a firm*

ii) Telling the time

The 24-hour clock is used for timetables. 'O'clock' is expressed in terms of *'the hours'* – **le ore**:

8.00: le otto   *2.15: le due e un quarto/e quindici*   *4.30: le quattro e mezza/e trenta*   *10.45: le undici meno un quarto/le dieci e quarantacinque*

Che ore sono?/Che ora è?   *What time is it?*

When you say the time, the word **ore** is dropped, leaving **sono + le +** number:

| sono | le otto | *it's* | *eight o'clock* |
| | le undici | | *eleven o'clock* |

But if you want to say *one o'clock* you use **è + l'**:

è' l'una   *it's one o'clock*

And midday or midnight is simply:

| è | mezzogiorno | *it's* | *midday* |
| | mezzanotte | | *midnight* |

For time past the hour you need to know the numbers up to 60 [see Ref. I, 1, p. 239] and use the word **e** – *and*:

sono	le due e mezza/e trenta	*it's*	*half past two/two thirty*
	le tre e un quarto/e quindici		*quarter past three/three fifteen*
	le sette e cinquantatrè		*seven fifty-three*

To say *half past,* Italians also use **e mezzo**.

iii) Arrivals and departures: at what time?

The key word is **a**, combined with **le** or **l'**:

Esco alle nove e torno all'una.   *I leave at nine and come back at one.*
Usciamo a mezzogiorno e torniamo a mezzanotte.   *We leave at midday and come back at midnight.*

See Systems, note 1 i, p. 93 for **uscire** *(to leave, to go out).*

Patterns 2

iv) From when to when?

The key words are **da** and **a**, combined with **le** and **l'**:

Lavoro dalle nove alle cinque   *I work from nine to five*

If it's a day of the week, **da/a** combine with **il** or **la**:

Lavoro | dal lunedì al venerdì
       | dal sabato alla domenica

v) Saying how often you do things

Ogni quanto | vieni?   *How often do you come?*
quanto spesso |
Vieni spesso qui?   *Do you often come here?*

Vengo . . . | sempre | *I come* | *always*
            | spesso | | *often*
            | di solito | | *usually*
            | qualchevolta, a volte | | *sometimes*
            | ogni tanto | | *occasionally*

Non vengo mai   *I never come*

vi) Saying how many times

The key word is **volta** followed by **a**, which combines with **la**, **il**, and **l'**.

quante volte | alla settimana?   *how many times* | *a week?*
             | al mese? | *a month?*
             | all'anno? | *a year?*

una volta | alla settimana   *once* | *a week*
due volte | al mese   *twice* | *a month*
tre volte | all'anno   *three times* | *a year*

vii) Saying when

To express *on* and *in*, all you need are the words for *'the'* – **il**, **la**, etc.

quando? | *when?* | la mattina | vado a lavorare | *in the morning* | *I go to work*
        | | il lunedì | | *on Mondays* |
        | | il pomeriggio | dormo | *in the afternoon* | *I sleep*
        | | la sera | | *in the evening* |
        | | il fine settimana | esco | *at the weekend* | *I go out*

However, for seasons it's **di** and **in**:

d'inverno | vado in vacanza | *in the winter* | *I go on holiday*
d'estate | | *in the summer* |
in primavera | rimango in città | *in the spring* | *I stay in town*
in autunno | | *in the autumn* |

From when to when?

1 Prepare a set of questions such as the following:

Qual'è l'orario di apertura delle banche?
Qual'è l'orario di apertura degli uffici postali?
A che ora apre l'edicola vicina a casa tua?
A che ora aprono e chiudono i pub?
A che ora si può sentire il notiziario alla radio?

2 Ask students to write the answers to the questions.

3 Tell students to ask you a question each on general opening and closing times in Italy.

The following can be practised in one single class activity.

Saying how often you do things
Saying how many times
Saying when

1 Tell students to go round the class to find out how often the other students do the following (write these on the board or hand out a copy):

andare	*al mercato/al supermercato/in piscina*
	al cinema/in banca/alla partita
	a teatro/all'ufficio postale/al mare
mangiare	*al ristorante/in mensa/al bar*
leggere	*il giornale/un settimanale/un romanzo*
scrivere	*una lettera/un romanzo/un memorandum*
guardare	*la televisione/la partita/il telegiornale*

2 Tell students to ask questions such as:

Ogni quanto . . .?
Quando . . .?
Quante volte al giorno/alla settimana . . .?

3 Students make a note of their findings.

4 Ask students at random: *Quante volte al mese student A va al cinema/ristorante?*

This point could be the end of the lesson. Revise the points covered so far. In the next lesson students will cover the following:

> **Structures:** prepositions
> **Functions:** understanding and telling the time
> **Vocabulary:** school subjects/travel and work

Practice 2

L'orario delle lezioni

Aim: to practise understanding and telling times

1 Secondary school in Italy is divided into Lower – *Scuola Media Inferiore* – and Upper – *Scuola Media Superiore*. Ten subjects on average are studied from the age of ten to the age of eighteen. School is mainly a morning affair in Italy.

2 The following subjects are studied in a *Scuola Media*. Write the list on the board and make sure the subjects are understood by all students.

Italiano	*Geografia*
Educazione artistica	*Educazione tecnica*
Lingua straniera	*Latino*
(inglese, francese, tedesco)	*Educazione fisica*
Storia	*Matematica*
Educazione musicale	*Scienze naturali*
Religione	

3 Read out the time and the day when each subject is taught, allowing students time to compile the timetable.

4 To simplify the task, give students a copy of this plan:

	lunedì	martedì	mercoledì	giovedì	venerdì	sabato
8.15 9.15						
9.15 10.15						
INTERVALLO						
10.30 11.30						
11.30 12.30						

Italiano	*martedì*	*dalle 11.30 alle 12.30*
	mercoledì	*dalle 9.15 alle 10.15*
		dalle 10.30 alle 11.30
	giovedì	*dalle 11.30 alle 12.30*
Storia	*mercoledì*	*dalle 8.15 alle 9.15*
	giovedì	*dalle 10.30 alle 11.30*
Geografia	*lunedì*	*dalle 8.15 alle 9.15*
	venerdì	*dalle 8.15 alle 9.15*
Educazione musicale	*lunedì*	*dalle 11.30 alle 12.30*
Educazione artistica	*venerdì*	*dalle 10.30 alle 12.30*
Lingua straniera	*martedì*	*dalle 9.15 alle 10.15*
	venerdì	*dalle 9.15 alle 10.15*
Latino	*sabato*	*dalle 11.30 alle 12.30*
Educazione tecnica	*sabato*	*dalle 8.15 alle 10.15*

Matematica	*lunedì*	*dalle 9.15 alle 10.15*
		dalle 10.30 alle 11.30
	martedì	*dalle 10.30 alle 11.30*
Scienze naturali	*martedì*	*dalle 8.15 alle 9.15*
	mercoledì	*dalle 11.30 alle 12.30*
Religione	*sabato*	*dalle 10.30 alle 11.30*
Educazione fisica	*giovedì*	*dalle 8.15 alle 10.15*

Scusi, sono un giornalista della Rai ...

Aim: oral and written practice of the main functions and structures of this unit

1 Tell students they are RAI journalists and their assignment is to find out how British people travel to work.

2 Ask them to copy out the questionnaire below, with the column on the left featuring job details, arrival and departure times and various means of transport. The names of at least half a dozen other students should be written in at the top of the other columns.

3 Students then interview each other, filling in the questionnaire with details of other students' occupations, times of travel to and from work and ticking the means of transport used. Remind students of the use of *viaggiare in* or *con* (refer them to the Patterns section).

	A	B	C	D	E	F
occupazione						
campo						
posto di lavoro						
partenza da casa						
arrivo al lavoro						
partenza dal lavoro						
arrivo a casa						
macchina						
treno						
metropolitana						
bicicletta						
autobus						
a piedi						
motocicletta						

4 Students can now write a short report on every other student they have interviewed.

e.g. *Student A è un ricercatore e lavora nel campo della farmacologia. Va a lavorare tutti i giorni in bicicletta. Parte da casa al mattino alle 7.30 e arriva al suo lavoro alle 8.15. La sera parte dal lavoro alle 4.15 e arriva a casa alle 5.00.*

Practice 2

I work for the State 10

Find out what the Bianciardis do for a living.

You	[Ask signor Bianciardi what job he does.]
Sig. B	Sono uno statale – un dipendente statale.
You	[He works for the state, but ask him where he works.]
Sig. B	Lavoro alle poste.
You	[Ah, he could be a postman, then. Ask him if he's a postman.]
Sig. B	No, non faccio il postino, sono il direttore delle poste in Emilia Romagna.
You	[Oh, the boss . . .! Better luck next time . . . Now ask his wife, dottoressa Bianciardi what she does.]
Dott.ssa B	Sono anch'io una dipendente statale. Lavoro in una scuola.
You	[Well that's easy, she's a teacher of course. Ask her if she's a teacher.]
Dott.ssa B	No, non insegno. Sono la preside di una scuola.
You	[Oh, she's the headmistress. Well, nearly right. Now you tell her what you do.]

What do you have?

For each day of the week say when you have a meal or drink. Take care how you express 'have'.

e.g. Il lunedì mattina al bar *(have a coffee)*
Il lunedì mattina prendo un caffè al bar.

1 Il martedì mattina a casa *(have breakfast)*
2 Il mercoledì a mezzogiorno *(have lunch)*
3 Il giovedì alle 4.30 *(have a snack)*
4 Il venerdì sera con i suoceri *(have an aperitif)*
5 Il sabato sera a casa *(have supper)*
6 La domenica alle 5 con amici inglesi *(have tea)*

Now say how frequently you do each of the above: always? often?

Identikit

If you work outside the home answer the following:
Che lavoro fa? Dove lavora? Come fa per andare al lavoro? Quante ore lavora al giorno? A che ora comincia e a che ora finisce?
If you're not employed, answer the following:
Cosa fa durante il giorno? Com'è la Sua vita?

Timetables

Look at the Bologna-Ferrara timetable below.
D stands for **diretto**, **Loc.** is short for **locale** and **IC** stands for **Intercity**.

a Which is the category of train to avoid when you're in a hurry? Complete the sentence.
Quando ho fretta devo evitare il . . .
b Is the **Intercity** faster than the **Diretto**? Delete as appropriate:
L'Intercity non è/è più rapido del Diretto.
c What do you think **andata** and **ritorno** mean?

BOLOGNA - FERRARA

ANDATA		D		D
BO		7.40		8.40
FE		8.10		9.10

RITORNO	D	Loc	D	IC
FE	16.53	17.37	18.53	19.33
BO	17.23	18.35	19.23	20.03

What time?

On Silvia's clocks are the times she does certain things during the day. Can you say when she does what?

e.g. A che ora si sveglia Silvia?
Si sveglia alle sette meno un quarto.

1 A che ora si alza?   2 A che ora fa colazione?

3 A che ora prende il treno la mattina?   4 A che ora va a letto?

Vocabulary

Time

quando	when
adesso	now
subito	at once
oggi	today
stasera	this evening
domani	tomorrow
già	already
dopo	afterwards, after
poi	then
presto	early
tardi	late

The time

l'ora	time, hour
il minuto	minute
il secondo	second
l'orologio	clock, watch
la sveglia	alarm
in ritardo	late
in anticipo	early
in orario	on time
avanti/indietro di x minuti	x minutes fast/slow

People jobs, and work

la professione	profession
il mestiere	trade, job
il/la collega	colleague
il capo	boss
il direttore	primary sch. head (m)
la direttrice	primary sch. head (f)
il proprietario	owner
l'autista	driver
l'avvocatessa	lawyer (f)
l'avvocato	lawyer (m)
la casalinga	housewife
il/la com- messo/a	shop assistant
il/la dattilo- grafo/a	typist
il/la dentista	dentist
il/la farmacista	chemist
il/la giornalista	journalist
l'idraulico	plumber
l'infermiere/a	nurse

l'ingegnere	engineer
l'insegnante	sec.-teacher
il/la maestro/a	primary teacher
il meccanico	meccanic
il medico	doctor (m/f)
l'operaio/a	worker (m/f)
il/la parruc- chiere/a	hair-dresser (m/f)
il/la poliziotto/a	policeman/woman
il postino	postman
il/la preside	sec. sch. head
il/la ragioniere/a	accountant (m/f)
la segretaria	secretary
il tassista	taxi-driver
lo studente	student (m)
la studentessa	student (f)
disoccupato/a	unemployed
in pensione	retired
il lavoro	work
il posto	job, place, seat
lo stipendio	salary
il salario	wage
guadagnare	to earn
spendere	to spend
risparmiare	to save
fare sciopero	to strike

Going places

andare	to go
venire	to come
uscire	to go out, to leave
partire	to leave
fermarsi	to stop
aspettare	to wait (for)
attraversare	to cross
tornare	to go/come back
rientrare	to get back
salire	to get into, to go up
scendere	to get out of, to go down
viaggiare	to travel

andare a trovare	to visit [person]
visitare	to visit [place]
andare/venire a piedi	to walk
fare il biglietto	to buy a ticket
fare un viaggio	to make a journey
fare una passeggiata	to go for a walk

Everyday activities

svegliarsi	to wake up
alzarsi	to get up
lavarsi	to wash
pettinarsi	to do one's hair
farsi la barba	to shave
fare il bagno	to have a bath
fare colazione	to have breakfast
fare il bucato	to do the washing
fare i compiti	to do homework
fare la doccia	to have a shower
fare la spesa	to go shopping
pranzare	to have lunch
cenare	to have supper
andare a letto	to go to bed

Adjectives

stesso	same
diverso	different
monotono	monotonous
noioso	boring
interessante	interesting
divertente	fun, enjoyable
piacevole	pleasant
affollato	crowded
libero	free, vacant
alto	high
basso	low

Vocabulary

1 The following is a story about an imaginary friend called Veronica which you can read to students.

2 Give them the following questions to answer but ask students to study them before they start reading:

How many hours per week does Veronica work at the shop?
How does Veronica go to work?
How does her work affect her social life?
What do Veronica and her friends usually do in the evening?
What are her plans for the next summer holiday?

3 Write on the board the difficult words for which help might be required, e.g. *abbigliamento, scomodo, pienozeppo*.

Veronica ha 22 anni e lavora in un negozio di abbigliamento. Il lunedì, il mercoledì e il venerdì lavora dalle due del pomeriggio alle otto di sera, mentre il martedì, il giovedì e il sabato lavora dalle otto del mattino alle due del pomeriggio. Il negozio è nel centro di Treviso, vicino alla piazza principale. L'autobus che va in centro è scomodo perché è sempre pieno zeppo e non è molto frequente. Per questo Veronica preferisce andare a lavorare in bicicletta, anche quando fa freddo, e prende l'autobus solo quando piove. La giornata lavorativa non è lunga ma il lavoro è stancante. La sera però Veronica è sempre disposta ad uscire con i suoi amici. In genere esce con la sua amica Luisa. Spesso vanno al ristorante o in pizzeria con Mario e Paolo. Il venerdì e il sabato vanno in discoteca o, se c'è un buon film, vanno a cinema. D'estate Veronica, se non va al mare per almeno due settimane, non è contenta, e anche quest'anno, vuole andare in Grecia con due sue amiche: Silvia e naturalmente Luisa.

4 When students have answered as many questions as they can, discuss any questions as required.

5 The following week, you could give a part of this passage as a short dictation exercise.

Scelta multipla

Aim: to expand and consolidate what has been dealt with during the unit

1 Tell students to choose the correct answer:

1 You get your *stipendio* or *salario* in it:
giacca   secchio   busta paga   borsa
2 You should normally address all complaints to him/her:
postino   direttore/direttrice   collega   pensionato
3 Sometimes they are unjustly referred to as *macellai*:
disoccupati   operai   tassisti   dentisti
4 You are not likely to do one of the following every day:
svegliarsi   lavarsi   prendere il sole   cenare
5 It is often associated with routine:
dalle 9 alle 5   fare sciopero   viaggio   giornalismo
6 You can ask for some special advice but don't take your film to be developed there:
tabaccheria   pasticceria   panetteria   farmacia
7 Which of these isn't connected with travel?
aspettare   salire   scendere   pettinarsi
8 Which one would you go to for a haircut?
barbiere   infermiere   sacerdote   commesso
9 Which one would not be connected with newspapers?
insegnante   redattore   editore   giornalista
10 Which is the correct version?
meglio presto che mai   meglio tardi che poi
meglio tardi che mai   meglio dopo che poi

Troubleshooting

1   In order to reinforce the meaning and usage of *ora*, *tempo* and *volta*, draw the attention of students to the examples below.

2   Write each word in Italian and elicit the meaning from students.

Ora tempo volta

Ora meaning a specific or particular time of the day:

ora	now – at this moment
ora di Greenwich	GMT
ora legale	summer time
ora locale	local time
ora di punta	rush or peak hour
a tutte le ore	at all hours
da ora in poi	from now on
è ora di agire	it is time to do something
fare le ore piccole	to stay up very late
non vedere l'ora	to look forward
è ora di . . .	it is time to . . .

Tempo meaning weather, space of time or period in more vague terms than *ora*:

tempo fa	some time ago
prima del tempo	before time
in tempo utile	in good time
tanto tempo	a long time
tempo perso	wasted time
non c'è tempo	there is no time
c'è tempo	there is no rush
quanto tempo?	how long?
fare il buono e il brutto tempo	to be all-powerful

Volta meaning time as a particular instance:

l'ultima volta	last time
la prossima volta	next time
quella volta	that time
poche volte	not often
ogni volta, tutte le volte	every time
una volta	once
una volta o l'altra	sooner or later
c'era una volta	once upon a time
una buona volta	once and for all
qualchevolta	sometimes

Review

Here is a checklist of the main points learned in this unit. For each point, ask the students to supply one or more examples by asking specific questions.

reflexive verbs (*alzarsi, scusarsi*)
andare, venire, uscire
dovere + infinitive
relative pronouns – *in cui, che*
infinitive + *da*
imperative (second person)
prepositions *a, in, con*
a + articles
asking and saying what something's like
asking and saying how often something happens
understanding and telling the time
talking about school subjects
expressing opinions
talking about jobs, professions and workplaces
travel to and from work
talking about routine daily activities

Troubleshooting

Ora tempo volta

In the expressions below, the English word *time* translates three Italian words:

a che **ora**?	*at what time?*
non ho **tempo**	*I haven't got time*
quante **volte**?	*how many times?*

Ora is the word for hour but it is also used when you're asking the time:

che ora è?	*what time is it?*

Tempo is the general word for time, and is used for weather too:

il tempo passa	*time passes*
da molto tempo	*for a long time*
fa bel tempo	*the weather is good*

Volta is used in connection with events:

un'altra volta	*another time*
è la prima volta	*it's the first time*
due volte al giorno	*twice (2 times) a day*

molto molto

Molto can mean *much/many*. In this case it is an **adjective** agreeing with the accompanying noun:

ci sono molt**e** macchine	*there are many cars*

However, **molto** can also be an **adverb** meaning *very*, in which case it never changes its form:

la giornata è molt**o** lunga	*the day is very long*

Vivere in città

Il Notai Palazzo (a sinistra) e il Palazzo Comunale, Piazza Maggiore, Bologna

Emilia Romagna · Ferrara
Borgotaro
Bologna
Rimini

In this unit you'll be introduced to the language of shops and shopping. You'll be asking about opening and closing times and making other simple enquiries, and you'll also be saying what you want and what needs to be done.

Since the mid 1980s Italy has become one of the most environmentally-conscious nations in Europe. It is now obvious that there has been a price to pay for its high-speed economic expansion in the 50s and 60s, especially as regards the quality of life in the town. During the post-war Economic Miracle, over 15 million Italians moved from the countryside to the towns in less than a decade. The result was a population explosion in the major cities, which doubled and sometimes even tripled in size.

By 1983, when the Ministry for the Environment was finally created, the environment had become a burning public issue. Membership of previously small organisations, such as **Italia Nostra** and **WWF** (Worldwide Fund for Nature), shot up: the Green movement took root and with other new organisations it campaigned vigorously to raise environmental awareness.

Il treno verde, co-sponsored by the **Lega Ambiente** and Italian Railways, toured the country, measuring and publicising levels of air and noise pollution; all over Italy green universities – **università verdi** – were organised to educate the public. The 'greening' of Italy can be judged a success, as there is now a lasting awareness of the need to protect the environment.

Vivere in città

Introduce the topic by reminding the students of some major differences between British and Italian cities.

Start from a linguistic point: tell the students that the word *la metropoli* is used to mean the largest cities in the world. *La città* is used for big cities, but it also means a town of the size of Bologna, for instance. Italians, therefore, will say *una cittadina* to mean a smaller town (as well as a female town dweller of course), of the size of Oxford, for instance, and *paese* to mean anything smaller than that, although the dividing line is a very fine one.

Describe how the High Street as a focal point is replaced by *la piazza,* or several of them. Usually on the central piazza, once a week, there is an open-air market. On market day, the piazza comes to life with a colourful display of fruit and vegetables, clothes and local products.

Talk to the students about how Italians, unlike the British, enjoy living close to the town centre (often in full view of *il centro storico*) and that the idea of living in the peripheral quieter suburbs doesn't really appeal to them. Many do have second homes *in campagna* or *in montagna,* but cities are places which are much 'lived in'. It is true that Italians do a lot of travelling to get to work but this is often from *città* to *città*. They do not move house frequently and the verb 'to move' – *traslocare* – has different connotations in Italy.

This attachment to home and neighbourhood has primarily economic reasons, but there are others. Since the end of the Dark Ages and the flourishing of arts Italian cities have competed in creating the best *chiese, piazze* or *palazzi*. Old hostilities have died down but *campanilismo* (provincialism) still inspires some jealousy and rivalry among Italians. Perhaps this is why football is taken so seriously in Italy.

1   Set the scene by asking the students to identify the geographical position of at least half a dozen major Italian cities. Draw a map on the board/OHP with the towns marked but not named.

2   Ask questions like *Dov'è Napoli? Nel nord, nel sud o nel centro Italia?*

3   Identify the geographical position of Bologna.

Video corner
In order of appearance
Aim: active viewing/vocabulary building

1   Tell students to look at the opening sequence. They will see shots of the following, but in a different order: *bambino/fontana con acqua che scorre/chiesa/statua/particolare di statua/orologio/torri*

2   Tell students to number the above items in order of appearance. (Some pictures appear more than once.)

3   Check answers and discuss any other questions.

In quale ordine?
Aim: active viewing
Video sequence: second part of Anna's interview with Fausto and Andrea in the Parco dei Cedri

1   Watch the video beforehand and write each line of the dialogue on flashcards.

2   Show students the video with the volume turned down and ask them to put the cards in the right order. Tell them to look at the hand movements for clues.

Interactions

> **Structures:** direct object pronouns/*potere* + infinitive
> **Functions:** asking permission/asking someone to do something/asking and saying prices
> **Vocabulary:** prices
>
> ### Help-phrases and instructions
>
> *Che cosa devo/dobbiamo fare?*
> *Vorrei fare una domanda a proposito di . . .*
> *Sarebbe una buona idea se leggessimo/scrivessimo/facessimo . . .*

Interaction 1 (036)

1 *Anna è in un erboristeria per comprare dello shampoo.*
What two things does Anna buy?
How much does she spend altogether?

2 Play the cassette/CD as required and ask further questions:
How much is the shampoo?
How much is the lotion?
Which type of shampoo can be used for frequent washes?

I'll have it

Aim: to practise the grammatical point *lo prendo*

1 Explain to students the use of the key phrase *lo prendo*.

2 Read out items from a shopping list and ask the students to put them into the four columns below. Tell students to guess any words they don't know.

| *la prendo* | *lo prendo* | *le prendo* | *li prendo* |

(There's no need for them to write the words, just the corresponding number.) Here is a sample shopping list:

1 *borsa*	6 *camicia*	11 *giornale*	16 *disco*
2 *orologio*	7 *funghi*	12 *birra*	17 *fagiolini*
3 *gelato*	8 *banane*	13 *spinaci*	18 *salsiccia*
4 *shampoo*	9 *giacca*	14 *pantaloni*	19 *scarpe*
5 *limoni*	10 *vestito*	15 *rivista*	20 *penna*

3 Check answers and discuss as necessary.

Quanto costa?

Aim: understanding and writing numbers

1 Tell students you are going to read out the prices of ten different items and that they should jot these down.

2 Read out, in full, the sentences below. On a first reading students could concentrate on writing the price only, filling in the item when they hear the list the second time. (Remind the students that a full stop, not a comma, separates more than three digits.)

1 *Una pizza quattro stagioni costa 12.000 lire.*
2 *Un biglietto per il cinema costa dalle 10.000 alle 13.500 lire.*
3 *Le banane costano 4.750 lire al chilo.*
4 *La benzina costa 1.340 lire al litro.*
5 *Il giornale costa 1.200 lire.*
6 *Lo shampoo alle erbe costa 9.000 lire.*
7 *I pantaloni costano 75.000 lire.*
8 *Un chilo di pane costa 3.500 lire.*
9 *Un francobollo per l'Europa costa 900 lire.*
10 *Le paste costano 450 lire l'una.*

Check answers by asking random questions such as:
Quanto costano le banane? or *Quanto costa la benzina al litro?*

3 Next, ask students to change all the prices on the list. They may have a ridiculously cheap or outrageously expensive price, as long as they know how to say it in Italian.

4 Play the role of the shopper. Ask several different students the price of the same item(s). When you hear the cheapest price, say that you'll have the item(s): *lo prendo/le prendo*, etc. Then, encourage a student to take the role of the shopper.

Germana	Costano lo stesso prezzo. Ottomila cinquecento lire.
Anna	Sì, prendo questo a base di mallo di noce.
Germana	Serve altro?
Anna	Sì. **Ha** per caso **una** lozione tonificante per il viso, senza alcool?
Germana	*[calling to the owner]* Signora, una lozione tonificante per il viso senza alcool . . .
Sig.ra Pironti	Sì, abbiamo questa a base di camomilla.
Anna	Uhm! Che buon odore!
Sig.ra Pironti	Sono buoni gli odori perché sono tutti prodotti naturali. [. . .] Va bene?
Anna	Sì, signora, **la prendo.**
Sig.ra Pironti	Desidera altro?
Anna	No, grazie, **basta così.**
Sig.ra Pironti	Sono ventimila lire.
Anna	Ecco a Lei.
Sig.ra Pironti	Grazie, buongiorno.
Anna	Buongiorno, grazie.

ecco [a Lei]	*here you are*
contiene	*it contains*
miglio	*millet*
mallo di noce	*walnut pulp*
serve altro?	*do you need anything else?*
per caso	*by any chance*
desidera altro?	*would you like anything else?*
sono ventimila lire	*that's 20 thousand lire*

Interactions

I   12

Bologna was the first Italian city to close its centre to traffic. In its busy pedestrian precinct Anna shops for shampoo and toning lotion in an environment-friendly **erboristeria**, a natural foods and beauty store.

First time round

i capelli *hair*	
il viso *face*	

Use the words given here plus a bit of guesswork – listen for words which resemble English ones. There are two people working in the shop.

a What two things does Anna actually buy?
b How much does she spend altogether?

Anna	Buongiorno, signorina. Come sta?
Germana	Bene, grazie. E Lei?
Anna	Bene, grazie.
Germana	Cosa desidera oggi?
Anna	Io ho bisogno di uno shampoo per capelli normali.
Germana	Sì. Ecco. Abbiamo questo che contiene miglio ed è adatto per lavaggi frequenti. Altrimenti abbiamo questo che contiene mallo di noce ed è adatto per lavaggi settimanali.
Anna	E **quanto costano?**

Key phrases

quanto costano?	*how much are they?*
ha . . . una . . . ?	*have you got a . . . ?*
la prendo	*I'll take it*
basta così	*that's all*

At the chemist's   12

You are in the chemist's shop waiting to ask for some shampoo. Listen and play your part in the conversation. You remember you also needed a tube of toothpaste . . .

2 CC CD 13

Bologna's **Centro informazioni comunali** provides information on all the city's services: there's even a computer which records levels of pollution – **inquinamento.** When Anna visits the Centre she asks if she can try the computer.

First time round

> l'inquinamento *pollution*

a Is Anna allowed to use the computer?
b Is everyone allowed to use the computer when they want to?

Anna	**Scusi. Posso?**
Ragazza	Sì, sì, **prego.**
Anna	**Che cosa si può** vedere esattamente?
Ragazza	Questo computer permette di vedere il grado di inquinamento nelle varie zone della città di Bologna.
Anna	E chi può usare questo computer?
Ragazza	È a disposizione di tutti. La gente lo può usare quando vuole per sapere se l'aria è inquinata.
Anna	E lo consultano spesso?
Ragazza	Sì, molti cittadini sono curiosi di sapere il livello di inquinamento della zona dove abitano.
Anna	Ah, è un'ottima iniziativa. [...]

la gente lo può usare quando vuole	*people can use it when they want to*
permette di vedere	*makes it possible to see*

> **Key phrases**
>
> | | |
> |---|---|
> | **scusi. Posso?** | *excuse me, may I?* |
> | **prego** | *go ahead* |
> | **che cosa si può...?** | *what can you...?* |

3 CC CD 14

The **Centro informazioni** also houses the tourist office. Anna checks she's in the right place and then enquires about opening hours.

First time round

aprire	*to open*
chiudere	*to close*

Use the words given here and what you studied in Unit 4.

a When is the office open?
b Are the Sunday opening hours the same?

Anna	Questo è l'ufficio turistico, vero?
Lucia	Certo.
Anna	Buongiorno.
Lucia	Buongiorno.
Anna	**Quando siete aperti?**
Lucia	Siamo aperti tutto il giorno. Non chiudiamo a mezzogiorno.
Anna	**A che ora aprite?**
Lucia	Apriamo alle nove e chiudiamo alle diciannove.
Anna	E siete aperti dalle nove alle diciannove anche di domenica?
Lucia	No, la domenica siamo aperti solo dalle nove alle tredici.
Anna	Ho capito. Qui vengono molti turisti?
Lucia	Sì, molti turisti italiani e anche stranieri.
Anna	Grazie, arrivederci.
Lucia	Arrivederci.

anche di domenica?	*on Sundays as well?*
ho capito	*I see*

> **Key phrases**
>
> | | |
> |---|---|
> | **quando siete aperti?** | *when are you open?* |
> | **a che ora aprite?** | *what time do you open?* |

Interaction 2 (163)

1 *Anna è nel 'Centro informazioni comunali' dove c'è un computer che registra il livello di inquinamento* – pollution level.

Is Anna allowed to use the computer?
Is everyone allowed to use the computer when they want to?

2 Play the cassette/CD as required.

Che cosa si può fare?

Aim: training in making 'guesses' and practising *si può* or *non si può*

1 Explain to students the use of the key phrase *Che cosa si può (fare)?*

2 Read out a list of activities like those below and ask students to put them into the following five categories, according to where they think it is possible to carry them out:

in ufficio   a casa   in treno   al cinema   in vacanza

3 Make sure students know the meanings of the five different locations **but do not give them the meanings of the activities before reading out the list**. Ask them to guess the meaning if it is not known.

1 *parlare al telefono*	6 *suonare la chitarra*	11 *dormire*
2 *prendere il sole*	7 *andare a gabinetto*	12 *fumare*
3 *giocare a tennis*	8 *guardare la televisione*	13 *leggere*
4 *giocare a scacchi*	9 *mangiare*	14 *ballare*
5 *ascoltare la radio*	10 *scrivere una lettera*	15 *sognare*

4 Ask students to check their answers in pairs while you write on the board the fifteen different activities.

5 Ask student A to say which answer student B has given. Explain the meaning of *secondo* followed by a name, and tell them to use this formula to say, for example: *Secondo (student B) si può fumare in treno.* Since some of the activities can be performed in more than one location, the students are bound to have different answers. This exercise will lead to interesting and lively discussion.

This point could be the end of the lesson. Revise the points covered so far. In the next lesson students will cover the following:

> **Structures:** *di* + article/*potere* + infinitive
> **Functions:** understanding opening and closing times/making requests
> **Vocabulary:** shops and shopping

Interaction 3 (197)

1 *Anna è ancora nel Centro informazioni comunali.*
Is the office open all day?
What are the opening hours?
Are Sunday opening hours the same?

2 Play the cassette/CD as required and ask one more question:
What type of tourists go there?

Patterns 1

Shopping

1   Remind students of the two ways in which you ask for goods:

Ha/Avete | del pane integrale?
della verdura organica?
dello sciroppo per la tosse?
delle pastiglie per la gola?

Mi dà | *una penna biro blu?*
un pacchetto di fiammiferi?

2   Give students names of items from a shopping list. (You may use the list given for the exercise immediately after Interaction 1.) Here it is again:

1 *borsa*	6 *camicia*	11 *giornale*	16 *disco*
2 *orologio*	7 *funghi*	12 *birra*	17 *fagiolini*
3 *gelato*	8 *banane*	13 *spinaci*	18 *salsiccia*
4 *shampoo*	9 *giacca*	14 *pantaloni*	19 *scarpe*
5 *limoni*	10 *vestito*	15 *rivista*	20 *penna*

3   Firstly, tell students to put the singular items on the list into the following four columns:

un   *uno*   *una*   *un'*

Then ask them to put all of the items into the following seven columns:

del   dello   della   dell'   dei   degli   delle

and again all of the items into the following two columns:

quanto costa?   *quanto costano?*

4   Finally, tell students to think of five different items and to write down the three most important questions or statements when shopping for them.

e.g. *Avete una crema per il viso?*
      Quanto costa?
      La prendo.

Patterns I

i) Shopping

Asking for goods

You can use the verb **avere** and the singular or plural *you*:

| Avete
Ha | una lozione tonificante? | *Have you got a toning lotion?* |

If you are asking for *some*, or *any*, rather than *a*, use **di** combined with the definite article:

| Avete
Ha | della pomata antisettica?
del dentifricio?
delle pastiglie per la gola?
dei cerotti? | *Have you got any* | *antiseptic cream?*
toothpaste?
throat pastilles?
plasters? |

If you know that they have what you want, use the phrase **mi dà**, literally '*will you give me*':

| Mi dà | uno shampoo per capelli normali
del dentifricio | *Can I have* | *a shampoo for normal hair?*
some toothpaste? |

[The verb **dare** (*to give*) is in Systems, note 1 ii, p. 97.]

Asking the price

All you need is the verb **costare** and the right word for *the*:

| Quanto costa | la birra?
il succo di frutta?
l'aperitivo?
l'aranciata? | *How much is* | *the beer?*
the fruit juice?
the aperitif?
the orangeade? |
| Quanto costano | le birre?
i succhi di frutta?
gli aperitivi?
le aranciate? | *How much are* | *the beers?*
the fruit juices?
the aperitifs?
the orangeades? |

If you want to know what everything adds up to, use the phrase **quant'è?** (*how much is it? how much is that?*).

| Quant'è? | Mille lire | *How much is it?* | *A thousand lire* |
| Quant'è? | Ottomila lire | *How much is it?* | *Eight thousand lire* |

[For more on numbers see Ref. I, 1, p. 239.]

Saying you'll take it or them

The key verb is **prendere**. The words for *it* and *them* depend on the words they replace:

| Va bene, | lo prendo (il vestito)
la prendo (la giacca) | *Fine, I'll take it* |
| Va bene, | li prendo (i fiori)
le prendo (le rose) | *Fine, I'll take them* |

Patterns I

ii) Asking permission

The key verb is **potere** (*to be able to*) [See Systems, note 1, p. 97.]

Posso?   *May I?*

| Posso | entrare?
guardare?
vedere? | *Can I* | *come in?*
look?
see? |

iii) Finding out what's possible

Again, the key verb is **potere:**

| Che cosa si può | vedere
fare | a Bologna? | *What can one/you* | *see*
do | *in Bologna?* |

iv) Asking someone to do something

Potere is useful for making requests:

Puoi ripetere, per favore? (*informal*)   *Can you repeat, please?*
Può parlare lentamente, per favore? (*formal*)   *Can you talk slowly, please?*

v) Opening and closing times

When making general enquiries, **voi,** the plural *you*, is often used:

Quando siete aperti?   *When are you open?*

| Siamo aperti | tutto il giorno
tutti i giorni
i giorni feriali
dalle 9 alle 19 | *We're open* | *all day*
every day
on weekdays
from 9 a.m. till 7 p.m. |

Siamo chiusi i giorni festivi   *We're closed on holidays*

To find out specific times the question to ask is:

| A che ora | aprite?
chiudete? | *What time do you* | *open?*
close? |

Apriamo alle nove   *We open at 9 a.m.*
Chiudiamo alle diciannove   *We close at 7 p.m.*

If you are asking when other places open and close, you use these forms of the verbs **aprire** and **chiudere:**

| A che ora | apre la posta?
aprono i musei? | *At what time* | *does the post office open?*
do the museums open? |

| A che ora | chiude?
chiudono? | *At what time* | *does it close?*
do they close? |

Asking permission

Explain *posso* + infinitive then ask students to write down something that they personally cannot eat, drink or do.

e.g. *Non posso mangiare cioccolata.*
Non posso bere caffè.
Non posso dormire più di sette ore.

Finding out what's possible

Ask students to write down a few examples of what is possible or allowed today but was not twenty years ago (or vice versa).

e.g. *Oggi si può parlare al telefono in macchina.*
Oggi non si può fumare al cinema.

Read out the most original sentences.

Asking someone to do something

Ask students to imagine trying to correct their partner's bad habits. Tell them to write down a few examples:

Puoi cercare di essere puntuale?!
Puoi smettere di fare briciole nel letto?!

Opening and closing times

1 Ask students if they know, or can guess, the meaning of the following eight types of public places and discuss as necessary.

*Discoteca Jerry   Caffè Gianduia   Pasticceria
Biblioteca Nazionale   Edicola   Ufficio Postale
Banca   Museo Egizio*

2 Below are the opening and closing times of the eight public places on the list (but in a different order). Read them out and ask the students to compile a timetable of opening and closing times, and possible lunch breaks and rest days. Tell them to make a note of the places.

1   L'edicola è aperta dal mattino presto fino all'una. Il pomeriggio riapre alle tre e mezzo e chiude alle sette e mezzo. È chiusa la domenica pomeriggio.

2   La banca è aperta dal mattino alle otto e trenta e fa orario continuato. Chiude per il pubblico alle due del pomeriggio.

3   Il Museo Egizio è aperto dal mattino alle nove fino all'una. Il pomeriggio è aperto dalle due e mezzo fino alle cinque e mezzo. È chiuso il lunedì.

4   Il Caffè Gianduia è aperto tutti i giorni della settimana dal mattino alle cinque fino a mezzanotte.

5   La Biblioteca Nazionale è nel centro di Roma. È aperta dal lunedì al sabato dalle nove all'una. Il pomeriggio è chiusa al pubblico.

6   L'ufficio postale è aperto dal lunedì al sabato dalle otto e mezzo alle tredici e trenta.

7   La Discoteca Jerry è aperta dalle dieci di sera fino alle due, le tre o anche le quattro del mattino.

8   La pasticceria, eccetto la domenica, è aperta tutti i giorni, dalle otto e trenta fino a mezzogiorno. Il pomeriggio apre alle quindici e trenta e chiude alle diciannove e trenta. La domenica è aperta solo al mattino.

Tell students to fit their answers into a grid of this kind:

	Opening time	Closing time	Lunch time	Rest day
1	early morning	19,30	13,00/ 15,30	Sunday pm
2				
3				
4				
5				
6				
7				
8				

Check answers and discuss any further questions.

Practice 1

La giornata di Giorgio

Aim: reading comprehension

Give students the following questions. Ask them to study them carefully before reading the passage:

Questions:
1 How far from the bus stop is Giorgio's house?
2 Describe Giorgio's routine from Monday to Friday.
3 How many times in one month will Giorgio have gone to
a) the cinema?
b) the restaurant?
4 What type of person is Giorgio?
5 How many brothers and sisters does Giorgio have and where do they live?

Lunedì mattina. Sono le otto e mezzo e Giorgio esce di casa per andare a lavorare. La fermata dell'autobus, che lo porta nel centro di Verona, è a circa un chilometro da casa sua. Giorgio lavora, dal lunedì al venerdì, dalle nove alle cinque. La giornata lavorativa in un agenzia di viaggi è molto stressante e per questo Giorgio, dopo le cinque, è molto stanco e ha bisogno di riposare. In genere quindi, dopo il lavoro preferisce andare in un bar a prendere un aperitivo e a leggere il giornale e rilassarsi. Una o due volte alla settimana va a mangiare al ristorante con qualche amico e almeno una volta ogni due settimane va al cinema. A Giorgio piace stare in compagnia di amici. Infatti ha una personalità molto socievole e per questo ha molti amici non solo a Verona, la sua città, ma anche in altre parti d'Italia. Ha anche molti amici stranieri perché Giorgio ha opportunità di viaggiare spesso e a buon mercato. In famiglia sono in cinque. Il padre, la madre e una sorella, di nome Agnese, abitano in una cittadina della provincia di Lecce, in Puglia, mentre un'altro fratello, che è sposato con una ragazza messicana, abita a Genova.

Role play

Divide the class into pairs and ask them to prepare a short dialogue set in an imaginary local tourist office. Student A asks student B:
a) What is there to see in town?
b) What are the opening and closing times of the places mentioned?
c) What is available at the tourist office in the way of literature?

Refresh your memory

1 Play Interaction 1 again.
2 Tell students to write down the Italian equivalent of:
a) Have you got a . . .?
b) How much is it . . .?
c) That's all.
3 Check answers and discuss any other points.

This point could be the end of the lesson. Revise the points covered so far. In the next lesson students will cover the following:

> **Structures:** present of *volere*
> **Functions:** understanding and asking for prices/ stating intentions
> **Vocabulary:** shops and shopping

Le torri Garisenda e Asinelli, Bologna

Practice I

The buildings of Bologna 15

You drop in to the tourist office and ask Lucia: What can one see in Bologna? Ask her in Italian. Listen to her answer. Now try to jot down the names of some of the buildings she mentioned.

Information seeking   15

Lucia now tells you what other items might be available in the tourist office:

posters (**i poster**), booklets (**gli opuscoli**), leaflets (**i dépliant**), information (**le informazioni**), map (**una pianta della città**).

Listen and repeat the words.

Now, can you ask if she has got any of these items:

> i poster della città   i dépliant sugli alberghi
> gli opuscoli sui musei   le informazioni sugli autobus   le piante di Bologna

e.g. i poster della città:
    Ha/Avete **dei** poster della città?

[Look at Unit 4 Systems, note 4, p. 94 if you need any help combining **di** with **il, la, i, le,** etc.]

When is it open?

Now try to ask what time the following buildings open and close:
    la posta   le banche   i musei

Refresh your memory

Play Interaction 1 again. This time listen out for the key shopping phrases: *have you got a . . . ?; how much is . . . ?; that's all.* And look at Patterns to remind yourself how you say: *Can I have . . . ?*

How much?   15

Below are items of food you can buy in a market. The prices of the fruit and vegetables are marked, but the groceries are not. Ask the stallholder how much each one costs and write the price underneath.

You'll find the following phrases helpful:

al chilo	*per kilo*
all'etto	*per 100 grammes*
al litro	*per litre*
mezzo chilo	*half a kilo*
mezzo litro	*half a litre*

L'alimentare   **Il fruttivendolo**

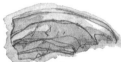

i pomodori
L. 900 Kg

1 il prosciutto

. . . .

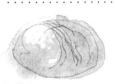

le pesche
L. 2.200 Kg

2 il pane

. . . .

l'uva
L. 2.500 Kg

3 il formaggio

. . . .

le mele
L. 2.300 Kg

gli spinaci
L. 3.000 Kg

4 il burro

. . . .

Il fruttivendolo CC CD 15

Listen to the cassette/CD and talk to the shopkeeper. The prices he quotes are from the price-list on the previous page.

Shopkeeper	Buongiorno. Desidera?
You	Buongiorno. *[Ask: have you got any peaches?]*
Shopkeeper	Sì, ecco.
You	*[Ask how much they cost.]*
Shopkeeper	Costano 2.200 lire al chilo.
You	*[Repeat the price. Ask for a kilo please.]*
Shopkeeper	Va bene. Desidera altro?
You	Sì, . . . *[Ask: can I have 2 kilos of spinach please?]*
Shopkeeper	Due chili di spinaci, sono 6.000 lire. Serve altro?
You	Sì . . . *[Ask: have you got any grapes?]*
Shopkeeper	Sì. Costa 2.500 lire al chilo.
You	Va bene, . . . *[Repeat the price. Ask: can I have half a kilo please?]*
Shopkeeper	Mezzo chilo, va bene. Sono 1.250 lire. Basta così?
You	*[Say yes, that's all and ask for the total.]*
Shopkeeper	Sono 9.450 lire.
You	*[Repeat price.]* Va bene, grazie.

You can use this dialogue for further practice – with a fellow learner or on your own. Choose your own items and use the prices from the previous exercise.

I'll have it

For each of the items below, say you'll have it or them. Make it absolutely clear what you want by then naming the item and the colour.

e.g. Va bene, **la** prendo. Sì, prendo la maglia rossa.

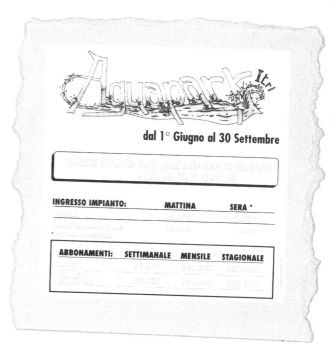

dal 1° Giugno al 30 Settembre

INGRESSO IMPIANTO:		MATTINA	SERA *

ABBONAMENTI:	SETTIMANALE	MENSILE	STAGIONALE

Aguapark

Look at the information leaflet advertising the summer-time prices and opening hours of the Aguapark swimming pool complex. Answer the questions in Italian – aloud or in writing.

1 L'Aguapark è aperto tutto l'anno?
2 È aperto tutti i giorni da giugno a settembre?
3 È aperto tutto il giorno?
4 A che ora apre la mattina?
5 A che ora chiude la sera?
6 Per un adulto quanto costa l'ingresso la mattina?
7 E per un bambino di 10 anni, quanto costa?
8 Quanti tipi di abbonamenti ci sono?

Shopping around

Aim: to encourage oral practice in pairs/to practise understanding and writing numbers and metrical measures

1 Tell students to imagine they have each invited four people for Sunday lunch. They are going to cook a three-course meal, followed by cheese, dessert and coffee. In order to cook the meal, they need to buy the following:

formaggio:	Dolcelatte	250 grammi
	Fontina	½ chilo
	Ricotta	200 grammi

pesce: merluzzo	1 chilo
pasta: penne	½ chilo
zucchini:	½ chilo
fagiolini:	½ chilo
insalata: rossa	300 grammi
pomodori:	½ chilo
limoni:	due
vino bianco:	un litro
una torta gelato:	confezione da sei
caffè:	100 grammi

2 Explain the meanings of ingredients in the recipes if necessary.

3 Choose four students, and give each of them a different price list.

4 The four students who are shopkeepers are bound to the price list given to them (i.e. they must quote their prices from their price lists and are not allowed to give discounts). The other students must shop around for the best prices. The quality of the food is the same in all shops. They must ask the cost of each item before they buy it and they should try to spend as little as possible.

5 Tell students to feel free to 'shop around', which means that they will have to move around the class in order to find out the information they need to complete the task.

6 Check answers and discuss as necessary.

Dolcelatte	Dolcelatte	Dolcelatte	Dolcelatte
Lit.	Lit.	Lit.	Lit.
7.500 Kg	7.800 Kg	7.200 Kg	7.400 Kg
Fontina	Fontina	Fontina	Fontina
Lit.	Lit.	Lit.	Lit.
5.600 Kg	5.500 Kg	5.300 Kg	5.700 Kg
Ricotta	Ricotta	Ricotta	Ricotta
Lit.	Lit.	Lit.	Lit.
6.500 Kg	6.400 Kg	6.400 Kg	6.600 Kg
Merluzzo	Merluzzo	Merluzzo	Merluzzo
Lit.	Lit.	Lit.	Lit.
9.800 Kg	9.500 Kg	9.700 Kg	9.400 Kg
Pasta	Pasta	Pasta	Pasta
Lit.	Lit.	Lit.	Lit.
1.300 Kg	1.500 Kg	1.100 Kg	1.300 Kg
Zucchini	Zucchini	Zucchini	Zucchini
Lit.	Lit.	Lit.	Lit.
2.100 Kg	1.900 Kg	1.800 Kg	2.200 Kg
Fagiolini	Fagiolini	Fagiolini	Fagiolini
Lit.	Lit.	Lit.	Lit.
2.500 Kg	2.300 Kg	2.700 Kg	2.600 Kg
Insalata	Insalata	Insalata	Insalata
Lit.	Lit.	Lit.	Lit.
700	800	600	750
Pomodori	Pomodori	Pomodori	Pomodori
Lit.	Lit.	Lit.	Lit.
2.300 Kg	2.100 Kg	2.400 Kg	2.500 Kg
Limoni	Limoni	Limoni	Limoni
Lit.	Lit.	Lit.	Lit.
200 l'uno	250 l'uno	200 l'uno	250 l'uno
Tocai	Tocai	Tocai	Tocai
Lit.	Lit.	Lit.	Lit.
5.400 litro	6.700 litro	5.900 litro	6.100 litro
Verdicchio	Verdicchio	Verdicchio	Verdicchio
Lit.	Lit.	Lit.	Lit.
6.300 litro	6.200 litro	6.400 litro	6.250 litro
Frascati	Frascati	Frascati	Frascati
Lit.	Lit.	Lit.	Lit.
5.200 litro	5.750 litro	5.900 litro	5.100 litro
Torta gelato	Torta gelato	Torta gelato	Torta gelato
Lit.	Lit.	Lit.	Lit.
12.000 Kg	13.000 Kg	12.500 Kg	12.800 Kg
Caffè	Caffè	Caffè	Caffè
Lit.	Lit.	Lit.	Lit.
11.300 Kg	12.400 Kg	12.200 Kg	11.700 Kg

Cultura e parole

1   Introduce the topic for this section by explaining that much of the terminology used to discuss environmental issues is similar in Italian and English and, to prove it, set the students a small task.

2   Ask students to try to think of the English equivalents of the following:

contaminazione dell'acqua
cambiamento del clima
effetto-serra
strato di ozono dell'atmosfera
combustibili non ecologici
protezione ambiente
depuratori dell'aria
inceneratori di rifuti
anidride carbonica
nuove tecnologie

3   Bring in newspaper articles which contain the above words in their titles. Show them to the students and discuss the meanings of the titles.

If the article is not too difficult, and if it talks about an issue which is familiar to the students, it is worth trying to read it in class.

1   Select difficult words and structures from the text and write them on the board.

2   Elicit their meanings from the students.

3   Give students a brief summary of what they are going to read.

4   Put students into small groups, give them copies of the articles and tell them to read and understand as much as they can by helping each other.

5   Supervise the activity by moving from group to group.

6   Ask each group to give a brief oral summary of the article in their own words to the rest of the class.

Cultura e parole

I n Italy environmental awareness has been translated into concrete action. Between 1986 and 1991, government spending on the environment – **l'ambiente** – went up tenfold and a spate of new legislation was introduced, such as the much-publicised 100-lira tax on plastic bags – **i sacchetti di plastica** – and the laws obliging every region to install a set quota of lead-free petrol pumps and waste recycling plants.

Much of the responsibility for implementing the legislation rests with the town councils – **i comuni.** Many town councils now have their own Environment Department – **l'Assessorato all'Ambiente,** though predictably some are better than others. Bologna is universally acknowledged to be a pioneer in the field. Recycling and waste disposal have been encouraged by installing different coloured disposal banks, called **campane** – bells – because of their shape: green for glass, blue for paper, yellow for plastic and grey for aluminium.

Bologna itself is traditionally linked with the colour red. It has been known as **Bologna la rossa,** both for the longstanding leftwing political affiliations of the city and for the brick with which much of the city is built. But the city is not only known for its efficiency and political militancy. It is also famous for its pleasures, both aesthetic and culinary. The Bolognese have flourishing restaurants and trattorias, as well as osterie.

Portici: arcades. There are 37 kilometres of arcades in Bologna, more than in any other Italian city. The first ones were originally built in the twelfth and thirteenth centuries, not as shelter from the elements, but to solve a housing problem; Bologna's university – the first in Europe – attracted over 2000 students to the city. Faced with this influx, the **comune** hit on the idea of using the space over the arcades for extra accommodation.

In Bologna, whatever the weather, it is always a pleasure to go for a stroll – **passeggiare.** In practice this usually refers to the custom of the **passeggiata,** the evening stroll in the main street or square of a town. The aim is to meet others, chat and be seen.

Osterie: Osterie have gone up in the world. Originally they were sordid taverns associated with drunkenness and low life. Nowadays they are carefully done up in traditional regional decor and are amongst the 'in' places to go and enjoy a vast range of wines, beers and spirits (mainly grappa and whisky). Food is available and sometimes entertainment as well.

Interactions

4 🔲 💿 16

On the outskirts of Bologna, in the **Parco dei Cedri** the Italian Worldwide Fund for Nature – **il WWF** – and the Bologna town council have set up a protected area within the park. Anna meets two people involved in the project and finds out what it's about.

First time round

le scuole elementari	*infant and junior schools*
le medie	*middle schools*
gli scopi didattici	*educational aims*
cercare di ottenere	*to try and achieve*

Remember to listen out for words which resemble English.

a Can you pick out who's the boss?
b What do they want people to learn about? Plants, or plants and animals?

Anna	Voi lavorate per il WWF, vero?
Fausto	Sì.
Anna	Lei come si chiama?
Fausto	Io mi chiamo Fausto Bonafede e sono il responsabile per il WWF di questo progetto.
Andrea	E io mi chiamo Andrea Sivelli e lavoro anch'io per il WWF.
Anna	Venite qui ogni giorno?
Andrea	Beh, ogni giorno no, però molto spesso.
Anna	E anche d'inverno?
Fausto	Anche d'inverno. Certo.
Andrea	Anche quando piove.
Anna	E cosa fate?

Fausto	Mah, accompagniamo spesso bambini e ragazzi delle scuole elementari e delle medie con scopi didattici.
Anna	E da quanto tempo esiste il progetto?
Andrea	Beh, questo progetto esiste dal novembre del 1989.
Anna	Che cosa cercate di ottenere con questo progetto?
Fausto	Cerchiamo di fare conoscere la flora ma anche la fauna caratteristiche di questa regione. E **vogliamo** studiare la natura abbandonata a sé stessa.

sono il responsabile . . . di questo progetto	*I'm in charge of this project*
che cosa cercate di ottenere?	*what are you trying to achieve?*
abbandonata a sé stessa	*left to itself*

Key phrase

vogliamo   *we want*

la Repubblica

Parchi e giardini bolognesi 8

Parco dei Cedri

Interaction 4 (339)

1 *Anna parla con Fausto e Andrea che lavorano per il World Wildlife Fund nel Parco dei Cedri vicino a Bologna.*
Can you pick out who's the boss?
What do they want to learn about? Plants, or plants and animals?

2 Play the cassette/CD as required and ask further questions:
How often do they go to the Parco dei Cedri?
Do they go there in wintertime too?
How do they help school children?
How long has the project been going on?
What other aims do Fausto and Andrea have?

Volere volare

Aim: to practise all verbal forms of *volere*

1 Give students a list of likely activities for the coming weekend and tell them to write them in one column. Tell them to write the names of at least half a dozen other students in the same number of columns alongside, so as to make up a chart like this:

STUDENTS

	A	B	C	D	E	F
leggere il giornale						
guardare un video						
andare a cinema						
fare la spesa						
riposare						
giocare a tennis						
andare al ristorante						
fare una passeggiata						
scrivere una lettera						
pulire la casa						
andare in campagna						
invitare amici a cena						
guardare la televisione						
dormire						
fare del giardinaggio						

2 Ask students to interview each other on what they intend to do at the weekend. Tell them to:
a) ask *Che cosa vuoi fare questo fine settimana?* or *Dove vuoi andare questo fine settimana?*
b) answer by saying, for example, *Questo fine settimana voglio andare in campagna.*
c) Record their findings on the chart by ticking each student's chosen activities.

3 When the students have finished their survey, check answers orally by asking: *Che cosa vuole fare student A questo fine settimana?* and so on for student B, C, etc. This time, tell students to answer by saying:

Student A vuole fare del giardinaggio, dormire, guardare la televisione; student B vuole guardare un video, leggere il giornale, etc.

4 Then pick out a popular activity and ask: *Chi vuole riposare questo fine settimana?* Tell students to answer by saying: *Student A e Student B vogliono riposare.*

5 Finally ask two students together:
Che cosa volete fare questo fine settimana? and tell them to start their answer by saying: *Vogliamo . . .*

At the end of this exercise all the verbal forms of *volere* will have been practised.

Interaction 5 (372)

1 *Anna è ancora in compagnia di Fausto e Andrea nel Parco dei Cedri.*
Ask students to pick out a couple of suggestions that Andrea and Fausto make for protecting the environment.

2 Play the cassette/CD as required and ask further questions:
Why do the people who visit the park respect the environment?
Are Andrea and Fausto optimistic about the future?

Che cosa bisogna fare?

Aim: vocabulary building and practice of *Che cosa bisogna fare?*

Divide the class into small groups and ask them to describe, with your help and with the help of a dictionary, what procedure needs to be followed in order to, for example, board a plane, go through a car wash, use a public phone, make a boiled egg (and soldiers), etc.

This point could be the end of the lesson. Revise the points covered so far. In the next lesson students will cover the following:

> **Structures:** impersonal constructions
> **Functions:** saying what must be done
> **Vocabulary:** cities/issues/amenities

Interaction 6 (389)

1 *A Bologna Anna chiede a tre persone perché è bello vivere a Bologna.*

2 Write on the board:

a) nightlife   b) walking around town   c) shopping

Ask students to sort out who is keen on what.

3 Play the cassette/CD as required and ask further questions:
Why are the shops in Bologna particularly attractive?
What can you do at night?
Why is it pleasant to walk around the town?

Città e paesi

Aim: to train understanding for gist and selecting information from a general context/guided note-taking

1 Four people talk about the towns in which they live. Tell students that the people will talk about the geographical position of their town or village and other important features.

2 Give students the list of words below, ensuring they know the meanings. Tell them to write the words in one column, leaving space for four more columns.

3 Read out the information on the different towns or villages (at least twice), allowing students time to make notes on what they hear in the appropriate spaces.

4 Ask students to write a short report from the information they have gathered on one town or village.

5 You could ask them to write about the other towns or villages for homework.

nome	*città più vicina*	*mare*
collina	*montagna*	*inquinamento*
tranquillità	*attività culturali*	*discoteche*
cinema/teatri	*bar/gelaterie*	*monumenti*
amici	*sciare*	*passeggiare*

Giaveno è una cittadina vicino a Torino, in collina. C'è prima di tutto poco traffico e quindi poco inquinamento e molta tranquillità. Ehmm . . . ci sono molti giovani. Specialmente d'estate, ehmm . . . si può uscire, andare in gelateria, passeggiare nella campagna circostante. D'inverno si può andare a sciare abbastanza facilmente. C'è un solo cinema però e i film non sono in genere molto belli.

Arezzano è un paesino rinascimentale su una collina vicino a Grosseto. Da vedere c'è un bellissimo panorama e da fare d'estate ci sono molte attività culturali come spettacoli e concerti. D'inverno invece, a parte gli amici, non c'è molto da fare, perché non ci sono cinema o teatri.

Varazze è una cittadina nell'Italia settentrionale a circa cinquanta chilometri da Genova. Il paesaggio è bellissimo ma d'inverno non si può fare o vedere molto . . . mentre d'estate c'è molta gente, molti turisti e molte attività anche culturali. Inoltre è un posto molto romantico e ci sono molti locali pubblici come bar, ristoranti e discoteche.

Verona non è una grande città come Milano, Roma o Napoli e quindi non ha problemi di inquinamento, traffico o sovraffollamento. La periferia non è molto attraente ma il centro storico con l'Arena è veramente stupendo. C'è molta attività culturale durante tutto l'anno, non solo durante la stagione turistica estiva.

5   cc   ◎ 17

When Fausto and Andrea have completed their work Anna finds out what still needs to be done.

First time round

tutelare l'ambiente	*to protect the environment*
cosa rimane da fare?	*what is left to do?*

What suggestions do Andrea and Fausto make for protecting the environment? Try to pick out two.

[...]

Anna	**Che cosa bisogna fare** per tutelare l'ambiente?
Andrea	Beh, **bisogna** imparare a vivere con la natura e non a combatterla.
Anna	Le persone che vengono qui, cosa fanno? Rispettano l'ambiente?
Andrea	Beh, in genere, sì, anche perché [...] capiscono che la natura è indispensabile per vivere.
Anna	Che cosa rimane da fare per la conservazione della natura?
Fausto	Qui in Italia e anche in altri paesi rimane tanto da fare, bisogna, io credo, estendere queste esperienze di natura libera, senza l'intervento dell'uomo, in altre parti, in altre aree. E poi **bisogna usare meno la macchina,** utilizzare meno l'energia, eccetera.
Anna	Ma siete ottimisti per il futuro?
Andrea	Sì.
Fausto	Moderatamente ottimisti.
Anna	Grazie.

estendere queste esperienze di natura libera ... in altre parti	*to extend these attempts at leaving nature alone ... to other places*

Key phrases

che cosa bisogna fare?	*what needs to be done?*
bisogna ...	*you need to ...*
bisogna usare meno la macchina	*you need to use cars less*

6   cc   ◎ 18

The inhabitants of Bologna are enthusiastic about their town. Anna finds out from three of them why it's so nice living there.

First time round

pieno di	*full of*
punto di vista	*point of view*

Sort out what each person is keen on and put the correct letter in the boxes below:

a nightlife   **b** walking around town   **c** shopping

Voice 1	Voice 2	Voice 3

Anna	Perché è bello vivere a Bologna?
Ragazza	Bologna è bella perché ha un bel centro pieno di negozi, pieno di vetrine, è sempre illuminata. È una bella città!
Giovane	Bologna è una città che offre molto, diciamo, anche da un punto di vista della vita notturna. C'è una 'cultura' di osterie, una 'cultura' di posti dove si mangia bene e si beve bene! [...]
Signora	È molto bello passeggiare anche sotto la pioggia a Bologna, perché abbiamo questi splendidi portici, che sono una delle caratteristiche principali di Bologna.

diciamo	*let's say*
si mangia bene	*you eat well*
si beve bene	*you drink well*
sotto la pioggia	*in [lit. under] the rain*

A meal out   cc   19

Bologna's night spots, in particular its restaurants, are much advertised on the local radio stations. There are two ads on the cassette/CD from Radio Sfera Regione. Listen for what's being advertised and then see if you can pick out the addresses.

74

Patterns 2

i) Saying what you want to do

The key verb is **volere** (*to want*) [see Systems, note 1 i, p. 97].

| Cosa | vuoi
vuole
volete | fare? | *What do you want to do?* |

| Voglio | studiare l'italiano | *I want* | *to study Italian* |
| Vogliamo | parlare italiano | *We want* | *to speak Italian* |

ii) Saying what must be done

The key verb is **bisognare** (*to be necessary*). The only form used when talking about the present is **bisogna** (*it is necessary, you/one must*).

Cosa bisogna fare? *What must one do?*

| Bisogna | lavorare per la pace
condannare la guerra | *You must* | *work for peace*
condemn war |

Practice 2

A better world?

Can you unscramble the phrases below to form a series of slogans? There's one word too many.
Per un mondo migliore BISOGNA...

ESSERE

la guerra!

RISPETTARE

tolleranti!

giovani!

LAVORARE

gli altri

CONDANNARE

per la pa

Patterns 2

Saying what you want to do

To practise the different verbal forms of *volere,* ask students to write out a few sentences based on the information they have gathered (and the chart they have filled in) on what their fellow students plan to do over the coming weekend. If they have not done the exercise from the Teacher's Book (which appears after Interaction 4), they could do it now.

Practice 2

Free writing

Ask students to write down:
a) a few more suggestions for *un mondo migliore.*
b) a plan of action for the coming weekend for themselves and other members of their household.

New Year resolutions

Aim: to practise all present tense forms of *dovere* and *volere*

1   Tell the students to find out what New Year resolutions the rest of the class want to make.

2   Give students a list of likely resolutions and tell them to write them down in one column. Some suggestions are below. Tell them to write the names of at least half a dozen other students alongside, to make up a chart like this:

STUDENTS

avere più tempo libero	A	B	C	D	E	F
lavorare di meno						
perdere cinque chili						
mangiare pochissimo						
fare più esercizio						
praticare uno sport						
imparare il tedesco						
risparmiare soldi						
spendere di meno						
essere più tollerante						
ascoltare gli altri						

3   Ask students to interview each other about the resolutions they intend to make. Tell them to ask: *Che cosa vuoi/Che cosa devi fare per l'anno nuovo?* giving the answer by saying, for example: *Devo spendere di meno* or *Voglio risparmiare soldi.*

4   Tell them to record their findings on the chart by ticking each student's chosen resolution.

5   When the students have finished their survey, check answers orally by asking: *Che cosa vuole fare student A?* and so on for student B, C, etc. This time, tell students to answer by saying:
Student A vuole or *deve . . .; student B vuole . . .* etc.

6   Then pick out a popular resolution and ask: *Chi vuole smettere di fumare?* Tell students to answer by saying: *Student A e student B vogliono smettere di fumare.*

7   Finally ask two students together:
Che cosa volete fare per l'anno nuovo? and tell them to start their answer by saying: *Vogliamo . . .*

New Year resolutions

First choose each resolution for yourself and say what you must do. Use **volere** and **dovere** each time.

e.g. avere più tempo libero *to have more free time*

    Io **voglio** avere più tempo libero
   lavorare meno   *to work less*
    Devo lavorare meno.

1 perdere 5 chili   *to lose 5 kilos*
   mangiare pochissimo   *to eat very little*

2 fare più esercizio   *to take more exercise*
   praticare uno sport   *to take up a sport*

3 imparare il tedesco   *to learn German*
   andare a un corso serale   *to go to an evening class*

4 risparmiare soldi   *to save money*
   spendere di meno   *to spend less*

5 essere più tollerante   *to be more tolerant*
   ascoltare gli altri   *to listen to others*

Now pick a few for a member of your family or a friend:

e.g. essere più sano/a   *to be healthier*

    Mio fratello **vuole** essere più sano.
   smettere di fumare   *to give up smoking*
    Deve smettere di fumare.

★ You can work with a fellow learner and use the dictionary to make up your own resolutions.

At the tobacconist's   19

On the tape/CD you'll hear an interview with Valerio Venturi, who runs a tobacconist's in the historic centre of Bologna. Listen to the statements and check whether they are true or false.

Identikit 19

Describe your home town or a town you know well. There's a model dialogue on the cassette/CD and below are some questions to guide you.

1 Di dov'è, Lei?
2 È grande, la Sua città?
3 Com'è la Sua città?
4 Che cosa c'è da vedere in centro?
5 È bello vivere a . . . ? – Che cosa si può fare a . . . ?

Vocabulary

Time

tutto il giorno	*all day*
tutto l'anno	*all year*
durante	*during*
i giorni festivi	*holidays*
i giorni feriali	*work days*

People

l'abitante	*inhabitant*
il cittadino	*citizen*
il poliziotto	*policeman*
la poliziotta	*policewoman*
il sindaco	*mayor*

Il campanile

Cityscape

l'edificio	*building*
il palazzo	*appartment block*
il municipio	*town hall*
il museo	*museum*
il campanile	*bell tower*
la torre	*tower*
il ponte	*bridge*
i portici	*arcades*
la statua	*statue*
la strada	*road*
il marciapiede	*pavement*
il traffico	*traffic*
il semaforo	*traffic light*
il segnale	*signpost*
il parco	*park*
la biblioteca	*library*
la pinacoteca	*art gallery*

Shopping

il prezzo	*price*
l'acquisto	*purchase*
i soldi	*money*
gli spiccioli	*small change*
il resto	*change*
caro/costoso	*expensive*
il negozio	*shop*
il supermercato	*supermarket*
il magazzino	*department store*
la vetrina	*shop window*
l'alimentare (*m*)	*grocer's*
la cartoleria	*stationer's*
l'erboristeria	*health shop*
la farmacia	*chemist's*
il fruttivendolo	*greengrocer*
la libreria	*bookshop*
la macelleria	*butcher's*
la pasticceria	*cake shop*
la panetteria	*bread shop*
il parrucchiere	*hairdresser*
la tabaccheria	*tobacconist*

Verbs

parcheggiare	*to park*
fare caldo	*to be hot*
fare freddo	*to be cold*
comprare	*to buy*
vendere	*to sell*
spendere	*to spend*
risparmiare	*to save*

Seasons

la stagione	*season*
la primavera	*spring*
l'estate (*f*)	*summer*
l'autunno	*autumn*
l'inverno	*winter*

La statua

Weather

il tempo	*weather*
il clima	*climate*
l'aria	*air*
inquinato	*polluted*
pulito	*clean*
il cielo	*sky*
sereno	*clear*
nuvoloso	*cloudy*
la nuvola	*cloud*
il vento	*wind*
la nebbia	*fog, mist*
che tempo fa?	*what's the weather like?*
fa bel/brutto tempo	*the weather's good/bad*
c'è sole	*it's sunny*
tira vento	*it's windy*
il caldo	*heat*
il freddo	*cold*
l'afa	*sultry heat*
la pioggia	*rain*
piovere	*to rain*
la neve	*snow*
nevicare	*to snow*
la grandine	*hail*
grandinare	*to hail*
il lampo	*lightning*
il tuono	*thunder*
il temporale	*storm*

Vocabulary

The following exercise provides one way of encouraging students to guess the meanings of words they have not met before.

1   Divide the students into four groups and give each one a different list of words (only some words should be familiar, the majority must be new). Each list should correspond to a particular place. Here are some suggestions:

guardiano	*cassa*	*stagno*	*silenzio*
gabbia	*commesso/a*	*spazio*	*guardiano*
bambini	*insegna*	*alberi*	*visitatori*
noccioline	*reparto*	*erba*	*un'altra epoca*
scimmia	*frutta*	*cani*	*studiosi*
leone	*verdura*	*aiuole*	*mummie*
giraffa	*salami*	*giardiniere*	*statue*
ippopotamo	*formaggi*	*picnic*	*reperti*

2   Each group writes the first word of the list in large letters and shows it to the rest of the class who must try to guess the place in question.

3   Playing goes on until all the places have been identified.

4   Students could use this vocabulary to play a game of Word Bingo.

Here are some suggestions for either oral or written work. Ask students to:

1   write up a weather chart for the previous seven days.

2   describe their town or city.

3   say what they do at weekends.

4   describe what types of shops there are in the neighbourhood.

Troubleshooting

Finally, here are some suggestions for either oral or written work based on the points raised in this section.

1   Tell students to go back to the resolutions and say what they need to do to implement them. For example: *Per smettere di fumare ho bisogno di fare agopuntura.*

2   Ask them to describe how people in town and people in the country live.

Review

Here is a checklist of the main points learned in this unit. For each point, ask the students to supply one or more examples by asking specific questions.

direct object pronouns
potere + infinitive
di + article
present tense of *volere*
impersonal construction
asking permission
asking someone to do something
asking and saying prices
understanding opening and closing times
making requests
stating intentions
saying what must be done
talking about problems of modern cities (pollution)

Troubleshooting

Aver bisogno di   bisogna

Don't confuse these two expressions.
Aver bisogno di literally means *to have need of.* (**il bisogno**
means *need*). It is used like an ordinary verb:

ho bisogno di	*I need*	abbiamo bisogno di	*we need*
hai bisogno di	*you need*	avete bisogno di	*you need*
ha bisogno di	*he/she/it needs*	hanno bisogno di	*they need/you need*

Bisogna is part of the verb **bisognare** (*to be necessary*) but **bisogna**
is the only form of the verb used. It can only be used in an
impersonal, general sense:

bisogna studiare   *one/you must study/ it is necessary to study*

La gente è people are

A singular form for a plural meaning.

La gente is used a lot in Italian. You need to remember to use
singular verbs and adjectives with it, even though the meaning
is plural. Look at these examples from Units 4 and 5.

molta gente [p. 51]   *lots of people*
la gentc lo può usare quando vuole [p. 67]   *people can use it
    when they want*

Systems I

1 Nouns

i) Masculine and feminine

bigliett**o**
guid**a**

Unlike English, all Italian nouns have a gender, – they are either masculine or feminine.
Nouns ending in **-o** are usually masculine:
   formaggio   ragazzo   figlio   bagno

Nouns ending in **-a** are usually feminine:
   pizza   ragazza   figlia   cucina

Other endings are possible. For example, masculine nouns can end in **-è**:
   caffè   tè

Feminine nouns can end in **à**:
   città   nazionalità

ii) Singular and plural

bigliett**o**   bigliett**i**
guid**a**   guid**e**

Masculine nouns usually form their plural in **-i**:
   formaggi   ragazzi   figli   bagni

Feminine nouns usually form their plural in **-e**:
   pizze   ragazze   figlie   cucine

Nouns ending with an accented letter do not change their form in the plural.

2 Definite articles

il biglietto   **i** biglietti
la guida   **le** guide

Definite articles are words for *the*.
The form depends on whether the accompanying noun is masculine or feminine, singular or plural.

il	i
il formaggio	i formaggi
il ragazzo	i ragazzi

la	le
la pizza	le pizze
la ragazza	le ragazze

If the noun ends in an accented letter the article changes in the plural, even though the noun stays the same.
   il tè   i tè   la città   le città
See also Unit 3, Systems, note 4, p. 88.

3 Indefinite articles

un biglietto
una guida

Indefinite articles are words for *a/an*.

un	una
un formaggio	una pizza
un ragazzo	una ragazza
un caffè	una città

As in English, there is often no need for an article in the plural:
   un formaggio *(a cheese)*   formaggi *(cheeses)*
   una pizza *(a pizza)*   pizze *(pizzas)*

To say *some* or *any* (the plural of *a*), see Unit 5, Systems, note 2iii, p. 98. See also Unit 3, note 4 p. 88 and Ref. I, 8 v, p. 240.

4 Adjectives

il   monumento famos**o**
i   monumenti famos**i**
la   basilica famos**a**
le   basiliche famos**e**

Adjectives change their endings to agree with the gender and number of the noun they accompany. This is always shown by the form of the article, whereas the noun ending is not necessarily a reliable guide.

   Unlike English, adjectives generally come *after* the noun, though quite a few common ones can also go before it. See Ref. V, 1, p. 244, for the position of adjectives.

Spelling note: Nouns and adjectives ending in **-ca**, **-ga** always add **h** before the plural ending:
   basilica   basiliche   antica   antiche
   lunga   lunghe

This is necessary to keep the original hard *k* sound of the singular ending.

Systems and Reinforcement

Although you may refer to this section at any time during the lesson to further explain any pattern included in the Interactions, you must encourage students to set time aside during homework periods to learn to recognise and use grammatical structures (and setting written homework on this section will give them some incentive). When you set homework in class, point out to the students that they can use the **Systems** as a reference section if they have any problems.

Section 1

In the following section each of the main points covered in the **Systems** is matched to the appropriate **Reinforcement** exercise. This is meant as a quick reference guide. The exercises aim to reinforce grammatical structures in a practical way, avoiding mechanical and 'autopilot' repetition. For this reason, you will mostly find that more than one grammatical point is tested in the same exercise.

Systems 1

STRUCTURES	PAGE NO.	REINFORCEMENT EXERCISES
1 Nouns	79	A B D E
2 Definite articles	79	A C E
3 Indefinite articles	79	B D
4 Adjectives	79	C D E
5 Demonstrative adjectives	80	D
6 *Essere*	80	B C D E F G
7 Sentence structure	80	B C D
8 Prepositions	80	G

Systems 2

STRUCTURES	PAGE NO.	REINFORCEMENT EXERCISES
1 Nouns	83	A B
2 Adjectives	83	B
3 Possessive adjectives	84	C D
4 Using the article	84	A B C D
5 Formal and informal speech	84	D
6 Regular verbs	84	E F
7 Using the present tense	85	E F
8 Irregular verbs	85	E
9 Sentence structure	85	E F G
10 A note on numbers	85	B

Systems 3

STRUCTURES	PAGE NO.	REINFORCEMENT EXERCISES
1 Regular verbs	87	A B F
2 Irregular verbs	87	C D
3 Using the present tense	88	A B C E F
4 Nouns and articles	88	G
5 Using the article	89	G I
6 Possessives	89	J
7 Interrogatives	90	E H
8 Object pronouns	90	K
9 *Vero?*	90	

Systems 4

STRUCTURES	PAGE NO.	REINFORCEMENT EXERCISES
1 Irregular verbs	93	A B C D
2 Using the present tense	93	D E
3 Prepositions	94	B H
4 Prepositions and definite articles	94	F G I
5 Variations in the use of prepositions	95	

Systems 5

STRUCTURES	PAGE NO.	REINFORCEMENT EXERCISES
1 Irregular verbs	97	C D
2 Prepositions	97	A E
3 Irregular nouns	98	B
4 Adjectives ending in *-ista*	98	B

Section 2

Suggestions are given here on how to make further use of the *Italianissimo* Course Book to reinforce points covered in the **Systems.** These are meant to be sample exercises which can be repeated at a higher and more complex level in the different units.

a) **Masculine and feminine/singular and plural**

1   Draw four columns on the board/OHP and ask students to do the same on a blank sheet of paper, giving them the following headings:

masculine   masculine   feminine   feminine
singular   plural   singular   plural

2   Ask students to put the words in the vocabulary section which refer to food (*Unità 1*) into the four columns above.

b) **Definite articles**   *il   la   i   le*

1   Ask students to put the appropriate definite article with the words in the **Odd one out** exercise on page 7.

c) **Feminine nouns beginning with a vowel**

Ask students to put the appropriate definite article with the nouns in the **Odd one out** exercise on page 29.

d) **Using the article**

Re-write the exercise **About Italy** on page 86 on a transparency, omitting the articles. Ask students to insert the missing articles. Go through the answers and discuss any points as required.

e) **Nouns ending in** *-e*

Ask students to look for the words which end in *e* in the vocabulary section (*Unità 2*) and put them into three categories according to whether they are:
masculine singular/feminine singular/feminine plural

f) **Adjectives**
i) **adjectives with** *-e* **nouns**
ii) **Adjectives ending in** *-e*
iii) *-issimo* **endings**

Ask students to describe a family in their neighbourhood by using as many words and adjectives as possible from the vocabulary section of *Unità 2*.

g) **Sentence structure**

Re-write an appropriate Interaction without question marks and let the students decide whether the sentences could be statements or questions.

The need for an **h** often applies to nouns and adjectives ending in **-co, -go**:

    tedesco tedeschi antico antichi
    lungo lunghi

There are a number of important exceptions:

    e.g. amico amici greco greci

For more on spelling see Ref. VI, 1, p. 245.

5 Demonstrative adjectives

questo monument**o**
questa basilic**a**
questi monument**i**
queste basilich**e**

Questo always precedes the noun. Its ending changes according to the gender and number of the noun it accompanies.

6 Essere (to be)

sono Anna
è il Colosseo
sono i Trulli

The present tense of **essere** is formed as follows:

(io)	sono	*I*	*am*
(tu)	sei	*you [informal]*	*are*
(lui, lei)	è	*he, she, it*	*is*
(Lei)	è	*you [formal]*	*are*
(noi)	siamo	*we*	*are*
(voi)	siete	*you [plural]*	*are*
(loro)	sono	*they*	*are*

i) Subject pronouns
In Italian the subject pronouns [*I, you, etc.*] are not strictly necessary to convey the meaning, whereas in English you have to use them. Italian subject pronouns are used mostly for emphasis or clarification:

    No, io non sono Stefano, lui è Stefano

ii) Understanding Lei
Lei means *she* and *you*. You use the same form of the verb and the same pronoun to talk about someone female and to talk formally to another person, whether female or male.

    Lei è inglese? *Are you English?*
          Is she English?
The context will tell you whether it's *you* or *she*.

iii) Two meanings of sono
Sono can mean *I am* or *they are*. **Essere** is the only verb where the **io** and the **loro** forms coincide. The context will tell you which form is which.

7 Sentence structures

i) Affirmative and negative statements

  è una casa
  non è una casa

Making a sentence negative is easy. Put **non** in front of the verb.

    sono case   *they are houses*
    non sono case *they aren't houses*

ii) Questions

  è una casa?
  non è una casa?

Remember, all statements can become questions with no change in word order. The rising intonation is all that's necessary.

    sono case?   *are they houses?*
    non sono case? *aren't they houses?*

8 Prepositions

i) Di

  la basilica **di** San Pietro

One of the meanings of **di** is *of*. It can be used with places:

    i Trulli di Alberobello

and also with people:

    le cartoline di Anna   *Anna's postcards*

ii) A and in

  siamo **a** Bologna
  in Emilia Romagna

A and **in** are both used to mean *in*:
a is used with towns, small islands and with some set expressions which you need to learn:

    a Rimini a Capri a Elba a casa a scuola

In is used with continents, countries, large islands and many set expressions which you can learn gradually:

    in Europa in Francia in Sicilia in Sardegna
    in città in campagna in montagna in salotto

Reinforcement I

A Your sitting-room

1 The contents of your sitting-room have all been labelled. Can you point out the objects in it to a friend?

e.g. Ecco la porta . . .

2 There are more than one of some of these objects. Can you also point these out?

e.g. Ecco le piante.

B Apples or pears?

Here are some more objects for you to identify to your friend.

e.g. È una mela. È una pera.   **1** *penna   matita*

2 *portafoglio   borsa*   **3** *libro   quaderno*

4 *pomodoro   cipolla*   **5** *ragazzo   ragazza*

But your friend's a bit confused and gets the wrong one of each pair, so you patiently correct him . . .

e.g. È una mela?
   No, non è una mela, è una pera.

1   È una matita?

. . . .

3   È un quaderno?

. . . .

5   È una ragazza?

. . . .

2   È un portafoglio?

. . . .

4   È un pomodoro?

. . . .

C The cathedral is famous

Match the adjectives to the phrases. Only one adjective will fit each phrase.

e.g. Il duomo è ...   fresca
Il duomo è famoso.   caldo

1	La frutta è ...	famoso
2	Il cappuccino è ...	fredda
3	La birra è ...	questo
4	Il ragazzo è ...	stanco
5	I giardini sono ...	pronti
6	Le paste sono ...	antiche
7	I caffè sono ...	buone
8	Le città sono ...	belli

The adjectives used are all in the Vocabulary on p. 15.

D This is a car!

Look at the objects below. Identify them, using **questo** and the word for *a*. Then define them further by using the adjective indicated. Remember to make any necessary changes to the ending.

nuovo

e.g.   Questa è una macchina. È una macchina nuova.

1 *vecchio*   **2** *rosso*

3 *nuovo*   **4** *buono*

5 *freddo*   **6** *vecchio*

E Check out your spelling!

Make these sentences plural.

e.g. Il monumento è antico.
I monumenti sono antichi.

1 La basilica è antica.
2 Il libro è lungo.
3 La strada è lunga.
4 La signora è stanca.
5 Il ragazzo è stanco.
6 La pesca è fresca.
7 Il pomodoro è fresco.

F I or they?

Which subject pronoun should be used in each of these sentences: **io** or **loro**?

e.g. Sono italiani.
Loro sono italiani.

1 Sono contento.
2 Sono australiana.
3 Sono americani.
4 Sono vecchie.

G Do you know your prepositions?

Complete the sentences using the prepositions **in**, **a** and **di** correctly.

e.g. La scuola ... lingue per stranieri è ... Perugia ... Umbria.
La scuola **di** lingue per stranieri è **a** Perugia **in** Umbria.

1 Anna è ... Rimini ... Emilia Romagna
2 Diego è ... Cagliari ... Sardegna.
3 I figli ... Sandra sono ... Italia ... Capri.
4 Il figlio ... Maria è ... scuola.
5 La tazza ... Cristiano è ... cucina.
6 Il portafoglio ... Angelo è ... casa ... salotto.

Systems 2

1 Nouns

i) Feminine nouns beginning with a vowel

l'amica
un'amica

When a feminine noun begins with a vowel, the definite article **la** and the indefinite article **una** are shortened to **l'** and **un'**. But the plural definite article, **le** does not change.

l'	un'	le
l'aranciata l'edicola	un'aranciata un'edicola	le aranciate le edicole

ii) Nouns ending in -e

il padre
la madre

Some nouns ending in **-e** are masculine and others feminine. Although the endings are the same, the articles vary according to the gender of the noun.

il	i	la	le
il dolce il signore	i dolci i signori	la canzone la chiave	le canzoni le chiavi

un	una
un nome un cognome	una notte una televisione

With a feminine noun ending in **-e**, use **l'** and **un'**:

l'	un'	le
l'opinione l'arte	un'opinione un'arte	le opinioni le arti

Nouns ending in **-zione** are always feminine:
la lezione

Apart from this rule, there are no clues as to the genders of nouns ending in **-e**, and it is advisable to note them down as you come across them. This is particularly important if the noun begins with a vowel: **l'estate** *(summer)* is feminine but **l'esame** *(exam)* is masculine.

For masculine nouns beginning with a vowel, see Unit 3, Systems, note 4 i, p. 88.

2 Adjectives

i) Adjectives with -e nouns

il pan**e** fresc**o**
la chiav**e** vecchi**a**

The spellings of the noun and adjective endings do not necessarily need to match. The adjectives agree with the number and gender of the noun, which is shown by the article.

ii) Adjectives ending in -e

il costum**e** tradizional**e**
il past**o** tradizional**e**
la lezion**e** tradizional**e**
la tort**a** tradizional**e**

There is a large category of adjectives which have only two forms: a singular and a plural.

singular: **-e**	*plural:* **-i**
il nipote intelligent**e** la nipote intelligent**e** il ragazzo intelligent**e** la ragazza intelligent**e**	i nipoti intelligent**i** le nipoti intelligent**i** i ragazzi intelligent**i** le ragazze intelligent**i**

iii) -issimo endings

molto   molt**issimo**
intelligente   intelligent**issimo**

Many adjectives, irrespective of whether they end in **-o** or **-e**, can have **-issimo** on the end. This adds the meaning of *very/extremely* to the adjective.

3 Possessive adjectives

la mia maestra
il mio maestro

masc.	*fem.*	
il mio	la mia	*my*
il tuo	la tua	*your*
il suo	la sua	*his/her*
il Suo	la Sua	*your*

i) The words for *my, your, his* and *her* are adjectives, and agree with the thing or person they describe. Unlike English, the definite article usually precedes them:

    questa è la mia amica
    questo è il mio vestito

If a *single* family member is described, then the article is dropped:

    questa è mia sorella
    questo è mio fratello

However, if there is a second adjective, or a suffix is added to the noun, the article comes back again:

    questa è la mia piccola sorella
    questa è la mia sorellina

ii) To say *your*, use **tuo/tua** if you're using **tu**, and **Suo/Sua** if you're using **Lei**.

iii) **suo/sua** is also used for *his/her:*

    questa è la sua gonna
    questo è il suo vestito

For further information on possessives, see Unit 3, Systems, note 6, p. 89.

4 Using the article

Unlike English, articles are used in Italian with surnames or titles, when talking *about* people:

Il signor Muratori è qui	*Mr M. is here*
Il dottor Viola è qui	*Dr V. is here*
Il professor Carli è qui	*Prof C. is here*

However, if you are talking directly *to* someone, you don't use the article:

    Buongiorno, signor Muratori
    Dottor Viola, cosa beve?
    Buonasera, professor Carli

In front of a name, **signore/dottore/professore** lose the **-e**.

For further uses of the article, see Unit 3, Systems, note 5, p. 89.

5 Formal and informal speech

Tu, Lei and **voi**

    tu sei Anna?
    Lei è la signorina Mazzotti?
    voi siete Carlo e Maria?
    voi siete i signori Manzi?

Tu (informal) and **Lei** (formal) both mean the singular *you*. **Voi** – the plural *you* – is used in informal and formal situations. There is a formal plural *you* – **loro**, but it is not used in everyday conversation.

Tu is always used with children, within the family and amongst friends. It is increasingly used amongst colleagues at work, although **Lei** is used by adults who don't know each other. It is best to use **Lei** when in doubt about the correct form of address.

6 Regular verbs

There are three main types of regular verbs: **-are, -ere** and **-ire**. The first two have appeared in this unit.

i) Present tense of -are and -ere verbs

The present tense is formed by substituting the **-are** and **-ere** endings with the following:

		-ARE		**-ERE**	
		portare	*to wear*	**mettere**	*to put*
I	(io)	port**o**		mett**o**	
you	(tu)	port**i**		mett**i**	
he	(lui)				
she	(lei)	port**a**		mett**e**	
you	(Lei)				
we	(noi)	port**iamo**		mett**iamo**	
you	(voi)	port**ate**		mett**ete**	
they	(loro)	port**ano**		mett**ono**	

Systems 2

ii) Reflexive verbs: the present tense

These follow the pattern of regular present tense verbs, with the addition of **mi, ti, si, ci, vi, si**. These reflexive pronouns are essential to the meaning and cannot be omitted, unlike the subject pronouns. The easiest equivalent in English is the addition of 'myself', 'yourself', etc.

-ARE	**-ERE**
chiamarsi *to be called*	**mettersi** *to put (oneself)*
mi chiam**o**	**mi** mett**o**
ti chiam**i**	**ti** mett**i**
si chiam**a**	**si** mett**e**
ci chiam**iamo**	**ci** mett**iamo**
vi chiam**ate**	**vi** mett**ete**
si chiam**ano**	**si** mett**ono**

Other common reflexive verbs are: **addormentarsi** *(to fall asleep)*, **alzarsi** *(to get up)*, **coricarsi** *(to go to bed)*, **fermarsi** *(to stop)*, **lavarsi** *(to wash)*, **pettinarsi** *(to do one's hair)*, **trovarsi** *(to be [somewhere], to find oneself)*, **riposarsi** *(to rest)*, **svegliarsi** *(to wake up)*, **perdersi** *(to get lost)*.

7 Using the present tense

beve vino?

The present tense can be used to say what happens in general and what is happening now:

cosa beve?	*what do you drink? [in general]*
	what are you drinking? [now]
cosa mangia?	*what do you eat? [in general]*
	what are you eating? [now]

8 Irregular verbs

Present tense

bere **bevo**
produrre **produco**

Some verbs do not always conform to a regular pattern in all tenses. Take, for example, **bere** and **produrre**. In the present tense, the regular **-ere** endings are added to **bev-** or **produc-**.

bere *to drink*	**produrre** *to produce*
bevo	produco
bevi	produci
beve	produce
beviamo	produciamo
bevete	producete
bevono	producono

9 Sentence structures

Word order

e la pasta, dov'è?
dov'è la pasta?

Word order is more flexible in Italian than in English. When a word is being emphasised, it is frequently put in front of the verb:

qui cosa c'è? *[lit.]*	*here what is there?*
e sua moglie, dov'è?	*and your wife, where is she?*
e tu, come ti chiami?	*and you, what is your name?*

10 A note on numbers

Look at the numbers from 20 upwards in Ref. I, 1, p. 239.

Cento *(a hundred)* is invariable in Italian:

100 – cento 200 – duecento 300 – trecento

Mille *(a thousand)* and **milione** *(a million)* are not invariable:

1000 – mille 2000 – duemila
1000000 – un milione 2000000 – due milioni

Reinforcement 2

A Memory game

Using the definitive article can you make these nouns plural?

1 amica   autostrada   attrice   autorità
2 edicola   entrata   emigrazione   età
3 isola   idea   immigrazione   indennità
4 offerta   opinione   occasione   opportunità
5 utopia   uscita   unione   università

B About Italy

You have been faxed some information about Italy and its population, etc. but some of the text is illegible. Using the list of key words, put it back together.

[1] **popolazione**   *[a]* **simile**
[2] **milione**   *[b]* **grande**
[3] **abitante** [m]   *[c]* **principale**
[4] **capitale**   *[d]* **importante**
[5] **regione**
[6] **fiume** [m]

[1] d'Italia è *[a]* alla *[1]* della Gran Bretagna. Ci sono circa 58 *[2]* di *[3]*. *[4]* d'Italia si chiama Roma. A Roma ci sono circa 3 *[2]* di *[3]*. È la città più *[b]* d'Italia. In Italia ci sono 20 *[5]* e circa 100 province. *[6]* più lunghi sono il Po e il Tevere; le montagne *[c]* sono le Dolomiti, le Alpi e gli Appennini. Ci sono circa 37 isole italiane e 22 laghi. Le isole più *[b]* sono la Sicilia e la Sardegna. I laghi più *[d]* sono il Lago di Garda e il Lago Maggiore.

Note: più   *most*; circa   *about*

C My brother

Which of the following phrases require the article before the possessive adjective?

1 mia famiglia è grande
2 mia amica è simpatica
3 mio fratello è simpatico
4 mia cugina è antipatica
5 mio fratellino è intelligente

D It's all yours

Complete the sentences by supplying the appropriate word for *your*, not forgetting the article.

1 Maria, come si chiama . . . amica?
2 Antonio, dov'è . . . giornale?
3 Signor Tagliaferri, questa è . . . penna?
4 Signora De Amicis, . . . borsa non è qui.
5 Dottor Corti, ecco . . . chiave.
6 Ecco, . . . dolce, signorina.

E Get it right!

Choose which of the two forms of the verbs given in the sentences below is correct.

**abitare   leggere   scrivere
studiare   produrre   bere**

1 Sua figlia, che cosa *[studia/studie]*?
2 Suo figlio, che cosa *[legga/legge]*?
3 Dove *[abitono/abitano]* i signori Cialdi?
4 Che cosa *[scrivono/scrivano]* Giacomo e Aldo?
5 Chi non *[beve/bevi]* vino? I bambini non *[bevano/bevono]* vino.
6 Chi *[produci/produce]* più vino – i francesi o i tedeschi? I francesi ne *[producono/producano]* di più.

F Using reflexives

Use the reflexive verbs given to complete the text.

Note: presto   *early*;   tardi   *late*

1 Mio padre *[chiamarsi]* Pietro. Lavora molto. *[alzarsi]* presto la mattina e *[coricarsi]* tardi la sera.
2 Noi siamo gemelle. *[chiamarsi]* Letizia e Patrizia. Siamo molto diverse. Io sono Letizia e la mattina *[svegliarsi]* presto. Poi *[alzarsi, lavarsi e pettinarsi]*. Patrizia *[riposarsi]* e non *[alzarsi]*!
3 I nonni *[chiamarsi]* Stefano e Stefania. Sono anziani e *[riposarsi]* molto. Qualchevolta *[addormentarsi]* dopo pranzo e *[svegliarsi]* solo per la cena!

G Try your hand at this multiple choice

Only one of the choices in the sentences below is correct: which is it?

1 *[Dov'è/Dove]* la pasta? *[C'è/È]* qui.
2 *[C'è/È]* molto lavoro oggi?
3 *[Ci sono/Sono]* molti bambini qui?
4 *[Cos'è/Cosa c'è]* qui? *[Ci sono/C'è]* gelati e torte

Systems 3

1 Regular verbs

i) Present tense of -ire verbs

There are two regular patterns. They are formed by substituting the **-ire** ending with the following:

preferire *to prefer*	**offrire** *to offer*
prefer**isco**	off**ro**
prefer**isci**	off**ri**
prefer**isce**	off**re**
prefer**iamo**	off**riamo**
prefer**ite**	off**rite**
prefer**iscono**	off**rono**

Other verbs like **preferire**: **capire** *(to understand)*, **finire** *(to finish)*, **gestire** *(to manage)*.
Offrire is like: **aprire** *(to open)*, **dormire** *(to sleep)*, **seguire** *(to follow)*, **servire** *(to serve)*.

Each time you come across a new **-ire** verb you need to learn which of the two patterns it follows. Refer to the list in Ref. VIII, A, 1i, p. 248.

ii) Reflexive verbs

You have come across **-are** and **-ere** reflexive verbs in Unit 2, Systems, note 6 iii, p. 85. The **-ire** reflexive verbs follow the pattern of verbs like **offrire**.

divertirsi *to enjoy oneself*
mi divert**o**
ti divert**i**
si divert**e**
ci divert**iamo**
vi divert**ite**
si divert**ono**

Vestirsi *(to get dressed)* is a common **-ire** reflexive verb.

2 Irregular verbs

i) avere and stare

The following are irregular in the present tense:

avere *to have*	**stare** *to be, to stay*
ho	sto
hai	stai
ha	sta
abbiamo	stiamo
avete	state
hanno	stanno

Avere is used with numerous basic idioms. [See Vocabulary, p. 47.]

There are fewer idioms with **stare**. Two important ones are: **stare attento** *(to be careful)*, **stare zitto** *(to be quiet)*.

ii) Other useful irregular verbs

rimanere *to stay, remain*	**tenere** *to keep, hold*
rimango	tengo
rimani	tieni
rimane	tiene
rimaniamo	teniamo
rimanete	tenete
rimangono	tengono

Tenere can be reflexive, as in **tenersi in forma** *(to keep fit)*:
Mi tengo in forma perché nuoto
I keep fit because I swim

Many verbs have the same pattern, e.g.
appartenere *(to belong)*:
appartengo a un circolo   *I belong to a club*

Rimanere can sometimes be used instead of **stare**:
domani rimango a casa
tomorrow I'm staying at home

3 Using the present tense

i) Saying 'for how long'

sono qui **da** un'ora

In Italian the present tense can be used with reference to the past to say for how long something has been going on. The word **da** means *for* and *since*:

Sono in Italia da un mese
I've been in Italy for a month
Sono in Italia da settembre
I've been in Italy since September

ii) Present + infinitive

è divertente **stare** qui
è bello **giocare** a golf

Many adjectives can be used with **è** in this way, followed directly by the infinitive, e.g.:
facile, difficile; possibile, impossibile; essenziale; necessario; interessante; noioso; utile; inutile

È facile imparare l'italiano
It's easy to learn Italian
È impossibile capire tutto
It's impossible to understand everything

ho bisogno **di** mangiare

Idioms which use **avere** need **di** in front of the infinitive:

Ho tempo di giocare

iii) Present + Reflexive infinitive

ho bisogno di divertir**mi**
hai bisogno di divertir**ti**

If the verb you are using is reflexive you need to vary the infinitive ending as follows:

divertirsi *to enjoy oneself*	
ho bisogno di divertir**mi**	abbiamo bisogno di divertir**ci**
hai bisogno di divertir**ti**	avete bisogno di divertir**vi**
ha bisogno di divertir**si**	hanno bisogno di divertir**si**

With expressions using **è . . . bello/necessario**, etc, the reflexive infinitive stays the same:

è bello divertir**si**
è necessario tener**si** in forma

4 Nouns and articles

i) Masculine nouns beginning with a vowel

l' gli un

l' *(the)*	**gli** *(the)*	**un** *(a)*
l'amico	gli amici	un amico
l'esercizio	gli esercizi	un esercizio
l'ospedale	gli ospedali	un ospedale

ii) Masculine nouns beginning with s- + consonant, z, ps and gn

lo gli uno

lo *(the)*	**gli** *(the)*	**uno** *(a)*
lo straniero	gli stranieri	uno straniero
lo zio	gli zii	uno zio
lo psicologo	gli psicologi	uno psicologo
lo gnocco	gli gnocchi	uno gnocco

You now know all the definite and indefinite articles. Here is the complete list:

	Definite		*Indefinite*	*Example*
Masc.	il	i	un	ragazzo
	l'	gli	un	amico
	lo	gli	uno	zio, studente
Fem.	la	le	una	ragazza
	l'	le	un'	idea, isola

Some and *any* is explained in Unit 5, p. 98 and Ref. I, 8v, p. 240.]

Systems 3

5 Using the article

In Italian, definite articles are needed with the following:

i) Places and languages

Continents:
   L'Europa   *Europe*; L'Asia   *Asia*
Countries:
   La Gran Bretagna   *Great Britain*; L'Italia   *Italy*
Regions:
   La Liguria   *Liguria*; Il Lazio   *Lazio*
Large islands:
   La Sicilia   *Sicily*; La Sardegna   *Sardinia*
Lakes:
   Il lago di Garda   *Lake Garda*
Languages:
   Il giapponese è difficile.   *Japanese is difficult.*
   Studio l'italiano.   *I study Italian.*
Note, however, that with **parlare** there is no need for an article:
   Parlo italiano.   *I speak Italian.*

ii) Nouns used in a general, collective sense

   Gli amici sono necessari   *Friends are necessary*
   Le lingue sono importanti
   Languages are important

iii) Abstract nouns

   la musica   la vita

iv) Substances, categories and species

   Lo zucchero è dolce
   Il tennis è uno sport popolare
   I gatti sono animali domestici

For further uses of the definite article see Unit 2, note 4, p. 84.

6 Possessives

In Unit 2 you learnt **mio**, **mia**; **tuo**, **tua**; **suo**, **sua**, which accompany singular nouns. There are other forms to accompany plural nouns. Here is the complete list:

Masc. Sing.	Pl.	Fem. Sing.	Pl.	
mio	miei	mia	mie	*my*
tuo	tuoi	tua	tue	*your*
suo	suoi	sua	sue	*his/her/its*
Suo	Suoi	Sua	Sue	*your*
nostro	nostri	nostra	nostre	*our*
vostro	vostri	vostra	vostre	*your*
loro	loro	loro	loro	*their*

i) Possessives and the definite article

As we saw in Unit 2, Systems, note 3, p. 84, the definite article is normally used in front of possessive adjectives. It is omitted with a singular family member (e.g. **mia figlia**) unless modified by an adjective or a suffix:
   questa è **la** mia figlia più piccola

Loro always takes the article:
   questa è **la** loro figlia

And in the plural the article is always used:
   queste sono **le** mie figlie

ii) Omitting possessives

Possessives are often omitted with parts of the body:
   Ho gli occhi azzurri
   My eyes are blue, I've got blue eyes
   Ho i capelli castani
   My hair is brown, I've got brown hair

iii) Possessives as pronouns

You can use possessives as pronouns. The article tends to be dropped except when needed for clarification or emphasis.
   Che bella macchina! È tua?
but:
   Questo è il mio e questo è il tuo.

7 Interrogatives

da **quanto** tempo?
quanti anni hai?

Quanto/a? *How much?*
Quanti/e? *How many?*
These are adjectives and pronouns. They agree with the person or thing they refer to:
Quanti libri e quante penne ci sono?

8 Object pronouns

lo   la

Lo and **la** can mean *it* or *him* and *her*.
Lo is used if the noun is masculine singular:
Chi lo gestisce?   [il giardino]
Chi lo aiuta?   [Carlo]

La is for feminine singular nouns:
Chi la gestisce?   [la galleria d'arte]
Chi la aiuta?   [Elisa]

9 Vero?

è qui in vacanza, **vero?**

Vero – which means *true* – can also be used on the end of negative sentences:
Non è difficile, vero?   *It isn't hard, is it?*
Lei non è italiano, vero?
You're not Italian, are you?

A Which pattern?

Look at the verbs in the sentences below. They are all **-ire** verbs, but which pattern do they follow? Tick the appropriate box and fill in the infinitive of each verb. If you need help, check the list in Systems, note 1, p. 87.

	Infin.	-isco	-o
1 Oggi offrite voi da bere?			
2 Non capiamo neanche noi.			
3 Preferite la coca cola?			
4 Perché non aprite la porta?			
5 Seguiamo un corso d'inglese.			
6 Quando finite il lavoro?			
7 Pulite la vostra camera.			
8 Dormite molto?			
9 Partiamo domani?			
10 Adesso servite la minestra.			
11 Perché non bolliamo l'acqua?			
12 Sentite il telefono?			

Check the meanings if necessary and make sure you know all the forms of the verbs.

B Reflexives

Complete the sentences using the appropriate present tense form of these reflexive verbs.
e.g. Io *[vestirsi]* lentamente perché sono stanco.
Io mi vesto lentamente perché sono stanco.

1   Mio figlio *[divertirsi]* in piscina.
2   Mio nonno *[riposarsi]* in giardino.
3   Le mie figlie *[divertirsi]* a scuola.
4   I miei genitori *[riposarsi]* in montagna.
5   Noi *[vestirsi]* rapidamente perché abbiamo fretta.

C Can you supply the questions?

Use the answers as cues.
e.g. Sì, rimango a Bordighera per una settimana.
Rimani/rimane a Bordighera per una settimana?

1   . . .? Sì, rimaniamo in Italia per un anno.
2   . . .? Sì, appartengo a un circolo.
3   . . .? Sì, tengo animali domestici in casa.
4   . . .? Sì, mi tengo in forma!

Reinforcement 3

D Basic needs

Say what you need or want to do when you are hungry, thirsty, etc., and then enquire about others. Choose from the following:

mangiare una brioche; prendere un toast; fare uno spuntino; bere un'acqua minerale; prendere un succo di frutta; fare colazione

e.g. [Io] – aver fame – aver bisogno di –
Ho fame, ho bisogno di mangiare una brioche.

1   [Noi] – aver caldo – aver voglia di –
2   [Voi] – aver sete – aver bisogno di – ?
3   [Tu] – aver fame – aver voglia di – ?

Now say what you have or haven't time for:
4   [Io] – aver fretta – non aver tempo di –
5   [Noi] – non aver fretta – aver tempo di –

E How long for?

You want to ask how long your friends have been in various places. Use **stare** and **da**.
e.g. Lei – in Italia – 20 anni?
Sta in Italia da vent'anni?

1   Tu – a Sanremo – 15 giorni?
2   Voi – in montagna – 3 settimane?
3   Loro – al mare – 2 mesi?
4   Lei – in campagna – molto tempo?
Now say how long you have been in a particular place.

F What do you do and why?

Say what people do in their spare time and why they do it, using both **per** and **perché ho bisogno di**.
e.g. Gioco a carte. Mi diverto.
Gioco a carte per divertirmi.
Gioco a carte perché ho bisogno di divertirmi.

1   Mia moglie nuota. Si rilassa.
2   I miei parenti giocano tutti a bridge. Si divertono.
3   Ascolto la musica. Mi riposo.
4   Giocate a squash? Vi tenete in forma?
5   Prendi il sole? Ti abbronzi?
Now say what you do in your spare time and why.

G Using the definite article

1   Look at the names of these countries. Which ones do you think require one of the following articles: **l'**, **lo**, **gli**. Beware when it comes to the ones beginning with **S**!

Egitto   Iran   Iraq   Stati Uniti   Spagna
Zaire   Zimbabwe   Zambia   Svezia   Svizzera
Sri Lanka   Sudafrica   Afghanistan

There is a list of countries in Ref. III, 5, pp. 242–3.

2   Find the correct definite article for each noun below and then make each plural.

straniero   straniera   svago   spiaggia   suocero
spumante*(m)*   zabaglione*(m)*   zia   zio
psicologo   hobby   animale*(m)*   isola
uccello   esercizio   origine*(f)*   ordine *(m)*
aperitivo   stato

H There's only one!

Ask how many there are and say there's only one each time. Use **quanto** and **uno, un, una, un'**.
e.g. *[Quanto]* studenti ci sono?
– C'è . . . studente soltanto.
Quanti studenti ci sono?
– C'è uno studente soltanto.

1   *[Quanto]* esercizi ci sono?   – C'è . . .
2   *[Quanto]* stranieri ci sono?   – C'è . . .
3   *[Quanto]* ragazze ci sono?   – C'è . . .
4   *[Quanto]* ragazzi ci sono?   – C'è . . .
5   *[Quanto]* isole ci sono?   – C'è . . .

I My friend Fabrizio

Insert articles where necessary.

mio amico Fabrizio ha occhi azzurri e capelli biondi. È italiano. Italia è un paese molto bello con tante montagne, Alpi, Appennini e Dolomiti. Il lago più grande d'Italia è lago di Garda. Fabrizio è ligure. Liguria è una regione che confina con Francia. Famiglia di Fabrizio non è grande: ha due sorelle. Sue sorelle studiano inglese, ma Fabrizio studia matematica. Suo padre è professore di matematica! Fabrizio ama molto sport e anche musica.

J Say it's yours

Using the cue in English, complete the sentences using possessive adjectives. As you do so, fill in the puzzle across. Can you spot an extra possessive and also a colour?

1 *[your – tu form]*
   Marco, ecco il . . . aperitivo.
2 *[your – Lei form]*
   Signora, dove sono i . . . figli?
3 *[your – voi form]*
   Signori, questo è . . . figlio?
4 *[our]*
   No, questo non è . . . figlio.
5 *[their]*
   Questo è Angelo e questa è Maria. Ti presento anche Marina, la . . . figlia.

n					
		t			
		v			
			s		
		1			

When you find the hidden words use them both in a short sentence.

K It and the

Each of the sentences below includes the words **lo** or **la**. Can you say which is a definite article *(the)* and which is an object pronoun *(it)*?
e.g. Nuoto perché lo trovo rilassante. *(pronoun)*

1 Dov'è Sandro? Non lo vedo.
2 Dov'è lo zucchero? Non lo trovo.
3 Ecco la pasta. La servo subito.
4 C'è Maria oggi? Non la vedo.

Systems 4

1 Irregular verbs

i) Andare, venire, uscire

vado a Bologna
vengo in autobus
esco di casa

andare *to go*	venire *to come*	uscire *to go out (of), to leave*
vado	vengo	esco
vai	vieni	esci
va	viene	esce
andiamo	veniamo	usciamo
andate	venite	uscite
vanno	vengono	escono

Andare, like many basic verbs, has a range of meanings. It crops up in a variety of common expressions:

> Come va?   *How's it going/how are things?*

Come va is an *informal* expression and is equivalent to **Come stai?**

> Va bene   *That's fine/all right [lit. it goes well]*

Using **uscire**: without a preposition it means to go out:

> Esco spesso la sera   *I often go out in the evening*

If you want to say what you go out and do, **uscire** can be used with the preposition **a**:

> Esco a fare la spesa   *I go out and do the shopping*

Uscire is used with the preposition **da** to mean *to leave, to go/to come out of*.

> Esco dall'ufficio alle cinque
> *I leave the office at five o'clock*
> Esco dalla stazione alle otto e mezza
> *I come out of the station at half past eight*

With the word **casa** *(home)*, **di** is used in preference to **da**:

> La mattina esco di casa alle sette e mezza
> *In the morning I leave the house at half past seven*

ii) **Fare** and **dovere**:

che lavoro **fa**?
devo partire

fare *to do, to make*	dovere *to have to*
faccio	dovere *to have to*
fai	devo
fa	devi
facciamo	deve
fate	dobbiamo
fanno	dovete
	devono

Fare has a wide range of meanings and is used in many common idioms:

> fare una domanda   *to ask a question;*
> fare la spesa   *to shop*

Dovere is always used in conjunction with another verb in the infinitive:

> Devo andare al lavoro
> Dobbiamo fare il biglietto

2 Using the present tense

i) Summary of uses so far

As we have seen, the present tense is used to express what is happening now; what happens in general; how long something has been happening:

> Cosa fai? Vado al mercato
> *What are you doing? I'm going to the market.*
> Vado al mercato ogni venerdì
> *I go to the market every Friday*
> Vado al mercato da nove anni
> *I've been going to the market for nine years*

ii) The immediate future

domani **vado** al mercato

The present tense is also often used to express the immediate future:

> Vengo in bicicletta   *I'll come/I'm coming by bike*
> Domani rimango a casa
> *Tomorrow I'll stay/I'm staying at home*

3 Prepositions

A or **in**?

sono/vado **a** Bologna
sono/vado **a** casa
sono/vado **in** centro
sono/vado **in** Italia

A and **in** each have two meanings: *in/at* and *to*. Here is a summary so far:

a) Use **in** with:
countries and regions:
 Vado in Gran Bretagna   *I go to Britain*
 Lavoro in Emilia Romagna   *I work in Emilia Romagna*

paese *country* and **posto** *place*:
 Vado in molti paesi/posti diversi
 I go to many different countries/places
 Lavoro in posti diversi   *I work in different places*

streets, piazzas, etc.:
 Vado in via Garibaldi   *I go to via Garibaldi*
 Conosco un bar in Piazza Maggiore   *I know a bar in Piazza Maggiore*

set expressions:
 vado in città   *I go to town*
 studio in biblioteca   *I study in the library*

b) Use **a** with:

towns and small islands:
 Vado a Capri   *I go to Capri*
 Arrivo a Londra   *I arrive in London*

set expressions:
 Torno a casa   *I go back home*
 Studio a scuola   *I study at school*

There's more on **in** and **a** in Ref. III, 1–4, p. 242.

4 Prepositions and definite articles

 dal lunedì **al** venerdì
 il treno **delle** 7.53
 un impiegato **dello** stato

When the prepositions **a**, **da**, **di**, **in** and **su** *(on)* precede a definite article, (the word for *the*), then they combine with it to form one word as follows:

	il	i	la	le	lo	l'	gli
a	al	ai	alla	alle	allo	all'	agli
da	dal	dai	dalla	dalle	dallo	dall'	dagli
di	del	dei	della	delle	dello	dell'	degli
in	nel	nei	nella	nelle	nello	nell'	negli
su	sul	sui	sulla	sulle	sullo	sull'	sugli

Not all prepositions combine with the article: **per** is never combined, and with **con** it's optional – you rarely see it in writing.
Never combine a preposition and an *indefinite* article:
 La lettera è **nella** borsa   *The letter is in the bag*
but:
 La lettera è **in una** borsa   *The letter is in a bag*

i) **A** and **in**

 mangia **alla** mensa
 abito **nel** centro di Ferrara

A is used with many other expressions of place, but with the article:
 Mangio al ristorante/alla mensa
 I eat at the restaurant/in the canteen
 Faccio la spesa al supermercato
 I shop at the supermarket

If a noun is modified by an adjective, or a specifying phrase, then you need the article:
 Abito in centro   *but*
 Abito **nel** centro di Ferrara
 I live in the centre of Ferrara
 Torno **alla** vecchia casa
 I'm going back to the old house
 Vado **nell'**Italia meridionale
 I go to Southern Italy

Casa, however, modified by a possessive adjective, is an exception:
 Torno a casa mia   *I'm going back to my home/house*
 Abiti a casa sua?   *Do you live in his/her house?*

Systems 4

ii) Da

parte **dal** binario 3
parto **dall'**Italia

Unlike **in** and **a**, **da** *(from)* nearly always requires the article:

Vado a teatro   *but* Torno **dal** teatro
Vado in ufficio   *but* Esco **dall'**ufficio

The only exceptions are towns, **casa** and **scuola**:

Vado a Roma   Parto **da** Roma
Vado a casa   Parto **da** casa
Vado a scuola   Parto **da** scuola

Da is also used in expressions of place meaning *to* and *in/at*. See Unit 5, Systems, note 2, p. 97.

5   Variations in the use of prepositions

The use of prepositions can be quite flexible. It depends on a number of things, including the region someone is from and the degree of familiarity with the place:

parcheggio alla stazione

is considered 'standard' Italian, but there are plenty of people who say:

parcheggio in stazione

if they are talking about a familiar station.

Reinforcement 4

A   Which verb makes sense?

1 Dove [*vai/vieni*] domani? – Domani [*vado/vengo*] a casa di un amico.
2 Chi [*va/viene*] qui stasera? – Stasera [*vanno/vengono*] Lucia e Filippo.
3 [*Esco/parto*] sempre di casa presto la mattina.
4 Il treno [*esce/parte*] dal binario 3.
5 Domani [*usciamo/andiamo*] al ristorante.
6 Come [*va/fa*]? – Non c'è male.
7 Come [*va/fa*] per arrivare al lavoro?

B   Do you come here often?

You are at a party and you ask various people whether they come regularly to the following places:

e.g. To a new acquaintance: Italia – ogni estate?
     Viene in Italia ogni estate?

To your friend Enrico: Bologna – ogni mese?
To a group of children: partita – ogni sabato?
To Marco and Elisabetta: mercato – ogni venerdì?
To your boss: ristorante – ogni sera?

C   I must go!

Rewrite the passage below using the appropriate form of the verb *dovere* plus the infinitive of the verbs marked.

Ogni mattina io e mio marito [**1** usciamo] di casa alle 7.15. Io [**2** vado] a Imola, mio marito [**3** va] a Cesena. Lui prende la macchina e io [**4** vado] a piedi alla stazione. Quando arrivo alla stazione [**5** faccio] il biglietto e poi [**6** trovo] un posto, che è difficile, perché il treno è sempre affollato. La sera torno tardi. [**7** vado] a letto presto perché [**8** mi alzo] alle 6.30.

D   Do you have to?

Answer the following questions using **fare**.
e.g. Dovete fare la spesa domani? [*sempre – il sabato*]
     No, facciamo sempre la spesa il sabato.

1 Deve fare il bucato dopo pranzo? [*di solito – la mattina*]
2 Devi fare il bagno la mattina? [*sempre – dopo cena*]
3 Dovete fare colazione adesso? [*non . . . mai*]

E Think of a reason

Answer the questions below by choosing the most appropriate expression with **fare** or **uscire**.

e.g. Perché non siete in ufficio?

> Fare: il biglietto/il bucato/sciopero/la doccia

Non siamo in ufficio perché facciamo sciopero.

1 Perché non studiate mai?

> Uscire: ogni tanto/spesso/a volte

Non studiamo mai perché . . .

2 Tua figlia si diverte la sera?

> Fare: un viaggio/la pendolare/i compiti

No, non si diverte la sera perché . . .

F The engineer's wife

Here is an exercise to remind you how definite articles and propositions are combined. Below, to help, are the definite articles plus a completed chart for the preposition **a**:

	Sing.	Plu.	Sing.	Plu.
Masc.	il	i	al	ai
	l'	gli	all'	agli
	lo	gli	allo	agli
Fem.	la	le	alla	alle
	l'	le	all'	alle

Read the sentences below and separate the combined articles and prepositions used into their component parts.

e.g. È la moglie dell'ingegnere.   di + l' = dell'.

1 Il portafoglio è nella borsa.
2 La chiave è nella porta oppure sul tavolo.
3 Lavoro dal lunedì al venerdì
4 Ogni domenica vado a casa dell'avvocato Bianchi.
5 Lo stipendio delle infermiere è molto basso.
6 Lo stipendio dei medici è abbastanza alto.

G From dawn to dusk

Now combine the prepositions given below with the definite article:

1 Mio fratello studia *[da]* mattina *[a]* sera.
2 La vita *[di]* studenti è dura.
3 La giornata *[di]* pendolare è lunga e faticosa.
4 Il film dura *[da]* otto *[a]* dieci e mezzo.
5 I libri sono *[in]* studio, *[su]* scaffale.

H Where do you live and work?

Choose between **in** and **a**.

1 Abito *in/a* Italia, *in/a* Ferrara, *in/a* via Madama.
2 Vado spesso *in/a* Irlanda, *in/a* Dublino: il mio amico abita *in/a* periferia, ma lavora *in/a* centro.
3 Di solito vado *in/a* vacanza *in/a* Capri, ma quest'anno vado *in/a* Emilia Romagna, *in/a* montagna.
4 Il lunedì non vado mai *in/a* lezione, ma studio sempre *in/a* biblioteca.

I The house in Garibaldi street

Combine the prepositions **in, a, da** and **di** with the definite article where necessary.

1 Abito *[in]* una bella casa *[in]* via Garibaldi. È *[in]* centro della città.
2 Abito *[in]* periferia, *[in]* periferia di Roma, *[in]* un appartamento moderno.
3 Qualchevolta vado *[in]* Italia, a trovare mio zio *[in]* campagna. I miei amici abitano vicino *[a]* casa sua.
4 I nonni abitano *[in]* Italia del nord, *[a]* Milano. Vanno spesso *[a]* teatro, *[a]* cinema e *[a]* concerti.
5 Domani parto *[da]* Roma. Parto *[da]* stazione Termini per tornare *[a]* casa mia.
6 Vado *[in]* ufficio la mattina alle 9.00 e la sera esco *[da]* ufficio alle 18.00.
7 Io scendo *[da]* autobus vicino *[a]* stadio, poi vado *[in]* Piazza Giulio Cesare per fare la spesa *[a]* supermercato.

Systems 5

1 Irregular verbs

i) potere and volere

posso vedere?
voglio vedere

potere *to be able to*	volere *to want*
posso	voglio
puoi	vuoi
può	vuole
possiamo	vogliamo
potete	volete
possono	vogliono

Potere is always used in conjunction with another verb in the infinitive:

> Può ripetere, per favore?   *Can you repeat, please?*
> (*Is it possible for you to repeat?*)

Use **potere** only for expressing possibility or requesting permission. In English 'I can see him now' expresses both possibility and the simple fact of seeing.

> Lo posso vedere adesso, perché ho tempo
> (i.e. *It is possible for me to see him now*)

But:

> Lo vedo adesso, vicino alla finestra
> (i.e. *I see him now, near the window*)

Volere is followed by another verb in the infinitive or by a noun. It can be preceded by a pronoun:

> Voglio partire
> Voglio un aumento *(a pay-rise)*, lo voglio presto

ii) Other irregular present tenses

dare *to give*	dire *to say*	sapere *to know*	contenere *to contain*
do	dico	so	contengo
dai	dici	sai	contieni
dà	dice	sa	contiene
diamo	diciamo	sappiamo	conteniamo
date	dite	sapete	contenete
danno	dicono	sanno	contengono

Contenere is conjugated in the same way as other verbs formed from **tenere**, e.g. **ottenere** (*to obtain, achieve*).

2 Prepositions

i) Da

Its various meanings include:

from:	vado da casa al lavoro	[place]
	parte dal binario 3	
	lavoro dal lunedì al venerdì	[time]
for:	sono qui da un'ora	[time]
since:	sono qui da lunedì	[time]
to:	ho molto da fare	[purpose]
	cosa prende da bere?	

In conjunction with names of people **da** means *to* or *at* [See **ii)** below.]

to:	vado da Mario. (*. . . to Mario's*)	[place]
	vado dal signor Rossi	
at:	abito da mia sorella (*. . . at my sister's*)	[place]
	abito dalla signora Mancini	

Da is also used with the names of shopkeepers and professional people.

to: vado dal macellaio   (*. . . to the butcher's*)
    vado dal medico   (*. . . to the doctor's*)

at: sono dal parrucchiere   (*. . . at the hairdresser's*)
    sono dal dentista   (*. . . at the dentist's*)

Note: You can only use **da** with people, not with names of shops and places. [See below.]

ii) A and in

A and **in** are both used with shops and public places to mean *to* or *at*. **In** is used if the place ends in **-ia**:

> vado in | macelleria   (*. . . to the butcher's*)
> | farmacia
> | osteria

In all other cases use **a** combined with the definite article:

> vado | al mercato
> | all'alimentare
> | alla Standa *[the name of a chain store]*

Note: For the other uses of **in** and **a** see Unit 4, Systems, note 3, p. 94.

iii) Di

So far the main meanings encountered are:

of:	il cugino	di Angela	[possession]
		del signor Brancati	
	l'orario	delle lezioni	[specification]
		dei treni	
	le strade	di Ferrara	[specification]
		della mia città	
	Di dov'è, Lei?	*(where from,*	[place]
		lit. of where?)	
	Sono di Edimburgo		

some/any: [quantity]
There are two kinds of '*some*':

Some/a bit of	*Some/a few*
del burro	dei ragazzi
della marmellata	degli studenti
dell'olio	delle ragazze
dello zucchero	
un po' di	alcuni, alcune

Di + the *singular* definite article is needed when you mean *a part/a bit of* something. You can also say **un po' di** (e.g. un po'di burro). **Di** + the *plural* definite article is needed when you mean *several/a few*. You can also use **alcuni/e** (e.g. alcuni ragazzi).

Sometimes you can use both:

| Oggi compro | del formaggio [= un po' di formaggio] |
| | dei formaggi [= alcuni formaggi] |

See Ref. I, 8vi and vii, p. 240 for *none/no, not any.*

3 Irregular nouns

i) Invariable nouns

These have the same form in the singular and the plural, but the articles change as usual. Some are foreign words:

il bar, i bar   lo shampoo, gli shampoo
il computer, i computer   l'autobus, gli autobus

You have also come across:
il golf, il dépliant, il poster, lo sport, il tennis
Accented words:
il caffè, i caffè
il tè, i tè
la città, le città
l'attività, le attività
la nazionalità, le nazionalità
l'università, le università

ii) Masculine nouns ending in -a

il programma, i programmi
il problema, i problemi

But some are invariable: il clima, i clima.

Some can be masculine or feminine:
il collega, i colleghi
la collega, le colleghe

iii) Nouns ending in -ista

Most can be masculine or feminine:
il turista, i turisti
la turista, le turiste

There are many nouns ending in **–ista.** Masculine versions tend to be more common, especially with male-dominated professions:
il barista, i baristi
il dentista, i dentisti
l'autista, gli autisti (*chauffeur/driver*)

An important irregular noun

l'uomo, gli uomini (*man, men*)

4 Adjectives ending in –ista:

ottimista, pessimista, socialista, comunista

There is one singular form, but two plural forms
un ragazzo ottimista, dei ragazzi ottimisti
una ragazza ottimista, delle ragazze ottimiste

Reinforcement 5

A To and at
Use the correct preposition in each sentence.

1 Da or a?
a È divertente andare . . . mercato perché c'è sempre tanta gente.
b È comodo fare la spesa . . . fruttivendolo perché è vicino a casa mia.
c Oggi devo andare . . . supermercato e dopo voglio andare . . . Carlo.
d Domani preferisco rimanere . . . mia zia perché stasera andiamo . . . ristorante.

2 In or a?
a La sera vado spesso . . . pizzeria, ma ogni tanto mangio . . . trattoria.
b La mattina, di solito prendo un caffè . . . bar e poi vado . . . tabaccheria per comprare le sigarette.

3 Da or a?
a C'è molto . . . fare oggi.
b Cosa c'è . . . bere?

B Nouns and adjectives
1 Make the following phrases plural:
a il turista straniero   b la città famosa
c il computer caro   d l'uomo pessimista

2 Now make these singular:
a gli autisti italiani   b i problemi importanti
c gli sport divertenti   d i partiti socialisti

3 Complete the sentences by translating the English.
a [The English socialist party] si chiama il partito laburista.
b [The Italian communist party] si chiama adesso il Partito Democratico della Sinistra.

C Can you come?
Which of the phrases below can be used with **potere**?
e.g. [Venire – noi] soltanto dopo le cinque:
      Possiamo venire soltanto dopo le cinque.
      [Vedere – io] l'autobus, ma [non vedere – io] il numero:
      Vedo l'autobus ma non vedo il numero.

1 È molto difficile, mi [aiutare – Lei]?
2 [Prendere – io] un opuscolo, per piacere?
3 [Sentire – io] il telefono, [rispondere – tu]?
4 [Non sentire – io] bene, [ripetere – Lei] per favore?

D Using the present tense
Match up the rules for the use of the present tense with each of the sentences below by writing the correct letter in the box. Then write the infinitive of the irregular verbs used in the second box.

The present tense is used for:
a a habitual action or permanent state;
b an action or state of affairs happening now;
c an action linked to the immediate future;
d saying how long something has been going on.

	Rule	Infinitive
e.g. Sono qui da mezzogiorno.	d	essere
1 Vado sempre in ufficio alle otto.		
2 Cosa bevi la mattina?		
3 Domani viene Carlo, vero?		
4 Da quanto tempo producete vino?		
5 Scusa, cosa dice Maria? – Non capisco.		
6 Rimango in Italia per quindici giorni.		
7 Il nostro vino non contiene mai zucchero.		
8 Lei sta a Roma da molto tempo?		
9 Cosa fate qui? Non potete tornare domani?		
10 Esce subito o vuole aspettare un po'?		

Now check you know the verbs in your completed list.

E Read, listen and speak
Read the questions below, then listen to Interaction 4. Answer in Italian using complete sentences:

1 Chi è il responsabile del progetto nel Parco dei Cedri?
2 Andrea Sivelli lavora anche lui per il WWF?
3 Fausto e Andrea lavorano tutti i giorni nel parco?
4 Lavorano tutto l'anno anche quando il tempo è brutto?
5 Da quando esiste il progetto?
6 Fausto e Andrea cosa vogliono studiare?

F Reading: what's on?

Below are four entries from the diary section of an ecological magazine. Try and do the following without looking anything up.

1 Skim through the text to find out what main activities each entry is publicising.
2 Which one appeals to you most?
3 Scan your favourite entry for any useful times or dates.

AGENDA
CHI? DOVE? QUANDO?

■ Anche quest'anno prende il via il **'Cammina-natura'**, una serie di itinerari guidati nella natura, a cura della Lega Protezione Uccelli e la Lega per l'Ambiente. Per cominciare, una serie di facili escursioni: l'11 marzo e il 15 marzo. Il 1 aprile è previsto un **birdwatching nell'oasi di Serre Presano**. Per ulteriori informazioni rivolgersi a: Davide Tufano, tel. (0832) 534324.

■ Lo studio fotografico 'Il fotogramma' di Salerno organizza il **V corso di fotografia naturalistica**. Il corso, tenuto da fotografi esperti, inizia il 6 marzo e si articola in dodici lezioni (due a settimana). Per ulteriori informazioni: 'Il fotogramma', (089) 121657.

■ **Università verde, Voghera**
Il primo corso è dedicato ai principi base di ecologia ed alle problematiche ambientali ed è organizzato in collaborazione con la Coop Lombardia. Le lezioni si tengono ogni martedì e sono aperte a tutti i cittadini. Ad aprile, il secondo corso ('Le immagini della natura nella filosofia occidentale'). Informazioni presso la Coop Lombardia. tel. 215602 o la Civica Biblioteca.

■ La Lega antivivisezione organizza una **manifestazione nazionale contro le pellicce** sabato 10 marzo a Pavia, sede della famigerata Pellicceria Annabella. L'appuntamento è alle 2.30. Per informazioni: tel. (06) 8356768 (Walter Gambini).

Review I

How well am I doing?

This section is designed to help you assess your progress and see how well you're doing. To do this effectively it is worth pausing to review what you set out to achieve.

Review your objectives

1 Which Track did you choose to follow and which skills did you prioritise? – Speaking? Listening? Reading? Writing?

2 What was your main concern? Fluency? Accuracy? Both? If you had not previously thought about this, think about it now and tick the chart below:

	Vital	Important	Quite important	Unimportant
Accuracy:				
Fluency:				

You may have found both equally important. Some **Track 2** learners may have focused on both from the beginning,' but many **Track 1** learners are likely to prioritise fluency. On the other hand, those mainly interested in reading and understanding Italian may feel no need to be especially fluent.

3 In achieving your goals, how important have the following been to you?

	Vital	Important	Quite important	Unimportant
Grammar:				
Vocabulary learning:				

4 Which aspect of language learning has proved hardest and which has been the easiest and most enjoyable?

Conclusions. When you assess yourself, it is important to bear in mind your *goals* – the needs and priorities you've analysed. For a realistic assessment you should also take into account the *means* – in other words the amount of time you have had, as well as the degree of help and guidance you received.

Review 1

Reviewing progress is essential for the teacher to assess the level not only of individuals, but also of the class as a whole. After the initial 'magical' rapid improvement the feeling most beginners have is one of slow progress, hindered by difficulty in remembering what has been learned. Constant reinforcement and repetition of the same structures, vocabulary and functions is, for this reason, one of the main aims of the course. Students, however, tend to lose sight of their linguistic objectives/achievements and many feel that they cannot adequately assess themselves. This section is intended as an opportunity for 'taking stock': making students aware of their achievements as well as of their deficiencies, so that they may develop their own strategies for improvement and become efficient learners.

The assessment of progress in the **Review** section may be carried out at home. However you could ask students to do a brief pre-assessment exercise in class. Ask them to jot down a quick off-the-cuff idea of the progress they have made so far – unsatisfactory, satisfactory, good, very good – in each of the four language skills, vocabulary and grammar. After students have completed the checklists, ask them to write a fuller diagnosis of their progress: they should compare this with their pre-assessment exercise and see how the two differ. Using their diagnosis, students should be able to see where they should now focus their attention: they should work out which specific areas need improvement and the steps they must take to effect this.

It may be useful for you to collect the students' diagnoses and check through them, to see whether the class as a whole has particular weaknesses which you need to be aware of in planning future activities.

Checklists

Now review your progress, using the checklists which follow. The first one is not exhaustive: it covers the main things you should be able to say, whatever track you are on.

A Speaking: Tracks 1 and 2

I can	Yes	No	Check
1 say hello and goodbye in various ways			Unità 1
2 ask for a drink or an ice-cream			
3 say who I am, spell my name, give my phone number, address and nationality			
4 ask someone's name and tell them mine			Unità 2
5 ask what something is, what it's called and where it is			
6 find out what's available and answer the same question			
7 introduce myself and others, respond when I'm introduced, and ask who someone is			
8 ask how someone is and answer the same question			Unità 3
9 ask someone where they're from and say where I'm from			
10 ask personal questions about someone's family, age, marital status etc., and give the same information			
11 say how long I've been studying Italian and ask the same question			
12 offer someone a drink or a snack			
13 say what I prefer doing and what's nice or enjoyable to do			
14 say what job I do, where I work and how I get there, and ask others the same questions			Unità 4
15 ask what someone's job/day is like and answer those questions myself			
16 tell the time, say when I do things and use the days of the week			
17 talk about how often I do things, how many times/hours per day/week I do them, and ask others the same questions			
18 ask for what I want in a shop, whether a particular item is available, and say I'll have something			Unità 5
19 ask the price and understand numbers – spoken slowly up to 50 000			
20 ask someone to repeat something			
21 ask what time places open and close			
22 ask permission to do something			
23 find out what it's possible to do			
24 say what I want to do, what I need to do and what needs to be done			

Review I

B Fluency: Tracks I and 2

At this stage it is probably more important to assess your fluency rather than your accuracy. Even if you have been working alone you should have been practising, using the cassette exercises and talking to yourself as much as possible! Work through the following checklist and say which statement you identify with at present:

* I need to construct each sentence in my head first.
* I construct sentences in my head first if they aren't stock phrases.
* I often have to pause and think about what I'm going to say, but I don't work it out exactly beforehand.
* I do/don't worry about making mistakes.
* I can only put together a sentence at a time.
* I can sometimes speak several sentences together in a connected way. I find it: Very hard   Difficult   Not too hard   Easy

If you are on Track 1 it would be unusual if you could easily use the language in new or unexpected situations, or be able to use several sentences at a time in a connected way. However, you should be able to recall a range of simple vocabulary and phrases and construct simple questions and answers.

Those on Track 2 should find it possible to put two or three short sentences together and begin to progress beyond the use of stock phrases by adapting them to their needs.

C Listening: Tracks I and 2

You should be able to:
* Understand the familiar stock questions listed in the speaking checklist above, if spoken clearly and not too fast, and make sense of variations.
* Understand the gist of the Course Book conversations on cassette or video without a transcript, playing them several times if necessary.
* Grasp the basic gist of very short conversations you've never heard before but which are on familiar topics.

If you are on Track 1 it would be unusual if you could follow the thread of conversations of over one or two minutes, especially if you don't know what they're about beforehand and if the sentences are long. This may be possible for a few Track 2 learners.

You can test yourself on unprepared conversations by listening to the Profile section of the cassette/CD – without reading the transcript, or by using the video and concentrating on the dialogues which are not in the Course book.

D Reading: Tracks I and 2

At this stage you are likely to read slowly and there will be few authentic texts where you will understand every word.

You should, however, be able to:
* Understand the Course Book dialogues without too much difficulty.
* Follow the poems and information given in the Culture section.

Whether on Track 1 or Track 2, you are unlikely to find the poems and biographies easy, and you will probably have to look up several words.

E Writing: Tracks I and 2

At this stage you are not expected to write much unless you find it helpful to write the exercises or use writing as a memory aid to learning vocabulary. You should, however, be able to write extremely basic messages or simple descriptions of your daily life in very short sentences, using familiar language. Those on Track 2 should be able to do this without meeting spelling difficulties except perhaps with double consonants.

F Grammar: Track 2

The checklist below uses grammatical terminology and is aimed primarily at those using Track 2. Nevertheless, it covers the language from both tracks. If you are using Track 1 and are familiar with the grammatical terms used (explained in the **Basics** section on pp. 237–8), you will find this list useful.

In assessing your grammar, be critical: grammar is a tool, not a straitjacket. The importance you place on particular points depends very much on what you are learning for. You may find it helpful to differentiate between understanding the grammar and producing it correctly. If your main aim in learning Italian is getting the basic message across – then the accuracy of your noun and adjective agreements is less important than knowing which preposition or possessive adjective to use, since misusing the latter could actually change the sense of what you are saying.

Checklist

	Yes	No	Check
1 I understand the singular and plural forms of regular nouns and adjectives (the **-o**, **-a** and **-e** endings)			Unità 1 & 2
2 I understand the definite and indefinite articles			Unità 1–3
3 I know when to use **tu** and when **Lei**			Unità 2
4 I can make a statement and ask a question			Unità 1
5 I can make a sentence negative			Unità 1
6 I can ask rhetorical questions (isn't it? aren't you? didn't you? etc.)			Unità 3
7 I can use possessive adjectives, pronouns			Unità 2–3
8 I understand when to use **a** and when to use **in**			Unità 1 & 4
9 I know how to join definite articles and prepositions			Unità 4
10 I know the present tense of most irregular verbs including reflexive verbs			Unità 2–4
11 I can use **da**			Unità 3 & 5
12 I know most of the following irregular present tenses: **andare, avere, bere, dire, dovere, essere, fare, potere, produrre, rimanere, salire, sapere, tenere, uscire, venire, volere**			Unità 1–5
13 I can deal with basic irregular nouns			Unità 5
14 Pronouns: I know the direct object pronouns **lo, la, li, le**			Unità 5

The above list is not exhaustive: for a thorough grammatical review go through the **Systems** exercises and check the answers in the back. On Track 2 you should aim to achieve a minimum 50% accuracy.

G Vocabulary: Tracks 1 and 2

The range of your vocabulary crucially affects what you can say and understand. By now you should be trying to consolidate a working vocabulary of everyday objects and topics, plus anything relating to your special needs. Level 1 has introduced about 800 words. You should aim to understand about half of these and use a quarter in conversation. Assess yourself by using the Vocabulary and Patterns sections and covering up the English. If you have been making your own vocabulary notebook use this too.

Working on your own I

Diagnosing difficulties

The ability to diagnose your weak spots and to devise ways of overcoming them is a crucial aspect of language learning. The 'menu' of language-learning activities below is designed to help you build up a useful repertoire of practice activities. In this Level the focus is on listening, speaking and acquiring vocabulary. Reading and grammar learning strategies are discussed after Level 2. Writing skills are developed in Book 2.

General advice

1 Keep a systematic record of your main difficulties, how you dealt with them and the extent to which you were satisfied.
2 Decide on the specific aim of each practice activity before you begin, e.g. *to improve speaking skills, especially pronunciation; to sort out my grammar, in particular the use of* **da**.
3 Set aside a regular time for practice. The best approach is 'little and often' rather than sporadic mammoth sessions which tire you out.
4 Don't get too bogged down if you encounter difficulties. Note them down and come back to them later with a fresh mind.

A Listening strategies

All learners need to spend time listening and absorbing the language: it helps enormously with speaking and is as necessary, if not more so, than speaking practice itself. If you practise regularly, your ear will become attuned to the language and you will rapidly learn to pick out key words and phrases. Without this skill you may become dependent on the visual word and find it hard to communicate orally. If your previous experience of language learning was based on reading and writing, allow yourself more time to develop your listening skills.

Reasons for listening include:
1 To practise guessing the meanings of words from the topic and follow the gist of what is said.
2 To identify sounds accurately and distinguish between one word and the next.
3 To improve your memory and concentration and extend your listening stamina, i.e. the length of time you can take things in.
4 To improve pronunciation, intonation and stress.

To improve your understanding of the gist, you could:

* Use prediction. Prepare the topic from the title or explanations accompanying the recording. Try and predict three or four words which might come up; look them up if you don't know them in Italian and then listen out for them.
* Break the language into manageable chunks by using the pause button and allowing your brain time to think through what's been said.
* Use grammatical clues. You will find, for example, that recognising the sounds of the verb endings gives you vital clues as to the meaning.
* Take notes. As you listen jot down key words you recognise. Use guesswork and try to piece together what's been said. Listen several times, noting down more words each time. Then refer to the transcript when you can't go any further.

It is important to realise that you don't need to understand every word in order to grasp the message. This is true in your native language as well, for example when you hear someone with an unfamiliar regional accent.

To practise identifying sounds and distinguishing between words, you could:

* Listen to a familiar recording without the transcript. Stop the tape and try to visualise the previous word by writing it down and checking it against the transcript.
* Read the transcript as you listen to the tape.
* Photocopy the transcript and delete every nth word (e.g. every 5th or 10th word). Listen again later and try to fill in the blanks.

Working on your own 1

The **Working on your own** section includes suggestions for encouraging students to work independently in class as well as consolidating their classroom learning at home and extending it into other areas of their lives.

In the classroom

The teacher can plan classroom activities which make students aware of what they need to study and how best to do it. Autonomy starts in class if students are given the opportunity to experiment with different ideas, discover how they learn and discuss the pros and cons of different learning strategies among themselves and with their teacher.

It is vital that learners become familiar with the Course Book, so that they are able to exploit it fully while working independently. Try the following exercise in class.

Which exercise?
Divide students into small groups. Give each group a different grammatical structure to practise and ask them to look for an appropriate exercise in the *Italianissimo* book. Each group should work independently. At the end of the session, each group in turn tells the others what their suggestions are and why.

You should set aside time in the classroom for students to try out the listening, speaking and vocabulary-learning strategies suggested in the **Working on your own** section in the Course Book.

Try this vocabulary-learning exercise:

Learning cards
1   Tell students that they might find it useful to write the words that they want to learn on little cards. They can write the Italian on one side and the English equivalent on the other side.
2   Ask students to divide (and cut) a size A4 sheet in halves until they have obtained 16 cards.
3   Ask them to write a word they know the meaning of or one which they can look up in the dictionary. All 16 words should be linked in some way; the student chooses the criterion which links the words.
4   Students learn the meaning of the words on each set of 16 cards by swapping their set each lesson with someone else. The same activity can be useful for encouraging students to learn short idiomatic sentences, collocations, phrasal verbs etc.

Outside the classroom

Encourage students to increase their learning skills by practising as much as possible outside the classroom situation. For example, they could:

● get into the habit of doing a little as often as possible at home: going over the last lesson, preparing for the following one
● keep a brief diary of work done at home and any difficulties experienced
● select words to learn that apply to their everyday experiences and write them on 'learning cards'.
● organise study groups: get together with other students and perhaps a bottle of Italian wine to do homework together or practise vocabulary
● carry a pocket-size dictionary so they can look up words as the need arises
● carry out tasks which force them to use the language for real purposes of communication, e.g. send postcards or short messages to each other, write shopping lists in Italian, visit an Italian restaurant and order a meal
● look at their surroundings, at home, at work or out shopping and see how many things they know the Italian names for.

Encourage students to report back to you and other students any other novel ideas they come up with for further practice of Italian outside the classroom.

To improve your memory and concentration you could:

* Stop the tape and repeat the last few words. Then try to repeat the last phrase.

To improve pronunciation, intonation and stress, you could:

* Shadow read. Turn the volume low on a familiar tape and read the transcript along with it.
* Record yourself on another tape.

B Speaking strategies

Your speaking will be helped by listening practice (see above), and by trying to communicate with native speakers. However, even if you cannot go to Italy or communicate with native speakers in the community, there is a lot you can do to improve on your own.

Reasons for speaking practice include:

1 To consolidate new language.
2 To improve fluency and confidence.
3 To improve pronunciation.

To improve your fluency and confidence, you could:

* Practise saying difficult phrases out loud.
* Act out imaginary dialogues – with yourself or another learner – recording yourself on cassette when you can.

To improve pronunciation, intonation and stress you could:

* Shadow-read [see listening section]
* Read a short course dialogue aloud, recording it on cassette, and then compare it with the original.

C Vocabulary learning strategies

Selecting what to learn

1 Be discriminating. Learn words for a purpose, *because you feel they are relevant to your needs.* Don't attempt to learn long lists of words which you might not use.
2 Set yourself some concrete situations, then target five to ten words which you feel are useful for the situation chosen. Use the Vocabulary sections of the Course, but consult a dictionary if the word you want isn't there.

To reinforce your vocabulary you could:

* Organise words into categories which are useful to you, such as travel, the home, etc.
* Pin up short lists to refer to.
* Record words – with a gap for the translation and listen in the car or on public transport.
* Test yourself regularly, from Italian to English and vice versa.

To widen your vocabulary you could:

* Regularly try to name objects around you: look up what you need in the dictionary – but not too much at a time.
* Find the opposites of words you know, especially adjectives, e.g. *grande – piccolo.* [See Ref. p. 244.]
* Learn words related to the ones you know, e.g. **lavoro – lavorare** or, **pranzo – pranzare**.

La famiglia Chiappini

The Chiappinis live in the old part of Ferrara and have chosen an unusual way of keeping the family together. When you've heard the profile, you can see how much you've understood by completing the true or false checklist.

[cc] [CD] 17

Presenter Anna Chiappini ha trentadue anni, e lavora come insegnante.

Anna La nostra famiglia ha, dunque, ha venti persone. Ci sono i miei genitori, mamma e papà; noi cinque, siamo tutte sorelle, tutte donne, e che abbiamo sposato naturalmente cinque ragazzi. In totale, abbiamo adesso ... un attimo ... eh ... quanti bimbi? ... dieci bambini più due in arrivo. Ecco qua quindi, questa è la famiglia:

Io sono qua, sulla sinistra. Vicino ad Antonio, ecco questo che vedi, vicino a me, è mio marito che ha in braccio Francesco, il primo figlio nostro. Noi, viviamo tutti nella stessa casa. È un palazzo molto grande con diversi appartamenti - sono sei. E quindi, sono sei famiglie, ci stiamo tutti per fortuna.

(Points to photo, *opposite above*) Questo è l'appartamento di mia sorella, Laura, e di suo marito Mario ... (*calls to Laura*) Laura, ecco, stiamo arrivando ... Ciao, ciao ... Questa è Laura.

Laura Piacere.

Presenter Laura è in cucina. Sta preparando un risotto molto grande ...

Laura Io mi chiamo Laura Chiappini. Abito a Ferrara, in Via Madama numero 31, in una casa dove abitano anche le famiglie delle mie sorelle e dei miei genitori. Io sono medico e lavoro in un ospedale. Questa sera abbiamo con noi a cena tre nipoti. Infatti i loro genitori sono fuori dalla città per una settimana e quindi noi zie e nonni li chiamiamo spesso a mangiare con noi.

Profile 1

The material in the **Profiles** provides extended listening and reading practice for students and gives them an opportunity to extend their listening and reading 'stamina'.

Students could work either on their own or in pairs or small groups. You could first of all ask students to read through the questions in the true or false checklist. Ensure that everyone has understood them.

Play the cassette/CD in sections. Students should have their books closed. Ask them just to listen the first time they hear the **Profile**. They should make brief notes on subsequent hearings. On each new hearing, they should be able to add to the notes they have made.

When students have answered all the true/false questions they can from hearing the cassette/CD, ask them to open their books again.

Students should now read through the text to complete any answers still missing. They could compare their notes with the printed version.

For oral practice, students could think up questions on the text and ask the teacher or other students for rapid answers.

Discuss any questions.

For homework, students could write a summary of the main points of the passage in English. They could also use the text to do some 'shadow-reading' to give them further speaking and reading practice. You could also ask them to make a note of any new vocabulary they have gleaned.

Presenter	Il marito di Laura si chiama Mario ...
Mario	Io mi chiamo Mario Bonatti. Sono insegnante. Insegno in una scuola professionale di Ferrara. Abbiamo due bambine, di nomi Elena e Maria. La più grande, Maria, ha dodici anni, Elena ne ha otto. E ce n'è un terzo in arrivo. Non so se è maschio o femmina. Ma la Laura, sì, ma non lo voglio sapere, voglio la sorpresa.
Presenter	E Laura sa?
Mario	Laura sa, sì, tutti in casa sanno. Io no.
Presenter	Quali sono i vantaggi e gli svantaggi della vita insieme?
Anna	È molto bello stare tutti insieme perché si parla, si chiacchiera, i bambini possono giocare assieme, e tutto è più facile. A volte gli adulti discutono per le macchine. Per esempio, in giardino ci sono uno, due, tre, quattro posti per le macchine ma le macchine sono cinque ... quindi una deve rimanere fuori dal garage.
Nicola	(*Nipote di Anna*) Sì, sì, penso che sia una grande fortuna vivere tutti insieme, tutti i parenti, ci aiutiamo molto, stiamo insieme.
Antonio	È molto divertente. Confusionario, ma molto divertente ... Come vedi qui è sempre un asilo con bambini che corrono, cani che abbaiano, zii che riparano le biciclette ... È veramente uno zoo.

	VERO O FALSO	V	F
1	Tutte le sorelle sono sposate.		
2	Il marito di Anna si chiama Francesco		
3	Laura è medico.		
4	Mario non vuole sapere se il figlio in arrivo è un maschio o una femmina.		
5	Non ci sono animali in casa.		
6	Gli abitanti di ogni appartamento hanno una macchina.		
7	È una vita molto tranquilla.		

Ambrogio Lorenzetti (c. 1285–1348)

'Effetti del Buon Governo in città'. (*The effects of good Government on the Town*) Palazzo Pubblico, Siena

Questo affresco fa parte di uno dei più importanti cicli pittorici profani del medioevo. Si trova nel Palazzo Pubblico *[Town hall]* di Siena, sede del governo senese a partire dall'inizio del Trecento. Rappresenta i benefici della pace, della giustizia e della sapienza nella città di Siena a quell'epoca.

Cercate di descrivere le persone, gli animali, le case e gli oggetti che vedete.

Culture 1

The **Culture** section of the book provides authentic material for students to read and enjoy at their leisure. This material gives learners a valuable opportunity for language practice: it should also stimulate and deepen interest in the Italian people and their culture. Cultural material can be in both printed or audiovisual form. Suggestions are given here on how you could use this material in class or at home and how to encourage students to share their (and your) material.

Printed material

Interested students will enjoy acquainting themselves with Italian literature. They should be able to find Italian novels either in translation, or in parallel texts. Material with plenty of illustration is particularly suitable for beginners and libraries sometimes have children's literature in foreign languages. You could devote some time during class for students to report back on any such reading they have done, perhaps giving a short presentation and passing the material around the class for comment.

Yet cultural material is not limited to literature alone and students should be encouraged to read magazines and books on football and fashion, food and wine, to reflect their own interests as far as possible.

Audiovisual material

It is difficult to find Italian available commercially, but you could ask your students to tap into the network of their Italian friends: some will almost certainly be able to provide good examples of modern Italian songs. Encourage your students to provide a commentary for the songs in *chiave comica, ironica o drammatica.*

Some songs – especially those which have a slow rhythm – are even suitable for a spot of simultaneous interpreting. Choose a suitable song and give an example of what you expect students to do. Ask students to think of any other songs they know that they would like to introduce to the class. On the other hand, Italian films are relatively easy to get hold of on video.

Film and video material can be presented in a number of ways: you could, for example, ask students to write subtitles for a short section, or to watch part of a video and briefly summarise events. Alternatively, you could play videos with the sound turned down and ask students to provice an oral commentary.

Encourage students to record Italian films from television, and circulate them among the class, for viewing at home. Ask students to use the video to practise the suggestions above. Or, they could simply watch for enjoyment and give a brief critique to the other class members next lesson.

Gianni Rodari (1920–80)

Nato a Omegna sul lago d'Orta in Piemonte, Gianni Rodari è autore di oltre venti libri per bambini ed è apprezzato e letto anche dagli adulti. Nel 1970 riceve il premio Andersen, il "Nobel della letteratura infantile". Rodari comincia la sua carriera come maestro e come giornalista per *l'Unità* di Milano, e ottiene il primo successo letterario scrivendo una rubrica per bambini. Nel 1950 pubblica la sua prima raccolta di canzonette, *Il libro delle filastrocche.* In seguito scrive molti racconti, e nel 1973 pubblica *La grammatica della fantasia,* un' interessante introduzione all'arte di inventare storie. L'opera di Rodari è spesso comica ma anche se la fantasia e l'assurdo ne costituiscono gli elementi principali, le sue storie rimangono legate in qualche modo al mondo reale. *Promemoria ['Memo']* è una delle poesie 'serie', di Rodari, pubblicata dopo la sua morte in *Il secondo libro delle filastrocche [1985].*

PROMEMORIA

Ci sono cose da fare ogni giorno:
    lavarsi, studiare, giocare
      preparare la tavola,
        a mezzogiorno.
    Ci sono cose da fare di notte:
    chiudere gli occhi, dormire,
      avere sogni da sognare,
    orecchie per non sentire.
Ci sono cose da non fare mai,
    né di giorno né di notte,
    né per mare né per terra:
    per esempio, la guerra.

> né ... né   *neither ... nor*

Primo Levi (1919–87)

Nato a Torino e laureato in chimica, nel 1943 Levi diventa partigiano e combatte nella Resistenza. Nel 1944 viene catturato e deportato ad Auschwitz ma sopravvive fino al gennaio 1945, quando le truppe sovietiche liberano il campo. Tornato in Italia, dopo lunghi viaggi, Levi riprende il suo mestiere di chimico e comincia a scrivere. La fama letteraria giunge con il primo libro, *Se questo è un uomo,* [1947]. Oltre ai libri che nascono dall'esperienza della prigionia, Levi scrive della narrativa d'invenzione, come *Il sistema periodico* [1975] e *Se non ora quando?* [1982], ed è autore di scritti, *L'altrui mestiere* [1985], di traduzioni, e anche di poesie pubblicate nella raccolta *Ad ora incerta* [1984]. I temi trattati da Levi sono spesso legati all'esperienza dei campi di concentramento, ma vanno al di là del personale, come per esempio nel grande libro di saggi intitolato *I sommersi e i salvati* [1986]. Poco dopo, nell'aprile 1987 Primo Levi si suicida a Torino: con la sua morte scompare uno dei più grandi scrittori e umanisti del secolo. La poesia 'Lunedì' viene scritta poco dopo il ritorno di Levi in Italia nel 1946.

LUNEDÌ

Che cosa è più triste di un treno?
Che parte quando deve,
Che non ha che una voce,
Che non ha che una strada.
Niente è più triste di un treno.

O forse un cavallo da tiro.
È chiuso fra due stanghe,
Non può neppure guardarsi a lato.
La sua vita è camminare.

E un uomo? Non è triste un uomo?
Se vive a lungo in solitudine
Se crede che il tempo è concluso
Anche un uomo è una cosa triste.

> un cavallo da tiro   *cart horse*
> stanghe   *shafts*
> a lato   *sideways*
> neppure   *not even*

Il mondo della musica

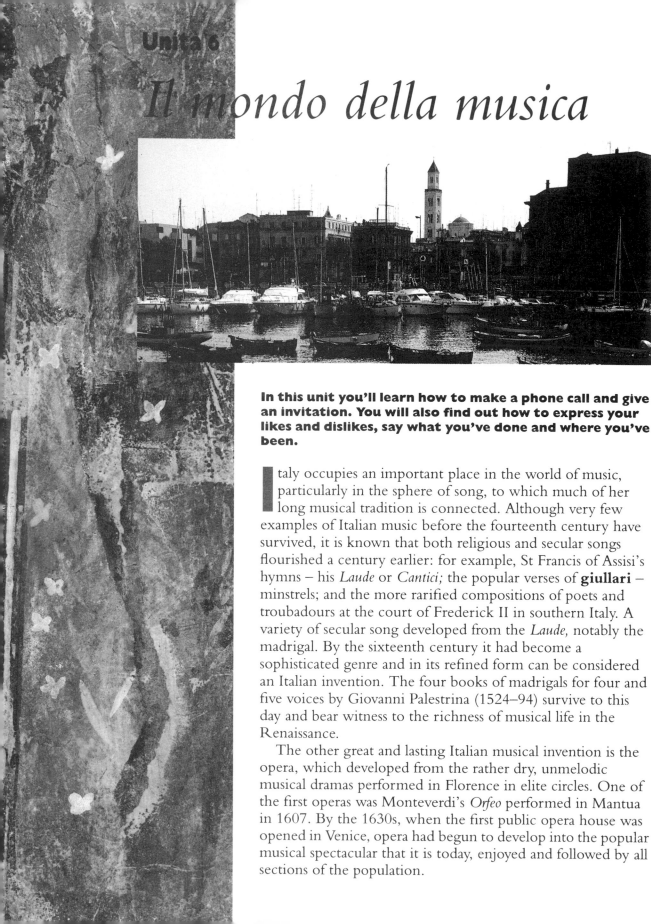

In this unit you'll learn how to make a phone call and give an invitation. You will also find out how to express your likes and dislikes, say what you've done and where you've been.

Italy occupies an important place in the world of music, particularly in the sphere of song, to which much of her long musical tradition is connected. Although very few examples of Italian music before the fourteenth century have survived, it is known that both religious and secular songs flourished a century earlier: for example, St Francis of Assisi's hymns – his *Laude* or *Cantici;* the popular verses of **giullari** – minstrels; and the more rarified compositions of poets and troubadours at the court of Frederick II in southern Italy. A variety of secular song developed from the *Laude,* notably the madrigal. By the sixteenth century it had become a sophisticated genre and in its refined form can be considered an Italian invention. The four books of madrigals for four and five voices by Giovanni Palestrina (1524–94) survive to this day and bear witness to the richness of musical life in the Renaissance.

The other great and lasting Italian musical invention is the opera, which developed from the rather dry, unmelodic musical dramas performed in Florence in elite circles. One of the first operas was Monteverdi's *Orfeo* performed in Mantua in 1607. By the 1630s, when the first public opera house was opened in Venice, opera had begun to develop into the popular musical spectacular that it is today, enjoyed and followed by all sections of the population.

Unità 6

Il mondo della musica

If you have opera fans among your students they will certainly appreciate your using lines of operatic Italian now and again as authentic material for lessons. The trouble with that, of course, is that, being very different from modern Italian, opera is of practically no value for language study, except for a few excerpts. Here is, however, the synopsis of *L'elisir d'amore* by Gaetano Donizetti. You won't have to sing any arias to your students (unless you happen to be an opera singer yourself) but you could make use of this simplified synopsis if, for example, you play a few comprehensible lines from the opera and ask the students to identify which part of the story it is and say what happens next.

1   Divide students into two groups. One group should read and summarise the *Atto primo,* the second group the *Atto secondo.* Each group reads their summary to the whole class.

Atto primo

Mentre Adina legge sotto un albero, Nemorino si sfoga cantando il suo amore. Intanto arriva un distaccamento di soldati capitanati da Belcore, arrogante e presuntuoso che, con grande sfoggio, offre ad Adina un mazzo di fiori. Vuole Adina sposarlo? Adina dice di non avere fretta; vuole pensarci un po'. Dopo che i soldati sono partiti, arriva Dulcamara, venditore ambulante, ciarlatano ed imbroglione che, con gran fanfara, offre in vendita una medicina miracolosa che cura ogni male. Nemorino ne compra una bottiglia perché è convinto da Dulcamare che la medicina (un vino Bordeaux) è un eccellente elisir d'amore. Nemorino incomincia a bere la medicina, cantando allegramente, e quando arriva Adina fa finta di non vederla. Sorpresa e indispettita da questo suo nuovo atteggiamento, Adina dichiara di voler sposare il sergente Belcore immediatamente ed invita tutti i presenti ad un banchetto per festeggiare.

Atto secondo

Nemorino la supplica invano di aspettare ancora un giorno e, disperato, chiede al dottore ancora una bottiglia di elisir per accellerare l'effetto. Ma come procurarsi i soldi? È Belcore stesso che da a Nemorino venti scudi. Nemorino deve però, in cambio, arruolarsi soldato. La festa è incominciata quando giunge notizia che lo zio di Nemorino è morto e gli ha lasciato un'immensa eredità. Mentre viene circondato dalle ragazze del villaggio (sempre di più convinto della bontà dell'elisir), Nemorino scorge una furtiva lacrima negli occhi di Adina, commossa perché è stata informata da Dulcamara su come Nemorino ha ottenuto i soldi necessari all'acquisto dell'elisir. Adina lo prega di non partire soldato perché è pur vero che lo ama. Belcore deve, quindi, rassegnarsi alla sorte. Cala il sipario mentre ognuno si affretta a comperare una bottiglia di elisir.

Video corner

You may like to draw the students' attention to the background music on the video. Giovanni Verga wrote the play *Cavalleria Rusticana* which was adapted for the musical stage by Mascagni.

What can you see?
Aim: vocabulary building through active viewing
Video sequence: opening sequence

1   Tell students to jot down which one of the following items they can spot in the opening sequence. Write the items on the board and ask students to guess the meaning. Help them if necessary.

aeroporto   fontana   chiavi   campi   porto   museo   tifosi edifici   motoscafo   cassetta   elicottero   concerto   negozi giardino   chiesa   trattore   autobus   negozio   stadio   barca

Guess what's in the picture
Aim: to encourage oral practice
Video sequence: From Anna dialling Rita's phone number to Rita's sister writing the message

1   Cover the screen (or turn the contrast and brightness down) and play the video sequence.

2   Ask students to imagine what is in the sequence. Elicit as much information as you can.

Di che colore è il telefono?
Quanti anni ha la sorella di Rita?

Interactions

> **Structures:** the past tense
> **Functions:** asking for information/asking someone
> to do something/arranging a meeting/talking about
> the past
> **Vocabulary:** on the telephone

Help-phrases and instructions

Sono (non sono) d'accordo.
Sono (non sono) completamente d'accordo.
Sei d'accordo?

Interaction 1 (041)

1 *Anna è in Puglia, il tacco dello stivale, per incontrare Rita
Jacobelli, una giovane musicista. La prima conversazione è al
telefono.*
Is Rita at home?
When would be a good time for Anna to ring back?

2 Play the cassette/CD as required and ask further
questions:
What is Rita's phone number?
What is the word for 'hello' when answering the phone?
How does Anna say 'Can I speak to . . .?'
Why is Rita not at home?
When is she coming home?
At what time of day does this phone call take place?

(If you use the video, you can press pause and ask what
Rita's sister writes in the message.)

Interactions

  2

Anna has written to a young violinist, Rita Jacobelli, who is studying music at the Bari Conservatorio. She wants to arrange an interview and is following up her letter with a phone call.

First time round

il prefisso	code
parlare	to speak
richiamare	to call back
prima di	before

Rita's sister Laura answers the phone.

a Is Rita at home?
b When would be a good time to ring back?

Anna	Allora, il prefisso zero otto zero (080). Ah! il numero di Rita, qual è? Ah, cinque uno due cinque tre zero.
Laura	**Pronto, chi parla?**
Anna	Buonasera. **Sono** Anna Mazzotti, **posso parlare con** Rita per piacere?
Laura	Mi dispiace, Rita **non c'è** in questo momento. È uscita. È andata in Conservatorio per una prova.
Anna	Ah! Ho capito. [. . .] E Lei **mi sa dire** quando torna?
Laura	Ma torna tardi, credo. Vuole lasciare un messaggio?

Anna	Sì. **Le può dire che** ha chiamato Anna Mazzotti per la questione dell'intervista e che la richiamo domani, se va bene.
Laura	Certo. Ma è meglio chiamare la mattina presto.
Anna	Verso che ora? Prima delle otto?
Laura	Anche dopo le otto va bene. Ma prima delle otto e mezzo.
Anna	D'accordo, La ringrazio. Buonasera.
Laura	Buonasera.

è uscita	*she's gone out*
ho capito	*I see [lit. I have understood]*
ha chiamato	*(she) called, phoned*
per la questione dell'intervista	*about the interview*
è meglio chiamare la mattina presto	*it's best to ring early in the morning*
d'accordo, La ringrazio	*all right, thank you*

Key phrases

pronto, chi parla?	*hello, who's speaking?*
sono . . .	*it's . . .*
posso parlare con . . .	*can I speak to . . .*
non c'è	*she's not in*
mi sa dire . . .	*do you know/can you tell me . . .*
le può dire che . . .	*can you tell her that . . .*

Ansaphone  2

See if you can leave a message on the Ansaphone.

2 3

The next morning Anna is more successful.

First time round

ieri sera	*yesterday evening*
La chiamo	*I'm calling you*
ha ricevuto?	*did you receive?*

This time Rita answers the phone.

a Did she get Anna's letter?
b When do they agree to meet?

Rita	Pronto.
Anna	Pronto? Sono Anna Mazzotti. **Ho chiamato** ieri sera. **Ho lasciato** un messaggio per Rita.
Rita	Sì, **sono io** Rita. Buongiorno.
Anna	Ah! Buongiorno. La chiamo a proposito dell'intervista. Ha ricevuto la mia lettera?
Rita	Sì, sì. Va bene. Ho organizzato tutto.
Anna	D'accordo. **Quando ci possiamo vedere** allora?
Rita	**Perché non ci vediamo** a casa mia, domani alle undici?
Anna	Sì.

a proposito di   *about*

Key phrases

ho chiamato	*I called*
ho lasciato	*I left*
sono io	*it's me*
quando ci possiamo vedere?	*when can we see each other?*
perché non ci vediamo	*why don't we meet*

3 4

The next day, as arranged, Anna and Rita meet up. Anna finds out about Rita's week and how she began her musical career.

First time round

studiando	*studying*
lo strumento	*instrument*
suonare per gioco	*to play for fun*
la sigla	*signature tune*

a How old is Rita now and how old was she when she began playing music?
b Name one thing she's done this week.

Rita	Il mio nome è Rita, ho diciannove anni e studio musica al Conservatorio Niccolò Piccinni di Bari dove frequento il settimo anno di violino.
Anna	**Cos' hai fatto** questa settimana?
Rita	Questa settimana, come tutte le mie settimane, l'ho trascorsa studiando in Conservatorio: musica da camera, storia della musica, armonia, orchestra, dove stiamo facendo una sinfonia di Mozart. E chiaramente, la mia lezione di violino, che è il mio strumento principale.
Anna	**Come hai cominciato** a studiare la musica?
Rita	Ho cominciato a suonare per gioco, all'età di nove anni. La prima musica che ho suonato al pianoforte è stata la sigla di un cartone animato che ho visto in televisione.

questa settimana . . . l'ho trascorsa	*I spent this week*
stiamo facendo	*we are doing*
un cartone animato che ho visto	*a cartoon I saw*

Key phrases

cos'hai fatto?	*what did you do?*
come hai cominciato?	*how did you begin?*

Interaction 2   (139)

1   *Il giorno dopo, Anna ritelefona a Rita.*
Did she get Anna's letter?
When do they agree to meet?

2   Play the cassette/CD as required and ask further
questions:
At what time of day does this phone call take place?
Does Anna address Rita formally or informally?
(Ask the students to change the telephone conversation
from formal to informal.)

Interaction 3   (170)

1   *Il giorno dopo durante l'intervista, Anna chiede a Rita di
parlare della sua carriera di musicista.*
How old is Rita now and how old was she when she
began playing music?
Name one thing she's done this week.

2   Play the cassette/CD as required and ask further
questions:
How many years has she been studying at the
Conservatorio?
Does she play any other instruments?

Anna Mazzotti has now changed to the informal means
of address. Take this opportunity to encourage further
discussion on the use of the formal/informal address.

Patterns 1

Getting in touch by phone

1   Give each student a telephone number written on a piece of paper.

2   Call out each number in turn and wait for a student to 'answer the phone'. Tell them to answer with *Pronto, chi parla?*

3   Improvise short role plays. Ask to speak to someone by name and tell them to answer *Sono io.* Ask to speak to their brother or sister and say *Posso lasciare un messaggio?*

Making suggestions

Tell students the class has one hundred pounds to spend and ask them to write down some suggestions on how to spend it.

Patterns 1

i) Getting in touch by phone

Identifying the speaker

Pronto, chi parla?   *Hello, who's speaking?*

Saying who you are

Sono	Rita	*It's/this is*	*Rita*
	il dottor Baldini		*Doctor Baldini*
	la signora Manzi		*Mrs Manzi*
	io		*me*

Asking to speak to someone

Posso parlare con	Anna?	*Can I speak to*	*Anna?*
	il signor Guerci?		*Mr Guerci?*
	la dottoressa Neri?		*Doctor Neri?*

Saying someone isn't in

Mi dispiace, non c'è   *I'm sorry, he/she isn't in*

Requesting information

Mi sa dire	quando torna?	*Can you tell me*	*when he/she will be back?*
	quando tornano?		*when they will be back?*

The phrase **mi sa dire** literally means *do you know how to tell me?* There's more on **sapere** *(to know)* in Systems 7, note 6, p. 198, Systems 8, note 4, p. 201 and Systems 9, note 6, p. 206.

Asking about leaving a message

Vuole/vuoi	lasciare un messaggio?	*Do you want to*	*leave a message?*
Posso		*Can I*	

Leaving a message

Le può dire che **la** richiamo domani?   *Can you tell her I'll call her tomorrow?*
Gli può dire che **lo** richiamo domani?   *Can you tell him I'll call him tomorrow?*
See Troubleshooting, p. 126 and Systems, note 1, p. 193 for **le, la, gli** and **lo**.

Ringing off: polite thanks

La ringrazio   *Thank you [lit. I thank you]*

Use **La** for both men and women.

ii) Making suggestions

To make a suggestion you can use **perché non**, plus the verb:

Perché non	ci vediamo a casa mia?	*Why don't we*	*see each other at my house?*
	andiamo al cinema?		*go to the cinema?*
	ceniamo insieme?		*have dinner together?*

You can also make a suggestion simply by using the **noi** form of the verb on its own:

Andiamo a teatro   *Let's go to the theatre*

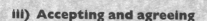

Patterns I

iii) Accepting and agreeing

| volentieri | *I'd like to* | va bene | *fine, all right* |
| mi fa piacere | *with pleasure* | d'accordo | *all right, agreed* |

iv) Arranging when to meet

Use the verb **potere** *(to be able to)* with either **vedersi** *(to see each other)* or **incontrarsi** *(to meet)*:

| Quando ci possiamo | vedere? | *When can we* | *see each other?* |
| | incontrare? | | *meet?* |

Perché non ci vediamo	stamattina	*Why don't we see*	*this morning*
ci incontriamo	oggi pomeriggio	*each other/meet*	*afternoon*
andiamo	stasera	*go*	*evening*
	questa settimana		*week*
	domani mattina		*tomorrow morning*
	dopodomani		*the day after tomorrow*
	la settimana prossima		*next week*
	sabato prossimo		*next Saturday*

v) Specifying times

A che ora? or   Verso che ora?   *At [about] what time?*

The answer can vary:

Ci vediamo	verso le undici	*See you*	*at about 11.00*
	alle cinque		*at 5.00*
	prima delle otto e mezzo		*before 8.30*
	dopo le otto		*after 8.00*
	fra le due e le tre		*between 2 and 3*

vi) Talking about the past (1)

To ask what someone has done, you need the past tense of **fare**. This is formed with the present tense of the verb **avere** and the past participle **fatto** *(done)*.

Che cosa	hai/ha	fatto?	*What*	*have you done/did you do?*
	avete			
Che cosa	ha	fatto?	*What*	*has he, she done/did he, she do?*
	hanno			*have they done/did they do?*

To reply, use part of the verb **avere** in the present tense plus the past participles of the verb describing the action. See Systems, notes 3 and 4 p. 194.

Most **-are** and **-ire** verbs have regular past participles ending in **-ato** and **-ito**:

[chiamare]	ho/abbiamo	chiam**ato** ieri sera	*I/we called*	*yesterday evening*
[lasciare]	ho/abbiamo	lasci**ato** un messaggio	*I/we left a*	*message*
[capire]	ho	cap**ito** tutto	*I (have)*	*understood everything*
[pulire]	ho	pul**ito** la macchina	*I (have)*	*cleaned the car*

Arranging when to meet

1 Ask students to make arrangements to see one another. Tell them to make entries in their diaries for the time (*stasera, domani mattina, domani sera,* etc.) and the place.

2 Students go round the class arranging meetings.

3 Ask each student individually who are they going to meet, when and where.

Specifying times

Repeat the exercise above but, this time, ask students to tell you the exact times they have arranged to meet.

Talking about the past

1 Start by telling students you're going to talk about what you ate and drank this morning. Ask them to tell you what they ate and drank.

2 Using familiar verbs, ask individual students simple questions such as:

Hai bevuto il caffè questa mattina?
Hai mangiato un panino oggi?
Hai sentito le notizie alla radio?
Hai comprato il giornale?

3 Tell students to listen for the clue in the question and to give full answers. e.g. *Sì, ho comprato il giornale . . .* When students have used the past tense orally, write their answers on the board.

4 Ask student A: *Hai mangiato colazione questa mattina?* Student A answers: *Sì, (No, non) ho mangiato colazione.* Ask student B: *Che cosa ha fatto student A?* Student B replies: *Student A ha mangiato colazione questa mattina.*

5 Carry on, varying the number of students and the meaning, e.g. *Che cosa avete comprato al negozio?* One student answers collectively: *Abbiamo comprato . . .* Ask a third student: *Che cosa hanno comprato . . .?*

6 Introduce some irregular past participles.
Hai letto il giornale? Hai visto il film ieri sera? Hai preso l'autobus oggi?

This point could be the end of the lesson. Revise the points covered so far. In the next lesson students will cover the following:

> **Structures:** the past tense
> **Functions:** talking about likes and dislikes
> **Vocabulary:** music, songs and instruments

Practice 1

Can I speak to ...?

Aim: written practice of the formal/informal address

After completing the exercise of the same title in the book, tell students to change whatever is necessary to make it informal.

Don Giovanni

Aim: to use the topic of music to enliven classwork

1 The famous Mozart opera offers a good opportunity to do some practice on numbers. Leporello has compiled a catalogue of his master's conquests. (You should briefly revise numbers over 100 before attempting this activity.)

> In Italia seicento e quaranta,
> In Almania duecento e trentuna,
> cento in Francia in Turchia novantuna,
> ma in Ispania son già mille e tre,
> V'han fra queste contadine
> cameriere, cittadine ...

2 Play a recording of the above (*Atto primo*) and ask students to jot down the number of Don Giovanni's conquests in each of the five countries. Again, you may like to play it several times, asking students to listen specifically for numbers the first time and countries the second time, or vice versa.

If the verb ends in **-ere** the regular pattern is:

[ricevere]   ho | ricev**uto** la lettera   *I (have)* | received the letter

But many **-ere** verbs have irregular past tense endings which have to be memorised individually as you need them:

[vedere]	ho	visto un programma	I	*saw a programme*
[leggere]	ho	letto un articolo	I	*read an article*
[prendere]	ho	preso il treno	I	*took the train*

There's more on the past tense in Patterns 2, p. 122 and Systems, notes 3, 4 and 5, p. 194.

Practice I

Can I speak to ...?

Here is the transcript of a telephone conversation but it's in the wrong sequence. Read it through and put it in the right order, beginning with **a**:

Speaker 1	Speaker 2
a Pronto, chi parla?	**1** Posso lasciare un messaggio?
b Sì, certo.	**2** Buonasera. Sono Ettore, posso parlare con Valerio?
c Torna tardi, credo.	**3** Gli può dire che lo richiamo domani?
d Mi dispiace, non c'è. È uscito.	**4** Mi sa dire quando torna?
e Chiama domani? Va bene.	**5** La ringrazio, buonasera.

Refresh your memory   ⌜cc⌝   ◎ 5

Listen again to Anna's phone conversation with Rita, without looking back at the text, and answer the questions on the cassette/CD.

Overbooking   ⌜cc⌝   ◎ 5

Giovanni Casanova arrives home to find three messages on his Ansaphone. Work out who called, why and what problem he is going to have.

Stop the cassette/CD as often as you like and have paper and pencil handy to jot down the messages.

Appointments

It's Monday morning. You're going through your appointments with a colleague who's in a muddle. Consult your diary and tell him the time of day you are seeing or ringing each person mentioned.

e.g. La dottoressa Muratori viene oggi pomeriggio, vero?
No, la vedo stamattina.

These are his other questions:
1 Aldo Carfagnini viene oggi pomeriggio, vero?
2 Devi chiamare Susanna Fallaci dopodomani?
3 Allora, quando vedi Letizia – mercoledì pomeriggio?
4 E chiami l'ingegner Vaccari giovedì mattina, vero?

Alibi

A Stradivarius violin was stolen on Tuesday evening. The Inspector – **il commissario** – has narrowed the suspects to two people. After he's heard the statements below, he is sure he's found the culprit. Can you spot him or her by reading the statements and checking the facts, using the radio and TV programmes?

Il com.	Signorina Agostini, dopo le sette, martedì sera, che cos'ha fatto?
Sig.na A.	Beh, non ho fatto molto. Ho letto il giornale, ho preparato la cena e ho ascoltato la radio.
Il com.	E che cos' ha sentito?
Sig.na A.	Ma . . . ho sentito un po' di musica al IV canale: il programma musicale delle otto.
Il com.	E quali cantanti ha sentito?
Sig.na A.	Mah, molti – Claudio Baglioni, Gianna Nannini, Venditti, Tozzi . . .
Il com.	La ringrazio, signorina.
Il com.	Allora, Signor Petronio, martedì sera, dopo le sette, che cos'ha fatto?
Sig. P.	Mah . . . ho fatto una telefonata, ho letto un po' e ho cenato. Dopo ho guardato la televisione. Ho visto *Blob* su Raitre.
Il com.	E che altro ha visto?
Sig. P.	Subito dopo, su Raidue, ho visto un film giallo, *Delitto sotto il Sole*.
Il com.	Signor Petronio, La ringrazio.

RAITRE
di. Margherita Lo....

11 **Mountain Bike.**
11,30 **Pallavolo femminile.**
12 **Tennis.**
14,45 **La scuola si aggiorna.**
17 **Vita col nonno,** telefilm.
17,45 **La rassegna** - Giornali e Tv estere.
18 **Bodymatters,** telefilm.
19,30 **Rai regione.**
19,45 **Cartoni animati.**
20 **Blob. Di tutto di più.**
20,25 **Una cartolina spedita da Andrea Barbato.**
20,30 **Un giorno in pretura.**
21,45 **Allarme in città.**
23,50 **Le mura di sabbia.** Texas: ricordi di guerra e di prigionia.
0,45 **Tg3 Nuovo giorno.**
1,10 **Fuori orario.**

1,20 **Mezzanotte e dintorni.**

RAIDUE

10 **Questa volta ti faccio ricco,** film comm. con Antonio Sabato (1974).
11,55 **I fatti vostri.**
13,50 **Quando si ama,** telefilm.
14,20 **Santa Barbara,** telefilm.
15,30 **Sale e pepe super spie hippy,** film comm. con Sammy Davis Jr (1968).
17,20 **Hill Street giorno e notte,** telefilm.
18,10 **Rock Cafè.**
18,35 **Il commissario Köster.**
20,30 **Senza limiti - Due casi per Sam Dietz,** film poliz. con Leo Rossi, 2° epis.
22,15 **Hunter,** telefilm.
23,10 **Tg2 Pegaso.**
0,20 **Delitto sotto il sole,** film giallo con Peter Ustinov, James Mason.

RAITRE

F I L O D I F

IV CANALE **Musica leggera**

6/**BUONGIORNO IN MUSICA**
8/**CONCERTO DEL MATTINO**
9/**CANTANDO IN ITALIANO**
10/**MUSICA DALLO SCHERMO**
11/**CANTAUTORI**
12/**ROCK & POP**
13/**JAZZ VARIETÀ**
14/**FOLKLORE DA TUTTO IL MONDO**
15/**PARATA DI STELLE**
16/**FACILE ASCOLTO**
18/**DISCOTECA**
20/**CONCERTO:** Claudio Baglioni - Antonello Venditti - Gianna Nannini - Pino Daniele - Umberto Tozzi - New Patetic «Elastic» - Gilbert Bécaud - Jair Rodrigues - Maria Bethania - Toquinho - Harry Belafonte - Jorge Ben - Count Basie - B. B. King - Mel Lewis - Duke Ellington - Benny Goodman - Woody Herman - Sonny Rollins - Stan Kenton - Buddy De Franco - Pee Wee Russell - Louis Armstrong
22-23,30/**MUSICA NELLA SERA**

Now you say what *you* did yesterday evening after seven o'clock. Did you . . . watch TV? prepare the supper? listen to the radio? read a book? write a letter? make a phone call? see a friend? have a bath?

Practise what you want to say, making notes if necessary. See if you can eventually do it from memory, perhaps into a cassette. Finally, write a brief report for the Inspector!

Alibi

1 Tell your students they are all suspects for the murder which took place on the Milano–Roma train, since they were all among the passengers. You are the *commissario* in charge of the enquiry and need to question them on what they did during the journey between 10 minutes to midnight and 10 minutes past midnight.

2 Prepare some flashcards to show each time you ask a question. Don't write the verb on the card, just a clue to the answer. Formal address is required. e.g. *Che cosa ha fatto ieri in treno intorno a mezzanotte?* (Show a card with the word *giornale*.)

3 Student A should answer: *Ho letto il giornale.*

4 Show a second clue (*sigaretta*). Student A: *Ho fumato una sigaretta.*
Here is a list of possible clues:

panino	birra	libro
lettera	zzz ...	paesaggio
walkman	cruciverba	telefono (cellulare)
fumetto	niente	caffè

5 After some oral practice of the above, you can ask the students to write and sign their own statements which should list the activities of half a dozen other passengers as well as their own. To do this, they have to ask each other questions and make sure there aren't any discrepancies in the statements. Split the class if necessary. (Arrest anyone claiming to be watching *il paesaggio* at midnight!)

Who did what?

Aim: to write full, meaningful sentences in the past tense

Ask students questions which require an answer in the past tense (go over irregular past tenses). Provide a verb and a choice of different objects and tell them to create an answer by using an appropriate object with the verb.

Perché Luisa ha fame questa mattina?
FARE   il compito, un errore, una foto, un tentativo, colazione
Luisa ha fame perché non ha fatto colazione.

Perché non hai fatto quello che ti ho detto?
LEGGERE   un libro, il giornale, il messaggio, una rivista, la lettera

Come mai conosci la trama se non conosci il libro?
VEDERE   un film, il telegiornale, il video, la televisione, lo spettacolo

Come mai sai già la notizia?
SENTIRE   la musica, la cassetta, il disco, la radio, il concerto

Come mai sei così bravo a giocare a tennis?
PRENDERE   il raffreddore, una sbornia, un influenza, lezioni, uno spavento

Cultura e parole

Il Festival di Sanremo is, without doubt, the most important contest in the world of *la canzone leggera italiana*. This is an annual event, much like the Eurovision Song Contest but on an Italian scale. It attracts a huge television audience (over 15 million) and is all fun, glitter and, inevitably, drama. Just as in the world of politics, *nel mondo della canzone leggera italiana* there are some old faces that never disappear from the scene and the *Festival di Sanremo* provides an opportunity to see quite a collection of these. You could perhaps discuss the reasons why with your students. What does this say about Italian society?

Although there is a token participation of *stranieri, il Festival di Sanremo* is an almost wholly Italian affair. It is here that the most authentic *vocalità pop latina* finds its expression, in the setting of a typical Italian show, full of drama and suspense.

According to De Crescenzo, author and philosopher, the most striking aspect for outsiders is that everyone takes this event so seriously. He says that what is important about this ritual is not that it should be enjoyable but that it gives everyone the opportunity to complain: *Quest'anno le canzoni non sono molto belle. L'anno scorso erano migliori . . .,* but, of course, the following year everyone is glued to their television screen (once again) ready to say the same things.

The lyrics of Italian songs, like many modern songs, do not always tell a logical or even comprehensible story, but the best of the *cantautori* manage to capture our imagination in a few words, without actually telling a story. On the whole, the most popular *canzoni* are *orecchiabili* and leave little to the imagination. The chief ingredients of these easy-listening songs are *le strofe rimate, i cori, il ritmo melodico e tanto, tanto sentimento.*

Bring in an example of Italian musical sentimentality for the students to hear. You could also make use of some of the lyrics for listening comprehension.

Cultura e parole

Italy's longstanding musical tradition, particularly in the field of popular song, is alive and well in the shape of her **cantautori** – writer singers: some of them have achieved the stature of poets rather like the troubadours of old, and the best of them attract a widespread following. Their songs are constantly in the charts alongside pop and rock stars. They vary in style from the philosophical and nostalgic to the humorous and irreverent, including biting satire and social or political comment. The music itself blends different influences: Dylan and rock music as well as the French chansonniers Brel and Bécaud. What the songs have in common is the importance of the words as well as the music and the fact that the themes concern ordinary people. The 'old guard' of **cantautori** which rose to fame in the golden era of the 1970s is still going strong: Lucio Battisti, Eduardo Bennato, Lucio Dalla, Fabrizio De André, Francesco De Gregori, Francesco Guccini, Gino Paoli, Antonello Venditti and Claudio Baglioni.

I Conservatori. Italy cultivates much of her musical talent in the **Conservatori**, her state music schools found in most major towns. The first one was set up in Bologna in 1808, though they existed in the seventeenth century as charitable institutions for the poor. Entry is by exam, usually at 11, and courses last 7 to 10 years depending on the main instrument chosen. Until the age of 14 all students study other subjects in the attached **scuola media.** They can then choose whether to devote all their time to music or to enrol at a **scuola superiore** where those wishing to go on to university will opt for enrolment, since the Diploma of the Conservatorio, although very hard to get, does not qualify a student for university entrance.

Italy's cultivation of her musical talent in the Conservatori has produced rebels like the rock singer Gianna Nannini and, of course, world-class musicians and performers – not just Luciano Pavarotti, but the conductors Claudio Abbado and Riccardo Muti, the pianist Maurizio Pollini and the contemporary composers Berio, Nono, Maderna and Togni.

The language of music

Be it **allegro** or **adagio**, **forte** or **piano**, the vast majority of expressive musical terms are in Italian. The practice of including indications of force and speed started in Italy in the seventeenth century and the enormous popularity of Italian music helped to spread these expressions. Many are familiar in colloquial Italian: you may know that **forte** means 'loud', **adagio** is 'slow', **piano** is 'soft', **vivace** is 'lively' and **presto** can mean 'quick'. But not all the terms coincide exactly with everyday Italian. In spoken Italian **piano** can also mean 'slow', whereas **presto** is also 'soon'. In music, **allegro** signifies 'lively and rather fast' while in spoken Italian it's 'happy' or 'jolly'. And if you take the diminutives of **allegro** or **andante** ('at a moderate pace'), there is room for confusion: **allegretto** instructs the musician to play a little more slowly, but if it's **andantino**, then he must play faster, not slower than **andante**. How fast, or slow, then, is **andante ma non troppo**?

Interactions

4 🔲 💿 6

In the course of the conversation with Rita, Anna finds out about her musical tastes.

First time round

ti piace	*you like*
il frastuono	*racket*
la batteria	*drums*

What sort of music does she like and what sort does she dislike?

Anna	**Quale** musica **ti piace?**
Rita	**Mi piace** principalmente la musica classica. Poi mi piace anche il jazz, sia nello stile moderno che classico. E poi anche la musica leggera.
Anna	E **quale** musica **non ti piace?**
Rita	La musica che non mi piace e che dà tanto fastidio alle mie orecchie è il frastuono che fanno le chitarre elettriche, il basso, la batteria. Una musica odiosa, terribile.

| sia nello stile moderno che classico | *both in the modern and the classic style* |
| che dà fastidio alle mie orecchie | *which bothers (offends) my ears* |

Key phrases

quale . . . ti piace?	*which . . . do you like?*
mi piace	*I like*
quale . . . non ti piace?	*which . . . don't you like?*
non mi piace . . .	*I don't like*

5 🔲 💿 7

Anna pays a visit to the Conservatorio where she meets several students. Marcello is a guitarist and Luciano is a violinist.

First time round

| il compositore | *composer* |

Who is Marcello's favourite composer?

Anna	Marcello, **quale** compositore **ti piace di più?**
Marcello	Io sono un musicista classico, suono la chitarra e quindi preferisco Mauro Giuliani.
Anna	Quale strumento ti piace di più?
Luciano	Lo strumento che **mi piace di più** è il violino, perché permette di esprimere meglio i propri sentimenti.
[Anna	E quando non suoni il violino, **che cosa ti piace fare?**
Luciano	Quando non suono il violino a me piace leggere e piacciono tante altre cose. come la fotografia.]

| esprimere | *to express* |
| a me piace | *I like [more emphatic than* mi piace*]* |

Key phrases

quale . . . ti piace di più?	*which . . . do you like most?*
mi piace di più	*I like most*
che cosa ti piace fare?	*what do you like doing?*

Interaction 4 (269)

1 *Anna parla con Rita dei suoi gusti musicali.*
What sort of music does she like and what sort does she dislike?

2 Play the cassette/CD as required.

This point could be the end of the lesson. Revise the points covered so far. In the next lesson students will cover the following:

> **Structures:** the past tense
> **Functions:** talking about likes and dislikes
> **Vocabulary:** music and instruments

Interaction 5 (293)

1 *Anna incontra alcuni studenti al Conservatorio di Rita.*
Who is Marcello's favourite composer?

2 Play the cassette/CD as required and ask further questions:
Which instrument does Luciano prefer and why?

De gustibus

Aim: to stimulate oral discussion and practice

1 Ask students to find out the most and the least liked activities at home, on holiday and at work. Tell them to write each student's name and the most or least liked activity in three other columns in this way:

Nome   a casa   in vacanza   al lavoro

2 Tell students to ask two types of question:

Che cosa ti piace fare di più al lavoro?
Che cosa ti piace fare di meno in vacanza?

Interaction 6 (311)

1 *Rita invita Anna a sentire un concerto.*
Where do they agree to meet?
What time do they decide on?

2 Play the cassette/CD as required and ask further
questions:
How does Rita invite Anna?
How does Anna say 'Fine. See you tomorrow'?

Interaction 7 (341)

1 *Anna chiede a Pietro e Mara che cosa hanno fatto il giorno
prima.*
Pick out one thing each of them did.

2 Play the cassette/CD as required and ask further
questions:
What else did they do?

6   8

Rita invites Anna to attend a chamber-music concert to be given on the seafront by a quartet she has formed with friends.

First time round

sul lungomare	on the seafront
dietro	behind

a Where do they agree to meet?
b What time do they decide on?

Rita	Allora vuoi venire domani?
Anna	Sì. Volentieri. **Dove ci incontriamo?**
Rita	Direttamente al Barion. È un club in centro, sul lungomare. Dietro il teatro Margherita.
Anna	E quando? Verso che ora? Alle due?
Rita	No. Prima delle due. Verso l'una e mezzo.
Anna	D'accordo. Ci vediamo domani, allora.
Rita	Va bene. Ciao.
Anna	Ciao.

Key phrase

dove ci incontriamo?   *where shall we meet?*

Rendez-vous   8

Listen to the cassette/CD and say you'll meet at the places associated with the sounds you hear.

7    9

Anna attends a rehearsal in the magnificent hall – **Aula Magna** – of the Conservatorio and talks to two more students about where they were yesterday.

First time round

ieri	yesterday
la musica d'insieme	ensemble music
il violoncello	cello

Pick out one thing each of them did.

Anna	Mara, **dove sei stata** ieri?
Mara	Ieri sono stata in Conservatorio a fare lezione di musica d'insieme. Poi **sono ritornata** a casa. Ho studiato violoncello e **sono uscita** con gli amici.
Anna	Ciao, Pietro.
Pietro	Ciao.
Anna	Pietro, dove sei stato ieri?
Pietro	**Sono stato** al Conservatorio a fare lezione di violoncello. Poi **sono andato** a casa. Ho cenato e poi sono andato a giocare a biliardo. [. . .]

Key phrases

dove sei stato/a?	*where were you/have you been?*
sono	
ritornato/a	*I returned*
sono uscito/a	*I went out*
sono stato/a	*I was/have been*
sono andato/a	*I went*

Patterns 2

i) Saying what you like

To say what you like, you use the verb **piacere** *(to like)*, which literally means *to be pleasing to.* The verb is used differently from most other verbs.

If you like one thing, you use the same form – **piace** – with a different pronoun for each person:

Mi piace	Pavarotti	*I like*	*Pavarotti*
Ci piace	il rock	*We like*	*rock*

If you like more than one thing, use the form **piacciono**:

Mi piacciono	i gialli	*I like*	*detective stories*
Ci piacciono	i western	*We like*	*westerns*

Saying you like it, her or them

Ti piace	Lucio Dalla?	Sì, mi piace	*Do you like*	*Lucio Dalla?*	*Yes, I like him*
Le piace	il jazz?	Sì, mi piace		*jazz?*	*Yes, I like it*
Vi piace	la professoressa di disegno?	Sì, ci piace		*the art teacher?*	*Yes, we like her*

Ti piacciono	i film dell'orrore?	Sì, mi piacciono	*Do you like*	*horror films?*	*Yes, I like them*
Le piacciono	i romanzi?	Sì, mi piacciono		*novels?*	*Yes, I like them*
Vi piacciono	i documentari?	Sì, ci piacciono		*documentaries?*	*Yes, we like them*

There is no need to use the words for *it, him, her* or *them* in your reply [see Troubleshooting, p. 174]. For more on **piacere** see Systems, note 2, p. 193.

Saying what you don't like

Put **non** in front of the verb and the pronoun:

Non mi piace la fantascienza   *I don't like science fiction*

Asking and saying which things you like best

The key phrases are **quale/i?** *(which?)* **che tipo di?** *(what sort of?)* and **di più** *(best)*:

Quale strumento	ti/Le vi	piace di più?	*Which instrument do you like best?*
Quali cantanti	ti/Le vi	piacciono di più?	*Which singers do you like best?*
Che tipo di film	ti/Le vi	piacciono di più?	*What sort of films do you like best?*

ii) Saying what you like doing

To say what you and others like doing you always use **piace** (with **mi, ci,** etc.) followed by the infinitive of the verb you want:

Cosa	ti Le vi	piace fare?	*What do you like doing?*	Mi piace suonare la chitarra	*I like playing the guitar*
				Ci piace giocare a biliardo	*We like playing billiards*

Patterns 2

Saying what you like

1   Put students into pairs and tell them they are going to practise 'Do you like?/I like'.

2   Write on the board a list of items for which students can express likes and dislikes. Make this into a grid for students to copy by adding columns for words which express varying degrees of like or dislike. e.g.

	sì	no	molto	abba-stanza	poco	per niente
lo sport						
il cinema						
il teatro						
la musica classica						
la musica jazz						
la musica pop						
la musica lirica						
la pizza						
il vino bianco						
il francese						
la moda italiana						
la carne						
gli spaghetti						
le canzoni italiane						
gli uomini sportivi						
le donne ambiziose						
le persone romantiche						
le fotografie in bianco e nero						
i lunghi viaggi in treno						
le auto veloci						
i film americani						
i quadri di Picasso						
i romanzi lunghi						
i compiti difficili						

3   When students have filled in the grid with their own likes and dislikes, they should find a partner. They then try to see how well they know one another, by taking turns to guess the other's likes and dislikes. They score a point for a correct guess.

Saying what you like doing

1   Ask students to think and write about what they like or dislike doing most:

e.g. *Mi piace vivere in città.*
Non mi piace lasciare messaggi telefonici.

2   Give them also the Italian for 'It's great/brilliant/ dreadful/boring', so that they can amplify their expression of likes and dislikes. Discuss also slang phrases.

This point could be the end of the lesson. Revise points covered so far. In the next lesson students will cover the following:

> **Structures:** the past tense
> **Functions:** understanding and leaving written and spoken messages
> **Vocabulary:** general – as chosen by students

Talking about the past

1 Here is a newspaper report of the tragic event which took place on the train your students were on. You may like to write it on the board, or give copies to the students to read.

Il treno Milano-Roma è partito da Milano alle ore 8,50 di sera. A Firenze il signor Poletti è salito, secondo alcuni testimoni, con una grossa valigia. La polizia ha confermato poche ore dopo, che il signor Poletti ha preso il treno da Firenze alle 11,30. Alla stazione di Roma, la polizia ha trovato il corpo senza vita sul pavimento. L'autopsia ha stabilito che la morte è stata causata da strangolamento e che è avvenuta intorno alla mezzanotte.

2 Ask students to guess the meanings of the new words and help them as required.

3 Tell students to write down where they got on and off the train.

4 Ask students to imagine what questions the newspaper reporter asked in order to compile the report.

Saying what others like doing

Gli	piace ballare in discoteca	*He*	*likes dancing at the disco*
Le	piace cantare nel coro	*She*	*likes singing in the choir*
Gli	piace suonare nell'orchestra	*They*	*like playing in the orchestra*

Gli piace means both *he likes* and *they like*.

iii) Talking about the past (2)

To talk about where you and others have been, you normally need verbs which form their past tense with **essere** rather than **avere**. For example, to form the past tense of **essere** itself, you use the present tense of **essere** with the past participle **stato/a** *(been)*.

| Piero, dove | sei stato? | *Where have you been/were you?* |
| Maria, | sei stata? | |

| Sono stato/a | a lezione | *I've been/I was* | *in class* |
| Sono stato/a | in ufficio | | *in the office* |

| Ragazze, dove siete state? | *Girls, where have you been/were you?* |
| Ragazzi, dove siete stati? | *Boys, where have you been/were you?* |

Siamo stati/e in Inghilterra   *We've been to England*

In talking about where you've been, you're also likely to need other verbs which form their past tense with **essere**:

| Sei andato/a | a casa | *You went/have gone* | *home* |
| È tornato/a | | *You, he, she came back* | |

Siamo usciti/e	presto	*We went out/have gone out*	*early*
Siete partiti/e		*You left/have left*	
Sono arrivati/e		*They arrived/have arrived*	

Some of these verbs are irregular, for example **rimanere** and **venire**:

| Sono rimasto/a | a casa ieri | *I stayed at home yesterday* |
| Sono venuto/a | subito | *I came at once* |

The endings of past participles used with the verb **essere** change according to the subject of the verb:

Posso parlare con	Rita? – È uscita	*Can I speak to*	*Rita? She's gone out*
	Piero? – È uscito		*Piero? He's gone out*
	Anna e Renzo? – Sono usciti		*Anna and Renzo? They've gone out*

See Systems, notes 3 i and iii and 4 ii, p. 194 for further explanations.

Patterns 2

iv) Arranging where to meet

To discuss venues, use the verb **incontrarsi** *(to meet)*:

Dove ci incontriamo? *Where shall we meet?*

Ci possiamo incontrare	dietro	il teatro	*We can meet behind*	*the theatre*
		la posta		*the post office*
	davanti	al cinema	*outside*	*the cinema*
		alla stazione		*the station*
	di fronte	al bar	*opposite*	*the bar*
		alla trattoria		*the trattoria*
	accanto	all'albergo	*next to*	*the hotel*
		al ristorante		*the restaurant*

Davanti a literally means *in front of.*

Some expressions of place need **in** or **a**:

Ci incontriamo	in centro/in piazza	*We'll meet*	*in town/in the square*
	a casa mia/tua/sua		*at my/your/his/her house*

And there are many expressions which need **a** combined with the definite article:

all'entrata del cinema	*at the entrance to the cinema*
all'uscita del teatro	*at the exit of the theatre*
all'angolo di via Manin	*on the corner of via Manin*

If you're meeting at someone's house, you need to use **da**, which, when followed by a person, means *at* or *to*. See Unit 5, Systems, note 2 i, p. 97.

Ci incontriamo	da Rita	*We'll meet*	*at Rita's*
	da mio fratello		*my brother's*
	dal mio amico		*my friend's*
	dalla mia amica		*my friend's*
	dai miei amici		*my friends'*
	dalle mie amiche		*my friends'*

Practice 2

Look at the map

You are arranging to meet a friend in a bar car park. He'll be arriving by bus and, as you show him your detailed plan of the town centre, you point out the exact location of the following landmarks:

1 the car park in relation to the bar
2 the bar in relation to the hotel
3 the bar in relation to the church
4 and the bus stop in relation to the hotel

Use the following phrases: **accanto a, dietro, davanti a, di fronte a**.

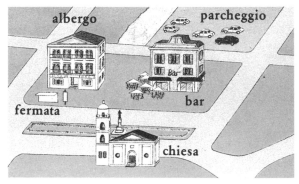

Now try to describe your local town square or similar location.

Arranging where to meet

1 Draw a diagram on the board of a wide open space (station, square, park, etc.). The diagram could look something like this:

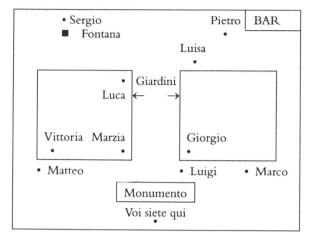

The two large squares could, for example, be identical parts of a larger area (e.g. forecourts of a train station/ departure lounges in an airport/sections of a park with special features).

2 Tell students they have arranged to meet someone somewhere in the area. They don't know the person and from where they are standing they can see several people who could be their person.

3 Here are the descriptions of the positions of all the people in the diagram except one. Who is missing?

a) fra il monumento e il giardino di destra (Luigi)
b) dietro la fontana (Sergio)
c) nel giardino di sinistra in basso a destra (Marzia)
d) fuori del giardino di sinistra in basso a sinistra (Matteo)
e) fuori del giardino di destra in alto a sinistra (Luisa)
f) nel giardino di sinistra in alto a destra (Luca)
g) davanti al bar (Pietro)
h) nel giardino di sinistra in basso a sinistra (Vittoria)
i) nel giardino di destra in basso a sinistra (Giorgio)
Answer: Marco is missing. His position is 'fuori del giardino di destra in basso a destra'.

4 Add a few more names (or letters) and ask students to describe the specific area of the diagram relating to the name.

Practice 2

Dove ci incontriamo?

Aim: to practise the prepositions *a, di, in* + articles

1 Draw on the board a diagram similar to the one in the previous exercise.

2 Change the names of the fixed features and tell the students to describe five to ten different positions in the diagram. (You could perhaps make it a plan of a library or music shop, with students looking for a book or record.)

Messaggio telefonico

Aim: understanding and preparing written and spoken messages

1 Give students a copy of the *Relazione telefonica* below, which can be used in both domestic and business situations, and make sure it is thoroughly understood.

2 Read a message (such as the one below) which you say was left on their answerphone and tell them to fill out the *Relazione telefonica*.

Sono Leonardo Malaguti e vorrei lasciare un messaggio per Laura Crispi. Non posso venire a cena venerdì sera perché devo andare a prendere mio fratello alla stazione. Ti ritelefono domani in giornata. Ora sono le sette di mercoledì sera. Ciao, bacioni.

Relazione telefonica

Per il/la signore/a . . . .

Data . . . .   Ore . . . .

Ha telefonato . . . .

delle società . . . .

e ha lasciato il seguente messaggio . . . .

. . . .

. . . .

. . . .

. . . .

La prega di richiamarlo/a

appena possibile

alle ore . . . .   data . . . .

al seguente numero . . . .   prefisso . . . .

Il ricevente

3 Check answers and discuss as required.

4 Divide your students into groups of four, with each group in turn divided into pairs. Tell each pair to write a message for the second pair on a blank *Relazione telefonica*.

5 Students swap *Relazioni telefoniche* and transform the written message into a spoken one which could be left on an answerphone.

6 They could use a tape recorder to record their messages for added realism.

Allora, ti/vi/gli piace/piacciono, sì o no?

Aim: to practise the use of *piacere*

1 Write the following on the board and tell students to reconstruct the questions which led to these answers.

Sì, gli piacciono i romanzi classici.
No, gli piaccioni i compiti facili.
Sì, le piace andare a passeggio.
Sì, gli piacciono gli articoli sportivi.
Sì, ci piace molto il tennis.
Sì, mi piacciono molto le fragole.
No, sia a Giorgio che a Luca non piace lo sport.
Sì, le piace la frutta matura.
No, non mi piacciono le canzoni di Bob Dylan.
Sì, gli piacciono i fumetti.

2 Check answers and discuss as necessary.

3 Give students a list of things to like and dislike and ask them to go around the class to find someone who likes Bob Dylan but doesn't like Bruce Springsteen, who likes tennis but doesn't like golf, etc. making a note of the person's name.

What did you do with it?

Aim: to practise the past tense

1 Write the following on the board and tell students to complete the questions below using the following verbs in the past tense.

COMPRARE FARE LAVARE VEDERE
METTERE PAGARE PRENDERE MANGIARE
LEGGERE BERE

. . . . *il vino?*
. . . . *la spesa?*
. . . . *la pizza?*
. . . . *il caffè?*
. . . . *il contò?*
. . . . *i piatti?*
. . . . *il film?*
. . . . *il giornale?*
. . . . *l'uva in frigo?*
. . . . *la lettera?*

2 Check answers and discuss as necessary.

When, where and how

Aim: to practise the past tense

1 Write the following on the board and tell students to ask the relevant questions. (Revise interrogatives briefly first.)

e.g. *È andato in vacanza in Marocco.*
Dove è andato in vacanza?

2 To help students, you could first ask a few questions and get them to read the correct answers from the board.

Abbiamo mangiato al ristorante.
Sono andato in campagna la scorsa settimana.
Ho incontrato tre amiche.
Hanno letto l'articolo questa mattina.
Abbiamo ballato per molto tempo.
Ha mangiato con gusto.
Ho telefonato ad un collega di lavoro.

3 Check answers and discuss as necessary.

Missing persons

1 Complete the following sentences with the appropriate direct object pronoun:

. . . . *vedo tutti i giorni.*	*Maria*
Michele . . . . vuole invitare alla sua festa.	*You*
. . . . *voglio salutare prima di partire.*	*You (Signor Frani)*
Hanno detto che . . . . vogliono assumere.	*You and Carlo*
. . . . *devi invitare.*	*Giovanni*
. . . . *vuole invitare se sei d'accordo.*	*Marta*

2 Complete the following sentences with the appropriate indirect object pronoun:

. . . . *voglio telefonare oggi.*	*To Maria*
Marco . . . . vuole chiedere un favore.	*To you*
. . . . *posso prestare la mia macchina.*	*To you (Signor) Frani*
Bisogna mandare . . . . una lettera.	*To you and Carlo*
. . . . *devi consegnare questo pacco.*	*To Giovanni*
. . . . *vuole comprare un regalo.*	*To Marta*

3 Complete the following sentences with the appropriate direct or indirect object pronoun:

. . . . *voglio ringraziare, Valeria, per l'ottima cena.*
. . . . *posso fare una domanda, Signor Monetti, se non sono indiscreto?*
Siete stati molto gentili ragazzi, ... ringrazio molto.
Diana, ... posso chiedere un favore?
I bambini hanno bisogno di aiuto, ... puoi aiutare.
. . . . *telefono in giornata Signor Manca.*

Half-baked

Translate part b) of the following sentences:
a) *Michele vuole invitarmi alla sua festa.*
   b) I must phone him to thank him.
a) *Voglio salutare Sarah prima di partire.*
   b) Can you tell her to call me?
a) *Ci vediamo tutti i giorni.*
   b) But I am not seeing her today.
a) *Devi invitare anche Monica.*
   b) Have you written to her yet?

What do you like?

You are hoping to arrange an outing to a concert or the cinema for your colleagues at work. But what would they like to go to? You start by asking them whether they like a) music and b) films.
e.g. Giulia, ti piace la musica?

1 Your friend Giulia
2 Signora Pacini
3 Anita and Miriam

Now you want them to be more specific. What kind of films or music do they like best?
e.g. Giulia, quali film ti piacciono di più?
or Che tipo di film ti piacciono di più?

Personal tastes

1 Say which you like in each of these three groups:
  a Poetry, novels, biographies
  b Documentaries, horror films, the news (TV/radio)
  c Going to the cinema, to the theatre, to concerts
2 Now say which you like best.
3 Which, if any, of the above do you dislike?
If you are learning in a group, ask each other what you like and dislike. [See Vocabulary, p. 125.]

An invitation   10

Answer the phone and speak to your friend Aldo who's just finished work.

You [Say hello and ask who's speaking.]
Aldo Ciao, sono io, Aldo.
You [Say hello and ask him how he is.]
Aldo Benissimo. Ho finito di lavorare per oggi. Senti, andiamo a cena stasera?
You [Say yes, you'd like to.]
Aldo Bene. Che cosa ti piace di più: la cucina italiana o la cucina francese?
You [Say you like Italian food.]
Aldo D'accordo. Andiamo al Cavallo Bianco, allora?
You [Say fine and ask him where you can meet.]
Aldo Ci possiamo incontrare in piazza alle 9.30 davanti al bar. Va bene?
You [You didn't get that. Ask, which bar?]
Aldo Il bar di fronte alla banca. Hai capito dove?
You [Ah, outside the bar opposite the bank . . . Say yes I see.]
Aldo D'accordo, a più tardi, allora. Ciao.

Now practise saying where you went yesterday.

Matchmaking

Rosanna and Susanna are looking for an Italian pen-friend. They've had some letters sent to them through a pen-friend agency and have narrowed the choice to Dino and Lino. Susanna is a bit of a wine buff and she likes cooking and listening to music into the early hours. Rosanna is a sporty type. She is a health freak but enjoys life in the fast lane. Who do they each choose?

Dino

Mi piace molto la musica rock e anche il jazz: suono il pianoforte e la chitarra. Quando ho tempo mi piace cucinare e invitare gli amici a cena. Lo trovo molto rilassante, e stiamo insieme fino a tardi. Qualchevolta gioco a tennis la domenica, ma gli unici sport che mi piacciono veramente sono il calcio e l'automobilismo... in televisione!

Lino

Mi piacciono i cantanti rock e vado spesso ai concerti. Mi piace soprattutto lo sport e stare all'aria aperta. Mi tengo sempre in forma: vado in palestra due volte alla settimana. Sono vegetariano e anche astemio, ma mi piace andare al ristorante! Mi piacciono tanto le macchine veloci e ho una Ferrari bellissima, un regalo di mio padre.

Vocabulary

Music

la musica classica	classical music
la musica leggera	light music
la musica pop	pop music
il jazz	jazz
la lirica	opera
il canto	singing, song
la canzone	song
il concerto	concert
la prova	rehearsal
la danza	dance, dancing
un ballo	a dance
il balletto	ballet
il complesso	group, band
il coro	choir
l'orchestra	orchestra
la sinfonia	symphony

il violino

Instruments

l'arpa	harp
la batteria	drums
la chitarra	guitar
il clarinetto	clarinet
il corno	horn
il contrab- basso	double bass
il fagotto	bassoon
il flauto	flute
l'oboe *(m)*	oboe
l'organo	organ
il pianoforte	piano
il sassofono	saxophone
la tromba	trumpet
il trombone	trombone
la viola	viola
il violino	violin
il violoncello	cello

Arts and mass media

l'arte *(f)*	art
la mostra	exhibition
lo spettacolo	show,
il teatro	theatre
la commedia	play, comedy
la tragedia	tragedy
la trama	plot
il cinema	cinema
il film giallo	detective film
il film ...	
comico	comedy
poliziesco	thriller
dell'orrore	horror film
il cartone animato	[film] cartoon
la televisione	television
il canale	channel
il programma	programme
il documen- tario	documentary
il telegiornale	TV news
il telefilm	TV film
la telenovela	'soap'
lo sceneggiato	TV serial
la puntata	episode
la radio	radio
il giornale radio	radio news
la letteratura	literature
l'articolo	article
la biografia	biography
la fanta- scienza	science fiction
il romanzo	novel
il foto- romanzc	photoromance
il fumetto	cartoon comic
il giallo	detective story
la poesia	poetry
la rivista	magazine

lo scultore	

People

l'artista	artist
l'attore	actor
l'attrice	actress
l'autore	author
il/la cantante	singer
il cantautore	singer composer
il composi- tore	composer
il conduttore	TV presenter (m)
la conduttrice	TV presenter (f)
il direttore/ la direttrice d'orchestra	conductor (m) conductor (f)
il/la musicista	musician
il/la pianista	pianist
il/la regista	producer
la star	star (m or f)
il soprano	soprano
lo scrittore	writer
la scrittrice	writer (f)
lo scultore	sculptor (m)
la scultrice	sculptor (f)
il/la violinista	violinist

Verbs

ballare	to dance
cantare	to sing
recitare	to act
suonare	to play [music]

Idioms

dare fastidio a	to bother, to be a nuisance to
dare una mano a	to give a hand, to help
dare un passaggio a	to give a lift to
fare una telefonata	to make a phone call
fare il numero	to dial

Vocabulary

1   Tell students you are going to read a short story on a particular topic.

2   Select ten to fifteen words and write them on the board in the order in which they appear in the text.

3   Tell students to work out what the story might be from the words given. Ask them to compare notes in pairs and then write the storyline.

4   Ask students to read aloud what they have written.

5   Make copies of the text and read it through with the students.

Here is an example:

colleghi	*vicini di casa*	*macchina*
Luigi	*bicicletta*	*Franco*
un passaggio	*rallentare e poi fermarsi*	*molto traffico*
ha proseguito	*10 minuti dopo*	*stanco e nervoso*

Franco e Luigi sono colleghi di lavoro e vicini di casa. Franco, che va al lavoro in macchina, esce di casa tutti i giorni alle otto del mattino e arriva in ufficio quaranta minuti dopo. Luigi invece prende l'autobus alle otto e mezzo e arriva in ufficio alle nove. Lunedì scorso Luigi ha deciso di andare al lavoro in bicicletta ed è uscito di casa anche lui alle otto. Franco gli ha offerto un passaggio ma Luigi ha preferito andare in bicicletta. 'Come vuoi!' gli ha detto Franco, e poi ha aggiunto: 'Dieci chilometri sono tanti!' Sono partiti nello stesso momento ma dopo qualche chilometro Franco ha dovuto rallentare e poi fermarsi perché a quell'ora c'è sempre molto traffico. Luigi invece ha proseguito senza fermarsi ed è arrivato in ufficio di buon'ora. Franco invece è arrivato dieci minuti dopo di lui, già stanco e nervoso.

Troubleshooting

Review

Here is a checklist of the main points learned in this unit.
For each point, ask the students to supply one or more
examples by asking specific questions.

talking in the past tense
asking for information
asking someone to do something
arranging a meeting
talking about likes and dislikes
understanding and writing messages
talking on the telephone
talking about music, songs and instruments

Troubleshooting

La: you   Le: to you

By now you will know that the subject pronoun **Lei** is used for the formal *you* as well as for *she*. Similarly the object pronouns **La** and **Le** mean *you* and *to you* as well as *her*. When **la** and **le** mean *you,* they are often written with a capital letter.

You	*To you*
La ringrazio *Thank you [lit. I thank you]*	**Le** presento mio marito *Let me introduce my husband to you*
La disturbo? *Am I interrupting? [lit. do I interrupt you?]*	**Le** posso offrire qualcosa? *Can I offer you anything? [lit. offer to you]*
La chiamo domani *I'll call you tomorrow*	**Le** telefono domani *I'll telephone [to] you tomorrow*

Le is used with verbs which require the preposition **a** before a person. Try and learn some of the following:

chiedere a *to ask*	dare a *to give*
dire a *to tell, to say to*	mandare a *to send to*
offrire a *to offer (to)*	parlare a *to speak to*
portare a *to bring (to)*	presentare a *to introduce to*
prestare a *to lend (to)*	regalare a *to give [as a present]*
restituire a *to give back (to)*	rispondere a *to reply (to)*
spiegare a *to explain to*	telefonare a *to telephone (to)*

Lo strumento   Il mio strumento

Remember that the article you use also depends on the initial spelling of the following word, not just on its gender and number. If an adjective precedes the noun this may change the article:

il treno	**il** ragazzo	**lo** specchio	l'apparta-mento
l'ultimo treno	**lo** stesso ragazzo	**il** tuo specchio	**il** nuovo app-partamento
l'idea	**i** ragazzi	**gli** amici	
la buona idea	**gli** altri ragazzi	**i** miei amici	

The changes also apply to the indefinite article:

un'idea	**un** ragazzo	**uno** specchio
una buona idea	**uno** stupido ragazzo	**un** vecchio specchio

A casa nostra

I Trulli di Puglia

Puglia

Bari •

Alberobello •

• Rionero

Matera •

B a s i l i c a t a

• Potenza

In this unit you'll find out more about telephone language, making plans and checking and confirming arrangements. You'll also learn to talk about houses and places you know.

The saying that an Englishman's home is his castle has no equivalent in Italian. Yet the home is very important in Italy. Despite rapid social change it remains the centre of the family: only 15 per cent of under-25s live away from home. In part this is due to the shortage and expense of rented accommodation, but it is also a question of choice. In the post-1968 shake-up of society, it is possible to live at home and enjoy personal freedom. Italians are among the world's top savers (22 per cent of disposable income). This may in part explain why there are many who choose to invest a lot of money in their homes. In the two-year period 1990–91, for example, 24 per cent of home-owners totally refurbished their bedroom and sitting-room; 19 per cent did the same to their kitchen and nearly 15 per cent acquired a new bathroom. However, what Italians change far less frequently is the home itself, which tends to be seen as a lifelong investment. A surprising 71 per cent of Italian houses are owner-occupied, despite the fact that buying a house is a costly affair, involving a deposit of up to a third of the total price and a mortgage – **un mutuo** – with interest rates not all that different from those of Britain. Italians take great pride in their home, which becomes, if not their castle, at least their **'palazzo'**.

A casa nostra

To introduce the topic of house and home in class, you may like to talk about the process of house buying in Italy. The following is intended to help you plan a few minutes of 'free talking' around the topic of this unit. To help students understand, you may like to use a mixture of Italian and English, but first pick out the difficult 'technical' words, write them on the board and elicit/explain the meanings.

According to Italian law, property is of two kinds: *beni mobili* – personal property and belongings – and *beni immobili* – land and buildings. The legal procedure for obtaining *il possesso del bene immobile* is fairly complex, but the crucial part, *il contratto di compravendita*, can be carried out without the expertise of a solicitor. Anyone can actually draw up *il contratto preliminare* or *compromesso* and this is often done by *l'agenzia di compravendita*. On signing the *compromesso*, the vendor undertakes to sell the property and the purchaser commits himself to buying it; a non-refundable deposit is paid by the purchaser at the time of signing. The fee to the estate agent is paid by both the buyer and the seller.

To complete the process, the assistance of a *notaio* is required, to register the deed of purchase with the competent authority: *l'ufficio del catasto urbano o rurale*. The notary is a solicitor who specialises mainly in conveyancing and inheritance, and because Italian law does not consider the procedure of house buying to involve a conflict of interests, there is no need for two *notai*. The official document on which you record the purchase in the *catasto* is called *il rogito notarile*. If the buyer or the seller cannot be present in person to sign the *rogito notarile* before the notary, they can be represented by someone else, as long as they are equipped with *una procura*, power of proxy, which has been pre-signed in front of another public official.

Italians regard house buying as a secure investment but not a speculative one. Buying a house is a big financial decision, because the house purchased is likely to be the one you live in for the rest of your life. The law does not provide for leaseholds, so the house or apartment Italians buy is passed onto their children, who, in turn, pass it on to their children. Only after all legal formalities have been concluded can the property become *la casa dolce casa* which Italians are proud not so much to possess but to furnish in style.

Video corner

Che regione?
Aim: to stimulate interest in the different Italian regions and their physical characteristics
Video sequence: opening sequence

1 Tell students that the opening sequence of the video (which they are going to watch with the volume turned down) shows the scenery typical of one Italian region.

2 Play the sequence, making sure you cover the bottom part of the screen, and ask students to guess which region it is . . . *Potrebbe essere . . .*

3 Engage students in discussion: *Non è il Piemonte perché c'è il mare . . .*

Che cosa c'è in casa?
Aim: vocabulary building around the topic of house furniture
Video sequence: From Lucia showing Anna her room to Peppe showing Anna the bathroom

1 Tell students they are going to see three different rooms. Ask them to jot down the names of the pieces of furniture they see.

2 Students compare and combine lists with two or three others.

3 Discuss as required.

A colazione
a) **Aim:** vocabulary building through active viewing
Video sequence: *Anna, Peppe e Lucia a colazione*

1 Tell students they are going to watch a sequence in which Anna, Peppe and Lucia are planning the day ahead. Ask them to concentrate on what they see.

2 Write the following questions on the board:

Che cosa c'è sul tavolo?
Dove sono i cuscini?
Di che colore sono gli orecchini di Lucia?
Che cosa si vede dietro Peppe?
Quanti quadri si vedono in tutto?

3 Ask students to answer the questions as they watch the sequence.

b) **Aim:** vocabulary building/revision of structures
Video sequence: *Anna, Peppe e Lucia a colazione*

1 Tell students they are going to watch the same sequence in which Anna, Peppe and Lucia are planning the day ahead.

2 Write some verbs on the board (some examples are given below) and discuss the meanings with students.

3 Students work out which of the verbs apply to what Anna, Lucia and Peppe do over breakfast:

cantare, bere, telefonare, disegnare, mangiare, litigare, parlare, fumare, mettersi d'accordo, ascoltare musica, cucinare, scrivere, pulire, sedersi

4   Ask students to describe in 50 words what Anna, Peppe and Lucia do over breakfast.

Qual è il contesto?

Aim: to stimulate discussion/writing/reading
Video sequence: final sequence in which three people (inset in boxes on screen) answer general questions

1   Play the sequence and ask students to tell you the questions each of the three people were asked, and the answers they gave (they will have to deduce the last question).

2   Put students into small groups and ask them to work out several new questions and answers for each of the three people.

3   Students role play their suggested mini-interview. (If you have access to a video camera you could ask your students to do the role play in front of the camera with as much professionalism as they can muster.)

Interactions

> **Structures:** impersonal *si/fare* + infinitive
> **Functions:** making arrangements on the phone/making suggestions/accepting or declining/asking and saying how things work
> **Vocabulary:** useful telephone phrases/house and home

Help-phrases and instructions

Potrebbe essere
Sono (Non sono) d'accordo
Sono (Non sono) completamente d'accordo
Sei d'accordo?
Dipende

Interaction 1 (406)

1   *Anna abita a Roma. Peppe e Lucia vogliono invitarla a passare qualche giorno a Rionero in Basilicata. Peppe le telefona.* Where has Anna gone, and what's her number?

2   Play the cassette/CD as required.

3   Tell students to re-write the telephone conversation, changing all that is necessary to imply that the two people in the conversation are:
a) female and old friends
b) female and do not know each other

4   Display the two correctly amended versions of the dialogue on the board.

Interaction 2 (429)

1   *Peppe telefona ad Anna in ufficio ma trova l'interno occupato.*

2   Write the questions on the board.
Has Anna ever been to Basilicata?
What date does she say she can go?
Remind the students that Peppe telephones Anna to invite her to visit Lucia and himself in their new apartment.

3   Ask the students to work in pairs and write a few lines they think would be in the dialogue, possibly on a transparency if you have an OHP.

4   Show what each pair of students has written on the OHP and ask everyone to comment.

5   Play the Interaction and discuss any questions.

Interactions

1   ⌷⌷ ◉ 12

Anna lives and works in Rome. Her friends Peppe and Lucia Leone want her to spend a few days at Rionero, in one of Italy's least known regions, the Basilicata.

First time round

un attimo	*hold on*	
ce l'ha?	*have you got [it]?*	Peppe tries to ring
l'interno	*extension*	Anna at her home.

Where has Anna gone, and what's her number?

Rudy   Pronto, chi parla?
Peppe   Buongiorno, sono Peppe. Chiamo da Rionero. **C'è Anna per caso?**
Rudy   No, Anna non c'è. Io sono il fratello. È uscita molto presto, questa mattina, per andare in ufficio. Se vuole, Le do il suo numero.
Peppe   Sì. Grazie. Molto gentile.
Rudy   Un attimo. Il prefisso di Roma, ce l'ha?
Peppe   Sì, sì. Zero sei, vero?
Rudy   Esatto: il numero è: tre tre quattro otto, **interno quattro tre due.**
Peppe   Allora, ha detto: **trentatrè, quarantotto,** interno quattro tre due. Grazie, buongiorno.
Rudy   Buongiorno. Prego.

molto gentile	*that's very kind of you*
esatto	*that's right*
ha detto	*you said*
prego	*that's all right, don't mention it*

Key phrases

c'è Anna per caso?	*is Anna in by any chance?*
interno 432	*extension four three two*
trentatrè, quarantotto	*three three four eight*

2   ⌷⌷ ◉ 13

Peppe next has a go at contacting Anna at work.

First time round

rimanere in linea	*to hold the line*	He talks
abbiamo comprato	*we've bought*	first to the
c'è posto	*there's room*	operator.

a Has Anna ever been to the Basilicata?
b What date does she say she can go?

Peppe   (to operator) Ah, l'interno **è occupato?** Sì, preferisco rimanere in linea.
Anna   Pronto, chi parla?
Peppe   Ciao Anna, sono Peppe. Come stai?
Anna   Ciao Peppe. Mah! insomma . . . non c'è male. E tu?
Peppe   Io sto benissimo e anche Lucia. Sai, abbiamo trovato un bellissimo appartamento in Basilicata e lo abbiamo comprato.
Anna   Che bello! Non conosco la Basilicata. Non ci sono mai stata.
Peppe   Allora, **perché non vieni a trovarci?** C'è posto nell'appartamento.
Anna   Eh, **mi dispiace, ma non posso.** Ho troppo lavoro.
Peppe   Ma dai, lavori troppo. Perché non vieni a trovarci per un paio di giorni?
Anna   Posso venire **verso il venti aprile.**
Peppe   Il venti aprile. Ma certo. Ti veniamo a prendere alla stazione di Rionero.
Anna   D'accordo. **Ci vediamo il** venti sera allora?
Peppe   OK, **a presto.** Ciao.
Anna   Ciao, Peppe.

non ci sono mai stata	*I've never been there*
ma dai	*go on*

Key phrases

è occupato?	*is it engaged?*
perché non vieni a trovarci?	*why don't you come and visit us?*
mi dispiace ma non posso	*I'm sorry, I can't*
verso il venti aprile	*about 20 April*
ci vediamo il . . .	*see you on . . .*
a presto	*see you soon*

Months of the year   🔲 📀 13

Listen to the months and repeat them after the speaker.

3   🔲 📀 14

On the evening of 20 April Anna arrives in Rionero.

First time round

i cassetti	*drawers*
sistemare	*to put, arrange*
la roba	*things, stuff*

She is shown to her room by Lucia.

a How do you turn on the television?
b What time are they having supper?

Lucia	Allora Anna, questa è la tua camera.
Anna	Ah, simpatica! Posso usare i cassetti?
Lucia	Certo! Puoi sistemare qui la tua roba. C'è la televisione.
Anna	E **come si accende?**
Lucia	È semplice. C'è il telecomando.
Anna	Ah, ecco il telecomando. Bene. Ah . . . che bella camera luminosa!
Lucia	Sono contenta. Senti, noi ceniamo alle nove stasera. **Ti va bene?**
Anna	Va benissimo! Grazie.
Lucia	**D'accordo. Ci vediamo dopo.**
Anna	**A più tardi.** Ciao.

ah, simpatica!   *oh, it's lovely! [lit. friendly]*

Key phrases

come si accende?	*how do you turn it on?*
ti va bene?	*does that suit you?*
d'accordo	*agreed, all right*
ci vediamo dopo	*see you in a while [lit. afterwards]*
a più tardi	*see you later*

4   🔲 📀 15

Later, in the well-equipped, modern kitchen, Lucia shows Anna the various appliances and how some of them work.

First time round

i fornelli	*gas burners*
girare	*to turn*
schiacciare	*to press*
il frigorifero	*fridge*

a How do you light the cooker?
b Can Anna help herself to what's in the fridge?

Lucia	Vieni, Anna. **Ti faccio vedere** il resto della casa.
Anna	Eh, sì, è molto utile se domani non ci siete.
Lucia	Certo. Questo è il piano di cottura, con quattro fornelli.
Anna	E come funzionano, i fornelli?
Lucia	Molto semplice, guarda. **Basta** girare, e schiacciare.
Anna	Ah, ecco!
Lucia	Questa, invece, è la lavastoviglie . . . Così, puoi aprire l'acqua.
Anna	E il frigorifero?
Lucia	Da questa parte. Vieni. Ecco. Se hai bisogno di qualcosa, serviti pure.
Anna	Grazie. Ma . . . la lavatrice, non c'è in cucina?
Lucia	No. La lavatrice è nel bagno di servizio. Adesso, Anna, io preparo un buon caffè. Peppe intanto ti fa vedere il bagno. Bene?
Anna	D'accordo. Torno subito. Ciao!

la lavastoviglie	*dishwasher*
la lavatrice	*washing machine*
se domani non ci siete	*if you're not there tomorrow*
il piano di cottura	*the hob*
da questa parte	*this way*
serviti pure	*do help yourself*
il bagno di servizio	*cloakroom/spare bathroom*

Key phrases

| **ti faccio vedere . . .** | *I'll show you* |
| **basta . . .** | *all you have to do is . . .* |

Interaction 3/4 (474/492)

1 *Anna non è mai stata a casa di Peppe e Lucia in passato. Peppe e Lucia le fanno vedere varie cose.*

2 Tell students they are going to listen to Peppe and Lucia showing Anna around the new house. Ask them to compile a list of pieces of furniture which may be found in each of the two rooms (three if you use the video).

3 Students compare and combine lists with the person sitting next to them.

4 Each pair tells you what is in their combined list. Write all the words on the board.

5 Remind students of the questions they have to answer:
How do you turn on the television?
What time are they having supper? (Interaction 3)
How do you light the cooker?
Can Anna help herself to what's in the fridge? (Interaction 4)

6 Play the cassette/CD as required and ask further questions:
Which is the first room?
What is the room like?
Where is the washing machine?
What does Lucia suggest? (Interaction 4)

This point could be the end of the lesson. Revise the points covered so far. In the next lesson students will cover the following:

> **Structures:** going over the patterns for impersonal *si/fare* + infinitive
> **Functions:** making arrangements on the phone/making suggestions/accepting or declining/asking and saying how things work
> **Vocabulary:** dates/on the telephone/useful numbers/house and home/general vocabulary, according to the situations you or your students choose

Patterns 1

Making a phone call

1 Tell students to imagine having to make a call to a very important person (the line is bound to be engaged and they are bound to be asked to hold on).

2 Ask students to choose a partner and prepare a telephone conversation together. Encourage students to use the functional words given and to build up a story around the telephone call.

Patterns I

i) Making a phone call

Asking if someone is in

Use **c'è?** [lit. *Is there?*]

C'è	Anna	per caso?	Is	Anna	in by any chance?
	la Signora Parisi			*Signora Parisi*	
	il dottor Rossi			*Doctor Rossi*	

Asking if the line is engaged

The word for *engaged* is **occupato**:

È occupato? *Is it engaged?*
La linea è occupata? *Is the line engaged?*

Asking someone to hold on

Just use the word for *moment*:

un attimo *hold on, one moment*

To ask whether someone wants to hold on you say:

Preferisce	rimanere in linea?	*Do you prefer*	*to hold the line?*
Vuole		*Do you want*	

Giving a phone number

The code – **prefisso** – and extension – **interno** – are generally said digit by digit, as in English:

Il prefisso	di Roma è zero sei
	per l'Inghilterra è zero zero quattro quattro

L'interno è quattro tre due

But when you give the actual phone number you group the digits in pairs:

Qual è il suo numero di telefono? *What's your phone number?*
Il mio numero è trentatrè quarantotto uno *My number is 33481*

If the number is three digits you generally say it as one number:

Per le ultime notizie RAI, si chiama il centonovanta *For the latest RAI news bulletin you call 190*

Patterns I

ii) Making plans and arrangements

Inviting someone to come and visit you

The verb to use is **venire a trovare** (**visitare** is only for places). The pronouns, **mi** *(me)* **ci** *(us)*, etc. go in front or on the end. See Systems, note 2 iii, p. 197.

Perché non	vieni/e a trovarmi?		Why don't	you come and visit me?
	mi vieni/e a trovare?			
	venite a trovarci?			you come and visit us?
	ci venite a trovare?			

Sì, va bene	*Yes, fine*			D'accordo	*All right*		
vengo	a trovarti	presto		ti	vengo a trovare	presto	*I'll come and visit you soon*
	a trovarLa			La			
	a trovarvi			vi			

Checking suitability and inclination

For making arrangements and giving invitations the following phrases may be useful:

Ti	va bene	cenare	fuori?	*Does it suit you to*	*have supper/eat/have lunch*	*out?*
Le		mangiare				
Vi		pranzare				

Ti	va di	andare	domani?	*Do you feel like*	*going/coming/leaving*	*tomorrow?*
Le		venire				
Vi		partire				

Agreeing and accepting

If you're emphasising that an arrangement suits you, you can say:

per me va bene	*that's fine by me*
mi va bene	*that suits me*

And if you are agreeing, you can say:

d'accordo	*agreed, all right*
va bene	*fine, all right*

See also Unit 6 Patterns 1 iii, p. 115.

Setting a date

Italians use cardinal numbers for the date except for the first of the month:

Quando puoi/può venire?		*When can you come?*	
Posso venire	il primo gennaio	*I can come*	*on the first of January*
	il cinque febbraio		*on the fifth of February*
	l'otto marzo		*on the eighth of March*
	l'undici aprile		*on the eleventh of April*

The months are listed on Reference p. 241 and you have heard them on the cassette/CD.

Making plans and arrangements

1   Ask students to write out a different invitation for each of half a dozen of their fellow students (these may range from an invitation to a night club or the cinema to a round-the-world trip).

2   Call out a student's name and ask the other students to read out their invitation to him/her.

3   Write on the board the functional language for agreeing, accepting and confirming an arrangement.

4   Ask students to read some of their invitations to you. Using the functional language, accept or decline a few and then encourage students to accept or decline one another's invitations in the same way.

Variation: ask students to think of one exciting event (a visit to another country, dinner with a celebrity, etc.) and one excruciatingly dull (a minor sporting event, or a visit to a boring town, perhaps). They can then invite other students who accept or decline with varying degrees of enthusiasm.

Setting a date

a) Revise months and dates by asking everyone their dates of birth and writing them on the board.

b) Obtain a list of important dates in the Italian calendar (diaries usually list these in the front pages). Make copies and give them to students, briefly discussing their significance.

1   Tell students they are all going to meet each other in the following 12 months.

2   Students go round the class arranging the dates on which they are going to meet. Tell them to list each meeting (not more than one a day).

3   Check answers by asking students at random who they are meeting and when.

Declining an invitation

Declining an invitation has a different cultural significance in Italian. Invitations may be offered or declined more than once and it is perhaps more polite to decline the first invitation sometimes. For example:

Vieni con noi?
No grazie, ho da fare.
Dai perché non vieni con noi?
Davvero non posso, devo finire un lavoretto.
Puoi finirlo più tardi. Eh dai, su vieni!!
Eh va bene, mi hai convinto.

Being hospitable: showing people round

1 Ask students to think of the literal meaning of *fare vedere* and discuss with them how to use *fare* + infinitive. Here are some examples. Ask students to think of the meaning of the following verbs on their own and then when preceded by *fare*:

osservare	*sapere*	*presentare*
entrare	*passare*	*funzionare*
venire	*tacere*	*avere*
capire	*arrabbiare*	*fare*
sentire	*provare*	*odorare*

Asking and saying how things work

1 *Basta* followed by a list of infinitives can also be used to explain simple procedures:

e.g. *Come si fa una macedonia di frutta?*
Basta
   pulire o sbucciare quattro o cinque tipi di frutta;
   tagliare la frutta a pezzi;
   mettere tutto in una terrina;
   aggiungere un po' di liquore (zucchero e panna a piacere).

2 Prepare a list of tasks:

telefonare da una cabina pubblica
controllare il livello dell'olio in un automobile
spedire un fax
prenotare la sveglia telefonica
spedire una lettera raccomandata espresso
mandare un mazzo di fiori ad una persona lontana
fare l'abbonamento per usare mezzi di trasporto pubblici

3 Give a pair or group of students a task on a slip of paper that the others don't see.

4 Each pair or group then works out the necessary steps for carrying out their task. (Give students help by supplying some extra vocabulary for each task.)

5 Check answers and discuss as necessary. Get each group to read out their answers to the class. The other groups then guess which task is being undertaken.

6 Give students individual tasks for homework based on their interests.

These homework exercises could become small presentations in the next class lesson if you give an OHP transparency to students who volunteer to do them.

Idiomatic point

Basta on its own or followed by *così*, is used to say 'that's enough', for example if someone is pouring wine into your glass.

You also use *basta* if you are doing the pouring:

Dimmi tu basta literally, 'tell me enough' – i.e. 'say when'.

Confirming an arrangement

If you're confirming or summing up an arrangement, use **ci vediamo** or simply **a**:

Allora,	sabato sera	*Right,*	*on Saturday evening*
ci vediamo	il venti aprile	*see you*	*on 20 April*
	la settimana prossima		*next week*

A	sabato sera	allora	*See you*	*on Saturday evening*	*then*
Al	venti aprile			*on 20 April*	
Alla	settimana prossima			*next week*	

Declining an invitation

The key phrase is **mi dispiace**, from the verb **dispiacere** *(to mind, to be sorry)* [see Systems, note 4, p. 198].

| Mi dispiace, non posso | *I'm sorry, I can't* |
| Ci dispiace, non possiamo | *We're sorry, we can't* |

If you want to give a reason you could say:

Ho da fare	*I've got a lot to do*
Sono impegnato/a	*I'm busy*
Ho un altro impegno	*I've got another engagement*

iii) Being hospitable: showing people round

Use the verb **far vedere a** *(to show)*. [See Systems, note 3 ii, p. 198.]

Ti	faccio vedere	la camera	*I'll show you*	*the bedroom*
Le		la cucina		*kitchen*
Vi		il soggiorno		*living-room*

iv) Asking and saying how things work

You need the verb **funzionare** *(to work)*.

Come funziona	il riscaldamento	*How does*	*the heating*	*work?*
	il ferro da stiro		*the iron*	
	la lavatrice		*the washing machine*	

The simplest explanation involves the verb **bastare** *(to be enough)*. Literally you say, *it is enough to.*

Basta	girare	*All you have to do is*	*turn*
	schiacciare/premere		*press*
	attaccare/staccare		*plug in/unplug*
	spingere/tirare		*push/pull*

Another way to find out how things work is to use the impersonal **si** *(one)* with a verb:

Come si	accende la luce?	*How does one/do you*	*turn on the light*
	spegne lo scaldabagno?		*turn off the water heater?*
	apre il rubinetto?		*turn on the tap?*
	apre il portone?		*open the front door?*
	chiude la porta a chiave?		*lock the door?*

Practice I

SIP service

Here are three services provided by SIP, the Italian telephone service. Try to understand the general meaning and consult the Lexis only if you have to.

1

110
Segreteria telefonica

NOTIZIE VARIE

Il servizio fornisce informazioni riguardanti: orari delle funzioni religiose; orari di musei e gallerie; ubicazione strade; itinerari autofilotranviari.
Il servizio dà luogo ad un addebito pari a cinque scatti.

dà luogo ad un addebito   *is subject to a charge*
pari a cinque scatti   *equivalent to five units.*

Can you pick out two or three of the services provided?

2

Informazioni elenco abbonati **12**

Il servizio fornisce gratuitamente:
● i numeri telefonici di nuovi abbonati non ancora compresi negli elenchi ufficiali
● l'orario dei posti telefonici pubblici.
Il servizio fornisce anche (con addebito pari a tre scatti per ogni singola richiesta):
● i numeri telefonici di abbonati già compresi negli elenchi ufficiali
● gli indirizzi ed i numeri civici degli abbonati
● i nominativi di abbonati dei quali sia noto il numero telefonico.

non ... ancora   *not yet*
compreso   *included*
nominativi = nomi

a Do you have to pay for directory enquiries if the subscriber is not in the phone book?
b Name one service you have to pay for: how much is the charge?

3

Informazioni interurbane e internazionali

Informazioni gratuite su:
● tariffe e relativi orari di applicazione
● indicativi (prefissi) nazionali e di Stati Esteri
● elenco abbonati esteri.

Per informazioni riferite al servizio interurbano   **175**
Per informazioni riferite al servizio internazionale europeo e del Bacino del Mediterraneo   **176**
Per informazioni relative al servizio intercontinentale   **170**
N.B. Per ulteriori informazioni vedere pagg 12, 15 e 17.

a What are the basic three services offered?
b For an international enquiry, what number should you ring?

Practice 1

Quale casa o appartamento?

Aim: discussion and vocabulary building

1 Tell students to imagine they are going to work in Italy for six months and the company they are working for has asked them to list their priorities as far as accommodation is concerned. The whole family is going to live there – mother, father, two children – including a three-year-old mongrel which is inseparable from your children.

2 Write on the board the following words and phrases which can be found in adverts for houses for rent or sale. Ask students to guess their meanings and help them if necessary.

terrazzo e giardino pensile
zona residenziale
stato di manutenzione buono e affitto alquanto alto
stato di manutenzione mediocre e affitto a buon mercato
cinque stanze + servizi e affitto alquanto alto
tre stanze + servizi e affitto a buon mercato
cucina attrezzata di tutto
citofono e porta blindata
casa d'epoca
doppi servizi
piscina e sauna
centrale
giardino
garage
balcone
cantina

3 From now on only Italian should be spoken. Make it absolutely clear that it is forbidden to utter a word in English throughout the rest of this activity.

4 Students have three minutes to write a priority number next to each item.

5 They then have a further three minutes to agree, in pairs, a common order of priority. (Go round checking that everyone is speaking Italian.)

6 Give students a further three minutes to discuss priorities again, this time in groups of four.

7 Carry on forming bigger groups until the class is divided into just two groups.

8 The two groups are bound to have different priorities. Ask one group to say which feature they have chosen first and then ask the second group to say whether or not they agree. If they do, carry on until you find a disagreement and then engage the two groups in discussion by asking them to justify their choices.

9 Don't take sides but be positive about anything any student might say. This will encourage someone from the other group to come back to add to the discussion. Encourage less talkative students to join in the discussion by calling out their name and giving them the opportunity to speak first. Push students to explain what their choices depend on.

Estate agent

1 Cut out pictures of houses and apartments from Italian magazines. In pairs, students take turns to play the part of an estate agent, who describes the place, and the client, who asks questions.

For written practice, ask students to imagine they are exchanging homes with an Italian family for the summer. Tell them to write a brief description of their house/flat, describing what mod. cons they have and in which rooms.

Che numero è necessario fare per ...?

Aim: writing numbers/vocabulary building

1 Write on the board the following list of public services and utilities:

Acquedotto segnalazione guasti
Aeroporto
Automobile Club d'Italia
Carabinieri
Elettricità
Ferrovie dello Stato
Guardia medica permanente
Gas
Municipio
Polizia
Poste e telecomunicazioni
Pronto soccorso ambulanze
SIP segnalazione guasti
Vigili del fuoco
Vigili urbani

2 Ask students to guess the meanings and help them if necessary.

3 Call out, at random, the phone number of each service and tell students to write them down. (Prepare three-digit numbers which you say in full, e.g. *centotredici – carabinieri*.)

With a telephone directory

1 If you can get hold of an Italian telephone directory, make a copy of the 'useful numbers' section. Separate the name and number of the service from the explanation of what the service provides.

2 Give each student the name and number of one service and the explanation of another.

3 Tell students to go round the class matching numbers and explanations.

This point could be the end of the lesson. Revise the points covered so far. In the next lesson students will cover the following:

Structures: *mi* + *potere* + infinitive/*ci* as an adverb of place
Functions: making/discussing plans and suggestions
Vocabulary: house and home/*conoscere, compreso*, etc.

Festivities   16

Listen to the tape and give the date of the following festivities in Italian.

1 Il giorno di Natale – Christmas Day.
2 L'Epifania – Twelfth Night.
3 La Festa dei Lavoratori – May Day.
4 Il pesce d'aprile – April Fool's Day.
5 Ferragosto – the Assumption of the Virgin Mary, – equivalent to our midsummer bank holiday.
6 Il tuo compleanno – when is your birthday?

Refresh your memory

Listen again to Interaction 2. Answer the questions in Italian. Don't refer to the written text but replay as often as you need to.

1 How does Peppe ask if the extension's engaged?
2 How does Anna say she doesn't know the Basilicata?
3 How does she say she's never been there?
4 How does Peppe say, 'Why don't you come and visit us?'
5 How many words and phrases conveying agreement can you pick out?

Hotel de luxe

You've booked into an expensive hotel but unfortunately nothing seems to work. You've called the manager to your room to sort things out.

Ask how the following work:

a the TV
c the iron
d the phone
e the heating

It's all a bit confusing! Here in the wrong order are the replies. Can you match them up with the right question?

1 Basta alzare il ricevitore e fare lo zero.
2 Basta aprire il rubinetto del termosifone!
3 Basta premere qui. C'è un pulsante rosso sulla destra dello schermo.
4 Basta attaccare qui: c'è una presa accanto al letto.

Party time   16

It's Maurizio's birthday and he has left you an invitation on the Ansaphone.

Jot down the occasion, the date and the extension number you are given.

R.S.V.P.   16

Unfortunately you can't come so you ring Maurizio back at work. Can you take part in the conversation?

Centralinista	Pronto . . .
You	*[Say hello and ask for the extension number he gave you.]*
Centralinista	Un attimo . . . È occupato. Vuole rimanere in linea?
You	*[Say yes.]*
Maurizio	Pronto . . .
You	*[Say hello to Maurizio and give him your name.]*
Maurizio	Ciao! Puoi venire alla festa, allora?
You	*[Say you're sorry but you can't.]*
Maurizio	Ah! Mi dispiace . . . Ma quando vieni a trovarci, allora? Senti, ho un'idea. Il mese prossimo facciamo un'escursione nel Parco Nazionale del Pollino. Ti va di venire?
You	*[Hmm, an excursion in the Pollino National Park: tell him yes, it suits you.]*
Maurizio	Ti va bene partire il dieci marzo?
You	*[Say yes, fine, see you on the tenth then.]*
Maurizio	Benissimo! Ciao, a presto.

Cultura e parole

THE **SASSI** OF MATERA, in the Basilicata region, derive their name from the word **sasso** – rock, because originally they were cave-like dwellings lining the two ravines between which Matera is built. They developed over the centuries into full-scale neighbourhoods with proper facades to the houses and churches, some of them with Byzantine frescoes going back to the ninth century. The **Sassi** have for centuries been notorious for their extreme poverty. With the recent greater prosperity, however, they were abandoned in the 1950s, although they are now in the process of being restored and done up. Once the site of flourishing Greek settlements, the mountainous Basilicata region has long been one of the poorest and most isolated parts of Italy, unknown to the majority of other Italians. Carlo Levi's famous book *Cristo si è fermato a Eboli (Christ stopped at Eboli)* (1945) is set in Lucania (as the Basilicata was called, hence the name of **lucani** for Basilicata's inhabitants), and it first brought the region to the attention of outsiders. The region is the least densely populated in the peninsula, afflicted by emigration and subject to earthquakes. Nevertheless, it has begun to attract some tourism and the buying of houses as second homes, precisely on account of its isolation. The Pollino park contains rare wildlife such as wolves, and examples of unusual species of trees such as the splendid **pino loricato**, which can grow at high altitudes.

   In the neighbouring and more prosperous region of Puglia, in the area known as the Murgia, the strange white single-storey conical houses known as **Trulli** are still built and lived in today. For centuries they have housed the **contadini** – the peasants who worked the land – although nowadays they are also used as holiday homes. They are built of limestone, without any mortar and the older ones are topped by traditional but often obscure symbols, some of them believed to be pre-Christian. Both Puglia and the Basilicata are famous for their castles – **castelli** – built during the Norman occupation of Sicily and Southern Italy, the most famous of which are at Melfi in Basilicata, where the Emperor Federico II was crowned, and at Castel del Monte in Puglia, designed by the Emperor himself.

IN TWENTIETH-CENTURY ITALY the majority of Italians live in **palazzi** – apartment blocks which generally operate under a system of joint ownership – **il condominio**. The **inquilini** – tenants, also known as **condomini**, pay a service charge and hold regular meetings. Many advertisements for flats make a feature of **il riscaldamento autonomo** – self-contained heating, because as a rule the heating is regulated for the whole building. Buying and selling property in Italy involves a bewildering variety of terms which may vary slightly according to the region. **Una villa, un villino** or **una villetta** usually refer to detached houses, but if they are **a schiera** this means terraced. Nowadays the term **un rustico** is much favoured to describe what might be called a cottage, although it is frequently modern, whereas **un casale** or **una cascina** both refer to older traditional farmhouses. Flats – **appartamenti** – are advertised according to the number of **locali** or **vani**, rooms not bedrooms: a bedsit is a **monolocale** while a one-bedroom flat is **2 locali** and so on. Beware of confusing terms: if there is **un box** advertised, this means there is a garage and if you spy **un attico**, don't expect a simple attic. It's a penthouse, which usually comes complete with alarm system – **impianto allarme** or **impianto di antifurto** – and roof garden – **terrazzo**.

Cultura e parole

Tell students you are going to talk about how the rented housing sector is regulated by law in Italy. The following is intended to help you with a few minutes of free discussion and, once again, a mixture of Italian and English is the most effective way of helping students follow your trail.

Although the development of council housing – *abitazioni di proprietà del comune* – goes back to the thirties, this type of dwelling is not very common in Italy, with rented accommodation almost entirely in the hands of the private sector. Housing is short especially where it is most needed, for instance where there is work. That is why, even in the private sector, Italians tend to live in the same house or apartment for a very long time and they are helped to do this by a set of laws which protect tenants' rights. Regaining possession of rented property can be a lengthy and costly affair, least painfully resolved with out-of-court settlements.

Since 1978, rents have been subject to the *'equo canone'* law, a sort of fair-rent scheme. This law set out to establish universal guidelines for the amount of rent – *la pigione* – that the tenant – *l'inquilino* – has to pay to the landlord – *il proprietario.* This amount is directly proportional to the value of the property in question and *l'equo canone* is, in effect, no more than a list of criteria against which the property is judged: its degree of *signorile o popolare,* for example, the standard of maintenance – *lo stato di conservazione: buono, mediocre o scadente* – and the area – *l'ubicazione: zona agricola, periferia, centro storico,* etc. As a result, the same type of building (*stessa grandezza, lussuosità e stato di conservazione*) in different localities can have very different values as far as the *equo canone* is concerned.

Interaction 5 (087)

1 *A colazione Lucia, Anna e Peppe discutono il programma per la giornata.*
What do they decide to do that day?
What about the following day?

2 Play the cassette/CD as required and ask further questions:
How does Lucia make her suggestion?
What does Anna say about Melfi's castle?

3 Students read the Interaction and write a short report based on what Anna, Peppe or Lucia would say two days later if they were to recount where they had been, and what they had done or seen.

4 Ask students to read what they have written and discuss as necessary.

Interactions

5 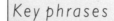 17

The next morning, at breakfast, plans are laid for the day. There's a great deal to see, both in Basilicata and in the neighbouring region of Puglia.

First time round

una gita	*an outing*
scegliere	*to choose*
i castelli . . . i laghi	*castles . . . lakes*
un giro per	*a tour round*

a What do they decide to do that day?
b What about the following day?

Anna   Ciao.
Lucia   Buongiorno.
Peppe   Dormito bene?
Anna   Sì. Bene, grazie.
Peppe   Allora, cosa facciamo oggi?
Lucia   Eh, perché non facciamo una gita?

Anna   E dove? Eh, Peppe, sei tu l'esperto, Lucia mi ha detto che **conosci** tutta **la Basilicata**. Ma **che cosa c'è di bello da vedere?**
Peppe   Tanto. Basta scegliere. Ci sono i laghi di Monticchio. C'è Matera con i Sassi. Ci sono i castelli di Federico.
Anna   Mmm . . .
Lucia   Io ho una proposta da fare. Oggi perché non facciamo un giro per la Basilicata. Domani, poi, andiamo in Puglia.
Anna   In Puglia?
Lucia   Sì. Ad Alberobello. Hai sentito nominare i Trulli, tu? Alberobello è famosa per i Trulli. Perché non andiamo lì?
Anna   Ma, interessante.
Peppe   **Non è una brutta idea.** Passiamo una giornata in Puglia e oggi ti facciamo vedere la zona qui intorno.
Anna   Ah, beh, per me va bene. Ho sentito nominare il castello di Melfi, ma **non ci sono mai stata.**
Lucia   Eh, allora, cosa aspettiamo? Andiamo?
Peppe   Perfetto.

hai sentito nominare . . .?   *have you heard of . . .?*

Key phrases

conosci la Basilicata	*you know the Basilicata*
che cosa c'è di bello da vedere?	*what is there worth seeing*
non è una brutta idea	*it's not a bad idea*
non ci sono mai stata	*I've never been there*

6   🔲   ⏺   18

After a day spent in the Basilicata, as planned, Lucia and Peppe take Anna to Alberobello where she visits a genuine Trullo. Afterwards she's keen to find out how much it would cost to rent one.

First time round

affittare	*to rent*	She visits an estate agent and talks to Maria Gargano.
da due posti letto	*which sleeps two*	
la biancheria	*linen*	
migliore	*best*	

a How much does a Trullo for four cost per week?
b Which season is the best, according to Maria Gargano?

Anna	Buongiorno.
Maria G.	Buongiorno.
Anna	Signora, **mi può dire** quanto costa affittare un Trullo?
Maria G.	Certo. Un Trullo, da due posti letto, costa cinquecentomila lire. Da quattro posti letto, invece, ottocentomila lire.
Anna	Alla settimana?
Maria G.	Alla settimana.
Anna	Ma, nel prezzo **è tutto compreso?**
Maria G.	Certo. È tutto compreso. È compresa la biancheria, è compreso il riscaldamento, è compresa la luce. È compreso tutto quello di cui uno ha bisogno per il soggiorno.
Anna	Bisogna pagare un anticipo?
Maria G.	Certo. Si dà un anticipo e poi, alla fine del soggiorno si dà il saldo.
Anna	E qual è la stagione migliore per venire qui?
Maria G.	Beh, tutte le stagioni sono buone perché d'inverno, per esempio, ci trova i Trulli con la neve. Qua di solito nevica ed è molto bello. D'estate, poi, è favoloso.
Anna	Grazie.

tutto quello di cui uno ha bisogno	*everything you need*
si dà un anticipo	*you pay an advance*
si dà il saldo	*you settle up / pay the difference*
alla fine del soggiorno	*at the end of the stay*

Key phrases

mi può dire . . .	*can you tell me . . .?*
è tutto compreso?	*is everything included?*

Interaction 6   (161)

1 *Anna va in un'agenzia immobiliare per chiedere quanto costa affittare un Trullo.*
How much does a Trullo for four cost per week?
Which season is the best, according to Maria Gargano?

2 Play the cassette/CD as required and ask further questions:
What exactly is included in the price?
Is it necessary to pay an advance?

3 Write the dialogue on the board, leaving out all the questions (or write the missing questions on the board). To help students a little, you could draw a line for each word in each question and underneath each line write the number of letters in the word. Ask students to provide the questions. Give extra help if needed by supplying the first and last word of each question.

Patterns 2

Discussing what there is to do

1   Put students into groups of four or five and tell them to think of different parts of the world.

2   Each group writes a few sentences on what is there to do or see in the city or country they have chosen and the others have to guess which part of the world they are talking about.

This point could be the end of the lesson. Revise the points covered so far. In the next lesson students will cover the following:

> **Structures:** go over *mi* + *potere* + infinitive/*ci* as an adverb of place/conjugation of *conoscere*
> **Functions:** saying where you have been/requesting information using the formal or informal means of address
> **Vocabulary:** countries/general and domestic/word maps

Talking about places

1   Divide students into small groups. Bring in an atlas, make copies of maps of the five continents and give them to students.

2   Each group discusses the places they know/have visited and chooses a spokesperson for the group.

3   The spokesperson makes a list of the countries known to the group:

Uno/a di noi conosce la Siria; un altro/a di noi conosce la Turchia.

4   The other groups, in turn, have to guess where each single student in that group has been:
Student A è stato/a in Siria; student B è stato/a in Turchia.

5   If a group fails to match all the students to the correct countries, another group gets the chance to guess.

Requesting information about renting

1   Divide students into small groups. Ask them to imagine they are members of a large extended family who are renting a *Trullo*. Tell them to work out questions about renting/hiring various pieces of equipment, such as cot/high chair/video recorder/bicycle/sports equipment and anything else they can think of.

Requesting information (using the formal or informal means of address)

1   Make sure students know the meaning of *mi può/puoi* followed by *incontrare, dare, dire, lasciare, indicare.*

2   Write the following ten words or phrases on the board:

la strada	*il ristorante*
alle sei	*in centro*
un messaggio	*in pace*
che ore sono?	*com'è il paese?*
un consiglio	*un'informazione*

3   Divide students into small groups and tell them to work out what to say in the following situations, using the structures and words and phrases given above:

You are looking for the restaurant
You are arranging to meet your boss
You have lost your way
You are asking your wife/husband to leave you a message
You need some information from a stranger
Your son/daughter keeps on bothering you with unimportant questions and you'd like five minutes' peace
You want to ask a passer-by the time
You are meeting a friend at a specific time
You are going on holiday to a foreign country and want to ask a friend who has just been there what it is like
You are at a friend's and would like some advice about a problem

Finding out what's included

1   Discuss other ways of saying *compreso*, e.g. *incluso* or *prezzo chiavi in mano.*

2   Obtain some Italian holiday brochures, if possible. Make copies of a particular page and distribute them to students. Ask them to study the page for a few minutes.

3   Divide students into groups and ask them to list a number of things which might be included in the price of a holiday, hotel, sightseeing trip, etc.

4   One group of students play the customers and ask the other group – the travel agent – what items are included in the price of the holiday.

Patterns 2

i) Discussing what there is to do

In Italian the question is literally *what is there of beauty to be done/seen?* etc.

Che cosa c'è di bello | da fare?   *What is there that's worth* | *doing?*
                   | da vedere? | *seeing?*

You can use different adjectives:

Che cosa c'è di interessante da vedere?   *What is there of interest to see?*

ii) Talking about places

Asking whether you know a place
The verb to use is **conoscere** *(to know)* [see Systems, note 6, p. 198].

Conosci/e la Basilicata? Sì la conosco   *Do you know the Basilicata? Yes I know it*
Conoscete Matera? No, non la conosciamo   *Do you know Matera? No we don't know it*

Saying you have been there
The key word to use is **ci** *(there)*:

Ci sono stato/a | un anno fa   *I went there* | *a year ago*
                | due settimane fa | *two weeks ago*
                | l'anno scorso | *last year*
                | la settimana scorsa | *last week*

Ci sono già stato/a   *I've already been there*
Non ci sono mai stato/a   *I've never been there*

For more information on **ci**, see Troubleshooting p. 142 and Systems, note 2 ii, p. 197.

iii) Requesting information about renting

Use the verb **potere**:

Mi può dire | affittare un Trullo?   *Will/can you tell me* | *to rent a Trullo?*
   quanto costa | noleggiare una macchina?   *how much it costs* | *to hire a car?*

iv) Finding out what's included

The key word is **compreso** *(included)*.

È tutto compreso?   *Is everything included?*
È compreso | il riscaldamento?   *Is* | *the heating included?*
   compresa | la luce? | *the electricity*
               | la biancheria? | *the linen*

Practice 2

Odd one out

Look up any words you don't know in the Lexis.

1 Which item is least likely to be found in the sitting-room?
la televisione   il televisore   il telegramma   il telecomando

2 Which of the following wouldn't you do at home?
fare la barba   fare il bucato   fare la spesa   fare il bagno

3 Which item couldn't fit easily through your letter-box?
il giornale   un francobollo   la bolletta del telefono   un tavolo da biliardo

4 Which of the following is unlikely to be found in your kitchen?
la lavastoviglie   la lavatrice   la lavagna   il lavandino

D'accordo    19

You are meeting a couple of Italian friends, Gianna and Ezio. The idea is to go on an outing to Puglia. You discuss what to do over breakfast in a bar.

You	[While you are waiting to be served, ask them what you're doing today.]
Ezio	Gianna vuole andare al mare, ma io voglio fare un giro in macchina fino a Castellana.
You	[Ask what's worth seeing at Castellana.]
Ezio	Ma ci sono delle bellissime grotte da visitare.
You	[Grotte . . . caves: say you have never visited a cave.]
Gianna	Ma io ci sono stata due volte l'anno scorso! Sono proprio delle belle grotte ma io preferisco il mare.
You	[Suggest going to Castellana this morning and going to the sea this afternoon.]
Gianna	Eh, sì, per me va bene.
Ezio	D'accordo, anche per me va bene.
You	[Suggest you all get going, then.]

Have you ever been to . . .?

You're staying with friends who want to be sure you don't miss any of the sights of Basilicata. This isn't your first visit, so they're checking on the places you know . . . You tell them if you've been there and if so, when.

1 Signore

Sei mai stato a Venosa?   Yes, two years ago.

2 Signora

E hai visto il posto dov'è nato il poeta romano Orazio?   Yes, I went last week.

3 Signora

Senti, sei già stato ai laghi di Monticchio?   Yes, last year.

4 Signore

E sei stato a Matera?   Yes, two weeks ago.

5 Signora

Andiamo al mare, allora? Sei stato a Maratea?   No, never.

Practice 2

Domestic row

Aim: to stimulate discussion and creative writing using an everyday situation

1 Make copies of the conversation below. Give one copy to one student and invite him/her to read it with you (you play Franco's part).

2 As soon as the student says *'Ciao, Franco'* you say your line with as much anger as you can muster. This will naturally surprise the students and in particular the one who is reading. Carry on reading and acting out the dialogue, showing anger and frustration (to the delight of the students).

3 Repeat this a number of times (each time give a copy of the dialogue to a different student and show even more anger and frustration).

4 Ask a student to volunteer for your part and give all the students a copy of the dialogue.

5 Tell students to practise the dialogue in pairs.

6 Discuss any questions raised.

7 Tell students to add their own ending to this domestic row.

8 Ask students to compare what they have written with other pairs.

9 Finally ask someone to volunteer their version of events.

If you have an OHP, you can ask students to write on transparent sheets. When projecting what they have written, be careful to show only one line at a time so as to keep students interested and amused.

- Ciao, Franco.
- Come!? 'Ciao, Franco'. Ti aspetto da tre ore. Perché non mi hai telefonato?
- Ho provato ma non sono riuscita a trovare un telefono.
- Ma si può sapere dove sei stata finora?
- Ma che modi! Sono appena entrata in casa, non mi hai neanche salutata e non mi dai neanche il tempo di spiegarti.
- Spiegare un cavolo. Lo sai che mi preoccupo e sto in pensiero.
- Ricominciamo con la stessa storia. Guarda che Luciano non l'ho più visto. Guarda che . . .
- A sì? E questo che cosa è?

A room of my own

Encourage students to write a short piece in which they describe their favourite room in the house and what they do in it.

Caccia agli oggetti

Aim: vocabulary building/revision of prepositions + articles – *nell'armadio, vicino al tavolo* – and of position words – *a destra/in alto/in basso,* etc.

1 Bring in a plan of a house or apartment. Make copies or display it on the OHP and discuss each room in detail (including the names of pieces of furniture).

2 Divide the class into two groups and ask each group to think of objects (not fixed features) generally found in the house, for example: *ferro da stiro, sapone, piatti, aspirapolvere,* etc.

3 The two groups make guesses in turn to find exactly where in the plan of the house or apartment a certain object is hidden.

Variation: show students a picture of a room taken from a magazine. Tell them there is a fifty pound note/bottle of champagne/diamond hidden somewhere in the room. Students take turns to guess its location until someone 'wins' the hidden object.

Home improvements

Below is a letter sent by a couple to a magazine specialising in country living. Read the letter, using the vocabulary given to help. Note that the couple write as one, using **io**, and that they address the magazine using the plural **voi**.

> Angela e Gianfranco Marese — Potenza
>
> Possiedo un piccolissimo rustico in una zona ancora molto bella e tranquilla. Prima, però, di iniziare i lavori di riadattamento, ho bisogno di un vostro parere. La casa deve servire solo per i fine settimana e le vacanze estive alla mia famiglia [padre, madre, più un bambino di sei anni] e ogni tanto a una coppia di amici. Ci sono già acqua e luce ma l'interno è tutto da rimettere a posto. Unisco uno schizzo con le misure approssimative che ho preso. Spero di poter avere un vostro aiuto e di potervi invitare per l'anno prossimo! Grazie di cuore

possiedo *I own;* un parere *an opinion;* riadattamento *renovating;* servire a *to be needed by;* una coppia *a couple;* unisco *I enclose;* uno schizzo *a sketch*

Now answer these questions in English:

a Why is the couple writing?
b Who is the house for?
c What amenities does it have at present?
d At the end of the letter what do Angela and Gianfranco Marese say they hope to do?

Identikit

Try and describe the contents and layout of the flat or house where you live, first to a friend and then to a potential buyer. Use the Vocabulary and some of the phrases given here. If possible, practise it out loud or on cassette; be prepared for questions on how things work.

al pianterreno *on the ground floor;* al primo/secondo piano *on the first/second floor;* di sopra, di sotto *upstairs, downstairs;* sopra *above;* sotto *under;* accanto a *next to;* vicino a *near*

Grand tour

You've just had a day out with a friend in the Vulture region of Basilicata and you're sending a postcard to a friend in Milan. Write the card saying where you've been and what you've done. Starting at Venosa, you visit all the places shown on the map, ending in Rionero before returning to Venosa.

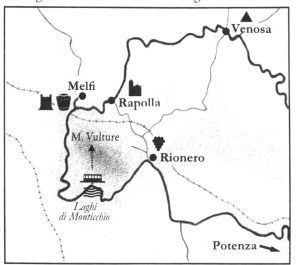

Legenda		castello	
duomo		terracotta	
vino		laghi	
funivia		abbazia	

partire da   arrivare a   andare   camminare   salire fino a   passare per   rimanere a   pranzare   fare il giro di   vedere   visitare   noleggiare

Now say what you did on *your* last day out.

Vocabulary

The phone

l'abbonato	subscriber
la bolletta del telefono	telephone bill
il/la centralinista	operator
la chiamata	call
il gettone	telephone token
l'elenco telefonico	telephone directory
le pagine gialle	yellow pages
il prefisso	code
il ricevitore	receiver
la teleselezione	automatic dialling
una telefonata interurbana	call long-distance
urbana	local
internazionale	international
la scheda telefonica	telephone card

The house [see also Unit 1]

l'appartamento	flat
l'attico	penthouse
il palazzo	block of flats
la villa	detached house
il tetto	roof
la soffitta	attic
il seminterrato	basement
la cantina	cellar
il box	garage
il balcone	balcony
il terrazzo	[roof] terrace
il citofono	entry-phone
il portone	front door
l'ingresso	entrance, hall
l'ascensore	lift
il corridoio	corridor, hall
la scala	stairs
il soggiorno	living-room
il tinello	dining-room
il muro	[outside] wall
la parete	[inside] wall
il pavimento	floor

il soffitto	ceiling
al pianterreno	on the ground floor
al primo/ secondo piano	on the first/second floor
all' ultimo piano	on the top floor

Furniture and house contents

i mobili	furniture
l'armadio	cupboard, wardrobe
il divano	sofa
il cassetto	drawer
il cassettone	chest of drawers
il comodino	bedside table
la credenza	sideboard
il letto	bed
la moquette	carpet [fitted]
le persiane	blinds
la poltrona	armchair
lo scaffale	shelf, bookshelf
la sedia	chair
il tavolo	table
le tende	curtains
la biancheria	linen
il lenzuolo (pl. le lenzuola)	sheet
il piumino	duvet
l'asciugamano	towel

Domestic appliances

gli elettrodomestici	domestic appliances
l'apriscatole	tin-opener
l'aspirapolvere	vacuum cleaner
il cavatappi	corkscrew
il congelatore /il freezer	freezer
il frigorifero	fridge
il ferro da stiro	iron
il forno a microonde	oven microwave
la lavastoviglie	dishwasher

la lavatrice	washing-machine
l'interruttore	[light] switch
la presa	socket
la spina	plug
il riscaldamento	heating
il rubinetto	tap

Verbs

festeggiare	to celebrate
invitare	to invite
ospitare	to put someone up
accettare	to accept
rifiutare	to refuse
affittare	to rent
noleggiare	to hire
fornire	to provide
fare un'escursione	to go on an excursion
fare una gita	to go on an outing
fare un giro per	to go on a tour of

Adjectives

comodo	comfortable
scomodo	uncomfortable
disordinato	untidy
ordinato	tidy
pulito	clean
sporco	dirty
tranquillo	quiet, peaceful
rumoroso	noisy
buio	dark
luminoso	light
spazioso	spacious, roomy
moderno	modern
ristrutturato	modernised
d'epoca	period
di lusso	luxury
signorile	elegant

Vocabulary

1 To make your house more homely you can do all of the following except:

appendere quadri   pitturare pareti   tagliare l'erba
tagliare la siepe   lasciare disordine dappertutto

2 Which one of the following jobs cannot be carried out from home?

parrucchiere   postino   insegnante   editore   giornalista

3 Which one of the following items cannot be delivered to your door?

palestra   latte   pizza   giornale   posta

4 Which one of the following items cannot be brought home in your shopping?

frutta   vini e liquori   suoceri   verdura   formaggi

5 Which one of the following items are you unlikely to use at home?

fucile da caccia   telefono   video   radio   televisione

6 Which of the following are you unlikely to plant in your garden?

lattuga   insalata   ravanelli   fiori   grano

7 Which of the following instruments are you unlikely to bring home to play?

viola   martello pneumatico   chitarra   violino   flauto

8 If you want to buy or sell your home you may do all the following except:

leggere gli annunci di compra-vendita case e terreni
telefonare ad un'agenzia immobiliare
fare ogni riparazione necessaria
litigare con il proprietario di un'agenzia di demolizioni
mettere un annuncio sul giornale locale

Troubleshooting

Review

Here is a checklist of the main points learned in this unit. For each point, ask the students to provide you with one or more examples by asking specific questions.

> impersonal *si*
> *fare* + infinitive
> making/discussing plans and suggestions
> accepting or declining
> asking and saying how things work
> *mi* + *potere* + infinitive
> *ci* as an adverb of place
> saying where you have been
> requesting information using the formal or informal
> means of address

Troubleshooting

Ci

Ci is used a lot in Italian. Here is a summary of its uses:

I *there*

C'è, **ci** sono	*There is, there are*
Ci sei stato?	*Did you go there?*
Non **ci** sono mai stato	*I've never been there*

Its use is wider than in English: it is often needed when talking about an activity:
Sei andato a ballare ieri? – Sì, **ci** sono andato   *Did you go dancing yesterday? Yes, I went (there)*

2 *Reflexive: ourselves, each other*

ci incontriamo   *we meet (each other)*   **ci** divertiamo   *we enjoy ourselves*   **ci** vediamo   *we see each other*

3 *Direct object: us*

Ci chiami domani?   *Will you call us tomorrow?*
Perché non vieni a trovar**ci** domani?   *Why don't you come and visit/see us tomorrow?*

4 *Indirect object: to us*

Ci può dire quanto costa?   *Will/can you tell us how much it costs? [lit. can you say to us]*
Ci piace la Basilicata   *We like Basilicata [lit. Basilicata is pleasing to us]*

5 *Pleonastic* **ci**

Ce l'hai il prefisso?   *Have you got the code? [lit. have you got it, the code?]*

Ci has become **ce** because it precedes another pronoun, **lo** [and **lo** has become **l'** in front of **hai**].
Ci here has no specific meaning. It is used for reasons of pronunciation:
    Hai il mio indirizzo? Sì **ce** l'ho   *Have you got my address? Yes,*

Che giornata!

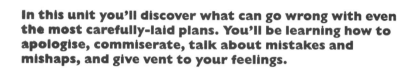

In this unit you'll discover what can go wrong with even the most carefully-laid plans. You'll be learning how to apologise, commiserate, talk about mistakes and mishaps, and give vent to your feelings.

Che giornata! – what a day! For the average Italian, a bad day could well be associated with the hazards of Italy's bureaucracy and public services: obtaining a certificate, renewing a driving licence or simply sending a parcel can all **cause** endless delay and frustration. Italy's ramshackle **bureaucracy** is in sharp contrast to her efficiency in other spheres: she is the fifth biggest world economy but is only eighth in the EC league of public services provision. The postal service is particularly bad, with an average 5.5 days for the receipt of a letter. This might explain why people never post their bills. For example, telephone bills – **bollette del telefono** – are paid in person or by direct debit. The nationalised Italian telephone company is known as **la SIP**, a throwback to the turn of the century when the main electricity company (from which the phone companies developed) was the **Società Idroelettrica Piemonte**. Italians often complain about **la SIP** but are avid users particularly of the **telefonino**, as portable telephones are affectionately called! Why, then, if public services are so frequently criticised is there no reform? One reason is that there is little political incentive. Italy's huge public sector has traditionally been run on a patronage system known as **la lottizzazione** – the allocation of the key jobs to political appointees.

Puglia

Basilicata

Lecce

Gallipoli

Che giornata!

This unit centres on the difficulties of day-to-day living in Italy and how to cope with them linguistically. It also discusses travelling through those southern parts of Italy which were formerly part of the Magna Graecia, one-time centre of civilization. You could take this opportunity to talk about Italy's rich past and, since most students will have reached a reasonably good level of comprehension by now, they should be able to follow a 'mini lecture', if the subject matter is not too difficult, if it is explained in simple words (with plenty of repetition) and, most of all, if the short exposé is supported by good visual aids. Historical topics provide ample scope for a talk of about eight to ten minutes, discussing various items such as coins, statues, temples, pottery, etc. This mini lecture could be quite a success, but it largely depends on generating interest in the topic from the start, which is why visual aids are essential. The aim, for students, is to listen for gist understanding, not to fight with words or worse, switch off.

In presenting the topic you might find the following suggestions useful:

1 Write difficult and technical words on the board.

2 Prepare some slides or pictures (diagrams and drawings are best shown on an OHP).

3 For each picture, slide, drawing or diagram, make up a card with a few key words to remind you of the features to discuss.

4 At the beginning, explain very briefly in English the main areas you are going to cover. Ask students to make notes on anything they do not understand and would like to question you about when you have finished.

Video corner

Una giornata di imprevisti

Aim: to stimulate free writing

Video sequence: the whole video sequence

1 Tell students the theme of the sequence they are going to watch is 'unexpected events'.

2 Play the video sequence and ask students to take note of the 'accidents'.

3 Divide the class into two groups – each group representing Anna or Alberto – and ask them to write one letter to a mutual friend to tell him or her about the day's misadventures.

4 Compare the two letters and discuss as required.

Che cosa vedi?

Aim: vocabulary building through active viewing

Video sequence: from opening titles to Anna speaking to camera

1 Write the words below on the board, discuss the meanings and ask students to note which of the following cannot be seen in the opening sequence:

treno, campanile, cartelli stradali, palazzo, mare, barche, autobus, chiesa, aereo, vespa, bosco, castello, montagne, cavalli, automobili, mercato, piazza, prati, frati, pizza, mulino

2 Play the sequence as required.

3 When the students are ready, ask for a volunteer to 'comment' on the sequence as you play it again, this time in slow motion.

Making arrangements

Aim: vocabulary building and writing through active viewing

Video sequence: from Anna's second attempt to phone Alberto to the end of the second telephone conversation

1 Write the following questions on the board, play the sequence and ask students to answer them.

Dov'è seduta Anna?
Dov'è seduto Alberto?
Che cosa c'è alle loro spalle?

2 Write the following adjectives on the board and ask students to choose which ones best describe Anna's and Alberto's mood:
agitato/a, compiaciuto/a, sorpreso/a, deciso/a, indeciso/a, nervoso/a, contento/a, imbarazzato/a

Interactions

> **Structures:** formal and informal imperative/*sperare di*/*pensare di*
> **Functions:** apologising/making plans for the future
> **Vocabulary:** useful telephone phrases/dates and the calendar/directions

Help-phrases and instructions

Oh no! Questa non ci voleva.
È un vero peccato.
E ora che si fa?
Scusa, ma non ho capito.
Scusa, ma non abbiamo sentito.
Scusa, ma non ti capisco.

To argue a point more forcibly:
Ma scusa, non hai detto che . . .
Scusa, ma è chiaro che non vuole farlo.

Excusing someone:
Sei scusato/a.

Interaction 1   (250)

1 *Anna telefona ad un suo amico che si chiama Alberto per invitarlo a visitare Lecce.*
Who does Anna get through to?
What number was she trying to dial?

2 Play the cassette/CD as required.

Interaction 2   (292)

1 *Anna riprova a telefonare ad Alberto.*
Has Alberto definitely decided to come?
What dates does Anna suggest?

2 Play the cassette/CD as required and ask further questions:
Has Anna spoken to Alberto before now?
Why is Alberto unable to confirm the arrangement right away?

3 Tell students that when Alberto checks his diary he discovers that he has pencilled in another engagement for that day. Ask students to write a dialogue between Alberto and his friend Nicola (on the phone) in which Alberto tells Nicola about Anna and asks him if they can meet the following week instead.

Interactions

1 [cc] [CD] 21

Anna is all set for more time off in the south, this
time with her friend Alberto. Arranging the trip to
the beautiful baroque town of Lecce, in Puglia, is
more difficult than she expects.

First time round

linea disturbata	*bad line*

She dials Alberto's
number.

a Who does Anna get through to?
b What number was she trying to dial?

Anna Cinque sette, sette due, sei uno. Pronto,
Alberto? **Con chi parlo, scusi?** Con chi,
scusi? La linea è disturbata. – Con Angelo!
Ma che numero ho chiamato? Ah, ho
capito! Cinque sette, sette due, sette uno. **Mi
dispiace! Ho sbagliato numero.**
Buonasera.

Key phrases

con chi parlo, scusi?	*excuse me, who am I speaking to?*
mi dispiace	*sorry*
ho sbagliato numero	*I've got the wrong number*

Wrong one [cc] [CD] 21

Listen to the cassette/CD and say you've got it
wrong.

2 [cc] [CD] 22

Anna gets through next time and suggests a
date.

First time round

ancora	*yet*
tra una settimana	*in a week*
fra poco	*soon*
l'agenda	*diary*

a Has Alberto definitely decided to come?
b What dates does Anna suggest?

Anna [. . .] Pronto? Alberto, **sei tu?**
Alberto Sì, sono io. Ciao Anna.
Anna Ciao Alberto. Allora hai deciso? Puoi venire?
Alberto Ma non lo so ancora. **Quando pensi di partire** esattamente?
Anna Mah! Veramente non ho ancora deciso.
Probabilmente la settimana prossima,
fra il due e il cinque maggio. Come vuoi
tu, insomma. Non ho deciso niente
ancora.
Alberto Ma, per me è lo stesso. Non ho molti
impegni in quel periodo.
Anna Ah, perfetto! Allora perché non partiamo
tra una settimana? Il tre maggio, per
esempio.
Alberto Benissimo. Ma **ti dispiace se** ti richiamo
fra poco per confermare? Sai, preferisco
controllare la data sulla mia agenda e non
ce l'ho qui con me.
Anna Va bene. A presto allora.
Alberto Sì, **ci sentiamo dopo.** Ciao.

per me è lo stesso	*it's all the same to me*
controllare la data	*to check the date*
non ce l'ho qui	*I haven't got it here*

Key phrases

Alberto, sei tu?	*Alberto, is that you?*
quando pensi di partire?	*when are you thinking of leaving?*
ti dispiace se . . .?	*do you mind if . . .?*
ci sentiamo dopo	*speak to you later*

Quando, quando, quando   22

Listen to the cassette/CD and say when you are thinking of leaving.

3   23

Alberto calls back having checked his dates.

First time round

la partenza	departure

He is unusually decisive . . .

a Where in Lecce does he suggest they meet?
b What time does he suggest?

Anna	Pronto?
Alberto	Ciao Anna, sono Alberto.
Anna	Ciao Alberto.
Alberto	Ti chiamo velocemente per confermare la partenza il tre maggio.
Anna	**Meno male.** E dove ci incontriamo?
Alberto	Davanti al Teatro dell'Opera di Lecce.
Anna	Davanti al Teatro dell'Opera di Lecce. A che ora?
Alberto	Verso le dodici.
Anna	A mezzogiorno, davanti al Teatro dell'Opera di Lecce. Ci rivediamo il tre. Ciao.

Key phrase

meno male *good, thank goodness*

4   24

On 3 May Anna arrives in Lecce to meet Alberto. The plan is to go on to Gallipoli near the southern tip of Italy to meet their friend Cioto.

First time round

per questa strada	along this road
ti accompagno io	I'll take you
figurati	it's no bother

Anna finds a theatre but Alberto isn't there, so she checks things out with a passer-by.

a Has Anna gone to the right place?
b What route is she told to take?

[Anna	Scusa, mi puoi dire se questo è il Teatro dell'Opera?]
Signorina	No, hai sbagliato teatro. Devi **continuare per questa strada**, devi **prendere la seconda a destra**, all'angolo c'è una bella chiesa barocca, devi continuare per quella strada.
Anna	Allora: prendere questa strada, la seconda a destra, alla chiesa barocca **sempre dritto**.
Signorina	Se vuoi ti accompagno io.
Anna	Ah, non voglio darti troppo fastidio.
Signorina	Figurati! Facciamo la strada insieme.
Anna	Grazie. **Mi fa piacere.** Sei gentile.
Signorina	Andiamo.
Anna	Sì.
[. . .]	

non voglio darti troppo fastidio
I don't want to give you too much bother

Key phrases

continuare per questa strada	carry on along this street
prendere la seconda a destra	take the second on the right
sempre dritto	straight on
mi fa piacere	it's a pleasure

Il teatro romano, Lecce

Interaction 3 (344)

1 *Questa volta Alberto telefona ad Anna per confermare l'accordo e stabilire dove incontrarsi.*
Where in Lecce does he suggest they meet?
What time does he suggest?

2 Play the cassette/CD as required.

3 Students work in pairs and role play the parts of Alberto and Anna, changing the date, the time and the meeting place.

Interaction 4 (367)

1 *Il tre maggio Anna è a Lecce davanti a un teatro ma Alberto non c'è.*
Has Anna gone to the right place?
What route is she told to take?

2 Play the cassette/CD as required and ask further questions:
Does Anna think the passer-by is impolite?
Was the young woman going in the same direction?

3 Make copies of the dialogue without the directions (i.e. leave only Anna's lines in). Give students time to supply all the missing words, first individually, then in pairs, then in small groups, until the class is divided into just two groups.

4 Ask students to write the missing lines on the board (take one line from each group), then play the Interaction again to check both groups have completed their task correctly.

5 Tell them to read the dialogue in pairs, then clear the board, line by line, starting from the top and giving students time to memorise each line.

6 Ask two volunteers to role play the whole interaction in front of the class. Ask the others to make a note of any mistakes.

This point could be the end of the lesson. Revise the points covered so far. In the next lesson students will cover the following:

> **Structures:** *ne* + verb + quantity
> **Functions:** expressing regret/playing down an accident
> **Vocabulary:** *come mi dispiace/pazienza/non importa/non è niente*

Interaction 5 (402)

1 *Alberto sta parlando con un suo amico quando arriva Anna. Tutti e tre vanno al bar . . .*

2 Play the cassette/CD as required and ask further questions:
What has actually happened?
What is the meaning of *ragazzi* in this context?
How does Anna react to the accident?

3 Ask students to write a dialogue, in pairs or small groups, in which an accident happens and they have to give vent to their feelings.

4 Discuss the use of slang.

5 [cc] [◎] 25

Anna eventually meets up with Alberto, who's been
chatting to the local doctor while waiting for her.
The doctor takes them to taste **arancini**, a local
cheese and rice savoury.

First time round

assaggiamo?	*shall we try it?*	But it's
macchiata	*stained*	not Anna's
		day . . .

How does Anna react to the accident?

[. . .]

[Anna	Allora, assaggiamo?
Alberto	Con cosa li fanno? Col riso e il formaggio anche?]
Dott. N.	Allora vi piacciono gli arancini?
Alberto	Sì! Sono buonissimi!
Anna	Mm! **Anche a me piacciono** tanto. Dopo **ne prendo un altro**. E tu, Alberto?
Alberto	No, io no. Basta così. Io non ho più fame.

[In her eagerness to take another arancino Anna drops one]

Anna	Ah! Oh no! Mi si è macchiata la gonna!
Alberto	**Come mi dispiace!**
Anna	Ah, uff, **pazienza! Non importa.** Mah, **non è niente.** Tanto non è nuova.
Alberto	Ragazzi, è ora di partire se vogliamo arrivare all'appuntamento con Cioto.
Anna	È vero. Andiamo.

non ho più fame	*I'm not hungry any more*
tanto non è nuova	*anyway it's not new*

Key phrases

anche a me piacciono	*I like them too*
ne prendo un altro	*I'll have another one*
come mi dispiace!	*I am sorry!*
pazienza!	*never mind!*
non importa	*it doesn't matter*
non è niente	*it's nothing*

*Santa Chiara,
Lecce*

Patterns I

i) On the phone
Checking who you're speaking to

Con chi parlo, scusi?   *Excuse me, who am I speaking to?*

If you think you know who it is, you say:

Sei tu, Alberto?   *Is that you, Alberto?*
È Lei, signor Abruzzi?   *Is that you, Mr Abruzzi?*

Setting a date
To find out what day someone has got in mind, use **pensare di**:

| Quando pensi di | partire? | *When are you thinking of* | *leaving?* |
| | pensa | venire? | | *coming?* |

The answer can vary in precision:

domenica/il 3 maggio	*on Sunday/on 3 May*
fra il 2 e il 5 maggio	*between 2 and 5 May*
fra una settimana/fra poco	*in a week/soon*

To say when you will next speak to someone, use **sentirsi** (lit. *to hear each other*):

Ci sentiamo	presto/dopo	*Speak to you*	*soon/later*
	il 18 luglio		*on 18 July*
	sabato		*on Saturday*

There is no article with a specific weekday but you always use the article with the date.
See Ref. II, 1, 3, p. 241. **Fra** or **tra** must be used to say *in* when you're referring to the future: you cannot use the Italian word **in**.

ii) A polite request

To ask whether someone minds if you do something:

| Ti dispiace se ti | chiamo più tardi? | *Do you mind* | *if I call you later?* |
| Le dispiace se La | | | |

To ask someone else to do something:

| Ti dispiace | venire più tardi? | *Do you mind* | *coming later?* |
| Le dispiace | darmi una mano? | | *giving me a hand?* |

iii) Excusing yourself and apologising

Scusi, ho sbagliato	numero	*Excuse me, I've got the wrong*	*number*
	strada		*street*
	porta		*door*

Ho sbagliato strada often means *I've gone the wrong way.*

Mi dispiace,	abbiamo bucato	*I'm sorry,*	*we've got a puncture*
	abbiamo finito la benzina		*we've run out of petrol*
	il telefono è guasto		*the phone is out of order*
	è (tutto) esaurito		*it's booked up, sold out, out of print*

Patterns 1

On the phone
Checking who you are speaking to
Excusing yourself and apologising

1 Prepare cards with names of famous people from the world of politics, finance, sport, etc.

2 Write on the board a title or a position associated with each of the names (the Italian foreign minister, the German Chancellor, the one hundred metres world champion).

3 Give each student a card which only he or she is allowed to see.

4 Students, in turn, look for the people associated with the titles by 'phoning' each other (tell students to say *Con chi parlo?* each time and to apologise with *Mi dispiace/Scusi, ho sbagliato numero* if they get the wrong number).

Setting a date

1 Write on the board a number of activities which your students are likely to do in future.

e.g. *fare il bucato   uscire*
guardare un film   telefonare a un amico
fare la spesa   fare un viaggio

Tell students to copy down the activities and write a day or date next to each one.

2 Tell students to go round the class to find out when each of them is going to do what, and to take brief notes.

3 Check their findings by asking student A *Quando pensa student B di fare . . .?*

A polite request

1 Tell students to imagine having to leave a written message to a flatmate requesting him or her to do something.

e.g. *innaffiare le piante   spedire la lettera*
telefonare domani   dar da mangiare al gatto
chiudere la porta a chiave   fare la spesa
mettere fuori la spazzatura   preparare la cena

2 In pairs or in small groups, students write a message in which they make a polite request and give a reason. Write an example on the board to help them:

Ti dispiace dar da mangiare al gatto questa sera perché vado a cena fuori dopo il lavoro e torno tardi?

3 If you're using an OHP, give students a transparent sheet on which to write their messages. Collect the sheets and show them on the OHP. Invite everyone to comment.

Expressing your feelings

1   Prepare some cards (at least one per student), each bearing a brief message.

2   Ask students to write, in one line, the expressions for communicating their feelings:

Come mi dispiace!/Accidenti!/Davvero?/Mi fa piacere!

3   Each time a student reads out a message from a card the others respond by ticking the appropriate expression(s). If, for example, the message is *Ho passato l'esame di guida,* the students will put a tick underneath *Davvero?* and *Mi fa piacere!*

Saying you like it too

1   Ask students to think of a particular preference of theirs and to write it, with their name, on a piece of paper which they give you.

e.g. *Mi piacciono/Non mi piacciono i cioccolatini ripieni.*

2   Read out what each student has written and ask the others to guess who wrote it.

3   Write each preference on the board and ask students at random *Che cosa piace anche a te?* Students answer *Anche a me/Neanche a me piace/piacciono . . .*

4   Tell students to make a chart with each other's names and preferences and to keep a record of the answers.

5   Ask student A *Che cosa piace a Student B?*

Talking about quantities

1   Tell students to imagine that they are journalists with a particular interest in finding out about the social behaviour of people in this country. They have to carry out surveys by asking each other questions about quantities and frequency.

2   Write these sample questions on the board:

Quanti libri leggi in un mese/anno?
Quante paia di scarpe compri in un anno?

3   Write also a list of items about which such questions could be asked and elicit the meanings from the students if they are not already known. You could also ask students to suggest some items.

tazze di tè/caffè – al giorno
film alla televisione – alla settimana
film al cinema – al mese
sigarette – al giorno
giornali – alla settimana
telefonate ad amici – alla settimana
vacanze – all'anno
mezzi pubblici – al giorno
spuntini – al giorno
lettere personali – al mese

4   Tell them to answer *Ne prendo/compro/faccio,* etc. + the number, or *Non ne prendo/compro/faccio nessuno/a.*

Asking and explaining the way

1   Discuss with the students the various ways of asking for directions:

Scusi.   Piazza Garibaldi?
          Dov'è il teatro . . .?
          Come faccio per andare al centro?
          Mi può indicare la strada per la stazione?
          Mi può dire dov'è il mercato?

2   Prepare a map with at least ten numbers marked, each corresponding to a place which has to be identified.

3   Make enough copies and distribute them to the students.

4   Put students into pairs and hand each student a list of the places indicated by numbers on the map. On the list for student A you will have identified the position of half the places by adding the correct map numbers alongside. On student B's list the other half will have been identified.

5   Students ask their partners for directions to the places not identified on their own list.

This point could be the end of the lesson. Revise the points covered so far. In the next lesson students will cover the following:

> **Structures:** formal and informal forms of address/past tense actions with verbs of movement/past tense of reflexive verbs
> **Functions:** giving directions
> **Vocabulary:** holidays/description of the local area/everyday actions

iv) Expressing your feelings

Come mi dispiace!	*I am so sorry!/Bad luck!*	Non è niente	*It's nothing.*
Che peccato!	*What a shame!*	Davvero?	*Really?*
Accidenti!	*Bother! Damn!*	Meno male!	*Good! Thank goodness!*
Pazienza!	*Ah well/Too bad/Never mind*		*(lit. less bad)*
Non importa	*It doesn't matter*	Mi fa piacere	*That's nice, I'd love to*

v) Saying you like it too

Gli arancini piacciono anche	a te?	*Do you like arancini too?*
	a Lei?	
	a voi?	

Piacciono anche	a me	*I like them too*	[See Systems, note 3, p. 201.]
	a noi	*We like them too*	

vi) Talking about quantities

The key word is **ne** (*of it, of them*), often not expressed in English:

Quanto/a ne ha?   *How much (of it) have you got?*
Quanti/e ne vuole?   *How many (of them) do you want?*

Ne ho	uno, due, tre	*I've got*	*one, two, three*
Ne voglio	alcuni, alcune	*I want*	*some, a few*
Ne prendo	un po', un altro po'	*I'll have*	*a bit, a bit more*
	una fetta, un pezzo		*a slice, a piece*

See Systems, note 1, p. 201.

vii) Asking and explaining the way

One simple way of asking for directions is to say *'Excuse me'* and name the place:

Scusi	il Teatro dell'Opera?
Scusa	viale Marconi?

The more complete question includes the phrase **come faccio?**

Scusi, per il Teatro dell'Opera, come faccio?   *Excuse me, how do I get to the Teatro dell'Opera?*

Deve/devi	seguire questa/quella strada	*You have to*	*follow this/that road*
	continuare per questa strada		*carry on along this road*
	fino al semaforo		*up to the lights*
	fino all'incrocio		*up to the crossroads.*
	andare sempre diritto/dritto		*go straight on*
	andare in fondo alla strada		*go to the end of the road*
	girare a destra/a sinistra		*turn right/left*
	prendere la prima strada/traversa		*take the first road/turning*
	la seconda a destra/sinistra		*the second on the right/left*

viii) Negative expressions

Non ho **più** fame	*I'm no longer hungry*
Non ho **ancora** deciso	*I haven't yet decided*
Non vado **mai** al mare	*I never go to the seaside*

148

Practice 1

When are you off?

You're being quizzed about when you're going to take a holiday. At first you hedge a bit – you haven't worked it out. Tell your friend you're thinking of leaving:

> soon
> in two weeks
> in a month
> between 8 June and 16 June

Finally you settle on a date:

> Thursday 15 June

When are you thinking of taking your next holiday?

Bad Blood   26

Anna and Michela are tucking into some exotic specialities in Lecce and you're their guest. Included on the menu are **lampasciumi** – cooked wild onions and **sanguinaccio** – a pork-based blood sausage, actually more delicious than it sounds (the name literally means 'bad blood'). Anna and Michela like everything: what about you?

Anna	Mmm, Michela, mi piacciono questi lampasciumi.
Michela	Mmm, che buoni! Sì, piacciono anche a me. A te piacciono?
You	*[You don't actually like onions. Be polite, though, and say you don't like them very much.]*
Anna	Ah, peccato, sono buoni, sai – io ne prendo un altro, allora. E dopo c'è il sanguinaccio.
You	*[You're a bit doubtful about this. Ask if it's good.]*
Anna	Ma sì! Il sanguinaccio è squisito, buonissimo! È una specialità di Lecce. Non ne vuoi?
You	*[You'll have to try some. Say yes thanks, you'll have a bit.]*
Michela	Ah, ne prendo anch'io, Anna. A me piace il sanguinaccio! E a te, piace allora?
You	*[Surprisingly, it's wonderful! Say you like it a lot and you'll have a bit more.]*
Anna	Bene, un altro po' per te . . . e un altro po' per me.
Michela	Eh, scusa, un altro po' anche per me!

Help!

You live in Italy and you have to go to England suddenly to visit a sick relative. At the airport you realise you've forgotten to do a few vital things. Luckily your elderly neighbour has a key. Ring her up and ask her if she minds helping you out. You've jotted down what you need to ask her:

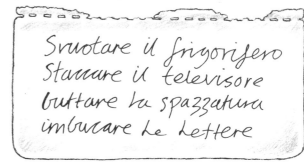

> Svuotare il frigorifero
> Staccare il televisore
> buttare la spazzatura
> imbucare le lettere

Here's how the first part of the conversation should go: can you carry on?

> Signora, Le dispiace svuotare il frigorifero?

You

Vicina

> Ma no, sono sempre contenta di aiutare.

You	*[Ask her if she minds unplugging the TV in the sitting room?]*
Vicina	Staccare la TV? Ma non c'è problema! Ha dimenticato altro?
You	*[Yes! Does she mind emptying the rubbish? It's behind the door.]*
Vicina	Buttare la spazzatura? Ma certo!
You	*[Oh, and does she mind posting the letters? They are on the table.]*
Vicina	Imbucare le lettere? Ma sì, vado subito. Buon viaggio!

Accident prone

Alberto is supposed to be coming to see you this morning but he's having his usual run of bad luck! Can you express how you feel when he rings up to tell you?

1 Mi dispiace, non posso venire stamattina.
2 La macchina è guasta.
3 Ho perso il treno delle undici . . .
4 Ma posso prendere un treno oggi pomeriggio.

Practice 1

Le mie vacanze

Aim: to practise free writing

1 Tell students to write a short piece about their next holiday in the form of a letter to a friend.

2 To give some encouragement, write one or two sentences on the board.

e.g. *Cara . . . ,*
L'estate è vicina e la voglia di andare in vacanza cresce. Non so ancora di preciso che cosa fare. Penso di andare in Grecia . . .

3 Go round the class giving advice and suggestions.

4 Ask students to read to the class what they have written.

5 If you have an OHP divide the students into groups and give each group a clean transparent sheet on which to write a piece collectively.

6 Collect the transparent sheets, show them on the OHP and ask the class to correct the mistakes.

Dove va il 34?

Aim: to practise giving directions

1 Divide students into small groups and ask each group to think of a local bus route.

2 Each group writes a description of the route (or part of it).

3 Elicit from the class the main verbs (*andare, girare a destra/sinistra*) and write them on the board. Add a few suggestions of your own, for example *passa da . . ./si ferma a . . ./percorre . . .*, etc.

4 Collect the work, read aloud what the students have written and ask the other students to guess which number bus it is.

Tu o Lei

Aim: to practise the formal address

Ask students to re-write Interaction 4 and change the form of address from informal to formal.

Dove sono?

Aim: to practise describing an area

1   Describe a short walk in the locality.
e.g. *Ieri ho camminato per 10 minuti. Ho girato a destra in Park Road e sono andato avanti fino all'incrocio. Qui ho girato a sinistra . . .*

2   Ask students to guess the various sites you covered during your walk.

Variation 1: Ask students to bring to the class maps of places they might have visited in Italy (or bring in one yourself, along with other *realia* such as postcards and photographs).

Variation 2: Make enough copies of a map and distribute them to the students. Ask one or more students to prepare a little talk about the places he/she has visited.

Vieni a trovarmi

Aim: to practise giving directions orally

Ask students to record a telephone message in which they give instructions on how to get from the nearest bus/tube/train stop to their home.

Mystery tour

  26

You've been sightseeing on your own in the centre of Lecce and you're in your car outside the church of Santa Croce waiting for your Italian friend. He has promised to guide you to a mystery spot. Listen to his instructions and follow the route on the map. Where do you end up?

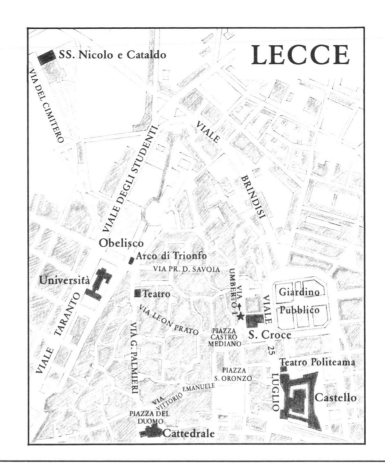

Which way please?

Now it's your turn to do some guiding. You've been in Gallipoli some time and people often ask you the way. Can you tell the following people how to get to their destination?

1 You are at the information office.

Ragazza Dov'è la posta, per favore?

2 You are outside the church of San Francesco.

Sig. anziano Scusi, per la cattedrale come faccio, per favore?

3 You are at the station.

Coppia Come facciamo per andare alla fontana ellenistica?

Back at home, can you now try to explain to a friend how to get to your nearest bus stop, post-office or chemist's?

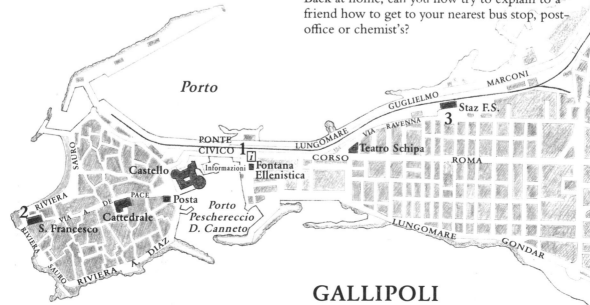

Cultura e parole

In Italy **l'ordine pubblico** – law and order – is the province of two bodies: the navy-blue uniformed **Arma dei Carabinieri** and the grey uniformed State Police, the **PS, la Polizia di Stato**. They both originated in the Kingdom of Piedmont before the unification of Italy. The carabinieri were originally the royal guard, the **Corpo dei Carabinieri Reali**, while the police were originally a civilian militia, the **Guardia Nazionale**. Nowadays the carabinieri are a special corps of the Italian army and are in part controlled by the **Ministero della Difesa** – the Ministry of Defence, and in part by the Interior Ministry. The **Polizia di Stato** have always been under the **Ministero degli Interni** – the Interior Ministry. The tasks of these two forces are not always easy to separate, since both deal with civilian crime: you can report a theft, for example, to either the **carabinieri** or the **polizia**. There have even been cases of the carabinieri and police both working independently on the same case unbeknown to each other, since there is no coordinating body. There are numerous carabinieri jokes in Italy which portray them as very stupid: in fact they are the most prestigious force and they have maintained their traditional right to provide the Presidential Guard of Honour and to be on duty in the Law Courts. Most important is the fact that the carabinieri are the institution most consistently trusted by Italians: recent surveys show that they come just ahead of the Church with over 31 per cent of Italians giving them their confidence. Since 1980, when the state police were reorganised, there have been women police and new words coined as a result: **poliziotta** – policewoman, **vigilessa** – traffic policewoman. There are no women carabinieri because at present women are not allowed to join the army. Bills have been put forward to change the law and if this happens it will be possible to become a **carabiniera**!

In most countries legal language and the language of bureaucracy tend towards the florid or even the impenetrable. In Italy people are so aware of the fact that they have a word for it: **il burocratese**. In 1988 the Italian Supreme Court, **la Corte di Cassazione**, actually ruled that if a law is incomprehensible there may be grounds for saying that citizens are not obliged to obey it! A project for simplifying the language of public administration was set up by the government and in 1991 its recommendations included the suggestion that it should use only the basic 7000 words known to the majority of Italians. The results of this recommendation have yet to be seen!

Cultura e parole

Just as in English, *Che giornata!* can be used to denote
either a very bad or a very good day, depending on the
intonation given to the expression. Besides *il compleanno,*
Italians enjoy another special day each year, the
onomastico – their saint's day. The unlucky ones are those
whose birthday falls on the same day as their *onomastico,*
or those whose name is not that of a *santo* the Vatican has
included in the calendar. Every so often this league of
saints is updated, with a few saints promoted and a few
demoted. There is even a proverb which metaphorically
uses the upgrading of saints to convey the idea of old
being replaced by new: *I santi nuovi mettono da parte i
vecchi.*

Modern life in Italy is not dictated by religious dogma,
as is often believed abroad, but religion still plays an
important part in keeping traditions alive. For further
discussion and class activities you might find the following
useful:

a) a list of the most common Italian names
b) *il culto dei santi/patroni* (one for every village or town)
c) *santi e idiomi*
e.g. *Impacciati coi fanti e lascia stare i santi.*
Fa scappare la pazienza anche a un santo.
Non sapere a che santo voltarsi.
Non c'è santo che tenga.
Avere qualche santo dalla propria parte.

Interaction 6 (462)

1 *Anna e Alberto vanno in macchina a Gallipoli. Nessuno dei due conosce la città.*
How long have they got before they are due to meet Cioto?
Has either of them got a map of Gallipoli?

2 Play the cassette/CD as required.

3 Write on the board and explain the grammatical structure *mi sono dimenticata*, giving other examples:

mi sono alzato/a   mi sono divertito/a

This point could be the end of the lesson. Revise all the points covered so far. In the next lesson students will cover the following:

> **Structures:** *stare* + gerund
> **Functions:** talking about what's wrong/expressing dismay
> **Vocabulary:** *conoscere, dimenticarsi, fare la multa*

Interaction 7 (480)

1 *Anna e Alberto non hanno molta fortuna. La macchina si ferma improvvisamente.*
Why have they stopped?

2 Play the cassette/CD as required.

3 Ask students to write a dialogue in which Anna and Alberto ring Cioto to tell him that they'll be arriving late.

Interactions

6 [cc] [CD] 27

Driving to the fishing port of Gallipoli, Anna and
Alberto are relieved to be getting there in good
time, because neither of them knows the place.

First time round

| il cartello | *signpost* |
| mi sono dimenticata di | *I forgot to* |

a How long have they got before they are due to
meet Cioto?
b Has either of them got a map of Gallipoli?

Alberto Siamo quasi arrivati. Hai visto il cartello per
        Gallipoli sulla destra?
Anna   Meno male. E che ore sono?
Alberto Sono le tre e mezza. A che ora abbiamo
        appuntamento con Cioto?
Anna   Alle quattro, vicino alla fontana greca.
Alberto E tu **conosci la strada**, Anna?
Anna   No, io non la conosco. Ah, mi sono
        dimenticata di portare la pianta della città.
        Tu ne hai una, Alberto?
Alberto Eh, non l'ho portata neanch'io.
Anna   Ah, pazienza. Quando arriviamo in città
        chiediamo la strada in centro.

Key phrases

conosci la strada?	*do you know the way?*
ne hai una?	*have you got one?*
chiediamo la strada	*we'll ask the way*

7 [cc] [CD] 28

So near and yet so far: the car grinds to a halt.

First time round

| controllo | *I'll check* |

Why have they stopped?

Anna   Alberto, perché ci fermiamo? **C'è qualcosa
        che non va?** Oddio! Che cosa abbiamo
        combinato adesso?
Alberto **Non lo so** Anna. Adesso controllo.
[Alberto gets out to see]
Anna   Stiamo qui un attimo, allora?
Alberto Sì.
Anna   Allora, mi puoi dire che **cos'è successo?**
Alberto **Che guaio!** Abbiamo bucato.
[...]

che cos'abbiamo combinato   *what have we done?*

Key phrases

c'è qualcosa che non va?	*is there something wrong?*
non lo so	*I don't know*
cos'è successo?	*what's happened?*
che guaio!	*what a disaster, bad luck!*

8 ▭ ◉ 29

They fix the puncture and arrive at Gallipoli. They park the car on the seafront and meet up with Cioto. But their troubles are not quite over . . .

First time round

la multa	*fine*
il vigile	*traffic policeman*

Why are they being fined?

Cioto   Ciao.
Alberto Ciao.
Anna   Ciao.
Cioto   Ragazzi, vi stanno facendo la multa. **Non si può** parcheggiare sul lungomare.
Anna   Oh no!

Alberto Ma tu conosci il vigile. Puoi fare qualcosa?
Cioto   Credo . . . non si può fare niente. [. . .]
Alberto Ah, ma allora è proprio vero. Non c'è due senza tre. Che giornata! [. . .]

vi stanno facendo la multa	*they're giving you a fine*
non c'è due senza tre	*disasters come in threes* [lit. *there isn't two without three*].

Key phrase

non si può . . .   *you can't, it's not allowed*

Interaction 8 (493)

1 *Finalmente Anna e Alberto arrivano a Gallipoli. I guai però non sono finiti.*
Why are they being fined?

2 Play the cassette/CD as required.

3 Ask students to suggest other places where you cannot park your car, for further practice of *non si può*.

Patterns 2

Talking about what's gone wrong

a)

1 Students should be able to provide a long list of things that have gone wrong for them in the recent past:

Ieri ho dimenticato l'ombrello.

Sono rimasto chiuso/a fuori casa il mese scorso.

2 Divide the students into small groups and tell them to make a list of things that went wrong for them (at least one per group member).

3 One student from each group reports to the rest of the class what has happened to the other students in his/her group.

b)

1 Tell students about an incident or accident in which you were involved. Show them a photograph of your arm in plaster, if you have one, or some other clear signs, a scar or mark on your body, etc. and tell students what happened (explain difficult words beforehand if necessary).

2 Divide the class into small groups and ask them to discuss their own personal incidents or accidents. Tell them to choose one example and to prepare a story to illustrate it.

3 One student from each group relates the story to the class without ever saying who was involved in the incident or accident. The class have to guess the student involved.

Being sure and unsure

1 Bring a large picture or object into the class.

2 Prepare a number of statements about it, some true and some false.

3 Divide the class into two groups and tell the students you are going to show them the picture or object for sixty seconds, before reading/showing them a number of statements about it. They can then comment on the statements in four different ways:

lo so   non lo so   penso di sì   non ho idea

4 Tell students to prepare a column for each comment and to tick which is most suitable for each statement you make. Each of the four comments has a score:

lo so/non lo so	one point
penso di sì	half a point
non ho idea	no points

If the answer is wrong the score is deducted from their total. *Non ho idea* does not gain or lose any points. *Non lo so* gains a point if the statement you have made cannot be said to be true on the basis of the information available.

5 Show the picture or the object again and discuss any questions raised.

Expressing dismay

1 Bring into the class a poem or song which describes a number of unfortunate events, all linked to each other.

e.g. *Il topo è stato mangiato dal gatto che viene inseguito dal cane che viene battuto con un bastone,* etc. Children's literature provides plenty of examples.

2 Read the poem/play the song and tell students to make a note of how many times they could express dismay (i.e. they should try to understand the gist of the events being described).

3 Discuss any questions raised.

What is not allowed

1 Divide the class into small groups and ask them to think of a team sport or game.

2 Tell students to make a list of the things you are not allowed to do in that game. Supervise the activity, moving from one group to another.

3 One student from each group reads the list to the class, who have to guess which sport or game it is.

Patterns 2

i) Asking about what happened

The verb *to happen* is **succedere**. In the past tense it takes **essere**:

Cos'è successo?   *What happened? What has happened?*

If you think there is something wrong, you can use the verb **andare**:

C'è qualcosa che non va?   *Is there something wrong?*

ii) Talking about what's gone wrong

Ho	rotto la torcia		I've	broken the torch
	perso la patente			lost my driving licence
	perso il treno			missed the train
	dimenticato l'apriscatole			forgotten the tin-opener
	lasciato il cavatappi a casa			left the corkscrew at home

It could be something that's happened to you: in this case you say literally *they have stolen/given*:

Mi hanno rubato	il portafoglio	*I've had my*	wallet	*stolen*
	la valigia		suitcase	
	la cartella		briefcase	

Mi hanno dato la camera sbagliata   *I've been given the wrong room*
Ci hanno dato il piatto sbagliato   *We've been given the wrong dish/order*

See Systems, note 5, p. 202.

It could be that something important is missing: use **mancare** (*to be lacking*):

Manca il sapone   *There's no soap*
Mancano le lenzuola   *There aren't any sheets*

See Unit 9, Systems, note 7 and Ref. I, 8, p. 240.

iii) Being sure and unsure

Lo so . . .	*I know* [lit. *I know it*]	Penso di sì	*I think so*
Non lo so	*I don't know (it)*	Non ho idea	*I don't have a clue*

See also Unit 5, Systems, note 1 ii, p. 97 and Unit 7, note 6, p. 198.

iv) Expressing dismay

Che guaio!   *What a disaster/bad luck!* [lit. *trouble*]
Che disastro!   *What a disaster!*
Che pasticcio!   *What a mess/mix up/muddle!*

v) What is not allowed

Non	è permesso	guidare a sinistra	*It's not allowed to*	drive on the left
	si può	sorpassare sulla destra	*You can't*	overtake on the right

You can also use the word **vietato**, from the verb **vietare** *(to forbid)*: **È vietato fumare.**

Practice 2

Odd one out

1 Which of these phrases wouldn't you use to express regret or dismay?
che pasticcio   che peccato   che bello   che guaio

2 Which of these couldn't you have lost from your briefcase?
un'agenda   un'agenzia   una carta di credito   una patente

3 Which one of the following could you do without?
un cavatappi   un apriscatole   un rompiscatole   una torcia

4 Which one of the following can't be used to give directions?
diritto   destra   davvero   dietro

5 Which of these wouldn't you eat?
cannelloni   carabinieri   sanguinaccio   arancini

Fawlty towers

The hard-pressed manager of a hotel is faced with a spate of disasters and complaints: would you give him a job? To make up your mind match up the complaints and his answers and see how he copes.

1 Ci hanno dato la stessa camera!
2 Ho perso la chiave!
3 Manca il sapone!
4 Mancano le lenzuola!
5 Il gabinetto/water è intasato!
6 Manca l'acqua calda!

a Ah! Non siete sposati? Che pasticcio. La camera è grande, però.
b Ah, che guaio! Ma scusi, perché non chiama l'idraulico? Le do subito il numero.
c Mi dispiace, non ne abbiamo altre. Basta entrare per la finestra.
d Davvero? Ma Lei non ne ha portato?
e Non c'è problema. Abbiamo anche l'acqua fredda.
f Che peccato! Ma oggi per fortuna non fa freddo.

Chapter of accidents   30

You've hired an idyllic **rustico** with a friend and are all set for a blissful week. You're nearing your destination and are looking forward to supper and a nice drink.

Amico   Ah! che bello! Siamo quasi arrivati.
You   [*Say thank goodness, you're tired.*]
Amico   Quando arriviamo, assaggiamo quel vino pugliese. A me piace tanto.
You   [*Say you like it too.*]
You   [*. . . Car splutters. Ask if there's something wrong.*]
Amico   Ma non lo so . . . Eh, penso di sì . . . Oh, no!
You   [*Ask what's happened.*]
Amico   Abbiamo finito la benzina!
You   [*Say really? – what a disaster!*]

But in the end you make it to the cottage. Now for that wonderful Pugliese wine . . .

Amico   Ah, eccoci finalmente! Prendiamo il vino?
You   [*Oh no . . . where can it be? Own up, say you've forgotten the corkscrew.*]
Amico   No! che disastro!

What people forget   30

Listen to the hotelier describing the things people leave behind. What are they?

Missing!

You have gone to the Pensione Millerose where your friend Jane Mitchell is supposed to be staying. But she isn't there. You start by asking the owner if he knows her and then try to find out what else he knows. Here are his answers: what were the questions you asked?

1 . . .? Sì, sì, la conosco. Ma è partita una settimana fa.
2 . . .? No, mi dispiace, non so dov'è andata.
3 . . .? Eh no. Non ha lasciato l'indirizzo.
4 . . .? Mi dispiace, non so neanche il numero di telefono.
5 . . .? Eh, no. Non so perché è partita. Non ho idea, mi dispiace.

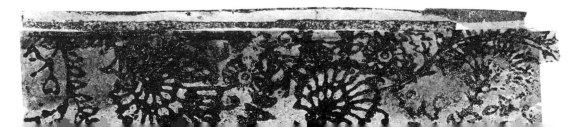

Practice 2

La multa

Aim: to practise describing what happened

1   Prepare a number of large cards of road signs.

2   Put students into pairs (each pair made up of a policeman or policewoman and a motorist who has contravened the highway code). Give one sign to each pair to work on.

3   Tell the student motorists to explain why they were fined and tell the students who represent *la forza dell'ordine* to write a short report of the incident. If, for example, the sign you give one pair of students is *Divieto di svolta a destra,* one student could say:

Non ho visto il divieto di svolta a destra perché era nascosto da un Tir, e ho girato a destra. Un carabiniere mi ha fermato e mi ha fatto una multa di 100.000 lire.

If the report written by the *carabiniere* differs, invite other students to be witnesses.

As well as jokes about national stereotypes, there are many about the Italian police force. Some are very funny, even though the underlying humour is still clearly based on the north-south division (many *carabinieri* come from southern Italy). Unfortunately, this humour is difficult to appreciate for linguistic and cultural reasons. You could, however, illustrate some jokes. There are some Italian magazines entirely devoted to jokes and puzzles. Make copies of these, leaving out the punchline which you ask students to supply. Comment and discuss as required.

Il codice stradale

Aim: to reinforce vocabulary used in road directions

1   Put students into pairs and give them a list of *divieto di* or *obbligo di* items from an Italian highway code manual.

2   Prepare a number of large cards featuring the corresponding road signs (one less than is on the list).

3   Show each card and ask students to tick off the description which corresponds to the sign. (At the end, all the pairs should be left with the same description.)

4   Discuss any questions raised.

Road sense

Can you match up the road signs with the descriptions given?

1 Doppia curva, la prima a destra
2 Animali domestici vaganti
3 Pericolo di incendio
4 Passaggio a livello senza barriere
5 Animali selvatici
6 Transito vietato ai pedoni

a
b
c
d
e
f

Before and after

Someone's broken into your house and items have been stolen. To find out what they are, compare the two pictures. Make an inventory, tell your flatmate what's missing (using **manca, mancano**), then tell the police what's been stolen (using **mi hanno rubato**).

Vocabulary

Documents

l'agenda	diary
il calendario	calendar
la carta assegni	cheque card
la carta di credito	credit card
la carta d'identità	identity card
il documento	document
il libretto degli assegni	cheque book
il modulo	form
il passaporto	passport
la patente	driving licence
la rubrica	address book
la tessera	card
i travellers cheques	travellers' cheques

People

il delinquente	criminal
il giudice	judge
il ladro	thief
la polizia	police
... doganale	border/customs police
... stradale	road police
il vigile, la vigilessa	traffic police

Adjectives

giusto	right
sbagliato	wrong
bucato	punctured
esaurito	out of print, booked up
guasto	out of order
intasato	blocked up
permesso	allowed
rotto	broken
scarico	flat [battery]
scaduto	expired, run out
vietato	forbidden

Crime, accidents and the law

la contravvenzione	fine [formal]
il danno	damage
il disguido	mix-up
la disgrazia	disaster
la fuga	[gas] leak
il furto	theft
l'incendio	fire
l'incidente	[car] accident
l'infortunio	[industrial] accident
l'infrazione	offence
la multa	fine
la questura	police station
la rapina	armed robbery
il reato	crime
il ritardo	delay
lo scippo	[handbag] snatching
il verbale	statement
divieto	
di sosta	no waiting
di transito	no thoroughfare

Personal property

la cartella	briefcase
la cinepresa	cine-camera
il compact disc	compact disc
la macchina fotografica	camera
il personal computer	word processor
lo stereo	stereo
il televisore	television set
la valigia	suitcase
il videoregistratore	video recorder

Verbs

bruciare	to burn
confermare	to confirm
controllare	to check
fissare un appuntamento	to make an appointment
fare un errore	to make a mistake
dimenticare	to forget
disdire	to cancel
firmare	to sign
guidare	to drive
lasciare cadere	to drop
mancare	to be missing, lacking
perdere	to lose; miss; leak
ricordare	to remember
riempire	to fill in [form]
rimandare/rinviare	to postpone
riparare	to mend
rompere	to break
rovesciare	to spill
rubare	to steal
sbagliare	to make a mistake; get it wrong
sorpassare	to overtake

Vocabulary

Practise collocation

1   Explain the meaning of collocation and give a couple of examples to illustrate this.

e.g. *fare la doccia, fare il bagno, avere sonno, avere paura*

2   Choose four to five verbs which can be used in collocation with different words and write them on the board.

e.g. *dare   fare   mettere   avere*

3   Write a number of different collocations for each verb on cards – at least one for each student.

e.g. *dare: un taglio/vitto e alloggio/causa/gusto*
fare: fortuna/da mangiare/una smorfia/la barba/la doccia
mettere: nel sacco/in difficoltà/in dubbio/al sicuro
avere: freddo/caldo/fretta/sonno/ragione

4   Distribute a card to each of the students who should try to form themselves into groups, according to the appropriate verb collocation.

5   When the groups are formed, discuss the exercise.

Troubleshooting

Review

Here is a checklist of the main points learned in this unit. For each point, ask students to provide you with one or more examples by asking specific questions.

formal and informal forms of address
imperative
apologising
making plans for the future
dates and calendar
asking and giving directions
ne + verb + quantity
expressing regret
past tense actions with verbs of movement
past tense of reflexive verbs
giving directions
description of the local area
everyday actions
stare + gerund
talking about what's wrong
expressing dismay

Troubleshooting

Non mi piace   Mi dispiace
Non mi dispiace

The above phrases have quite distinct meanings.
Non mi piace is the opposite of **mi piace**. It means *I don't like, I dislike*:

> Non mi piace questa città

Mi dispiace is used to express regret and sympathy.
It means *I'm sorry* [*lit. it is displeasing to me*].

> Mi dispiace, non posso venire
> Hai perso il passaporto? – Mi dispiace

Non mi dispiace means *I quite like, don't mind something*:

> Non mi dispiace cucinare

Mi dispiace   Scusi Scusa

Scusi [formal] and **scusa** [informal] mean *excuse me, sorry, forgive me.*
They are used both to interrupt or attract attention and also to apologise for what you've done:

> Scusi, può ripetere?
> Scusa, mi puoi dire se c'è Maria?
> Scusi se La disturbo
> Scusi, ho rovesciato il caffè!

Mi dispiace is also used to say sorry, but for something which is not directly your fault:

> È tutto esaurito. – Mi dispiace!

It is possible to use both expressions together:

> Ho rotto il piatto! Scusi! Mi dispiace!
> *I've broken the plate! Forgive me! I'm sorry!*

A caccia di funghi

In this unit you'll find out about the language of the Italian countryside: you'll be learning about some of the flora and fauna, indulging in country pursuits and expressing your own enthusiasms and fancies, pet hates and phobias.

Although Italy had become an industrialised nation by the 1930s, over 40 per cent of the work-force was employed on the land until the 1950s. The countryside was considered a place for work rather than leisure. Nowadays, however, countryside leisure pursuits such as riding, rambling and hiking – **il trekking** – are gaining in popularity. In the mid 1980s, the **Sentiero Italia** project was set up under the auspices of the **Club Alpino Italiano,** to provide 4000 km of path to cover the length and breadth of Italy. Over half has been completed and it is possible to walk from the Trentino in the North right down to Sicily. The practical attitude inherited from a relatively recent agricultural past still survives in more traditional pastimes as mushroom-picking and hunting – **la caccia. La caccia** is mainly about shooting birds rather than hunting animals: it is a sport which appeals to all classes and has a body of passionate supporters as well as dedicated opponents. Growing environmental awareness in Italy has led to **la caccia** being a controversial issue since the 1970s: the indiscriminate shooting of birds has given rise to fears that whole species will be wiped out. There have been four attempts to hold a national referendum to ban the sport. When a referendum was finally held and won in 1990, it was ruled invalid since the turnout was only 43 per cent – under the 50 per cent required to make a referendum legally binding.

Emilia Romagna

Borgotaro

Bologna

A caccia di funghi

Essere in contatto con la natura is not an alien concept to Italians. The mountains which cover most of the country are areas where people can freely wander in search of wild fruits and berries or simply enjoy the peace and tranquillity of the countryside. Mushroom-picking is one of a number of outdoor activities which vary according to the season. Mushrooms grow in springtime but are mainly found at the end of the summer. *Mirtilli* (whortleberries/bilberries) and other wild fruits are picked in the summer and the autumn is the time for *castagne* and, of course, *la vendemmia*. The hot weather, congenial for outdoor activities, makes a visit to the country the favourite pastime of all classes and it is not uncommon to see large groups of people eating and drinking around picnic tables by the side of country roads. Often, religious festivals are excuses for thousands to make excursions to the countryside and local harvests, too, are celebrated with a *scampagnata*. There are hundreds of such gatherings on any given day of the summer up and down the country and, whether it is a saint or a local agricultural product which is being celebrated, enjoyment of the countryside is at the heart of the festivities.

Video corner

What are they wearing?

Aim: vocabulary building through active viewing
Video sequence: Anna, Paolo, Michela and Toto walking through the forest at dawn

1 Tell students they are going to see a sequence in which they have to pay attention to the items of clothing worn by the four people going mushroom-picking.

2 Write the following chart on the board and ask students to copy it:

	Paolo	Anna	Michela	Toto
scarpe				
camicia				
giacca				
foulard				
pantaloni				
gonna				
maglione				

3 Ask students to tick the right clothing for each person and possibly write the colour of each item.

4 Similarly ask students to describe the mood of each of the four by ticking one of the following (explain and discuss as necessary):

	Paolo	Anna	Michela	Toto
allegro/a				
stanco/a				
scettico/a				
entusiasta				
pessimista				
ottimista				

About mushrooms

Aim: guided note-taking
Video sequence: interview with the mushroom expert

1 Tell students that *un esperto di funghi* is going to talk about mushrooms. Ask them to listen out for the three questions below (a, b, c) and help them take notes using the guidelines given.

a) Mushrooms grow especially in the proximity of three kinds of trees – which ones?
Write the following on the board, discuss the meanings and ask students to copy them.

*quercia pioppo cedro pino gaggia
frassino platano cipresso castagno faggio*

b) Which of the following conditions does the expert say there should be a balance of?
Write the following on the board, discuss the meanings and ask students to copy them.

*inquinamento clima fauna
temperatura flora luce*

c) Why is the position crucial?

2 Play the video sequence and ask students to tick/write the right answer

Making your own video

Aim: to encourage students to make their own video

The video sequence showing the recipe is a good starting point if you want to encourage students to make a video of their own, should you or any of your students have the use of a video camera.
Ask students to write a plan for a video. Give them a few ideas.
e.g. how to make a dish (their favourite perhaps)
how to change a spark plug in a car engine
how to knit a jumper

You can either choose something that can be filmed in class or you can ask the students to do it at home and bring it to the class to show the others.

Interactions

> **Structures:** agreement of past participle when *avere* is preceded by a direct object pronoun/*non* + verb + *niente*
> **Functions:** inviting/accepting/asking permission/urging on
> **Vocabulary:** *funghi porcini, segreto, esperto,* Saturday night activities

Help-phrases and instructions

Il mio punto di vista è il seguente:
Discutiamone

Interaction 1 (025)

1 *Anna telefona, da una cabina telefonica, ad una sua amica, Michela Alberti, per invitarla ad andare a cercare funghi.* Michela agrees to come. Why?

2 Play the cassette/CD as required and ask further questions:

What did Anna do the previous week?
How many people are going to go mushroom-picking and when?

3 After students have listened and answered all the questions, give them a copy of the dialogue with Michela's lines erased. Michela speaks seven times. Give the total number of words (55 in all) for each line and ask the students to supply the missing words.

4 Students work individually for a few minutes, then in pairs, then they join in groups of four and so on until the class is divided into just two groups.

5 Students carry on working in two groups. At this stage they can ask for the number of letters in each word. Here they are

1)   6   4   7
2)   4   9   1 2
3)   4   3   10 2   6
4)   2   5   4 3 10 2 6
5)   1   4   2 5   1 4 7   5 2 8   1 3 2 9 5 1 7
6) 10   5   7 2   3 5 1 14 1 2 10 1 4 5 3
7)   2   2   1 2 10 1 4   3 1 4   6

6 Draw 55 lines on the board and ask each group to send a student to the board to fill in the words.

7 Discuss any questions raised.

Interactions

Anna is staying in Borgotaro, the 'mushroom capital' of Emilia Romagna in the mountains of the Val Taro region, about 65 km from Parma. She's discovered a good place for finding the prized **porcino** mushroom and rings up her friend Michela Alberti to see if she feels like mushroom-picking.

First time round

a caccia di funghi	*mushroom-picking*
proprio stufa	*really fed up*
posto segreto	*secret place*

Anna is in a phone box in a noisy street.

Michela agrees to come. Why?

Michela	Pronto, casa Alberti.
Anna	Ciao Michela. Sono Anna. Come stai?
Michela	Ciao! Benissimo, e tu?
Anna	Anch'io, grazie. Senti, ti ho telefonato per sapere **se hai voglia di** andare a caccia di funghi.
Michela	**Dove hai intenzione di** andare?
Anna	**Come hai detto? Non ti sento bene.**
Michela	Ho detto: dove hai intenzione di andare?
Anna	Beh, conosco un posto segreto, molto bello. La settimana scorsa ci ho trovato moltissimi funghi porcini.
Michela	L'idea mi piace e sono proprio stufa di studiare. E poi mi piacciono tanto i porcini.
Anna	Bene. Allora vieni?
Michela	Volentieri. **Posso portare un mio amico?** È simpaticissimo. L'ho conosciuto a Roma dagli zii.
Anna	Certo. Perché no! Viene anche un altro mio amico, Paolo. Lo conosci?
Michela	Sì, sì. L'ho conosciuto a casa tua, l'anno scorso.
Anna	Ah! già, è vero. Bene, allora, ci troviamo tutti a casa mia sabato mattina.

[...]

casa Alberti	*one way of identifying the house when answering the phone: you never say your number*
l'ho conosciuto	*I met him*
già, è vero	*that's right, it's true*

Key phrases

se hai voglia di ...	*if you feel like ...*
dove hai intenzione di ...?	*where do you intend to ...?*
come hai detto?	*what did you say?*
non ti sento bene	*I can't hear you properly*
posso portare un mio amico?	*can I bring a friend of mine?*

2 [cc] [CD] 3

Anna, Paolo, Michela and her friend Totò have met up early; it's damp and misty but Anna makes light of Michela's ironic comment about the weather.

First time round

speriamo	let's hope
senz'altro	definitely

a Is Anna confident about finding mushrooms? Why?
b What is Paolo's particular interest in them?

Michela	Che bella giornata per andare a funghi!
Anna	Sì, siamo proprio fortunati.
Michela	**Speriamo di trovare** funghi, almeno.
Anna	Ne troviamo senz'altro. Ne ho visti tanti l'altro giorno.
Paolo	Meno male! Stasera li mangiamo tutti.
Totò	Ma li sai preparare, Paolo?
Paolo	Certo. Sono un esperto, io!
Totò	Benissimo! Allora Anna, dove li hai visti questi funghi? **Da che parte andiamo** per trovarli?
Anna	Bisogna andare **di qua**. Sempre dritto. Andiamo!

andare a/per funghi	to go mushroom-picking
siamo proprio fortunati	we're really lucky
almeno	at least
ne ho visti tanti	I saw lots
li sai preparare?	do you know how to prepare them?
dove li hai visti?	where did you see them?

Key phrases

speriamo di trovare	let's hope we find
da che parte andiamo?	which way do we go?
di qua	this way

3 [cc] [CD] 4

The boys are fairly hopeless, but Anna turns out to be quite an expert at finding mushrooms.

First time round

guardare	to look
il cestino pieno	full basket
quell'albero	that tree

a What advice does Michela give the boys?
b Where does Anna go off to?

Anna	Che bello! Ne ho trovati tanti!
Paolo	Ma dove? Io non ne ho visti.
Totò	Neanch'io. **Non ho visto niente.** [...]
Michela	Ma voi ragazzi non sapete come fare. Bisogna avere pazienza per trovarli. I funghi ci sono. Basta guardare bene.
Totò	Ho guardato. **Non ce ne sono.**
Michela	Ci sono. **Ce ne sono tantissimi.** Guarda, ho il cestino pieno. [...]
Totò	Forza Paolo, ne dobbiamo trovare anche noi. Perchè non provi? Non si sa mai!
Paolo	Ma non trovo mai niente io. A me piace soprattutto mangiare i funghi. Ma Anna dov'è?
Michela	È andata **un po' più avanti, lì in fondo** a sinistra, dietro quell'albero. Non la vedi? Lei conosce i posti migliori.
Totò	E noi i posti peggiori!
[...]	

non sapete come fare	you don't know how to do it
forza	come on!
non si sa mai	you never know
non trovo mai niente	I never find anything
migliori/peggiori	best/worst

Key phrases

non ho visto niente	I haven't seen anything
non ce ne sono	there aren't any
ce ne sono tantissimi	there are lots
un po' più avanti	a bit further on
lì in fondo	right over/down there

Interaction 2 (077)

1 *Il sabato mattina all'alba Anna, Michela, Paolo e Toto sono già in cerca di funghi.*
Is Anna confident about finding mushrooms? Why?
What is Paolo's particular interest in them?

2 Play the cassette/CD as required.

3 Ask students to predict the outcome (who will, if anyone, find some mushrooms?), and to put their suggestions in writing.

Interaction 3 (114)

1 *I ragazzi che non sono molto bravi a trovare funghi sono un po' scoraggiati. Anna invece è una vera esperta e ne trova molti.*
What advice does Michela give the boys?
Where does Anna go off to?

2 Play the cassette/CD as required and ask further questions as required.

3 Tell students to imagine they are either Paolo or Toto and write an account of the day so far.

Interaction 4 (147)

1 *Anna ha trovato molti funghi fra cui anche alcuni porcini.*
How many *porcini* has Anna found?
Does Paolo manage to find any?

2 Play the cassette/CD as required and ask further questions:
Where did Anna find the porcini?
How big are they?
What is foremost in Paolo's mind?

4 ⌜cc⌝ ◉ 5

Anna is rejoined by the others. She's found plenty of mushrooms – and a few of the prized **porcini.** They're so enormous you only need a few to make a meal.

First time round

in tutto	*in total*
solo	*only*
altri	*more*

a How many **porcini** has Anna found?
b Does Paolo manage to find any?

Anna	Avete visto quanti funghi si trovano nel bosco? Io ho anche trovato alcuni porcini.
Michela	Ma dove?
Anna	Là, a sinistra sotto l'albero.
Totò	**E già!** Sono porcini! belli, grossi! Sei fortunata, Anna.
Michela	Quanti ne hai trovati in tutto?
Anna	**Non lo so.** Il cestino è pieno. Però ho trovato solo tre porcini. **Forse** ne troviamo altri fra poco.
Paolo	Ragazzi! Porcini! Ne ho trovati altri tre!
Michela	Altri porcini? **Sei sicuro?**
Paolo	**Certo**, è facile riconoscerli. Anche se non è facile trovarli. Sono enormi! Giganteschi! E stasera li mangiamo tutti!

ne ho trovati altri tre	*I've found three more*
è facile riconoscerli	*it's easy to recognise them*

Key phrases

e già!	*that's right!*
non lo so	*I don't know*
forse	*maybe*
sei sicuro?	*are you sure?*
certo	*of course*

Patterns I

i) Asking for clarification

If you can't hear what someone has said, you can say:

Come hai detto?/Cos'hai detto, scusa?   *What did you say?*
Come ha detto?/Cos'ha detto, scusi?
Non ti/La sento bene   *I can't hear you properly*
Puoi/può ripetere, per piacere?   *Can you please repeat?*

ii) Wishes and intentions

To find out what someone feels like doing, use **avere voglia di** (*lit. to have desire to*):

Hai voglia di | andare per funghi?   *Do you feel like* | going mushroom picking?
              | prendere qualcosa? | having something?
              | uscire stasera? | going out tonight?

To say you plan to do something use **avere intenzione di** (*lit. to have intention to*):

Dove hai intenzione di andare?   *Where do you plan to go?*
Cosa ha intenzione di fare?   *What do you intend to do?*

To say what you're thinking or hoping of doing use **pensare di** or **sperare di**:

Penso di | andare in montagna   *I think I'll* | go to the mountains
Speriamo di | fare una scampagnata   *We hope to* | go on a picnic, country outing

iii) Bringing a friend of yours

The verb **portare** has various meanings including *to bring*.

Posso portare | un mio amico?   *Can I bring a friend of mine?* (lit. a my friend)
              | una mia amica?
              | un altro mio amico? *Can I bring another friend of mine?*
              | un'altra mia amica?

See Systems, note 2, p. 205.

iv) Talking about place

Da che parte andiamo?   *Which way do we go?*   Di qua/da questa parte   *Over here/this way*

Andiamo | avanti   *Let's go* | on, forward
        | lì in fondo | over, down there
        | lassù, laggiù | up there, down there
Torniamo indietro   *Let's turn back, round*

v) Nothing and no-one

In Italian you say: *I haven't seen nothing/no-one.*

Non ho visto | niente   *I haven't seen* | anything
                | nessuno | anyone

Non hai trovato | niente?   *Didn't you find* | anything?
                | nessuno? | anyone?

Patterns 1

Asking for clarification

Students should already be familiar with these useful help-phrases.

Wishes and intentions

1 Tell students to think of a possible activity for a Saturday night and to write it, together with their name, on a large piece of paper which you pass round. (Fold the paper each time so that students do not know what the others have written.)

2 Students go around the class finding out what most people have thought of doing. Tell them to ask questions such as:

Che cosa hai voglia/intenzione di fare in genere il sabato sera?

and to answer by saying:

Spero/Penso di . . .

3 Each student should try to convince as many others as possible to do something that he/she feels like doing. Tell students to make suggestions by saying:

Hai voglia/intenzione di . . .?

4 Compare what each student has finally decided to do with the suggestions originally written on the piece of paper.

This point could be the end of the lesson. Revise the points covered so far. In the next lesson students will cover the following:

> **Structures:** *ce n'è, ce ne sono/non* + verb + *mai, niente* or *nessuno*
> **Functions:** asking permission
> **Vocabulary:** words related to the building you are in/hand gestures and facial expressions/*alimenti*

Bringing a friend of yours

1 Ask students to divide a piece of paper into four columns as follows:

(Non) posso portare:

un amico	un amica	amici	amiche

2 Tell students you are going to read out a list of activities. For each one they have to ask themselves the question: *Posso o non posso portare un amico/a o degli amici?* and write *sì* or *no* in the appropriate column.

3 Tell students that if they cannot work out the meaning of what you are reading they should guess. Here is a sample list. Each activity is preceded by *andare*:

a vedere una casa da comprare
a parlare con il direttore della banca
in ufficio
in discoteca
all'esame di guida
al ristorante
dal dottore
dallo psichiatra
in viaggio di nozze

4 Since some of the activities are deliberately open to interpretation, the students might have different answers. If this is the case, encourage them to discuss their answers and justify their choices.

Talking about place

1 Draw a map of the building you are in on a large piece of paper. Put students into pairs and give them copies of the map.

2 Tell students to imagine showing a visitor around the building. Tell them to start their sentences with *se*. e.g. *Se andiamo da questa parte . . . Se torniamo indietro . . .*

3 Give students time to practise the presentation amongst themselves, then draw the same map on the board and ask one volunteer to do the presentation in front of the class.

4 Ask each student to present his or her own map of a place they know well.

Nothing and no-one

1 Tell students that you are a suspect for a jewellery shop robbery. The students, in pairs, are detectives and work out questions to ask you. But you are uncooperative and reply to everything in the negative. Reverse roles and ask the students questions.

2 Play a game with students. Choose one student and interrogate him/her on anything you like for about a minute. The student must reply without saying *sì* or *no*.

Talking about quantity

Divide students into two groups and give each group a
card with the name of a place on it. One group has to
guess where the other group is by asking questions such
as *c'è ...?* or *ci sono ...?* If the question is not
grammatically correct, it automatically becomes the other
group's turn to ask questions.

Start with easily guessed places, then go on to more
difficult ones.

e.g. *scuola*	*casa*	*stazione*
parco	*autostrada*	*negozio di abbigliamento*
banca	*stadio*	*ufficio*
ospedale	*mare*	*montagna*

Being sure and unsure

1 Think of hand gestures and facial expressions which
would go with the following:

certo   senz'altro   penso di sì   forse   non lo so

2 Write these on the board and elicit meanings (help
when required). Add a few more expressions.

e.g. *ma cosa dici   sei matto/a   è ottimo   è caro   fa caldo*

3 Tell students you are going to communicate the above
expressions without talking and ask them to match your
hand gestures and facial expressions to the words.

vi) Talking about quantity

Some of it

To say 'there is some', you combine **c'è** with **ne**, which becomes **ce n'è**:

| C'è dell'acqua qui? | *Is there any water here?* | No, non ce n'è | *No, there isn't any* |

Sì,	ce n'è	Yes,	there is (some)
	ce n'è molta, un po'		there's lots, a little
	ce n'è poca		there isn't much

| C'è | un rifugio qui? | *Is there* | *a hut here?* | No, non ce ne sono | *No, there aren't any [i.e.* |
| | una locanda qui? | | *an inn* | | *isn't one]* |

| Sì, | ce n'è uno | *Yes, there is one* |
| | ce n'è una | |

Some of them

You combine **ci sono** with **ne**, which becomes **ce ne sono**:

Ci sono animali selvatici qui?	*Are there wild animals here?*	No, non ce ne sono	*There aren't*
Sì,	ce ne sono	Yes,	there are		*any*
	ce ne sono molti/alcuni		there are many/a few	
	ce ne sono pochi		there aren't many	

See Systems, note 1, p. 205.

More

To talk about another, or more of something, you use **altro**.

un altro tartufo   *another truffle*   altre castagne   *more chestnuts*

To specify how much more, you can use the following with **altro**:

Ho visto	tantissime	altre bacche	*I've seen*	lots	*more berries*
	molte			many	
	alcune			a few	

With numbers or **un po'**, the quantity comes last:

Ne prendo un altro po'   *I'll have a bit more*

Ho trovato	un altro po' di	mirtilli	*I've found*	a few more	*bilberries*
	altri due	lamponi		two more	*raspberries*
	altre cinque	more		five more	*blackberries*

vii) Being sure and unsure

Sei sicuro?	*Are you sure?*	Forse	*Maybe, perhaps*
Certo	*Of course*	Dipende	*It depends*
Senz'altro	*Definitely*	Non lo so	*I don't know*
Penso di sì	*I think so*		

If you're acknowledging something is true you can say:

| Già | *[That's] right* | Note: you are familiar with **già** meaning *already*. |
| È vero | *It's, that's true* | |

Practice I

Hold up   6

How effective are you when it comes to holding up the proceedings? Listen to the cassette/CD and find out.

NB Some of the expressions you'll need have come in previous units. Can you remember them?

1 You're on the phone: ask someone to hold on.
2 How do you tell someone it's a bad line and you can't hear them properly?
3 You didn't catch what someone's just said: ask what did you say?
4 And what if you've heard, but haven't understood? How do you say: Sorry I haven't understood.
5 Ask someone if he minds repeating.

Wrong spot   6

It's a lovely day and you're taking some Italian guests on a picnic. You're carrying the food and looking for a picnic spot. Play the host or hostess and take part in the conversation.

You	[Say what a lovely day it is.]
Patrizia	Sì, siamo proprio fortunati!
Carlo	Senti, dove andiamo adesso? Di qua o di là?
You	[Tell him, this way.]
Carlo	D'accordo, andiamo.
Patrizia	È pesante questa roba! Siamo quasi arrivati?
You	[The stuff **is** heavy: tell her you're nearly there.]
Patrizia	Meno male!
You	[The picnic spot is at the end of the path: say it's down there.]
Carlo	Ah, che bello! Io ho fame.
You	[Oh dear, he'll have to wait a bit. This isn't the right place: tell them you're sorry, you've gone the wrong way, you'll have to turn back.]
Patrizia	Ah, che pasticcio!

Point it out

Look at the picture below. Using the words given to help, point out where things are.

accanto a   lì in fondo   lassù   laggiù   avanti   indietro

1 A wants to get to the church. Point out where it is.
2 B is there already and wants to get back to the river. Point out where it is.
3 C wants to know where D is. You tell her exactly.
4 On the way to the tree, C wants to stop at the inn. Tell her she must keep going.
5 When she gets there, D tells C she wants something to eat. Tell C she must go back.

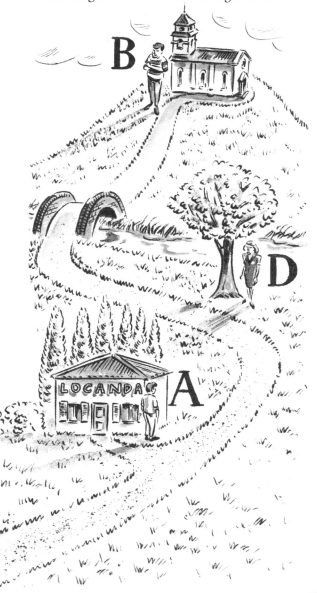

Practice 1

Diete e alimenti

Aim: vocabulary building through exchange of information

1 Tell students they are going to make up a dietary chart on the basis of the information you give them.

2 Prepare two sets of cards: one with types of food, the other with names of different foods. Distribute the cards among the students and tell them to match them up. (Food is divided here into six main categories but you may wish to give a more elaborate classification.)

Latte e derivati	*latte di mucca/pecora*
	formaggi
Carne, pesce, uova	*vitello manzo maiale agnello*
	pollame selvaggina
	pesce uova
Legumi secchi	*lenticchie fagioli fave piselli*
	ceci
Cereali e derivati	*pane pasta*
	riso farina
	biscotti fiocchi d'avena
Grassi e oli vegetali	*burro olio di oliva olio di semi*
	margarina lardo strutto
Ortaggi e frutta	*bietole cavoli cavolfiori*
	spinaci fagiolini piselli
	zucchine patate
	albicocche
	banane mele pere agrumi
	pomodori

3 On another set of six cards write the contents of each type of food. For example, following the same order:

Grassi, proteine e calcio
Proteine di alto valore nutritivo
Proteine di buona qualità
Calorie proteine e vitamine
Grande quantità di calorie
Vitamine di vari tipi   Sali minerali zuccheri   Scarse proteine

Give these to students and ask them to match them with the types and names of food.

4 Write on three more cards the different functions of food. Give these to students and ask them to match each one with two different types of food.

Costruire e rinnovare i tessuti
Fornire energia
Regolare e proteggere

The same activity can be carried out with other subjects which can be classified in this way, such as animals, plants (flowers), and musical instruments. Ask one student to present his or her own special classification of a subject.

C'è/Ci sono?

For each of the objects listed below, ask the question *c'è. . .?/ci sono . . .?* and tell students to provide the answer by looking around the classroom in the way shown in the following examples:

C'è un bicchiere/libro?	*Sì, ce n'è uno.*
C'è una penna?	*Sì, ce n'è una.*
C'è un telefono/una scarpa?	*No, non ce n'è.*
Ci sono calze/libri?	*Sì, ce ne sono.*
Ci sono scarpe/dischi?	*No, non ce ne sono.*

una borsa	*una radio*	*un libro*	*guanti*
una matita	*libri*	*sigarette*	*un dizionario*
pantofole	*macchine*	*oggetti*	*giornali*
ombrelli	*una palla*	*calze*	*occhiali*

This point could be the end of the lesson. Revise the points covered so far. In the next lesson students will cover the following:

> **Structures:** *stare* + gerund/agreement of past participle when *avere* is preceded by a direct object pronoun
> **Functions:** describing something as difficult or easy/expressing likes and dislikes, loves, hates and fears
> **Vocabulary:** idioms related to a life on the land

A friend of mine

You're having a party to welcome the Italian couple who've come to stay. Introduce them to your friends:

e.g. Allora, vi presento Charles, un mio amico.

Now here's who the others are:
1 Margaret, a colleague of yours.
2 Francesca, a neighbour of yours.
3 Andrew, a cousin of yours.
4 John, another colleague of yours.
5 Simon, another friend of yours.

Making tracks

You're leading a group on a hike and are collecting the equipment and provisions at your place. One of the participants calls in to check everything first: he's the anxious type.
First tell him about the equipment so far:

e.g. Quante tende ci sono? *[5]*
Ce ne sono cinque.

1 Quanti zaini ci sono? *[8]*
2 E quanti sacchi a pelo ci sono? *[9]*

Now he asks you about the provisions you've packed. Can you answer his questions?
e.g. La cioccolata c'è? *[molto]*
Ma sì, ce n'è molta.

3 Le mele ci sono? *[abbastanza]*
4 I biscotti ci sono? *[tanto]*

Finally, reassure him that if all else fails there is shelter at the end of the road:

5 C'è un rifugio se il tempo è brutto? *[uno]*
6 C'è anche una locanda? *[uno]*

Inquisition

You're notoriously vague and your friends are trying to check up on your plans. Try to answer their questions, using phrases in Italian such as:

> I don't know   of course   maybe   definitely
> it depends   I think so   I hope so

1 Hai intenzione di andare alla festa?
2 Hai deciso di invitare gli Alberti?
3 Hai intenzione di prenotare i biglietti?
4 Pensi di venire con noi?
5 Hai intenzione di lavorare domani?
6 Pensi di partire presto?

Mushrooms and the Law

Collecting mushrooms is subject to strict regional regulations. Can you answer the questions on the regulations below in Italian?

Disciplina della raccolta dei funghi

ART.12 – Nel territorio della regione è consentita la raccolta dei funghi spontanei soltanto per le specie commestibili e per una quantità giornaliera non superiore a due chilogrammi per persona.

commestibili

velenosi

È altresì consentita, per scopi didattici e scientifici, la raccolta giornaliera di due esemplari per persona di ciascuna specie dei funghi non commestibili.

1 Di solito è permesso raccogliere i funghi velenosi?
2 Qual è la quantità di funghi permessa per persona?
3 Se qualcuno vuole studiare i funghi non commestibili, quanti ne può raccogliere?

Cultura e parole

*Emilia e Romagna. If you were to ask people from Emilia Romagna where they are from, some would be likely to say, '***sono emiliano***', while others might reply '***sono romagnolo***'. This reflects the fact that until 1947 Emilia and Romagna were two regions, with separate histories and distinct culinary traditions.*

La cucina regionale. It is difficult and frequently impossible to translate culinary terms from one language to another, hence the existence in English of many Italian words, from pasta and spaghetti to ravioli, maccheroni, or, more recently, radicchio. The problem of translating food, however, also exists within Italy itself. It is not uncommon in a restaurant to hear a customer from another region asking for a dish to be explained. 'Italian' food, in fact, still remains to a large extent regional and often provincial. It is true that some erstwhile regional foods have become 'national': **pizza** from Naples, **grissini** breadsticks from Piedmont, **mortadella** salami from Bologna and so on. It is also true that international influences have crept in – **fast food, hamburger** and **il self service** for example – but none of this has changed the essentially regional face of Italian cooking. Even very basic items such as bread, pasta or cheese come in a bewildering variety of forms: there is **coppie** bread in Ferrara, Rome has **ciriole**, the Romagna area has **piadine**, while in Sardinia there is **carasau.** Food varies within regions themselves, especially pasta dishes: the famous **tortellini** from Bologna, known as early as the fifteenth century, gave rise to variants throughout Emilia Romagna: **tortelli, cappelletti** – little hats – and **cappellacci** – 'ugly big hats'. Again from Bologna, there are **tagliatelle**, said to have been inspired by the long blond tresses of Lucretia Borgia and created for her wedding in 1487. These have versions in other regions, such as the Piemontese **tajarin.** Even parmesan cheese – **il parmigiano** – is not unique to Parma: there is for example the **parmigiano reggiano**, from Reggio nell'Emilia.

The countryside and the culinary use of its natural resources have always been an important element in Italy's cuisine, from wild herbs and salads to mushrooms. Nowadays mushrooms – fresh or dried – are expensive to buy, particularly the **porcini**, so for many, going mushroom-picking is a favourite autumn pastime. The danger of being poisoned is very real – some porcini are lethal – and most local authorities have trained personnel (sometimes the local **vigili!**) to check pickers' findings and the market produce. The countryside is also the source of edible wildlife, for example snails, whose nutritional virtues are nowadays extolled in cooking magazines. The rearing of **le lumache** – or **chiocciole**, as the edible species are more properly called – has been an agricultural activity recognised by law since 1986, but eating them goes back at least as far as Roman times.

Popular food festivals and celebrations – **sagre** – have long been associated with much of Italy's countryside produce and wild-life, from the chestnut or wild boar festivals – **sagre della castagna** or **del cinghiale** – to the festival of the humble snail itself.

Cultura e parole

The number of people employed in agriculture is very small in Italy today, as in any other developed country, but the way in which Italians relate to the countryside is still very heavily influenced by the country's recent transition from a mainly agricultural economy to a fully industrial one. Strong links with the peasant culture – anti-industrial and anti-capitalistic – are very obvious even in the dynamic, economically developed areas of northern Italy. It is here more than anywhere else that unchecked urban development is seen as the curse of modern times. (The metaphor *spuntare come i funghi* – to grow suddenly and very quickly – was often used to describe the sudden, rushed development of *blocchi di cemento*.) Another idiom using *funghi, fare le nozze con i funghi* – to do big things with limited resources – is a linguistic example of the links between the former, rural peasant way of life and modern-day living. There are many such examples, in the form of idioms and metaphors, of Italians' continued attachment to the land, to the *civiltà contadina*. Some can be found in English too. Give the students a copy of the following expressions and ask them to guess which ones have equivalents in English.

Brutta bestia
cacciarsi in un ginepraio
darsi la zappa sui piedi
forte come un toro
la botte dà il vino che ha
lana caprina
mettere il carro davanti ai buoi
ritornare all'ovile
uscire dal seminato
pecora nera
campa cavallo che l'erba cresce
come i cavoli a merenda
far di ogni erba un fascio
come la gramigna
scarpe grosse cervello fino
coda di paglia
cervello di gallina
chi di gallina nasce convien che razzoli
far ridere i polli
tagliare la testa al toro
fare il galletto
cercare l'ago in un pagliaio
dare frutti

Interaction 5 (232)

1 *La selezione e confezione di funghi secchi è un importante settore dell'economia di Borgotaro. Anna parla con due donne che lavorano in questo settore.*
How much must each box weigh?

2 Play the cassette/CD as required.

3 Do several things: write on the board, read silently, pretend to smoke. Ask students *Cosa sto facendo?*

Interaction 6 (258)

1 *Anna chiede ad un esperto di funghi, il sindaco di Borgotaro, se i funghi sono difficili da preparare.*
What else does Anna want to know?

2 Play the cassette/CD as required.

3 Make outrageous statements to elicit a *sì* or *no* response from students.

e.g. *A tutti piacciono:*

i calciatori	*le noci*
gli uomini politici	*i rospi*
i bambini	*le mosche*
i cantanti pop	*i grissini*

4 Ask students to give a brief description of a dish they know how to cook and describe the process in the same way as Signor Ferrari.

Interaction 7 (265)

1 *Paolo prepara un piatto di tagliatelle ai funghi.*
Did Paolo produce a good meal?

2 Play the cassette/CD as required.

3 Ask students to list as many dishes as they can which contain *funghi,* e.g. omelette. Tell them to use Interaction 7 as a basis for writing a similar dialogue, changing the dish, people's opinions of it, and asking people to pass them something different during the meal.

Interactions

5   7

Mushrooms are vital to the economy of Borgotaro and the surrounding valley. Anna visits a factory where dried mushrooms are selected and packaged. She finds out what some of the workers are doing.

First time round

scegliere	to choose, select	
pesare	to weigh	How much must
la scatola	box, packet	each box weigh?

Anna	Signora, **cosa sta facendo?**
Rina	**Sto scegliendo** i funghi per poter confezionare il cestino.
	[...]
Anna	E Lei, signora, cosa sta facendo?
Silvana	Devo pesare queste scatole, perché devono avere il peso di cento grammi. Un etto.
	[...]

per poter confezionare   *to be able to make up*

Key phrases

cosa sta facendo?	*what are you doing?*
sto scegliendo	*I'm selecting*

6   8

The mayor of Borgotaro, Pier Luigi Ferrari, is something of an expert on mushrooms. Anna asks him if they are hard to prepare.

First time round

tagliare	to cut	velenosi	*poisonous*
far cuocere	to cook	commestibili	*edible*

What else does Anna want to know?

Anna	**A tutti piacciono i funghi.** È difficile prepararli?
Sig. Ferrari	No. C'è una ricetta semplice. Trifolati. Bisogna tagliarli a pezzi e farli cuocere in padella.
[Anna	È difficile riconoscere i funghi velenosi?
Sig. Ferrari	Può essere difficile riconoscere i funghi velenosi dai funghi commestibili. L'importante è chiedere l'aiuto di un esperto.
Anna	Ecco. Chiedere l'aiuto di un esperto.]

trifolati	*sliced and cooked with oil, garlic and parsley*
in padella	*in a pan*
l'importante è	*what's important is*

Key phrase

a tutti piacciono i funghi	*everyone likes mushrooms*

7   8

Paolo, that other mushroom expert, prepares a dish of **tagliatelle ai funghi**.

First time round

Did Paolo produce a good meal?

Paolo	Ecco le tagliatelle.
Anna	Allora, **buon appetito!**
Tutti	Buon appetito!
Michela	Uhm! Che buone!
Paolo	Ti piacciono, Toto?
Toto	Sì mi piacciono moltissimo. Ma **le hai cucinate proprio tu?**
Paolo	Certo! Sono un esperto io!
Anna	**Mi passi un po' di vino.** [...]

Key phrases

buon appetito!	*good appetite!*
le hai cucinate proprio tu?	*did you really cook them yourself?*
mi passi un po' di vino?	*can you pass me some wine?*

Patterns 2

i) Saying what you are doing

To say what you are in the process of doing right now use the present tense of the verb **stare**, plus the '-ing' form of the verb.

Cosa	stai	facendo?	*What are you doing?*
	sta		
	state		

Sto	parlando al telefono	*I am/we are*	*talking on the phone*
Stiamo	scegliendo un regalo		*choosing a present*
	pulendo la casa		*cleaning the house*

See Systems, note 4, p. 206.

ii) Saying who likes what

A tutti	piacciono	i funghi	*Everyone*	*likes*	*mushrooms*
A nessuno		le castagne	*No-one*		*chestnuts*
A Giacomo		le nocciole	*Giacomo*		*hazelnuts*
A mia madre		le noci	*My mother*		*walnuts*
Ai miei amici		i pinoli	*My friends*		*pine-nuts*

See Unit 6, Systems, note 2 iii, p. 193.

iii) Talking about your loves, hates and fears

| La campagna | mi piace | parecchio | *I like* | *the countryside* | *a lot* |
| La montagna | | tanto | | *the mountains* | *a great deal* |

Le farfalle	mi piacciono	da morire	*I'm crazy about*	*butterflies*
I gufi		da impazzire	*I'm mad about*	*owls*
I daini		tantissimo	*I adore*	*deer*
Gli scoiattoli		moltissimo	*I love*	*squirrels*

This is how you express your dislike of something:

Non mi piace per niente	l'anguilla	*I don't like*	*eel*	*at all*
	il buio		*the dark*	
	la pioggia		*rain*	

| Non mi piacciono per niente | le mosche | *I don't like* | *flies* | *at all* |
| | le formiche | | *ants* | |

If you hate or dislike something intensely, use the verb **odiare** *(to hate)*:

| Odio | il freddo | *I hate* | *the cold* |
| | il caldo | | *the heat* |

You might hear the expression **fare schifo** *(to be disgusting, revolting)*:

| Mi fanno schifo | i lumaconi | *I find* | *slugs* | *revolting* |
| | i rospi | | *toads* | |

See Systems, note 7, p. 207.

Patterns 2

Saying what you are doing

1 Bring in pictures of yourself, your family and friends. Tell students what you are doing in each picture before showing it. Do the same with large pictures from magazines.

2 Give each student a card with a different action on it. The student mimes the action and the others guess what he/she is doing.

Saying who likes what

1 Prepare some cards (one for each student) on which you write three or four things which students like (types of drink, flavours of ice-cream, etc.). Each card must be different but they should all have at least one item in common.

2 Ask students to say which items they like, i.e. reading aloud the items on their card.

3 Write all the items on the board. Ask which students like which items and tell them to begin their answer with *a* followed by a name or *tutti* or *nessuno*.

Talking about your loves, hates and fears

1 Write a selection of animals, insects, places, foods, types of music, even personalities on the board. Tell students your personal reaction to a few of them. Ask a student if he/she loves or hates a particular thing. Ask students to ask one another about their loves and hates, and to find someone with identical loves/hates.

2 With some help from you, students write down something they are afraid of. The others try to guess what it is. If they are unsuccessful after three guesses, the first student reveals his/her fear and everyone tries to guess the next person's fear. You could compile a class 'top ten' fears list on the board.

Saying you did it, etc.

Try the avoiding Yes/No game again: ask students slightly bizarre questions.

e.g. *Ha cucinato Lei i ragni?*
Ha assaggiato delle vespe?

This point could be the end of the lesson. Revise the points covered so far. In the next lesson students will cover the following:

> **Structures:** *stare* + gerund
> **Functions:** describing what something is used for
> **Vocabulary:** as required

To say you're frightened of something use **avere paura di**:

| Ho paura | del fuoco/del lampo | *I'm frightened of* | *fire/lightning* |
| | delle vespe/dei ragni | | *wasps/spiders* |

If something really scares you, use the phrase **avere il terrore di**:

| Ho il terrore | dei topi/dei pipistrelli | *I'm terrified of* | *mice/bats* |
| | degli scorpioni/delle vipere | | *scorpions/vipers* |

iv) Saying you did it, etc.

Hai preparato tu	il dolce?	Sì, l'ho preparato io	*Yes I prepared it*
	l'insalata?	Sì, l'ho preparata io	
Ha cucinato Lei	i fusilli?	Sì, li ho cucinati io	*Yes I cooked them*
	le tagliatelle?	Sì, le ho cucinate io	

Notice how the ending of the past participle changes after **lo, la, li, le**.

v) Saying you tasted some, visited some, etc.

Hai assaggiato	del vino?	Sì, ne ho assaggiato	*Yes, I tasted some*
preso	della grappa?	Sì, ne ho presa	*Yes, I had some*
Ha visitato	dei castelli?	Sì, ne ho visitati	*Yes, I visited some*
visto	delle chiese?	Sì, ne ho viste	*Yes, I saw some*

Notice how the ending of the past participle changes after **ne**. See Systems, note 5, p. 206.

vi) Mealtime conversation

In Italy you always begin your meal with a greeting:
Buon appetito!   *Good appetite!*
The standard reply is:
Grazie, altrettanto   *Thank you and you too*

You can also say **Buon appetito** back.

You frequently need to compliment the host:
Che buono, buoni, buona, buone!   *How nice!*
È ottimo/a   *It's excellent!*   Sono squisiti/e!   *They are delicious!*

You need to ask for things:

Mi passi	il vino?	*Will you pass me*	*the wine? [informal]*
Mi passa	l'acqua?		*the water? [formal]*
Ti/Le dispiace passarmi	il pane?	*Do you mind passing me*	*the bread?*
	il sale?		*the salt?*

And you need to offer things:

| Ne vuole | ancora? | *Do you want* | *some more?* |
| Ne prende | un altro po'? | *Are you having* | *a bit more?* |

Practice 2

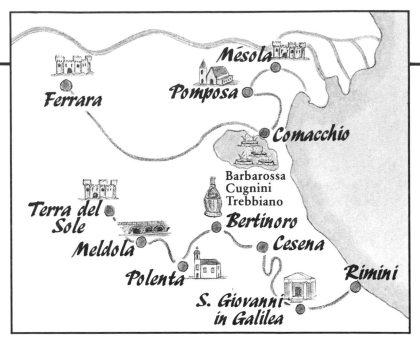

Legenda

vino
chiesa
castello
abbazia
acquedotto
ponte
museo
isole

Emilia and Romagna:

You've been visiting parts of Emilia Romagna, stopping mostly at lesser-known places (shown on the map). On the way back to Ferrara you meet an elderly couple on the train (he's from Emilia and she's from Romagna) who ask you about your trip.

Signore emiliano

1 Ha visitato Comacchio? – la chiamano 'la Venezia dei poveri'. *[Sí, . . .]*
2 Ha visto tutte le isolette – le piccole isole – a Comacchio? *[Sì, . . .]*
3 Ha mangiata dell'anguilla? *[Sì, . . . tanta!]*
4 Ha visto l'abbazia di Pomposa? *[Sì, . . .]*
5 E ha visitato tutti i monumenti di Ferrara? *[Sì, . . . tutti]*

Signora romagnola

6 A Bertinoro ha bevuto dei vini romagnoli? *[Sì, . . . alcuni]*
7 Ha assaggiato la piadina – il pane romagnolo? *[Sì, . . .]*
8 Ha visitato i castelli di Terra del Sole? *[No, . . .]*
9 Ha visto l'acquedotto e il ponte di Meldola? *[Sì, . . .]*

Now use the map to answer their general questions:

10 Ha visitato alcuni musei? *[Sì, . . . uno]*
11 Ha visto alcune belle chiese? *[Sì, . . . una]*

Imagine you are talking to a friend who has just had an interesting trip. Work out the questions you would ask, and see if you can answer them.

Fads and fancies

It's Ferragosto and you're helping your Italian friend sort out what to get for the festive picnic. Here's who's coming:

Giovanni, i gemelli, la zia, lo zio, gli amici di Giovanni.

And here are their fads and fancies:

Giovanni:

Mi piace parecchio la pasta al forno

1 *I gemelli:* La ricotta ci piace da morire!
2 *La zia:* Non mi piace per niente l'insalata di riso.
3 *Lo zio:* Mi piace tantissimo il vino Trebbiano!
4 *Gli amici:* Ci piacciono molto le patatine!

Now you go through everyone's likes and dislikes with your friend – you've already begun with Giovanni:

A Giovanni piace parecchio la pasta al forno.

Can you talk about the likes and dislikes of people you know? Use the Vocabulary to help.

Practice 2

Album di famiglia

Aim: practice of *stare* + gerund

Ask students to bring in their own pictures and show them to the class, saying what they are doing in each picture.

Dallo psichiatra

Aim: practice of *stare* + gerund

1 Set the scene by explaining to students that you are a psychiatrist working on a very difficult case. In order to help your patient to remember an event which he/she has erased from his/her memory, you have hypnotised him/her. Your patient, under hypnosis, does not speak coherently, in fact he/she says only names of objects.

2 Tell students that, in turn, they are going to play the part of the patient, and try to help you make sense of the patient's answers.

3 Write the objects on cards. Here is a sample list:

sapone	*ricetta*	*forbici*
televisione	*disco*	*telefono*
penna	*piatto*	*pennello e colori*
libro	*negozio*	*chiave*

4 Divide the students into two teams. Give a student from one team a card and ask him or her to read out the word. (Remind them they are under hypnosis.)

5 Ask the question: *Che cosa stai facendo?* The student answers, using *sto* + gerund with the name of the object on the card.

Award points to the team, on the basis of how good the answer is. If a student gives a grammatically correct answer unaided – and one which makes sense – the team scores full marks. If he/she turns to his/her team for help, take away a few points from the team's total if the answer is correct, more if they make mistakes.

Pubblicità

Aim: practice of *stare* + gerund

Bring in several well-known newspaper or magazine advertisements. Stick them on cards, give them to the students and ask them to describe what is going on.

Video mime

Aim: practice of *stare* + gerund

Watch part of the video for *Unità 6* with students, with the sound turned down. Give a commentary on what is happening, using *stare* + gerund. From time to time, make a deliberate mistake. Students have to spot the discrepancy and correct you. If one student is particularly confident with the structure, suggest that he/she takes over the role of the commentator.

Strong reactions   9

Listen to the sounds and say how you feel about what you hear. [See Patterns 2 iii, p. 171]

Table talk

Can you sort out who's talking to who?

1 Buone queste tagliatelle!
2 Buon appetito!
3 Le dispiace passarmi il sale?
4 Ti verso un altro po' di vino?
5 Ottimi questi funghi, mi dà la ricetta?

a) Grazie, altrettanto.
b) Ma no, eccolo qua.
c) Ne vuoi ancora?
d) Ma certo, è semplice.
e) No, grazie, basta così.

Better luck next time   9

Here's the sequel to your blunder earlier on. You've found the picnic spot and have settled down to eating.

You	*[Wish everyone a good meal.]*
Carlo	Grazie, altrettanto.
Patrizia	Mm, ottima quest'insalata di riso. L'hai preparata tu?
You	*[Tell her yes, you did and ask her if she wants a bit more, there's lots.]*
Patrizia	Va bene, sì, grazie.
You	*[You'd like some ham: ask Carlo to pass you the ham.]*
Carlo	Va bene, eccolo . . . Oh no!
Patrizia	Che c'è? – C'è qualcosa che non va?
Carlo	Ma ci sono formiche dappertutto . . .
You	*[Ugh: say you're scared of ants.]*
Patrizia	Andiamo! Troviamo un altro posto!
Carlo	Ragazzi, non c'è due senza tre (= *third time lucky*)!

Early bird   9

Listen and answer the questions about this mushroom expert, Mario Ugolini.

In Defiance of Death!

Read this passage from a magazine about one of Italy's greatest mushroom experts. Remember, you don't need to understand every word.

PER AMORE DEI FUNGHI A TAVOLA SFIDO LA MORTE

San Paolo di Morsano (Pordenone), ottobre

"Ho sessantasei anni e da quasi trenta rischio, se non la vita, almeno grandi sofferenze tutti i giorni per provare su di me le reazioni dei funghi velenosi. Ma non ho paura perché questa è molto più di una passione, è una vera e propria missione: andando incontro a pericoli non indifferenti, infatti, permetto agli specialisti di fare gli studi sull'avvelenamento da funghi e così, in futuro, potranno salvare molte vite umane".

Chi parla è Umberto Nonis: quelli che si intendono di funghi e che in questo periodo dell'anno vagano per i boschi alla ricerca di porcini, sanno che non c'è esperto più esperto di lui. Ne ha assaggiate, cucinate e mangiate millecinquecento specie. Buone e cattive, tossiche e non, commestibili e perfino mortali.

È talmente bravo che è in grado di riconoscere un porcino o un ovulo soltanto dall'odore. Così i suoi amici giocano spesso con lui nelle sere di autunno, lo bendano ben bene e gli mettono sotto il naso un'infinità di tipi di funghi. E non ne sbaglia uno.

Can you answer these questions?

1 How long has Umberto Nonis been eating poisonous mushrooms?
2 How does he explain the fact that he isn't afraid of eating them?
3 How many types of mushrooms has he tasted, cooked and eaten?
4 Does he have to see a mushroom to tell what type it is?

sfido *I defy;* potranno *they will be able to;*
chi *he who;* quelli che *those who;* vagare per
to wander through; bendare *to blindfold*

Vocabulary

Countryside

il bosco	wood
il campo	field
la cascata	waterfall
la collina, il colle	hill
il fiume	river
il lago	lake
la montagna	mountain
la palude	marsh, bog
il panorama [inv.]	view
la pianura	plain
il sentiero	path, track
il ruscello	stream
la valle/ vallata	valley
la caccia	hunting
il cacciatore	hunter
la pesca	fishing
il pescatore	fisherman

Equipment

il binocolo	binoculars
la bussola	compass
il campeggio	camping; campsite
la giacca a vento	wind-cheater
la tenda	tent
il sacco a pelo	sleeping-bag
lo zaino	rucksack

Trees and plants

la pianta	plant
l'erba	grass
il prato	meadow

l'albero	tree
il tronco	trunk
il ramo	branch
il ramoscello	twig
la foglia	leaf
l'abete (m)	fir
il castagno	chestnut
il cipresso	cyprus
il faggio	beech
il pino	pine
il pioppo	poplar
il platano	plane
la quercia	oak
il fiore selvatico	wild flower

Animals

l'animale (m)	animal
l'agnello	lamb
l'asino	donkey
il bue (pl. buoi)	ox
la capra	goat
il cavallo	horse
il cervo	stag
il cinghiale	wild boar
il coniglio	rabbit
il daino	deer
la lepre	hare
la lumaca	snail
il lumacone	slug
il lupo	wolf
la mucca, vacca	cow
la pecora	sheep
il pipistrello	bat
il porco, maiale	pig
la rana	frog
il ratto	rat
il rospo	toad
lo scoiattolo	squirrel
il serpente	snake
il topo, topolino	mouse
il toro	bull
la vipera	adder
la volpe	fox

Birds

l'uccello	bird
l'anatra	duck
l'aquila	eagle
il gufo	owl
l'usignolo	nightingale

Insects

l'ape (f)	bee
la farfalla	butterfly
la formica	ant
la mosca	fly
il ragno	spider
lo scorpione	scorpion
la vespa	wasp
la zanzara	mosquito

Feelings

ridere	to laugh
piangere	to cry
sorridere	to smile
gridare	to shout
litigare	to quarrel
arrabbiarsi	to be angry
annoiarsi	to get bored
stufarsi	to be fed up
seccarsi	to be annoyed
arrabbiato	angry
contento	happy, pleased
scontento	displeased
felice	happy
triste	sad
stufo	fed up
aver paura di	to be afraid of
aver il terrore di	to be terrified of

Vocabulary

A che cosa serve?

1 Bring in a number of pictures (one for each student) of obscure or mysterious objects (or the objects themselves if you can). Put them on display.

2 On one set of cards write the name of each object, on another set of cards write what each object is used for and on a third set write a brief description of the object.

3 Distribute one card from each set to students so that they each have three cards – name, description and purpose – which do not match.

4 Ask students to go round the class swapping cards with one another to obtain a complete matching set.

5 When students are ready, tell them to explain what each object is called and what it is used for.

DIY tools, for instance, can prove useful for the above activity.

Troubleshooting

Review

Here is a checklist of the main points learned in this unit. For each point, ask the students to provide you with one or more examples by asking specific questions.

---

agreement of past participle when *avere* is preceded by
    a direct object pronoun
non + verb + *niente*
inviting/accepting/asking permission/urging on
ce n'è, ce ne sono
non + verb + *mai, niente* or *nessuno*
asking permission
stare + gerund
describing something as difficult or easy
expressing likes and dislikes, loves, hates and fears
describing what something is used for

Troubleshooting

else another more other

The word **altro** is used in a variety of contexts.

1 Adding to what you've got

> Vuole altro?   *Do you want anything else?*
> Sì, mi dà . . .   *Yes, give me . . .*
>   altre due arance   *two more oranges*
>   un altro po' di formaggio   *a bit more cheese*

Another way of expressing more of the same is to use **ancora** (which literally means *again*):

> Ne vuole ancora?   *Do you want some more?*

2 Referring to something which is different

> Preferisco vedere un altro colore – un colore diverso
> *I prefer to see another colour – a different colour*

piace piacciono

1

> mi piacciono i porcini   *I like porcini*
> mi piace mangiare i porcini   *I like eating porcini*

Piacciono is used if you're naming several items you like. **Piace** is used if it's one item you like or if you're saying what you like doing, whether this is more than one thing or not.

2 *It* and *them* with **piacere**. Compare **piacere** with **preferire**:

> Mi piace la pasta – mi piace   Preferisco la pasta – la preferisco
> *I like pasta – I like it*   *I prefer pasta – I prefer it*
> Mi piacciono i funghi – mi piacciono   Preferisco i funghi – li preferisco
> *I like mushrooms – I like them*   *I prefer mushrooms – I prefer them*

You may wonder why there seems to be no word for *it* and *them* when **piacere** is used. This is because:

> **piace** on its own means *it is pleasing*
> **piacciono** on its own means *they are pleasing*

La moda

Rome

In this unit you'll be introduced to the world of Italian fashion and design, and investigating the clothing industry. You'll be choosing clothes and discussing price and quality, asking people's opinions and giving your own.

In Italy it could be said that style, not manners maketh man – and woman. Looking good permeates everyday life: it is important for the person in the street and it has also become big business. Italy dominates the international designer clothes market and clothing, textiles and shoes are her biggest exports. But the largest consumers of high quality fashion are the Italians themselves. Some 50 per cent of Italian designer clothes are sold in Italy, where **la moda** is the concern of ordinary people, not simply of the rich. Compared with the rest of Europe, Italians are prodigal in their consumption of high-quality clothes and jewellery. Almost 28 per cent own designer clothes and nearly 20 per cent of men own tailor-made shirts. Italy's nearest European rival, Spain, comes a poor second in this respect. So why the high consumption and what lies behind Italy's huge business success in the sphere of fashion? **La bella figura** – cutting a good figure, keeping up appearances – has always been a way of life, as has the long and proud tradition of craftsmanship associated with it. Fashion is not seen as pure frivolity, it is to be taken seriously. The artisan spirit and the cult of **la bella figura** have combined to produce a seemingly unerring sense of style plus unbeatable quality.

Milan is the capital of **il prêt à porter** – designer ready-to-wear fashion – and its financial capital, but Rome is the centre of **l'alta moda** – haute couture.

La moda

Food and fashion are two areas in which cultural differences between Italians and other nationalities are clearly evident. Stereotyped images of the Italian people as an exquisitely-dressed, food-loving nation strolling along tree-lined streets and squares with pavement cafés are found in every travel brochure or magazine. They should provide plenty of *realia* which can be exploited in class. Fashion could be used for both controlled activities and less structured discussions. Students, especially young ones, will have definite views on the subject. How do they perceive fashion? How do they think their perception is different from that of Italians? Are there points in common? Why do Italians take so much pride in the way they dress?

Fashion is big business in Italy and an important source of exports. The industry, as anywhere else, in order to prosper, exploits vanity and frivolity, qualities incompatible with the more puritanical view held by northern European cultures which equates worldly pleasures with superficiality. For Italians, striving to reach perfection of form is a deeply rooted cultural element. What pleases the eye, *la bella figura,* is not thought of as frivolous or vain. Fashion is only part of a general aspiration to uphold the rich historical tradition of not regarding art as ephemeral. This cultural heritage speaks for itself in Italy, where Tuscany alone has more classified historical buildings than any other country in the world.

Food and fashion are topics which provide ample opportunity to learn important linguistic functions. They are both major cultural elements — where else in the world would there be a need for pasta designers? — and can generate much discussion in class, allowing students to look beyond the stereotyped image of a nation obsessed with self-image.

Video corner

What's the price?

Aim: active viewing, note-taking

Video sequence: Anna interviewing three women in via Condotti, after the interview with Signor Balestra

1 Write on the board a number of words which refer to items of clothing, or prepare some flashcards. Ask students to guess the meaning of each word. Here is a sample list:

pantaloni	maglione	camicia	giacca	foulard
maglietta	gonna	bermuda	cappotto	calze
pigiama	cardigan	cappello	mutande	scarpe

2 Play the sequence and for each mini-interview ask students to say which item of clothing from the list is involved and the price. Write the following on the board, as a checklist:

	articolo	prezzo
1		
2		
3		

In Bandini's house and studio

Aim: active viewing, vocabulary building

Video sequence: Anna's interview with Bandini in his flat

1 Play the sequence and ask students to make a list of the objects they see.

2 Re-play the sequence in slow motion and ask students to call out when they see an object on their list.

3 Write the names of the objects on the board.

Fashion show

Aim: to practise giving opinions

Video sequence: after the interview with Signor Bandini, Anna and Signor Bandini watch a fashion show

Tell students they are going to see a mini fashion show and ask them to give their opinions on each of the three items, judging the following qualities:

	1	2	3
vestito			
stoffa			
colore o disegno			
taglio			

Interactions

> **Structures:** comparative adjectives
> **Functions:** asking for someone's opinion/giving
> opinions/making judgements and comparisons
> **Vocabulary:** *stilista, fresco, incamerare, canoni, vivace,*
> *settori, artigianali, sarti, tessuto, confezione*

Help-phrases and instructions

Qual è il significato letterale della frase?
Conosco il significato delle parole ma non capisco il significato
della frase.
Ti dispiacerebbe . . .?/Non mi dispiace.

Interaction 1 (033)

1   *Anna Mazzotti è a colloquio con lo stilista Renato Balestra*
che è anche il coordinatore della Camera Nazionale della Moda
Italiana. Balestra pensa che la moda italiana sia più dinamica
di quella francese.
Ask students what they think he means when he talks of
angel's hands?

2   Play the cassette/CD as required and ask further
questions:

How many questions does Anna ask?
How do Italian designers manage to have so much success?
Is Italian craftsmanship a key element?
Does Anna say anything else not in the form of a question?

3   Ask students to discuss the best shops in town for
clothes, according to:

stile   prezzo   qualità   varietà

Interactions

I 🔲 🔘 11

The Fashion Designer's Guild – **La Camera Nazionale della Moda Italiana** – has its headquarters in Rome. Anna Mazzotti talked to its coordinator, the designer Renato Balestra, who, like many famous fashion designers, began his career in another field, in his case engineering.

First time round

l'artigianato	*craftsmanship*
le mani d'angelo	*angel's hands*
i sarti	*tailors*
i tessuti	*textiles*
le case di confezione	*clothing manufacturers*

Balestra thinks that Italian fashion is more dynamic than its French rivals.
What do you think he means when he talks about the importance of 'angel's hands'?
[. . .]

[*Anna*   La moda italiana è diventata un fatto economico importante. A tutti piacciono gli stilisti italiani. **Secondo Lei,** come sono riusciti ad avere tanto successo?]

Balestra   La moda italiana forse è **più fresca della moda francese**, io trovo. La moda francese ha una lunga tradizione, è un po' incamerata in certi canoni, forse. La moda italiana è più viva, è più colorata, è più giovane, forse, è più vivace e forse anche gli stessi stilisti sono, sono . . . provengono da vari settori. Non tutti hanno cominciato con la moda o col disegno. [. . .]

Anna   **Secondo Lei**, l'artigianato italiano è un fattore fondamentale?

Balestra   Certamente è un fattore molto importante. Noi abbiamo in Italia quello che chiamiamo – che io chiamo – 'le mani d'angelo'. Cioè, **le mani** più, **più brave**, più, più artigianali forse **del mondo**. Tant'è vero che anche i sarti stranieri, per esempio, i sarti francesi, vengono a iniziare e a collaborare con le case italiane di tessuti, di confezione, italiane perché ci sono queste mani favolose.

cioè	*that is to say*
un po' incamerata in certi canoni	*a little hidebound by certain rules*
gli stessi stilisti	*the designers themselves*
quello che	*what [lit. that which]*
tant'è vero che	*so much so that*

Key phrases

più fresca della moda francese	*fresher than French fashion*
secondo Lei	*in your opinion [lit. according to you]*
le mani più brave del mondo	*the cleverest hands in the world*

2 $\boxed{\text{cc}}$ $\boxed{\text{CD}}$ 12

Out in the elegant via Condotti, in Rome's main fashion district, Anna finds out what sort of clothes people actually buy and how much they pay for them.

First time round

Here are two of the women she speaks to.
What has each of them bought and how much have they paid? The prices are higher than you might think.

Anna	Signora, che cosa ha comprato?
Signora	Ho comprato una giacca da MaxMara.
Anna	E . . . si può dire **quanto l'ha pagata?**
Signora	L'ho pagata tre e ottantasette. [. . .]

Anna	Che cosa hai comprato?
Ragazza	Ho comprato un pantaloncino, un bermuda.
Anna	E **di che colore?**
Ragazza	Grigio.
Anna	E . . . quanto l'hai pagato?
Ragazza	L'ho pagato centotrenta.

si può dire?   *is it possible to say?*

Key phrases

quanto l'ha pagato/a?	*how much did you pay for it?*
di che colore?	*what colour?*

Price is right $\boxed{\text{cc}}$ $\boxed{\text{CD}}$ 12

Listen to the cassette/CD and try and make the prices fit the items.

Interaction 2 (103)

1 *In una via del centro di Roma Anna intervista due donne che hanno appena fatto spese.*
What has each of them bought and how much have they paid?

2 Play the cassette/CD as required.

3 Write some higher numbers on the board. Give each one a letter. Read the numbers out and ask students to write down the letters in order.

Interaction 3 (149)

1 *La casa/studio di Francesco Maria Bandini, un'altro designer intervistato da Anna, è nel centro di Roma.*
When did Bandini start his career as a fashion designer and what did he do before?

2 Play the cassette/CD as required and ask further questions:

What does Anna know about Bandini?
Where is his studio?

Interaction 4 (193)

1 *Anna continua l'intervista con Bandini nel suo studio.*
Apart from clothes, what else has he designed?

2 Play the cassette/CD as required and ask further questions:

How much time does he spend in the studio?
Is Bandini satisfied with his work?

3   13

Francesco Maria Bandini is a young and much-sought-after designer of haute couture who lives in the artistic quarter of Rome a stone's throw away from his smart salon in via Condotti.

First time round

la carriera	*career*
prima di	*before*
cominciare	*beginning*

Anna arrives to interview him at his home.

a When did Bandini start his career as a fashion designer?
b What did he do before?

Anna	Signor Bandini, Lei è uno dei designers più conosciuti in Italia e senz'altro quello più giovane. Quando esattamente ha cominciato la Sua carriera di designer?
Bandini	Ho cominciato **nel millenovecentoottantaquattro.**
Anna	E che cosa ha fatto prima di cominciare a disegnare i vestiti?
Bandini	Ho fatto molte cose, per esempio architettura. [...]
Anna	Ho capito. E dove lavora? Qui nel Suo appartamento?
Bandini	Sì, qui sopra. Andiamo, Le faccio vedere.

qui sopra   *here upstairs*

Key phrase

nel millenovecentoottantaquattro   *in 1984*

Year in question 13

Listen to the cassette/CD. Can you give in Italian the years of the important events mentioned?

4 14

Bandini takes Anna up to his studio.

First time round

| finora | *so far* |
| ho realizzato | *I've created* |

Apart from clothes, what else has he designed?

Bandini	Ecco, questo è il mio studio. E qui è dove disegno.
Anna	E quante ore lavora al giorno?
Bandini	Cinque ore.
Anna	E **che cos'altro** ha fatto nel campo del design?
Bandini	Mah, finora ho realizzato un orologio e questa casa. [...]
Anna	Tra le cose che ha disegnato, quale preferisce, quale Le piace di più?
Bandini	Mah, tutte e nessuna.

Key phrase

che cos'altro?   *what else?*

Patterns I

i) Expressing opinions

Use **Secondo** (*lit. according to*):

Secondo	te/Lei voi	gli stilisti italiani sono bravi?	*In your opinion, are Italian designers good?*

Sì, secondo	me noi	sono molto bravi	*Yes, in my opinion they're very good*

ii) Making judgements and comparisons

The most and the least

Use the definite article, plus **più** or **meno**:

Quel vestito è	il più il meno	elegante di tutti	*That dress is*	*the smartest* *the least smart*	*of all*

Quei sandali sono	i più comodi i meno comodi	di tutti	*Those sandals are*	*the most comfortable* *the least comfortable*	*of all*

The article is often separated from **più** or **meno**:

È la giacca	più bella meno bella	di tutte	*It's*	*the nicest* *least nice*	*jacket of all*

The best and the worst

Use the definite article plus **migliore** (*best*) or **peggiore** (*worst*):

Il vino francese è	il migliore il peggiore	del mondo	*French wine is*	*the best* *the worst*	*in the world*

La cucina italiana è	la migliore la peggiore	del mondo	*Italian food is*	*the best* *the worst*	*in the world*

Notice that in these examples **di** is used to mean *in*.

See Systems, note 3, p. 211.

More and less

When you compare things, you need the words **più** and **meno** without the article:

Le scarpe nere sono	più care meno care	delle scarpe marrone
The black shoes are	*more expensive* *less expensive*	*than the brown shoes*

Quei pantaloncini sono	più belli meno belli	degli altri	*Those shorts are*	*nicer* *not as nice*	*than the other ones* *as*

Patterns 1

Expressing opinions

Secondo . . . has been practised at several points in these notes.

Divide the students into two groups. Ask them to think of a number of divergent opinions in the areas of politics, economics, or history. Tell one group to state the first of two opinions, for example:
Secondo gli antichi, il sole gira intorno alla terra.

The other group has to provide the second opinion:
Secondo Galileo, la terra gira intorno al sole.

Making judgements and comparisons

1 Elicit the meaning of the following adjectives from students (help when required):

piacevole	duro/a	difficile	complicato/a
stimolante	noioso/a	interessante	disastroso/a
tranquillo/a	simpatico/a	caotico/a	divertente

2 Tell them to link one of the adjectives, preceded by *il più* or *il meno*, with one of the last twelve months and ask them to justify their choice with a short explanation, for example: *dicembre è stato il mese più piacevole perché ho passato molto tempo in poltrona a leggere e ad ascoltare musica.* They could do a similar exercise based on the past week.

This point could be the end of the lesson. Revise the points covered so far. In the next lesson students will cover the following:

> **Structures:** comparative adjectives
> **Functions:** asking for someone's opinion/giving opinions/making judgements and comparisons/finding out more
> **Vocabulary:** adjectives that can describe cities or other suggested topics/talking about cost, colour and material of garments

More and less

1 Give students the names of ten cities.

e.g.	Città del Messico	Nuova Deli	Dallas
	Melbourne	Firenze	Casa Blanca
	Pekino	Mosca	Parigi

If you can, show a picture of a famous monument associated with the city first of all. Ask students to tell you the name of the city and write it on the board.

2 (Optional) Ask students what they know about particular cities:

Dov'è Atene? Qual è l'immagine tipica di Atene? Come si chiamano gli abitanti di Atene?

3 Ask students to think of ten different adjectives which can describe a city.

inquinata	affollata	moderna	romantica
antica	pulita	giovane	austera
attiva	vasta		

4 Students give a score from one to ten against each adjective for each of the cities.

5 Ask students to discuss their marking scheme with each other, for example: *Parigi è più romantica di Melbourne. Firenze è meno austera di Dallas.*

Variation: Instead of cities, you could ask students to score different types of cars, for instance (*veloce, economica, spaziosa,* etc.), sports (*spettacolare, violento, duro*) or television programmes (*simpatico, interessante, stupido*). Students don't have to give precise reasons for their choices but now and again you could ask them to justify their scores to stimulate discussion.

Talking about price

1 Give students simple mathematical problems to solve.

e.g. *Quesito: la signora Simonetti è andata dal macellaio e ha comprato 750 grammi di carne di manzo e mezza dozzina di uova. La carne costa 15.000 lire al chilo e le uova 1.700 lire la dozzina. Quanto ha speso in tutto?*

2 Show pictures of various objects – clothes, records, fashion or household items – and ask students to guess how much you paid for each one. If they need more help, write three possible prices on the board and ask them to choose the right one.

Better and worse
Use **migliore** and **peggiore** without the articles:

| La cucina italiana è | migliore | della cucina francese | Italian food is | better | than French food |
| | peggiore | | | worse | |

Note that in these examples **di** means *than*. It is used when directly comparing two things.

But if you compare two activities use **che**:

È meglio risparmiare soldi che spendere troppo   *It's better to save money rather than spend too much*

See Systems, note 2, p. 210.

iii) Talking about price

What you paid
The verb **pagare** means *to pay for*.

Che bella camicetta, l'hai pagata molto?   *What a lovely blouse, did you pay a lot for it?*
Che begli occhiali, li hai pagati molto?   *What lovely glasses, did you pay a lot for them?*

See Systems, note 4, p. 211 for the spelling changes of **bello**.

Quanto	l'hai pagato?	*How much did you*	*pay for it?*
	l'hai pagata?		
	li hai pagati?		*pay for them?*
	le hai pagate?		
L'ho pagato/a	centoventi	*I paid*	120 000	*for it*
Li/le abbiamo pagati/e	sette e cinque	*we paid*	7500	*for them*

In Italian the word **mila** is sometimes omitted when saying the price, especially if it's quite high. The word **cento** for talking about the hundreds is also often left out, along with the word **lire**.

How much you've spent
Use **spendere** which has an irregular past participle:

Quanto ha speso in tutto?   *How much did you spend altogether?*

iv) Colours and materials

If you want to know what colour or material something is, you say, literally, *of which colour, material?*

| Di che colore | è l'abito da sera? | *What colour* | *is the evening dress?* |
| | sono i cappotti? | | *are the coats?* |

| L'abito da sera è | rosa | *The evening dress is* | *pink* |
| | viola | | *purple* |

| I cappotti sono | marrone | *The coats are* | *brown* |
| | blu scuro | | *dark blue* |

Some adjectives of colour, such as the ones above, are invariable.

Patterns I

Di che stoffa	è l'abito da sera?	What	is the evening dress	made of?
	sono i cappotti?		are the coats	
Gli abiti da sera sono	di seta	The evening dresses are made	of silk	
	di raso		of satin	
I cappotti sono	di lana	The coats are made	of wool	
	di cachemire		of cashmere	

v) Finding out more

The key word is **altro**:

Che cos' altro	ha fatto?	What else	did you	do?
	ha comprato?			buy?
	ha scelto?			choose?
Chi altro	hai visto?	Who else	did you	see?
	hai incontrato?			meet?
	sei andato a trovare?			visit?

vi) Saying the year

In Italian, the year is always accompanied by the definite article. You literally say *the 1993*, etc.

Il milleottocentosessantuno (1861) è una data importante   *1861 is an important date*
Il millenovecentoquarantasei (1946) è una data importante   *1946 is an important date*

To say *in 1861, 1946* etc., join **in** to the article:

Nel 1861 il regno d'Italia è stato creato   *In 1861 the Kingdom of Italy was created*
Nel 1946 gli italiani hanno votato per la Repubblica   *In 1946 the Italians voted for a Republic*

For more on dates, see Ref. II, 3, p. 241.

Practice I

Good advice?

You've arrived in a new place and want to know which are the best clothes shops. You ask the hotel receptionist for her opinion:

> Mah, il migliore è La Capanna, secondo me. Hanno dei bellissimi vestiti d'alta moda – un po' cari, forse.

> Secondo Lei, quali sono i migliori negozi di abbigliamento qui vicino?

But maybe it would be too expensive. Can you put the same question to a couple in the hotel and then to their teenage daughter? What do you think they would say?

Finding out more

1 Divide the class into two groups.

2 Prepare some cards featuring one sentence which gives some general information about a pop group, sports personality, fiction writer, etc. Write the subject of the sentence in brackets.

e.g. *(I Beatles) sono famosi per Let it Be.*

3 Give one card to a student in group A who reads it aloud, leaving out the name inside the brackets.

4 The students in group B have to guess the name and ask a question using *altro*:

e.g. *Che cosa altro hanno cantato i Beatles?*

5 If the question is relevant (right subject and verb), give a new card to group A and ask them to carry on. If the question is wrong, give the new card to group B and ask them to take over.

Saying the year

1 Ask students to make a list of half a dozen important years in recent history.

e.g. *Il 1896 è un anno importante nella storia del cinema. Nel 1969 l'uomo è atterrato sulla luna.*

2 Describe some fashion items and ask students to give them an approximate date

e.g. platform shoes (c.1973)
ripped jeans and leather jackets (1976–80)
long, flowered skirts and beads (1966–70)

If possible, show some pictures.

Practice 1

What are the British most famous for?

Aim: to stimulate a controlled discussion

1 Ask students to think of our ten most important national characteristics and write them down in order of priority.

2 Tell them to compare their order with the person sitting next to them, discuss as required and come to an agreement.

3 Build up the pairs into larger groups until the class is split into just two groups. Although the two groups will largely agree on the priorities there are bound to be differences and you must exploit these.

4 Ask one group to say which characteristics they consider to be most important and why. Ask the second group the same question and carry on until you find a discrepancy.

5 Having found one, engage students in a discussion. Ask the first group to state again their reasons and expand on them. Be very positive (. . . *ah certo, è vero . . . sì, benissimo, è proprio così!*) and make it sound as if they have won the argument over the other group.
Ask the other group to give reasons to counter the arguments of the first group and be equally impressed by what they say (. . . *è un punto molto importante . . . è assolutamente indispensabile*). To stimulate further discussion, pretend you are now convinced by this argument until someone from the other group takes up the challenge and gives more reasons for their choice. (Be ready to calm any heated arguments which might develop.)

Cost, colour and material

Aim: vocabulary building

1   Cut some pictures out of a fashion magazine and show them to the students. For each one, ask students to state the name of the garment (or write some names on the board and ask them to link names and pictures).

2   Say the price, the colour and the material of each of the garments. Students have to guess which garment you are talking about. When they guess correctly, a student takes over the describing role.

When did it happen?

Quando sono successi questi avvenimenti?

When did these events take place? Choose from these years:

1776   1492   1861   1957   1939   1989

1 Cristofero Colombo ha scoperto l'America.
2 Il Belgio, La Francia, la Germania, l'Italia, il Lussemburgo e l'Olanda hanno firmato il trattato di Roma per fondare la Comunità Economica Europea.
3 L'America ha dichiarato la sua indipendenza.
4 È scoppiata la seconda guerra mondiale.
5 È caduto il muro di Berlino.
6 Il Conte Camillo di Cavour è diventato il primo Primo Ministro dell'Italia unita.

Figure conscious   15

Buying anything involves some rapid thinking when it comes to figures. How quick off the mark are you? Listen and write down the prices mentioned.

Shopping spree   15

You're entertaining an Italian acquaintance. She's come back laden from a shopping spree. Listen and join in the conversation.

Sig.ra P. Sono proprio stanca! Ho comprato tante cose.
You [Express interest and ask her what she's bought.]
Sig.ra P. Beh, sono riuscita a trovare due golf di cachemire, e un cappotto di lana pura.
You [Ask her to show you the sweaters].
Sig.ra P. Ma certo … Eccoli. Belli, vero?
You [They're lovely. You've always wanted a cashmere sweater. Ask if she paid a lot for them.]
Sig.ra P. Ma … non tanto. Mi hanno fatto un piccolo sconto. Adesso Le faccio vedere il mio cappotto.
You [Mm, it's a lovely coat, is it black or navy blue? Ask her what colour it is.]
Sig.ra P. È blu marino.
You [See if she'll tell you what she paid for it.]
Sig.ra P. Ah, questa è stata una vera occasione. L'ho pagato soltanto 765.000 lire!
You [Well, for some people it's a bargain: ask her what else she's bought.]
Sig.ra P. Ah, ho comprato un bellissimo foulard di seta, un paio di stivali, delle camicette di puro cotone, due gonne scozzesi favolose …

Can you remember?   15

You are being asked to do certain things. What are they? Listen to the cassette/CD and try to remember what they are.

Home truths

Think about the places you know. Can you tell your Italian guests which is:
1 the best restaurant
2 the most friendly pub
3 the most interesting market
4 the least expensive clothes shop.
Now give some further advice. Tell them:
5 It's more fun to go by bus than by tube.
6 It's better to shop at the supermarket than in small shops.
7 It's cheaper and easier to travel after nine than before.

A whiff of astrology

Read the descriptions of the designer perfumes below. Choose one for a man and one for a woman. Can you say what it is about that person which made you choose the perfume?

eg. Ho scelto … perché … Tony è un uomo sensibile.

Now answer the following questions:

1 Secondo Lei, si può veramente scegliere il profumo secondo il segno dello zodiaco?
2 Lei crede nell'astrologia?
3 Lei sa di che segno è?
4 Lei ha mai regalato un profumo? A chi?
5 Le piace ricevere un profumo per regalo?
6 Qual è il profumo che Le piace di più?

VERGINE'

❝ **Intelligente e razionale, non è facile agli innamoramenti, ma quando incontra l'uomo giusto…** ❞

Il suo profumo è…
Ferrè by Ferrè: un bouquet ricco e persistente, pensato per la donna anni '90. Il flacone è unico: sferico, avvolto in una preziosa rete di seta (da L. 45.000).

CANCRO

❝ **È difficile prevedere le sue mosse. Ma è proprio questo a renderlo straordinariamente affascinante.** ❞

Il suo profumo è…
Romeo Gigli: un bouquet complesso che fa riscoprire il fascino di aromi esotici, addolciti dalle fresche fragranze del bosco, (da L. 48.000).

PESCI

❝ **È un uomo sensibile, sempre pronto ad aiutare chi si trova in difficoltà. S'innamora difficilmente.** ❞

Il suo profumo è…
Ungaro Pour l'Homme, dove primeggiano i freschi aromi della lavanda, dell'abete e del bergamotto, dando vita a una fragranza che evoca mille emozioni. (da L. 48.000).

BILANCIA

❝ **Non è soltanto la più bella dello zodiaco, ma anche la più raffinata. Vive attorniata da molti ammiratori.** ❞

Il suo profumo è…
Via Spiga: un sapiente mix di note fiorite, tra cui la rosa e il neroli, che sfumano nelle note calde della vaniglia (da L. 46.000).

L'altra metà

Aim: to stimulate an exchange of information

Divide the class into two groups and give them some fashion pictures cut in half (give one half to each group). One group has to ask the other for more information in order to complete the details of each picture.

This point could be the end of the lesson. Revise the points covered so far. In the next lesson students will cover the following:

> **Structures:** *ce pleonastico*
> **Functions:** making polite requests
> **Vocabulary:** shopping for clothes

Cultura e parole

From a very young age, Italians are encouraged to develop a positive sense of their own image – *'Sei il bambino/la bambina più bello/a del mondo',* proud parents often say. In order that they appear spotlessly clean, children are even prevented from doing the very things that make them different from adults – *'Non ti sporcare il vestito/i pantaloni . . .'* you will hear mothers warn as often as *'Comportati bene'.* On occasions such as religious ceremonies – *battesimo, prima comunione,* etc. – children receive jewellery as well as new clothes (but this is also a convenient opportunity for the adults to renew their wardrobe).

'Farsi' un vestito, una giacca or *un pantalone nuovo* is a male as well as female compulsion. Shopping is not something that women do on their own, or followed by unwilling men, but rather a leisurely way of spending a couple of hours, going from small boutiques to big department stores. Many bargains can be found in open-air markets too, next to the fruit and vegetable stalls. It is frequently an opportunity to meet friends who will have a say in what you purchase – *'Questo ti sta meglio'* – and spend a pleasant afternoon together. Freedom to wander in and out of shops, however, is limited and the English idiom 'window shopping' is much more appropriate for describing the way in which you shop in Italy, i.e. if you don't want to buy anything in particular, you do not go inside shops to browse: you literally just look at what is in the window.

Fashion is also imported from abroad but it is adapted to Italian tastes. 'Casual', for instance, still means the opposite of 'formal', but in an Italian context it certainly does not mean any combination of loosely fitting clothes to be worn in the garden, rather a look which requires careful preparation in front of the mirror in order to match colours, hairstyle, shoes, etc.

Individuality is a strong Italian trait and, as one would expect, it is reflected in fashion. Schools do not have uniforms. This would be seen as the equivalent of being in prison. And yet there seems to be so much uniformity in the way young people dress that, seen from far away, Italian youths appear almost indistinguishable in their Benetton sweaters and designer jeans.

Whether in their Sunday best or in carefully coordinated casual garments, Italians are well aware that appearances can deceive, and that *Non è l'abito che fa il monaco.* In other words; in Italy, it is not enough to dress well – but dress well you must!

Cultura e parole

The language of fashion. In comparison with French fashion, which was established at the turn of the century, Italian fashion is very young. Yet over the past twenty years it has established itself as a leader in haute couture – **l'alta moda** – and has conquered the mass market of **il prêt à porter** – ready-to-wear. Nevertheless, despite Italy's leading international position, French and English dominate the language of fashion: it is the language of exclusivity and snob appeal, and uses words rarely found in everyday conversation. Colours are a case in point: **foncé** is often preferred to **scuro** – dark, while **rouge** [rosso], **jaune** [giallo], **marron** [marrone], **orange** [arancione], and **gris** [grigio] are just a few of the unnecessarily gallicised words. If you are well off you wear **bijoux** not **gioielli** – jewels, and amongst the garments you might wear are **tailleurs, gilets, chemisiers,** and **blousons. Lo chic** and **l'aplomb** are what every modern woman hopes to have – along with **il glamour** and **il sex-appeal**, which comes from having the right **look** as well as clothes carefully chosen to suit **il mood** of the day, be it **casual** or not! **Il T-shirt, il top, il blazer, il cardigan** and even **il bomber** have all become stylish creations in Italian hands, worn by **le top model** on the catwalk – **la passerella**. And then, of course, there are **i blue jeans** … The name, however, is Italian in origin! It comes from **blu di Genova**, the name used to describe the heavy-duty material produced since the thirteenth century in Genoa and commonly worn by the Ligurian peasantry in the eighteenth and nineteenth centuries. The export of the cloth to the USA eventually paved the way to its mass production by the famous Levi Strauss.

Interactions

5   [cc]   [CD]   16

Bandini shows Anna the busy workshop in via Condotti where his designs are made up by skilled women seamstresses.

First time round

misurare	*to measure*
le maniche	*sleeves*
tagliare	*to cut*

a What is Antonietta doing?
b Has she ever made a mistake?

Bandini	Prego, **si accomodi**. Questa è la sartoria. Loro sono le persone che lavorano con me. Lei è Antonietta che sta preparando un vestito.
Anna	Buongiorno, signora Antonietta.
Antonietta	Buongiorno.
Anna	**Le dispiace spiegarmi** cosa sta facendo?
Antonietta	Sto misurando il tessuto per tagliare delle maniche.
Anna	Ho capito. Quindi prima di tagliare, di cominciare a cucire l'abito, Lei ha molto da fare, eh?
Antonietta	Eh, abbastanza.
Anna	Ma Lei ha mai sbagliato?
Antonietta	Sì, e gli errori costano cari! [. . .]

la sartoria	*workshop*
cucire	*to sew*

Key phrases

si accomodi	*come this way; make yourself at home*
Le dispiace spiegarmi?	*do you mind explaining?*

6   [cc]   [CD]   17

Bandini's mother, Alba Bandini, directs the business and runs the salon where clients come for fittings.

First time round

A client rings up to check up on a dress.
a Is it ready?
b Why is the client going to ring back in a week?

Sig.ra Alba	Pronto, sartoria Bandini. Buongiorno, sono la signora Alba. Sì, il Suo vestito è già pronto. Però un attimo che controllo in sartoria . . .
	She speaks through the intercom.
	Antonietta, è pronto l'abito della contessa Pecci?
	Now she speaks to the client
	Sì, signora, l'abbiamo qui. Vuol passarlo a prendere o vuole che lo mandiamo noi? Scusi, non La sento bene. Può ripetere? Ah, ho capito, Lei non può prenderlo oggi perché è rimasta a Milano. Eh, se Lei non è sicura quando può tornare a Roma, perché non ci richiama? Fra una settimana? **Ce l'ha, il nostro numero?** Grazie, molto gentile, buongiorno.

vuol passarlo a prendere . . .?	*do you want to drop by and collect it?*

Key phrase

ce l'ha il nostro numero?	*have you got our number?*

Interaction 5 (266)

1 *Bandini fa vedere ad Anna il negozio in via Condotti dove vengono fatti i vestiti.*
What is Antonietta doing?
Has she ever made a mistake?

2 Play the cassette/CD as required.

3 Ask students what mistakes they have made in the past.

Interaction 6 (296)

1 *La signora Bandini, la madre di Francesco, dirige la sartoria e tratta con i clienti quando vengono alla sartoria o per telefono.*
A client rings up to check up on a dress.
Is the dress ready?
Why is the client going to ring back in a week?

2 Play the cassette/CD as required and ask further questions:

Who is the client?
Has the client an urgent need to collect the new dress?

Interaction 7 (325)

1 *Anna fa qualche domanda alla signora Bandini.*
Who are the Bandini's clients?
What does Anna ask permission to see?

2 Play the cassette/CD as required and ask further questions:

Are Bandini's clients very busy?
Why are they happy with the service they get?

Interaction 8 (342)

1 *La signora Bandini fa vedere ad Anna alcuni modelli.*
Does Anna like both dresses equally?
What do Bandini and the model think of the suit Anna models?

2 Play the cassette/CD as required.

3 Show the students fashion pictures and ask them to make similar comments on the clothes.

7 ⌷⌷ ◎ 18

Anna asks Signora Alba about their clients.

First time round

| trattare con | to deal with |
| consigliare | to advise |

a Who are the Bandini's clients?
b What does Anna ask permission to see?

Anna	Signora Alba, Lei è la direttrice della sartoria Bandini?
Sig.ra Alba	Sì, io sono la direttrice e mio figlio è lo stilista.
Anna	Vedo che riesce ad accontentare le Sue clienti. Chi sono?
Sig.ra Alba	Sono delle clienti italiane e abbiamo anche delle clienti straniere importanti.
Anna	E vengono sempre qui, in via Condotti, per scegliere?
Sig.ra Alba	Sì, riescono anche a stare tutto il giorno da noi.
Anna	Ah, beate loro! Signora, è difficile trattare con le Sue clienti?
Sig.ra Alba	No, debbo dire che le nostre clienti diventano sempre amiche, perché sappiamo consigliarle bene.
Anna	**Mi permette di** vedere i nuovi vostri vestiti?
Sig.ra Alba	Cosa preferisce vedere?
Anna	Degli abiti da sera.
Sig.ra Alba	Prego, si accomodi.
Anna	Grazie.

debbo	an alternative for devo, I must
beate loro!	lucky them!
accontentare	to keep happy

Key phrase

mi permette di ...? would you let me ...?

8 ⌷⌷ ◎ 19

Anna sits down with Bandini to watch a mini fashion show and then takes part herself.

First time round

a Does she like both dresses equally?
b What do Bandini and the model think of the suit Anna models?

Anna	[looking at a bright red, purple and yellow dress] Mm . . ., **quello lì mi piace molto!**
Bandini	Davvero? Le piace?
Anna	Sì, **è proprio bello!** [Looking at a chiffon dress with a grey skirt and purple bodice] Quel vestito . . . **mi piace un po' meno**.
Bandini	Non Le piace il colore?
Anna	Sì, mi piace, ma preferisco l'altro. Now Anna has a go at modelling a bright blue and red suit. She's watched by Bandini and the model.
Modella	Che bel modello! **Le sta proprio bene!**
Bandini	Eh, sì. Effettivamente le sta proprio bene.

effettivamente le sta proprio bene it really does suit her

Key phrases

quello lì mi piace molto	I like that one a lot
è proprio bello	it's really lovely
mi piace un po' meno	I like it a bit less
le sta proprio bene	it really suits her

186

Patterns 2

i) Asking if someone has got something

| Ce l' | hai
ha
avete | il numero?
il prefisso?
l'indirizzo? | *Have you got the* | *number?*
code?
address? |

Sì, ce l'ho   *Yes, I've got it*
No, non ce l'abbiamo   *No, we haven't got it*

The literal translation is: *the number/code/address, have you got it?* In speech it is much more common to use this expression than simply **'hai il nostro numero?'**

Ce l'hai un abito da sera?   *Have you got an evening dress?*
Ce l'ha una giacca di pelle?   *Have you got a suede-leather jacket?*
Ce l'avete una cintura di cuoio?   *Have you got a leather belt?*

See Troubleshooting, Unit 7, p. 142.

ii) Making polite requests [see also Unit 8, Patterns ii, p. 154.]

| Le dispiace | spiegarmi
dirmi
farmi vedere | cosa sta facendo? | *Do you mind* | *explaining to me*
telling me
showing me | *what you are*
doing? |

To ask permission to do something, say:

| Mi permette di | vedere
provare | quel vestito? | *Would you let me* | *see*
try on | *that dress?* |

iii) In the clothes department

Pointing out what you want

Quale vestito?	– Quello lì	*Which dress?*	*– That one*
Quale giacca?	– Quella lì	*Which jacket?*	*– That one*
Quali pantaloni?	– Quelli lì	*Which trousers?*	*– Those ones*
Quali scarpe?	– Quelle lì	*Which shoes?*	*– Those ones*

The word **proprio** (*really*) is handy for emphasis:

| Quella borsa lì è proprio bella | *That bag* | *is really nice* |
| Quelle cinture lì sono proprio belle | *Those belts* | *are really nice* |

What suits you?

Come mi sta?   *How does it suit me?*
Quel vestito ti sta proprio bene   *That dress really suits you*
Quelle scarpe Le stanno proprio bene   *Those shoes really suit you*

To suit is **stare bene a**. See Systems, note 6, p. 211.

Patterns 2

Asking if someone has got something

Divide students into two groups. Give a different picture to each group, for example one of a soldier and the other of a priest.

Each student knows what the other picture is about but does not know the exact details, so one group asks the other, for example:

Ce l'ha il fucile?

Students may use dictionaries for this exercise.

This point could be the end of the lesson. Revise the points covered so far. In the next lesson students will cover the following:

> **Structures:** conditional tense *(ti starebbe bene)/ stare* + gerund
> **Functions:** making polite requests
> **Vocabulary:** shopping for clothes/describing clothes

Making polite requests

1 Tell students they have been appointed head of a large office. They have a lot to do and are under a great deal of pressure. The office is new to them, which does not make things easy, but the secretarial assistance they receive is superb.

2 Write on the board:

Le dispiace farmi . . .?

vedere	*sentire*	*sapere*	*entrare*
cominciare	*osservare*	*passare*	*capire*
avere	*pervenire*	*ascoltare*	*telefonare*

3 One group plays the part of the boss and asks questions, using the above constructions, the other group plays the part of an efficient secretary who has ready answers for everything, for example:
  Boss: *Le dispiace farmi vedere la lettera?*
  Secretary: *Eccola/benissimo/nessun problema.*

In the clothes department

1 Cut out a number of items of clothing from a fashion magazine and stick them on large cards.

2 Show them to the students and discuss the name of each item, its pattern, colour, etc.

3 Pin them up on the board (put a letter or number next to each one) and give students a few minutes to choose an item of clothing for themselves and one for each of the other students.

4 Starting with student A, ask at random which items other students think suit him/her. Encourage students to use the pattern given as much as possible. (Point out the use of the conditional *ti starebbe bene*.)

What you like best

1   Show students half a dozen fashion pictures from magazines, and display them on the board.

2   Ask them to number the pictures in order of preference.

3   Starting with student A, ask which items he/she likes best and least and ask students to continue the discussion.

What you like best

Quell' impermeabile mi piace	(di) meno di più	*I like that raincoat*	*less* *more*
Quelle camicie mi piacciono	(di) meno di più	*I like those shirts*	*less* *more*

Saying what size you take

Che numero porta?	*What size [shoe, shirt] do you take?*
[Porto] il 38	*I take a 38*
Che taglia ha?	*What size [coat, trousers, jacket etc.] do you take?*
[Porto] la 40	*I take a 40*
La mia taglia è 38	*My size is 38*

General clothes sizes (including chest/hip measurements)

GB	USA	Europe	ins	cms
8	6	36	30/32	76/81
10	8	38	32/34	81/86
12	10	40	34/36	86/91
14	12	42	36/38	91/97
16	14	44	38/40	97/102
18	16	46	40/42	102/107
20	18	48	42/44	107/112
22	20	50	44/46	112/117

iv) Being hospitable

The following are much–used all-purpose phrases deriving from the verb **accomodarsi** (*to settle oneself, make oneself comfortable*). They can mean, *do come in; do sit down; this way please.*

Accomodati	*[tu]*
Si accomodi	*[Lei]*
Accomodatevi	*[voi]*

Practice 2

Lucky you!

Here's some things you might love to have:

Choose three and ask the following people whether they have one. If so, can you tell them each time how lucky they are using **beato te, Lei** or **voi**?

1 a female friend
2 the couple next door
3 a male acquaintance

Sales talk

You are trying on a jacket but it's definitely too large! Which of the following remarks by the sales assistant would be inappropriate in the circumstances?

1 Le sta molto bene.
2 Quel modello lì è proprio bello.
3 Il colore Le sta bene.
4 È proprio la Sua taglia.
5 Ma possiamo accorciare le maniche.
6 Le giacche larghe vanno di moda quest'anno.
7 No, non è troppo stretta.

Footloose   20

You've just spied a lovely pair of shoes in the shop window – **in vetrina**. They're not cheap, but you want to try them on. Listen to the cassette/CD and take part in the conversation.

Commesso	Buongiorno, desidera?
You	*[Say hello and ask if you can see the black shoes in the window.]*
Commesso	Ma certo. Mi fa vedere quali?
You	*[Say of course and point out the shoes you want.]*
Commesso	Ho capito. Va bene. Che numero porta?
You	*[Tell him you take size 38.]*
Commesso	*[He comes back but with a different black pair]* Mi dispiace, ma nel 38 abbiamo solo queste. Le vuole provare?
You	*[Bother, you'd rather have the others. Still these are nice too: say yes, that's fine.]*
Commesso	Ah, è proprio un bel modello. Le stanno proprio bene ...
You	*[Actually, they're too tight: tell him.]*
Commesso	Troppo strette? È sicura?
You	*[You're quite sure – they're killing you: ask if he's got a bigger size.]*
Commesso	In questo modello, no, mi dispiace.
You	*[Say what a pity, then thank him and say goodbye.]*

Getting what you want 20

Can you remember the various ways you've come across so far for getting what you want? Listen to the cassette/CD to find out.

1 You want the man in the information office to tell you what time the museum opens.
2 You ask the woman at the bus stop if she can tell you when the next bus is due.
3 You ask the man on the train if he minds opening the window.
4 You ask the sales-assistant to show you another style.
5 You ask the greengrocer to give you a few more apples.
6 You ask your host if he will let you see the house.

Practice 2

Love your neighbours

Aim: to practise making polite requests

Tell students to imagine having to ask very difficult neighbours to do certain things. Tell them to write notes in which they have to ask their neighbours politely to do something about the noise, for example – a dog barking at all hours, loud music, children crying and screaming – or about any other problem likely to arise between neighbours – a fence falling down, overgrowing trees, etc.

Every picture tells a story

Aim: to practise *stare* + gerund

1   Bring in several pictures of people doing different things (from newspapers, magazines and travel brochures).

2   Pin up the pictures on the board and ask students to write sentences about them, using *stare* + gerund. The complexity will vary according to the student's ability.

Buying clothes

Aim: to practise clothes and colours vocabulary

Put students into pairs or small groups. Ask them to imagine they are buying clothes and to write a short conversation for the situation. They could incorporate one or more of the following characters:

a) A very persuasive sales assistant.

b) A customer who is worried about the price of everything.

c) A customer who likes the next thing he/she sees better than the previous items.

d) A friend who thinks that nothing suits the customer.

e) A friend who is very enthusiastic about everything the customer tries on.

f) A customer who is difficult and always wants a different colour or style.

Comparing styles

Read the extract below from an article on language. Style, it seems, is not only a question of how things look. It's reflected in your speech and it's a gender issue. Do you agree?

Se dici 'fantastico' sei donna.

Lui è volgare e rispetta poco la grammatica, lei usa molto i superlativi ed è pignola; c'è una differenza di linguaggio fra i due sessi. Lo provano alcune indagini scientifiche.

Lo stile della donna

- Dice le cose in maniera indiretta, fa cioè dei giri di parole prima di arrivare alla conclusione.

- Parla molto correttamente usando parecchi aggettivi e eufemismi.

- Usa i superlativi 'bellissimo', 'fantastico', 'delizioso', 'adorabile' in molte situazioni, anche poco entusiasmanti.

- Usa espressioni neutre come 'forse' 'non è vero?' 'ma chissà' per prendere tempo e organizzare le frasi successive.

Lo stile dell'uomo

- Quando parla è molto obiettivo e va direttamente al nocciolo del discorso e non si perde in mille particolari.

- Rispetta poco la grammatica

- Usa i superlativi come 'bellissimo' e 'facilissimo' soltanto nelle situazioni di minore importanza; per esempio riesce a lanciare un 'bellissima' a qualsiasi donna che passa per strada e a essere imbarazzato se deve dirlo a una che lo interessa davvero ...

- Mentre parla fa delle pause per organizzare ciò che dirà in seguito

---

Secondo me è assurdo!
Non sono d'accordo!
Sono d'accordo! E giusto!

Using some of the adjectives given below, express your views on each of the eight statements you've just read.

assurdo   falso/vero   giusto/sbagliato   ridicolo   buffo

Gender games

How many comparisons between men and women can you make? Use the text above and the words below to help, but you don't need to restrict yourself to this. Be as outrageous as you like!

---

obiettivo   *objective;* equilibrato   *balanced*
razionale   *rational;* irrazionale   *irrational*
sensibile   *sensitive;* insensibile   *insensitive*
sicuro di sè   *confident;* timido   *shy*
spendaccione   *extravagant*
tirchio   *mean;* generoso   *generous*
aver buon senso   *to have common sense*
esprimersi   *to express oneself*

---

e.g. Gli uomini sono più obiettivi delle donne!
Le donne sanno esprimersi meglio degli uomini!

---

pignola   *particular, precise*
l'indagine *[f]   survey*
il nocciolo del discorso   *the heart of the matter*
qualsiasi   *any;* chissà   *who knows*
ciò che dirà   *what he'll say*

Vocabulary

Clothes and accessories

l'abbiglia- mento	clothing
l'abito	man's suit, dress
l'abito da sera	evening dress
i blue jeans	jeans
la calzamaglia	tights
le calze	stockings
i calzini	socks
la camicia da notte	nightdress
la canottiera	vest
il cappello	hat
il cappotto	coat
il cardigan	cardigan
il costume da bagno	bathing- costume
la cravatta	tie
il fazzoletto	handkerchief
il foulard	headscarf
il gilè	waistcoat
il golf	jumper
i guanti	gloves
l'imperme- abile	raincoat
il maglione	sweater
le mutande	underpants
le mutandine	panties
la pelliccia	fur coat
il pigiama	pyjamas
il reggiseno	bra
lo slip	briefs
il tailleur	woman's suit
la vestaglia	dressing-gown
la taglia	size [clothes]
il numero	shoe/shirt size
il bottone	button
la chiusura lampo, la zip	zip
il colletto	collar
la manica	sleeve
l'orlo	hem
la tasca	pocket
il sandalo	sandal
lo scarpone	ski, walking- boot
lo stivale	boot

lo zoccolo	clog
il tacco	heel
la stringa	shoe-lace

Jewellery and other accessories

la gioielleria	jewellery
l'anello	ring
il bracciale, braccialetto	bracelet
la collana	necklace
l'orecchino	earring
la spilla	brooch
il diamante	diamond
l'argento	silver
l'oro	gold
gli occhiali da sole	sunglasses
la pelletteria	leather goods
il borsellino	purse
la borsetta a tracolla	shoulder-bag
la cintura	belt
la profumeria	perfumery
il profumo	perfume
il trucco	make-up
la cipria	face-powder
il rossetto	lipstick

Materials

la stoffa	material
il tessuto	textile, fabric
il cachemire	cashmere
il cotone	cotton
il feltro	felt
la lana	wool
il lino	linen
il nailon	nylon
la paglia	straw
il pizzo	lace

il raso	satin
la seta	silk
il velluto	velvet, corderoy
il camoscio	suede
il cuoio	leather
la pelle	soft leather, suede
a maglia	knitted
il metallo	metal
l'acciaio	steel
l'ottone	brass
il rame	copper
la carta	paper
il legno	wood

Colours and patterns

blu	blue
blu marino	navy blue
turchino	dark blue
turchese	turquoise
rosa	pink
viola	purple
chiaro	light
scuro	dark
a righe	striped
a quadretti	checked
a fiori	flowered

Adjectives

corto	short
lungo	long
largo	loose
stretto	tight
bravo	good [at s.thing]
assurdo	absurd
buffo	funny
falso	false, untrue
giusto	right, fair
ridicolo	ridiculous
sbagliato	wrong, mistaken
strano	strange

Verbs

accorciare	to shorten
allungare	to lengthen
restringere	to take in
provare	to try on

Vocabulary

Labelling a drawing

1 Divide the class into groups of three or four students.

2 Give each group a large drawing (at least A3 size) of a complex object, a car, for example.

3 Ask each group to label each part of the object according to various criteria, such as:
a) moving parts
b) electrical parts
c) non-metal parts
d) parts which the car has in common with another vehicle, a lorry, for example.

4 As well as asking for your help, make sure each group has a good dictionary at their disposal.

5 Each group comments on their picture.

Semantic fields

Aim: to encourage students to develop personal ways of building their vocabulary

1 Divide students into groups and provide each group with a poster-size sheet of blank paper, a marker pen and a dictionary.

2 Prepare a list of words linked to a central theme. Write these words on the board in a spider's web.

3 Give students a central theme on which to develop their own personal spider's web, for example *vacanze, divertimenti, nutrizione, movimento* (transport), etc.

4 Pin up the finished pieces of work and gather students around to discuss the meanings of all the new words.

Troubleshooting

Review

Here is a checklist of the main points learned in this unit.
For each point, ask the students to provide you with one
or more examples by asking specific questions.

asking someone's opinion
giving opinions
making judgements and comparisons
finding out more
talking about cost, colour and material of garments
ce pleonastico
making polite requests
shopping for clothes
conditional tense (*ti starebbe bene*)
stare + gerund
describing clothes

Troubleshooting

meglio migliore   peggio peggiore

Learn to distinguish between the use of **meglio** (adverb) and
migliore (adjective). Both words can mean *better* and *best*.

Rita conosce Bari **meglio** di me	*Rita knows Bari better than me*
È **meglio** chiamare la mattina presto	*It's best to call early in the morning*
Questa pasta è **migliore** dell'altra	*This pasta is better than the other*
Lei conosce i posti **migliori**	*She knows the best places*

Similarly, **peggio** is an adverb and **peggiore** is an adjective. Both
words can mean *worse* and *worst*:

Lui parla inglese **peggio** di me	*He speaks English worse than me, than I do*
Lui parla **peggio** di tutti	*He speaks worst of all*
La situazione è **peggiore** del previsto	*The situation is worse than expected*
Tu conosci i posti **peggiori**	*You know the worst places*

bravo   buono   bene

These words can all mean *good*.

Bravo implies good at something, clever:
    È un designer molto bravo.
    Lui è bravo in matematica.

It can be used to express praise and say 'well done':
    Hai finito? – Bravo!

Buono refers to the quality of something:
    Il film è molto buono

If it is used with reference to a person it tends to imply kindness:
    È una persona molto buona

Bene is an adverb meaning *well*, but it is also used for expressing
approval and saying 'good':
    Hai finito? – Bene

Systems 6

1 Object pronouns

La richiamo
Le può dire?

i) Direct and indirect
Object pronouns are so called because they stand in for the noun objects of verbs. Indirect object pronouns are used with verbs which normally require the preposition **a** before a person. In Italian, some direct and indirect object pronoun forms are different:

Direct object		Indirect object	
mi	me	mi	to me
ti	you	ti	to you
lo	him, it	**gli**	to him
la	her, it	**le**	to her
La	you	**Le**	to you
ci	us	ci	to us
vi	you	vi	to you
li/le	them	**gli**	to them
		loro	to them★

★ **Loro** is not common in speech and comes after the verb: Do loro un libro

Compare direct and indirect forms:

Direct him, her, it:	Indirect
lo vedo stasera **la** vedo stasera	**gli** telefono stasera **le** telefono stasera
them: **li** vedo stasera *(m)* **le** vedo stasera *(f)*	**gli** telefono stasera *(m & f)*
Formal *you:* **La** vedo stasera	**Le** telefono stasera

ii) Position of pronouns
These generally come before the verb. If a verb is used with **potere, volere** and **dovere**, the pronoun can precede the whole phrase:
> le può dire che . . .
> la voglio invitare

In some cases pronouns go after the verb. See Unit 7, note 2 ii and iii, p. 197 for further information.

2 Piacere (to like)

mi piace la musica
mi piacciono i concerti
mi piace andare ai concerti

Piacere is a difficult verb. One way to get it right is to remember what it means literally:
> mi piace la musica *music is pleasing to me*
> mi piacciono i concerti *concerts are pleasing to me*
> mi piace andare ai concerti *going to concerts is pleasing to me*

i) Form
There are only two basic present-tense forms: **piace** if you like (doing) one thing, and **piacciono** if you like several things.

ii) Use of pronouns
Piacere doesn't use the usual subject pronouns. The indirect object pronouns are used instead. Here's how the present tense of **piacere** looks in full:

mi piace/piacciono	*I like*
ti piace/piacciono	*you like*
gli piace/piacciono	*he likes*
le piace/piacciono	*she likes*
Le piace/piacciono	*you like*
ci piace/piacciono	*we like*
vi piace/piacciono	*you like*
gli piace/piacciono	*they like*
piace/piacciono loro	*they like* [mostly written form]

iii) Using piacere:
If the subject is a noun, e.g. **Maria, il signor Porrino, la gente, i miei amici,** then **a** must go in front, combined with the article if there is one:
> A Maria piace la letteratura *Mary likes literature [lit. literature is pleasing to Mary]*
> Al signor Porrino piacciono i gialli
> Alla gente piace guardare la televisione
> Ai miei amici piace uscire la sera

With pronouns such as **tutti, nessuno, molti** and **tanti, a** is also needed:
> A tutti piace ascoltare la musica
> A nessuno piace il rumore

Take care using **piacere** with the following:
> mi piacciono gli spaghetti *[spaghetti is plural]*
> mi piace l'uva *[grapes are singular]*

See also Unit 8, Systems, note 3, p. 201.

Systems and Reinforcement

Section I
For notes on using this section, please refer to page 79.

Systems 6

STRUCTURES	PAGE NO.	REINFORCEMENT EXERCISES
1 Object pronouns	193	B D E
2 *Piacere*	193	A B C
3 The past: *il passato prossimo*	194	G H I
4 Verbs with regular past participles	194	G
5 Verbs with irregular past participles	194	H I

Systems 7

STRUCTURES	PAGE NO.	REINFORCEMENT EXERCISES
1 Stressed pronouns	197	A B C
2 Position of pronouns	197	D E F
3 Object pronouns with compound verbs	198	H I
4 *Dispiacere*	198	J K
5 Impersonal *si*	198	
6 *Conoscere* and *sapere*	198	L
7 Irregular present	198	

Systems 8

STRUCTURES	PAGE NO.	REINFORCEMENT EXERCISES
1 The pronoun *ne*	201	A
2 Prepositions in questions	201	B
3 *Piacere* with *a*	201	C D
4 *Sapere*	201	E
5 Double object verbs	202	F
6 Double negatives	202	G H I
7 Irregular verbs	202	J

Systems 9

STRUCTURES	PAGE NO.	REINFORCEMENT EXERCISES
1 Pronouns combining *ci ne*	205	A
2 Possessives	205	B C D
3 Demonstratives	205	E F
4 Present progressive	206	G
5 *Passato prossimo* with *avere*	206	J
6 *Conoscere* and *sapere*	207	H K
7 Impersonal verbs and expressions	207	
8 Negatives	207	L M
9 Irregular verbs	207	

Systems 10

STRUCTURES	PAGE NO.	REINFORCEMENT EXERCISES
1 Comparative and superlative adjectives	210	A B C
2 Comparative and superlative adverbs	210	E
3 Making comparisons	211	A B C
4 A note on *bello, buono* and *grande*	211	D H
5 Relative pronouns	211	F G
6 Verbs used with indirect object pronouns	211	
7 Verbs and prepositions	212	K
8 Review of prepositions	212	
9 Irregular nouns	212	K
10 Irregular verbs	212	L
11 A note on numbers	212	

Section 2

The following section includes suggestions for classroom activities which aim to reinforce some of the grammatical structures covered in the **Systems**.

Sentence structure (Affirmative and negative statements/Questions)

1   Bring some pictures (or write the names on cards) of famous people.
2   Stick a picture or card on the back of each student with Sellotape.
3   Revise all the necessary vocabulary.
4   In turn, students will ask questions to guess the identity of the *personaggio* on their back. The others should give a yes or no answer followed by a statement in the affirmative or the negative.

Possessive adjectives

Ask students to give you something of theirs, for example, a pen or a pencil, a wrist watch, a brooch, etc.
Collect all the items and display them on a desk.
Call the name of a student and invite the others to say what belongs to him or her.

La penna è sua or *questa è la sua penna.*
L'orologio è suo or *questo è il suo orologio . . .* etc.

Section 3

In the following section suggestions are given on how to help students deduce grammatical rules, and take a more analytical approach to language.

Reflexives

1   Write on the board the grammatical structure *mi sono dimenticata* and explain it, giving other examples:

mi sono   alzato/a divertito/a stancato/a lavato/a
ci siamo   alzati/e divertiti/e stancati/e lavati/e

Ask students to deduce two types of reflexive, i.e.
a) I enjoyed/washed/prepared myself
b) I got tired/dirty/fed up/drunk

Analisi grammaticale

1   Explain to students the aim of the exercise. Tell them, for example, that labelling each part of the sentence will help them to make sense of the structure of the language.
2   On the board/OHP write one or two simple (from a grammatical point of view) sentences. If at all possible, try to use a simple newspaper headline or advertisement, for example:

Il viaggio in treno è caro, i ritardi sono frequenti
Il vota a Brescia è un segno di protesta

3   Put students in groups and ask them to write each part of the sentence in columns, for example:

article	noun	adjective	verb	preposition etc.
il	viaggio	caro	è	in
i	ritardi	frequenti	sono	
	treno			
il	voto		è	a
un	Brescia			di
	segno			
	protesta			

4   Check answers and discuss as necessary.

Review 2

For general suggestions on using the **Review** in class, please see page 101.

Ask students to complete the section on learning styles. They should then discuss their answers in groups. The differences of opinion should stimulate lively discussion and give students the opportunity to discover strategies which have proved successful for other students. Hopefully they will also get some insight into the ways in which they themselves learn best.

Students could complete the **Checklists** section in pairs. It may be useful for you to discuss the results individually with students if possible.

Working on your own 2

For general suggestions on **Working on your own**, please see page 105.

Having completed the **Review**, students should have a clearer idea of the areas in which they are most and least successful, and what they need to work on.

Encourage students to read the suggestions in the **Working on your own** section of the Course Book on listening, speaking vocabulary and grammar strategies. Provide opportunities for students to try out the techniques suggested in class if possible.

Ask students to set themselves a target or goal: they could give themselves a specified time limit to work on and improve one particular skill, for example, memorising grammar details. After the specified time they should complete the **Review** again, aiming for a better result.

Profile 2 and Culture 2

Please see the suggestions on pages 107 and 109.

3 The past: il passato prossimo

| ho |
| sono |

↑
auxiliary

lasciato un messaggio
andata in Conservatorio

↑
past participle

The **passato prossimo** expresses simple past actions. It is made up of an auxiliary verb in the present – **avere** or **essere** – plus the past participle of the verb you are using. Some verbs take **avere** while others require **essere**.

i) Which auxiliary?
There is no simple answer. Many more verbs require **avere** than **essere**. It may be helpful to learn that many verbs of movement require **essere**, but there are exceptions. It is best to learn the main verbs which require **essere**. [See the list in Ref. p. 250]. You can then assume the rest take **avere**.

ii) The regular past participle
To form the regular past participle you drop the **–are**, **–ere** and **–ire** infinitive ending and substitute **-ato**, **-uto**, **-ito**. To form the complete verb, use part of the present tense of **avere** or **essere**, whichever is appropriate, in front of the past participle.

iii) Using the passato prossimo
This tense corresponds to three English tenses:
Ho chiamato   *I have called/I called/I did call*
Sono andato   *I have gone/I went/I did go*
The way it is translated depends on the context.

4 Verbs with regular past participles

i) Verbs with avere

	lasci**are** *to leave*	ricev**ere** *to receive*	cap**ire** *to understand*
ho	lasci**ato**	ricev**uto**	cap**ito**
hai	lasci**ato**	ricev**uto**	cap**ito**
ha	lasci**ato**	ricev**uto**	cap**ito**
abbiamo	lasci**ato**	ricev**uto**	cap**ito**
avete	lasci**ato**	ricev**uto**	cap**ito**
hanno	lasci**ato**	ricev**uto**	cap**ito**

The verb **avere** is regular in the past and takes the auxiliary **avere**:

ho avuto	abbiamo avuto
hai avuto	avete avuto
ha avuto	hanno avuto

ii) Verbs with essere

	and**are** *to go*	cad**ere** *to fall*	usc**ire** *to go out*
sono	and**ato/a**	cad**uto/a**	usc**ito/a**
sei	and**ato/a**	cad**uto/a**	usc**ito/a**
è	and**ato/a**	cad**uto/a**	usc**ito/a**
siamo	and**ati/e**	cad**uti/e**	usc**iti/e**
siete	and**ati/e**	cad**uti/e**	usc**iti/e**
sono	and**ati/e**	cad**uti/e**	usc**iti/e**

Verbs which have no direct object [intransitive verbs], tend to require **essere**:
e.g. arrivare, tornare, partire
But there are some exceptions which require **avere**:
e.g. camminare, cenare, pranzare, dormire
See list in Reference, p. 251.

Past participle agreement
If a verb uses **essere** as the auxiliary, the participle agrees with the subject of the verb:
Rita è uscita
Le ragazze sono riuscite a prendere il treno

5 Verbs with irregular past participles

i) Verbs with avere

Many common verbs have irregular past participles. Here are 12 key ones:

bere	bevuto	leggere	letto
chiedere	chiesto	mettere	messo
dare	dato	prendere	preso
decidere	deciso	rispondere	risposto
dire	detto	scrivere	scritto
fare	fatto	vedere	visto

See list in Reference, pp. 251–2.

ii) Verbs with essere

The verb **essere** itself is irregular in the past and takes the auxiliary **essere**:

sono stato/a	siamo stati/e
sei stato/a	siete stati/e
è stato/a	sono stati/e

The verb **stare** *(to be, to stay)* takes the auxiliary **essere** and has the same past participle as **essere**:
sono stato/a da mia zia per due giorni

Reinforcement 6

Here are four more key irregular verbs requiring **essere**:

nascere	nato	morire	morto
rimanere	rimasto	venire	venuto

And here are three which can take **essere** but also **avere**:

correre	corso	scendere	sceso
vivere	vissuto		

For a full explanation see Reference p. 250.

6 Interrogatives: which? what?

i) Quale? Quali?

> **Quale** musica preferisce?
> **Quali** strumenti preferisce?

Quale means *which? what?* Like all adjectives ending in **-e** it has only one singular and one plural form:
Quale rivista ti piace?   Quali riviste ti piacciono?
Quale libro ti piace?   Quali libri ti piacciono?

Quale can also be used as a pronoun:
> Quale libro vuole? – Quale?   *Which one?*
> Quali libri vuoi? – Quali?   *Which ones?*

In front of **è** the final **-e** is dropped:
> Il numero di Rita, qual è?

ii) Che

The word **che** is sometimes used as an interrogative adjective, meaning *what?* It is quite colloquial:
> Che libri vuoi?   *What (which) books do you want?*

Unlike **quale**, **che** cannot be used as a pronoun.

7 A note on ordinal numbers

> il mio **primo** strumento
> frequento il **settimo** anno

Ordinal numbers are used for numbering things in order: first, second, third, etc. There is a list of these in Reference, p. 239.

A Piace *or* piacciono?

Fill in the correct form.
1 Ti . . . il teatro?
2 Le . . . le commedie di Dario Fo?
3 Vi . . . andare a teatro?
4 Ti . . . l'uva?
5 Le . . . gli spaghetti?
6 Vi . . . mangiare gli spaghetti?

B What do they like?

You ask a friend about the tastes of members of his family and friends.
e.g. Tuo fratello: la lirica?
    Gli piace la lirica?

1 Tua sorella: il balletto?
2 Le tue amiche: la chitarra?
3 Antonio: i documentari?
4 Norma: le telenovele?
5 I tuoi figli: i cartoni animati?
6 Il professore: i fumetti?

C They don't like anything!

Your friend answers in the negative each time.
e.g. La lirica: tuo fratello?
    No, la lirica non piace a mio fratello.

1 Il balletto: tua sorella?
2 La chitarra: le tue amiche?
3 I documentari: Antonio?
4 Le telenovele: Norma?
5 Cartoni animati: i tuoi figli?
6 Fumetti: il professore?

D Check your pronouns

Say whether the pronoun in each of the sentences below is a direct object or an indirect object.

1 Signor Petrucci, *La* ringrazio.
2 Dov'è la mia borsa? Non *la* vedo qui.
3 Hai visto Angela? *La* devo vedere subito.
4 Hai visto Maria? *Le* devo parlare subito.
5 Dottor Alberoni, *Le* presento mia moglie.
6 Dove sono le riviste? Non *le* trovo qui.
7 Mario, dov'è? *Gli* voglio parlare.
8 I tuoi cugini dove sono? *Gli* devo dire una cosa.
9 Edda *ci* chiede di venire presto domani.
10 Aldo *ci* richiama dopodomani.

E I'll phone you tomorrow

Complete the following sentences using the appropriate direct object pronoun.

e.g. Carla, . . . chiamo domani, se vuoi. *[you]*
Carla, ti chiamo domani, se vuoi.

1 Non ho visto il film. . . . vedo domani. *[it]*
2 Non ho letto la rivista. . . . leggo più tardi. *[it]*
3 Va bene, dottore, . . . richiamo martedì. *[you]*
4 Gemma e Lucio sono simpatici. . . . invito per domani. *[them]*
5 Le chiavi dove sono? Non . . . vedo. *[them]*
6 Devo scappare, ragazzi. . . . saluto. *[you]*
7 Non abbiamo capito. . . . puoi aiutare? *[us]*

F I'll give him the book back

Substitute the phrase in brackets with an appropriate indirect object pronoun. Check it is in the right place.

e.g. Domani restituisco il libro *[a mio fratello]*.
Domani gli restituisco il libro.

1 Posso offrire *[a Lei]* qualcosa da bere?
2 Devo chiedere *[a Monica]* di venire più tardi.
3 Dobbiamo rispondere *[a Alberto]*.
4 Perché non dai una mano *[a Marta e a Susanna]*?
5 Per favore, Alessio, non vedi che dai fastidio *[a me]*?
6 Se volete, do un passaggio *[a voi]*.
7 Perché non spiegate *[a noi]* il problema?
8 Perché non mando un fax *[a te]*? – È più rapido.

G Use the past tense

Complete the questions below, choosing an appropriate verb from this list.

ricevere, uscire, vendere, suonare, capire, cantare, dormire, arrivare, cadere.

e.g. Hai suonato il flauto?

1 Hai . . .	la canzone?
2 Sei . . .	in ritardo?
3 Ha . . .	una lettera?
4 Ha . . .	la macchina?
5 È . . .	per strada?
6 Avete . . .	la trama?
7 Avete . . .	tutta la mattina?
8 Siete . . .	con gli amici?

H Daily routine

Here is an account of someone else's daily routine. Can you adapt it to your own routine and say what you have done today?

> Di solito . . .
> faccio colazione alle sette. Esco di casa alle sette e mezzo. Prendo il treno e arrivo in ufficio alle nove. Verso le undici bevo il caffè, poi lavoro fino all'una, e pranzo con i colleghi. Rimango in ufficio fino alle sei, perché vedo molti clienti. Poi viene il mio amico: mi dà un passaggio fino alla stazione. Torno a casa verso le sei e mezzo.

Start: Oggi . . .

I Viva Verdi

A class is doing a project on Giuseppe Verdi's life. They've been asked to read through the biographical notes below and prepare questions for a quiz. Can you make up 5–10 questions for the quiz, using the *passato prossimo*?

e.g. Quando è nato Giuseppe Verdi?

Giuseppe Verdi nasce nel 1813, a Roncole vicino a Busseto, in Emilia Romagna. Impara a suonare l'organo a 11 anni, ma non riesce ad entrare nel Conservatorio di Milano. Diventa ben presto comunque uno dei compositori più famosi nella storia della musica lirica italiana. La prima delle 22 opere di Verdi è *Oberto*, [1839], scritta a appena 26 anni. Il successo internazionale arriva nel 1842 con la sua terza opera, il *Nabucco*. Giuseppe Verdi ha una vita triste e difficile. Sua moglie muore giovane nel 1840. Soltanto due mesi dopo, muoiono anche i due figli e Verdi è sul punto di abbandonare la musica. Continua però per il resto della sua vita a comporre altre opere che sono destinate a diventare grandi successi. L'ultima, dopo oltre 50 anni dalla prima, è *Falstaff*, [1893]. Muore a Milano nel 1901 all'età di 87 anni.

Biographies, historical events and stories often make use of the 'historic present'.

Systems 7

1 Stressed pronouns

per me va bene
vengo **con te**

These pronouns are used after prepositions. They are exactly the same as the subject pronouns, except for **me** and **te**.

me	*me*
te	*you*
lui, lei	*him, her*
Lei	*you*
noi	*us*
voi	*you*
loro	*them*

Carlo ha parlato **di** te
Gina è venuta **da** me

Stressed pronouns are also used to replace direct or indirect object pronouns when two of them are contrasted:

lo vedo domani   *But:*
vedo **lui**, non **lei**   *I'm seeing him, not her*
gli telefono domani   *But:*
telefono a **lui**, non a **lei**   *I'm phoning him, not her*

For a complete list of pronouns, see Reference p. 243.

2 Position of pronouns

i) Pronouns before the verb

lo abbiamo comprato
ci sono stato

Pronouns generally precede the verb. In the case of the past tense, this means they go in front of the auxiliary:

gli hai telefonato?
Ci sei andato?

In front of the auxiliary **avere**, the direct object pronouns **lo** and **la** are frequently shortened to **l'**:

Tu l'hai visto?

These are the only pronouns elided in this way:

L'ha vista (Maria) *but* Le ha parlato (a Maria).

ii) Pronouns after the verb

ecco**lo**
preferisco telefonar**gli** dopo

Pronouns used with **ecco** are always joined on the end, to form one word:

Dove sono i ragazzi? Ecco**li**.   *Here they are [lit. behold them].*

With expressions using the infinitive, the final **–e** is dropped and the pronouns are attached to form one word:

preferisco far**lo** subito   *[direct object]*
è meglio spiegar**gli** la situazione   *[indirect obj.]*
sono qui per divertir**mi**   *[reflexive]*
basta andar**ci** una volta   *[ci]★*

There are other cases when pronouns follow the verb: you will come across them in Book 2.

★ Strictly speaking, in the examples used here, **ci** is an adverb, but it is used like a pronoun.

iii) Optional position of pronouns

posso telefonar**gli**?
gli posso telefonare?
sai far**lo**
lo sai fare?

With modal verbs such as **volere, potere, dovere**, and with **sapere**, the position of the pronoun is optional: it can precede the verb or be attached to the infinitive:

Modal verbs
ti voglio vedere   *or* voglio vederti
la posso aiutare   *or* posso aiutarla
le devo telefonare   *or* devo telefonarle

Sapere
Lo sai spiegare?   *or* sai spiegarlo?

The pronoun position is also optional with some **compound verbs**:

andare a trovare	*to go and visit*
venire a trovare	*to come and visit*
andare a prendere	*to go and collect*
venire a prendere	*to come and collect*

perché non vieni a trovar**ci**?
or perché non **ci** vieni a trovare?
domani andiamo a trovar**lo**
or domani **lo** andiamo a trovare.
vengo a prender**ti** subito
or **ti** vengo a prendere subito.

3 Object pronouns

Le va bene
La vengo a trovare?

It is important to learn which verbs require direct
object pronouns and which need indirect object
pronouns.

i) Direct object pronouns
These are used with **andare/venire a trovare**, and
andare/venire a prendere [see **2iii**]:

I figli tornano domani, li vado a prendere alla
stazione.
Claudia è tornata, la vado a trovare domani

ii) Indirect object pronouns
These are used with many common verbs:

andar bene a qlcu.	*to suit, be fine*
andare a qlcu. di	*to feel like*
far vedere a	*to show*

Le va bene venire con noi?
Gli va di partire domani?
Le faccio vedere l'ufficio domani.

Look back at the list in Unit 6 Troubleshooting,
p. 126.

4 Dispiacere

mi dispiace, non posso
Le dispiace se vengo?

Dispiacere *(to be sorry, to mind)* is formed exactly
like **piacere**. It is used to express regret or sympathy:
Mi dispiace, non posso venire   *I'm sorry . . .*
Stai male? Mi dispiace!

It is also used to make a request:
Le dispiace se porto un amico?   *Do you mind
if . . .?*

In the negative – **non dispiacere** – the verb means
I don't mind, I quite like . . .:
Non mi dispiace uscire stasera, ho poca voglia di
studiare.
Non gli dispiace aiutare, ha molto tempo libero.

Dispiacere is only used in singular **dispiace**.
See also Unit 8 Troubleshooting, p. 158.

5 Impersonal si

si dà un anticipo
come **si** accende?

Si is a pronoun used in a general sense, *meaning one,
you, people*. It is used a lot in Italian:
qui si parla italiano   *here one speaks Italian [i.e.,
Italian is spoken]*

If **si** is used with plural objects, the verb must be
plural:
Questo libro si vende solo in Italia
Questi libri si vendono solo in Italia
Come si accende il gas?
Come si accendono i fornelli?

6 Conoscere and sapere

non **conosco** la Basilicata
sai, ho comprato una casa

Conoscere and **sapere** both mean *to know* but they
are not interchangeable. **Conoscere** is used to say
you know a place:
Conosce la zona? Conoscete l'Italia?

or a person:
Conosci mio cugino? Conoscete Daniela?

Sapere is used for knowing a fact:
Lei sa se lui conosce Alberobello?   *Do you know
if he knows Alberobello?*

or for saying what you know how to do:
So nuotare   *I can swim*

There's more on these verbs in Units 8 and 9.

7 Irregular present

Continue to learn the irregular present tense of
useful verbs. In Practice 2 p. 140 the exercise 'Home
improvements' includes the verb **possedere**:

possiedo	possediamo
possiedi	possedete
possiede	possiedono

A verb like **possedere** is **sedersi** *(to sit)*:

mi siedo	ci sediamo
ti siedi	vi sedete
si siede	si siedono

Reinforcement 7

A Partners

You want to find out if it's all right for you to join up with the following people:
Can you reconstruct the sentences to make sense.

1 Beppe, ti | va bene se gioco | con Lei?
2 Signor Bruni, Le | va bene se vengo | con voi?
3 Carlo e Anna, vi | va bene se pranzo | con te?

B One not the other!

Try and put your friend right. He needs to know who you have in mind:

e.g. Mi aiuti domani? Li aiuti domani?
   Aiuto te domani, non loro!

1 Lo inviti a cena?   La inviti a cena?
2 Gli *[pl.]* telefoni stasera?   Mi telefoni stasera?
3 Le fai un regalo? Gli fai un regalo?
4 Gli dai una mano?   Ci dai una mano?

C Pronoun practice

Use the right Italian word for the formal *you* (**Lei, le, la**).

1 Ma signore, . . . ho mandato una lettera espresso!
2 Per . . . va bene, professore?
3 D'accordo signora, . . . vengo a trovare giovedì prossimo.

Now use the right word for *them* (**li, gli, loro**).

4 I Bianchi sono esperti: perché non ha parlato con . . . prima di decidere?
5 I signori Valenti sono tornati: . . . chiamo dopo il telegiornale.
6 Gli studenti non lo sanno: . . . avete spiegato il problema?

Use the correct words for *her* (**la, le, lei**).

7 Ma, no, ho prestato il libro a . . . non a Roberto.
8 Per il suo compleanno . . . abbiamo regalato un telefonino!
9 Monica ha comprato una villetta in campagna. . . . vado a trovare il sedici giugno.

Finally, fill in the correct words for *him* (**lo, gli, lui**).

10 Il compleanno di Angelo è domani: . . . hai comprato un regalo?
11 C'è posto nell'appartamento di Antonio – perché non rimani da . . . domani sera?
12 Il marito di Carlotta è simpatico, . . . conosco da anni.

D Your advice, please

Read each pair of sentences then rewrite the last one, beginning with the word given.

e.g. Ho rovesciato il caffè sul divano!
   L'hai pulito con un po' d'acqua?   *[Bisogna]*
   Bisogna pulirlo con un po' d'acqua.

1 Non trovo il numero di Paolo.
   L' hai cercato sull'elenco telefonico?   *[Basta]*
2 Non ho voglia di accettare l'invito.
   L'hai rifiutato, allora?   *[Basta]*
3 Luca mi ha invitato al matrimonio.
   Gli hai risposto subito?   *[Bisogna]*
4 Giovanna non mi ha spiegato come funziona la lavatrice.
   Le hai chiesto come funziona?   *[Bisogna]*

E Quite contrary

Say you haven't done any of the following:

e.g. Hai studiato la lezione? – No, non ho cominciato a . . .
   No, non ho cominciato a studiarla.

1 Hai letto l'articolo? – No, non ho finito di . . .
2 Hai fatto i compiti? – No, non sono riuscito a . . .
3 Hai parlato al professore? – No, non mi piace . . .
4 Hai scritto a Maria? – No, non ho bisogno di . . .
5 Hai pulito la moquette? – No, preferisco . . . domani.

F Both are right

There's more than one way of saying the same thing. Rewrite the sentences below, putting the pronouns in the alternative position.

e.g. Mi può dire come funziona lo scaldabagno?
   Può dirmi come funziona lo scaldabagno?

1 La biancheria è sporca, la devo lavare.
2 È un bellissimo castello, lo voglio visitare.
3 Mia cugina è simpatica, la vado a trovare domani.
4 Mi sa dire se la mostra è aperta domenica?
5 Giovanni arriva il dieci marzo: lo vado a prendere alla stazione.
6 Non ho la macchina, mi puoi dare un passaggio?

G Coming and going

Answer these questions using **ci** in two alternative positions:

e.g. Volete andare a ballare? – Sì, . . .
    Sì, ci vogliamo andare.
    Sì vogliamo andarci.

1 Potete andare al cinema? – Sì, . . .
2 Dovete andare a fare la spesa? – Sì, . . .
3 Volete venire con noi in piscina? – Sì, . . .

H Preferences

You're checking out your guests' preferences. Can you use one phrase from each part to make meaningful sentences?

Ti va di	partire presto	o preferite mangiare dopo?
Le dispiace	cenare adesso	o preferisci andare a teatro?
Vi va bene	andare al cinema	o preferisce partire più tardi?

I Houseproud

You're delighted with your new home and possessions and lose no opportunity to show them off.

e.g. nuovo divano – molto comodo.
    Ti faccio vedere il nuovo divano – è molto comodo. Ti piace?

Show your best friend the following:
1 nuove tende – molto belle
2 nuova cucina – molto pratica

Show your new neighbour the following:
3 nuovi tappeti – molto raffinati
4 nuovo specchio – molto antico

And get your in-laws to look at the following:
5 nuovi scaffali – molto belli
6 nuovo quadro – molto originale.

J Excuses excuses

No one really wants to come to the party. As the diplomat you've got the task of making the excuses. Using **dispiacere**, pass on your friends' regrets, choosing a plausible reason why they can't come.

e.g. Annalisa non può venire.
    [avere: molto da fare/molti impegni/molta fame]
    Annalisa non può venire. Le dispiace, ma ha molti impegni.

1 Alessia non può venire.
   [essere: molto impegnata/molto stanca/molto in gamba]
2 Beppe non può venire.
   [avere: un altro appuntamento/un'altra ragazza/un altro impegno]
3 Elisa e Franco non possono venire.
   [avere: l'influenza/fretta/ospiti in casa]

K Is it all right if . . .?

You tend to put things off but you know how to get round others! Try it on with these people.

e.g. Signora Monetti – se vengo più tardi?
    Signora Monetti, Le va bene se vengo più tardi? Le dispiace?

1 Ragazzi – se lo faccio la settimana prossima?
2 Signor Arbasino – se La chiamo domani?
3 Giorgio – se arrivo in ritardo?

L Do you know?

Can you remember when to use **conoscere** and when to use **sapere?**

1 Non *[conosco/so]* dove ci incontriamo.
2 La Basilicata è molto interessante, è una zona che *[conosco/so]* bene.
3 Scusi, Lei *[conosce/sa]* a che ora parte il treno?
4 Scusa, tu *[conosci/sai]* il marito di Elena?

M False friends, double meanings

Can you give the correct meaning of each of the following words, and give the Italian for the English word which it sounds like:
1 attico; 2 pavimento; 3 box

The following Italian words all have more than one meaning. How many can you give?
4 Il soggiorno *(×2)*; 5 il palazzo *(×2)*; 6 il posto *(×3)*

Systems 8

1 The pronoun ne

ne hai una?
ne prendo un altro

Ne is a pronoun meaning *of it, of them*. It can replace singular and plural, masculine and feminine nouns. You use it with expressions of quantity:

Quanto/a **ne** prende?
How much [of it] will you have?
Ne prendo un chilo/una fetta
I'll have a kilo/a slice [of it]
Quanti/e **ne** prende?
How many [of them] will you have?
Ne prendo dieci/una ventina
I'll have 10/about 20 [of them]

Although **ne** may not appear in the question, it is required in the answer:

Quanto pane mangi al giorno?
Ne mangio molto/un po'/poco

The position of ne
Ne comes before the verb unless it is used with **ecco** or an infinitive [See Unit 7, Systems, note 2 ii, p. 197.]
For more on **ne** see Unit 9, Systems, note 1, p. 205 and Ref. I, 8vc, p. 240.

2 Prepositions in questions

con chi parlo?
con cosa li fanno?

Prepositions precede the question words **chi? (che) cosa? dove? che?/quale?**:

A chi scrivi?
Per che cosa lo fai?
Da dove parte il treno?
Di che colore è?
In quale città sei nato?

Note the following useful expressions:
Di chi è?   *Whose [of whom] is it?*
Di chi sono?   *Whose [of whom] are they?*

3 Piacere with a

piacciono anche **a me**
piacciono anche **a lui**

In Unit 6, you learned that **piacere** is used with the indirect object pronouns: **mi, ti, gli**, etc.

However, it is sometimes used with **a**, plus the stressed pronouns, **me, te, lui, lei, noi, voi, loro** [See Unit 7, Systems, note 1 i, p. 197.].

When to use a + stressed pronoun
a) With **anche**:
   Piace anche a te? Piace anche a Lei?
   Do you like it too?

b) For contrast and comparison:
   A me piace la carne, ma a lui piace il pesce.
   A te piace il mare, ma a me non piace.

c) When emphasising the subject:
   A Lei piace la cucina italiana?

You could equally well say, less emphatically:
   Le piace la cucina italiana?

In colloquial speech it is common to hear both pronouns used together with **piacere**, but, strictly speaking, this is incorrect:
   A me mi piace la cucina italiana.

4 Sapere

lo sai che non è permesso?
sì, **lo so**

Common uses include

a) Knowing a fact:
   Lo so   *I know [lit. I know it]*
   Non lo so   *I don't know*

Although not strictly necessary, **lo** is often used for emphasis:
   Lo sai che è vietato fumare?

b) Finding out a fact:
   Ti chiamo per sapere se puoi venire

c) Knowing how to do something:
   So scrivere a macchina   *I can type*
   Mi sa dire dov'è la posta   *Can you tell me . . .?*
Mi sa dire is used in preference to **mi può dire** when you are not sure the person has the information.
There is more on **sapere** in Unit 9.

5 Double object verbs

mi hanno rubato **la macchina**
gli hanno rubato **lo stereo**

Many verbs can be used with two objects: direct and indirect.
Verbs of this type include:

comprare	*to buy something for someone*
mandare	*to send something to someone*
portare	*to bring something to someone*
regalare	*to give something to someone*
rubare	*to steal something from someone*

Gli hanno rubato la macchina
He had his car stolen [lit. they stole the car from him]

Note that in expressions of this type, you use the indirect object pronoun for the person.

For a list of similar verbs, see Ref. VII, 4ii, p. 247.

6 Double negatives

non è **niente**
non ho **più** fame

A simple negative is made by putting **non** in front of the verb:
    Non vengo

A double negative contains **non** plus a second negative word.
Here are the main ones:

non . . . nessuno	*no-one*
non . . . niente/nulla	*nothing*
non . . . ancora	*not yet*
non . . . mai	*never*
non . . . più	*no longer, not any more*
non . . . affatto	*not at all*

non . . . neanche/
    nemmeno/
    neppure
	not even

non . . . mica	*not really*

Non vedo nessuno
Non capisco niente

Word order

Non always precedes the verb.
a) Present tense. The verb goes between **non** and the second part of the negative:
    Non studia mai
    Non mi diverto affatto

If the verb is part of a phrase, e.g. **aver fame, avere voglia di, essere in ritardo**, the second negative word tends to come between the verb and the rest of the verbal phrase.
    Non ho più fame
    Non ho affatto voglia di venire
    Non sono mai in ritardo

However, **niente** and **nessuno** are exceptions:
    Non ho voglia di fare niente
    Non ho voglia di vedere nessuno

b) Past tense. If the verb is in the **passato prossimo** tense, the second negative word tends to come after the auxiliary:
    Non ho ancora deciso
    Non ho mica capito
    Non mi ha neanche salutato

But, again, the exceptions are **niente** and **nessuno**:
    Non ho deciso niente
    Non ha visto nessuno

The word order can vary with double negatives, but for the learner it is helpful to grasp a basic pattern. There is more on negatives in Unit 9.

7 Irregular verbs

The following new verbs with irregular past participles have been used in this unit:

decidere	deciso	*to decide*
perdere	perso	*to lose, miss*
permettere	permesso	*to allow*
rompere	rotto	*to break*
succedere	successo	*to happen*

Reinforcement 8

A Escalation
Your friends and acquaintances have twice as much as you have. Can you complete the mini dialogues?
e.g. Ho una figlia. E Lei . . .?
     E Lei, quante ne ha? – Ne ho due.

1 Bevo cinque caffè al giorno. E tu . . .?
2 Prendo due vacanze all'anno. E voi . . .?
3 Fumo tre sigari alla settimana. E Lei?
4 Leggo quattro riviste al mese. E tu?

B Nosey parker
You're curious about your glamorous new neighbour, so you ask your home help about her. Below is what she told you. What were your questions?
e.g. . . .?   *[chi?]*
     Lavora per una grande società straniera.
     Per chi lavora?

1 . . .?   *[chi?]*
  È sposata con un avvocato molto ricco.
2 . . .?   *[che cosa?]*
  Con suo marito parla di soldi e di affari.
3 . . .?   *[quali?]*
  Ha vissuto in vari paesi, in Giappone, negli Stati Uniti.
4 . . .?   *[dove?]*
  Il suo cane strano viene dalla Cina.
5 . . .?   *[che]*
  Dorme nella stanza che dà sul giardino.
6 . . .?   *[che]*
  La sua biancheria è tutta rosa.
7 . . .?   *[chi?]*
  La Lamborghini rossa è sua.

C Soul mates
Here are some like-minded people, who enjoy the same things. Bring them closer together by making a single sentence out of each pair.
e.g. Gli piace andare al mare. Le piace andare al mare.
     A lui piace andare al mare e piace anche a lei.

1 Ci piace viaggiare. Gli *(he)* piace viaggiare.
2 Mi piacciono le orecchiette. Le piacciono le orecchiette.
3 Vi piacciono lunghe passeggiate sulla spiaggia. Gli *(they)* piacciono lunghe passeggiate sulla spiaggia.
4 Ti piace leggere poesie. Mi piace leggere poesie.

D Incompatible
Now here are some pretty incompatible people. They just don't like the same things. Sum up the sorry situation each time:

e.g. *Girl:* Mi piace la lirica!
     Boy: Non mi piace la lirica!
     A lei piace la lirica ma a lui no.
1 *Class:* Ci piacciono i fumetti!
  Male teacher: Non mi piacciono i fumetti!
2 *Wife:* Mi piacciono le macchine veloci.
  Husband: Non mi piacciono le macchine veloci.
3 *Parents:* Ci piace visitare i musei.
  Daughter: Non mi piace visitare i musei!

E Do you know it?
Have you got to grips with **sapere**?
How well can you cope in the following situations?

1 You tell Enrico that you've called to find out if he can come. What do you say?
2 Your son wants an expensive computer game. You tell him you need to know how much it costs.
3 You're wondering whether this passer-by can tell what time the banks close.
4 You want to explain that you can't type but you can drive.

F Nice or nasty?
Match up the two parts of the sentences below to discover which are the pleasant experiences and which not so pleasant. Link each part with the pronoun **mi, le/Le, gli** or **ci** as appropriate.

1 Davvero, signore,	**mi**	ho regalato un computer.
2 Lisa è malata,	**le**	hanno rubato l'orologio?
3 È il compleanno di Angelo,	**gli**	hanno mandato dei fiori.
4 Sono disperata,	**ci**	ho portato un po' di frutta.
5 I Fortunato sono così gentili,	**Le**	hanno rubato la collana.

G What next?

Complete the sequel by translating the second part into Italian.

e.g. Mario la conosce da anni.
  But he doesn't love her any more.
  Ma non la ama più.

1 Devo invitare anche Norma.
  But I haven't written to her yet.
2 Non gli piace andare al mare.
  He never goes.
3 Sono molto stanco.
  I don't want to see anyone.
4 Ma non importa.
  It's nothing.
5 Le sue feste sono sempre noiose.
  I don't feel at all like going.
6 Renata è veramente antipatica.
  She doesn't even say hello to me. [*Use* salutare]
7 Ho mangiato troppo.
  I'm not really hungry.

H Making sense

Can you reorder these sentences to make sense?

1 Deciso non ancora ho.
2 Non mai sono stato ci.
3 Più venuto sono non.
4 Niente non preso ho.
5 Non nessuno arrivato è.

I Chalk and cheese

These two are total opposites. They always contradict each other.

e.g. Vado sempre al cinema – Non vado mai al cinema.

1 Ho già mangiato.
2 Ho visto arrivare qualcuno.
3 Ho fatto qualcosa oggi.
4 Ho ancora fame.

J Irregular past participles

Below are parts of irregular verbs which have appeared in this unit. Match up the two parts of the past participle and give the infinitive and meaning of each verb.

VISS   SUC   PER   AP   CHI   R   P

erto   erso   uso   otto   cesso   uto   messo

K Pardon me

Complete the sentences using the phrases given.

scusa   scusi
mi dispiace   non mi piace
non mi dispiace

1 . . ., signora, per il Teatro dell'Opera come faccio?
2 No Carlo, . . . è impossibile uscire domani.
3 L'idea . . ., il tempo è ideale per fare una gita.
4 Oh, . . . Laura! Colpa mia! Ti ho macchiato la gonna?
5 La proposta . . ., non sono mai stato/a a Gallipoli.

L Word perfect

How well do you know the irregular past tense? Can you give the past participle of the verbs listed here? They have all appeared in the course so far.

bere	morire
chiedere	nascere
correre	prendere
dare	rispondere
decidere	scendere
dire	stare
fare	scrivere
leggere	vedere
mettere	venire

M Fra o Fa?

Do you remember which is which?

e.g. Quando hai incontrato Delio?   *[20 anni]*
  Ho incontrato Delio 20 anni fa.
  Quando vi vedete?   *[10 giorni]*
  Ci vediamo fra 10 giorni.

1 Quando pensate di venire?   *[15 giorni]*
2 Quando sei venuto a Bari per la prima volta?   *[15 anni]*
3 Quando ha cominciato a studiare l'italiano?   *[6 mesi]*
4 Quando vengono i tuoi genitori?   *[un paio di giorni]*
5 Quando siete venuti per l'ultima volta?   *[molto tempo]*

Systems 9

1 Pronouns: combining ci and ne

ce n'è uno qui
ce ne sono alcuni qui

The expressions **c'è [ci è]** (*there is*) and **ci sono** (*there are*) are often used in conjunction with **ne**. **Ci** always precedes **ne**, and both pronouns must come before the verb: **ci** becomes **ce** in front of **ne**.

Ce n'è derives from:	**ci + ne + è**
This becomes:	**ce + ne + è**
And finally:	**ce n'è**

(**Ne** elides with the verb **è** to make the expression pronounceable.)

The expression **ce ne sono** derives from:

ci + ne + sono

This becomes: **ce ne sono**

Using ce n'è, ce ne sono

Ce n'è, ce ne sono must be used with expressions of quantity:

Quanto/a ce n'è?
Ce n'è molto/a, un chilo, un litro
Quanti/e ce ne sono?
Ce ne sono molti/e, 2 chili, 3 litri

2 Possessives

i) Possessive adjectives with indefinite articles

è un mio amico: sono amici **miei**
è un tuo amico: sono amici **tuoi**

È			He, she is a friend of mine
un mio, una mia			
un tuo, una tua			of yours
un suo, una sua			of his, hers
un Suo, una Sua	amico/a		of yours
un nostro, una nostra			of ours
un vostro, una vostra			of yours
un loro, una loro			of theirs
Sono amici, amiche miei, mie tuoi, tue ecc.			*They are friends of mine of yours, etc.*

ii) Position of the possessives

In singular expressions they tend to come before the noun and in plural expressions they often come after it. However, the position depends to some extent on emphasis and region.

iii) Possessive adjectives with other quantifiers

ho visto **degli** amici **tuoi**
ho visto **alcuni** amici **suoi**
ho visto **molti** colleghi **vostri**

You can use many other quantifiers with possessive adjectives:

Sono venuti pochi amici miei
Ho parlato con due amici tuoi

3 Demonstratives

quel cespuglio
quell'albero
quella pianta

i) Quello as an adjective

Quello always precedes the noun. Like the definite article, its form varies according to the initial spelling of the noun as well as its number and gender.

	sing.	*plu.*
masc.	quel ragazzo quello studente quell'uomo	quei ragazzi quegli studenti quegli uomini
fem.	quella ragazza quell'arancia	quelle ragazze quelle arance

ii) Quello as a pronoun

The forms are simpler:

masc. sing. quello *fem. sing.* quella	*masc. pl.* quelli *fem. pl.* quelle

Quale ragazzo/uomo/studente? – Quello lì
Quali ragazzi/uomini/studenti – Quelli lì
Quale ragazza/arancia? – Quella lì
Quali ragazze/arance? – Quelle lì

4 Present progressive

sto scegliendo i funghi
stiamo lavorando molto

This is formed from the present tense of the verb
stare and the gerund of the verb required.
There are only two gerund endings: **–ando** for **–are**
verbs and **–endo** for the rest. These are added to
the stem of the infinitive.

i) Regular gerunds

stare	*gerund*	*infinitive*
sto		
stai	parl**ando**	*(parlare)*
sta	legg**endo**	*(leggere)*
stiamo	part**endo**	*(partire)*
state	fin**endo**	*(finire)*
stanno		

ii) Irregular gerunds

A few verbs with 'contracted' infinitives have
irregular gerunds. Most of them use the **–endo** form
of the gerund added to an 'expanded' stem of the
verb:

infinitive	*gerund*
bere	**beve**ndo
dire	**dice**ndo
fare	**face**ndo
attrarre	**attrae**ndo
produrre	**produce**ndo
proporre	**propon**endo

★ All verbs ending in **–arre**, **–urre** or **–orre** form
the gerund in the same way:
   estrarre (*to extract*) **estrae**ndo;
   tradurre (*to translate*) **traduc**endo;
   supporre (*to suppose*) **suppon**endo.

★ **Dare** and **stare** use the **–are** form of the gerund:
   dando   stando

iii) Uses of the present progressive

In Italian the present progressive has a far more
restricted use than in English and is only used to
focus on an activity taking place at the time of
speaking. In the following examples, the English
'What are you doing?' is not **'Cosa sta facendo?'**,
though it would be possible in the third example.
   Cosa fai domani?   Vado a Roma
   What are you doing tomorrow?   I'm going to Rome
   Cosa fai qui?   Sono qui in vacanza
   What are you doing here?   I'm here on holiday
   Cosa fai con i funghi?   Li sto tagliando
   *What are you doing with the mushrooms?   I'm cutting
   them up*

5 Passato prossimo with avere

le hai cucinate tu?
ne ho visti tanti

Past participle agreement

Verbs which use **avere** as the auxiliary in the **passato
prossimo** past tense normally require no changes
in the past participle:
   Ho visto tanti porcini

However, if the verb is preceded by a direct object
pronoun, **lo, la, li, le** or **ne**, the participle must
agree with it:
   Ne ho visti tanti   Li ho visti tutti
   Ho conosciuto Maria.   L'ho conosciuta
   Ho conosciuto le ragazze.   Le ho conosciute

With **ne** the form of the agreement depends on
what **ne** stands for:
   Hai mangiato un po' di pizza?
   Sì, ne ho mangiata molta
   Hai mangiato delle mele?
   Sì, ne ho mangiate due

Note: There are occasions when **ne** is not a direct
object and no agreement of the past participle is
made. See Book 2.

Agreements with the direct object pronouns **mi, ti,
ci, vi** and **La** are less consistently made:
   Quando ci ha visto? is very common instead of:
   Quando ci ha visti?

With the formal direct object **La** (*you*) the
agreement, if made, must be feminine even if you
are formally addressing a man:
   L'ho vista ieri, signor Marini.

Systems 9

Beware: never make past participles agree with a preceding *indirect* object pronoun. Compare:

Ho visto Marina. L'ho vista   *[direct]*
Ho telefonato a Marina. Le ho   *[indirect]*
telefonato

6 Conoscere and sapere

Here is a summary of the uses of each verb:

i) Conoscere

Knowing a place:	Conosce Bari
	Conosce i posti migliori
Knowing a person:	Conosce il signor Fanfani?
Knowing a work –	Conosce *La Primavera* di
a painting or book:	Botticelli?
In the past: meeting	L'ho conosciuto a Roma.
somebody:	

ii) Sapere

Knowing a fact:	So che viene domani
	So il suo numero
Knowing a language:	So quattro lingue
Knowing by heart:	Lo so a memoria
Finding out:	Ho telefonato per sapere ...
Knowing how to do	Li so preparare
something:	So parlare italiano

iii) Comparing conoscere and sapere

Conoscere implies being acquainted with, while **sapere** implies complete knowledge of something. Sometimes the same phrase can be used with either **sapere** or **conoscere**, but with a different meaning:

La sai quella poesia di Carducci?
[i.e. have you studied the poem, learned it?]
Conosci quella poesia di Carducci?
[i.e. have you heard of the poem?]

The use of **sapere** and **conoscere** can be subject to individual and regional differences. Both verbs are used for knowing the way:

Conosci la strada? *or* La strada la sai?

The learner should nevertheless follow the basic guidelines.

7 Impersonal verbs and expressions

mi fa paura il fuoco
gli fanno paura le vipere

There are many common verbs other than **piacere** which can be used impersonally, i.e. with the third person of the verb:

fare piacere (a)	*to give pleasure*
fare schifo (a)	*to disgust*
fare paura (a)	*to frighten*
bastare (a)	*to be enough*
mancare (a)	*to be missing*

As with **piacere**, indirect object pronouns are used:

Le manca qualcosa?   *Is anything missing (for you)?*
Le bastano due chili?   *Are 2 kilos enough (for you)?*

For similar verbs see Ref. VIIIB, l ii and iii, p. 250.

8 Negatives

non trovo **mai niente**
non vedo **più nessuno**

When negative expressions such as **non ... mai, non ... più, non ... ancora** are combined with **niente** or **nessuno**, the order of negatives can vary, but there are some basic rules. [See also Unit 8, Systems, note 6, p. 202.]

a) **Non** always comes before the verb.
b) In the present tense the two negatives come together:
Non c'è **ancora nessuno**
c) In the past tense, **niente** and **nessuno** tend to come after the participle:
Non ha **mai** trovato **niente**
Non abbiamo **più** visto **nessuno**

9 Irregular verbs

Continue to learn irregular verbs:

scegliere *to choose*	**togliere** *to remove*	**salire** *to go up*
scelgo	tolgo	salgo
scegli	togli	sali
sceglie	toglie	sale
scegliamo	togliamo	saliamo
scegliete	togliete	salite
scelgono	tolgono	salgono

Scegliere and **togliere** have irregular past participles:

scegliere: scelto   togliere: tolto

Reinforcement 9

A Down your way

You're being asked what amenities you have in your area. Give the answers, following the guidelines below and using **per fortuna** (*luckily*) if the answer is yes and **purtroppo** (*unfortunately*) if the answer is no.

e.g. C'è un buon ristorante vicino a casa Sua? *[Sì – molti]*

Sì, per fortuna ce ne sono molti.

1 C'è un parco nel tuo quartiere? *[Sì – 1]*
2 Ci sono dei cinema nella Sua città? *[Sì – alcuni]*
3 C'è una macelleria nel tuo quartiere? *[No]*
4 C'è una banca vicino a casa Sua? *[Sì – 1]*
5 C'è una piscina nella tua città? *[Sì – 2]*
6 Ci sono scuole nel tuo quartiere? *[No]*

B Who's that?

You're showing your holiday snapshots and are explaining who everyone is in relation to you. You need to rewrite the sentences below:

e.g. Giacomo è un collega. Giacomo è un mio collega.

1 Susanna è un'amica.
2 I Moro sono amici.
3 Lidia e Marta sono colleghe.
4 Gianni è un cugino.

C Who's who?

You've gone through a round of introductions but you're still a little unsure about who Sandro and Giovanna are. You ask Pino, signor Bruni and a couple of friends about them.

e.g. Pino, Sandro . . . parente?

Pino, Sandro è un tuo parente?

1 Signor Bruni, Sandro . . . collega?
2 Ragazzi, Sandro . . . amico?
3 Pino, Giovanna . . . sorella?
4 Signor Bruni, Giovanna . . . cugina?
5 Ragazzi, Giovanna . . . collega?

D Who came?

You and your partner are explaining who came to the barbecue last night.

e.g. tanti amici

Ieri sera sono venuti tanti amici nostri.

Continue using the following:
1 molti colleghi   4 una zia
2 alcuni cugini   5 un vicino
3 pochi parenti   6 quattro amiche

E Point it out

Last night you had guests and cleared up in a hurry, putting things in odd places. No-one can find anything, so point out where you put things, using the correct form of **quello**.

e.g. Le matite? – nella tazza

Ho messo le matite in quella tazza.

1 Il giornale? – sotto il cuscino.
2 Le foto? – dietro lo specchio.
3 I vestiti? – nei cassetti.
4 Le scarpe? – nell'armadio.
5 Le riviste? – sugli scaffali.
6 I giocattoli? – nelle borse.

F Spell it out

Which do you prefer? You're being asked to pick out the item you want. The one you want is always different:

e.g. Quale pasta vuole?   Questa?

No, quella lì.

1 Quali panini preferisce?   Questi?
2 Quale salame prende?   Questo?
3 Quali caramelle vuole?   Queste?
4 Quale arancia preferisce?   Questa?

G Otherwise engaged

All the following invitations and requests are turned down. The reasons are given in English. Put these into Italian: all but two of them are to do with what's going on right now.

e.g. Possiamo vederci fra poco?

No, I'm sorry, I'm preparing the supper.

No, mi dispiace, sto preparando la cena.

1 Avete voglia di venire a prendere un caffè?
We're sorry, we can't, we're studying.
2 Senti, vuoi venire a cena con noi?
No, I can't, I'm waiting for my friends.
3 Carlo e Pietro possono venire da noi stasera?
I'm sorry, they can't, they're going to their grandmother's.
4 Pronto, posso parlare con Francesca?
I'm sorry, but she's sleeping.
5 Posso parlarti adesso?
I'm sorry, but I'm going out right now.
6 Venite al cinema con noi?
We can't, we're going out tonight.

Reinforcement 9

H The first time

Where and when did you first meet these people?

e.g. I miei vicini – a una festa 3 anni fa.

Li ho conosciuti a una festa 3 anni fa.

1 La suocera – a casa sua 5 anni fa.
2 La moglie – in casa di parenti 20 anni fa.
3 Gina e Franco – in casa di amici l'altro giorno.
4 Il nuovo collega – in ufficio l'anno scorso.

I Killjoy

You're at a loose end: here's what your various friends suggest you do. Say you've done it all already. There's one sentence which doesn't fit the pattern below: which is it?

e.g. Andiamo a vedere la mostra?

No, mi dispiace, l'ho già vista.

1 Vuoi visitare l'abbazia di Pomposa?
2 Perché non leggi quelle nuove riviste?
3 Ti va di visitare i musei?
4 Non hai voglia di scrivere alla tua ragazza?
5 Perché non senti questi dischi nuovi?

J Not yet

You have joined a group of friends on holiday. When you ask what they've been up to so far, it doesn't amount to much!

e.g. Giovanni, hai fatto alcune gite?

No, non ne ho ancora fatte.

1 Anita e Paolo, avete fatto delle passeggiate?
2 Emilio, hai assaggiato i vini locali?
3 Franca, hai mandato delle cartoline?
4 Rosaria e Carmelo, avete visto alcuni monumenti?
5 Riccardo, hai comprato delle specialità del paese?

K What do you know?

Using **conoscere** and **sapere** can be tricky. Try and complete the sentences using the words below:

sa conosce sappiamo conosci
sapete so sanno ho conosciuto

1 Tu . . . Lucio? – Certo, l' . . . a Parma.
2 Lei . . . quella poesia? – Certo la . . . anche a memoria.
3 Scusi, . . . se è permessa la caccia?
4 Noi . . . riconoscere tutti i funghi velenosi.
5 I miei figli . . . due lingue.
6 Ragazzi, lo . . . il mio indirizzo e il telefono?

L Black list

These people are all on the black list. Why? Match up the sentences to find out.

e.g. Perché non chiedi a Antonella di dare una mano?

Ma lei non aiuta mai nessuno!

1 Perché non dici a Giorgio di fare la spesa oggi?
2 Perché non chiedi a Giulio di spiegare la lezione?
3 Perché non dici a Stefania di stare a casa?
4 Perché non chiedi a Francesca di preparare la cena?

a Ma lui non fa mai niente!
b Ma lei non cucina mai niente!
c Ma lei non aiuta mai nessuno!
d Ma lui non capisce mai niente!
e Ma lei non ascolta mai nessuno!

M Nobody loves me

Nothing ever goes right. Can you reorder the sentences to explain?

e.g. Quando telefono in ufficio *[c'è non mai nessuno]*

Non c'è mai nessuno

1 Quando telefono in Inghilterra *[risponde nessuno non mai]*
2 Quando telefono a casa tua *[non nessuno mai trovo]*

Things have even got worse. Can you explain?

3 Quando vado in ufficio *[più nessuno mi parla non]*
4 Quando ho bisogno di aiuto *[nessuno più non mi aiuta]*

Systems 10

1 Comparative and superlative adjectives

è **più bravo**
è **meno bravo**
i designer **meno bravi**
le mani **più brave**

Superlatives (*most, -est, least*) generally differ from comparatives (*more, less*) only in the use of the article with **più** and **meno**.

Regular adjectives

Adj.	Comparative	Superlative
bello	più bello meno bello	il/la/i/le più bello/a/i/e meno bello/a/i/e
facile	più facile meno facile	il/la/i/le più facile meno facile

Irregular adjectives

buono	migliore/i	il/la/i/le migliore/i
cattivo	peggiore/i	il/la/i/le peggiore/i

Note: **più/meno buono/cattivo** can be used instead of **migliore/peggiore,** e.g. in relation to food:

Questi spaghetti sono più buoni   (*nicer*)
Queste tagliatelle sono le più buone   (*the nicest*)

Here are some examples of superlatives:
Roma è la città più grande d'Italia
Carlo è il ragazzo meno bravo della classe
È il risultato peggiore della stagione

The article can also go next to **più**, **migliore** and **peggiore**:
Roma è la più grande città d'Italia
È il peggiore risultato della stagione

Examples of comparatives:
Sandro è più bravo di lui
Giorgio è meno simpatico di Susanna

2 Comparative and superlative adverbs

Regular comparative and superlative forms differ only in the use of the article:

Regular adverbs

Adverb	Comparative	Superlative
rapidamente	più rapida- mente meno rapida- mente	il più rapida- mente il meno rapida- mente
forte	più forte meno forte	il più forte il meno forte

Here are some examples of superlatives:
Gaetano parla il più forte possibile
Vittorio lavora il meno rapidamente possibile

Examples of comparatives:
Anita legge più rapidamente di Edda
Patrizio parla meno forte di Mario

Irregular adverbs

With irregular adverbs the comparative and superlative forms are often the same, but the context will tell you whether the adverb is comparative or superlative:

Adverb	Comparative	Superlative
molto (*very*)	di più (*more*)	di più (*most*)
poco (*not very*)	di meno (*less*)	di meno (*least*)
bene (*well*)	meglio (*better*)	meglio (*best*)
male (*badly*)	peggio (*worse*)	peggio (*worst*)

Examples of superlatives:
Mario mangia più di/meno di tutti   (*most/least of all*)
Venezia è la città che mi piace di più/di meno   (*most/least*)

Comparatives:
Mario mangia più/meno di me   (*more/less*)
Mi piace Roma, ma Venezia mi piace di più   (*more*)

Systems 10

3 Making comparisons

è più vivace **della** moda francese
è più bello vivere qui **che** a Parigi

When making a comparison of inequality you need to know how to translate *than*:
Di is used to express *than* if you are directly comparing people or objects:

Piero è più alto di te
Elisabetta è meno intelligente di Mina
Questa casa è più bella dell'altra
Gianna fuma meno di me.

Di is also used where numbers are involved:
Abbiamo più di tre milioni da spendere
Sara ha meno di cinque anni

Che is used
When two activities are compared:
È meno divertente andare da Marco che rimanere qui
È più bello vivere a Berlino che a Atene
Bero più tè che caffè

When two items are related to a single person or thing:
A Roma ci sono più chiese che parchi
Pino ha più nemici che amici

When there is a comparison between two adjectives:
Quel vestito è più elegante che comodo
Paola è più intelligente che simpatica

4 A note on bello, buono and grande

Bello follows the spelling changes of **quello** when it is used before a noun [See Unit 9, Systems, note 3, p. 205.]

un bel modello	bei modelli
un bello specchio	begli specchi
un bell'appartamento	begli appartamenti
una bell'estate	belle estati

Buono becomes **buon** before a noun whose indefinite article is **un**:
un buon caffè   un buon amico

Grande can optionally become **gran** with a noun whose indefinite article is **un**, unless it begins with a vowel where **grand'** can be used:
un gran romanzo *or* un grande romanzo
un grand'amico *or* un grande amico

5 Relative pronouns

il designer **che** mi piace
il modello **che** ho visto
quello che io chiamo ...

The pronoun **che** means *who, whom, which/that*:
È l'amico che mi piace di più
L'amico che ho visto si chiama Andrea
È il film che mi piace di meno
Il film che ho visto si chiama 'Novecento'.

It is possible to omit relative pronouns in English but never in Italian.

Quello che, or **ciò che** mean *what*:
Ho capito quello che vuoi dire
Quello che Lei dice è interessante.

For more on relative pronouns, see Book 2.

6 Verbs used with indirect object pronouns

le sta bene
gli permette di vedere?

Stare bene a (*to suit*) requires an indirect object pronoun:
Quelle scarpe Le stanno bene, signore.

Permettere a qualcuno di (*to allow someone to*) is also used with an indirect object pronoun:
Gli permette di uscire?

There are several similar verbs, such as **proibire a qualcuno di** (*to prohibit someone to*), **vietare a qlcu. di** (*to forbid s.one to*).

See the list in Ref. VII, 5, pp. 247–8.

7 Verbs and prepositions

cominciare **a** disegnare
finire **di** lavorare
quanto l'ha pagato?

Many common verbs require either **a** or **di** after them. Often the English equivalent is *to*:

Sono riuscito a studiare   *I managed to*
Ho deciso di venire   *I decided to*

It is worth gradually learning which prepositions accompany the common verbs. See Ref. VII, pp. 246–8.

Some common Italian verbs require no prepositions, unlike their English equivalents:

Quanto l'avete pagato?   *How much did you pay for it?*

Similar verbs include:

ascoltare	*to listen to*	cercare	*to look for*
aspettare	*to wait for*	guardare	*to look at*

See Ref. VII,1, p. 246.

8 Review of prepositions

i) Per

Its various meanings include:

for:	Sono qui per tre giorni	[time]
	Lo preparo per domani	[time]
	L'ho comprato per poco	[cost]
	Lo faccio per te	[purpose]
	È partito per Roma	[place]
to:	Sono qui per divertirmi	[purpose]
in:	L'ho incontrato per strada	[place]
through:	Ho camminato per i campi	[place]
around:	Hanno camminato per la città	[place]
along:	Continuiamo per questa strada	[place]
by:	L'hanno mandato per posta	[means]
because of:	Non sono venuto per la neve	[cause]
	È famoso per la sua importanza economica	[reason]

ii) Da

Apart from the meanings listed in Unit 5, **da** can describe the purpose of an object:

Una sala da pranzo, una stanza da letto
Un abito da sera, un ferro da stiro

It can also be used to describe the quality of something:

La ragazza dai capelli rossi.
Una fame da lupo

iii) Fra/tra

between:	Arrivo fra l'una e le due	[time]
	È seduto fra Pino e Carlo	[place]
amongst:	Fra le cose che ha disegnato	[relations]
in:	Arrivo fra due giorni	[future time]

9 Irregular nouns

i) Invariable nouns

Apart from the ones mentioned in Unit 5, the following are also invariable:

a) Nouns ending in **-isi** [they are always feminine].
   la crisi, le crisi   l'analisi, le analisi   la tesi, le tesi
b) Nouns ending in **-ie**.
   la specie, le specie   la serie, le serie
   But: la moglie, le mogli

ii) Nouns which change gender

These include:

l'uovo, le uova	*egg, eggs*
il lenzuolo, le lenzuola	*sheet, sheets*
il paio, le paia	*pair, pairs*
il braccio, le braccia	*arm, arms*
il dito, le dita	*finger, fingers*
il ciglio, le ciglia	*eyelash, eyelashes*
il labbro, le labbra	*lip, lips*
il ginocchio, le ginocchia	*knee, knees*

iii) Also irregular are:

la mano, le mani	*hand, hands*
il bue, i buoi	*ox, oxen*
il dio, gli dei	*god, gods*

10 Irregular verbs

Spendere (*to spend*) has an irregular past participle: **speso**.

Costare (*to cost*) and **diventare** (*to become*) take the auxiliary **essere**.

Mi è costato tanto
La moda italiana è diventata famosa

11 A note on numbers

The definite article is required with:

the year:	il 1999
percentages:	il 20 per cento
half:	la metà

See Ref. I, 3, 4; II, 3, p. 239.

Reinforcement 10

A Pros and cons

Make your own comparisons using the adjective indicated, with either **più** or **meno**, depending on your view. Can you use **di** and **che** correctly?

e.g. Il nuoto   il tennis   *[rilassante]*
   Il nuoto è più rilassante del tennis

1 L'alpinismo   il parapendismo   *[pericoloso]*
2 gli inglesi   gli scozzesi   *[simpatico]*
3 Fare la spesa   fare il bucato   *[noioso]*
4 Vivere in città   vivere in campagna   *[sano]*

B How are you feeling?

Specify which of the two possibilities is most relevant by rewriting the sentences.

e.g. Ma, sei contento o scontento?
   Sono più contento che scontento.

1 I bambini sono stufi o stanchi?
2 Gaetano è nervoso o irritato?
3 Sei triste o arrabbiato?
4 Avete fame o avete sete?

C Appraisal

Two of you are comparing the merits of your colleagues and you don't agree with each other. Complete your friend's part of the dialogue using **di** or **che**, and then say what *you* think, using one of the following adjectives:

   simpatico   cortese   coscienziosa
   intelligente   nevrotica

e.g. Valerio è più pigro *[di]* Carlo.
   Certo, ma Valerio è più *[cortese!]*

1 Sara è meno intelligente . . . Anna.
   Sì, forse, però Sara è meno . . .
2 Adalgisa ha più esperienza . . . Maria.
   Lo so, ma Maria è più . . .
3 Lisa sbaglia più spesso . . . Rita.
   È vero, però Lisa è più . . .
4 Franco lavora meno . . . Enzo.
   Sì, ma Franco è più . . .

D Recommendations

Advise your friend on the items below by saying they are the best – or worst, and repeat what you've said for emphasis.

e.g. Quegli stivali sono senz'altro   *[comodo]*
   Quegli stivali sono senz'altro i più comodi. Sono gli stivali più comodi.

1 Quella giacca è indubbiamente   *[bello]*
2 Quei pantaloni sono sicuramente   *[elegante]*
3 Quelle scarpe sono senz'altro   *[caro]*
4 Quelle camicette sono probabilmente   *[brutto]*
5 Quel prezzo è sicuramente   *[buono]*
6 Quel modello è sicuramente   *[cattivo]*

E For better or worse

Things have turned out differently from what you expected. Complete the sentences, using **meglio, migliore, peggio** or **peggiore**.

1 Il tempo è stato *[worse]* del previsto.
2 La riunione è andata *[better]* del previsto.
3 Lo spettacolo è stato *[better]* del previsto.
4 Ha recitato *[worse]* del previsto.

F Relating

Rewrite the pairs of sentences as one, using a relative pronoun.

e.g. Il tailleur di lana è troppo caro.
   Ho provato il tailleur di lana.
   Il tailleur di lana che ho provato è troppo caro.

1 L'appartamento è molto spazioso.
   L'appartamento è al quinto piano.
2 L'amica è molto simpatica.
   L'amica mi ha accompagnato al cinema.
3 Il collega è un tipo allegro.
   Ho incontrato il collega.
4 I pantaloni di velluto sono un po' stretti.
   Hai voluto comprare i pantaloni di velluto.

G What? or What

See if you can distinguish between the interrogative *what?* and the relative *what*. Complete the sentences, using **che cosa** or **quello che**.

1 Non capisco . . . vogliono fare.
2 . . . vogliono fare?
3 . . . dicono?
4 . . . dicono è assurdo.
5 Mi fai vedere . . . hai comprato?
6 . . . hai comprato?

H Good

Can you fill in the right word for *good* in each case?

1 È un ragazzo molto .... Aiuta sempre gli altri.
2 È una ragazza molto .... Sa quattro lingue.
3 Possiamo finire presto oggi. ...!
4 Ho preso il voto più alto in matematica. ...!
5 Angela è ... in inglese.

I Saying 'to'

Can you decide which prepositions, if any, are needed to translate *to*? Choose between **a** or **di**, but note that not all the sentences require a preposition.

1 Abbiamo cominciato ... lavorare presto stamattina.
2 Mi piace ... dormire dopo pranzo.
3 È necessario ... partire presto.
4 Siete riusciti ... finire in tempo?
5 Sono molto contento ... aiutare.
6 Mi dispiace ... disturbarLa.
7 L'importante è ... analizzare il problema.
8 Sono andato ... trovarli ieri.

J Per/fra

Use **per** or **fra**, as appropriate to complete the sentences.

1 Vengo a trovarti ... un'ora
2 Passa a prenderci ... le due e le tre
3 Il bar si trova ... l'albergo e il ristorante
4 Sono qui ... una settimana
5 Arrivo ... una settimana
6 L'ho incontrato ... strada
7 Siete venuti ... la festa?
8 Pisa è famosa ... la sua torre pendente.
9 Bologna è ... le città che mi piacciono di più.
10 Ho trovato la lettera ... le mie cose.

K Irregular noun practice

What's the singular of the following nouns?
le crisi   le analisi   le mogli   le mani
le paia   le ginocchia

What's the plural of the following?
il dio   il bue   il braccio   l'uovo

Now say:
1 My hands are dirty (*sporco*).
2 I need six fresh (*fresco*) eggs.
3 I want to buy two pairs of shoes.

L Procrastination

You haven't got round to doing anything. Let your friend know, using the verbs given here:
decidere   comprare   scegliere   scrivere   leggere

Scusa, ma non ho ancora deciso niente

Review 2

Refine and review your objectives

Before assessing your progress and performance, review your objectives: have they remained the same? Are you satisfied with the Track you have chosen? If not, do you need to review the way you are using the course? Use the chart below to focus your thoughts.

	Important:			Enjoyable:			Making progress:		
	Yes	No	why?	Yes	No	why?	Yes	No	why?
Speaking									
Listening									
Reading									
Writing									
Vocabulary learning									
Grammar									

Try and answer the 'why?' question each time, as this will help you analyse your methods as well as your aims. Being aware of *how* you learn best is as important as knowing *what* to learn.

Learning styles: what kind of a learner am I?

Are *you* a successful learner? By and large the most successful learners are curious and motivated, build on what they know and relate what they learn to their own needs and experience. 'Good' learners, therefore, can vary enormously in their methods, but what they have in common is self-awareness: they think about how and why they learn and experiment to find language learning strategies which work for them.

How much do *you* think about language learning? What do you think it entails? Below are some common views regarding language learning. They express one of two opposing assumptions: language is something you learn through analysis and conscious effort [A]; language is acquired naturally through immersion, by some kind of osmosis. [O]. What's your reaction?

1 You can only really learn a language by living in the country.   *I agree . . . I disagree . . . Not sure . . . [O]*
2 You can only really learn a language if you learn all the grammar. *I agree . . . I disagree . . . Not sure . . . [A]*
3 If you're over 11 there's no hope of learning a foreign language properly.   *I agree . . . I disagree . . . Not sure . . . [O]*
4 It's embarrassing to make mistakes.   *I agree . . . I disagree . . . Not sure . . . [A]*
5 There's no point in guessing what something means.   *I agree . . . I disagree . . . Not sure . . . [A]*
6 It's fun trying to get the message across even if you make the odd 'howler'.   *I agree . . . I disagree . . . Not sure . . . [O]*
7 It's boring learning by heart.   *I agree . . . I disagree . . . Not sure . . . [O]*
8 It's vital to have someone to correct all your mistakes.   *I agree . . . I disagree . . . Not sure . . . [A]*

Is your learning 'profile': *a*) mainly analytical? *b*) mainly 'osmosis'? *c*) a mixture? Whichever it is, does it reflect your learning methods so far? If not, are you inclined to reconsider your views, or do you think you should modify your methods instead? You might in any case consider modifying your approach, especially if your profile was either entirely 'analytical' or entirely 'osmosis'. If you are predominantly 'analytical' you could benefit by relaxing a little and allowing yourself to make mistakes, while if you believe in 'picking up' a language, you would probably improve by paying more attention to detail! If you were consistently unsure, try to think more carefully about how you are learning.

Conclusion

It is important to think about *how* you are learning – and *why,* not only about *what* you are learning. If you can, discuss your views, exchange ideas and relate this to your personal learning strategies.

A Speaking: Tracks 1 and 2
Checklist

I can	Yes	No	Check
1 say hello on the phone, ask to speak to someone, ask when he/she'll be back and leave a message			Unità 6
2 suggest doing something in two ways and accept in two ways			
3 ask at what time to meet, and where, and answer the same questions			
4 ask someone what he/she has done recently and say what I've done			
5 say what I like/dislike and ask others what they like			
6 ask someone to visit, find out if an arrangement suits, say what suits me and turn down an invitation			Unità 7
7 ask if someone is in, get someone to hold on, ask who I'm speaking to on the phone and say when we'll speak next			Unità 7 & 8
8 use dates when making an arrangement and confirm when I'm seeing someone			Unità 7 & 10
9 ask someone to show me something and say I'll do the same			Unità 7
10 ask how something works and explain it simply myself			
11 ask what's worth doing or seeing			
12 ask someone if he/she knows a place, has ever been there and answer these questions myself			
13 ask someone if he/she minds if I do something, or minds doing something for me			Unità 8
14 ask what's happened and what's wrong, and answer these questions – say you've gone the wrong way, lost something or had it stolen, missed a bus or train			

Review 2

15 apologise, express sympathy, dismay, displeasure as well as pleasure and relief		
16 say how much or how many I require and ask the same question		
17 ask and explain the way and point out where things are	Unità 8 & 9	
18 ask people what they feel like doing and what they intend to do and answer the same questions	Unità 7 & 9	
19 ask for more of something, and how much of something there is and answer the same questions	Unità 9	
20 Talk about what others like and what I love or hate		
21 Talk about my fears and phobias and ask others about theirs		
22 say what I think and ask others for their opinions	Unità 10	
23 compare things and say what's best		
24 ask to see and try on clothes, point out which items I require, and talk about what suits me and others		

B Fluency: Tracks 1 and 2

Look at the Level 1 **Review** section on p. 101 to help you assess your progress. For those on Track 1 it should now be easier to use more than one sentence at a time in fairly stock situations and you should be beginning to try to express yourself more independently.

You will probably still find it difficult to talk in new situations, but on Track 2 you should be capable of this, albeit with some hesitation.

C Listening: Tracks 1 and 2

You should be able to:
* Understand the stock questions from Checklist A if spoken clearly and at a reasonably normal speed.
* Follow the Course Book conversations on cassette or video without a transcript, if necessary playing them several times.
* Grasp the basic gist of short conversations on familiar topics you haven't heard before, and find it easier to guess the meaning of words.
* Find it easier to concentrate and understand for longer periods.

D Reading: Tracks 1 and 2

Reading becomes increasingly important as you progress.
You should be able to:
* Follow the Course Book dialogues with ease.
* Extract basic information from menus and simple leaflets or posters.
* Follow the gist of the transcript in the **Profile** section on p. 221, and the material in the **Culture** section on p. 223.

If you are on Track 2 you should be finding it possible to follow the gist of some short articles on familiar topics in mass market magazines, such as *Oggi* or *Gente,* even though they will contain a lot of language you haven't covered. You will not find it easy to read a newspaper, but it is worth scanning them for items of news or entertainment you recognise.

E Writing: Tracks I and 2

It should be possible for you at this stage to write a simple postcard or message and give an account of what you have done in fairly short sentences.

On Track 1 you may be finding it difficult to analyse or express your views. On Track 2 you should find it possible to express simple views with relative ease.

F Grammar: Track 2

If you are on Track 1 you might wish to use this list selectively.

Checklist

	Yes	No	Check
1 I can recognise and use direct object pronouns			Unità 6
2 I can recognise and use indirect object pronouns			Unità 6/7
3 I am familiar with the position of pronouns, can use them with **venire/ andare a trovare, dovere, potere, volere, sapere**			Unità 7 & Systems 7
4 I can use **ci** and **ne** and **ce n'e/ce ne sono**			Unità 7/8 Unità 9
5 I can recognise and use stressed pronouns and relative pronouns			Unità 7/10
6 I know the present tense of **piacere**			Unità 6
7 I know the present tense of **possedere, sedersi, scegliere, togliere** and **salire**			Systems 6/ 7/9
8 I can use **conoscere** and **sapere**			Unità 6–9
9 I can form and use the present progressive tense			Unità 9
10 I can form the **passato prossimo** and use the correct auxiliary			Unità 6
11 I know the rules for the agreement of past participles with **essere** and **avere**			Unità 6 & Systems 9
12 I have learnt the important irregular past participles			Unità 6/7/8
13 I can use the impersonal **si**			Unità 7
14 I can use double negatives			Unità 8/9
15 I can form and use **quello** and I know the changes of **bello, buono, grande**			Systems 9/10
16 I know how to make adjectives and adverbs superlative			Unità 10
17 I can make adjectives and adverbs comparative and know when to use **di** or **che** to express *than*			Unità 10
18 I know the meanings of **per, fra, da**			Unità 6–10
19 I have begun to learn which key verbs take **di** and which **a**			Systems 10
20 I have learnt some invariable nouns plus those which change gender in the plural			Systems 10

G Vocabulary

The number of words introduced has approximately doubled. By now you should have acquired an active vocabulary of approximately 500 words, and a passive vocabulary roughly twice as large.

Working on your own 2

At this stage the language-learning strategies you use should be influenced by your ability to diagnose not just your objectives, but the reasons for your success or failure.

Analysing success and failure

Try and review the areas in which you feel most confident. Can you find reasons for your success? Bear these in mind when organising your practice. Now review your least successful areas. Try and pinpoint the reasons for your difficulties: *e.g., I find listening to speech at normal speed hard because:*
1 *I still sometimes have difficulty hearing each word distinctly.*
2 *I cannot concentrate for long.*
3 *I lack vocabulary.*
Action. Decide what to do next, for example:
1 *Learn five new words per day.*
2 *Spend half an hour, Monday, Wednesday, Friday on improving ability to distinguish sounds.*
3 *Practise building up concentration for 20 mins, Tuesday and Sunday.*

A few more learning strategies

At this stage you will probably still be trying out some of the suggestions from Level 1, but here are a few more to add to your repertoire.

A Listening strategies

To develop your ability to understand the gist, you could:
* Stop the tape and try to predict what the speaker will say or talk about next. [You'll need a transcript to be able to check: the **Profile** on p.221 is suitable material].
* Try to take notes and write a short summary in English, again checking it against the transcript.
* Listen in stages. If a dialogue is long, concentrate on one speaker first, then replay for the next speaker and finally play again and listen to both.
* Exploit every opportunity to hear Italian: you can use video films, especially if they have subtitles. Play short sequences, with the subtitles in view and then after an interval – of 10 minutes, say – cover them up and see what you can grasp. As you improve, extend the interval.

For further training in recognising sounds and words, you could:
* Use the TV dialogues not in the Course Book and write a transcript of what you hear – initially just a few sentences – and check it against the real one.

To develop your concentration and memory, you could:
* Listen for about a minute, stop the tape and summarise the points – in English. Extend the length of time and see how you get on.

B Speaking strategies

See Level 1. Remember you can make progress even without the opportunity to speak to native Italians.

To improve your confidence, you could:
* Read aloud.

To develop fluency, you should:
* Avoid translating in your head from English to Italian. This can be demoralising and frustrating and will certainly slow you down. It is best to express yourself simply, using what you know.

C Vocabulary learning strategies

To reinforce your vocabulary, you could:
* Build up a word-file of small cards you can carry around: put the translation on the other side, with a short sentence in which the word is used.
* Associate words. You often learn words best in groups which have something in common. The links can be phonetic or grammatical as well as semantic. Make your own associations, e.g. **lezione** can be linked to **stazione** and **televisione** or to **classe, imparare, studiare,** etc.

To extend your vocabulary:
* Associate along the lines mentioned above.

D Grammar strategies

Reasons for grammar practice include:

1 Difficulties with understanding the rules
2 Problems in memorising details
3 Difficulties in applying the grammar in new contexts

To improve your understanding of a difficult point, you could, if on Track 1:

★ Look up the point in **Systems**. If this is unhelpful or if you're on Track 2:

★ Do the **Reinforcement** exercises first, with the aid of the answers. Look at the completed, correct exercise and see if you can discover a pattern which makes sense to you. Now try and say what the rule is, in your own words, then go back to the explanations and see if they make more sense.

To improve your capacity to memorise detail, such as agreements or verb endings, you could:

★ Do plenty of exercises, checking the answers carefully.

★ Try out the structures frequently in short sentences.
Don't divorce grammar from meaning. Never do an exercise mechanically – make sure you know what it's testing and what it means.

To improve your ability to apply the grammar learned you could:

★ Take a couple of examples which interest you from a Patterns section in the course and write them down. A day later, come back to them and see how many similar examples of your own you can create.

E Reading strategies

What to read

★ When selecting material, focus on familiar topics or on subjects of interest to you: the former is good for your confidence and the latter sustains motivation.
Some learners also find parallel texts motivating and useful.

Reading for meaning

★ At this stage, particularly if you are on Track 1, you need to focus on basic comprehension and build up your speed.
You should:

★ Use the dictionary sparingly, rely as much as possible on guesswork using the layout, pictures, headlines or titles as clues.

★ Avoid details. Focus on the beginning of paragraphs and on words you recognise to help piece together the gist.

Reading for language

You can use reading for vocabulary and grammar consolidation. If you are on Track 1 this should not be your priority. If you are on Track 2 you could begin to read familiar texts for language [e.g. to look at pronoun position], but at this stage your focus should still be on the general meaning.

Giordano Mazzolini

Giordano Mazzolini is an officer in the Corpo Forestale dello Stato: The Italian Forestry Service. He lives in Abetone, a Tuscan ski resort high in the Appenines, and his work involves both protecting forest habitats and educating people in ways of enjoying them. He gives talks and classes, runs guided tours of the protected Nature Reserves, is in charge of Abetone's 'Orto Botanico' and has written books about the local flora and fauna as well as guides to the footpaths of Abetone. Giordano took Mick Webb on one of his forest trails, and their journey began in the car.

21

Giordano	Allora Mick, come vedi, ci sono i torrenti, che sono ricchi di acqua perché ha piovuto tantissimo. Però bisogna dire che negli ultimi dieci anni, è piovuto poco all'Abetone, è piovuto poco. Oggi, quattordici giugno, c'è ancora neve sulle montagne. È una stazione dove nevica tanto e piove anche tanto. Oggi è una bella giornata. Oggi ho guidato, questa mattina, un gruppo di escursionisti di Firenze. Le mie gite sono indirizzate a far capire alle persone i problemi della montagna, del bosco, e della natura. Parlo dei fiori, parlo degli animali della zona, parlo dell'ambiente. Parlo a queste persone come ci si deve comportare nell'ambiente in montagna, nell'ambiente naturale. Ora andiamo, su, e ci fermiamo e poi andiamo a fare anche una camminata nel bosco. Mettiamo la macchina all'ombra e possiamo anche scendere.
Presenter	**Scendono dalla macchina, davanti a un cartello:**
Giordano	Ecco qui, Mick, vedi un cartello con scritto 'La natura è un patrimonio. Non distruggetela.' È stata fatta una campagna per l'ambiente nel milleottocento, nel mille, . . . scusate, nel millenovecentottantanove. È buona l'aria, è buona anche l'acqua che troviamo in questa zona. Questa è la viola biflora. È una bellissima viola, questa qui, che, sì sì che non è viola. Perché le viole non sono solo viola. Ma possono essere gialle e possono essere anche un colore più bianco, ecco.

Presenter   **Giordano ha scritto diversi libri.**

Giordano   Nel 1990 ho scritto un libro sui fiori dell'Abetone. Quest'anno, a Firenze, proprio il 3 giugno, ho presentato un libro – sempre sul trekking – che s'intitola *Abetone trekking* che sono ventotto itinerari naturalistici che la gente può percorrere quando viene all'Abetone. Ah guarda . . . ti faccio vedere una pianta velenosa o mortale. Questa qui, si chiama . . . si chiama Mezzereo o Fior di Stecco. Il nome scientifico è Dafne Mezzereum e le bacche sono velenose . . . sono rosse, rosse, molto rosse . . . sì.

Vogliamo continuare per questo sentiero . . . Ah, guarda. Poi ci sono anche le orchidee. Attenzione . . . le vedi? Stanno per fiorire. Ecco, sono orchidee selvatiche, chiaramente, e protette dalla legge. I funghi si trovano da tutte le parti. A cominciare da marzo i primi funghi, che si chiamano dormienti. Il fungo più ricercato è il porcino, quello che abbiamo mangiato oggi noi . . . Boletulus Edulis. Edulis vuol dire . . . buono da mangiare. Qui fra qualche giorno cominciamo a trovare i porcini eh . . . ma ci sono anche i funghi velenosi e . . . quelli . . . bisogna fare attenzione!

Presenter   **Per la gente che va in montagna, Giordano offre questi consigli:**

Giordano   Bisogna mettere nello zaino, prima di tutto, energetici: cioccolata, marmellata, zucchero. Bisogna portarsi dietro dello zucchero in montagna. Non salame o salsicce eh? Perché salame e salsicce non si digeriscono – viene mal di stomaco. Poi nello zaino metterci senz'altro un binocolo per osservare gli animali, acqua sempre, giacca a vento, perché è utile. Poi, può anche piovere . . .

come ci si deve . . .	*how you should . . .*
stanno per . . .	*they are about to . . .*
metterei . . .	*I would put . . .*

The following statements are based on what Giordano Mazzolini said. Are they true or false?

Vero o Falso?	V	F
1 A Giordano piace molto la natura.		
2 C'è sempre sole ad Abetone.		
3 Si possono mangiare le bacche del Fior di Stecco.		
4 Si possono mangiare i porcini.		
5 Giordano e Mick trovano qualche porcino.		
6 Bisogna portare salsicce in montagna.		

Vittore Carpaccio
(1460–c. 1526)

'Storie di S. Orsola: Arrivo dei Pellegrini a Colonia' (*Arrival of the Pilgrims in Cologne*) Accademia, Venezia

Questo quadro fa parte di un ciclo di nove dipinti che rappresentano la triste storia di sant'Orsola, massacrata a Colonia dagli Unni, con il fidanzato e il papa, durante il ritorno da un pellegrinaggio a Roma. L'arrivo a Colonia è il preludio al martirio: a sinistra si vedono Orsola e il papa nella prima nave, e a destra ci sono gli Unni che assediano la città. Cercate di descrivere il quadro e di dire che cosa stanno facendo i vari personaggi. Vi piace il quadro? Perché?

Giuseppe Ungaretti (1888–1970)

Nato a Alessandria d'Egitto da genitori toscani (di Lucca), Giuseppe Ungaretti si afferma rapidamente come uno dei poeti più importanti del Novecento. Nella sua lunga carriera di poeta scrive centinaia di poesie e traduce anche sonetti di Shakespeare, *Phèdre* di Racine e poesie di Góngora e William Blake. La conoscenza di varie lingue deriva da un'esistenza cosmopolita: dopo l'infanzia e la gioventù passate in Egitto studia per due anni a Parigi. Negli anni Trenta viaggia molto in Europa e in Africa, e per alcuni anni insegna letteratura italiana all'università di San Paolo in Brasile. Nel 1942 torna in Italia dove insegna all'università di Roma fino al 1958. L'opera poetica di Ungaretti è priva di retorica, e il linguaggio, a prima vista, è semplice, perché sembra avvicinarsi alla lingua di tutti i giorni. Nelle poesie, spesso brevissime, il fascino delle immagine poetiche sta nella loro sorprendente semplicità: Ungaretti è il maestro della concentrazione della lingua poetica e attraverso questa riesce a condensare i sentimenti ed a esprimersi con un'intensità a volte straziante. La vita del poeta è segnata da due tragedie: la prima guerra mondiale e la morte del figlio di nove anni. La prima lo porta a scrivere il diario poetico che lo rende famoso: *l'Allegria* [1914–19] e la seconda ispira la terza raccolta di poesie, *Il Dolore* [1937–46].

Le poesie 'Veglia' e 'Sono una creatura' vengono da *l'Allegria:* raccontano la sua esperienza di soldato al fronte. Ungaretti scrive queste poesie sul monte San Michele del Carso, una regione nel nord-est d'Italia, luogo di feroci battaglie al fronte. Nella prima poesia racconta una notte passata accanto a un compagno morto, e nella seconda il poeta diventa il simbolo dell'umanità, sconvolta dal dolore.

VEGLIA

Cima Quattro il 23 dicembre 1915

Un'intera nottata
buttato vicino
a un compagno
massacrato
con la sua bocca
digrignata
volta al plenilunio
con la congestione
delle sue mani
penetrata
nel mio silenzio
ho scritto
lettere piene d'amore

Non sono mai stato
tanto
attaccato alla vita

Giuseppe Ungaretti

digrignata	*grinning*
volta al plenilunio	*turned to the full moon*

SONO UNA CREATURA

Valloncello di Cima Quattro il 5 agosto 1916

Come questa pietra
del S. Michele
cosí fredda
cosí dura
cosí prosciugata
cosí refrattaria
cosí totalmente
disanimata

Come questa pietra
è il mio pianto
che non si vede

La morte
si sconta
vivendo*

Giuseppe Ungaretti

* You pay for death by living

Reference Section

Answers

Unit 1 – Practice 1

Odd one out (p. 7)
1 cin cin. **2** Olivetti. **3** vermicelli. **4** dolcevita.

Places (p. 8)
Irlanda.

Spot the city (p. 8)
1 Roma. **2** Firenze. **3** Napoli. **4** Venezia. **5** Torino.

Hello or goodbye? (p. 8)
1 hello. **2** goodbye. **3** goodbye. **4** hello. **5** goodbye.

Buying breakfast (p. 8)
Buongiorno./Una pasta, per favore./Sì./Mille lire. Grazie, arrivederci [or Buongiorno].

Numbers (p. 8)
1 quattro. **2** cinque. **3** sette. **4** otto. **5** nove (o sette, in Italia). **6** tre. **7** dieci.

Ordering drinks (p. 8)
Buonasera./Un caffè e tre birre, per favore./Grazie – e due cappuccini, per favore.

Unit 1 – Practice 2

Where? (p. 14)
Sono ... **1** in bagno. **2** in cucina. **3** a casa. **4** in biblioteca. **5** a scuola.

What's this? (p. 14)
1 Questa è una macchina. **2** Questo è un quadro. **3** Questa è una pasta. **4** Questo è un ragazzo.

What are these? (p. 14)
1 Queste sono macchine. **2** Questi sono quadri. **3** Queste sono paste. **4** Questi sono ragazzi.

Buying an ice-cream (p. 14)
Buonasera, un gelato, per favore./Sì grazie. Questo è caffè?/Questo è pistacchio?/Pistacchio e caffè, per favore./Grazie, arrivederci [or Grazie, buonasera].

What's in a name? (p. 14)
1 Guglielmo Marconi/Benito Mussolini/Luciano Pavarotti/Enzo Ferrari. **2 a)** la lirica – Pavarotti. **b)** la radio – Marconi. **c)** la macchina – Ferrari. **d)** il fascismo – Mussolini. **3** They all come from the region of Emilia Romagna.

Unit 2 – Practice 1

What's your name (p. 22)
1 Ciao, come ti chiami? **2** Buongiorno, come si chiama? **3** Come vi chiamate?

What about you? (p. 22)
Io mi chiamo ... **1** E Lei? **2** E tu? **3** E voi?

Who is it? (p. 22)
Giancarlo.

Spot the relations (p. 22)
Suocera, zia. e.g., *Susanna:* 'Giovanni è mio suocero'. *Lucia:* 'Maria è mia zia'.

Guess who? (p. 22)
1 Bianca. **2** Maria. **3** Patrizio. **4** Giovanni.

What's in it? (p. 23)
Ci sono pomodori./C'è mozzarella./Sì, c'è basilico.

House with all amenities (p. 23)
e.g., **1** Sì, c'è un parco grande. **2** Sì, c'è una bella piscina. **3** Sì, c'è una vecchia chiesa. **4** Sì, c'è una piccola trattoria.

What's on today? (p. 23)
Buongiorno. Oggi, che cosa c'è?/La stracciatella che cos'è?/Gli spaghetti all'amatriciana che cosa sono?/Gli spaghetti, per favore.

Home cooking (p. 23)
1 Grandmother. **2** Here is your vol. on free trial. **3** 103. **4** 320. **5** 505.

Unit 2 – Practice 2

What's this? (p. 28)
1 È un orologio. Si chiama 'Orbis'. **2** Sono caffettiere. Si chiamano 'La Cupola'.

Odd one out (p. 29)
1 elefante. **2** pomeriggio. **3** pesce. **4** giallo. **5** acciaio.

Where is everyone? (p. 29)
1 Mia madre è a scuola. Studia lingue. **2** Mio padre è in cucina. Prepara la cena. **3** Mio figlio è in camera. Ascolta la musica. **4** Mio nonno è in salotto. Guarda la televisione.

Friends and neighbours (p. 29)
1 Questa è la mia amica Gina e questo è suo fratello Paolo. **2** Questa è la mia vicina Sandra e questa è la sua amica Susanna. **3** Questo è il mio amico Giuseppe e questo è suo fratello Enrico. **4** Questo è il mio vicino Manlio e questa è sua cugina Cristina.

I too ... (p. 29)
1 Anch'io abito in Gran Bretagna. **2** Anch'io lavoro molto. **3** Anch'io sono di nazionalità britannica.

You too? (p. 29)
1 Anche Lei abita a Bologna? **2** Anche Lei lavora in via Cavour? **3** Anche Lei studia lingue? *For the couple, your questions should be:* **1** Anche voi abitate a Bologna? **2** Anche voi lavorate in via Cavour? **3** Anche voi studiate lingue?

Colour associations (p. 30)
1 La bandiera italiana à rossa, bianca e verde. **2** azzurro: un azzurro *is an Italian international sportsman.* **3** giallo: *the early detective novels, published by Mondadori, had yellow covers, hence the name.* **4 a)** rosso [essere in rosso]. **b)** nero [essere in nero]. **c)** bianco. **d)** verde.

Unit 3 – Practice I

How are you all? (p. 38)
Ciao, Roberto. Come stai?/Bene, grazie. E tu?/Sto bene anch'io.
E tua moglie?/Sta bene anche lei./E i figli?/Stanno bene anche
loro./Allora, voi state tutti bene!/Sì, stiamo tutti bene.

Getting to know you (p. 38)
Buonasera. Come sta?/Sto bene anch'io./Sono di . . . Lei, di
dov'è?/È sposato?/Sua moglie, di dov'è?/Ha figli?/Quanti anni
ha Sua figlia?/E i Suoi figli?

Kindred spirits (p. 39)
Ah, davvero? . . . **1** Non ho fratelli neanch'io! **2** Non sono
sposato neanch'io! **3** Non ho figli neanch'io! **4** Non gioco
a golf neanch'io!

Tea or coffee? (p. 39)
1 Andrea, cosa preferisci . . .? **2** Signor Fante, cosa preferisce
. . .? **3** Signori, cosa preferite . . .?

What you'd rather do (p. 39)
1 Andrea, cosa preferisci fare . . .? **2** Signor Fante, cosa
preferisce fare . . .? **3** Signori, cosa preferite fare . . .?

Choosing a holiday (p. 40)
piacevole   divertente

Golf in Italy (p. 40)
1954: 1.200 giocatori e 18 campi. 1960: 2.500; 25 campi. 1970:
7.000; 30 campi. 1980: 13.000 giocatori; 1985. 25.000
giocatori. Nowadays: 40.000 e 137 campi.

Unit 3 – Practice 2

May I introduce . . .? (p. 45)
Ti presento . . . **1** mia madre. **2** mio fratello. **3** le mie
sorelle. **4** il mio vicino/la mia vicina. Le presento . . . **5** i
miei genitori. **6** mia zia. **7** la mia amica. **8** i miei nonni.

How lovely! (p. 45)
1 Che bella macchina! È Sua? **2** Che bel bambino! È
Suo? **3** Che belle scarpe! Sono Sue? **4** Che bel cane! È Suo?

It's on me (p. 45)
Signor Giustini, cosa prende da bere?/Cosa prende da
mangiare?/Sandra, cosa prendi?/Prendi qualcosa da mangiare?/
Anch'io. E prendo un Cinzano.

How long for? (p. 46)
1 Gioco a carte . . . **2** Nuoto . . . **3** Canto . . . **4** Gioco a
tennis . . . *e.g.* da un'ora; da tre settimane; da diciotto mesi; da
sette anni.

Give your reasons (p. 46)
Choose from the following: Ho bisogno di/È bello/È importante/È
necessario/È essenziale . . . **1** imparare una lingua straniera.
2 stare con la famiglia.
È divertente/È interessante . . . **3** lavorare in un paese
straniero. **4** essere socio di un circolo. **5** giocare a scacchi.

Who does what? (p. 46)
Speaker 1: read novels, watch TV or video, listen to classical
music, be with friends, play chess, belong to a club.
Speaker 2: play tennis, do yoga, belong to a gym, do gardening,
cooking.

Unit 4 – Practice I

Excuses! Excuses! (p. 55)
1 Ogni martedì vado in piscina. **2** Ogni mercoledì vado al
supermercato. **3** Ogni giovedì vado in ufficio. **4** Ogni
venerdì vado all'istituto. **5** Ogni sabato vado allo stadio.
6 *e.g.* Ogni domenica vado a messa/vado in campagna.

Refresh your memory (p. 55)
1 Esco di casa. **2** Prendo la macchina. **3** Arrivo a
Bologna. **4** Prendo un autobus. **5** Vado a lavorare.

Getting to work (p. 55)
1 Vado in aereo. Sì, prendo l'aereo. **2** Vado in autobus. Sì,
prendo l'autobus. **3** Vado in bicicletta. Sì, prendo la
bicicletta. **4** Vado in macchina. Sì, prendo la macchina.

How do you get there? (p. 55)
Esco di casa e vado alla fermata dell'autobus./No, non devo
aspettare molto./Quando arrivo a Manchester vado in ufficio a
piedi./Sì, è vicino alla stazione.

Where's everybody? (p. 56)
1 . . . vanno al parco. **2** . . . va al mercato. **3** . . . andiamo al
bar. **4** . . . va alla fermata. **5** . . . vanno al cinema. **6** Tutti
vanno allo stadio.

Memory test (p. 56)
1 venerdì. **2** mercoledì. **3** lunedì. **4** domenica.
5 sabato. **6** giovedì. **7** martedì.

What's it like? (p. 56)
La sua vita è veramente **1** . . . poco divertente. **2** . . . molto
noiosa. **3** . . . tanto interessante.

Unit 4 – Practice 2

I work for the state (p. 62)
Lei, che lavoro fa?/Dove lavora esattamente?/Lei fa il postino?/
Lei, signora, che lavoro fa?/Lei è insegnante?/Io sono . . . *or,*
faccio il/la . . .

What do you have? (p. 62)
1 Il martedì mattina faccio colazione a casa. **2** Il mercoledì
pranzo a mezzogiorno. **3** Il giovedì faccio uno spuntino alle
4,30. **4** Il venerdì sera prendo un aperitivo con i suoceri. **5** Il
sabato sera ceno a casa. **6** La domenica alle 5 prendo il tè con
amici inglesi. [*To say how often you do the above, choose from:* sempre
(*always*); spesso (*often*); di solito (*usually*); qualchevolta (*sometimes*);
ogni tanto (*occasionally*); raramente (*rarely*). *e.g.* Il martedì mattina
faccio sempre colazione a casa.]

Timetables (p. 62)
a) Il diretto **b)** L'Intercity è più rapido . . . **c) andata** =
outward journey, **ritorno** = *return journey.* **Un'andata e ritorno**
is *a return ticket.*

What time? (p. 62)
1 Si alza alle sei e cinquantacinque. **2** Fa colazione alle sette e
un quarto/e quindici. **3** Prende il treno alle sette e
cinquantatrè. **4** Va a letto a mezzanotte.

Unit 5 – Practice I

The buildings of Bologna (p. 70)
1 Che cosa si può vedere a Bologna?   2 la chiesa di San
Petronio; la chiesa di Santo Stefano; il santuario di San Luca;
l'università; le due torri; i palazzi e i monumenti in Piazza
Maggiore; la fontana di Nettuno.

Information seeking (p. 70)
Avete/Ha . . . dei poster della città?/dei dépliant sugli
alberghi?/degli opuscoli sui musei?/delle informazioni sugli
autobus?/delle piante di Bologna?

When is it open? (p. 70)
A che ora apre la posta? A che ora chiude la posta?/A che ora
aprono le banche? A che ora chiudono la banche?/A che ora
aprono i musei? A che ora chiudono i musei?

How much? (p. 70)
1 L. 4.500 all'etto.   2 L. 650 al chilo.   3 L. 2.000 all'etto.
4 L. 2.000 all'etto.

Il fruttivendolo (p. 71)
Ha delle pesche?/Quanto costano?/Duemiladuecento lire al
chilo. Mi dà un chilo, per favore?/ Sì. Mi dà due chili di spinaci
per favore./Sì. Ha dell'uva?/Duemilacinquecento lire. Mi dà
mezzo, chilo, per favore./Sì, basta così.
Quant'è?/Novemilaquattrocentocinquanta lire. Va bene, grazie.

I'll have it (p. 71)
Va bene . . .   1 li prendo. Sì, prendo i pantaloni grigi.   2 la
prendo. Sì, prendo la camicia azzurra.   3 le prendo. Sì, prendo
le scarpe nere.   4 la prendo. Sì, prendo la giacca verde.   5 lo
prendo. Sì, prendo il vestito arancione.   6 lo prendo. Sì, prendo
il cappotto marrone.

Aguapark (p. 71)
1 Sì, l'Aguapark è aperto tutto l'anno per matrimoni,
comunioni, lauree, battesimi e compleanni.   2 Sì. Da giugno a
settembre è aperto tutti i giorni.   3 No, non è aperto tutto il
giorno. È chiuso dalle 18,30 alle 20,30.   4 La mattina apre alle
9,30.   5 La sera chiude alle 01,00.   6 Per un adulto l'ingresso
costa quindicimila lire.   7 Per un bambino di dieci anni costa
lo stesso prezzo, quindicimila lire.   8 Ci sono tre tipi di
abbonamenti: settimanale, mensile e stagionale.

Unit 5 – Practice 2

A better world! (p. 75)
1 Per un mondo migliore bisogna . . . rispettare gli altri! . . .
condannare la guerra! . . . lavorare per la pace! . . . essere tolleranti!

New Year resolutions (p. 76)
1 Voglio perdere 5 chili. Devo mangiare pochissimo.   2 Voglio
fare più esercizio. Devo praticare uno sport.   3 Voglio imparare
il tedesco. Devo andare a un corso serale.   4 Voglio risparmiare
soldi. Devo spendere di meno.   5 Voglio essere più tollerante.
Devo ascoltare gli altri. *e.g., for family:* Mia madre vuole dimagrire.
Deve mangiare di meno.

At the tobacconist's (p. 76)
1 No. Lavora con la moglie, il cognato e la cognata.
2 No. Viene in bicicletta. D'inverno prende l'autobus.
3 No. Il negozio è aperto tutto il giorno dalle 6,30 alle 7,30 di
sera.
4 Sì. Il quartiere è abbastanza silenzioso perché non ci sono
molte macchine.

SYSTEMS LEVEL I

Unit I

A   Your sitting room (p. 81)
1 Ecco . . . la finestra, la sedia, la poltrona, la lampada, la tazza,
il tavolo, il piatto, il divano, il vaso, il quadro, il tappeto, il
camino.   2 Ecco . . . le finestre, le sedie, le piante, le tazze, i
piatti, i quadri.

B   Apples or pears? (p. 81)
1 È una penna. È una matita.   2 È un portafoglio. È una
borsa.   3 È un libro. È un quaderno.   4 È un pomodoro. È
una cipolla.   5 È un ragazzo. È una ragazza.
1 No, non è una matita, è una penna.   2 No, non è un
portafoglio, è una borsa.   3 No, non è un quaderno, è un
libro.   4 No, non è un pomodoro, è una cipolla.   5 No, non
è un ragazzo, è una ragazza.

C   The cathedral is famous (p. 82)
1 La frutta è fresca.   2 Il cappuccino è caldo.   3 La birra è
fredda.   4 Il ragazzo è stanco.   5 I giardini sono belli.   6 Le
paste sono buone.   7 I caffè sono pronti.   8 Le città sono
antiche.

D   This is a car! (p. 82)
1 Questa è una casa vecchia.   2 Questo è un telefono
rosso.   3 Questa è una guida nuova.   4 Questi sono gelati
buoni.   5 Queste sono birre fredde.   6 Questi sono biglietti
vecchi.

E   Check out your spelling (p. 82)
1 Le basiliche sono antiche.   2 I libri sono lunghi.   3 Le
strade sono lunghe.   4 Le signore sono stanche.   5 I ragazzi
sono stanchi.   6 Le pesche sono fresche.   7 I pomodori sono
freschi.

F   I or they? (p. 82)
1 Io.   2 Io.   3 Loro.   4 Loro.

G   Do you know your prepositions? (p. 82)
1 a . . . in.   2 a . . . in.   3 di . . . in . . . a.   4 di . . . a.   5 di
. . . in.   6 di . . . a . . . in.

Unit 2

A   Memory game (1) (p. 86)
1 l'amica, le amiche; l'autostrada, le autostrade; l'attrice, le
attrici; l'autorità, le autorità.   2 l'edicola, le edicole; l'entrata,
le entrate; l'emigrazione, le emigrazioni; l'età, le età.   3 l'isola,
le isole; l'idea, le idee; l'immigrazione, le immigrazioni;
l'indennità, le indennità.   4 l'offerta, le offerte; l'opinione, le
opinioni; l'occasione, le occasioni; l'opportunità, le opportunità.
5 l'utopia, le utopie; l'uscita, le uscite; l'unione, le unioni;
l'università, le università.

B   About Italy (p. 86)
(*1*) La popolazione   (*a*) simile   (*1*) popolazione   (*2*) 58
milioni   (*3*) abitanti   (*4*) la capitale   (*2*) 3 milioni
(*3*) abitanti   (*b*) grande   (*5*) 20 regioni   (*6*) i fiumi
(*c*) principali   (*b*) grandi   (*d*) importanti

C   My brother (p. 86)
1 la mia famiglia.   2 la mia amica.   3 mio fratello.   4 mia
cugina.   5 il mio fratellino.

D   It's all yours (p. 86)
1 la tua amica.   2 il tuo giornale.   3 la Sua penna.   4 la Sua borsa.   5 la Sua chiave.   6 il Suo dolce.

E   Get it right (p. 86)
1 studia.   2 legge.   3 abitano.   4 scrivono.   5 beve, bevono.   6 produce, producono.

F   Using reflexives (p. 86)
1 Si chiama . . . si alza . . . si corica.   2 Ci chiamiamo . . . mi sveglio . . . mi alzo, mi lavo, mi pettino . . . si riposa . . . si alza.
3 Si chiamano . . . si riposano . . . si addormentano . . . si svegliano.

G   Multiple choice (p. 86)
1 Dov'è la pasta? È qui.   2 C'è molto lavoro oggi?   3 Ci sono molti bambini qui?   4 Cosa c'è qui? Ci sono gelati e torte.

Unit 3

A   Which pattern? (p. 90)
1 offrire: offro.   2 capire: capisco.   3 preferire: preferisco.   4 aprire: apro.   5 seguire: seguo.   6 finire: finisco.   7 pulire: pulisco.   8 dormire: dormo.   9 partire: parto.   10 servire: servo.   11 bollire: bollo.   12 sentire: sento.

B   Reflexives (p. 90)
1 Mio figlio si diverte in piscina.   2 Mio nonno si riposa in giardino.   3 Le mie figlie si divertono a scuola.   4 I miei genitori si riposano in montagna.   5 Noi ci vestiamo rapidamente perché abbiamo fretta.

C   Can you supply the question? (p. 90)
1 Rimanete in Italia per un anno?   2 Appartieni/e a un circolo?   3 Tieni/e animali domestici in casa?   4 Ti tieni in forma?/Si tiene in forma?

D   Basic needs (p. 91)
N.B. Some phrases suit more than one sentence.
1 Abbiamo caldo – abbiamo voglia di prendere un succo di frutta.   2 Avete sete? – Avete bisogno di prendere un'acqua minerale?   3 Hai fame? – Hai voglia di prendere un toast?   4 Ho fretta – non ho tempo di fare colazione.
5 Non abbiamo fretta – abbiamo tempo di fare uno spuntino.

E   How long for? (p. 91)
1 Stai a Sanremo da 15 giorni?   2 State in montagna da 3 settimane?   3 Stanno al mare da 2 mesi?   4 Sta in campagna da molto tempo? *Personal examples:* Sono in salotto da un'ora./ Abito a Winchester da 12 anni. etc.

F   What do you do and why? (p. 91)
1 Mia moglie nuota per rilassarsi/perché ha bisogno di rilassarsi.   2 I miei parenti giocano a bridge per divertirsi/perché hanno bisogno di divertirsi.   3 Ascolto la musica per riposarmi/perché ho bisogno di riposarmi.   4 Giocate a squash per tenervi in forma?/perché avete bisogno di tenervi in forma?   5 Prendi il sole per abbronzarti?/perché hai bisogno di abbronzarti?

G   Using the definite article (p. 91)
1 l'Egitto   l'Iran   l'Iraq   gli Stati Uniti   la Spagna   lo Zaire   lo Zimbabwe   la Zambia   la Svezia   la Svizzera   lo Sri Lanka   il Sudafrica   l'Afghanistan.   2 lo straniero, gli stranieri; la straniera, le straniere; lo svago, gli svaghi; la spiaggia, le spiagge; il suocero, i suoceri; lo spumante, gli spumanti; lo zabaglione, gli zabaglioni; la zia, le zie; lo zio, gli zii; lo psicologo, gli psicologi; l'hobby, gli hobby; l'animale, gli animali; l'isola, le isole; l'uccello, gli uccelli; l'esercizio, gli esercizi; l'origine, le origini; l'ordine, gli ordini; l'aperitivo, gli aperitivi; lo stato, gli stati.

H   There's only one! (p. 91)
1 Quanti esercizi ci sono? C'è un esercizio soltanto.   2 Quanti stranieri ci sono? C'è uno straniero soltanto.   3 Quante ragazze ci sono? C'è una ragazza soltanto.   4 Quanti ragazzi ci sono? C'è un ragazzo soltanto.   5 Quante isole ci sono? C'è un'isola soltanto.

I   My friend Fabrizio (p. 91)
Il mio amico Fabrizio ha **gli** occhi azzurri e **i** capelli biondi. [. . .] **L'**Italia è un paese molto bello, con tante montagne, **le** Alpi, **gli** Appennini e **le** Dolomiti. Il lago più grande d'Italia è **il** lago di Garda. [. . .] **La** Liguria è una regione che confina con **la** Francia. **La** famiglia di Fabrizio non è grande. [. . .] **Le** sue sorelle studiano [**l'**] inglese, ma Fabrizio studia [**la**] matematica. [. . .] Fabrizio ama moltissimo **lo** sport e anche **la** musica.

J   Say it's yours (p. 92)
1 tuo.   2 Suoi.   3 vostro.   4 nostro.   5 loro. *Reading down, the extra possessive is* tuo *and the colour* rosso. *e.g.* Dov'è il tuo vestito rosso?/È bello il tuo cappotto rosso.

K   It and the (p. 92)
1 pronoun.   2 article; pronoun.   3 article; pronoun.
4 pronoun.

Unit 4

A   Which verb makes sense? (p. 95)
1 vai vado.   2 viene vengono.   3 esco.   4 parte.
5 andiamo.   6 va.   7 fa.

B   Do you come here often? (p. 95)
1 Vieni a Bologna ogni mese?   2 Andate alla partita ogni sabato?   3 Andate al mercato ogni venerdì?   4 Va al ristorante ogni sera?

C   I must go! (p. 95)
1 dobbiamo uscire.   2 devo andare.   3 deve andare.   4 devo andare.   5 devo fare.   6 devo trovare.   7 devo andare a letto.   8 devo alzarmi.

D   Do you have to? (p. 95)
1 No, di solito faccio il bucato la mattina.   2 No, faccio sempre il bagno dopo cena.   3 No, non facciamo mai colazione.

E   Think of a reason (p. 96)
1 . . . perché usciamo spesso.   2 . . . perché fa i compiti.

F   The engineer's wife (p. 96)
1 in + la = **nella**.   2 su + la = **sulla**; su + il = **sul**.   3 da + il = **dal**; a + il = **al**.   4 di + l' = **dell'**.   5 di + le = **delle**.
6 di + i = **dei**.

G From dawn to dusk (p. 96)
1 dalla alla. **2** degli. **3** del. **4** dalle alle. **5** nello sullo.

H Where do you live and work? (p. 96)
1 in a in. **2** in a in in. **3** in a in in. **4** a in.

I The house in Garibaldi street (p. 96)
1 in in nel. **2** in nella in. **3** in in a.
4 nell' a a al ai. **5** da dalla a.
6 in dall'. **7** dall' allo in al.

Unit 5

A To and at (p. 99)
1 a al mercato. **b** dal fruttivendolo. **c** al supermercato
da Carlo. **d** da mia zia al ristorante. **2 a** in pizzeria
in trattoria. **b** al bar in tabaccheria. **3 a** da fare.
b da bere.

B Nouns and adjectives (p. 99)
1 a i turisti stranieri. **b** le città famose. **c** i computer
cari. **d** gli uomini pessimisti. **2 a** l'autista italiano. **b** il
problema importante. **c** lo sport divertente. **d** il partito
socialista. **3 a** il partito socialista inglese. **b** il partito
comunista italiano.

C Can you come? (p. 99)
1 mi può aiutare? **2** Posso prendere un opuscolo . . .?
3 Sento il telefono, puoi rispondere? **4** Non sento bene, può
ripetere . . .?

D Using the present tense (p. 99)
1 a andare. **2 a** bere. **3 c** venire. **4 d** produrre.
5 b dire. **6 c** rimanere. **7 a** contenere. **8 d** stare.
9 b fare; potere. **10 c; b** uscire; volere.

E Read, listen and speak (p. 99)
1 Il responsabile del progetto nel Parco dei Cedri è Fausto
Bonafede. **2** Sì, anche Andrea Sivelli lavora per il WWF.
3 No, non lavorano tutti i giorni nel parco, ma molto spesso.
4 Sí, lavorano tutto l'anno, anche d'inverno e anche quando
piove. **5** Il progetto esiste dal novembre del 1989.
6 Vogliono studiare la natura abbandonata a sé stessa – la flora
e anche la fauna.

F Reading: what's on? (p. 100)
1 The activities are: **a** Nature rambles, including
birdwatching. **b** A nature photography course. **c** Two
Green university courses: basic ecology and environmental
problems; nature in Western philosophy. **d** An antivivisection demonstration outide a well-known fur shop.

Profile Level I

La famiglia Chiappini (p. 101)
1 vero. **2** falso. **3** vero. **4** vero. **5** falso. **6** vero.
7 falso.

LEVEL 2 (Units 6–10)

Unit 6 – Practice 1

Can I speak to . . .? (p. 116)
a 2, **d** 4, **c** 1, **b** 3, **e** 5.

Refresh your memory (p. 116)
1 Sono io. **2** La chiamo a proposito dell'intervista.
3 Quando ci possiamo vedere?

Overbooking (p. 116)
Mirella called to invite him to a jazz concert; Letizia asked him
to come to the cinema and Marinella called to suggest dinner.
His problem is that they all suggest the same day: next Saturday
evening.

Appointments (p. 116)
1 No, lo vedo stasera. **2** No, la chiamo domani mattina.
3 No, la vedo domani pomeriggio. **4** No, lo chiamo
mercoledì mattina.

Alibi (p. 117)
The culprit is Signor Petronio. *Delitto sotto il sole* was not shown
immediately after *Blob*.

Unit 6 – Practice 2

Look at the map (p. 123)
1 Il parcheggio è dietro il bar. **2** Il bar è accanto
all'albergo. **3** Il bar è di fronte alla chiesa. **4** La fermata è
davanti all'albergo.

What do you like? (p. 124)
1 Giulia, ti piace la musica?/ti piacciono i film? **2** Signor
Pacini, Le piace la musica?/Le piacciono i film? **3** Anita e
Miriam, vi piace la musica?/vi piacciono i film? **1** Quale
musica/che tipo di musica ti piace di più? Quali film/che tipo
di film ti piacciono di più? **2** Quale musica/che tipo di musica
Le piace di più? Quali film/che tipo di film Le piacciono di
più? **3** Quale musica/che tipo di musica vi piace di più? Quali
film/che tipo di film vi piacciono di più?

Personal tastes (p. 124)
1 a Mi piace la poesia. Mi piacciono i romanzi/le biografie.
b Mi piacciono i documentari/i film dell'orrore. Mi piace il
telegiornale/il giornale radio. **c** Mi piace . . . andare al
cinema/a teatro/ai concerti. **2** *Your preferences will be personal.*
Here are examples: Mi piace di più . . . la poesia; Mi piacciono di
più i romanzi; Mi piace di più andare a teatro. **3** *Examples of*
dislikes: Non mi piace la poesia; Non mi piacciono i
documentari.

An invitation (p. 124)
Pronto. Chi parla?/Ciao, come stai?/Sì, volentieri/Mi piace la
cucina italiana/Va bene. Dove ci possiamo incontrare
allora?/Non ho capito. Quale bar?/Davanti al bar di fronte alla
banca. Sì, ho capito.
   To practise saying where you went yesterday, begin: Ieri . . . *You could*
use some of the following phrases: Sono andato/a da mia sorella/dagli
amici; sono rimasto/a a casa; sono stato/a in piscina/a scuola;
sono uscito/a con gli amici/i figli; sono tornato/a presto/tardi.

Matchmaking (p. 124)
Rosanna chooses Dino and Susanna chooses Lino.

Unit 7 – Practice 1

SIP service (p. 133)

1 Among the services offered are information on religious services, street directory, public transport, and opening times of museums and galleries. **2 a** No. **b** Telephone numbers of subscribers whose names *are* in the directory, addresses of subscribers, names of subscribers whose telephone numbers are known. **3 a** The basic three services are long distance, international and intercontinental calls. **b** For international enquiries the number is 176.

Festivities (p. 134)

1 il venticinque dicembre. **2** il sei gennaio. **3** il primo maggio. **4** il primo aprile. **5** il quindici agosto. **6** *To check on your birthday look at the date section in Ref. II, 3, p. 241.*

Refresh your memory (p. 134)

1 L'interno è occupato? **2** Non conosco la Basilicata. **3** Non ci sono mai stata. **4** Perché non vieni a trovarci? **5** Certo; d'accordo; OK.

Hotel de luxe (p. 134)

Come funziona . . . **a** la TV? **b** il ferro da stiro? **c** il telefono? **d** il riscaldamento?
1 d. 2 e. 3 a. 4 c.

Party time (p. 134)

The occasion is a party for his birthday on 18 February and the number given is his extension at work: 359.

R.S.V.P. (p. 134)

Pronto, interno 359 per favore./Sì./Ciao, sono . . ./Mi dispiace ma non posso./Sì, va benissimo./Va bene. Ci vediamo il dieci allora.

Unit 7 – Practice 2

Odd one out (p. 139)

1 il telegramma. **2** fare la spesa. **3** un tavolo da biliardo. **4** la lavagna.

D'accordo (p. 139)

Allora, cosa facciamo oggi?/Cosa c'è da vedere a Castellana?/Non ho mai visitato una grotta./Perché non andiamo a Castellana stamattina e poi stasera andiamo al mare?/Andiamo allora.

Have you ever been to . . .? (p. 139)

1 Sì, ci sono stato/a due anni fa. **2** Sì, sì, ci sono stato/a la settimana scorsa. **3** Sì, ci sono stato/a l'anno scorso. **4** Sì, ci sono stato/a due settimane fa. **5** No, non ci sono mai stato/a.

Home improvements (p. 140)

a The couple is writing to get advice on how to plan their second home. **b** The house is for themselves, their six-year-old and a few friends now and again. **c** There is water and electricity. **d** They hope to invite the magazine editors to visit their home the following year.

Identikit (p. 140)

To a friend your description will be a personal one, e.g. Al pianterreno c'è la cucina, il soggiorno e uno studio. La cucina è un po' buia, ma mi piace perché è abbastanza grande e ci possiamo mangiare. In cucina c'è . . . [*say where everything is, using* accanto a, davanti a, *etc.*]. Il soggiorno è in fondo al corridoio: è molto disordinato. C'è . . . [*describe position of objects*]. Accanto al soggiorno c'è lo studio. È piccolissimo con scaffali pieni di libri. Al primo piano ci sono due camere da letto e il bagno. Il bagno è spesso sporco ma è abbastanza luminoso . . . [*describe position of contents*].

To a potential buyer the picture will look rosier, e.g., Questa è una casa d'epoca. Al pianterreno abbiamo la cucina, il soggiorno e lo studio. La cucina è spaziosa e molto carina: è anche attrezzata molto bene . . . Abbiamo un soggiorno elegante . . ., *etc.*

Grand tour (p. 140)

Caro . . . [*give a name*] Siamo partiti da Venosa e siamo arrivati a Rapolla verso le undici – siamo andati a vedere il duomo. Siamo rimasti a pranzare in una trattoria molto simpatica. Poi siamo partiti per Melfi dove abbiamo visitato il castello. Abbiamo fatto il giro della città e abbiamo visto della bella terracotta. Dopo siamo andati ai laghi di Monticchio e abbiamo noleggiato una barca. Abbiamo salito il monte Vulture in funivia. Al ritorno siamo passati per Rionero e abbiamo bevuto dell'ottimo vino.

Unit 8 – Practice 1

When are you off? (p. 149)

Penso di partire . . . presto/fra poco; fra due settimane; fra un mese; fra l'otto e il sedici giugno. Parto giovedì quindici giugno. Penso di andare in vacanza il . . .

Bad Blood (p. 149)

A me non piacciono molto./È buono?/Sì, grazie, ne prendo un po'./Mi piace molto, ne prendo un altro po'.

Help (p. 149)

Le dispiace staccare la televisione in salotto?/Le dispiace buttare la spazzatura? È dietro la porta./Le dispiace imbucare le lettere? Stanno sul tavolo.

Accident prone (p. 149)

There are various possible reactions: **1** Davvero?/Che peccato. **2** Mi dispiace. **3** Che peccato/pazienza/non importa. **4** Meno male.

Mystery tour (p. 150)

Follow *Via Umberto 1* – take second left – go as far as *l'Arco di Trionfo* then straight on towards *l'obelisco.* Then turn right into *Viale degli Studenti* and immediately left. Go right to the end of the street and there you are! You end up at the church of *SS Nicolò e Cataldo,* one of the most interesting churches in Lecce.

Which way please? (p. 150)

1 Bisogna andare sempre diritto fino al castello, poi prendere la prima a sinistra. La posta si trova sulla destra. **2** Bisogna andare sempre diritto. La cattedrale si trova dopo la quarta traversa a destra. **3** Bisogna seguire questa strada e andare sempre diritto fino a corso Roma. Poi deve girare a destra, andare avanti fino all'ufficio informazioni e girare a sinistra. La fontana ellenistica si trova vicino, sul lungomare.

Unit 8 – Practice 2

Odd one out (p. 155)
1 che bello. 2 un'agenzia. 3 un rompiscatole. 4 davvero.
5 carabinieri.

Fawlty towers (p. 155)
1 a. 2 c. 3 d. 4 f. 5 b. 6 e.

Chapter of accidents (p. 155)
1 Meno male, sono stanco/a. Piace anche a me./C'è qualcosa
che non va?/Cos'è successo?/Davvero? Che disastro! or Che
guaio!/Ho dimenticato il cavatappi.

What people forget (p. 155)
i costumi da bagno, i documenti, le cose più strane, più personali.

Missing (p. 155)
1 Conosce Jane Mitchell? 2 Sa dov'è andata? 3 [Sa se] ha
lasciato l'indirizzo? 4 Sa il suo numero di telefono? 5 Sa
perché è partita?

Road sense (p. 156)
1 a. 2 e. 3 d. 4 f. 5 c. 6 b.

Before and after (p. 156)
Manca la macchina fotografica, la televisione, il vaso, il video [*or*
il televisore] e la mia cartella. Mancano i due quadri e i due
orologi. Mi hanno rubato . . .

Unit 9 – Practice I

Hold up (p. 165)
1 Un attimo. 2 La linea è disturbata, non La/ti sento
bene. 3 Scusi, Come ha detto? *or, informally,* Scusa, Come hai
detto? *You can also say,* Cosa ha/hai detto? 4 Scusi/scusa, non
ho capito. 5 Le/ti dispiace ripetere?/Può ripetere per favore?

Wrong spot (p. 165)
Che bella giornata!/Di qua/Siamo quasi arrivati/È lì in
fondo/Mi dispiace, ho sbagliato strada. Dobbiamo tornare
indietro.

Point it out (p. 165)
1 La chiesa è lassù. 2 Il fiume è laggiù. 3 È lì in fondo,
accanto all'albero. 4 Devi/bisogna andare avanti.
5 Devi/bisogna tornare indietro.

A friend of mine (p. 166)
Allora vi presento . . . 1 Margaret, una mia collega.
2 Francesca, una mia vicina. 3 Andrew, un mio cugino.
4 John, un altro mio collega. 5 Simon, un altro mio amico.

Making tracks (p. 166)
1 Ce ne sono otto. 2 Ce ne sono nove. 3 Ma sì, ce ne sono
abbastanza. 4 Ma sì, ce ne sono tanti. 5 Ma sì, ce n'è uno.
6 Ma sì, ce n'è una.

Inquisition (p. 166)
The phrases in Italian to choose from are: non lo so; certo; forse;
senz'altro; dipende; penso/credo di sì; spero di sì.

Mushrooms and the Law (p. 166)
1 No, di solito non è permesso. 2 Ogni persona può
raccogliere due chili di funghi commestibili al giorno. 3 È
permesso raccogliere soltanto due esemplari di ciascuna specie.

Unit 9 – Practice 2

Emilia and Romagna (p. 171)
1 Sì, l'ho visitata. 2 Sì, le ho viste. 3 Sì, ne ho mangiata
tanta. 4 Sì, l'ho vista. 5 Sì, li ho visitati tutti. 6 Sì, ne ho
bevuti alcuni. 7 Sì, l'ho assaggiata. 8 No, non li ho
visitati. 9 Sì, li ho visti. 10 Sì, ne ho visitato uno. 11 Sì,
ne ho vista una.

Fads and fancies (p. 171)
1 Ai gemelli piace da morire la ricotta. 2 Alla zia non piace
per niente l'insalata di riso. 3 Allo zio piace tantissimo il vino
Trebbiano. 4 Agli amici piacciono molto le patatine. [*It is
possible to change the order and say, e.g.* Ai gemelli la ricotta piace
da morire, *etc.*]

Strong reactions (p. 172)
1 Mi fanno schifo le zanzare (*or* non mi piacciono per niente, *or*
mi fanno paura). 2 Mi piacciono gli uccelli. 3 Mi piacciono
tantissimo gli usignoli. 4 Mi fa paura il tuono. 5 Mi
piacciono i gatti (*or* mi fanno paura).

Table talk (p. 172)
1 to c. 2 to a. 3 to b. 4 to e. 5 to d.

Better luck next time (p. 172)
Buon appetito/Sì. Ne vuoi un altro po'? Ce n'è tanta. [*You could
also say:* ne vuoi ancora?]/Mi passi il prosciutto?/Le formiche
mi fanno paura *or* Ho paura delle formiche.

Early bird (p. 172)
1 Mario Ugolini is a waiter. 2 The mushroom season is from
June to September. 3 He gets up early to avoid walking too
far in the heat of the day.

In Defiance of Death! (p. 172)
1 For almost 30 years. 2 He says he has a mission to help
studies on poisonous mushrooms and hence save lives.
3 1,500. 4 No, he can tell by the smell, and even blindfold.

Unit 10 – Practice I

Good Advice! (p. 181)
Secondo voi, quali sono i migliori negozi di abbigliamento qui
vicino? Secondo te . . .

When did it happen? (p. 182)
1 nel 1492. 2 nel 1957. 3 nel 1776. 4 nel 1939. 5 nel
1989. 6 1861.

Figure conscious (p. 182)
1 silk scarf: 125.000 lire. 2 sunglasses: 75.000 lire.
3 cashmere sweater: 455.000 lire. 4 wool coat: 565.000 lire.
5 boots: 350.000 lire.

Shopping spree (p. 182)
Ah, davvero? Che cos'ha comprato?/Mi fa vedere i golf?/Li hai
pagati molto?/Di che colore è?/Quanto l'ha pagato?/Che
cos'altro ha comprato?

Can you remember? (p. 182)
1 Come in. 2 Sit down. 3 Help yourself. 4 Can you pass
me the water please? 5 Would you like to come to
supper? 6 Do you feel like going out this evening?

Home truths (p. 182)
The specific answers depend on you, but here's how they should begin: **1** Il ristorante migliore è . . . **2** Il pub più simpatico è . . . **3** Il mercato più interessante è . . . **4** Il negozio di abbigliamento meno caro è . . . **5** È più divertente andare in autobus che andare in metropolitana. **6** È più economico/meno caro e più semplice/facile viaggiare dopo le nove che prima.

A whiff of astrology (p. 183)
The answers you give depend on your own tastes. Here are some possibilities: **1** Secondo me non si può scegliere il profumo secondo il segno dello zodiaco. **2** Qualchevolta sì, credo nello zodiaco/No, non ci credo. **3** Sì, sono del segno del Pesce. **4** Sì, ho regalato un profumo a mia madre, alla zia e alle mie sorelle. **5** Mi piace tantissimo ricevere il profumo. **6** Il profumo che mi piace di più è . . .

Unit 10 – Practice 2

Lucky you! (p. 189)
1 Ce l'hai . . . un cavallo/un pianoforte/una spider/un forno a microonde/un personal computer/un orologio d'oro? Beata te! **2** Ce l'avete . . .? Beati/e voi! **3** Ce l'ha . . . ? Beato Lei!

Sales talk (p. 189)
1 It really suits you. **4** It's exactly your size.

Footloose (p. 189)
Buongiorno, posso vedere (*or* mi fa vedere) le scarpe nere in vetrina?/Certo, sono quelle lì/Porto il 38/Sì, va bene/Sono troppo strette/Sì. Ha un numero più grande?/Che peccato. Grazie, buongiorno.

Getting what you want (p. 189)
1 Mi può dire a che ora apre il museo? **2** Mi sa dire quando arriva il prossimo autobus? **3** Le dispiace aprire la finestra? **4** Mi fa vedere un altro modello? **5** Mi dà un altro po' di mele? **6** Mi permette di vedere la casa?

Comparing styles (p. 190)
The answers depend on your views. Here are some possibilities: È assurdo/ridicolo/falso/giusto dire . . . che gli uomini sono più obiettivi delle donne./ . . . che le donne non sanno arrivare ad una conclusione/ . . . che gli uomini non si perdono in particolari/ . . . che le donne parlano molto correttamente e che gli uomini rispettano poco la grammatica/ . . . che le donne esagerano e che usano molti superlativi/ . . . che gli uomini usano i superlativi soltanto quando non gli interessa una donna, *etc.*

SYSTEMS LEVEL 2

Unit 6

A Piace or piacciono? (p. 195)
1 ti piace. **2** Le piacciono. **3** vi piace. **4** ti piace. **5** Le piacciono. **6** vi piace.

B What do they like? (p. 195)
1 le piace il balletto? **2** gli piace la chitarra [piace loro]? **3** gli piacciono? **4** le piacciono? **5** gli piacciono [piacciono loro]? **6** gli piacciono?

C They don't like anything! (p. 195)
1 No, il balletto non piace a mia sorella. **2** No, la chitarra non piace alle mie amiche. **3** No, i documentari non piacciono ad Antonio. **4** No, le telenovele non piacciono a Norma. **5** No, i cartoni animati non piacciono ai miei figli. **6** No, i fumetti non piacciono al professore.

D Check your pronouns (p. 195)
1 direct. **2** direct. **3** direct. **4** indirect. **5** indirect. **6** direct. **7** indirect. **8** indirect. **9** indirect. **10** direct.

E I'll phone you tomorrow (p. 196)
1 lo. **2** la. **3** La. **4** li. **5** le. **6** vi. **7** ci.

F I'll give him the book back (p. 196)
1 Le posso offrire. **2** le devo chiedere. **3** gli dobbiamo rispondere. **4** gli dai una mano. **5** mi dai fastidio. **6** vi do un passaggio. **7** ci spiegate. **8** ti mando un fax.

G Use the past tense (p. 196)
1 Hai cantato. **2** Sei arrivato. **3** Ha ricevuto. **4** Ha venduto. **5** È caduto/a. **6** Avete capito. **7** Avete dormito. **8** Siete usciti.

H Daily routine (p. 196)
Oggi ho fatto colazione alle sette. Sono uscito/a di casa alle sette e mezzo. Ho preso il treno e sono arrivato/a in ufficio alle nove. Verso le undici ho bevuto il caffè, poi ho lavorato fino all'una, e ho pranzato con i colleghi. Sono rimasto/a in ufficio fino alle sei, perché ho visto molti clienti. Poi è venuto il mio amico: mi ha dato un passaggio fino alla stazione. Sono tornato/a a casa verso le sei e mezzo.

I Viva Verdi! (p. 196)
Possible 10 questions include: **1** Quando è nato Verdi? **2** Dov'è nato Verdi? **3** Quale strumento ha imparato a suonare? **4** È riuscito a entrare nel Conservatorio di Milano? **5** Qual è stata la prima opera di Verdi? **6** Quando ha ottenuto il successo internazionale – e con quale opera? **7** Quante opere ha scritto Verdi? **8** Ha avuto una vita sempre felice? **9** Verdi ha pensato di abbandonare la musica – quando e perché? **10** Quand'è morto Verdi? – dove?

Unit 7

A Partners (p. 199)
1 Beppe, ti va bene se pranzo con te? **2** Signor Bruni, Le va bene se gioco con Lei? **3** Carlo e Anna, vi va bene se vengo con voi?

B   One not the other! (p. 199)
1 Invito lui a cena, non lei!   **2** Telefono a loro stasera, non a te!   **3** Faccio un regalo a lei, non a lui!   **4** Do una mano a lui, non a voi!

C   Pronoun practice (p. 199)
1 Le.   **2** Lei.   **3** La.   **4** loro.   **5** li.   **6** gli.   **7** lei.
8 le.   **9** la.   **10** gli.   **11** lui.   **12** lo.

D   Your advice, please (p. 199)
1 Basta cercarlo sull'elenco telefonico.   **2** Basta rifiutarlo, allora.   **3** Bisogna rispondergli subito.   **4** Bisogna chiederle come funziona.

E   Quite contrary (p. 199)
1 No, non ho finito di leggerlo.   **2** No, non sono riuscito a farli.   **3** No, non mi piace parlargli.   **4** No, non ho bisogno di scriverle.   **5** No, preferisco pulirla domani.

F   Both are right (p. 199)
1 devo lavarla.   **2** voglio visitarlo.   **3** vado a trovarla.   **4** sa dirmi?   **5** vado a prenderlo.   **6** puoi darmi un passaggio?

G   Coming and going (p. 200)
Sì, . . .   **1** ci possiamo andare/possiamo andarci.   **2** ci dobbiamo andare/dobbiamo andarci.   **3** ci vogliamo venire/vogliamo venirci.

H   Preferences (p. 200)
1 Ti va di andare al cinema o preferisci andare a teatro?   **2** Le dispiace partire presto o preferisce partire più tardi?   **3** Vi va bene cenare adesso o preferite mangiare dopo?

I   Houseproud (p. 200)
1 Ti faccio vedere le nuove tende – sono molto belle. Ti piacciono?   **2** Ti faccio vedere la nuova cucina – è molto pratica. Ti piace?   **3** Le faccio vedere i nuovi tappeti – sono molto raffinati. Le piacciono?   **4** Le faccio vedere il nuovo specchio – è molto antico. Le piace?   **5** Vi faccio vedere i nuovi scaffali – sono molto belli. Vi piacciono?   **6** Vi faccio vedere il nuovo quadro – è molto originale. Vi piace?

J   Excuses excuses (p. 200)
1 Le dispiace ma . . . è molto impegnata/è molto stanca.   **2** Gli dispiace ma . . . ha un altro appuntamento/ha un altro impegno.
3 Gli dispiace ma . . . hanno l'influenza/hanno ospiti in casa.

K   Is it all right if . . .? (p. 200)
1 Ragazzi, vi va bene se lo faccio la settimana prossima? Vi dispiace?   **2** Signor Arbasino, Le va bene se La chiamo domani? Le dispiace?   **3** Giorgio, ti va bene se arrivo in ritardo? Ti dispiace?

L   Do you know? (p. 200)
1 so.   **2** conosco.   **3** sa.   **4** conosci.

M   False friends, double meanings (p. 200)
1 attico – *penthouse. An attic is* una soffitta.   **2** pavimento – *floor. The pavement is* il marciapiede.   **3** box – *garage. A box is* una scatola.   **4** Soggiorno – *stay, residence; living room.*   **5** il palazzo – *block of flats; palace. [In political terms it can also mean The Establishment].*   **6** Il posto – *place; seat; job.*

Unit 8

A   Escalation (p. 203)
1 Ne bevo dieci.   **2** Ne prendo quattro.   **3** Ne fumo sei.   **4** Ne leggo otto.

B   Nosey parker (p. 203)
1 Con chi è sposata?   **2** Di che cosa parla con suo marito?   **3** In quali paesi ha vissuto/è vissuta?   **4** Da dove viene il suo cane strano?   **5** In che stanza dorme?   **6** Di che colore è la sua biancheria?   **7** Di chi è la Lamborghini rossa?

C   Soul mates (p. 203)
1 A noi piace viaggiare e piace anche a lui.   **2** A me piacciono le orecchiette e piacciono anche a lei.   **3** A voi piacciono lunghe passeggiate sulla spiaggia e piacciono anche a loro.   **4** A te piace leggere poesie e piace anche a me.

D   Incompatible (p. 203)
1 A loro piacciono i fumetti ma a lui no.   **2** A lei piacciono le macchine veloci ma a lui no.   **3** A loro piace visitare i musei ma a lei no.

E   Do you know it? (p. 203)
1 Ho chiamato per sapere se puoi venire.   **2** Ho bisogno di sapere quanto costa il gioco.   **3** Mi sa dire a che ora chiudono le banche?   **4** Non so scrivere a macchina ma so guidare.

F   Nice or nasty? (p. 203)
1 Davvero signore, Le hanno rubato l'orologio?   **2** Lisa è malata, le ho portato un po' di frutta.   **3** È il compleanno di Angelo, gli ho regalato un computer.   **4** Sono disperata, mi hanno rubato la collana.   **5** I Fortunato sono così gentili, ci hanno mandato dei fiori.

G   What next? (p. 204)
1 Ma non le ho ancora scritto.   **2** Non ci va mai.   **3** Non voglio vedere nessuno.   **4** Non è niente.   **5** Non ho affatto voglia di andarci.   **6** Non mi saluta nemmeno.   **7** Non ho mica fame.

H   Making sense (p. 204)
1 Non ho ancora deciso.   **2** Non ci sono mai stato.   **3** Non sono più venuto.   **4** Non ho preso niente.   **5** Non è arrivato nessuno.

I   Chalk and cheese (p. 204)
1 Non ho ancora mangiato.   **2** Non ho visto arrivare nessuno.   **3** Non ho fatto niente oggi.   **4** Non ho più fame.

J   Irregular past participles (p. 204)
vissuto [*vivere*], successo [*succedere*], permesso [*permettere*], aperto [*aprire*], chiuso [*chiudere*], rotto [*rompere*], perso [*perdere*]

K   Pardon me (p. 204)
1 scusi.   **2** mi dispiace.   **3** non mi dispiace.   **4** scusa.
5 non mi piace.

L   Word perfect (p. 204)
bevuto chiesto corso dato deciso detto fatto letto messo morto nato preso risposto sceso stato scritto visto venuto

M   Fra or fa? (p. 204)
1 fra quindici giorni.   **2** quindici anni fa.   **3** sei mesi fa.
4 fra un paio di giorni.   **5** molto tempo fa.

Unit 9

A   Down your way (p. 208)
1 Sì, ce n'è uno.   2 Sì, ce ne sono alcuni.   3 No, non ce n'è.   4 Sì, ce n'è una.   5 Sì, ce ne sono due.   6 No, non ce ne sono.

B   Who's that? (p. 208)
1 Susanna è una mia amica.   2 I Moro sono amici miei.
3 Lidia e Marta sono colleghe mie.   4 Gianni è un mio cugino.

C   Who's who? (p. 208)
1 un Suo collega?   2 un vostro amico?   3 una tua sorella?   4 una Sua cugina?   5 una vostra collega?

D   Who came? (p. 208)
Ieri sera sono venuti …   1 molti colleghi nostri.   2 alcuni cugini nostri.   3 pochi parenti nostri.   4 È venuta una nostra zia.   5 È venuto un nostro vicino.   6 Sono venute quattro amiche nostre.

E   Point it out (p. 208)
Ho messo …   1 il giornale sotto quel cuscino.   2 le foto dietro quello specchio.   3 i vestiti in quei cassetti.   4 le scarpe in quell'armadio.   5 le riviste su quegli scaffali.   6 i giocattoli in quelle borse.

F   Spell it out (p. 208)
1 No, quelli lì.   2 No, quello lì.   3 No, quelle lì.   4 No, quella lì.

G   Otherwise engaged (p. 208)
Numbers 3 and 6 refer to the immediate future so it is not possible to use the present progressive.
1 Ci dispiace, non possiamo, stiamo studiando.   2 No, non posso, sto aspettando i miei amici.   3 Mi dispiace, non possono, vanno dalla nonna.   4 Mi dispiace, ma sta dormendo.   5 Mi dispiace ma sto uscendo adesso.   6 Non possiamo, usciamo stasera.

H   The first time (p. 209)
1 L'ho conosciuta.   2 L'ho conosciuta.   3 Li ho conosciuti.
4 L'ho conosciuto.

I   Killjoy (p. 209)
No, mi dispiace …   1 l'ho già visitata.   2 le ho già lette.   3 li ho già visitati.   4 le ho già scritto.   5 li ho già sentiti. [*Number 4 is the odd one out. In this context* le *is an indirect object, 'to her', and the past participle does not agree.*]

J   Not yet (p. 209)
No, non …   1 ne abbiamo ancora fatte.   2 ne ho ancora assaggiati.   3 ne ho ancora mandate.   4 ne abbiamo ancora visti.   5 ne ho ancora comprate.

K   What do you know? (p. 209)
1 conosci, l'ho conosciuto.   2 conosce, so.   3 sa.
4 sappiamo.   5 sanno.   6 sapete.

L   Black list (p. 209)
1 a.   2 d.   3 e.   4 b.

M   Nobody loves me (p. 209)
1 non risponde mai nessuno.   2 non trovo mai nessuno.
3 non mi parla più nessuno.   4 non mi aiuta più nessuno.

Unit 10

A   Pros and cons (p. 213)
1 L'alpinismo è meno/più pericoloso del parapendismo.   2 Gli inglesi sono più/meno simpatici degli scozzesi.   3 È meno/più noioso fare la spesa che fare il bucato.   4 Vivere in città è meno/più sano che vivere in campagna.

B   How are you feeling? (p. 213)
1 I bambini sono più stufi che stanchi.   2 Gaetano è più nervoso che irritato.   3 Sono più triste che arrabbiato.   4 Ho più fame che sete.

C   Appraisal (p. 213)
1 di Anna; nevrotica.   2 di Maria; più coscienziosa/intelligente.
3 di Rita; più intelligente/coscienziosa.
4 di Enzo; simpatico.
[*None of the comparisons here require* che *as in each case two people are being directly compared.* Che *would be necessary in the following examples:* Anna è più simpatica che intelligente. Lina ha più esperienza che conoscenza.]

D   Recommendations (p. 213)
1 la più bella. È la giacca più bella.   2 i più eleganti. Sono i pantaloni più eleganti.   3 le più care. Sono le scarpe più care.   4 le più brutte. Sono le camicette più brutte.   5 il migliore. È il prezzo migliore.   6 il peggiore. È il modello peggiore.

E   For better or worse (p. 213)
1 peggiore.   2 meglio.   3 migliore.   4 peggio.

F   Relating (p. 213)
1 L'appartamento che è al quinto piano è molto spazioso.
2 L'amica che mi ha accompagnato al cinema è molto simpatica.
3 Il collega che ho incontrato è un tipo allegro.   4 I pantaloni di velluto che hai voluto comprare sono un po' stretti.

G   What? or What (p. 213)
1 quello che.   2 che cosa?   3 che cosa?   4 quello che.
5 quello che.   6 che cosa?

II   Good (p. 214)
1 buono.   2 brava.   3 Bene!   4 Bravo!   5 brava.

I   Saying 'to' (p. 214)
1 a.   4 a.   5 di.   8 a. *No prepositions are needed with the other questions.*

J   Per/fra (p. 214)
1 fra.   2 fra.   3 fra.   4 per.   5 fra.   6 per.   7 per.
8 per.   9 fra.   10 fra.

K   Irregular noun practice (p. 214)
la crisi   l'analisi   la moglie   il paio   il ginocchio   gli dei
i buoi   le braccia   gli uova
1 Ho le mani sporche/le mie mani sono sporche.   2 Ho bisogno di sei uova fresche.   3 Voglio comprare due paia di scarpe.

Procrastination (p. 214)
Scusa ma non ho ancora … comprato/scelto/scritto/letto … niente.

Profile Level 2

Giordano Mazzolini (p. 222)
1 vero.   2 falso.   3 falso.   4 vero.   5 falso.   6 falso.

Basics

These notes are meant as a guide for those learners who have little or no experience of the terminology of grammar.

1 Noun

A noun is a word used for naming people, animals, places, objects and concepts, e.g., *Mary; cat; Italy; table; justice.*
Number and gender: the number of a noun refers to whether it is singular or plural. The gender refers to whether it is masculine, feminine or neuter. In English nouns have no gender, but in Italian they are either masculine or feminine. In Italian the gender and number of a noun is shown by the article.

2 Article

Articles are words meaning *the, a, an.* They are used before a noun or its accompanying adjective. *The* is a **definite** article and is used with specific objects, e.g. *the boy, the flowers. A* and *an* are **indefinite** articles and are used with non-specific objects, e.g. *a cat, an idea.*

3 Adjective

Adjectives are words which describe or 'modify' nouns or pronouns. There are four main kinds:

Descriptive: *the happy boy, a black cat, he is sad, it is difficult.*
Possessive: *his book, your cat, my boy, their problems*
Demonstrative: *this book, that cat, these boys, those problems*
Interrogative: *how much bread? how many books? which cat? what sort?*

4 Pronoun

This is a word which replaces a noun. There are different kinds of pronouns.

i) Personal pronouns

These include **subject** pronouns and **object** pronouns.

Subject			Object	
Subject	*Reflexive*	*Disjunctive*	*Direct Object*	*Indirect Object*
I	myself	me	me	me
you	yourself	you	you	you
he	himself	him	him	him
she	herself	her	her	her
we	ourselves	us	us	us
you	yourselves	you	you	you
they	themselves	them	them	them

Although in English the forms are frequently identical, it is worth knowing how they are used because in Italian the forms vary far more.

A **subject** pronoun denotes the subject or doer of a verb: *I read, you write, it works.*
A **reflexive** pronoun denotes what you do to yourself: *I wash myself.*
A **disjunctive** or **stressed** pronoun is used mainly with prepositions: *come with me, speak to her.*

An **object** pronoun denotes the object of an action, and there are two types of object, **direct** and **indirect**. A **direct** object pronoun denotes what is directly affected by the action of the verb and it immediately follows the verb: *Mary saw me; Charles invited you. Susan met him; Anna thanked them; the children ate it.* An **indirect** object pronoun is less directly linked to the action of the verb and generally answers the questions of whom? of what? to whom? etc. It follows a preposition linked to the verb: *John spoke to me, Alex wrote to you.*

ii) Other types of pronoun

Relative: words like *who, whom, which, that* and *what: the boy who is here; the man whom I saw; the book which is on the table; what I want is a drink.*
Interrogative: words like *who? whom? what? which [one/ones]? how much/many?.* They introduce questions: *who did you say was coming? What/which one do you want? How many are there?* In English the forms of relative and interrogative are in most cases identical. This is not true of Italian and it is important to distinguish between the two.
Demonstrative: words like *this [one] these [ones] that [one] those [ones].* They refer to nouns which have been pointed out: *I'll take this one; I like that one; these ones are best; I'll have those.*
Possessive: words like *mine, yours, his, hers, ours, theirs.* They replace a phrase containing a possessive adjective: *this is mine [my book]; show me yours [your book].*

5 Preposition

This is a word or words indicating the position of one object in relation to another in space or time: *on, in, from, with, at, of, in front of, next to,* etc.

Prepositions are often differently used in English and Italian, which means that they need to be studied carefully.

6 Verb

This is a word used for denoting a physical or mental action or state: *to eat, to drink, to think, to be* [these are the **infinitive** forms of a verb]. In Italian the infinitive is a single word, not two as in English.

i) Tenses

A verb has different tenses. A tense indicates the time when the action of the verb takes place, e.g. now – the **present**: *I sing, he sings,* etc.; later – the **future**: *I will sing;* in the past – the **perfect**: *I sang, I have sung, I did sing.*

ii) Compound tenses

A tense can be made up of two or more parts: e.g. an **auxiliary** verb and a **past participle**: *I have eaten; he has finished.*

The **auxiliary** is the 'helper' verb which in English is usually *to have.* The **past participle** of English verbs often ends in *-ed* *-en* and forms part of various tenses: *I have written; he had played; we will have started.* Many English past participles are irregular, e.g. *thought, sung, run.* In Italian the auxiliary can be *to have (avere)* or *to be (essere).* As in English, many past participles are irregular.

iii)   The person of a verb

The shorthand way of referring to the form of a verb is to talk about the **first, second** and **third person singular** or **plural**.

	Sing.	**Plural**
First person: [the speaker]	I	we
Second person: [person spoken to]	you	you
Third person: [person spoken about]	he she it	they

In the verb *to go, I go* and *we go* are the first persons singular and plural; *you go* is the second person singular and plural; *he/she/it goes* is the third person singular and *they go* is the third person plural.

iv)   Transitive and intransitive verbs

A **transitive** verb is a verb which can take a direct object [see 4i. above]: *I saw her; they ate pasta; he wrote a letter.* In these examples the direct objects are: *her, pasta, letter.* A verb defined as transitive is not always used with a direct object: *they ate quickly; he wrote to her.* Nevertheless, if a verb can be used with a direct object it is generally defined as transitive.

An **intransitive** verb can never be used with a direct object: *Mary arrived late; I lay down.* In Italian it can be useful to understand these broad distinctions when learning about which auxiliary to use with a verb: *essere* or *avere.*

7   Adverb

This is a word used to give extra information about, or 'modify', verbs, other adverbs or adjectives.

When used with a **verb,** an adverb describes an action: *they eat quickly; he runs fast; Ann sings well.*
When **two adverbs** come together, the degree or intensity of that action is described: *they eat too quickly; he runs very fast; Anne sings extremely well.*
Adverbs can also modify **adjectives**: *Mary is very good; my car is too old; this is extremely difficult.*

Reference

I QUANTITY

I Cardinal numbers: numbers for counting

I numeri da zero a duecento [0–200]

0	zero	31	trentuno, *etc.*
1	uno	40	quaranta
2	due	41	quarantuno, *etc.*
3	tre	50	cinquanta
4	quattro	51	cinquantuno, *etc.*
5	cinque	60	sessanta
6	sei	61	sessantuno, *etc.*
7	sette	70	settanta
8	otto	71	settantuno, *etc.*
9	nove	80	ottanta
10	dieci	81	ottantuno, *etc.*
11	undici	90	novanta
12	dodici	91	novantuno, *etc.*
13	tredici	100	cento
14	quattordici	101	cento uno [centuno]
15	quindici	108	cento otto [centotto]
16	sedici	111	centoundici
17	diciassette	120	centoventi
18	diciotto	121	centoventuno
19	diciannove	128	centoventotto
20	venti	130	centotrenta, *etc.*
21	ventuno	140	centoquaranta, *etc.*
22	ventidue	150	centocinquanta, *etc.*
23	ventitrè	160	centosessanta, *etc.*
24	ventiquattro	170	centosettanta, *etc.*
25	venticinque	180	centoottanta, *etc.*
26	ventisei	190	centonovanta, *etc.*
27	ventisette	200	duecento
28	ventotto		
29	ventinove		
30	trenta		

Notes

a) When **uno** and **otto** are part of numbers above 20, the final vowel of **venti, trenta,** etc. is omitted: **quarantuno** – 41; **sessantotto** – 68; **centoventuno** – 121; **centoventotto** – 128; **duecentotrentuno** – 231; **duecentotrentotto** – 238, etc.
When **uno** and **otto** are part of 101, 108, 201, 208, 301, 308, etc., it is common to pronounce the final **–o** of **cento: cento uno, duecento uno, trecento uno.**

b) When **tre** is part of another number it must be written with an accent: **ventitrè** – 23; **trentatrè** – 33.

c) Odd and even numbers: 2, 4, 6 sono numeri **pari**; 1, 3, 5 sono numeri **dispari**.

I numeri da duecento a due miliardi [200–2000.000.000]

200	duecento	1001	milleuno
201	duecento uno, *etc.*	1008	milleotto
300	trecento	1528	millecinquecentoventotto
301	trecento uno	2000	duemila
400	quattrocento, *etc.*	2001	duemilauno
500	cinquecento	2008	duemilaotto
600	seicento	10.000	diecimila
700	settecento	15.000	quindicimila
800	ottocento	100.000	centomila
900	novecento	1.000.000	un milione
999	novecentonovantanove	2.000.000	due milioni
1000	mille	1000.000.000	un miliardo
		2000.000.000	due miliardi

Notes

a) **Cento** is invariable.
The plural of **mille** is **mila**:
  mille lire; duemila lire
The plural of **milione** and **miliardo** is regular: **milioni, miliardi**.

b) **Mille** and **mila** retain the final **-e** and **-a** in front of **uno** and **otto**.

c) **Milione/i, miliardo/i** require **di** before a noun:
  un milione di sterline   tre miliardi di dollari
This is not the case when additional numbers are used:
  un milione [e] duecentomila sterline   tre miliardi [e] cinquecentomila dollari

2 Ordinal numbers: numbers for indicating order

1st	primo	11th	undicesimo
2nd	secondo	12th	dodicesimo
3rd	terzo	13th	tredicesimo
4th	quarto	14th	quattordicesimo
5th	quinto	15th	quindicesimo
6th	sesto	16th	sedicesimo
7th	settimo	17th	diciassettesimo
8th	ottavo	18th	diciottesimo
9th	nono	19th	diciannovesimo
10th	decimo	20th	ventesimo

Notes

a) Roman numerals are used to abbreviate ordinal numbers:
  I – 1st   II – 2nd   XX – 20th

b) Alternatively ordinal numbers can be abbreviated thus: 1° 2° 20°, etc.

c) Like adjectives, they agree with the accompanying noun. They generally precede the noun except in the case of monarchs and popes:
  la terza pagina *but* Enrico terzo

3 Fractions (*le frazioni*)

With the exception of *a half,* fractions are expressed by combining cardinal and ordinal numbers, as in English:

un quarto **di**	*a quarter of*
tre quarti **di**	*three quarters of*
un terzo **di**	*a third of*
due terzi **di**	*two thirds of*
un decimo **di**	*a tenth of*
la metà **di**	*half*

Notes
a) **Di** is always required:
la metà del mio stipendio   *half my salary*
tre quarti del mio stipendio   *three quarters of my salary*
b) **Mezzo** (not **metà**) is used for units of measure:
mezzo chilo per favore   *half a kilo please*
c) **Metà** can also mean *mid*:
Arrivo a metà settimana   *I'm coming midweek*
Parto a metà luglio   *I'm leaving in mid July*

4   Percentages (*le percentuali*)
The definite article is always used:
il cinquanta per cento   *fifty per cent*
To indicate a decimal point, a comma (**virgola**) is used in Italian:
1,5 – uno virgola cinque   1.5 – *one point five*
99,9 – novantanove virgola nove   99.9 – *ninety nine point nine*

5   Collective numbers
un paio **di**	*a pair, a couple*
due paia **di**	*two pairs*
una decina **di**	*about ten*
una decina di libri	*about ten books*
una dozzina **di**	*a dozen*
una trentina **di**	*about thirty*
una quarantina **di**	*about forty*
una cinquantina **di**	*about fifty*
un centinaio **di**	*about a hundred*
centinaia **di**	*hundreds of*
un migliaio **di**	*about a thousand*
migliaia **di**	*thousands of*

6   Basic arithmetic
L'addizione:	3 più/e 2 fa 5	$3 + 2 = 5$
La sottrazione:	10 meno 6 fa 4	$10 - 6 = 4$
La moltiplicazione:	6 per 6 fa 36	$6 \times 6 = 36$
La divisione:	10 diviso 2 fa 5	$10 \div 2 = 5$

7   Basic measurement
La stanza è **lunga** 4 metri e **larga** 3 metri
The room is 4 metres by 3
La stanza è **alta** 5 metri   *The room is 5 metres high*
La valigia **pesa** 20 chili   *The suitcase weighs 20 kilos*

Note
The words **lungo** (*long*), **largo** (*wide*), **alto** (*high*) agree with the noun.

8   Useful expressions of quantity
i) *Double, treble:* il doppio di; il triplo di
il doppio/il triplo del mio stipendio

ii) *Twice, 3,4 times, etc:* due, tre, quattro volte
È due volte più grande   *It's twice as big*

iii) *Both:* tutti e due *[m/m & f]*; tutte e due *[f]*
Vengono tutti e due i bambini   *Both children are coming*
Sono arrivate tutte e due le ragazze   *Both girls arrived*

iv) *All 3/4/5, etc:* tutti/e e tre/quattro/cinque
Vengono tutti e tre   *All three are coming [m/m & f]*
Sono arrivate tutte e quattro   *All four came [f]*

v) *Some, any* [see Systems 5, 2 iii, p. 98]:

To express *some/any* in Italian it is necessary to distinguish between countable and non-countable nouns. *[Non-countable nouns have no plurals, e.g. substances and some foods.]* The partitive article [**di** + definite article] is used to express unspecific quantity:

Countable nouns	Non-countable nouns
dei/degli/delle	**del/dello/della/dell'**
Ci sono dei francobolli	C'è del pane
Ci sono delle buste?	C'è della marmellata?
There are some stamps	*There is some bread*
Are there any envelopes?	*Is there any jam?*

To express the idea of an unspecific quantity more clearly, the following are used:

Countable nouns	Non-countable nouns
un po' di + *plu.*	**un po' di**
alcuni/e + *plu.*	
qualche + *sing.*	
Mi dà un po'/alcune ciliegie?	Mi dà un po' di formaggio?
Mi dà qualche ciliegia?	*Will you give me some/a bit of cheese?*
Will you give me some/a few cherries?	

Notes
a) The above are all used only when amount is in focus, otherwise they can be omitted, as in English:
C'è pane e burro da mangiare   *There's bread and butter to eat*
Ci sono riviste e giornali da leggere   *There are magazines and newspapers to read*
b) **Qualche** is followed by a singular verb as well as a singular noun, despite the plural meaning:
Ieri è venuto qualche amico   *Yesterday a few friends came*
c) On its own, as a pronoun, *some/any* is **ne**:
Ne vuoi?   *Do you want some/any?*
Ne ho, grazie   *I've got some, thanks*
[See Systems 8, 1, p. 201.]

vi) *No, Not any:*
In negative expressions the partitive article is dropped. However, with non-countable nouns the definite article is needed:
La carta non c'è   *There isn't any paper*
but: Non ci sono guide   *There aren't any guides*
Alternatively, **mancare** (*lit. to be lacking*) can be used:
Manca la carta   *There isn't any paper*
Mancano guide   *There aren't any guides*

vii) *No, Not a single:*
If the negative is emphatic, **nessun** can be used, with countable nouns only [*i.e. nouns with plurals*].
Non c'è . . . nessun problema/errore
nessuno sbaglio
nessuna difficoltà
nessun'aspirina

Note
The spelling changes of **nessun** follow the rules for the indefinite article.
[See Systems 1, 3, p. 79 and 2, 1, p. 83.]

II TIME

For notes on telling the time see Unit 4, Patterns 2, note 2 ii–iv, p. 60.

I Days of the week (*i giorni della settimana*)

(il)	lunedì	*Monday*	(il)	venerdì *Friday*
(il)	martedì	*Tuesday*	(il)	sabato *Saturday*
(il)	mercoledì	*Wednesday*	(la)	domenica *Sunday*
(il)	giovedì	*Thursday*		

Notes

a) Weekdays are written without capitals in Italian.

b) The article is only used to express habitual action:
La domenica vado a Roma e il lunedì vado a Napoli   *On Sundays I go to Rome and on Mondays I go to Naples*

c) To say on a specific day drop the article:
Domenica vado a Roma e lunedì vado a Napoli   *On Sunday I'm going to Rome and on Monday I'm going to Naples*

d) Di is sometimes used to express habitual action:
Siete aperti anche di domenica?   *Are you open on Sundays too?*

2 Months of the year (*i mesi dell'anno*)

gennaio	*January*	luglio	*July*
febbraio	*February*	agosto	*August*
marzo	*March*	settembre	*September*
aprile	*April*	ottobre	*October*
maggio	*May*	novembre	*November*
giugno	*June*	dicembre	*December*

Notes

a) Months are written without capitals in Italian.

b) To express *in*, either **a** or **in** is used:
Arrivo **a** luglio   *I'm arriving in July*
Sono nato **in** luglio   *I was born in July*

c) **In** is more common if habitual action is involved:
In gennaio vado sempre in montagna   *In/every January I always go to the mountains*

3 Dates (*le date*)

The year is written as one word and the definite article is required:
Il millequattrocentonovantadue   *1492*
Il millenovecentosessantotto   *1968*
Il 1992 è un anno bisestile   *1992 is a leap year*

Notes

a) To express *in*, **in** plus the article is required:
Sono nato nel millenovecentocinquantuno   *I was born in 1951*

b) Another way of saying when you're born is to use **di**:
Di che anno sei/è? – Sono del '50/1950   *lit. of what year are you? – I'm of '50/1950.*

c) With complete dates there is no article before the year:
Sono nato il 13 agosto, 1946

d) Apart from the 1st of the month, dates are expressed with cardinal numbers:
il primo maggio   *May 1st*
il due aprile   *April 2nd*
l'otto luglio   *July 8th*
l'undici febbraio   *February 11th*
il ventun marzo   *March 21st*
il trentuno agosto   *August 31st*

e) There is more than one way of asking the date:
Qual è la data (di) oggi? – È il 3 ottobre
Quanto ne abbiamo oggi? – Ne abbiamo 3

f) To express *on*, use the article:
Arrivo il 26 ottobre

g) If you use the day with the date the article is dropped:
Arrivo giovedì 26 ottobre

h) **Ventuno** and **trentuno** tend to drop the **–o** before months beginning with consonants.

4 Centuries (*i secoli*)

B.C.: **ac [avanti Cristo]**   A.D.: **dc [dopo Cristo]**
In Italian, as in English, ordinal numbers are used:
il terzo secolo ac   *the third century BC*
From the thirteenth century on, there are two possibilities in Italian:

il Duecento	il tredicesimo secolo	13th c.
il Trecento	il quattordicesimo secolo	14th c.
il Quattrocento	il quindicesimo secolo	15th c.
il Cinquecento	il sedicesimo secolo	16th c.
il Seicento	il diciassettesimo secolo	17th c.
il Settecento	il diciottesimo secolo	18th c.
l'Ottocento	il diciannovesimo secolo	19th c.
il Novecento	il ventesimo secolo	20th c.

Note

The alternative form – **Duecento**, etc. – is especially common in art and literature. Capital letters are always used.

5 Seasons (*le stagioni dell'anno*)

la primavera	*spring*	l'autunno	*autumn*
l'estate (f)	*summer*	l'inverno	*winter*

Notes

a) The definite article is required:
Mi piace l'autunno

b) To express *in*, **in** is used, without the article:
Sono nato **in** . . . primavera/estate/autunno/inverno   *I was born in spring/summer/autumn/winter*
Siamo **in** estate   *It's summer*

c) With **estate** and **inverno** only, **di** can also be used, especially where habitual action is involved:
D'estate vado al mare   *In the summer I go to the seaside*
D'inverno fa freddo qui   *In the winter it's cold here*
but:
In autunno il tempo è ancora bello   *In the autumn the weather is still fine*

III PLACE

I Geographical position

Il nord; del nord/settentrionale   *the north; northern*
Il sud; del sud/meridionale   *the south; southern*
L'est; dell'est/orientale   *the east; eastern*
L'ovest; dell'ovest/occidentale   *the west; western*

Notes

a) To express *in*, the definite article plus **in** is used:
Torino è nell'Italia del nord, Pescara è nell'Italia orientale
La Finlandia è nel nord dell'Europa

b) **A** and **di** are used to express the relationship between 2 places:
Frascati è a nord di Roma   *Frascati is north of Rome*

c) **A** or **verso** express the direction:
Bisogna andare a/verso sud   *You have to go south*

2 Continents (*i continenti*)

The definite article is normally required.

l'Africa   l'Asia   l'Australasia   l'Europa   l'America
Africa   Asia   Australasia   Europe   America

Notes

a) The definite article must be combined with prepositions:
Parla molto **dell'**Africa
Parte **dall'**Africa

b) The article is not required with **in** to express *in* and *to*:
Vado **in** Africa   *I go to Africa*
Vivo **in** Africa   *I live in Africa*

c) The article is needed when the noun is modified:
Vado **nell'**Africa del sud   *I'm going to southern Africa*

3 Countries, regions, large islands and island groups

The article is usually required:

l'Italia   **la** Gran Bretagna   **il** Belgio   **lo** Zaire
gli Stati Uniti   **i** Paesi Bassi *but:* Israele
il Piemonte   **la** Toscana   **gli** Abruzzi   **le** Marche
la Sicilia   **la** Sardegna   **la** Corsica   **le** Eolie
le Tremiti

Notes

a) *In* and *to* is usually expressed by **in**, without the article:
Vivo in Italia, in Toscana
Vado in Italia, in Toscana
Sono nato in Sicilia ma lavoro in Belgio

b) If the country or region is masculine, the article is sometimes used with **in**. This is less common nowadays, but some Italian regions retain the article:
il Molise – vado nel Molise
il Veneto – abito nel Veneto
but:
il Piemonte – vado/abito in Piemonte

c) Countries or islands which are identified with their main town do not require the article and follow the rules set out in section 4 below:
Cuba   Haiti   Malta   Trinidad   Bahrain
Hong Kong   Monaco   San Marino
This is also the case with many large non-Italian islands:
Bali   Cipro   Corfu   Creta   Malta   Taiwan

d) Plural countries, regions or islands require the article:
Quest'anno vado nei Paesi Bassi e negli Stati Uniti
Vivo nelle Marche ma sono nato negli Abruzzi
Ho visitato le Bahamas, le Bermuda e le Canarie

e) Countries, regions and islands modified by an adjective or adjectival phrases require the article:
Vado nell'Italia meridionale
Vivo nella Sicilia occidentale

4 Towns and small islands

The article is normally not required:
Edimburgo   Parigi   Berlino
Capri   Elba   Giglio   Ischia   Lipari   Stromboli   Lampedusa
Exceptions:
L'Aia [*The Hague*]   L'Aquila   l'Avana [*Havana*]   Il Cairo
La Mecca   Il Pireo [*Piraeus*]   La Spezia   Le Tremiti [*a group of small islands off the coast of Puglia*]

Notes

a) *To* and *in* are expressed by **a**:
Lavoro a Roma e passo le ferie a Capri o a Cuba

b) Geographical names normally taking **a** require the article if they are modified:
M'interessa la Berlino del secolo scorso/la vecchia Roma

5 Countries and nationalities

In Italian capital letters are only used for the name of the country.

	il paese	*la nazionalità*
Afghanistan	l'Afghanistan [m]	afgano
Albania	l'Albania	albanese
Algeria	l'Algeria	algerino
America (USA)	l'America / gli Stati Uniti	americano / statunitense
Angola	l'Angola	angolano
Argentina	l'Argentina	argentino
Australia	l'Australia	australiano
Austria	l'Austria	austriaco
Bangladesh	il Bangladesh	★
Barbados	le Barbados	★
Belgium	il Belgio	belga
Bolivia	la Bolivia	boliviano
Botswana	il Botswana	★
Brazil	il Brasile	brasiliano
Bulgaria	la Bulgaria	bulgaro
Burma	la Birmania	birmano
Cameroon	il Cameroon	camerunense
Canada	il Canadà	canadese
Chile	il Cile	cileno
China	la Cina	cinese
Colombia	la Colombia	colombiano
Cuba	Cuba	cubano
Cyprus	Cipro	cipriota
Czechoslovakia	la Cecoslovacchia	cecoslovacco
Denmark	la Danimarca	danese
Egypt	l'Egitto	egiziano
El Salvador	El salvador [m]	salvadoregno
England	l'Inghilterra	inglese
Ethiopia	l'Etiopia	etiope
Fiji	le isole Figi	figiano
Finland	la Finlandia	finlandese
France	la Francia	francese
Germany	la Germania	tedesco
Ghana	il Ghana	ganese
Great Britain (UK)	la Gran Bretagna / il Regno Unito	britannico
Greece	la Grecia	greco
Guatamala	il Guatemala	guatemalteco
Guyana	la Guyana	guyanese
Haiti	Haiti	haitiano
Hong Kong	Hong Kong	★
Hungary	l'Ungheria	ungherese
India	l'India	indiano
Indonesia	l'Indonesia	indonesiano
Iran	l'Iran	iraniano
Iraq	l'Iraq	iracheno
Ireland	l'Irlanda	irlandese
Israel	Israele	israeliano

Italy	l'Italia	italiano
Jamaica	la Giamaica	giamaicano
Japan	il Giappone	giapponese
Jordan	la Giordania	giordano
Kenya	il Kenya	keniota
Korea	la Corea	coreano
Kuwait	il Kuwait	kuwaitiano
Lebanon	il Libano	libanese
Libya	la Libia	libico
Luxembourg	il Lussemburgo	lussemburghese
Madagascar	il Madagascar	malgascio
Malawi	il Malawi	★
Malaysia	la Malesia	malese
Mauritius	Maurizio	mauriziano
Malta	Malta	maltese
Mexico	il Messico	messicano
Monaco	Monaco	monegasco
Morocco	il Marocco	marocchino
Mozambique	il Mozambico	mozambicano
Namibia	il Namibia	nambibiano
Nepal	il Nepal	nepalese
Netherlands	l'Olanda/i Paesi Bassi	olandese
New Zealand	la Nuova Zelanda	neozelandese
Nicaragua	il Nicaragua	nicaraguense
Nigeria	la Nigeria	nigeriano
Norway	la Norvegia	norvegese
Pakistan	il Pakistan	pakistano
Paraguay	il Paraguay	paraguayano
Peru	il Perù	peruviano
Philippines	le Filippine	filippino
Poland	la Polonia	polacco
Portugal	il Portogallo	portoghese
Puerto Rico	Porto Rico	portoricano
Rumania	la Romania	rumeno
Russia	la Russia	russo
San Marino	San Marino	sanmarinese
Saudi Arabia	l'Arabia Saudita	saudita
Scotland	la Scozia	scozzese
Senegal	il Senegal	senegalese
Seychelles	le Seychelles	★
Somalia	la Somalia	somalo
South Africa	il Sudafrica	sudafricano
Spain	la Spagna	spagnolo
Sri Lanka	lo Sri Lanka	★
Sudan	il Sudan	sudanese
Sweden	la Svezia	svedese
Switzerland	la Svizzera	svizzero
Syria	la Siria	siriano
Taiwan	Taiwan	taiwanese
Tanzania	la Tanzania	tanzaniano
Thailand	la Tailandia	tailandese
Trinidad	Trinidad [m]	trinidadiano
Tunisia	la Tunisia	tunisino
Turkey	la Turchia	turco
Uganda	l'Uganda	ugandese
Uruguay	l'Uruguay	uruguayano
Wales	il Galles	gallese
Yemen	lo Yemen	yemenita
Yugoslavia	la Iugoslavia	iugoslavo
Zaire	lo Zaire	zairese
Zambia	la Zambia	zambiano
Zimbabwe	lo Zimbabwe	zimbabwiano

★ Adjectives of nationality are not commonly used. Reference tends to be made to **un abitante di . . .**

IV PRONOUN REVIEW

Below is a summary of the pronouns mentioned in the Course:

Subject		Stressed	
I	io	*me*	me
you	tu	*you*	te
he, she	lui, lei	*him, her*	lui, lei
you [formal]	Lei	*you*	Lei
we	noi	*us*	noi
you	voi	*you*	voi
they	loro	*them*	loro
See Systems 1, note 6, p. 80		See Systems 7, note 1, p. 197	

Reflexive		Direct obj.		Indirect obj.	
myself	mi	*me*	mi	*to me*	mi
yourself	ti	*you*	ti	*to you*	ti
him/herself	si	*it, him, her*	lo, la	*to him, her*	gli, le
yourself	si	*you*	La	*to you*	Le
ourselves	ci	*us*	ci	*to us*	ci
yourselves	vi	*you*	vi	*to you*	vi
themselves	si	*them*	li, le	*to them*	gli/loro★
See Systems 2, note 6, p. 85		See Systems 6, note 1, p. 193		See Systems 6, note 1, p. 193	

★ **gli** is usual especially in speech. **Loro** is formal and comes after the verb.

V ADJECTIVES

I Position of adjectives
There are no hard and fast rules for this, but the following are generally applicable:

i) Before the noun
Demonstrative adjectives like **quella**:
    quella ragazza
Interrogative adjectives like **quale?**:
    quale ragazza?
Possessive adjectives like **mia**:
    la mia ragazza

Note:
In set phrases possessives can come after:
casa mia (*my home*) colpa mia (*my fault*)

ii) After the noun
Adjectives of colour, religion, nationality and most other descriptive adjectives:
    l'esame difficile   la gonna rossa   il ragazzo italiano
    la fede cristiana

iii) Using two adjectives
The two are separated if one of them is demonstrative, possessive or interrogative:
    quell'esame **difficile**   *that difficult exam*
    la **mia** gonna **rossa**   *my red skirt*
    quale ragazzo **italiano?**   *which Italian boy?*
The same is true with many descriptive adjectives:
    una **grande** casa **antica**   *a large old house*
    un **piccolo** quaderno **giallo**   *a small yellow exercise book*
    un **nuovo** romanzo **tedesco**   *a new German novel*
    una **vecchia** sedia **rotta**   *an old broken chair*
    un **bel** vestito **nuovo**   *a beautiful new dress*
    una **brutta** maglia **vecchia**   *a horrible old jumper*
Beware: if an adverb like **molto** or **tanto** is used with an adjective, they both follow the noun. Adverbs do not agree with the noun, while adjectives do:
    una casa **molto antica**   *a very old house*
    ragazzi **tanto simpatici**   *extremely nice boys*
Sometimes two adjectives are placed together but they are usually linked by **e** – *and*. It is more common for them to go after the noun:
    un uomo **alto e bello**   *a tall handsome man*
    una donna **snella e bionda**   *a slim blonde woman*
However, they can also precede it. The effect is more emphatic:
    il **giovane e simpatico** atleta   *the charming young athlete*

iv) Variable position and changes in meaning
Many descriptive adjectives can go before the noun as well as after it. The most common are:
    antico   vecchio   nuovo   giovane
    bello   brutto   buono   cattivo
    grande   piccolo   lungo   breve
    povero   caro   diverso

The position of some adjectives can determine slight changes in meaning. After the noun they can have a more literal meaning.

La minestra è cattiva	*The soup is horrible/bad*
È una cattiva idea	*It's a bad idea*
La carne è buona	*The meat is nice/good*
È una buona cosa	*It's a good thing*

Sometimes the changes in meaning are more than slight:

	Before the noun	After the noun
caro	*dear, lovely*	*expensive*
diverso	*several*	*different*
grande	*great*	*large*
nuovo	*another*	*new*
povero	*unfortunate*	*poor*
vecchio	*old [for many years]*	*old [age]*

È un vecchio amico di mio figlio   *He is an old friend of my son's*
Sì, il mio amico è vecchio   *Yes, my friend is old*
Ci sono diversi problemi   *There are various problems*
Ci sono problemi diversi   *There are different problems*

2 Opposites
One way of vocabulary building is to learn basic opposites:

beautiful; ugly	bello; brutto [*people/objects*]
good; bad	buono; cattivo [*food*]
good; naughty	buono; cattivo [*people*]
nice; unpleasant	simpatico; antipatico [*people*]
young; old/elderly	giovane; vecchio/anziano
big; little	grande; piccolo
fat; thin	grasso; magro
heavy; light	pesante; leggero
tall; short	alto; basso [*people*]
high; low	alto; basso [*objects/sound*]
long; short	lungo; corto [*objects*]
	breve [*book/speech*]
wide; narrow	largo; stretto
square; round	quadrato; rotondo
clean; dirty	pulito; sporco
hot; cold	caldo; freddo
wet; dry	bagnato; asciutto
sweet; dry	dolce; secco [*wine*]
greasy; dry	grasso; secco [*hair/skin*]
hard; soft	duro; morbido
loud; soft	forte; piano
fast; slow	rapido; lento/piano
sweet; bitter	dolce; amaro [*coffee, etc.*]
sweet; sour	dolce; agro
open; closed	aperto; chiuso
on; off	acceso; spento [*light, etc.*]
up; down	su; giù
upstairs; downstairs	di sopra; di sotto
inside; outside	dentro; fuori
easy; difficult	facile; difficile
happy; sad	felice; triste, infelice
pleased; displeased	contento; scontento
polite; rude	educato; maleducato

VI SPELLING AND PRONUNCIATION

I Plurals of nouns and adjectives ending in:

i) –ca, –ga

To keep the hard sound an **h** is always needed in the plurals of
-ca,/-ga words:

l'amica simpatica   le amiche simpatiche
la strada larga   le strade larghe

ii) –co, –go

The hard sound of **–co** nouns is kept unless it is preceded by a
vowel:

il mio ami**co** pola**cco**   i miei ami**ci** polac**chi**
il tedes**co** simpati**co**   i tedes**chi** simpati**ci**

Exceptions include:

bu**co**, bu**chi**   *hole*
fuo**co**, fuo**chi**   *fire* [**-co** preceded by a vowel, but ending is
-chi]
por**co**, por**ci**   *pig* [**-co** preceded by a consonant, but ending
is **-ci**]

The hard sound of the **–go** ending is kept:

il lago lungo   i laghi lunghi

But if the ending is **–ologo** and the word refers to a profession,
the ending tends to be **-gi**:

il biologo   i biologi   l'archeologo   gli archeologi
lo psicologo   gli psicologi

Otherwise it is **-ghi**:

il catalogo   i cataloghi   il dialogo   i dialoghi

iii) –cia, –gia

The **-i-** is usually dropped from the plural if the endings are
preceded by a consonant:

l'aran**cia**, le aran**ce**   *orange, oranges*
la spia**ggia**, le spia**gge**   *beach, beaches*

Otherwise the **-i-** is usually retained:

la cilie**gia**, le cilie**gie**   *cherry, cherries*
la cami**cia**, le cami**cie**   *shirt, shirts*

If a noun has a consonant preceding the **–cia** or **–gia** ending,
but is pronounced with the stress on the **-i**, then the **-i** is retained
in the plural:

l'aller**gia**, le aller**gie**   *allergy, allergies*

Note
You may encounter individual variations on the above rules: it is possible
to spell the plural of **ciliegia, ciliege** [instead of **ciliegie**] and the plural
of **provincia, provincie** [instead of **province**]. For the learner, however,
it is best to use the guidelines given.

iv) –cio, –gio

There is no need for two **i**'s in the plural:

il ba**cio**, i ba**ci**   *kiss, kisses*
l'orolo**gio**, gli orolo**gi**   *watch, watches*

v) –io

There is only one **i** in the plural:

il figlio, i figli   *son, sons/children*
lo studio, gli studi   *study, studies*

If the **i** in the singular is stressed, then there are two **i**'s in the
plural:

lo zio, gli zii   *uncle, uncles*

The exception is **il tempio**   *temple*

Its plural should be **tempi**, but, in order to distinguish it from
the plural of **tempo** *(time)*, the form **i templi** is generally used.

2 Stress patterns

i) General guidelines

It is not always easy to know where to stress a word. As a general
guideline, the stress comes on the last but one vowel and on the
end of a word if this is marked by an accent:

ami**co**   scar**pe**   farma**cia**   cit**tà**   per**ché**

Exceptions to this are numerous. It is worth marking where the
stress comes when you learn new vocabulary: many dictionaries
indicate stress.

ii) Accents

Rules for the use of accents exist, but by and large the convention
is to use a grave accent [`] for most words apart from those ending
in **-che**:

perché   *because/why*   benché   *although*

and also

né . . . né   *neither . . . nor*   sé   *self*

Accents are also used to distinguish between words with the same
spelling but different meanings:

né . . . né, *neither . . . nor*   ne, *of it/them*
sé, *self*   se, *if*
tè, *tea*   te, *you*
dà, *he/she gives*   da, *from, by*
 you give   etc.

Parla molto di sé   *He talks a lot about himself*
Se vieni, ci divertiamo   *If you come we'll have fun*
Mi dà un etto di formaggio?   *Can you give me 100 gr of cheese?*
Vado da mia nonna   *I'm going to my grandmother's*

VII VERBS AND PREPOSITIONS

Prepositions can be tricky for the language learner, as their meaning and use in different languages frequently differ.

I Verbs requiring no preposition in Italian

chiedere qlco.	to ask **for** s.th.
pagare qlco.	to pay **for** s.th.
aspettare qlcu./qlco.	to wait **for** s.o./th.
cercare qlcu./qlco.	to look **for** s.o./th.
guardare qlcu./qlco.	to look **for** s.o./th.
ascoltare qlcu.qlco.	to listen **to** s.o./th.
sognare qlcu./qlco.	to dream **about** s.o./th.

Notes

a) *To ask for or after **someone** is chiedere di:*
   Ho chiesto di Aldo   *I asked after Aldo*
   Di chi devo chiedere?   *Who must I ask for?*
b) *To pay for **someone** is pagare per:*
   Ho pagato io per Aldo   *I paid for Aldo*

2 Verbs with no preposition before an infinitive

i) Verbs used impersonally [See Ref. VIIIB ii and iii, p. 250 for definitions]

bastare	to be enough
bisognare	to be necessary
convenire	to be a good idea
importare	to matter, to mind
interessare	to be interested in
occorrere	to need, be necessary
piacere	to like
sembrare	to seem
servire	to be of use

Le conviene arrivare in anticipo   *It would be a good idea [for you] to arrive early*
Gli dispiace non venire   *He is sorry not to come*
Occorre partire presto   *It's necessary to leave early*

ii) Impersonal expressions with essere

essere ...	To be ...
semplice/facile/difficile	*simple/easy/difficult*
giusto/ingiusto	*fair/unfair*
interessante/importante	*interesting/important*
meglio/peggio	*better, best/worse*
permesso/vietato/proibito	*allowed/forbidden*
utile/inutile	*useful/useless*

È meglio partire presto   *It's best to leave early*
È facile parlare italiano   *It's easy to speak Italian*

3 Verbs and expressions with di

The following require **di** before an infinitive, noun or pronoun:

avere bisogno	to need
avere fretta	to be in a hurry
avere tempo	to have time
avere intenzione	to intend
avere paura	to be afraid
avere vergogna	to be ashamed
avere voglia	to feel like
essere contento	to be pleased
essere curioso	to be curious
essere felice	to be happy

essere stanco	to be tired of
essere stufo	to be fed up with
accorgersi	to notice
ammettere	to admit
aspettare	to wait
aspettarsi	to hope, to expect to
augurarsi	to hope
cercare	to try
cessare	to cease, stop
chiedere	to ask
credere	to believe
decidere	to decide
diffidare	to distrust
dimenticare/si	to forget
dire	to say
domandare	to ask
dubitare	to doubt
fare a meno	to do without
fare finta	to pretend
fidarsi	to trust
fingere	to pretend
finire	to finish
lagnarsi	to complain
lamentarsi	to complain
meravigliarsi	to be surprised at
minacciare	to threaten
non vedere l'ora	to look forward to
offrirsi	to offer
pensare	to plan, think of
pentirsi	to regret
pregare	to beg
promettere	to promise
rendersi conto	to realise
ricordarc/si	to remember
rifiutare/si	to refuse
sapere	to know
sentirsi	to feel like
sforzarsi	to try hard
smettere	to stop, give up
sognare	to dream of doing
sperare	to hope
stancarsi	to be tired of
stupirsi	to be amazed
temere	to fear, be afraid
tentare	to try, attempt
vantarsi	to boast
vergognarsi	to be ashamed
vivere	to live on

Mi fido di te   *I trust you*
Si vergogna di me   *He's ashamed of me*
Non vedo l'ora di partire   *I'm looking forward to leaving*
Ha smesso di parlare   *He stopped talking*
Mi rendo conto delle difficoltà   *I realise the difficulties*
Penso di partire domani   *I'm thinking of leaving tomorrow*
Cosa pensi del film?   *What do you think of the film?*

Note the expressions:
    Ho detto di no/di sì   *I said no/yes*
    Penso/credo/spero di sì   *I think/believe/hope so*
    Penso/credo/spero di no   *I don't think/believe so, I hope not*

4   Verbs and expressions with a

i)   The following require **a** before infinitive, noun or pronoun:
abituarsi★   *to get used to*
affrettarsi   *to hurry*
aiutare   *to help*
assistere   *to attend, participate in*
assomigliare★   *to resemble, look like*
andare   *to go (and)*
annoiarsi   *to be bored*
avere ragione   *to be right*
avere torto   *to be wrong*

cominciare   *to begin*
continuare   *to continue*
convincere   *to persuade*
costringere   *to force/compel*
dare fastidio★   *to bother*
decidersi   *to make up one's mind*
dedicarsi★   *to devote oneself*
divertirsi   *to enjoy oneself*

esitare   *to hesitate*
essere deciso   *to be determined*
essere disposto   *to be prepared*
essere pronto   *to be ready*

fermarsi   *to stop*
forzare   *to force*

giocare   *to play*

imparare   *to learn*
impegnarsi   *to undertake to*
incoraggiare   *to encourage*
insegnare★   *to teach*
invitare   *to invite*
mandare★   *to send*
mettersi   *to set about, to begin*

obbligare   *to oblige/force*

parlare★   *to talk*
persuadere   *to persuade*
prepararsi   *to get ready to*
provare   *to try*

rassegnarsi   *to resign oneself*
rinunciare   *to give up*
rispondere★   *to answer, reply*
riuscire   *to succeed*
rivolgersi★   *to address oneself to*

sparare★   *to shoot at*
sopravvivere★   *to survive, to outlive*

telefonare★   *to telephone*
tornare   *to return, to do again*

voler bene★   *to be fond of, to love*

Ho pensato al problema   *I've thought about the problem*
Mi sono preparato a partire   *I got ready to leave*
Si è messa a studiare   *She began to study*
Ho provato a capire   *I tried to understand*

Notes
a) Verbs marked ★ require **a** before a person and hence an indirect object pronoun: this is not the case for the others on the list:
    Gli insegno a leggere   *I teach him to read*
    Le assomigli molto   *You resemble her a lot*
but:
    Lo aiuto a leggere   *I help him to read*
    La devi convincere a venire   *You must persuade her to come*
b) Note the following expressions:
    andare a trovare qualcuno   *to visit someone*
    mandare a chiamare qualcuno   *to send for someone*
    tornare a fare qualcosa   *to do something again*

ii)   The following double object verbs require **a** before a person and hence an indirect object pronoun:

chiedere qlco. a qlcu.	*to ask s.o. for s.th.*
comprare qlco. a qlcu.	*to buy s.th. for s.o.*
consegnare qlco. a qlcu.	*to deliver s.th. to s.o.*
consigliare qlco a qlcu.	*to recommend s.th. to s.o.*
dare qlco. a qlcu.	*to give s.o. s.th.*
dire qlco. a qlcu.	*to tell s.o. s.th.*
far sapere qlco. a qlcu.	*to let s.o. know s.th.*
far vedere qlco. a qlcu.	*to show s.o. s.th.*
insegnare qlco. a qlcu.	*to teach s.o. s.th.*
inviare qlco. a qlcu.	*to send s.o. s.th.*
leggere qlco. a qlcu.	*to read s.o. s.th.*
mandare qlco. a qlcu.	*to send s.th. to s.o.*
offrire qlco. a qlcu.	*to offer s.o. s.th.*
portarc qlco. a qlcu.	*to bring s.o. s.th.*
presentare qlco../qlcu. a qlcu.	*to present s.th. or s.o. to s.o.*
prestare qlco. a qlcu.	*to lend s.o. s.th.*
promettere qlco. a qlcu.	*to promise s.o. s.th.*
proporre qlco. a qlcu.	*to propose s.th. to s.o.*
regalare qlco. a qlcu.	*to give s.th. to s.o. [gift]*
restituire qlco. a qlcu.	*to give s.th. back to s.o.*
rubare qlco. a qlcu.	*to steal s.th. from s.o.*
scrivere qlco. a qlcu.	*to write s.th. to s.o.*
spiegare qlco. a qlcu.	*to expain s.th. to s.o.*
suggerire qlco. a qlcu.	*to suggest s.th. to s.o.*

Ho chiesto un aumento al direttore   *I've asked the director for a rise*
Gli ho chiesto un aumento   *I've asked him for a rise*

5   Verbs taking a and di
Many common verbs require **a** with the person and **di** before an infinitive:

chiedere a qlcu. di	*to ask s.o. to*
comandare a qlcu. di	*to order s.o. to*
consentire a qlcu. di	*to allow s.o. to*
consigliare a qlcu. di	*to advise s.o. to*
dire a qlcu. di	*to tell s.o. to*
domandare a qlcu. di	*to ask s.o. to*
impedire a qlcu. di	*to prevent s.o. from*
ordinare a qlcu. di	*to order s.o. to*
permettere a qlcu. di	*to allow s.o. to*
proibire a qlcu. di	*to prohibit s.o. from*
proporre a qlcu. di	*to propose s.o. should*
ricordare a qlcu. di	*to remind s.o. to*

sconsigliare a qlcu. di   *to advise s.o. not to*
suggerire a qlcu. di   *to suggest s.o. should*
vietare a qlcu. di   *to forbid s.o. to*

A few verbs used impersonally are also in this category:
andare a qlcu. di   *to be fine/all right for s.o. to*
capitare a qlcu. di   *to happen to s.o. to*
succedere a qlcu. di   *to happen to s.o. to*

Ho chiesto al direttore di darmi un aumento
I've asked the director to give me a rise
Gli ho chiesto di darmi un aumento
I've asked him to give me a rise
A Lina capita qualchevolta di perdere il treno?
*Does Lina ever miss the train? [lit. does it ever happen to her
    to miss the train?]*
Sì, le capita ogni tanto   *Yes, it happens to her occasionally*

6 Verbs and expressions requiring da
There are not many of these and they do not often cause
confusion.

derivare **da**   *to derive from*
diverso/differente **da**   *different from/to*
difendere **da**   *to defend from/against*
dipendere **da**   *to depend on*
giudicare **da**   *to judge by/on*
indipendente **da**   *independent of*

7 Verbs and expressions requiring per
Note the following linked with place:

camminare **per** strada   *to walk **along** the street*
girare **per** il mondo   *to go **around** the world*
incontrare qlcu. **per** strada   *to meet s.o. **in** the street*
partire **per** . . . Londra   *to leave **for** London*
passare **per** . . . Londra   *to pass **through** London*

8 Verbs and expressions requiring in, su, con
The following can cause confusion with English:

entrare **in**   *to enter*
incidere **su**   *to affect*
congratularsi **con**   *to congratulate s.o.*

Sono entrato **in** una stanza enorme
I entered an enormous room
Questo non incide **sulla** decisione
This doesn't affect the decision
Mi sono congratulato **con** lui   *I congratulated him*

VIII VERBS

The emphasis in this section is on helping you deal with problems
and irregularities of the Present and Passato Prossimo tenses.
The regular forms, plus notes on how to use the tenses are in
the Systems sections.

A PRESENT TENSE

I Regular forms
See Systems 2, note 6, p. 84 for **-are** and **-ere** verbs.
See Systems 3, note 1, p. 87 for **-ire** verbs. The uses of the
present are on p. 88 [Systems 3, note 3].

i) -ire verbs
The majority of regular **-ire** verbs take the **-isco** pattern [like
finire and **capire**]. Below is a list of the main verbs which do
not take the **-isco** pattern.

aprire	*to open*	investire	*to invest*
avvertire	*to warn, notify*	offrire	*to offer*
bollire	*to boil*	partire	*to leave*
consentire	*to consent*	pentirsi	*to regret*
convertire	*to convert*	scoprire	*to discover*
coprire	*to cover*	seguire	*to follow*
divertire	*to amuse*	sentire	*to feel*
dormire	*to sleep*	servire	*to serve, be useful*
fuggire	*to run away, escape*	soffrire	*to suffer*
		vestire	*to dress*

Notes
a) Verbs which are compounds of any of the above follow the same
pattern: e.g. riaprire, ricoprire, risalire, riscoprire, risentire.
b) Some **-ire** verbs can take either pattern. The most common of these
are:
applaudire   *to applaud* [applaudo/applaudisco]
assorbire   *to absorb*
inghiottire   *to swallow*
mentire   *to lie*
tossire   *to cough*

2 Irregular forms

i) -are verbs

Infinitive	Present	Meaning
andare	vado vai va andiamo andate vanno	*to go*
dare	do dai dà diamo date danno	*to give*
fare[1]	faccio fai fa facciamo fate fanno	*to make, to do*
stare	sto stai sta stiamo state stanno	*to be, to stay*

Other verbs of this type:
1. soddisfare   *to satisfy*

ii) -ere verbs

Infinitive	Present	Meaning
Auxiliaries:		
avere	ho hai ha abbiamo avete hanno	*to have*
essere	sono sei è siamo siete sono	*to be*

Modal verbs:

dovere	devo devi deve dobbiamo dovete devono	*to have to*
potere	posso puoi può possiamo potete possono	*to be able*
volere	voglio vuoi vuole vogliamo volete vogliono	*to want*

Other:

cogliere[1]	colgo cogli coglie cogliamo cogliete colgono	*to catch, gather*
cuocere	cuocio cuoci cuoce cociamo cocete cuociono	*to cook*
muovere[2]	muovo muovi muove muoviamo muovete muovono	*to move*
parere	paio pari pare paiamo parete paiono	*to appear*
piacere	piaccio piaci piace piacciamo piacete piacciono	*to like, please*
rimanere	rimango rimani rimane rimaniamo rimanete rimangono	*to stay, to remain*
sapere	so sai sa sappiamo sapete sanno	*to know*
scegliere	scelgo scegli sceglie scegliamo scegliete scelgono	*to choose*
sedere[3]	siedo siedi siede sediamo sedete siedono	*to sit*
tacere	taccio taci tace tacciamo tacete tacciono	*to be silent*
tenere[4]	tengo tieni tiene teniamo tenete tengono	*to hold, to have*
bere	bevo bevi beve beviamo bevete bevono	*to drink*

Other verbs of this type:

1 accogliere *to welcome;* raccogliere *to pick up, to gather, pick;* sciogliere *to melt, dissolve;* togliere *to remove, take off*
2 commuovere *to move [emotions];* promuovere *to promote*
3 possedere *to possess*
4 appartenere *to belong;* contenere *to contain;* mantenere *to keep, maintain;* ottenere *to obtain;* ritenere *to claim, to maintain*

Note: For **piacere** see Systems 6, note 2, p. 193. It is possible to use parts of the verb other than **piace** or **piacciono** as follows:

Io gli piaccio *He likes me [I am pleasing to him]*
Tu gli piaci *He likes you*

iii) –ire verbs

Infinitive	Present	Meaning
apparire	appaio appari appare appariamo apparite appaiono	*to appear*
cucire	cucio cuci cuce cuciamo cucite cuciono	*to sew*
dire[1]	dico dici dice diciamo dite dicono	*to say*
morire	muoio muori muore moriamo morite muoiono	*to die*
salire[2]	salgo sali sale saliamo salite salgono	*to go up, get into*
scomparire	scompaio scompari scompare scompariamo scomparite scompaiono	*to disappear*
udire	odo odi ode udiamo udite odono	*to hear*

uscire[3]	esco esci esce usciamo uscite escono	*to go out*
venire[4]	vengo vieni viene veniamo venite vengono	*to come*

Other verbs of this type:

1 contraddire *to contradict;* disdire *to cancel*
2 risalire *to date from; to go up/to get into again*
3 riuscire *to manage, succeed*
4 avvenire *to happen;* intervenire *to intervene*

Note

Apparire and **scomparire** can also take the **–isco** ending.

iv) Verbs based on –trarre:

These all have a similar pattern:

Infinitive	Present		Meaning
attrarre	attraggo attrai attrae attraiamo attraete attraggono		*to attract*

See also: distrarre: distrarsi *to entertain, to distract, to amuse oneself;* estrarre *to extract;* sottrarre *to take away;* trarre *to draw, to pull*

v) Verbs based on –porre:

Infinitive	Present		Meaning
comporre	compongo componi compone componiamo componete compongono		*to compose*

See also: esporre *to expose;* imporre *to impose;* opporre *to oppose;* porre *to place;* proporre *to propose;* supporre *to suppose.*

vi) Verbs based on –durre:

Infinitive	Present		Meaning
condurre	conduco conduci conduce conduciamo conducete conducono		*to lead, to conduct*

See also: dedurre *to deduce;* introdurre *to introduce;* produrre *to produce;* ridurre *to reduce;* sedurre *to seduce;* tradurre *to translate*

B PRESENT PERFECT – PASSATO PROSSIMO

Regular forms
See Systems 6, notes 3–4, p. 194.
There are notes on its use in Systems 6, note 5, p. 195.
Remember, there are two parts to the verb – an auxiliary verb and a past participle.

Which auxiliary? Essere or avere?
The majority of verbs take **avere**. If you learn the important ones taking **essere** then you can assume the others take **avere**.

I Verbs taking essere

i) Many intransitive verbs

andare	*to go*	morire	*to die*
apparire	*to appear*	nascere	*to be born*
arrivare	*to arrive*	partire	*to leave*
bastare	*to be enough*	pervenire	*to arrive, come to*
cadere	*to fall*	restare	*to stay*
costare	*to cost*	rimanere	*to stay*
crollare	*to collapse*	ritornare	*to return*
dipendere	*to depend*	riuscire	*to manage, succeed*
divenire	*to become*	scadere	*to run out, expire*
diventare	*to become*	scappare	*to dash, to escape*
durare	*to last*	sparire	*to disappear*
emergere	*to emerge*	stare	*to stay, be*
entrare	*to come in*	svenire	*to faint*
esistere	*to exist*	tornare	*to return*
essere	*to be*	uscire	*to go out*
intervenire	*to intervene*	venire	*to come*

Notes
a) For a definition of intransitive see Basics, note 6iv, p. 235.
b) Beware: do not assume that all verbs of movement take **essere**. There are some which don't. [See Ref. VIII, 2i and 3, pp. 250 and 251.]

ii) Impersonal verbs
These verbs express actions which cannot be attributed to a specific person or thing, for example, verbs for the weather. These are always used in the *it* form [third person singular].

balenare	*to flash with lightning*	nevicare	*to snow*
diluviare	*to pour*	piovere	*to rain*
grandinare	*to hail*	tonare	*to thunder*
lampeggiare	*to lighten*		

Note: In speech it is common to use **avere** as well as **essere** as the auxiliary. You can say **è** piovuto or **ha** piovuto. [See Profile 2, p. 221]

iii) Verbs used impersonally
There are a number of verbs, like **piacere**, whose *it* and *they* forms [third person, singular and plural] tend to be used, often in conjunction with **mi, ti, gli, le, Le, ci, vi**.

accadere	*to happen*	importare	*to matter, to mind*
avvenire	*to happen*	mancare	*to lack, be missing*
bastare	*to be enough*	occorrere	*to be needed*
bisognare	*to be necessary*	parere	*to seem*
capitare	*to chance, happen to*	piacere	*to like*
convenire	*to be advisable,*	rincrescere	*to regret*
	advantageous	sembrare	*to seem*
dispiacere	*to be sorry*	succedere	*to happen*

mi **è** piaciuto; gli **è** bastato; le **è** sembrato; Le **è** successo? ci **è** capitato, etc.

iv) Reflexive verbs
If a verb is reflexive it always takes **essere**.

Infinitive	Passato prossimo	Meaning
alzarsi	mi sono alzato/a	*to get up*
divertirsi	mi sono divertito/a	*to enjoy oneself*
fermarsi	mi sono fermato/a	*to stop*
lavarsi	mi sono lavato/a	*to wash oneself*

Note
Beware: many reflexive verbs can also be non reflexive – and take **avere**:
alzare ho alzato la voce *I raised my voice*
lavare ho lavato il pavimento *I washed the floor*
fermare ho fermato la macchina *I stopped the car*

2 Essere and avere
Some verbs take **essere** if they are being used intransitively. Otherwise they take **avere**:
cominciare finire salire scendere:
Il film è cominciato/finito tardi [*intransitive*]
Sono salito in treno/sono sceso dal treno
Ho cominciato/finito il lavoro [*transitive*]
Ho salito le scale/ho sceso le scale

i) Other verbs of this type include:

aumentare	*to increase*	passare	*to pass, to spend [time]*
cambiare	*to change*	peggiorare	*to worsen*
correre	*to run*	salire	*to go up/get in*
dimagrire	*to lose weight, make thin*	saltare	*to jump*
		scendere	*to go down, get out of*
guarire	*to get well/cure*	volare	*to fly*
migliorare	*to improve*		

Notes
a) Transitive and intransitive verbs are defined in Basics 6 iv, p. 238.
b) A few verbs can take **avere** as well as **essere** when being used intransitively: **correre, saltare, volare** take **essere** when they express movement to a place.
sono corso a casa; **sono** volato a vederlo; **sono** saltato dal treno
However, in other intransitive expressions they take **avere**:
ho corso per due ore; **ho** saltato per cinque minuti; **ho** volato in un elicottero
Like all the other verbs in the list they take **avere** when there is a direct object:
ho corso un chilometro

ii) Modal verbs: dovere, potere, volere
These can take either **avere** or **essere**. This depends on the auxiliary required by the infinitive which follows:
ho potuto studiare [studiare takes avere]
sono potuto/a partire [partire takes essere]
In spoken Italian **avere** is often used instead of **essere**:
ho dovuto partire

If **dovere, potere** or **volere** are used with a reflexive verb there are two possible constructions:

With **avere**:	With **essere**:
Gina ha voluto sposarsi	Gina si è voluta sposare
Le ragazze hanno potuto divertirsi	Le ragazze si sono potute divertire

These are both used in spoken Italian.

3 Avere

Avere is used with transitive verbs. It is also used with the intransitive verbs below:

arrossire	*to blush*	parlare	*to speak*
abitare	*to live*	partecipare	*to participate*
brillare	*to shine*	passeggiare	*to walk/stroll*
camminare	*to walk*	piangere	*to cry*
chiacchierare	*to chat*	piovere★	*to rain*
cenare	*to have supper*	pranzare	*to have lunch*
collaborare	*to collaborate*	respirare	*to breathe*
dormire	*to sleep*	ridere	*to laugh*
esagerare	*to exaggerate*	sciare	*to ski*
esitare	*to hesitate*	sopravvivere★	*to survive*
giocare	*to play*	sorridere	*to smile*
girare	*to turn*	starnutire	*to sneeze*
insistere	*to insist*	telefonare	*to 'phone*
litigare	*to quarrel*	tossire	*to cough*
lottare	*to struggle*	viaggiare	*to travel*
nevicare★	*to snow*	vivere★	*to live*
pattinare	*to skate*		

★**Essere** can be used with the verbs marked ★, but it is less usual in everyday speech.

4 Past participles: 124 irregular verbs

Verbs with irregular participles are often common ones. You will need to learn them gradually:

	Infinitive	Participle	Meaning
anto	piangere	pianto	*to cry*
	rimpiangere	rimpianto	*to regret*
arso	apparire	apparso	*to appear*
	parere	parso	*to seem*
	scomparire	scomparso	*to disappear*
	spargere	sparso	*to spread*
asto	rimanere	rimasto	*to stay/remain*
aso	evadere	evaso	*to escape*
	invadere	invaso	*to invade*
	persuadere	persuaso	*to persuade*
ato	essere	stato	*to be*
	nascere	nato	*to be born*
	stare	stato	*to stay, to be*
atto	fare	fatto	*to make, do*
	soddisfare	soddisfatto	*to satisfy*
	attrarre	attratto	*to attract*
	distrarre	distratto	*to distract, entertain take mind off*
elto	scegliere	scelto	*to choose*
ento	spegnere	spento	*to turn off, put out*
	redimere	redento	*to redeem*
erso	sommergere	sommerso	*to submerge*
	perdere	perso	*to lose*
erto	aprire	aperto	*to open*
	offrire	offerto	*to offer*
	scoprire	scoperto	*to discover*
	soffrire	sofferto	*to suffer*

eso	accendere	acceso	*to light, put on*
	comprendere	compreso	*to include*
	difendere	difeso	*to defend*
	offendere	offeso	*to offend*
	rendere	reso	*to give back, to make*
	scendere	sceso	*to descend, get out of*
	sorprendere	sorpreso	*to surprise*
	spendere	speso	*to spend*
esso	succedere	successo	*to happen*
	ammettere	ammesso	*to admit*
	mettere	messo	*to put*
	permettere	permesso	*to permit*
	promettere	promesso	*to promise*
	smettere	smesso	*to stop, cease*
	esprimere	espresso	*to express*
esto	chiedere	chiesto	*to ask*
	richiedere	richiesto	*to request*
etto	contraddire	contraddetto	*to contradict*
	dire	detto	*to say*
	disdire	disdetto	*to cancel*
	costringere	costretto	*to force*
	stringere	stretto	*to squeeze, to shake [hand]*
	correggere	corretto	*to correct*
	leggere	letto	*to read*
	proteggere	protetto	*to protect*
into	distinguere	distinto	*to distinguish*
	convincere	convinto	*to convince, persuade*
	dipingere	dipinto	*to paint*
	fingere	finto	*to pretend*
	spingere	spinto	*to push*
	vincere	vinto	*to win*
iso	decidere	deciso	*to decide*
	dividere	diviso	*to divide*
	ridere	riso	*to laugh*
	sorridere	sorriso	*to smile*
	uccidere	ucciso	*to kill*
isto	prevedere	previsto	*to arrange, foresee*
	vedere	visto	*to see*
itto	descrivere	descritto	*to describe*
	iscrivere	iscritto	*to enrol*
	scrivere	scritto	*to write*
	friggere	fritto	*to fry*
	sconfiggere	sconfitto	*to defeat*
issuto	sopravvivere	sopravvissuto	*to survive*
	vivere	vissuto	*to live*
iuto	conoscere	conosciuto	*to know, meet*
	compiere	compiuto	*to undertake*
	dispiacere	dispiaciuto	*to mind, be sorry*
	piacere	piaciuto	*to like*
	tacere	taciuto	*to be silent*

ito	This regular **-ire** ending is used for a group of **-ere** verbs:		
	assistere	assistito	*to attend*
	esistere	esistito	*to exist*
	insistere	insistito	*to insist*
	resistere	resistito	*to resist*
olto	accogliere	accolto	*to welcome*
	[rac]cogliere	colto	*to pick, gather*
	togliere	tolto	*to remove*
	sciogliere	sciolto	*to dissolve*
	risolvere	risolto	*to resolve*
	rivolgersi	rivolto	*to address, speak to*
	svolgere	svolto	*to carry out, take place*
	seppellire	sepolto	*to bury*
orso	correre	corso	*to run*
	trascorrere	trascorso	*to spend [time]*
	mordere	morso	*to bite*
orto	accorgersi	accorto	*to notice, realise*
	sporgersi	sporto	*to lean out of*
	morire	morto	*to die*
oso	esplodere	esploso	*to explode*
	rodere	roso	*to gnaw*
osso	commuovere	commosso	*to move [emotion]*
	muovere	mosso	*to move*
	promuovere	promosso	*to promote*
	scuotere	scosso	*to shake*
osto	comporre	composto	*to compose*
	imporre	imposto	*to impose*
	opporre	opposto	*to oppose*
	proporre	proposto	*to propose*
	nascondere	nascosto	*to hide*
	rispondere	risposto	*to reply*
otto	introdurre	introdotto	*to introduce*
	produrre	prodotto	*to produce*
	ridurre	ridotto	*to reduce*
	tradurre	tradotto	*to translate*
	cuocere	cotto	*to cook*
	interrompere	interrotto	*to interrupt*
	rompere	rotto	*to break*
unto	aggiungere	aggiunto	*to add*
	giungere	giunto	*to arrive at, reach*
	raggiungere	raggiunto	*to reach, attain*
uso	confondere	confuso	*to confuse, muddle mix up, merge*
	diffondere	diffuso	*to spread*
	chiudere	chiuso	*to close*
	deludere	deluso	*to disappoint*
	escludere	escluso	*to exclude*
usso	discutere	discusso	*to discuss*
utto	distruggere	distrutto	*to destroy*
uto	This regular **-ere** ending is used for:		
	venire	venuto	*to come*

Index of Grammar

This index refers to the material in Systems, Troubleshooting, Basics and Reference.

LEXIS (Italian–English)

Notes:

1 The English translations apply to the words as used in the course.

2 Stress patterns: see Reference VI, 2, p. 245. Irregular stress patterns and those in words ending in two vowels are marked by a dot under the stressed vowel.

3 Abbreviations: m = masculine; f = feminine; s = singular; pl = plural; pp = past participle; inv. = invariable; pr = present; adj = adjective; adv = adverb.

4 Symbols: † = irregular present; ★ = takes **essere** [see Reference VIIIB, 1, p. 250]; (★) = takes **essere** and **avere**, depending on how the verb is used [see Reference VIIIB, 2, p. 250]; (pr −o) = the present tense of the **-ire** verb is like **dormire**, not **finire** [see Systems 3, note 1, p. 87 and Reference VIIIA, 1i, p. 248].

5 Countries and nationalities are listed in Reference III, pp. 242–3.

A

a *to; at; in*
abbaiare *to bark*
abbandonare *to abandon; to leave*
abbandonato/a *abandoned, left*
abbastanza *fairly, quite*
l'abbazia *abbey*
abbiamo *see avere*
l'abbigliamento *clothes*
l'abbonamento *subscription, season ticket*
    fare un abbonamento *to get a season ticket*
l'abbonato *subscriber*
abbronzarsi★ *to get a tan*
l'abete (m) *fir*
l'abitante (m/f) *inhabitant*
abitare *to live*
l'abito *dress; suit*
    l'abito da sera *evening dress*
abituarsi★ *to get used to*
gli Abruzzi *Abruzzi (Italian region)*
accadere★ *to happen*
accanto (a) *next to, beside*
accendere (pp acceso) *to light; to switch on*
accettare *to accept*
l'acciaio *steel*
accidenti! *bother! damn!*
accogliere (pp accolto) *to welcome*
accomodarsi★ *to make oneself comfortable*

accompagnare *to accompany*
accontentare *to keep happy*
accorciare *to shorten*
l'accordo *agreement*
    d'accordo *fine*
accorgersi★ (pp accorto) *to notice; to realise*
l'acqua *water*
    l'acqua minerale *mineral water*
acquatico/a (m pl −ci) *aquatic*
l'acquisto *purchase*
ad = a
adagio *slowly*
adatto/a *suitable*
l'addebito *charge*
addolcito/a *sweetened*
addormentarsi★ *to fall asleep*
adesso *now*
adorabile *adorable*
l'adulto *adult*
l'aereo *aeroplane*
aerobico/a (m pl −ci) *aerobic*
l'aeroporto *airport*
l'afa *sultry heat*
gli affari (pl) *business*
affascinante *fascinating*
affatto *at all*
    non ... affatto *not at all*
affermarsi★ *to make oneself known*
affittare *to rent*
affollato/a *crowded*
l'affresco *fresco*
affrettarsi★ *to hurry*
l'agenda *diary*
l'agenzia *agency*
l'aggettivo *adjective*
aggiungere (pp aggiunto) *to add*
l'aglio *garlic*
l'agnello *lamb*
agro/a *sour*
aiutare *to help*
l'aiuto *help*
l'albergo *hotel*
l'albero *tree*
l'albicocca *apricot*
l'alcool (m) *alcohol*
alcuni/e *some, a few*
al di là *beyond*
l'alimentare (m) *grocer; grocer's*
l'allarme (m) *alarm*
    impianto allarme *burglar alarm*
l'allegria *cheerfulness*
allegro/a *cheerful, happy*
allenarsi★ *to train*
allora *so, then, in that case*
l'alluminio *aluminium*
allungare *to lengthen*

almeno *at least*
le Alpi *Alps*
l'alpinismo *climbing*
alpino/a *alpine*
alto/a *high*
altresì *also*
altrettanto! *the same to you!*
altrimenti *otherwise*
altro/a *other, another, more*
altro (inv) *else*
    che altro *anything else?*
    senz'altro *definitely*
altrui *of others, of other people*
l'alunno/l'alunna (m/f) *pupil*
alzare *to lift up*
alzarsi★ *to get up*
amare *to love*
amaro/a *bitter*
l'amaro *bitter after-dinner liqueur*
l'amatriciana *amatriciana sauce*
ambientale *environmental*
l'ambiente (m) *environment*
    la Lega Ambiente *Environment League*
l'amico/l'amica (m pl −ci) *friend*
l'ammiratore (m) *admirer*
ammettere (pp ammesso) *to admit*
l'amore (m) *love*
l'anagrafe (f) *registry office*
analcolico/a (m pl −ci) *non-alcoholic*
l'analisi (f) (inv) *analysis*
analizzare *to analyse*
l'anatra *duck*
anche *also, too, as well; even*
    anch'io *I also, me too*
ancora *still; again; some more*
andare†★ *to go*
    come va? *how's it going? how are things?*
    c'è qualcosa che non va? *is something wrong?*
l'andata *single (ticket)*
    l'andata e ritorno *return (ticket)*
l'anello *ring*
l'anfiteatro *amphitheatre*
l'angelo *angel*
l'angolo *corner*
l'anguilla *eel*
l'animale (m) *animal*
    gli animali domestici *pets*
    gli animali selvatici *wild animals*
animato/a *animated*
l'animazione (f) *liveliness*
l'anno *year*
    quanti anni hai/ha? *how old are you?*
annoiarsi★ *to be bored*

l'antіcipo (f)   *advance*
   in anticipo   *early*
antico/a   *old, ancient*
l'antipasto   *starters, hors d'oeuvre*
antipаtico/a (m pl –ci)   *nasty, unpleasant*
antisеttico/a (m pl –ci)   *antiseptic*
l'antivivisezione (f)   *antivivisection*
anziano/a   *elderly*
l'ape (f)   *bee*
l'aperitivo   *aperitif*
aperto/a   *open*
   all'aperto   *in the open*
apparire†★ (pp apparso)   *to appear*
l'appartamento   *apartment, flat*
appartenere★   *to belong*
gli Appennini   *Apennines*
l'appetito   *appetite*
   buon appetito!   *good appetite!*
applaudire   *to applaud*
applicato/a   *applied*
apprezzato/a   *appreciated*
approssimativo/a   *approximate*
l'appuntamento   *appointment*
aprile (m)   *April*
aprire (pr –o) (pp aperto)   *to open*
   aprire il rubinetto   *to turn on the tap*
l'apriscаtole (m)   *tin opener*
l'аquila   *eagle*
l'arаncia   *orange*
l'aranciata   *orangeade*
l'arancino   *rice and cheese savoury*
arancione   *orange*
l'architettura   *architecture*
l'archeоlogo (pl –gi)   *archaeologist*
l'arco   *bow*
   il tiro con l'arco   *archery*
l'аrea   *area*
l'argento   *silver*
l'аria   *air*
   all'aria aperta   *in the open air*
l'armаdio   *cupboard; wardrobe*
l'armonіa   *harmony*
l'aroma (m)   *aroma, fragrance*
l'arpa   *harp*
arrabbiato/a   *angry*
l'arredamento (m)   *interior design; furnishings*
arrivare★   *to arrive*
arrivederci   *goodbye*
l'arrivo   *arrival*
   in arrivo   *on the way*
arrossire   *to blush*
arrosto/a   *roasted*
l'arte (f)   *art*
l'Arte (f)   *medieval guild*
articolarsi★ (in)   *to be made up of*
l'artіcolo   *article*
l'artigianato   *artisan, craftsmanship*
l'artista (m/f) (m pl gli artisti, f pl le artiste)   *artist*
l'ascensore (m)   *lift*

l'asciugamano   *towel*
asciutto/a   *dry*
ascoltare   *to listen to*
l'asilo   *nursery*
l'аsino   *donkey*
gli aspаragi (pl)   *asparagus*
l'aspirapоlvere (m)   *vacuum cleaner*
aspettare   *to wait*
aspettarsi★   *to hope, to expect to*
l'aspetto   *aspect*
l'aspirina   *aspirin*
assaggiare   *to taste*
assediare   *to besiege*
l'assegno   *cheque*
   la carta assegni   *cheque card*
   il libretto degli assegni   *cheque book*
l'Assessorato all'Ambiente (m)   *Environment Department*
assieme = insieme   *together*
l'assistente (m/f)   *assistant*
   l'assistente sociale   *social worker*
assistere   *to attend; to participate in*
assomigliare   *to resemble, to look like*
assorbire   *to absorb*
assurdo/a   *absurd*
astеmio/a   *teetotal*
l'astrologіa   *astrology*
Atene   *Athens*
l'atleta (m/f)   *athlete*
l'atmosfera   *atmosphere*
attaccare   *to plug in*
attaccato/a   *attached*
attento/a   *careful*
   stare attento   *to be careful*
l'аttico   *penthouse*
l'аttimo   *moment*
   un attimo   *hold on (a moment)*
l'attività (inv)   *activity*
   svolgere un'attività   *to do an activity*
l'attore/l'attrice   *actor/actress*
attorniato/a   *surrounded*
attrarre† (pp attratto)   *to attract*
attraversare   *to cross*
attraverso   *through*
attrezzato/a   *well-equipped*
attualmente   *at present*
augurarsi★   *to hope to*
aumentare⁽★⁾   *to increase*
l'aumento   *payrise*
l'autista (m/f) (m pl gli autisti, f pl le autiste)   *driver*
l'аutobus (m) (inv)   *bus*
autofilotranviario/a (adj.)   *overground public transport*
l'automobilismo   *motor racing*
autоnomo/a   *self-contained*
l'autore (m)   *author*
l'autorità (inv)   *authority*
l'autostrada   *motorway*
l'autunno   *autumn*
   in autunno   *in the autumn*
avanti   *ahead; forward*
   avanti di   *fast (time)*

   avanti di cinque minuti   *five minutes fast*
avere†   *to have*
   avere fame/sete   *to be hungry/thirsty*
   avere caldo/freddo   *to be hot/cold*
   avere fretta   *to be in a hurry*
   avere voglia di   *to feel like*
   avere tempo di   *to have time to*
   avere bisogno di   *to need*
   avere da fare   *to be busy, to have a lot to do*
l'avvenimento   *event*
avvenire†★   *to happen*
avvertire (pr –o)   *to warn, to notify*
avvicinarsi★   *to approach*
l'avvocato/l'avvocatessa (m/f)   *lawyer*
avvolto/a   *wrapped*
l'azienda   *firm*
   azienda vinіcola   *wine-making firm*
azzurro/a   *blue*

B

la bacca   *berry*
il bаcio   *kiss*
bagnato/a   *wet*
il bagno   *bathroom*
   fare il bagno   *to have a bath*
   il bagno di servizio   *cloakroom/spare bathroom*
il balcone   *balcony*
ballare   *to dance*
il balletto   *ballet*
il ballo   *dance*
la bambina   *child, baby, little girl*
il bambino   *child, baby, little boy*
la banana   *banana*
la banca   *bank*
la bandiera   *flag*
il bar (inv)   *bar*
la barba   *beard*
   farsi la barba   *to shave*
il bаrbecue   *barbecue*
il barista   *barman*
barocco/a   *baroque*
la barriera   *barrier*
la base   *base, foundation*
   di base   *basic*
la basіlica   *basilica*
la Basilicata   *Basilicata (Italian region)*
il basіlico   *basil*
basso/a   *low; short*
il basso   *bass; bass guitar*
bastare★   *to be enough*
   basta così?   *is that all?*
i bastoni (pl)   *clubs (in cards)*
la battаglia   *battle*
la batterіa   *drums (drum kit)*
il battеsimo   *christening*
beato   *lucky*
   beato/a me/te!   *lucky me/you!*
bei   *see bello*
bel   *see bello*

la bellezza *beauty*
    l'istituto di bellezza *beauty salon*
bello/a (bel) *beautiful, nice;* che
    bello! *how lovely!*
benché *although*
bendare *to blindfold*
bene *well fine*
    va bene *okay, that's fine*
    sto bene *I'm fine*
il beneficio *benefit*
la benzina *petrol*
    finire la benzina *to run out of petrol*
bere† (pp bevuto) *to drink*
il bergamotto *bergamot*
Berlino *Berlin*
il bermuda (inv) *Bermuda shorts*
la bevanda *drink*
la biancheria *linen*
bianco/a *white*
la bibita *cold drink*
la biblioteca *library*
il bicchiere *glass*
la bicicletta *bicycle*
    con la bicicletta *by bike*
il biglietto *ticket*
    fare il biglietto *to get a ticket*
la Bilancia *Libra*
il biliardo *billiards*
il bimbo *child*
il binario *platform*
il binocolo *binoculars, field glasses*
la biografia *biography*
il biologo (m pl –gi) *biologist*
biondo/a *blond(e)*
la birra *beer*
il biscotto *biscuit*
bisognare★ *to be necessary*
il bisogno *need*
    avere bisogno (di) *to need*
la bistecca *steak*
blu (inv) *blue*
    blu scuro *dark blue*
    blu marino *navy blue*
il blu di Genova (inv) *denim*
i blue jeans (pl) *jeans*
le bocce (pl) *bowls*
la bolletta *bill*
    la bolletta del telefono *telephone
    bill*
bollire (pr –o) *to boil*
la borsa *bag*
il borsellino *purse*
la borsetta a tracolla *shoulder bag*
il bosco *wood* (m pl –ci)
    botanico/a *botanic*
    i giardini botanici *botanic gardens*
la bottiglia *bottle*
il bottone *button*
il box (inv) *garage*
il bracciale/il braccialetto *bracelet*
il braccio (pl le braccia) *arm*
    in braccio *in one's arms*
bravo/a *good, expert*

breve *short*
il bridge (inv) *bridge (game)*
brillare *to shine*
la brioche (inv) *croissant*
la briscola *briscola (card game)*
il brodo *broth, stock*
bruciare *to burn*
la bruschetta *bruschetta (garlic bread)*
brutto/a *ugly; nasty; unpleasant*
    fa brutto tempo *the weather's nasty*
    non è una brutta idea *it's not a bad
    idea*
bucare *to puncture*
    bucato/a *punctured*
il bucato *washing*
    fare il bucato *to do the washing*
il buco *hole*
il bue (pl i buoi) *ox*
buffo/a *funny*
buio/a *dark*
il buio *dark, darkness*
buonanotte *good night*
buonasera *good afternoon; good
    evening*
buongiorno *good morning*
buono/a *good*
il burocratese *language of bureaucracy*
il burro *butter*
la bussola *compass*
la busta *envelope*
    la busta paga *wage packet*
buttare *to throw out*
    buttare la spazzatura *to throw out
    the rubbish*

C

la caccia *hunt*
il cachemire *cashmere*
cadere★ *to fall*
    lasciare cadere *to drop*
il caffè (inv) *coffee*
la caffettiera *coffee pot*
la Calabria *Calabria (Italian region)*
il calcio *football; kick*
caldo/a *hot*
    avere caldo *to be hot*
il caldo *heat*
il calendario *calendar*
il calore *warmth*
la calzamaglia *tights*
le calze (pl) *stockings*
i calzini (pl) *socks*
cambiare(*) *to change*
la camera *room, chamber*
    la camera da letto *bedroom*
    la musica da camera *chamber music*
il cameriere *waiter*
la camicia *shirt*
    la camicia da notte *nightdress*
la camicetta *blouse*
il camino *fire-place*
camminare *to walk*
la camminata *walk*

la camomilla *camomile*
il camoscio *suede*
la campagna *country(side); campaign*
la campana *bell; disposal bank*
la Campania *Campania (Italian region)*
il campanile *bell tower*
il campeggio *camping; campsite*
campestre *rural, country*
il campo *field, court; camp*
    nel campo di *in the field of*
    il campo di concentramento
    concentration camp
il canale *channel*
il cancello *gate*
il cane *dog*
la canoa *canoeing*
il canone *rule*
la canottiera *vest*
il/la cantante *singer*
cantare *to sing*
il cantautore *writer singer, singer-
    songwriter*
il cantico (m pl –ci) *canticle*
la cantina *cellar; wine-cellar*
il canto *singing; song*
la canzone *song*
la canzonetta *little poem, ditty*
CAP (codice di avviamento
    postale) *postal code*
la capanna *hut*
i capelli (pl) *hair*
capire *to understand*
    ho capito *I see*
la capitale *capital*
il capitano *captain*
capitare★ *to chance, to happen to*
il capo *boss*
il capolavoro *masterpiece*
il capolinea *terminus*
il capoluogo *regional/provincial capital*
la cappella *chapel*
il cappello *hat*
il cappotto *coat*
il cappuccino *cappuccino (white coffee)*
la capra *goat*
il carabiniere *Carabiniere (semi-military
    police officer)*
la caramella *sweet*
caratteristico/a (m pl –ci)
    characteristic
il cardigan (inv) *cardigan*
la carne *meat*
caro/a *expensive (after the noun);
    lovely, dear (before the noun)*
la carota *carrot*
la carriera *career*
la carta *paper, card*
    le carte da gioco *playing cards*
    le carte napoletane *Neapolitan
    cards*
    la carta assegni *cheque card*
    la carta di credito *credit card*
    la carta d'identità *identity card*

la cartella   *briefcase*
il cartello   *signpost*
la cartoleria   *stationer's*
la cartolina   *postcard*
il cartone   *cartoon*
  il cartone animato   *(film) cartoon*
la casa   *house*
  a casa   *at home*
  la casa di confezione   *clothing manufacturer*
il casale   *farmhouse*
la casalinga   *housewife*
  casalingo/a   *home-made*
la cascata   *waterfall*
la cascina   *farmhouse*
il casello   *toll station*
il caso   *chance*
  per caso   *by chance*
la cassa   *till*
il cassetto   *drawer; bag*
il cassettone   *chest-of-drawers*
la castagna   *chestnut*
il castagno   *chestnut tree*
  castano/a   *brown*
il castello   *castle*
il catalogo   *catalogue*
il catamarano   *catamaran*
la cattedrale   *cathedral*
  cattivo/a   *bad*
la cattura   *capture*
  catturare   *to capture*
il cavallo   *horse*
  a cavallo   *on horseback*
  il cavallo da tiro   *cart horse*
il cavatappi   *corkscrew*
il cavolo   *cabbage*
  c'è   *see ci 2*
  ce   *see ci 1*
il cedro   *cedar*
il cellulare   *portable telephone*
la cena   *supper, dinner*
  cenare   *to dine*
il centinaio (pl le centinaia)   *about a hundred*
  cento   *hundred*
  per cento   *per cent*
il centro   *centre*
il/la centralinista   *telephone operator*
il centralino   *exchange, switchboard*
  cercare   *to look for*
  cercare di   *to try to*
la cerniera   *zip*
il cerotto   *sticking-plaster*
  certamente   *certainly*
  certo   *certainly, yes indeed*
  certo/a   *certain*
il cervo   *stag*
il cespuglio   *bush, shrub*
  cessare   *to cease, to stop*
il cestino   *basket*
il cetriolo   *cucumber*
lo champagne (m)   *champagne*
  che   *that, which, who, whom; than*

che!   *what! how!*
  che fortuna!   *what luck! how lucky!*
chi?   *who? those/people who*
  chiacchierare   *to chat*
  chiamare   *to call; to telephone*
  chiamarsi★   *to be called*
la chiamata   *call*
il Chianti   *Chianti (wine)*
  chiaramente   *clearly*
  chiaro/a   *clear; light*
la chiave   *key*
  chiudere a chiave   *to lock*
  chiedere (pp chiesto)   *to ask*
la chiesa   *church*
il chilo/chilogramma   *kilo*
il chilometro   *kilometre*
la chimica   *chemistry*
il chimico (m pl –ci)   *(research) chemist*
la chiocciola   *snail*
  chissà   *who knows*
la chitarra   *guitar*
  la chitarra elettrica   *electric guitar*
  chiudere (pp chiuso)   *to close*
  chiudere a chiave   *to lock*
la chiusura lampo   *zip*
  ci 1   *us; ourselves; each other; to us*
  ci 2   *here; there*
  c'è   *there is*
  non c'è   *he/she's not here*
  c'è l'hai/ha?   *have you got it?*
  ciao   *hello, goodbye*
  ciascuno/a   *each, every*
il cibo   *food*
il ciclismo   *cycling*
il ciclo   *cycle*
il cielo   *sky*
il ciglio (pl le ciglia)   *eyelashes*
la ciliegia   *cherry*
  cin-cin!   *cheers!*
il cinema (inv)   *cinema*
la cinepresa   *film camera*
il cinghiale   *wild boar*
la cintura   *belt*
il cioccolato/la cioccolata   *chocolate*
  i cioccolatini   *individual chocolates*
  cioè   *that is, in other words*
la cipolla   *onion*
il cipresso   *cypress*
la cipria   *face powder*
  circa   *about, around*
il circolo   *club*
il citofono   *entryphone*
la città (inv)   *town, city*
il cittadino   *citizen, townsperson*
la civetta   *owl*
  civico/a   *civic*
il clarinetto   *clarinet*
la classe   *class*
  classico/a (m pl –ci)   *classic(al)*
  la musica classica   *classical music*
la classifica   *classification, league table*
il clavicembalo   *harpsichord*

il/la cliente   *client*
il clima (inv)   *climate*
il club (inv)   *club*
  tessera club   *club membership card*
il cocco   *coconut*
  cogliere[†] (pp colto)   *to catch; to gather*
il cognato/la cognata   *brother/sister-in-law*
il cognome   *surname*
la colazione   *breakfast*
  fare colazione   *to have breakfast*
  collaborare (con)   *to collaborate, to work with*
la collaborazione   *collaboration*
la collana   *necklace*
i collant (pl)   *tights*
il colle   *hill*
il collega/la collega   *colleague (m/f)*
  collettivo/a   *collective, general*
il colletto   *collar*
la collina   *hill*
  Colonia   *Cologne*
  colorato   *coloured*
il colore   *colour*
  di che colore?   *what colour?*
il Colosseo   *Coliseum*
la colpa   *fault; blame*
  colpa mia   *my fault*
il coltello   *knife*
  comandare   *to order*
  combattere   *to fight*
  combinare   *to do*
  che cos'abbiamo combinato?   *what have we done?*
  come   *like; as*
  come?   *how? what?*
  com'è?   *what's (something) like?*
  come va?   *how's it going? how are things?*
  comico/a (m pl –ci)   *comic*
  cominciare(★)   *to start, to begin*
la commedia   *play; comedy*
  commerciale   *commercial, trade*
il commesso/la commessa   *shop assistant*
  commestibile   *edible*
il commissario   *police inspector*
  commuovere[†] (pp commosso)   *to move (emotion)*
il comodino   *bedside table*
  comodo/a   *comfortable; convenient*
il compact disc (inv)   *compact disc*
la compagnia   *company*
il compagno   *companion*
  compiere (pp compiuto)   *to undertake*
il compito   *duty, job*
  i compiti   *home-work*
  fare i compiti   *to do home-work*
il compleanno   *birthday*
il complesso   *group, band*
  complesso/a   *complex*
  comporre[†] (pp composto)   *to compose*

comportarsi★ *to behave*
il compositore *composer*
comprare *to buy*
compreso/a *included*
il computer (inv) *computer*
comunale *municipal*
il comune *town council*
la comunicazione *communication*
la comunione *communion*
comunista (m/f) *communist*
la comunità (inv) *community*
    la Comunità Economica
    Europea *EEC*
comunque *however, anyhow*
con *with*
    con la bicicletta *by bike*
la concentrazione *concentration*
il concerto *concert*
concludere (pp concluso) *to end*
la conclusione *conclusion*
condannare *to condemn*
condensare *to condense*
condividere (pp condiviso) *to share*
il condominio *jointly-owned block of flats*
il condomino *joint owner*
condurre† (pp condotto) *to conduct, to lead*
il conduttore/la conduttrice *TV presenter*
confermare *to confirm*
confezionare *to make up (package)*
la confezione *clothing*
confinare (con) *to border (on)*
confondere (pp confuso) *to confuse; to merge*
confusionario/a *chaotic*
il congelatore *freezer*
la congestione *congestion*
congratularsi★ con *to congratulate*
il coniglio *rabbit*
il cono *cone*
la conoscenza *knowledge*
conoscere (pp conosciuto) *to know (someone or something); to meet*
conosciuto/a *well-known*
consegnare *to deliver, hand in*
consentire (pr –o) *to consent*
consentito/a *allowed*
il Conservatorio *state music school*
la conservazione *conservation*
consigliare *to advise*
il consiglio *advice*
consultare *to consult*
il contadino *peasant*
il contatto *contact*
    a contatto *in touch*
il conte *Count*
contenere† *to contain*
contento/a *happy*
la contessa *Countess*
contraddire† (pp contraddetto) *to contradict*

la contravvenzione *fine (formal)*
contro *against*
controllare *to check*
continuare(★) *to continue*
il contrabbasso *double bass*
convenire†★ *to be advisable, advantageous*
convertire (pr –o) *to convert*
convincere (pp convinto) *to convince, to persuade*
la coppa *cup*
la coppia *couple*
coprire (pr –o) (pp coperto) *to cover*
il coraggio *courage*
    che coraggio! *how brave! you're brave!*
cordiale *cordial*
coricarsi★ *to go to bed*
il corno *horn*
il coro *choir*
il corpo *corps*
correggere *to correct*
correre(★) (pp corso) *to run*
correttamente *correctly*
il corridoio *corridor, hall*
la corsa *trip, journey*
    la corsa semplice *single ride*
    la corsa campestre *cross-country running*
il corso *course*
la corte *court;* la Corte di Cassazione *Supreme Court*
cortese *courteous, polite*
corto/a *short*
la cosa *thing*
    cosa?/che cosa? *what?*
coscienzioso/a *conscientious*
così *thus, so, like this*
    basta così? *is that all?*
cosmopolita (m/f) *cosmopolitan*
costare★ *to cost*
costituire *to constitute*
costoso/a *expensive*
costringere (pp costretto) *to force*
il costume *costume, dress*
    il costume da bagno *bathing costume*
il cotone *cotton*
la cottura *cooking*
    il piano di cottura *hob*
la cravatta *tie*
la creatura *creature*
la credenza *sideboard*
credere *to believe, to think*
il credito *credit*
    la carta di credito *credit card*
la crema *egg custard*
la crisi (inv) *crisis*
crollare★ *to collapse*
il crostino *crostino (a starter)*
crudo/a *raw*
    prosciutto crudo *cured ham*
il cucchiaio *spoon*

la cucina *kitchen; cuisine*
cucinare *to cook*
cucire† *to sew*
il cugino/la cugina *cousin*
cui *which; whom; whose*
    in cui *in which*
    di cui *of which*
la cultura *culture*
culturale *cultural*
cuocere† (pp cotto) *to cook*
    fare cuocere *to cook*
il cuoio *leather*
il cuore *heart*
la cupola *dome*
la cura *treatment, care*
    a cura di *care of*
curioso/a *curious*
la curva *bend*
il cuscino *cushion*

D

da *by; from; since/for; at*
    da otto anni *for eight years*
    da Rita *at Rita's*
il daino *deer*
dando *giving; see dare*
il danno *damage*
la danza *dance; dancing*
dappertutto *everywhere*
dare† *to give*
    dare su *to look out on, to open onto*
    dai! *go on!*
la data *date*
il dattilografo/la dattilografa *typist*
davanti a *in front of, outside*
davvero *really*
decidere (pp deciso) *decide*
decidersi★ *to make up ones mind*
il decimo *tenth*
deciso/a *determined*
dedicarsi★ *to devote oneself*
dedicato/a *dedicated*
dedurre† (pp dedotto) *to deduce*
il delinquente *criminal*
il delitto *crime*
delizioso/a *delicious; delightful*
deludere (pp deluso) *to disappoint*
demaniale *State*
democratico/a (m pl –ci) *democratic*
il denaro *money*
il dente *tooth*
    lavarsi i denti *to brush one's teeth*
il dentifricio *toothpaste*
il /la dentista *dentist (m/f)*
dentro *in, inside*
il dépliant (inv) *leaflet*
deportato/a *deported*
il deposito *deposit*
depresso/a *depressed*
derivare *to derive*
descrivere (pp descritto) *to describe*
desiderare *to wish, to want*
il design (inv) *design*

il designer (inv) *designer*

la destra *right*

  a destra *on the right*

  devo, devi, deve, devono *see* dovere

di *of; than*

  di dove sei/dov'è? *where are you from?*

il dialetto *dialect*

il dialogo *dialogue*

il diamante *diamond*

il diametro *diameter*

il diario *diary*

dichiarare *to declare*

didattico/a (mpl −ci) *teaching, educational*

  gli scopi didattici *educational aims*

dietro *behind*

difendere (pp difeso) *defend*

la difesa *defence*

  il Ministero della Difesa *Ministry of Defence*

differente *different*

la differenza *difference*

difficile *difficult, hard*

la difficoltà (inv) *difficulty*

diffidare *to trust*

diffondere (pp diffuso) *to spread*

digerire *to digest*

il digestivo *after-dinner drink*

digrignato/a *grinning*

dimagrire⁽★⁾ *to lose weight*

dimenticare (di) *to forget*

dimenticarsi★ (di) *to forget*

dinamico/a (m pl −ci) *dynamic*

il dio (pl gli dei) *god*

il/la dipendente *employee*

dipendere★ (pp dipeso) *to depend*

  dipende *it depends*

dipingere (pp dipinto) *to paint*

il dipinto *painting*

dire† (pp detto) *to say, to tell*

direttamente *directly*

diretto/a *direct*

  il programma in diretta *live programme*

il diretto *average-speed stopping-train*

il direttore/la direttrice *director, primary school head*

  il direttore/la direttrice d'orchestra *conductor*

il diritto *right*

disanimato/a *inanimate*

il disastro *disaster*

la disciplina *regulation*

il disco *record*

il discorso *speech; conversation*

la discoteca *discotheque*

discutere (pp discusso) *to discuss; to argue*

disdire† (pp disdetto) *to cancel*

disegnare *to draw*

disegnato/a *designed*

il disegno *drawing; design*

la professoressa di disegno *art teacher*

la disgrazia *disaster*

il disguido *mix-up*

il disgusto *disgust*

disoccupato/a *unemployed*

disordinato/a *untidy*

dispari *uneven (numbers)*

disperato/a *desperate*

dispiacere★ *to be sorry; to mind*

  mi dispiace *I'm sorry*

  Le dispiace se . . . ? *would you mind if . . . ?*

la disposizione *disposal*

  a disposizione *available, at s.o's disposal*

disposto/a *prepared, willing*

distinguere (pp distinto) *to distinguish*

distrarre† (pp distratto) *to entertain, to distract*

distrarsi†⁽★⁾ (pp distratto) *to have fun, to amuse oneself*

distruggere (pp distrutto) *to destroy*

disturbare *to trouble, to interrupt*

  la linea disturbata *bad line*

la ditta *firm*

il divano *sofa*

divenire★ (pp divenuto) *to become*

diventare★ *to become*

diverso/a *different (after the noun); various, several (before the noun)*

divertente *fun, amusing, entertaining*

il divertimento *entertainment*

divertire (pr −o) *to amuse*

divertirsi★ (pr −o) *to enjoy oneself*

dividere (pp diviso) *to divide*

il divieto *prohibition, no . . .*

  il divieto di sosta *no waiting*

  il divieto di transito *no thoroughfare*

dobbiamo *see* dovere

la doccia *shower*

  fare la doccia *to have a shower*

il documentario *documentary*

il documento *document*

doganale *customs*

dolce *sweet*

il dolce *dessert*

il dolcelatte *dolcelatte (cheese)*

il dollaro *dollar*

le Dolomiti *Dolomites*

il dolore *pain; grief*

la domanda *question*

  fare una domanda *to ask a question*

domandare *to ask*

domani *tomorrow*

la domenica *Sunday*

domestico/a (m pl −ci) *domestic, household*

la donna *woman*

dopo *after, afterwards*

dopodomani *the day after tomorrow*

doppio/a *double*

  il doppio lavoro *double work*

il dormiente *sleeper*

dormire (pr −o) *to sleep*

il dottore/la dottoressa *doctor*

dove? *where?*

  dov'è? *where is?*

dovere†⁽★⁾ *to have to, must*

dritto *straight on*

dubitare *to doubt*

due *two*

dunque *now, therefore*

il duomo *cathedral*

durante *during*

durare★ *to last, to go on (for)*

duro/a *hard*

E

e *and*

è *see* essere

ecc. *etc. (etcetera)*

eccetera *etcetera*

ecco *here is, here are*

  eccolo/la *here it is*

  eccoli/le *here they are*

l'ecologia (f) *ecology*

economico/a (m pl −ci) *cheap, economic*

ed = e

l'edicola *news-stand*

l'edificio *building*

l'editore/l'editrice *publisher*

l'editoria *publishing*

educato/a *polite*

effettivamente *effectively; in fact*

l'effetto *effect*

efficace *effective*

l'elefante (m) *elephant*

elegante *elegant, smart*

elementare *elementary*

  le scuole elementari *infant and junior schools*

l'elemento *element*

l'elenco *list, directory*

  l'elenco telefonico *telephone directory*

elettrico/a (m pl −ci) *electric*

l'elettrodomestico (pl −ci) *domestic appliance*

l'elicottero *helicopter*

ellenico/a (m pl −ci) *Greek*

emergere★ (pp emerso) *to emerge*

l'emigrazione (f) *emigration*

l'emozione (f) *emotion*

l'energetico *energy-giving food*

l'energia *energy*

enorme *enormous*

entrambe *both*

entrare★ *to enter, go in*

l'entrata *entrance*

entusiasmante *exciting*

l'Epifania *Twelfth Night*

l'epoca   *era*
   una casa d'epoca   *period house*
equilibrato/a   *balanced*
l'equitazione (f)   *horse-riding*
erano   *see* essere
l'erba   *herb; grass*
l'erboristeria   *health food and beauty store*
l'errore (m)   *mistake*
   fare un errore   *to make a mistake*
esagerare   *to exaggerate*
l'esame (m)   *exam*
esattamente   *exactly*
esatto   *that's right*
esaurito/a   *out of stock/print*
escludere (pp escluso)   *to exclude*
esco, esci, esce, escono   *see* uscire
l'escursione (f)   *excursion*
   fare un'escursione   *to go on an excursion*
l'escursionista (m/f)   *walker, tripper*
l'esempio   *example*
   per esempio   *for example*
l'esemplare (m)   *specimen*
l'esercizio   *exercise*
l'esistenza   *existence*
esistere★ (pp esistito)   *to exist*
esitare   *to hesitate*
esotico/a   *exotic*
l'esperienza   *experience, experiment, attempt*
l'esperto   *expert*
esplodere (pp esploso)   *to explode*
esporre (pp esposto)   *to expose*
l'espressione (f)   *expression*
espressivo/a   *expressive*
espresso/a   *express*
   la lettera espresso   *express letter*
esprimere (pp espresso)   *to express*
essenziale   *essential*
essere†★ (pp stato)   *to be*
essi/esse   *they (m/f)*
esso/essa   *it (m/f)*
l'estate (f)   *summer*
estendere (pp esteso)   *to extend*
l'estero   *abroad*
estivo/a   *summer*
   le vacanze estive   *summer holidays*
estrarre† (pp estratto)   *to extract*
l'età (inv)   *age*
l'etto   *hectogramme (100 grammes)*
   all'etto   *per 100 grammes*
l'eufemismo   *euphemism*
europeo/a   *European*
evadere (pp evaso)   *to escape*
evitare   *to avoid*
evocare   *to arouse, to evoke*

F

fa   *ago*
   un anno fa   *a year ago*
faccio, facciamo   *see* fare
facile   *easy*

facile a   *prone to*
il faggio   *beech*
il fagiolo   *bean*
il fagiolino   *green bean*
il fagotto   *bassoon*
falso/a   *false, untrue*
la fama   *fame*
la fame   *hunger*
   avere fame   *to be hungry*
famigerato/a   *infamous*
la famiglia   *family*
familiare   *(of a) family*
famoso/a   *famous*
i fans (pl)   *fans*
la fantascienza   *science fiction*
la fantasia   *imagination*
fantastico/a (m pl –ci)   *fantastic*
fare† (pp fatto)   *to do; to make*
   fare il bucato   *to do the washing*
   fare colazione   *to have breakfast*
   fare il biglietto   *to get a ticket*
   fare un abbonamento   *to get a season ticket*
   fa bel/brutto tempo   *the weather's good/bad*
   fare vedere a   *to show*
   fare piacere a   *to please*
   fare il numero   *to dial*
   fare parte di   *to belong to*
   fare sapere a   *to let someone know*
   fare a meno di   *to do without*
   fare finta di   *to pretend*
la farfalla   *butterfly*
la farmacia   *chemist's*
il /la farmacista   *chemist*
il fascino   *fascination, attraction*
il fascismo   *fascism*
il fastidio   *annoyance*
   dare fastidio a   *to bother, to be a nuisance to*
faticoso/a   *tiring*
il fatto   *fact*
il fattore   *factor*
la fauna   *fauna*
favoloso/a   *fabulous, amazing*
il favore   *favour*
   per favore   *please*
il fax (inv)   *fax machine*
il fazzoletto   *handkerchief*
febbraio (m)   *February*
la fede   *faith*
la federa   *pillow-case*
la federazione (f)   *federation*
il fegato   *liver*
felice   *happy*
il feltro   *felt*
la femmina   *girl; female*
le ferie   *holidays*
feriale   *working*
   i giorni feriali   *working days, weekdays*
fermarsi★   *to stop*
la fermata   *stop*

la fermata dell' autobus   *bus-stop*
feroce   *ferocious*
il Ferragosto   *Ferragosto (August 15 Bank holiday)*
il ferro   *iron*
   il ferro da stiro   *(flat) iron*
la ferrovia   *railway*
la festa   *holiday, festival*
festeggiare   *to celebrate*
festivo/a   *holiday*
   i giorni festivi   *holidays*
la fetta   *slice*
le fettuccine (pl)   *fettucine (pasta)*
il fiammifero   *match*
il fidanzato/la fidanzata   *fiancé/fiancée*
fidarsi★ di   *to trust*
la figlia   *daughter*
il figlio   *son*
   i figli   *children*
   figli di papà   *Daddy's boys*
la figura   *figure*
   fare bella figura   *to cut a fine figure*
figurati!   *not at all!*
la filastrocca   *nursery rhyme, nonsense rhyme*
il film (inv)   *film*
la filosofia   *philosophy*
finalmente   *finally*
la finanza   *finance*
   le finanze   *(state) finances*
la fine   *the end*
   il fine settimana (inv)   *weekend*
la finestra   *window*
fingere (pp finto)   *to pretend*
finire(★)   *to finish*
fino a   *until, as far as*
il finocchio   *fennel*
finora   *till now*
il fiore   *flower*
   il fiore selvatico   *wild flower*
   a fiori   *flowered*
fiorire   *to bloom*
fiorito/a   *flowery*
Firenze   *Florence*
la firma   *signature*
firmare   *to sign*
il fitness   *fitness*
il fiume   *river*
il flacone   *small bottle*
il flauto   *flute*
la flora   *flora*
la foglia   *leaf*
folle   *mad*
fondamentale   *fundamental*
fondare   *to establish, to found*
il fondo   *bottom, base*
   lì in fondo   *right over/down there*
la fontana   *fountain*
la forchetta   *fork*
il formaggio   *cheese*
il formato   *size, format*
la formica   *ant*
la formula   *formula*

il fornello   *burner*
fornire   *to provide*
il forno   *oven*
   il forno a microonde   *microwave oven*
forse   *maybe*
forte   *strong; loud*
la fortuna   *luck*
   per fortuna   *luckily*
fortunato/a   *lucky, fortunate*
forza!   *come on!*
forzare   *to force*
la foto (inv)   *photograph*
la fotografia   *photography; photograph*
fotografico/a (m pl –ci)   *photographic*
   la macchina fotografica   *camera*
il fotografo   *photographer*
il fotoromanzo   *photoromance*
il foulard (inv)   *headscarf*
   fra   *between, among, in (period of time)*
   fra poco   *soon*
la fragola   *strawberry*
la fragranza   *fragrance*
il francobollo   *stamp*
il Frascati   *Frascati (wine)*
la frase   *phrase; sentence*
il frastuono   *racket, din*
il fratello   *brother*
   il fratellino   *little brother*
la frazione   *fraction*
freddo/a   *cold*
   avere freddo   *to be cold*
il freddo   *cold*
il freezer   *freezer*
frequentare   *to frequent, to attend*
frequente   *frequent*
fresco/a   *fresh*
la fretta   *hurry, haste*
   avere fretta   *to be in a hurry*
friggere (pp fritto)   *to fry*
il frigorifero   *fridge*
frizzante   *sparkling; exciting*
il fronte   *front*
   di fronte a   *opposite, in front of*
la frutta/il frutto   *fruit*
   i frutti del bosco   *forest fruits (nuts and berries)*
il fruttivendolo   *greengrocer, fruiterer*
la fuga   *(gas) leak*
fuggire(*)   *to run away, to escape*
fumare   *to smoke*
il fumetto   *cartoon comic*
il fungo   *mushroom*
la funivia   *cable car*
funzionare   *to work*
il fuoco   *fire*
fuori   *outside*
il furto   *theft*
i fusilli (pl)   *fusilli (pasta)*
la fusione   *casting*
il futbol   *football*
il futuro   *future*

G

il gabinetto   *toilet*
la galleria   *gallery*
   la galleria d'arte   *art gallery*
la gallina   *hen*
il gallo   *cock*
la gamba   *leg*
   essere in gamba   *to be able, capable*
il garage   *garage*
il gatto   *cat*
la gelateria   *ice-cream shop*
il gelato   *ice-cream*
i gemelli/le gemelle   *twins*
generale   *general*
generalmente   *generally*
il genere   *kind, sort*
   in genere   *in general, as a rule*
il genero   *son-in-law*
generoso/a   *generous*
il genitore (m)   *parent*
gennaio (m)   *January*
la gente   *people*
gentile   *kind*
gestire   *to run, to manage*
il gettone   *telephone token*
il ghiaccio   *ice*
già   *already; that's right*
la giacca   *jacket*
   la giacca a vento   *windcheater*
giallo/a   *yellow*
   il film giallo   *detective film*
il giallo   *detective story*
il giardinaggio   *gardening*
   fare il giardinaggio   *to garden*
il giardino   *garden*
   i giardini pubblici   *public gardens*
   i giardini botanici   *botanic gardens*
gigantesco/a   *gigantic*
il gilè (inv)   *waistcoat*
la ginnastica   *gymnastics*
   la ginnastica aerobica   *aerobics*
il ginocchio (pl le ginocchia)   *knee*
giocare (a)   *to play*
il giocatore   *player*
il giocattolo   *toy*
il gioco   *game; fun*
   suonare per gioco   *to play for fun*
il gioiello   *jewel*
il giornale   *newspaper*
   il giornale radio   *radio news*
giornaliero/a   *daily*
il /la giornalista   *journalist*
la giornata   *day*
il giorno   *day*
giovane   *young*
il giovane   *young man*
giovanile   *youthful*
il giovedì   *Thursday*
la gioventù (inv)   *youth*
girare   *to turn; to go round*
il giro   *tour*
   fare un giro per   *to go on a tour of*
   fare il giro di   *to go round*

la gita   *outing*
   fare una gita   *to go on an outing*
giù   *down*
giudicare   *to judge*
il giudice   *judge*
giugno   *June*
il giullare   *minstrel*
giungere (*) (pp giunto)   *to arrive, to reach*
la giustizia   *justice*
giusto/a   *right, fair*
gli 1   *the*
gli 2   *to him; to them*
lo gnocco   *gnocco (dumpling)*
la gola   *throat*
il golf (inv)   *golf; cardigan, jumper*
il /la golfista   *golfer*
la gondola   *gondola*
la gonna   *skirt*
il gorgonzola (inv)   *gorgonzola (cheese)*
il governo   *government*
il grado   *degree*
   essere in grado di   *to be capable of*
la grammatica   *grammar*
il grammo   *gramme*
grande (gran)   *big, large (after the noun); great (before the noun)*
grandinare(*)   *to hail*
la grandine   *hail*
grasso/a   *greasy*
gratis   *free*
grazie   *thank you*
gridare   *to shout*
grigio/a   *grey*
il grissino   *breadstick*
grosso/a   *big, large*
la grotta   *cave*
il gruppo   *group*
guadagnare   *to earn*
il guanto   *glove*
guardare   *to look at, to watch*
la guardia   *guard*
   la guardia delle finanze   *customs and excise office*
guarire(*)   *to get well; to cure*
guasto/a   *out of order*
il guaio   *trouble*
la guerra   *war*
il gufo   *owl*
la guida   *guide*
guidare   *to drive; to guide*
guidato/a   *guided*

H

hanno   *see avere*
l'hit-parade (inv)   *hit-parade*
ho   *see avere*
l'hobby (m) (inv)   *hobby*

I

i   *the*
IC   *Intercity (train)*
l'idea   *idea*

non ho idea   *I haven't a clue*
ideale   *ideal*
l'identità (inv)   *identity*
   la carta d'identità   *identity card*
l'idraulico (pl –ci)   *plumber*
l'idromassaggio   *water massage*
ieri   *yesterday*
il   *the*
illuminato/a   *illuminated*
illustrativo/a   *illustrative*
imbarazzato/a   *embarrassed*
imboccare   *to take*
   imboccare una strada   *to turn into a street*
imbucare   *to post*
l'immagine (f)   *image*
l'immigrazione (f)   *immigration*
imparare   *to learn*
impazzire★   *to go mad*
   mi piace da impazzire   *I'm crazy about it*
impedire   *to prevent*
impegnarsi★   *to undertake to*
impegnato/a   *busy*
l'impegno   *engagement; commitment*
l'impermeabile (m)   *raincoat*
l'impianto   *system*
   l'impianto allarme   *alarm system*
l'impiegato   *employee*
imporre† (pp imposto)   *to impose*
importante   *important*
importare★   *to be important, to matter*
   non importa   *it doesn't matter*
impossibile   *impossible*
in   *in; into*
incamerato/a   *hidebound*
l'incendio   *fire*
incerto/a   *uncertain*
l'incidente (m)   *(car) accident*
incidere (pp inciso)   *to affect*
includere (pp incluso)   *to include*
l'incomprensione (f)   *incomprehension*
incontrare   *to meet*
incontrarsi★   *to meet with (someone)*
incoraggiare   *to encourage*
l'incrocio   *crossroads*
l'indagine (f)   *survey*
indeciso/a   *undecided*
l'indennità (inv)   *indemnity*
indietro   *behind*
   indietro di   *slow (time)*
   indietro di cinque minuti   *five minutes slow*
indipendente   *independent*
l'indipendenza   *independence*
indiretto/a   *indirect*
indirizzare   *to aim*
l'indirizzo   *address*
indispensabile   *indispensable*
indubbiamente   *undoubtedly*
infantile   *juvenile, children's*
l'infanzia   *childhood*
infatti   *as a matter of fact, in fact*

infelice   *unhappy*
l'infermiere/l'infermiera   *nurse*
informale   *informal*
l'informatica   *information technology; computers*
l'informazione (f)   *information*
l'infortunio   *(industrial) accident*
l'infrazione (f)   *offence*
l'ingegnere (m)   *engineer*
ingiusto/a   *unfair*
l'ingresso   *entrance; hall; admission fee*
iniziare(★)   *to begin, to start (on)*
l'iniziativa   *initiative*
l'inizio   *beginning*
innaffiare   *to water*
l'innamoramento   *falling in love*
inoltre   *besides, in addition*
l'inquilino   *tenant*
l'inquinamento   *pollution*
inquinato/a   *polluted*
l'insalata   *salad*
l'insegnante (m/f)   *secondary school teacher*
insegnare   *to teach*
insensibile   *insensitive*
insieme   *together*
   la musica d'insieme   *ensemble music*
insistere (pp insistito)   *to insist*
insomma   *in short; well*
intanto   *meanwhile*
intasato/a   *blocked up*
intelligente   *intelligent*
l'intensità (inv)   *intensity*
l'intenzione (f)   *intention*
   avere intenzione   *to intend*
intercontinentale   *intercontinental*
interessante   *interesting*
interessare   *to interest*
l'interesse (m)   *interest*
interno/a   *internal*
l'interno   *extension (telephone)*
   il Ministero degli Interni   *Interior Ministry*
intero   *whole, entire*
interrompere (pp interrotto)   *to interrupt*
l'interruttore (m)   *light switch*
l'interurbano/a   *between cities*
   la telefonata interurbana   *long-distance call*
intervenire†★ (pp intervenuto)   *to intervene*
l'intervento   *intervention; interference*
l'intervista   *interview*
intitolare (si★)   *to call (to be called: book, article, etc.)*
intorno   *around*
introdurre† (pp introdotto)   *to introduce*
l'introduzione (f)   *introduction*
inutile   *useless*
invadere (pp invaso)   *to invade*
invece   *instead, on the other hand*

inventare   *to invent*
l'invenzione (f)   *invention*
l'inverno (m)   *winter*
   d'inverno   *in the winter*
investire (pr –o)   *to invest*
inviare   *to send*
invitare   *to invite*
io   *I*
irritato/a   *irritated*
l'iscritto   *(paid-up) member*
iscritto/a   *enrolled*
iscrivere (pp iscritto)   *to enrol*
l'isola   *island*
ispirare   *to inspire*
l'istituto   *institute*
   l'istituto di bellezza   *beauty salon*
l'Italiese (m)   *anglicised Italian*
l'itinerario   *route, tour*
   l'itinerario naturalistico   *nature trail*

J

il jazz   *jazz*

K

il karatè   *karate*

L

l'   *the*
là   *there, over there*
   di là   *that way*
la; La   *her; you*
laburista   *Labour*
   il partito laburista   *the Labour party*
il ladro   *thief*
laggiù   *down there*
lagnarsi★   *to complain*
il lago   *lake*
la laguna   *lagoon*
lamentarsi★   *to complain*
la lampada   *lamp*
i lampasciumi (pl)   *wild onions*
il lampo   *lightning*
   la chiusura lampo   *zip*
il lampone   *raspberry*
la lana   *wool*
lanciare   *to throw*
largo/a   *loose; wide*
le lasagne   *lasagne (pasta)*
lasciare   *to leave*
   lasciare cadere   *to drop*
lassù   *up there*
il latte   *milk*
la lattina   *tin, can*
il lato   *side*
   a lato   *sideways*
la lauda   *medieval hymn*
la laurea   *university degree*
laureato/a in   *with a degree in*
il lavabò   *bathroom sink*
il lavaggio   *washing*
la lavagna   *blackboard*

la lavanda   *lavender*
il lavandino   *kitchen sink*
   lavare   *to wash*
   lavarsi★   *to wash (oneself)*
la lavastoviglie   *dishwasher*
la lavatrice   *washing machine*
   lavorare   *to work*
il lavoratore   *worker*
il lavoro   *work*
   il lavoro nero   *moonlighting*
il Lazio   *Lazio (Italian region)*
   le 1   *the; them*
   le; Le 2   *to her; to you*
la lega   *league*
   la Lega Ambiente   *Environment League*
   legare   *to link*
   leggere (pp letto)   *to read*
   leggero/a   *light*
il legno   *wood*
il legume   *legume, pulse*
   lei   *she; you*
   lentamente   *slowly*
la lenticchia   *lentil*
   lento   *slow*
il lenzuolo (pl le lenzuola)   *sheet*
la lepre   *hare*
la lettera   *letter*
la letteratura   *litarature*
   letterario/a   *literary*
il lettino   *sunbed*
il letto   *bed*
la lezione (f)   *lesson*
   li   *them*
   lì   *there*
   lì in fondo   *right over there*
la libreria   *bookshop*
   liberare   *to free*
   libero/a   *free*
il libretto   *(small) book, booklet*
   il libretto degli assegni   *cheque book*
il libro   *book*
   ligure   *Ligurian*
la Liguria   *Liguria (Italian region)*
il limone   *lemon*
la linea   *line*
   la linea disturbata   *bad line (telephone)*
   rimanere in linea   *to hold the line*
la lingua   *language, tongue*
il linguaggio   *language*
   linguistico/a (m pl –ci)   *linguistic*
il lino   *linen*
la lira   *lira*
la lirica   *opera*
   lirico/a (m pl –ci)   *operatic*
   litigare   *to quarrel*
   litoraneo/a   *coastal*
il litro   *litre*
il livello   *level*
   il passaggio a livello   *level crossing*
   lo   *the; it*
   locale   *local*

il locale   *room*
la locanda   *inn*
la Lombardia   *Lombardy*
   Londra   *London*
   lontano/a (da)   *far (from)*
   loro   *they; to them; their; theirs*
   lottare   *to struggle*
la lottizzazione   *lotting (political patronage)*
la lozione   *lotion*
   lucano/a   *from the Basilicata*
la luce   *light; electricity*
la lucertola   *lizard*
la lucidatrice   *floor polisher*
   lui   *he; him*
la lumaca   *snail*
il lumacone   *slug*
   luminoso/a   *light*
il lunedì   *Monday*
   dal lunedì al venerdì   *from Monday to Friday*
   lungo/a   *long*
   a lungo   *for a long time*
il lungomare   *the seafront*
il luogo   *place*
   dare luogo a   *to give rise to, is subject to*
il lupo   *wolf*
il lusso   *luxury*
   di lusso   *luxury*

M

   ma   *but*
   macchiato/a   *stained*
la macchina   *car; machine*
   andare in macchina   *to go in the (by) car*
   la macchina fotografica   *camera*
la macedonia   *fruit salad*
il macellaio   *butcher*
la macelleria   *butcher's*
la madre   *mother*
il maestro/la maestra   *primary school teacher; coach*
il magazzino   *department store*
il magistrato   *magistrate*
   maggio (m)   *May*
la maggiorana   *marjoram*
la maglia   *jumper*
   lavorare a maglia   *to knit*
   a maglia   *knitted*
la maglietta   *T shirt*
il maglione   *sweater*
   magro/a   *thin*
   mai   *ever*
   non . . . mai   *not ever, never*
il maiale   *pork, pig*
   malato/a   *ill*
   male   *bad, unwell, badly*
   non c'è male   *not bad*
   meno male!   *good!*
   maleducato/a   *rude*
la malinconia   *melancholy*

il mallo   *pulp*
   il mallo di noce   *walnut pulp*
la mamma   *mum*
il mammismo   *close attachment between mother and son*
il/la manager   *manager*
   mancare★   *to lack*
   mancano le lenzuola   *there aren't any sheets*
   mandare   *to send*
   mangiare   *to eat*
la manica   *sleeve*
il manico   *handle*
la maniera   *way, style, fashion*
la manifestazione (f)   *demonstration*
la mano (pl le mani)   *hand*
   dare una mano   *to lend a hand, to help*
   mantenere†   *to keep, to maintain*
il manzo   *beef*
il marafone   *marafone (card game)*
   le Marche   *Marche (Italian region)*
il marciapiede   *pavement*
il mare   *sea*
   marino/a   *navy*
il marito   *husband*
il marketing   *marketing*
la marmellata   *jam*
   marmorizzato/a   *marbled*
   marrone   *brown*
il martedì   *Tuesday*
il martirio   *martyrdom*
   marzo (m)   *March*
il maschio   *boy; male*
   massacrato/a   *massacred*
la matematica   *maths*
la matita   *pencil*
il matrimonio   *marriage, wedding*
il mattino/la mattina   *morning*
   maturo/a   *ripe*
il meccanico (pl –ci)   *mechanic*
   medicinale   *medicinal*
   medico/a (m pl –ci)   *medical*
il medico (pl –ci)   *doctor*
   medio/a   *middle*
   le medie   *middle schools*
il medioevo   *Middle Ages*
   meglio   *better, best*
la mela   *apple*
la melanzana   *aubergine*
il melone   *melon*
la memoria   *memory*
   a memoria   *by heart*
   meno   *less; minutes to*
   le sette meno un quarto   *a quarter to seven*
   di meno   *less*
   meno male!   *good!, thank goodness!*
   il/la meno   *the least*
la mensa   *canteen*
   mentire   *to lie*
   mentre   *while*
   meravigliarsi★   *to be surprised at*

meraviglioso/a *marvellous*
il mercato *market*
il mercoledì *Wednesday*
meridionale *southern*
  l'Italia meridionale *Southern Italy*
il mese *month*
la messa *mass*
il messaggio *message*
il mestiere *trade, job*
la metà (inv) *half; mid*
il metallo *metal*
la metropolitana *tube (underground)*
mettere (pp messo) *to put*
mettersi★ *to set about, to begin*
la mezzanotte *midnight*
mezzo/a *half*
  le . . . e mezzo *half past*
il mezzogiorno *midday*
mi *me; to/for me; myself*
mica: non . . . mica *not really*
la microonda *microwave*
  il forno a microonde *microwave oven*
il miglio *millet*
migliorare *to improve*
migliore(★) *better*
  il/la migliore *the best*
mila *see mille*
il milione *million*
mille (pl mila) *thousand*
minacciare *to threaten*
minerale *mineral*
  l'acqua minerale *mineral water*
la minestra *minestra (soup)*
  minestra in brodo *clear soup*
la miniatura *miniature*
il ministero *ministry*
il ministro *minister*
la minoranza *minority*
minore *less*
il minuto *minute*
mio/a *my; mine*
il miracolo *miracle*
il mirtillo *bilberry*
la missione *mission*
la misura *measurement*
misurare *to measure*
i mobili (pl) *furniture*
la moda *fashion*
  l'alta moda *haute couture*
  andare di moda *to be in fashion*
la modella *model*
il modello *style*
moderatamente *moderately*
moderno/a *modern*
il modo *way, manner*
il modulo *form*
la moglie (pl le mogli) *wife*
molto *very; very much*
molto/a *much, a lot (of), many*
moltissimo *very much*
il momento *moment*
  in questo momento *at the moment*

mondiale *world*
il mondo *world*
il monolocale *bedsit; studio flat*
monotono/a *monotonous*
la montagna *mountain*
il monte *mountain*
il monumento *monument*
la moquette *(fitted) carpet*
la mora *blackberry*
morbido/a *soft*
mordere (pp morso) *to bite*
morire†★ (pp morto) *to die*
  mi piace da morire *I adore it*
la mortadella *mortadella (salame)*
mortale *deadly*
la morte *death*
la mosca *fly*
la mossa *move*
la mostra *exhibition*
la motocicletta *motorbike*
la mountain bike (inv) *mountain bike*
la mozzarella *mozzarella (cheese)*
la mucca *cow*
la multa *fine*
  fare la multa a *to fine*
il municipio *town hall*
muovere† (pp mosso) *to move*
il muro *(outside) wall*
il museo *museum*
la musica *music*
  la musica classica *classical music*
  la musica da camera *chamber music*
  la musica d'insieme *ensemble music*
  la musica pop *pop music*
musicale *musical*
il /la musicista *musician*
le mutande (pl) *underpants*
le mutandine (pl) *panties*
il mutuo *mortgage*

N

il nailon *nylon*
napoletano/a *Neopolitan*
la narrativa *narrative; fiction*
nascere★ (pp nato) *to be born*
nascondere (pp nascosto) *to hide*
nascosto/a *hidden*
il Natale *Christmas*
la natura *nature*
la nave *ship*
nazionale *national*
la nazionalità (inv) *nationality*
la nazione *nation*
ne *of it, of them*
né . . . né *neither . . . nor*
neanche *neither, not even;*
  neanch'io *me neither*
la nebbia *fog*
necessario *necessary*
il negozio *shop*
il nemico (m pl −ci) *enemy*

nemmeno: non . . . nemmeno *not even*
neppure: non . . . neppure *not even*
nero/a *black*
il nerdi *orange flower oil*
nervoso/a *nervous*
nessuno: non . . . nessuno *no-one*
neutro/a *neutral*
la neve *snow*
nevicare(★) *to snow*
nevrotico/a (m pl −ci) *neurotic*
niente: non . . . niente *nothing*
  per niente *at all*
il /la nipote *nephew; grandson/niece; granddaughter*
no *no*
la nocciola *hazelnut*
il nocciolo *heart (of the matter)*
la noce *walnut*
  il mallo di noce *walnut pulp*
noi *we*
noioso/a *boring*
noleggiare *to hire*
il nome *name*
nominare *to mention*
  hai sentito nominare . . .? *have you heard of . . .?*
il nominativo *name [formal]*
non *not*
il nonno/la nonna *grandfather/ grandmother*
nonostante *despite, notwithstanding*
il nord *north*
il nord-est *north-east*
normale *normal*
nostro/a *our; ours*
la.nota *tone; note*
la notizia *news*
la nottata *night (long)*
la notte *night*
notturno/a *night*
  la vita notturna *nightlife*
il Novecento *twentieth century*
novembre (m) *November*
le nozze *wedding, marriage*
nulla: non . . . nulla *nothing*
il numero *number; size*
  fare il numero *to dial*
  che numero porta? *what size do you take?*
la nuora *daughter-in-law*
nuotare *to swim*
il nuoto *swimming*
Nuova York *New York*
nuovo/a *new (after the noun); another (before the noun)*
la nuvola *cloud*
nuvoloso/a *cloudy*

O

l'oasi (f) (inv) *oasis*
obbligare *to force, to oblige*
obbligatorio/a *obligatory, compulsory*

obiettivo/a   *objective*
l'oboe (m)   *oboe*
l'oca   *goose*
l'occasione (f)   *occasion; bargain*
gli occhiali   *glasses*
   gli occhiali da sole   *sunglasses*
l'occhio   *eye*
occidentale   *western*
occorrere★   *to be needed*
occuparsi★   *to deal with, to be interested in, to be in (profession)*
   mi occupo di editoria   *I'm in publishing*
occupato/a   *busy*
l'oculista (m/f)   *optician*
oddio!   *oh dear!*
odiare   *to hate*
odioso/a   *hateful, odious*
l'odore (m)   *smell*
offendere (pp offeso)   *to offend*
l'offerta   *offer*
offrire (pp offerto)   *to offer*
l'oggetto   *object*
oggi   *today*
ogni   *every, each*
   ogni tanto   *every so often*
   ogni quanto?   *every how often?*
l'olio   *oil*
l'oliva   *olive*
oltre   *beyond, over*
   oltre a   *apart from*
l'ombra   *shade*
   all'ombra   *in the shade*
l'ombrellone (m)   *beach-umbrella*
onesto/a   *honest*
l'opera (f)   *work; opera*
   il teatro dell'opera   *opera house*
l'operaio/operaia (m/f)   *worker*
l'opinione (f)   *opinion*
opporre† (pp opposto)   *to oppose*
l'opportunità (inv)   *opportunity*
oppure   *or else*
l'opuscolo   *booklet*
ora   *now*
l'ora   *hour*
   che ora è?/che ore sono?   *what time is it?*
l'orario   *timetable*
   in orario   *on time*
Orazio   *Horace*
l'orchestra   *orchestra*
l'orchidea   *orchid*
ordinare   *to order*
ordinato/a   *tidy*
l'ordine (m)   *order*
   l'ordine pubblico   *law and order*
le orecchiette (f)   *orecchiette (ear-shaped pasta)*
l'orecchino   *earring*
l'orecchio (pl gli orecchi/le orecchie)   *ear*
organizzare   *to organise, to arrange*
l'organo   *organ*

originale   *original*
l'origine (f)   *origin*
l'orlo   *hem*
l'oro   *gold*
l'orologio   *clock; watch*
   orologio da parete   *wall-clock*
l'orrore (m)   *horror*
   i film dell'orrore   *horror films*
Orsola   *Ursula*
l'orto   *garden*
l'ospedale (m)   *hospital*
ospitare   *to put someone up*
l'ospite (m/f)   *guest*
osservare   *to observe, to watch*
l'osteria   *tavern*
ottenere†   *to obtain; to achieve*
ottimista   *optimistic*
l'ottimista (m/f)   *optimist*
ottimo/a   *excellent*
l'ottone (m)   *brass*
l'ovulo   *ovule, spore (bot.)*

P

la pace   *peace*
la padella   *pan*
il padre   *father*
il padrone   *owner*
il paese   *country; village*
la paga   *pay*
   la busta paga   *wage packet*
pagare   *to pay (for)*
la pagina   *page*
   le pagine gialle   *yellow pages*
la paglia   *straw*
il paio (pl le paia)   *pair, couple*
   un paio di giorni   *a couple of days*
il palazzo   *block of flats; palace; the Establishment*
la palestra   *gymnasium*
la pallavolo   *volley-ball*
il pallone   *ball*
   giocare a pallone   *to play ball*
la palude   *marsh, bog*
il pane   *bread*
la panetteria   *bread shop*
il panino   *bread roll*
la panna   *cream*
il panorama (inv)   *view*
il pantaloncino   *shorts*
i pantaloni   *trousers*
il papà   *dad*
il Papa   *Pope*
il paragone   *comparison, parallel*
il parapendismo   *hang-gliding*
parcheggiare   *to park*
il parcheggio   *car park*
il parco   *park*
parecchio   *a lot*
il/la parente   *relative*
parere†★ (pp parso)   *to seem*
il parere   *opinion*
la parete   *(inside) wall*

pari   *equal, equivalent; even (number)*
parlare   *to speak*
il parmigiano   *parmesan (cheese)*
la parola   *word*
il parrucchiere/la parrucchiera   *hairdresser*
la parte   *part; side*
   da che parte?   *which way?*
   da questa parte   *this way*
   fare parte   *to form part*
partecipare   *to participate*
la partenza   *departure*
il particolare   *particular, detail*
il partigiano   *partisan*
partire★ (pr –o)   *to leave*
   a partire da   *starting from*
la partita   *match (sport)*
il partito   *party (political)*
il passaggio   *lift*
   dare un passaggio a   *to give someone a lift*
   il passaggio a livello   *level crossing*
il passaporto   *passport*
passare(★)   *to pass; drop by*
   passare il tempo   *to spend time*
la passerella   *catwalk*
il passatempo   *pastime*
passeggiare   *to go for a stroll*
la passeggiata   *walk, stroll*
   fare la passeggiata   *to go for a walk*
la pasta   *pasta, cake*
il pasticcio   *mess, muddle*
la pastiglia   *pastille, lozenge*
il pasto   *meal*
la pasticceria   *cake shop*
la patata   *potato*
le patatine (pl)   *crisps*
la patente   *driving licence*
il patrimonio   *heritage*
il pattinaggio   *skating*
pattinare   *to skate*
la paura   *fear*
   avere paura di   *to be afraid/frightened of*
   fare paura a   *to frighten*
la pausa   *pause*
il pavimento   *floor*
la pazienza   *patience*
   pazienza!   *oh well! too bad! never mind!*
peccato   *pity, shame*
   che peccato!   *what a shame!*
la pecora   *sheep*
il pecorino   *pecorino (cheese)*
il pedaggio   *toll*
pedalare   *to pedal*
il pedone   *pedestrian*
peggio   *worse, worst*
peggiorare(★)   *to worsen*
peggiore   *worse*
   il/la peggiore   *the worst*
la pelle   *soft leather, suede*
il pellegrinaggio   *pilgrimage*

il pellegrino   *pilgrim*
la pelletteria   *leather goods*
la pellicceria   *fur shop*
la pelliccia   *fur coat*
pendente   *leaning*
il /la pendolare   *commuter*
   fare il pendolare   *to commute*
penetrato/a   *penetrated*
la penisola   *peninsula*
la penna   *pen*
   le penne   *penne (pasta)*
pensare   *to think*
   quando pensa di partire?   *when are you thinking of leaving?*
   penso di sì   *I think so*
la pensione   *pension; guest house*
   in pensione   *retired*
pentirsi★ (pr −o)   *to regret*
il pepe   *pepper (spice)*
il peperone   *pepper*
il peperoncino   *hot pepper, chilli*
per   *for; in order to; through; around; by; because of*
   per esempio   *for example*
   per strada   *in the street*
la pera   *pear*
perché?   *why?*
perché   *because*
la percentuale   *percentage*
percorrere (pp percorso)   *to go along*
perdere (pp perduto or perso)   *to lose*
   perdere il treno   *to miss the train*
perfetto   *perfect*
il pericolo   *danger*
pericoloso/a   *dangerous*
la periferia   *outskirts, suburbs*
   abitare in periferia   *to live in the suburbs*
periodico/a   *periodic*
il periodo   *period*
permesso   *allowed*
permettere (pp permesso)   *to permit, to allow*
però   *but, however*
la perplessità (inv)   *perplexity, bewilderment*
le persiane (pl)   *blinds*
persistente   *long-lasting*
la persona   *person*
personale   *personal*
il personale   *staff*
persuadere (pp persuaso)   *to persuade*
pervenire†★ (pp pervenuto)   *to arrive, to come to*
pesante   *heavy*
pesare   *to weigh*
la pesca 1   *peach*
la pesca 2   *fishing*
il pescatore   *fisherman*
il pesce   *fish*
il peso   *weight*
pessimistico/a   *pessimistic*
pettinarsi★   *to do one's hair*

il pezzo   *piece*
   pezzettini   *small pieces*
piacere†★ (a)   *to please; to like*
   mi piace   *I like*
   fare piacere a   *to please*
piacere   *how do you do? pleased to meet you*
   per piacere   *please*
piacevole   *pleasant*
piangere (pp pianto)   *to cry*
il /la pianista   *pianist*
piano   *softly; slow*
il piano 1   *piano*
il piano 2   *floor*
   al primo piano   *on the first floor*
   l'ultimo piano   *top floor*
   il piano di cottura   *hob*
il pianoforte   *piano*
la pianta 1   *plant*
la pianta 2   *map*
il pianterreno   *ground floor*
il pianto   *weeping*
la pianura   *plain*
il piatto   *plate, dish*
la piazza   *square*
piccante   *hot, spicy*
piccolo/a   *small, little*
il picnic: fare un picnic   *to go on a picnic*
il piede   *foot*
   a piedi   *on foot*
   andare/venire a piedi   *to walk*
pieno/a   *full*
la pietà (inv)   *compassion, pity*
la pietra   *stone*
il pigiama   *pyjamas*
pignolo/a   *particular, precise*
pigro/a   *lazy*
il /la pilota   *pilot (m/f)*
la pinacoteca   *art gallery*
il ping-pong   *table-tennis*
il pino   *pine*
il pinolo   *pine-nut*
la pioggia   *rain*
   sotto la pioggia   *in the rain*
il pioppo   *poplar*
piovere(★)   *to rain*
il pipistrello   *bat*
la piscina   *swimming-pool*
i piselli   *peas*
il pistacchio   *pistachio*
pittorico/a   *pictorial*
più   *more; most; plus*
   il/la più   *the most*
   di più   *more/best*
   in più   *in addition*
   non … più   *no longer*
il piumino   *duvet*
la pizza   *pizza*
la pizzeria   *pizzeria*
il pizzo   *lace*
la plastica   *plastic*
plastificato/a   *plastic-coated*
il platano   *plane (tree)*

il plenilunio   *full moon*
un po'   *a little; some*
   un altro po'   *a bit more/a few more/some more*
poco   *little, not much (adj.); not very (adv.)*
la poesia   *poetry; poem*
il poeta/la poetessa   *poet*
poetico/a   *poetic*
poi   *then*
la poliammide   *polyamide*
la polizia   *police*
   la polizia doganale   *border/customs police*
   la polizia stradale   *road police*
poliziesco/a   *of the police*
   il film poliziesco   *thriller*
il poliziotto/la poliziotta   *policeman/policewoman*
il pollo   *chicken*
la poltrona   *armchair*
la pomata   *cream, ointment*
   la pomata antisettica   *antiseptic cream*
il pomeriggio   *afternoon*
il pomodoro   *tomato*
il pomolo   *knob*
il pompelmo   *grapefruit*
il ponte   *bridge*
popolare   *popular*
la popolazione   *population*
il porcino   *porcino mushroom, cep*
il porco   *pig*
porre† (pp posto)   *to put*
la porta   *door*
il portafoglio   *wallet*
il portamonete   *purse*
portare   *to wear; to bring*
portatile   *portable*
   il telefono portatile   *portable telephone*
il portico (pl −ci)   *arcade*
il portone   *front door*
possedere†   *to possess, to own*
possibile   *possible*
posso, possiamo   *see potere*
le poste   *Post Office*
il poster (inv)   *poster*
il postino   *postman*
il posto   *place; seat; job*
   prenotare un posto   *to book a seat*
   da due posti letto   *which sleeps two*
potente   *powerful*
potere†★   *to be able to*
povero/a   *poor (after the noun); unfortunate (before the noun)*
pranzare   *to have lunch*
il pranzo   *lunch*
   a pranzo   *at lunchtime*
praticamente   *virtually, basically*
il/la praticante   *participant*
praticare   *to practise*
   praticare uno sport   *to play a sport*

pratico/a (mpl –ci) *practical*
preferire *to prefer*
preferito/a *preferred*
il prefisso *code (telephone)*
pregare *to beg*
prego *don't mention it, go ahead*
il preludio *prelude*
premere *to press*
il premio *prize, award*
prendere (pp preso) *to take; to collect; to have (to) eat/drink*
cosa prendi/e? *what will you have (to eat/drink)?*
prendere la macchina/il treno *to take the car/train*
prenotare *to book*
preparare *to prepare*
prepararsi★ *to get ready to*
la presa *socket*
presentare *to present; to introduce*
il /la preside *head-teacher*
presso *care of*
prestare *to lend*
presto *quickly; early; soon*
a presto *see you soon*
il prêt-à-porter *ready-to-wear fashion*
prevedere (pp previsto) *to predict; to envisage, to foresee*
prezioso/a *precious; valuable*
il prezzemolo *parsley*
il prezzo *price*
la prigionia *imprisonment*
prima (di) *before*
la prima colazione *breakfast*
la primavera *spring*
in primavera *in the spring*
primeggiare *to dominate*
primo/a *first*
il primo *first course*
principale *principal*
principalmente *principally*
il principio *principle*
privo/a *devoid of*
probabilmente *probably*
il problema (pl i problemi) *problem*
non c'è problema *no problem*
la problematica *problems (pl)*
il prodotto *product*
produrre† (pp prodotto) *to produce*
profano/a *profane, secular*
professionale *professional*
la scuola professionale *vocational school*
la professione *profession*
il professore/la professoressa *professor, teacher*
la profumeria *perfumery*
il profumo *perfume*
il progetto *project*
il programma (pl i programmi) *programme; routine*
proibire *to prohibit*
il promemoria *memo*

promesso/a *promised*
I Promessi Sposi 'The Betrothed' (novel)
promettere (pp promesso) *to promise*
promuovere† (pp promosso) *to promote*
pronto *hello (on the telephone)*
pronto/a *ready*
proporre† (pp proposto) *to propose*
la proposta *proposal, suggestion*
la proprietà (inv) *ownership*
il proprietario *owner*
proprio *really; precisely, exactly*
proprio/a *one's own*
il proposito *subject*
a proposito di *about, on the subject of*
prosciugato/a *dried up*
il prosciutto *ham*
la prossimità *proximity, nearness*
prossimo/a *next*
proteggere (pp protetto) *to protect*
la protezione *protection*
Prov. (la provincia) *province*
la prova *rehearsal; test*
provare *to try; to try on*
provenire† (pp provenuto) *to originate from*
la provincia *province*
lo psicologo (pl –gi) *psychologist*
pubblicare *to publish*
pubblico/a (m pl –ci) *public*
i giardini pubblici *public gardens*
le pubbliche relazioni *public relations*
la Puglia *Puglia (region)*
pugliese *from Puglia*
pulire *to clean*
pulito/a *clean*
il pulsante *button*
la puntata *episode*
il punto *point*
il punto di vista *point of view*
puramente *purely*
pure *also; by all means*
puro/a *pure*
purtroppo *unfortunately*

Q

quà *here*
di quà *this way*
il quaderno *exercise-book*
quadrato/a *square*
i quadretti *small squares*
a quadretti *checked*
il quadro *picture*
qualche *some, a few*
qualchevolta *sometimes*
qualcosa *something*
qualcosa da bere *something to drink*
qualcuno *someone*
quale? *which (one)? what (one)?*
qualsiasi *any*

quando *when*
la quantità (inv) *quantity*
quanto/a? *how much how many?*
quanti anni hai? *how old are you?*
da quanto tempo? *for how long?*
ogni quanto? *every how often?*
quant'è? *how much is it? how much is that?*
il quartiere *district*
il quarto *quarter*
un'ora e un quarto *an hour and a quarter*
quasi *almost*
quattordicesimo/a *fourteenth*
quello/a *that (one)*
la quercia *oak tree*
questo/a *this (one)*
questi/e *these (ones)*
la questione *question*
per la questione di … *about the …*
la questura *police station*
qui *here*
quindi *so, therefore*
quinto/a *fifth*

R

raccogliere† (pp raccolto) *to pick; to collect; to gather*
la raccolta *picking, gathering; collection*
il racconto *short story*
il radicchio *radicchio lettuce*
la radio (inv) *radio*
raffinato/a *refined*
la ragazza *girl*
il ragazzo *boy*
raggiungere (pp raggiunto) *to reach; to attain*
la ragione *reason*
avere ragione *to be right*
il ragioniere/la ragioniera *accountant*
il ragno *spider*
il rame *copper*
il ramo *branch*
il ramoscello *twig*
la rana *frog*
rapidamente *quickly*
rapido/a *fast*
la rapina *armed robbery*
rappresentare *to represent*
raramente *rarely*
il raso *satin*
rassegnarsi★ *to resign oneself*
il ratto *rat*
razionale *rational*
reagire *to react*
realizzare *to create; to accomplish*
reale *royal; real*
il reato *crime*
recitare *to act*
redimere (pp redento) *to redeem*
refrattario/a *refractory*
regalare *to give (as a present)*

il regalo   *gift, present*
il reggiseno   *bra*
regionale   *regional*
la regione   *region*
il /la regista   *producer*
il regno   *kingdom*
regolarmente   *regularly*
la relazione   *relation*
   le pubbliche relazioni   *public relations*
rendere (pp reso)   *to render, to make*
   rendersi★ conto   *to realise*
la repubblica   *republic*
resistere   *to resist*
la Resistenza   *Resistance*
respirare   *to breathe*
responsabile   *responsible*
il responsabile   *the one responsible, in charge*
restare★   *to stay*
restituire   *to give back*
il resto   *rest; change (money)*
restringere (pp restritto)   *to take in*
la rete   *net*
la retorica   *rhetoric*
il riadattamento   *renovating*
riaprire (pr –o) (pp riaperto)   *to reopen*
ricco/a   *rich; lavish*
   ricco di   *full of*
ricercato/a   *sought-after*
il ricercatore/la ricercatrice   *researcher*
la ricetta   *recipe*
ricevere   *to receive*
il ricevimento   *reception; welcome*
il ricevitore   *receiver (telephone)*
richiamare   *to call back*
richiedere (pp richiesto)   *to request*
riconoscere   *to recognise*
ricoprire (pr –o) (pp ricoperto)   *to recover*
ricordare   *to remember; to remind*
la ricotta   *ricotta cheese*
ridere (pp riso)   *to laugh*
ridicolo/a   *ridiculous*
ridurre† (pp ridotto)   *to reduce*
riempire (pr –o)   *to fill in (form)*
rientrare★   *to get back*
il rifugio   *hut*
rifiutare   *to refuse*
la riga   *stripe*
   a righe   *striped*
rilassante   *relaxing*
rilassarsi★   *to relax*
la rilegatura   *binding*
rimandare   *to postpone*
rimanere★ (pp rimasto)   *to stay, to remain*
   rimanere in linea   *to hold the line*
rimettere (pp rimesso)   *to put back*
   rimettere a posto   *to put back into place*

rimpiangere (pp rimpianto)   *to regret*
rinascimentale (adj)   *Renaissance*
rincrescere★   *to regret*
ringraziare   *to thank*
rinunciare   *to give up*
rinviare   *to postpone*
riparare   *to mend*
ripetere   *to repeat*
riposarsi★   *to rest*
riprendere (pp ripreso)   *to resume*
risalire†★   *to climb up again*
il riscaldamento   *heating*
il rischio   *risk*
riscoprire (pr –o) (pp riscoperto)   *to rediscover*
risentire (pr –o)   *to hear again; to feel again*
la riserva   *reserve*
   la riserva naturale   *nature reserve*
il riso   *rice*
risolvere (pp risolto)   *to resolve; to solve*
il risotto   *risotto*
risparmiare   *to save*
rispettare   *to respect*
rispettivamente   *respectively*
rispondere (pp risposto)   *to answer, to reply*
il ristorante   *restaurant*
ristrutturato/a   *modernised*
il risultato   *result*
il ritardo   *lateness, delay*
   essere in ritardo   *to be late*
ritenere†   *to claim; to maintain*
ritornare★   *to return, to come back*
il ritorno   *return*
   l'andata e ritorno   *return (ticket)*
la riunione   *reunion*
riuscire†★   *to succeed; to manage to*
la rivista   *magazine*
rivolgersi★ (pp rivolto)   *to apply to, to contact*
la roba   *things, stuff, belongings*
il rock (inv)   *rock music*
rodere (pp roso)   *to gnaw*
il rognone   *kidney*
romagnolo/a   *from Romagna*
romano/a   *Roman*
il romanzo   *novel*
   il romanzo rosa   *romantic fiction*
rompere (pp rotto)   *to break*
il rompiscatole   *nuisance, pest*
rosa (inv)   *pink*
la rosa   *rose*
il rospo   *toad*
il rossetto   *lipstick*
rosso/a   *red*
rotondo/a   *round*
rovesciare   *to spill*
rubare   *to steal*
   mi hanno rubato il portafoglio   *I've had my wallet stolen*
il rubinetto   *tap*

   aprire il rubinetto   *to turn on the tap*
la rubrica   *column (in newspaper)*
il rumore   *noise*
rumoroso/a   *noisy*
il ruscello   *stream*
il rustico (pl –ci)   *cottage*

S

il sabato   *Saturday*
il sacchetto   *(small) bag*
   il sacchetto di plastica   *plastic bag*
il sacco   *sack, bag*
   il sacco a pelo   *sleeping bag*
il sacerdote   *priest*
il saggio   *essay*
la sagra   *village festival*
la sala da pranzo   *dining-room*
il salame   *salame*
il salario   *wage*
il saldo   *the difference*
il sale   *salt*
salire†★   *to get into (vehicle), to go up*
il salotto   *sitting-room*
la salsa   *sauce*
la salsiccia   *sausage*
saltare(★)   *to jump*
salutare   *to greet, say hello/goodbye*
Salute!   *Your health! Cheers!*
salvato/a   *saved*
San Marco   *Saint Mark*
San Pietro   *Saint Peter*
il sandalo   *sandal*
il sanguinaccio   *pork blood sausage*
sano/a   *healthy*
sapere†★   *to know; to know how to*
   sai guidare?   *can you drive?*
   non lo so   *I don't know*
sapiente   *masterly*
la sapienza   *wisdom*
il sapone   *soap*
la Sardegna   *Sardinia*
il sarto   *tailor*
la sartoria   *tailor's workshop*
il sasso   *rock; cave-like dwelling of Matera in Basilicata*
il sassofono   *saxophone*
sbagliare   *to make a mistake, to get it wrong*
   sbagliare numero   *to dial a wrong number*
sbagliato/a   *wrong*
   la camera sbagliata   *the wrong room*
sbattuto/a   *beaten*
gli scacchi (pl)   *chess*
scadere★   *to expire, to run out*
lo scaffale   *shelf, bookshelf*
la scala   *stairs*
lo scaldabagno   *water heater*
la scampagnata   *country outing; picnic*
lo scantinato   *basement*
scappare★   *to flee, to dash off*
scarico/a (m pl –ci)   *flat (battery)*

la scarpa   *shoe*
lo scarpone   *ski/walking boot*
la scatola   *box, packet*
lo scatto   *unit*
scegliere† (pp scelto)   *to choose*
la scelta   *choice*
la scena   *scene*
scendere(*) (pp sceso)   *to come down, to get out (vehicle)*
lo sceneggiato   *TV serial*
la scheda   *card*
   la scheda telefonica   *telephone card*
lo scheletro   *skeleton*
lo schermo   *screen*
lo scherzo   *joke*
schiacciare   *to press, to crush*
la schiena   *back*
la schiera   *group*
   a schiera   *terraced (houses)*
lo schifo   *disgust*
   fare schifo a   *to disgust*
lo schizzo   *sketch*
lo sci   *skiing*
   sciare   *to ski*
la sciarpa   *scarf*
scientifico/a (m pl −ci)   *scientific*
lo scienziato/la scienziata   *scientist*
sciogliere† (pp sciolto)   *to melt; to dissolve*
lo scioglilingua   *tongue-twister*
lo sciopero   *strike*
   fare sciopero   *to strike*
lo scippo   *(handbag) snatching*
lo scoiattolo   *squirrel*
scomodo/a   *uncomfortable*
scomparire†* (pp scomparso)   *to disappear*
sconfiggere (pp sconfitto)   *to defeat*
sconsigliare   *to advise not to*
scontarsi*   *to expiate, to pay for*
scontento/a   *dissatisfied, discontented*
lo sconto   *discount*
lo scontrino   *ticket, receipt*
sconvolto/a   *overcome, disturbed, troubled*
lo scopo   *aim*
   gli scopi didattici   *educational aims*
scoppiare*   *to break out*
scoprire (pr −o) (pp scoperto)   *to discover*
scorso/a   *last*
scozzese   *Scottish; tartan (material)*
lo scritto   *writing*
lo scrittore/la scrittrice   *writer*
scrivere (pp scritto)   *to write*
   scrivere a macchina   *to type*
lo scultore/la scultrice   *sculptor*
la scuola   *school*
   le scuole elementari   *infant and junior schools*
   le (scuole) medie   *middle schools*
   la scuola superiore   *upper school*

la scuola professionale   *vocational school*
scuotere (pp scosso)   *to shake*
scuro/a   *dark*
scusare   *to excuse*
   scusa!/scusi!/ scusate!   *excuse me!/sorry!*
la sdraia   *deck-chair*
se   *if*
sé: sé stesso   *himself, herself, yourself, itself*
secco/a   *dry*
il secolo   *century*
secondo   *according to*
   secondo Lei   *in your opinion*
il secondo   *second ; main course*
il sedano   *celery*
la sede   *seat; centre*
sedersi†*   *to sit*
la sedia   *chair, seat*
sedurre† (pp sedotto)   *to seduce*
il segnale   *signpost*
segnare   *to mark*
il segno   *sign*
la segretaria   *secretary*
la segreteria telefonica   *telephone answering machine, Ansaphone*
segreto/a   *secret*
seguire   *to follow*
il seguito   *sequence*
   in seguito   *subsequently*
selvatico/a (m pl −ci)   *wild*
il semaforo   *traffic light*
sembrare*   *to seem*
il seminterrato   *basement*
semplice   *simple; single*
   una corsa semplice   *a single ride*
la semplicità   *simplicity*
sempre   *always*
senese   *Sienese*
sensibile   *sensitive*
il senso   *sense*
   aver buon senso   *to have common sense*
il sentiero   *path, track*
il sentimento   *feeling*
sentire (pr −o)   *to feel, to hear*
   senti!/senta!   *listen!*
sentirsi (pr −o)*   *to feel like*
senz'altro   *definitely*
senza   *without*
seppellire (pp sepolto)   *to bury*
la sera   *evening*
serale   *evening*
   il corso serale   *evening class*
sereno/a   *clear*
il serpente   *snake*
la serie (inv)   *series*
serio/a   *serious*
la serra   *greenhouse*
servire (pr −o)(*)   *to serve; to be needed*
   serve altro?   *do you need anything else?*

il servizio   *service*
   il bagno di servizio   *cloakroom/ spare bathroom*
il sesso   *sex*
la seta   *silk*
la sete   *thirst*
settembre (m)   *September*
la settimana   *week*
   il fine settimana (inv)   *weekend*
settimanale   *weekly*
settimo/a   *seventh*
il settore   *sector*
sferico/a   *spherical; round*
sfidare   *to defy; to challenge*
sforzarsi*   *to try hard*
sfumare in   *to blend into*
lo shampoo (inv)   *shampoo*
si   *oneself; yourself; yourselves; herself; himself; itself; themselves; (to) each other*
   si mangia bene   *you eat well (one eats well)*
sì   *yes*
sia: sia . . . che   *both . . . and*
siamo   *see essere*
la Sicilia   *Sicily*
sicuramente   *surely*
la sicurezza   *safety*
sicuro/a   *sure*
   sicuro di sé   *confident*
la sigaretta   *cigarette*
il sigaro   *cigar*
la sigla   *signature tune*
la signora   *lady, Mrs, madam*
il signore   *man, Mr, sir*
signorile   *elegant*
la signorina   *young lady, Miss*
il silenzio   *silence*
silenzioso/a   *silent*
il simbolo   *symbol*
simile   *similar*
simpatico/a (m pl −ci)   *nice, pleasant*
il sindaco   *mayor*
la sinfonia   *symphony*
la sinistra   *left*
   a sinistra   *on the left*
sintetico/a (m pl −ci)   *synthetic*
SIP   *Italian Telephone Company*
il sistema (pl i sistemi)   *system*
sistemare   *to put; to arrange*
la situazione   *situation, position*
lo slip   *briefs*
smettere (pp smesso)   *to stop; to give up*
   smettere di fumare   *to give up smoking*
snello/a   *slim*
so   *see sapere*
sociale   *social*
   l'assistente sociale   *social worker*
socialista (m/f)   *socialist*
la società (inv)   *society; company*
il socio   *member*

soddisfare† (pp soddisfatto) *to satisfy*
la sofferenza *suffering*
la soffitta *attic*
il soffitto *ceiling*
soffrire (pr −o) (pp sofferto) *to suffer*
il soggiorno *stay; sitting-room*
sognare *to dream*
il sogno *dream*
il soldato *soldier*
i soldi (pl) *money*
il sole *sun*
   c'è sole *it's sunny*
solito/a *usual*
   di solito *usually*
la solitudine *solitude*
solo *only*
   da solo *by oneself*
soltanto *only*
la soluzione *solution*
sommergere (pp sommerso) *to submerge*
il sonetto *sonnet*
il sonno *sleep*
   aver sonno *to be sleepy*
sono *see essere*
sopra *above*
   di sopra *upstairs*
il soprano (inv) *soprano*
soprattutto *above all, chiefly*
sopravvivere(*) (pp sopravvissuto) *to survive*
la sorella *sister*
   la sorellina *little sister*
sorpassare *to overtake*
sorprendente *surprising*
sorprendere (pp sorpreso) *to surprise*
la sorpresa *surprise*
sorridere (pp sorriso) *to smile*
la sosta *halt*
   il divieto di sosta *no waiting*
sotto *under, beneath*
   di sotto *downstairs*
la sottoveste *petticoat, slip*
sottrarre† (pp sottratto) *to take away, remove*
sovietico/a (m pl −ci) *Soviet*
S.p.A. (Società per Azioni) *Joint-Stock Company*
la spada *sword*
   le spade *spades (cards)*
gli spaghetti *spaghetti*
sparare *to shoot*
spargere (pp sparso) *to spread*
sparire★ *to disappear*
lo spazio *space*
spazioso/a *spacious, roomy*
la spazzatura *rubbish*
lo specchio *mirror*
la specialità (inv) *speciality*
specialmente *especially*
la specie (inv) *species*
spedire *to send; to post*
spegnere (pp spento) *to put out, to*

extinguish; to turn off
spendaccione *extravagant*
spendere (pp speso) *to spend*
sperare *to hope*
   sperare di trovare *to hope to find*
la spesa *shopping*
   fare la spesa *to go shopping*
spesso *often*
lo spettacolo *show; performance*
la spiaggia *beach*
   in spiaggia *on the beach*
gli spiccioli *small change*
lo spider (inv) *convertible sports-car*
spiegare *to explain*
la spilla *brooch*
la spina *plug*
gli spinaci *spinach*
spingere (pp spinto) *to push*
splendido/a *splendid, magnificent*
sporco/a *dirty*
sporgersi★ (pp sporto) *to lean out of*
lo sport (inv) *sport*
sportivo/a *sporting*
sposarsi★ *to get married*
sposato/a *married*
   sposato con *married to*
gli sposi *married couple*
   I Promessi Sposi *'The Betrothed' (novel)*
lo spot (inv) *TV advertising spot*
la spremuta *freshly squeezed juice*
lo sprint (inv) *sprint*
lo spumante *sparkling wine*
lo spuntino *snack*
   fare uno spuntino *to have a snack*
la squadra *team*
lo squash *squash*
   giocare a squash *to play squash*
squillare *to ring (telephone)*
squisito/a *delicious*
staccare *to unplug*
lo stadio *stadium*
la stagione *season*
stamattina *this morning*
la stampa *press*
stancarsi★ *to be tired of*
stanco/a *tired*
la stanga *shaft*
la stanza *room*
la star (inv) *star (celebrity m/f)*
stare†★ *to be; to stay*
   come stai/sta? *how are you?*
   stare attento *to be careful*
   stare zitto *to be quiet*
   stare bene a *to suit*
starnutire *to sneeze*
stasera *this evening*
statale *(of the) state*
lo statale *state employee, civil servant*
gli Stati Uniti *United States*
lo stato *state*
la statua *statue*

la stazione *station; resort*
lo stereo *stereo*
la sterlina *pound (money)*
lo stesso/la stessa *the same*
   sé stesso/a *himself, herself, yourself, itself*
lo stile *style*
lo /la stilista *designer (m/f)*
lo stipendio *salary*
stiro: il ferro da stiro *(flat) iron*
lo stivale *boot*
la stoffa *material*
lo stomaco *stomach*
   il mal di stomaco *stomach-ache*
la storia *history; story*
la stracciatella *chicken and egg soup*
la strada *road*
straniero/a *foreign*
lo straniero, la straniera *foreigner*
strano/a *strange, unusual*
straordinariamente *extraordinarily*
straziante *excruciating*
stressante *stressful*
stretto/a *tight; narrow*
la stringa *lace*
stringere (pp stretto) *to squeeze; to shake (hand)*
lo strumento *instrument*
lo strutto *lard*
lo studente/la studentessa *student*
studiare *to study*
lo studio *studio*
stufo/a *bored, fed up*
stupendo/a *stupid*
stupido/a *stupid*
stupirsi★ *to be amazed*
su *on, upon; up*
subito *straight away, at once, immediately*
succedere★ (pp successo) *to happen*
   che cos'è successo? *what's happened?*
successivo/a *successive, following*
il successo *success*
il succo di frutta *fruit juice*
   il succo d'arancia *orange juice*
suddetto/a *afore-mentioned*
suggerire *to suggest*
suicidarsi★ *to commit suicide*
suo/a *his; her; hers; its; your; yours*
il suocero/la suocera *father-/mother-in-law*
suonare *to play (an instrument); to ring (telephone)*
il suono *sound*
la superficie *surface*
superiore *superior*
   la scuola superiore *upper school*
il superlativo *superlative*
il supermercato *supermarket*
il supplemento *supplement*
supporre† (pp supposto) *to suppose*
lo svago *entertainment; relaxation*
lo svantaggio *disadvantage*

la sveglia   *alarm-clock*
svegliarsi★   *to wake up*
svenire†★ (pp svenuto)   *to faint*
svolgere (pp svolto)   *to carry out;*
   svolgere un'attività   *to carry out an*
   activity

T

il tabaccaio   *tobacconist*
la tabaccheria   *tobacconist's shop*
il tacco   *heel*
il taccuino   *note book*
tacere† (pp taciuto)   *to be silent*
la taglia   *size (clothes)*
tagliare   *to cut*
le tagliatelle   *tagliatelle (pasta)*
il tailleur (inv)   *(woman's) suit*
talmente   *so (adv)*
tanti/e   *so many*
tanto   *so much; a lot; anyway*
   tantissimo   *lots*
tanto/a   *a lot (of), extremely*
   ogni tanto   *every so often*
il tappeto   *carpet, rug*
tardi   *late*
   a più tardi   *see you later*
il tartufo   *truffle*
la tasca   *pocket*
il tassì (inv)   *taxi*
il/la tassista   *taxi-driver*
il tavolo/la tavola   *table*
la tazza   *cup*
il tè (inv)   *tea*
il teatro   *theatre*
   il teatro dell'opera   *opera house*
il telecomando   *remote control*
il telefilm (inv)   *TV film*
telefonare a   *to telephone*
la telefonata   *telephone call*
   la telefonata interurbana   *long-distance call*
   la telefonata urbana   *local call*
il telefonino   *portable telephone*
il telefono   *telephone*
il telegiornale   *TV news*
il telegramma (pl i telegrammi)   *telegram*
la telenovela   *'soap'*
la teleselezione   *automatic dialling*
la televisione   *television*
il televisore   *television set*
il tema (pl i temi)   *theme*
il tempio   *temple*
il tempo   *time; weather*
   da quanto tempo?   *how long?*
   avere tempo   *to have time*
   da molto tempo   *for a long time*
   fa bel/brutto tempo   *the weather's good/bad*
il temporale   *storm*
la tenda   *curtain; tent*
tenere†   *to hold; to keep*
tenersi†★ in forma   *to keep fit*

il tennis (inv)   *tennis*
tentare   *to try, to attempt*
il termosifone   *radiator*
la terra   *earth*
   la terra rossa   *clay*
la terracotta   *terracotta*
il terrazzo   *(roof) terrace*
terribile   *terrible*
il terrore   *terror*
   avere il terrore di   *to be terrified of*
il terzo   *third*
il tesoro   *treasure*
la tessera   *ticket, card*
   tessera club   *club membership*
   avere la tessera per   *to belong to, to have a ticket for*
il tessuto   *textile, fabric*
il tetto   *roof*
il Tevere   *Tiber*
ti   *you; to/for you; yourself*
il tifoso   *fan (sports)*
il tinello   *dining-room*
il tipo   *kind, type; chap*
tirare   *to pull*
   tira vento   *it's windy*
il tiro   *shooting*
   il tiro con l'arco   *archery*
   il cavallo da tiro   *cart-horse*
il toast (inv)   *toasted sandwich*
togliere† (pp tolto)   *to remove*
tollerante   *tolerant*
tonificante   *toning*
il topo/il topolino   *mouse*
tornare★   *to return, to go/come back; to do again*
   tornare indietro   *to turn back/round*
il torneo   *tournament*
il toro   *bull*
la torre   *tower*
il torrente   *river, stream*
la torta   *cake*
i tortelli   *tortelli (pasta)*
i tortellini   *tortellini (pasta)*
il torto   *wrong*
   avere torto   *to be wrong*
toscano/a   *Tuscan*
tossico/a (m pl −ci)   *toxic*
tossire   *to cough*
il totale   *total*
   in totale   *in total*
totalmente   *totally*
la tovaglia   *table-cloth*
il tovagliolo   *napkin*
tra   *see fra*
tradizionale   *traditional*
la tradizione   *tradition*
tradurre† (pp tradotto)   *to translate*
la traduzione   *translation*
il traffico   *traffic*
la tragedia   *tragedy*
il traghetto   *ferry*
la trama   *plot*

il tramezzino   *sandwich*
il tramonto   *sunset*
tranne   *except*
la tranquillità   *tranquillity, calm*
tranquillo/a   *quiet, peaceful*
trarre† (pp tratto)   *to pull, to draw*
il transito   *thoroughfare*
   il divieto di transito   *no thoroughfare*
trascorrere (pp trascorso)   *to spend, to pass*
   trascorrere il tempo   *to use time*
il trasporto   *transport*
trattare (con)   *to deal with*
il trattato   *treaty*
la trattoria   *trattoria (modest restaurant)*
traversare   *to cross*
il Trebbiano   *Trebbiano (wine)*
il Trecento   *fourteenth century*
tredicesimo/a   *thirteenth*
il trekking   *hiking*
il treno   *train*
   prendere il treno   *to take the train*
   il treno delle 7.53   *the 7.53 train*
il trentino   *person from Trento*
trifolato   *truffled (sliced and cooked with oil, garlic and parsley)*
triste   *sad*
la tristezza   *sadness*
la tromba   *trumpet*
il trombone   *trombone*
il tronco   *(tree) trunk*
troppo   *too much*
trotterellare   *to trot*
trovare   *to find*
   andare a trovare   *to visit (person)*
trovarsi★   *to be (somewhere); to find oneself*
il trucco   *make-up*
il trullo   *trullo (ancient conical house in Puglia)*
le truppe   *troops*
tu   *you*
il tuffo   *dive*
tuo/a   *your; yours*
il tuono   *thunder*
turchese   *turquoise*
turchino/a   *dark blue*
il /la turista   *tourist*
turistico/a (m pl −ci)   *tourist*
   l'ufficio turistico   *tourist office*
tutelare   *to protect*
tutto   *all, everything*
   in tutto   *altogether*
tutti/e   *all, everyone*
   tutti e due   *both*
   tutti e trentatré   *all 33*

U

l'ubicazione (f)   *location*
l'uccello   *bird*
uccidere (pp ucciso)   *to kill*
l'ufficio   *office*

l'ufficio turistico   *tourist office*
ulteriore   *further (adj.)*
ultimo/a   *last; latest*
    l'ultimo piano   *top floor*
l'umanista (m/f)   *humanist*
l'umanità   *humanity*
un, un', uno, una   *a, an, one*
    è l'una   *it's one o'clock*
undicimila   *eleven thousand*
unico/a   *only; unique*
    sono figlio unico   *I'm an only child*
l'unione (f)   *union*
unire   *to join; to unite; to enclose*
l'unità (inv)   *unit*
unito/a   *united*
l'università (inv)   *university*
gli Unni   *the Huns*
l'uomo (pl gli uomini)   *man*
l'uovo (m) (pl le uova)   *egg*
    uova sbattute   *beaten eggs*
urbano/a   *city, urban*
    la telefonata urbana   *local call*
usare   *to use*
uscire†★   *to go out, to exit*
    uscire di casa   *to leave the house*
l'uscita   *exit*
l'usignolo   *nightingale*
utile   *useful*
utilizzare   *to use*
l'utopia   *utopia*
l'uva   *grapes (pl)*

V

va bene   *okay, that's fine*
    mi va bene   *that suits me*
la vacanza   *holiday*
    in vacanza   *on holiday*
la vacca   *cow*
vado, vai, va, vanno   *see* andare
vagare   *to wander*
    vagare per   *to wander through*
la valigia   *suitcase*
la valle/la vallata   *valley*
i valori   *valuables*
    il deposito valori   *safety deposit*
la vaniglia   *vanilla*
il vano   *room*
il vantaggio   *advantage*
vantarsi★   *to boast*
il vaporetto   *waterbus*
vario/a   *various, different*
il vascellaro   *vatmaker*
il vaso   *vase*
vecchio/a   *old*
vedere (pp visto *or* veduto)   *to see*
    fare vedere a   *to show*
    non vedere l'ora   *to look forward to*
vedersi★ (pp visto *or* veduto)   *to see one another; to meet*
    ci vediamo!   *see you later!*
vegetariano/a   *vegetarian*
la veglia   *(night) watch*

la vela   *sail*
velenoso/a   *poisonous*
il velluto   *velvet, corduroy*
veloce   *fast*
velocemente   *quickly*
vendere   *to sell*
il venerdì   *Friday*
Venezia   *Venice*
vengo, vieni, viene, vengono   *see* venire
venire†★ (pp venuto)   *to come*
ventidue   *22*
la ventina   *about 20*
il vento   *wind*
    tira vento   *it's windy*
veramente   *really*
il verbale   *statement*
verde   *green*
la verdura   *vegetables*
la vergogna   *shame*
    avere vergogna   *to be ashamed*
vergognarsi★   *to be ashamed*
il verme   *worm*
i vermicelli   *vermicelli (pasta)*
vero?   *true? right?*
versare   *to pour*
verso   *towards; at about*
la vespa   *wasp*
la vestaglia   *dressing-gown*
vestire (pr −o)   *to dress*
vestirsi★ (pr −o)   *to get dressed*
il vestito   *dress*
la vetrina   *shop-window*
vi   *you (pl); to/for you; yourselves*
la via   *street*
viaggiare   *to travel*
il viaggio   *journey*
il vicino/la vicina   *neighbour*
vicino   *nearby, close*
    qui vicino   *near here*
il video   *video*
il videoregistratore   *video*
vietare   *to forbid*
vietato/a   *forbidden*
    è vietato fumare   *it is forbidden to smoke*
il vigile/la vigilessa   *traffic policeman/woman*
la villa   *detached house*
il villaggio   *village*
la villetta   *cottage*
il villino   *cottage*
vincere (pp vinto)   *to win*
vinicolo/a   *(relating to) wine*
il vino   *wine*
viola (inv)   *purple*
la viola 1   *viola*
la viola 2   *violet*
il /la violinista   *violinist*
il violino   *violin*
il violoncello   *cello*
la vipera   *adder, viper*
la virgola   *comma*

la visione   *vision*
visitare   *to visit (place)*
il viso   *face*
la vista   *view*
    il punto di vista   *point of view*
    a prima vista   *at first sight*
la vita   *life*
il vitello   *veal; calf*
vivace   *lively*
vivere(★) (pp vissuto)   *to live, to live on*
vivo/a   *alive*
la voce   *voice*
la voglia   *desire, wish*
    avere voglia di   *to feel like*
voglio, vogliamo, vogliono   *see* volere
voi   *you (pl)*
volare(★)   *to fly*
volentieri   *willingly, with pleasure*
volere†★   *to want*
    voler bene   *to be fond of, to love*
volgare   *vulgar, coarse*
il volo   *flight*
la volpe   *fox*
la volta   *time*
    a volte   *sometimes*
il volto   *face*
volto/a   *turned to*
il volume   *volume*
vostro/a   *your (pl); yours (pl)*
votare   *to vote*
il voto   *mark*
vuoi, vuole   *see* volere
vuotare   *to empty*
vuoto/a   *empty*

W

il waltzer (inv)   *waltz*
il water (inv)   *toilet*
il weekend (inv)   *weekend*
il western (inv)   *western film*
il whisky (inv)   *whisky*
il windsurfing   *windsurfing*

Y

lo yoga   *yoga*

Z

lo zabaglione   *zabaglione, syllabub (dessert)*
lo zaino   *rucksack*
la zanzara   *mosquito*
la zia   *aunt*
lo zio   *uncle*
la zip   *zip*
zitto/a   *quiet, silent*
    stare zitto   *to be quiet*
lo zoccolo   *clog*
lo zodiaco   *zodiac*
la zona   *area, district*
lo zoo (inv)   *zoo*
lo zucchero   *sugar*
la zucchina/lo zucchino   *courgette*

Picture Credits

BBC Books would like to thank the following for providing photographs and for permission to reproduce copyright material. While every effort has been made to trace and acknowledge all copyright holders, we would like to apologize should there have been any errors or omissions.

Julian Baldwin pages iii, 1 (*right*), 2, 3 (*left*), 10, 11 (*bottom right*), 18 (*bottom*), 33, 34, 43, 48, 58, 73, 120, 136 (*bottom*), 137, 144, 145, 152, 153, 160, 162 (*left*), 175, 176, 177, 178, 184 (*bottom right*), 185 and 186; **J. Allan Cash** pages 65 and 167 (*top*); **Chiappini family** pages 107 and 108; **Giangiacomo Feltrinelli Editore, Milano** page 24; **Robert Harding Picture Library** pages 17 (Gascoigne) and 135 (Giulio Veggi); **Image Bank** pages 49 (Guido Rossi), 127 (Giuliano Colliva) and 146 (Giuliano Colliva); **Andrew Oliver** pages 16 (*bottom right*), 32 and 174; **Jeremy Orlebar** pages 19, 51, 52, 66, 136 (*top*), 137 (*inset*), 162 (*right*) and 168; **Picturepoint** pages 70 and 159; **Scala** pages 109 and 223; **David Simson** pages 57 (*bottom*), 151 (*bottom*) and 184 (*bottom left*); **Spectrum** pages 1 (*left*), 78 and 143; **Mick Webb** pages 72, 76, 221 and 222; **Zefa** page 142.

The following photographs were taken for the BBC by: **Benedict Campbell** pages i, 24, 41, 57 (*top*), 64, 118, 126 and 192; and **Daniel Thistlethwaite** pages 11 (*top left*) and 167 (*bottom*).

Front cover photos: **Julian Baldwin**
Back cover photo: **Andrew Oliver**

Notes

Notes